Life Histories of
NORTH AMERICAN
WILD FOWL

Arthur Cleveland Bent

Two Parts Bound as One

DOVER PUBLICATIONS, INC.
NEW YORK

Published in Canada by General Publishing Company, Ltd., 30 Lesmill Road, Don Mills, Toronto, Ontario.
Published in the United Kingdom by Constable and Company, Ltd., 10 Orange Street, London WC2H 7EG.

This Dover edition, first published in 1987, is a republication in one volume of the 1962 two-volume Dover edition, an unabridged and unaltered republication of the work first published by the United States Government Printing Office. Part I was originally published in 1923 as Smithsonian Institution United States National Museum *Bulletin 126*; Part II was originally published in 1925 as Smithsonian Institution United States National Museum *Bulletin 130*.

Manufactured in the United States of America
Dover Publications, Inc., 31 East 2nd Street, Mineola, N.Y. 11501

Library of Congress Cataloging-in-Publication Data

Bent, Arthur Cleveland, 1866–1954.
Life histories of North American wild fowl.

Bibliography: p.
Includes index.
1. Anatidae. 2. Anatidae—Behavior. 3. Birds—Behavior. 4. Birds—North America—Behavior. I. Title.
QL696.A52B46   1987   598′.41′097   87-580
ISBN 0-486-25422-4 (pbk.)

PART I

INTRODUCTION

Nearly all those who contributed material for former volumes have rendered similiar service in this case. In addition to those whose contributions have been previously acknowledged, our thanks are due to the following new contributors:

Photographs have been contributed by A. A. Allen, J. H. Bowles, A. D. Dubois, J. Labarthe, C. W. Townsend, and W. Raine.

Notes and data have been contributed by A. A. Allen, G. M. Allen, H. W. Brandt, L. Griscom, J. F. Honecker, W. J. Hoxie, J. C. Phillips, and G. M. Sutton. Mr. Wharton Huber has written the life history and the distribution of his new species, the New Mexican duck.

Dr. John C. Phillips has furnished the references for the life history of the falcated teal and very kindly placed at the author's disposal his entire unpublished manuscript on this species.

The information previously furnished by Dr. T. S. Palmer, on bird reservations belonging to the United States, and a lot of data recently furnished by Mr. Hoyes Lloyd, on Canadian bird reservations and sanctuaries, form such a voluminous mass that it seems best to leave it for future publication by itself, rather than attempt to do but scant justice to it in this volume.

The distributional part of this volume is the work of the author; but it has been examined by Mr. James H. Fleming, Mr. P. A. Taverner, and Mr. F. Seymour Hersey. Mr. Hersey also figured the egg measurements, after collecting a lot of additional measurements from some of the large egg collections, notably those of the California Academy of Sciences (Mailliard collection), the Colorado Museum of Natural History (Bradbury collection), Mr. Richard C. Harlow, Col. John E. Thayer, and the University of California (Grinnell collection).

In outlining the breeding ranges of the ducks, no attempt has been made to mention all of the many cases recorded of northern breeding species which have lingered for the summer and bred far south of their normal breeding ranges, as such birds are often cripples; only a few cases have been mentioned which seemed to be casual breeding records of normal birds.

The author regrets that, in a general work of this kind, he did not feel justified in giving detailed descriptions of the interesting plumage changes of the ducks; so the sequences of molts and plumages have been only briefly indicated with sufficient descriptions to make them recognizable. The reader, who wishes to make a more thorough study of this subject, is referred to the splendid monographs of the ducks by Mr. John G. Millais and to the full and accurate descriptions of the various plumages by Miss Annie C. Jackson, in A Practical Handbook of British Birds, edited by Mr. H. F. Witherby.

The old check list is now so far out of date that it seems unwise to follow it in the use of scientific names. Therefore, Dr. Charles W. Richmond and Dr. Harry C. Oberholser have kindly furnished the scientific names for this volume, which, according to their best judgment, most satisfactorily represent our present knowledge.

THE AUTHOR.

TABLE OF CONTENTS.

Page.

Family Anatidae... 1
  Mergus merganser americanus... 1
  American merganser... 1
    Habits... 1
    Distribution... 12
  Mergus serrator... 13
  Red-breasted merganser... 13
    Habits... 13
    Distribution... 21
  Lophodytes cucullatus... 22
  Hooded merganser... 22
    Habits... 22
    Distribution... 29
  Mergellus albellus... 30
  Smew... 30
    Habits... 30
    Distribution... 34
  Anas platyrhyncha... 34
  Mallard... 34
    Habits... 34
    Distribution... 46
  Anas novimexicana... 48
  New Mexican duck... 48
    Habits... 48
    Distribution... 50
  Anas rubripes tristis... 50
  Black duck... 50
    Habits... 50
    Distribution... 63
  Anas rubripes rubripes... 64
  Red-legged black duck... 64
    Habits... 64
  Anas fulvigula fulvigula... 68
  Florida duck... 68
    Habits... 68
    Distribution... 72
  Anas fulvigula maculosa... 72
  Mottled duck... 72
    Habits... 72
    Distribution... 75
  Eunetta falcata... 75
  Falcated teal... 75
    Habits... 75
    Distribution... 77
  Chaulelasmus streperus... 77
  Gadwall... 77
    Habits... 77
    Distribution... 84
  Mareca penelope... 86
  European widgeon... 86
    Habits... 86
    Distribution... 88
  Mareca americana... 89

Family Anatidae—Continued.   **Page.**

Baldpate... 89
   Habits.. 89
   Distribution.. 97
Nettion crecca... 98
European teal.. 98
   Habits.. 98
   Distribution.. 101
Nettion carolinense.. 102
Green-winged teal.. 102
   Habits.. 102
   Distribution.. 109
Querguedula discors.. 111
Blue-winged teal... 111
   Habits.. 111
   Distribution.. 120
Querquedula cyanoptera... 122
Cinnamon teal.. 122
   Habits.. 122
   Distribution.. 129
Casarca ferruginea... 130
Ruddy sheldrake.. 130
   Habits.. 130
   Distribution.. 131
Tadorna tadorna.. 132
Sheld duck... 132
   Habits.. 132
   Distribution.. 135
Spatula clypeata... 135
Shoveller.. 135
   Habits.. 135
   Distribution.. 142
Dafila acuta tzitzihoa... 144
American pintail... 144
   Habits.. 144
   Distribution.. 154
Poecilonetta bahamensis.. 156
Bahama pintail... 156
   Habits.. 156
   Distribution.. 158
Aix sponsa... 158
Wood duck.. 158
   Habits.. 158
   Distribution.. 170
Netta rufina... 171
Rufous-crested duck.. 171
   Habits.. 171
   Distribution.. 175
Nyroca americana... 175
Redhead.. 175
   Habits.. 175
   Distribution.. 184
Aithyia ferina... 185
European pochard... 185
   Habits.. 185
   Distribution.. 189
Aristonetta valisineria.. 189
Canvasback... 189
   Habits.. 189
   Distribution.. 201
Fuligula fuligula.. 202
Tufted duck.. 202
   Habits.. 202
   Distribution.. 206
Fulix marila nearctica... 207
American scaup duck.. 207
   Habits.. 207
   Distribution.. 215

Family Anatidae—Continued.   **Page.**
    Fulix affinis..   217
    Lesser scaup duck..   217
        Habits..   217
        Distribution..   223
    Perissonetta collaris..   224
    Ring-necked duck..   224
        Habits..   224
        Distribution..   229
References to bibliography..   231
Index...   241

LIFE HISTORIES OF NORTH AMERICAN WILDFOWL, ORDER ANSERES (PART).

By ARTHUR CLEVELAND BENT,
Of Taunton, Massachusetts.

Family ANATIDAE, Ducks, Geese, and Swans.

MERGUS MERGANSER AMERICANUS Cassin.

AMERICAN MERGANSER.

HABITS.

Spring.—This large and handsome duck has always been associated in my mind with the first signs of the breaking up of winter. Being a hardy species, it lingers on the southern border of ice and snow and is the very first of our waterfowl to start on its spring migration. We may confidently look for it in New England during the first warm days in February or as soon as the ice has begun to break up in our rivers and lakes. We are glad to greet these welcome harbingers of spring, for the sight of the handsome drakes flying along our water courses or circling high in the air over our frozen lakes, with their brilliant colors flashing in the winter sunshine, reminds us of the migratory hosts that are soon to follow. They are looking for open water in the rivers, for rifts in the ice or open borders around the shores of the lakes, where the first warm sunshine has tempted the earliest fish to seek the genial shallows, but they are often doomed to disappointment, for winter lingers in the lap of spring and again locks the lakes with solid ice driving the hardy pioneers back to winter quarters. The drakes are always the first to arrive and the females follow a few weeks later. Mr. Fred A. Shaw writes to me that in Maine—"The males generally make their appearance in March and in a short time select their mates, leaving early in April for their breeding grounds."

Courtship.—Perhaps the best account of the courtship of this species is given by Dr. Charles W. Townsend (1916), as follows:

A group of five or six male mergansers may be seen swimming energetically back and forth by three or four passive females. Sometimes the drakes swim in a compact mass or in a file for six or seven yards or even farther, and then each turns abruptly

1

and swims back. Again they swim in and out among each other, and every now and then one with swelling breast and slightly raised wings spurts ahead at great speed by himself or in the pursuit of a rival. The birds suggest swift motor boats by the waves which curl up on either side, and by the rapidity with which they turn and swash around. Again they suggest polo ponies, as one in rapid course pushes sidewise against a rival, in order to keep him away from the object of the quest. They frequently strike at each other with their bills, and I have seen two splendid drakes rise up in the water breast to breast, and, amid a great splashing, during which it was impossible to see details, fight like gamecocks. The pursuit is varied by sudden, momentary dives and much splashing of water.

The smooth iridescent green heads, the brilliant carmine bills tipped with black nails, the snowy white of flanks and wing patches and the red feet, which flash out in the dive, make a wonderful color effect, contrasting well with the dark water and white ice. The smaller females, with their shaggy brown heads, their neat white throat bibs, their quaker blue-gray backs and modest wing patches, which are generally hidden, are fitting foils to their mates. I have reserved for the last the mention of the delicate salmon yellow tint of the lower breast and the belly of the male, a coloration of which he is deservedly proud, for, during courtship, he frequently raises himself up almost onto his tail with or without a flapping of the wings and reveals this color, in the same way that the eider displays his jet-black shield. Most of the time he keeps his tail cocked up and spread, so that it shows from behind a white center and blue border. Every now and then he points his head and closed bill up at an angle of 45° or to the zenith. Again he bows or bobs his head nervously and often at the same time tilts up the front of his breast from which flashes out the salmon tint. From time to time he emits a quickly repeated purring note, "dorr-dorr" or "krr-krr."

The most surprising part of the performance is the spurt of water fully 3 or 4 feet long which every now and then is sent backward into the air by the powerful kick of the drake's foot. It is similar to the performance of the whistler but much greater, and while the foot of the whistler is easily seen and is plainly a part of the display, it is difficult to see the red foot of the merganser in the rush of water, although it is evident, doubtless, to the females. The display of the brilliantly colored foot in both species is probably the primary sexual display, and the splash, at first incidental and secondary, has now become of primary importance.

During all this time the female swims about unconcernedly, merely keeping out of the way of the ardent and belligerent males, although she sometimes joins in the dance and bobs in a mild way. At last she succumbs to the captivating display and submerges herself so that only a small part of her body with a bit of the crest appear above the water, and she swims slowly beside or after her mate, sometimes even touching him with her bill. Later she remains motionless, flattens herself still more, the crest disappears, and she sinks so that only a line like that made by a board floating on the water is seen. One would never imagine it to be a live duck. The drake slowly swims around her several times, twitches his head and neck, picks at the water, at his own feathers, and at her before he mounts and completely submerges her holding tightly with his bill to her neck meanwhile. Then she bathes herself, washes the water vigorously through her feathers and flaps her wings; the drake stretches himself and flaps his wings likewise. From the beginning of submergence by the female the process is the same in all the duck family that I have observed.

Nesting.—On the nesting habits of the American merganser there has been much discussion and many conflicting opinions, some asserting that it always nests in hollow trees or that it never nests on the ground. As a matter of fact it does both, for its nesting habits vary greatly in different localities or even with different individuals in the same locality. Major Bendire carried on an extensive correspondence with Mr. Manly Hardy on this subject and the latter was finally convinced that the goosander, as he called it, does occasionally nest on the ground. On June 12, 1891, Mr. Hardy wrote that, in passing through Caribou Lake, June 8, he found three nests, containing 26 eggs, on ledges under low fir bushes, which settled the controversy. I believe, however, that in the Eastern States and Provinces this merganser prefers to nest in hollow trees where it can find suitable cavities, which are usually scarce. Mr. Fred A. Shaw, who has had 30 years' experience with this species in the vicinity of Sebago Lake, Maine, contributes the following notes on its nesting habits:

A few breed around Sebago, especially near the mouth of Songo River, the principal tributary, where there is a large area of bog, flooded in spring, through which are scattered large hollow trees providing safe nesting places for them. The nest of this species is commonly placed in a hollow tree standing near the water and is composed of feathers and down from the breast of the parent bird. A nest of this bird near Whites Bridge at the outlet of Sebago Lake was shown me in May, 1897. It was in a white birch stub which was broken off about 15 feet from the ground and was hollow for about 10 feet from the top and contained 10 eggs, which were laid at the bottom of the hole on a warm bed of soft down from the breast of the mother bird.

Mr. Hardy wrote that it nested in hollow trees, usually hardwood trees, such as maples and ashes, and often in green trees. Mr. John H. Sage (1881) found a nest on an island in Moosehead Lake. Maine, on June 19, 1881—

in a hollow under the roots of a standing tree, roots, earth, and moss forming a perfect roof, so that the nest, after the heavy shower of that day, seemed well protected and was quite dry. The eggs were covered with leaves, moss, and feathers—mostly feathers. The old bird was seen to leave the nest.

On Lake Winnipegosis and Waterhen Lake, Manitoba, we found the American merganser very common and nesting on the numerous islands, wherever suitable nesting sites could be found among the piles of loose bowlders along the shores. Mr. Walter Raine found as many as 30 nests of this species on Gun Island, a large island in Lake Winnipegosis. On one island that we visited the Indians had collected about 60 eggs of the "saw bills," as they call them, a short time previously. The nests were very well hidden in remote crevices under the piles of large bowlders; many of them were quite inaccessible, where the bowlders were too large for us to move them. We often saw mergansers flying away from islands where we felt sure that they were nesting, but where we were unable to find or reach the nests. A few nests were found in the dense tangles of gooseberry bushes and nettles on the tops of the islands where hunting for them was difficult and painful unless a telltale path, strewn with feathers and droppings, told us just where to look.

Near the north end of Lake Winnipegosis, on Whiskey Jack Island, we visited, on June 18, 1913, a deserted ice house where we were told that we might find the "little saw bills," hooded mergansers, nesting. It was an old tumbled-down affair, with the roof nearly gone and partly filled with loosely piled bales of hay; there did not seem to be any suitable nesting sites for "saw bills" anywhere in the vicinity, so we sat down to eat our luncheon. While so occupied we were surprised to see a female American merganser fly up and alight on the landing and gaze longingly into the ice house. We then began an exhaustive search by moving the bales of hay and crawling into the crevices between them. While peering into a dark cavity I thought I saw something moving regularly like a breathing duck; we pulled away some more bales and there sat a female merganser on her nest within 2 feet of my face; I reached in to catch her but she slipped away and escaped through another passage way. There were 15 eggs under her in a nest profusely lined with white down, mixed with hay. Further search revealed another nest near by, similarly located; the bird had left the nest and had carefully covered the 12 eggs which it contained with a soft blanket down. Lieut. I. T. Van Kammen (1915) found two nests in an old, abandoned lighthouse tower; the nests were about 3 feet apart and "each nest was placed in a depression, perhaps 5 inches deep, scraped out of the soft dirt of the lighthouse floor."

Audubon (1840) gives an attractive account of finding the nest of a goosander on a marshy island. He describes the nesting site and nest as follows:

The islands on which the goosander is wont to breed are mostly small, as if selected for the purpose of allowing the sitting bird to get soon to the water in case of danger. The nest is very large, at times raised 7 or 8 inches on the top of a bed of all the dead weeds which the bird can gather in the neighborhood. Properly speaking, the real nest, however, is not larger than that of the dusky duck, and is rather neatly formed externally of fibrous roots and lined round the edges with the down of the bird. The interior is about 7½ inches in diameter and 4 inches in depth.

Mr. W. L. Dawson (1909) says of its nesting habits in Washington:

Now and then a crevice in the face of a cliff does duty, and old nests of hawk or crow have been pressed into service. Moderate elevations are favored, but Mr. Bowles once found a nest near Puget Sound in a decayed fir stub at a height of over a hundred feet. The cavity, wherever found, is warmly lined with weeds, grasses, and rootlets, and plentifully supplied with down from the bird's breast.

Mr. Fred H. Andrus (1896) thus describes a nest which he found in Oregon:

May 26, 1895, I collected a set of 10 American merganser's eggs from a hole in the rocks about 100 feet above the Umpqua River. The nest was about 15 feet from the top of a nearly perpendicular cliff about 50 feet in height, and was found by watching the bird. In going to the nest the bird would fly up and down the river in an oval course several times, and finally, coming close to the water as if to light, would rise to the nest. The entrance to the hole was 6 inches by 12, and the inside dimensions 4 feet long, 2 feet deep, and 18 inches high. The nest was about 1 foot in diameter, of down mixed with moss, one-half inch thick in the center and thicker around the edges.

Eggs.—The American merganser raises but one brood in a season and lays from 6 to 17 eggs; some writers say that it lays from 6 to 10 eggs, but I think these small sets must have been incomplete or second attempts; I should say that the commonest numbers would run between 9 and 12, but I have personally taken sets of 15 and 16. The eggs are usually distinctive, and typical eggs are not easily mistaken for anything else. The female is difficult to distinguish from the female red-breasted merganser when she flies from the nest, though she is a decidedly heavier looking bird and has more white in the wings. The down, however, in the American merganser's nest is much whiter than that in the nest of the red-breasted and the color of the eggs is different. The down is grayish white in color, about No. 10 gray of Ridgway, or "pale gull gray," and it is usually mixed with numerous pure white breast feathers and considerable rubbish or bits of straw. The eggs of the American merganser are very pale buff or "ivory yellow." The shell is thick and strong, with little, if any, luster. The shape varies from elliptical ovate to elliptical oval.

The measurements of 93 eggs in various collections average 64.3 by 44.9 millimeters; the eggs showing the four extremes measure **72** by 46, 64 by **50, 55.4** by 38.5 and 56.7 by **37** millimeters.

The drakes desert the ducks and usually disappear from the breeding grounds entirely as soon as the eggs are laid, leaving the females to perform the duties of incubation and care for the young alone. In Newfoundland we saw only females on the lakes, where they were busy with family cares, but we saw plenty of males on the swift-water rivers, playing in the rapids and fishing in the pools. Several observers in Maine have said that the males are not seen during the summer, but this may be due to the fact that the males are in eclipse plumage at this time and are very shy and retiring. Mergansers which nest in hollow trees are usually very close sitters, and it is often impossible to drive a sitting bird from her nest by pounding the tree; on the other hand those which nest on the ground on islands usually slip away long before the intruder reaches the vicinity of the nest, often before a boat lands on the island; a deviation from either of these habits would, in either case, tend to reveal the nest. Fresh eggs, taken from incomplete sets in Manitoba and hatched in our incubators, showed an incubation period of 28 days.

Young.—Several writers state that the young mergansers are carried from a nest in a hollow tree to the water, in the bill of the parent bird; Millais (1913) says that Mr. Oswin Lee has seen a female goosander carry down nine young ones out of the nest, and that she "carried them partly in her beak, partly between the beak and the breast."

Mr. Shaw, however, offers the following evidence to the contrary:

An interesting occurrence in connection with the breeding of this bird was related to me by Mr. G. H. Moses, who while in camp at Songo River had exceptional opportunity to observe them. In the spring of 1896 a nest was located in a tall hollow tree where it could be readily seen from his camp door. After the young were hatched Mr. Moses saw the mother bird alight in the water at the foot of the stub in which the nest was located and commence to call to the young birds in the nest. Immediately the little ones came tumbling down one after another from the hole in the tree top to the water and at once swam away with their mother.

Mr. William S. Post (1914) has twice witnessed a similar performance; the following is his account of it:

It was my good fortune to witness twice the emerging of a young brood of mergansers from an extreme situation of this kind, an old pileated woodpecker's hole about 40 feet high in the limb of a live elm, standing about 15 feet from the edge of the Tobique River in New Brunswick.

On June 18, 1910, I fished the famous salmon pool at the fork of the river, and having incidentally run the canoe close to the shore near where this old elm stands, I landed and rapped several times sharply on the tree with a stick, for I had been told that a wood duck—which on the Tobique means a golden eye—nested there the previous spring. The female merganser immediately flew out and having circled about over the river, alighted on the water. After assuring myself of the identification, which caused me some astonishment on account of the size of the bird in proportion to the entrance of the hole, I returned to my fishing.

In a few moments I noticed a small bird drop down apparently from the hole, and in a few more seconds another and then a third. My first thought was that a bank swallow, of which there are many on the river, had flown up near to the hole and down again three times in succession. This caused me to stop fishing and to watch, when to my astonishment a small bird with white breast appeared in the hole, jumped out, and was followed by another, and again another. I then lost no time in reaching a point in the river opposite the tree, where I saw in the water against the bank, swimming around, a brood of 11 young ducks. I was much surprised, as I had been under the impression from what I had read that the old duck would certainly carry down the young from such an inaccessible position, and though I believe the young birds must have landed in the water, I was yet astonished that they could withstand the shock of such a drop, and I presumed that by rapping on the tree I had caused the old bird to leave in such fright that her fear had been communicated to the young and they had followed her example, and that the whole procedure was therefore an unnatural one.

The clubhouse is situated directly across the river, and on June 12, 1913, two years later, I was sitting on the piazza when my attention was attracted by seeing something large drop from the top of this same elm into the water. I immediately saw that it was the old sheldrake and that she was swimming around close to the shore.

In a few seconds another dropped from the hole to the ground and I could see it run down the bank and join its mother who was calling loudly and turning round and round in the water. This one was quickly followed by others in succession until there were seven. By this time I had called my guide and in company of one of the members of the club was crossing the river, provided with trout-landing nets.

The old bird seeing us immediately swam upstream and around the point with her brood and this was the last we saw of her. We landed and stood under the tree where we could hear distinctly more young ducks peeping in the hole. Looking up we saw one tottering on the edge, and before we could take stations where we could properly observe the actual drop he had struck the ground close to my friend and made such rapid progress toward the water that he escaped in spite of landing nets. In a few seconds another, which proved to be the last, followed, falling on the other side of the tree, and I promptly made him captive. The first bird was in the water and had immediately dived. It is strange that he should have known enough to seek the water, and also to dive immediately.

After a day or two of rest in the nest, probably longer in tree nests than in those on the ground, the young have dried off their down and gained sufficient strength to take to the water, where they are very precocious. The downy young are very handsome and attractive. It is a beautiful sight to see a female merganser swimming in the clear calm water of some mountain lake or wilderness stream, where the mirrored reflections of picturesque scenery and forest trees make a splendid setting for the picture of a swiftly gliding, graceful duck followed by a procession of pretty little balls of down, with perhaps one or two of them riding on her back. If danger threatens she quickens her pace, but the little fellows are good swimmers and keep right at her heels; even if she dives they can follow her under water, working their little paddles vigorously and darting along like so many fish. If too hard pressed she rises and flaps along the surface, half flying; they can almost keep up with her at this pace, for they can run along the surface as fast as we can paddle our canoe. They soon become exhausted with some exertion, so she leads them into some sheltered cove, where they can run up on the shore and hide in the grass, or even up into the thick woods, where it is almost hopeless to hunt for them; it is surprising to see how quickly the young and even the mother bird can disappear. Millais (1913) relates the following interesting incident:

When rushing down the swift rivers of Newfoundland in my canoe, I have often wondered at the resource or natural instinct of the broods of goosander and their mothers which remain perfectly still when suddenly confronted with danger. As the little boat flies down a rapid, swiftly passing silent pools in the rock eddies at the sides, I have often turned my head and noticed a female goosander and her nearly full-grown young. On a lake or open stretch of the river, knowing that concealment was impossible, the mother would have dashed out in the open, and either hurried by flapping along the surface to the middle of the lake, or, in the case of the river, downstream, and so endeavor to escape. When suddenly confronted within a few yards in the eddies of the rapids, she felt that such a method of escape was useless, and with swift intuition remained perfectly still, each member of the brood keeping the neck held stiffly, so that the whole party looked like the stiff twigs of an upturned tree. This sudden assimilation to surroundings, so wonderfully exhibited in the common or little bittern amid the rushes, seems to be a natural instinct in all birds, and they often adopt it as a last resort.

Plumages.—Downy young mergansers are beautiful creatures; the upper parts, including the crown, down to the lores and eyes, hind neck, and back, are rich deep "bister" or "warm sepia," relieved by the white edging of the wing and a large white spot on each side of the rump; the sides of the head and neck are "mikado brown" or "pecan brown", shading off on the neck to "light vinaceous cinnamon" or "buff pink;" a pure white stripe extends from the lores to a point below the eyes and it is bordered above and below by dark-brown stripes; the rest of the lower parts are pure white. The nostril is in the central third of the bill, instead of in the basal third, as in the red-breasted merganser.

In the juvenal plumage, which is acquired at about the time that the young bird attains its growth, the sexes are practically indistinguishable except that the male is slightly larger. This plumage is similar to that of the adult female except that, in the young bird, the white throat extends down to the chest, whereas, in the adult female, the lower throat is brown. The wing pattern is also different in young males, which have the outer secondaries white and the inner secondaries gray. During the fall and winter an almost continual molt is in progress, black feathers appearing in the head and neck, producing a mottled effect, and vermiculated feathers appearing in the flanks. The tail is renewed in the spring but not the wings. The first postnuptial molt, which can hardly be said to involve an eclipse plumage, takes place in August and September; this molt is complete and is prolonged through October at least; by November, when the bird is nearly a year and a half old, the adult plumage is complete.

Millais (1913) says:

In May the adult male goosander begins to assume its eclipse plumage. The adult male in August has the crown reddish brown, with a gray tinge; chin white, and the rest of the head and upper neck rich red brown. There is a black mark in front of the eye, and a whitish line from this to the lower angle of the upper mandible. The lower neck is blue gray, interspersed with creamy white; mantle, flanks, scapulars, back, and tail blue gray; the flanks have a few white feathers on the outer sides, vermiculated with brownish gray; the last inner secondaries only change from black to black; wings as in winter, and now changing as usual only once; under parts not so rosy as in winter. In early September the wings and tail are renewed, and the black feathers on the mantle come in. After this the whole plumage proceeds to molt slowly, the full winter dress not being assumed until early December.

Subsequent molts of adult males consist of a postnuptial molt of the contour feathers early in the summer into the eclipse plumage, a molt of the flight feathers in August or September, and a complete molt of the contour feathers out of the eclipse plumage in the fall. Females probably do not make the double molt of the contour feathers but have a complete molt in the late summer.

Food.—The merganser is primarily a fishing duck, at which it is very skillful and a voracious feeder. It pursues under water and catches successfully the swiftest fish. Often a party of sheldrakes may be seen fishing together, driving the panic-stricken fish into the shallows or into some small pool where they may be more easily caught. Mr. Hardy writes:

They fish in companies; as fast as they come up the hind ones run ahead of those in front of them and dive again, being in turn succeeded by others. I have seen them fishing on quick water in very cold weather until January 7. They feed exclusively on fish, several often uniting to capture one of large size. Last year we took a pickerel from a party of them which measured 14 inches in length; also took from one's throat a chub which, with head decomposed, measured 10 inches.

One of these gluttonous birds will often attempt to swallow a larger fish than it can dispose of, leaving the tail of the fish protruding from its mouth while the head is digesting. Mr. Shaw found in the "stomach" of one bird "13 perch, a few of which were nearly 3 inches in length."

Audubon (1840) says:

I have found fishes in its stomach 7 inches in length, and of smaller kinds so many as to weigh more than half a pound. Digestion takes place with great rapidity, insomuch that some which I have fed in captivity devoured more than two dozen of fishes about 4 inches in length, four times daily, and yet always seemed to be desirous of more.

Mr. Harry S. Swarth (1911) describes the following manner of feeding, which is unusual for this species:

I was concealed in the shrubbery at the water's edge examining a large flock of ducks for possible rarities, when a dozen or more mergansers (both *M. americanus* and *M. serrator*) began swimming back and forth but a very short distance from my blind. They swam slowly, with neck outstretched, and with the bill held just at the surface of the water, and at a slight angle, so that the head was submerged about to the level of the eyes. The water was evidently filtered through the bill, as a slight "gabbling" noise was quite audible, and obviously something was being retained as food, though just what it was I could not tell. This is rather remarkable, as it is exactly the manner of feeding usually employed by the shoveller (*Spatula clypeata*), a species which, as regards bill structure, is further removed from the mergansers than any other member of the Anatidae.

Mr. Ora W. Knight (1908) says:

Along the coast in winter they eat many mussels and allied species of mollusks, swallowing them shell and all. The shells are soon ground to pieces in their intestines and stomachs, and in dead birds dissected out I have traced the entire process from entire mussel shells down to impalpable mud at the lower end of the intestinal tract.

In the early spring, when live fish are difficult to obtain, they seem to enjoy frozen, rotten fish with the same gusto as fresh, picking them out of the floating ice. They also feed to some extent on frogs, small eels, aquatic salamanders, crawfish, and other small crustaceans, various bivalve mollusks and snails, leeches, worms, water insects and larvae, and the stems and roots of aquatic plants.

Behavior.—The American merganser is a heavy-bodied bird and sometimes experiences considerable difficulty in rising from the water; if the circumstances are not favorable, it has to patter along the surface for a considerable distance; when flying off an island it often does the same thing unless it gets a good start from some high place, so that it can swoop downward. In swift water it has to rise downstream, as it can make no headway against the current; but it generally prefers to fly upstream if it can. Mr. Aretas A. Saunders writes to me, in regard to the flight of mated pairs, noted in Montana, "that they flew off, with the male in the lead in each case," also "that they left the water flying in a long, low slant upstream, not rising high enough to see them above the willows that lined the stream until they had flown a considerable distance." When well under way the flight of this species is strong, swift, and direct; on its breeding grounds it usually flies low, along the courses of rivers or about the shores of lakes, seldom rising above the tree tops; but on its migrations it flies in small flocks, high in the air with great velocity. The drake may be easily recognized in flight by its large size, loonlike shape, its black and white appearance above, dark green head and white underparts; its flight is said to resemble that of the mallard. The female closely resembles the female red-breasted merganser, but it is a more heavily built bird, has a more continuous white patch in the wings, the white tips of the greater coverts overlapping the black bases of the secondaries, giving the appearance of a large white speculum, whereas in the red-breasted merganser the black bases of the secondaries show below the greater coverts, forming a black stripe through the middle of the white speculum. When flying to its nest cavity in a tree or cliff it rises in a long upward curve and enters the hole with speed and precision. Mr. Harry S. Swarth (1911) refers to—

a peculiar habit which made this species quite conspicuous throughout the summer, was that of individuals rising high in the air and circling about for hours at a time, uttering at frequent and regular intervals a most unmelodious squawk. Both sexes were observed doing this, and the habit was kept up until about the end of August.

This sheldrake is probably the most expert diver of its tribe, being built somewhat like a loon and approaching it in aquatic ability. It can sink quietly down into the water like a grebe or dive quickly with a forward curving plunge, clearing the water for a foot or more, as it does so. It swims swiftly on the surface, but can attain even higher speed below it, where few fish can escape it. Dr. Charles W. Townsend (1909) infers from its method of diving, that the wings are not used when swimming under water and he quotes a statement from Selous to the same effect; he says:

The American and the red-breasted merganser both dive like the cormorant. They often leap clear of the water, in graceful curves, with their wings cleaving closely to the sides. At other times the leap is much curtailed, or they sink beneath the surface without apparent effort. I should infer, therefore, that the wings were not used under water.

On the other hand I quote from Mr. Walter H. Rich (1907) as follows:

Seen under the water in pursuit of a breakfast or dodging about to escape capture when wounded the resemblance to some finny dweller of the sea is very marked— head and neck outstretched, every feather hugged closely to the body, the half-opened wings like large fins aiding the feet in their work, he goes shooting through the water like a flash.

Probably both observers are correct, for birds are not bound by hard and fast rules. The rapidity with which this species can dive from the air is remarkable. While in full flight it plunges into the water, swims below the surface for a distance and then suddenly emerges and continues its flight. Millais (1913) says of its behavior on land:

The walk is very heavy and rolling, and the feet are placed on the ground deliberately, whilst the bill is pointed downward, and each step taken as if the bird was afraid of tripping or falling. They seldom go more than a yard or two from the water's edge, but can run quite swiftly for a few yards if suddenly surprised. In winter it is a very rare event to see goosanders ashore, but in spring they often leave the water, and will spend hours sleeping and preening on some small island or point of land. No birds are more industrious in their toilet than the mergansers in spring, and most of their time, when not feeding, flying, or sleeping, is spent in polishing up their plumage and bathing.

Of the vocal performances of this species I know very little; I have never heard a sheldrake utter a sound, so far as I can remember, and very little seems to have been written on the subject. Audubon (1840) describes the notes of the goosander as "harsh, consisting of hoarse croaks, seldom uttered unless the bird be suddenly startled or when courting."

Game.—As they live almost exclusively on fish, sheldrakes are not considered good table birds and so are not much sought after by gunners. But young sheldrakes are not unpalatable, and many gunners shoot them regularly for food. They do not come to decoys, but, as they are swift fliers and hard to kill, shooting them is good sport. Many sportsmen feel justified in killing them on account of the large numbers of trout which they consume; but this is hardly justifiable, for they also destroy many predatory fish, such as pickerel and thus help to preserve the balance of nature.

Fall.—The name "pond sheldrake" has been applied to this species because it shows more preference for fresh water than its relative, the red-breasted merganser, its fall migration is more inland, where it flies along our larger water courses and frequents our lakes and ponds until it is forced coastwise by the freezing of its favorite resorts.

Winter.—But even in winter it still lingers wherever it can find open water near its summer home and its migration is one of the shortest. Mr. Shaw says that, at Sebago Lake, Maine—

a few remain through the winter in the coldest weather spending the day in the open water at the foot of the lake and in the upper part of Presumpscot River, its outlet, and at night leaving for the salt water.

It is more common on the coast of New England than in the interior in the winter, but it winters in large numbers in some of the Great Lakes and on the large rivers of the interior, especially in the rapids and about the cascades of clear-water streams. The icy waters of our northern streams have no terrors for this hardy fisherman provided it can find open water and plenty of food. Rev. Manley B. Townsend writes to me:

Every winter during my residence in Nashua, N. H., 1912–1918, I noted considerable numbers of these "fish ducks" as they are locally called, between Manchester and Nashua. Even in the coldest, most inclement weather, when the Merrimack was frozen several feet deep, these birds could be seen sitting on the ice about the rapids, where the swiftly flowing water kept the river free from ice, or swimming and diving in careless abandon. I once counted 40 on the ice or in the water at a single rapid. Fish seemed to be abundant. The birds apparently wintered well.

DISTRIBUTION.

Breeding range.—Northern States and Canada entirely across the continent. South to west central Nova Scotia (Gaspereaux Lakes), southern Maine (Washington to Cumberland Counties), central New Hampshire (White Mountain region), central Vermont (Windsor County), central New York (Adirondacks and Cayuga County), southern Ontario (Parry Sound and Red Bay), central Michigan (Josco County), northeastern Wisconsin (Dorr County), southwestern Minnesota (Heron Lake), southwestern South Dakota (Black Hills), northern New Mexico (near Santa Fe), north central Arizona (Fort Verde), and central California (Tulare County). South formerly, and perhaps casually now, to the mountain regions of western Massachusetts, central Pennsylvania and in Ohio. North to the base of the Alaska Peninsula (Iak Lake), southern Yukon (Lake Tagish), southern Mackenzie (Great Slave Lake), Hudson Bay (York Factory and Norway House), southern Ungava, central Labrador (Hamilton River), and Newfoundland (Humber River).

Winter range.—Mainly within the United States, including practically all of them. South to central western Florida (Tampa Bay); the Gulf coasts of Alabama, Louisiana, and Texas; northern Mexico (Sonora and Chihuahua); and northern Lower California (Colorado delta). North to the Aleutian Islands, rarely to the Pribilof Islands, regularly to southern British Columbia (Chilliwack and Comox), the Great Lakes, the St. Lawrence valley, and Prince Edward Island.

Spring migration.—Early dates of arrival: Ontario, Ottawa, February 25; Labrador, Hamilton River, May 28; Minnesota, Heron Lake, March 17; Wisconsin, Milwaukee, March 1. Average dates of arrival: Vermont, St. Johnsbury, March 17; Quebec, Montreal, April 5; Ontario, Ottawa, April 16; Prince Edward Island, April 21; Iowa, Hillsboro, March 28; Minnesota, Heron Lake, March 26; Manitoba, Aweme, April 11. Dates of departure: Maryland, March 29; Pennsylvania, Erie, April 7; Connecticut, April 17; Rhode Island, Newport, April 25.

Fall migration.—Average dates of arrival: Massachusetts, October 5; Chesapeake Bay, October 15 (earliest September 29). Average dates of departure: Prince Edward Island, November 1; Quebec, Montreal, November 6; Ontario, Ottawa, November 21 (latest November 26).

Casual records.—Accidental in the Aleutian Islands (Unalaska, May 26, 1906).

Egg dates.—Maine and Nova Scotia: Five records, May 22 to June 8. Michigan: Six records, May 13 to 30. Manitoba: Four records, June 16 to 19. California and Oregon: Three records, April 2, May 21 and June 20.

MERGUS SERRATOR Linnaeus.

RED-BREASTED MERGANSER.

HABITS.

Contributed by Charles Wendell Townsend.

The red-breasted merganser, or sheldrake, as it is commonly called in New England, the "bec-scie" or "saw bill" of the Acadians, although often hunted, is generally classed as a fish duck and considered almost worthless. But there are other things in life besides bread and meat and dollars and cents, and the esthetic appreciation of this, as well as of many other "worthless" birds, is surely increasing.

The drake in his newly acquired nuptial plumage is resplendent with a metallic green headdress and waving crest, the whole set off by a long coral-red bill. The white ring about his neck, the reddish brown and speckled breast, the snowy flanks and wing patches, and the dark back all go to create a picture of great beauty as he swims or dives or restlessly flies to and fro among the breakers. The females and young in their more modest suits of drab and brown are not to be despised from an esthetic point of view. They, too, like the drakes, are furnished with crests.

The great multitudes of these birds off the New England coast in winter is a wonderful sight and most satisfying to the bird lover, especially as there seems to be no doubt that the numbers have increased of late years. This increase is doubtless due partly to the better enforcement of game laws and to the stopping of spring shooting, but also to the fact that the great island of Anticosti in the Gulf of St. Lawrence has become a veritable haven for breeding birds since M. Meunier, the French chocolate king, has debarred all guns from this, his domain.   During the last of October and the first part of November for several miles off Ipswich Beach the water is covered with these birds, and I have no doubt that the multitude at times numbers 25,000.

Spring.—The spring migration of this bird is at its height on the New England coast in March and April, but it also continues through May.   Although it does not, as a rule, breed south of southern Maine, it is not uncommon to find two or three nonbreeding birds from place to place along the coast in summer as far south as Cape Cod.

Courtship.—The courtship of the red-breasted merganser is a spectacular performance.   I (1911) have described it as observed at Ipswich as follows:

The nuptial performance is always at its best when several drakes are displaying their charms of movement, voice, and plumage, before a single duck, and each vies with the other in the ardor of the courtship.   The drake begins by stretching up his long neck so that the white ring is much broadened, and the metallic green head, with its long crest and its narrow red bill, makes a conspicuous object.   At once the bill is opened wide and the whole bird stiffly bobs or teeters, as if on a pivot, in such a way the breast and the lower part of the neck are immersed, while the tail and posterior part of the body swing upward.   This motion brings the neck and head from a vertical position to an angle of 45°.   All the motions are stiffly executed, and suggest a formal but ungraceful courtesy.

This song, emitted when the bill is opened, is a difficult one to describe, but easily recognized when once heard, and remains long in the memory after one has heard it repeated over and over again by a number of merganser suitors.   It is a loud, rough, and purring, slightly double note which I wrote down "da-ah," but the note is probably insusceptible of expression by syllables.

The bobbing and the love note may be given twice in rapid succession, although at times the performance is a single one, or may consist of an extensive bob, preceded by a slighter but similar one.   The performance is, however, repeated at frequent or infrequent intervals, depending on the ardor and number of the suitors, and, no doubt, on the attitude of the modestly dressed lady.

Although the female merganser may remain passive and coyly indifferent, as is the habit of her sex, she sometimes responds by a bobbing which is similar to that of the male, but of considerably less range.   That is to say, the neck is not stretched so straight up, and the breast is not so much depressed during the bob.   She emits a single note at this time, which is somewhat louder than that of the male and is of a different quality as it is decidedly rasping.   As nearly as I can remember this note is similar to the rough croaks I have heard given by these birds in Labrador when they were flying to and from their nests.

When the female responds in this manner she appears to be very excited, and the ardor of the drakes is correspondingly increased, if one may judge by the frequent repetition of the love antics and notes, and by the fact that they crowd about the duck.   Every now and then she darts out her neck and dashes at the ring of suitors, just as the female English sparrow does under similar circumstances.

The bobbing up of the stern of the male is the more conspicuous as the wings are then apparently slightly arched upwards, so that the white secondary feathers are very prominent.   These show at all times as the male swims in the water, but in the female they are generally, but not always, invisible.

The drakes, in their eagerness, often rush through the water with slightly opened wings making the water foam about them. Again they rise in the water with wings close to the side until they almost seem to stand on tip-toe.

Nesting.—The nest of the red-breasted merganser is built on the ground, and, although the bird is marine in its haunts, the nest is generally situated in the borders of fresh-water ponds, pools, or rivers, often, however, in close proximity to the seacoast. Occasionally it is found on the shore of the ocean itself or on coastal islands. The bird also breeds throughout the interior at long distances from the sea. According to Macoun (1909) " it does not breed in the prairie region, but prefers the clear lakes and streams of the north." The nest is generally built within 25 yards of the water.

The nest, although sometimes built in the open, is generally placed under some shelter, as the overhanging and prostrate branches of dwarfed spruces, firs, or willows, or among the roots of trees or in a pile of driftwood, and is so well concealed and the female lies so close that the intruder often nearly steps into the nest before he is aware of its presence. Macfarlane (1908) mentions a nest near the Anderson River " on the border of the ' Barrens ' to the east, under a fallen tree, close to a small lake. It was a scooped-out hole lined with feathers and down, and it contained six eggs. "

[Author's note: The red-breasted merganser breeds abundantly in the Magdalen Islands, Quebec, where numerous nests have been found by others, as well as by me. An island near Grosse Isle, known as Seal Island, is a famous breeding resort for this species. It is a high island of red sandstone, nearly covered with a dense forest of spruces and firs, under which the nests are concealed. A typical nest, shown in the accompanying photograph, was located in the thick woods, about 1 rod from the edge and about 40 yards from the shore; it was perfectly concealed under a dense thicket of balsam firs and would never have been discovered except that we saw the bird fly out and a few pieces of down indicated where to look. The nest was a hollow in the ground, profusely lined with gray down and a few white breast feathers; it measured 14 by 12 inches in outside and 8 by 7 inches in inside diameter. Several pieces of dry egg membrane in the nest suggested the idea that it might have been used the previous season also. It contained eight fresh eggs on June 21, 1904.

On the previous day we had found a nest of this species in a very different situation, on what is locally known as the Gully Flats, a long stretch of beaches and sand dunes with numerous marshy or grassy hollows scattered among the sand hills. The nest was in one of these small marshy hollows, which was overgrown with coarse sedges or marsh grasses; it was well concealed in the thickest grass and was made of the dry stalks of this grass, scantly arranged under, around, and partially over the eggs; very little down had been added, as the six eggs were perfectly fresh and the set was probably incomplete.

The down in the nest of the red-breasted is much darker than that found in the nest of the American merganser; it is "mouse gray" with paler centers and usually pure white breast feathers and more or less rubbish are mixed with it. When the set is complete a thick blanket of down and rubbish is provided in sufficient quantity to entirely conceal the eggs when the bird has time to cover them before leaving the nest.

Eggs.—This merganser usually lays from 8 to 10 eggs, sometimes as many as 16. The eggs are quite different from those of the American merganser. The shape varies from elliptical ovate or elliptical oval to elongate ovate. The shell is smooth but without much luster. The color varies from a rich "olive buff" or "pale olive buff" to "cartridge buff"; the olive shades are commoner than the lighter shades. The measurements of 85 eggs in the United States National Museum average 64.5 by 45 millimeters; the eggs showing the four extremes measure **67.5** by 46, 67 by **46.5**, **56.5** by 43 and 60.5 by **41** millimeters.]

Young.—Incubation lasts from 26 to 28 days and is performed entirely by the female; the drakes are rarely seen in the neighborhood during this period. P. L. Hatch (1892), who has found this bird breeding within a few miles of both Minneapolis and St. Paul, says:

Only a very few individuals have seen these ducks during the summer, for the obvious reason that, like all other locally breeding ducks, they are rarely found on the wing.

The young are active within a few hours of hatching, as has been well described by R. M. Strong (1912), and wriggle in a prostrate manner over the ground like a snake. They are soon able to run about on their feet and climb easily to the mother's back.

The food of the young consists of small fish, water insects and larvae, worms, crustaceans, and sometimes frogs. Both parents are assiduous in caring for the young. The young mergansers are carefully fed and guarded by their parents, and the family group keeps together until the young are fully grown. At the slightest sign of danger the young conceal themselves under the bushes and among the reeds of the banks of the river or pond, while the adults do their best to entice the intruder away. When suddenly disturbed in the open the young are able to make their way over the surface of the water with surprising rapidity by the combined action of the wings and legs. The noise of such a flight often confuses the enemy. On open shores I have known the young to flee from the approaching canoe, creep ashore, and, trusting to their protecting coloring, crouch motionless among the rocks and small plants.

Rev. Manley B. Townsend contributes the following pretty picture of a family party:

One summer day, toward evening, as I sat upon the shore of a wilderness lake, drinking in the beauty of the forest and the mountain, a flock of red-breasted mergansers came sailing around a rocky point, close inshore. There were 10, led by a wary old male in full adult plumage. The other nine were much duller of color. I took them for the mother and her eight children. How alert! How wary! How incomparably wild! Suspiciously they scanned me, but I sat immovable. Plainly they were nonplussed. Yet they were taking no chances. Silently they submerged until only their heads and upper necks were above the surface, and turning swam quietly off out into the lake. A calculated movement on my part, and off went the whole family, led by the father, leaving a foamy wake to mark their tumultuous passage.

Plumages.—[Author's note: The downy young red-breasted merganser is exactly like the young American merganser except for two very slight differences in the head; the nostrils in the red-breasted are in the basal third of the bill, whereas in the American they are in the central third; and the white loral stripe is tinged with brownish or fluffy but with a more or less distinct white spot under the eye.

The down is worn for a long time. The first of the plumage appears on the under parts, then comes the tail, the flanks, and the scapulars in the order named; the remainder of the body plumage follows, then that of the head and neck; the wings appear last, and the bird is fully grown before it can fly. The last of the down is on the hind neck or central back.

Millais (1913) says that in its first plumage the young male—

resembles the adult female, but the crest is less, the bill much shorter, and the plumage of the upper parts more slaty and not nearly so brown, and the cheeks more red with less white. The ends of the tail are also worn. By the end of October young males are easily recognized by their superior size and bill. It is not until December that much change takes place. The red-brown crest is then abundant, and black feathers begin to appear on the sides of the crown and cheeks, chin, mantle, and scapulars. The tail and rump also begin to molt to blue gray, and many vermiculated feathers mixed with slaty-brown ones come in on the thighs and flanks. By the end of March some white feathers appear on the scapulars and the first white, broadly black-edged feathers come in on the sides of the breast overlapping the wings. These prominent feathers are, however, never complete as in the case of the adult males, but are always divided in color, the lower halves being red and vermiculated with black from the broad black edge to the white above. The nape is now very dark-brown edged with worn blue gray, and not a clear rich red brown, as in the female. The long inner secondaries, similar to adult males, now also appear.

I have seen young males in this plumage, with immature backs and wings, and with more or less black mottling in the heads and necks, in March, April, May, and June, during which time the old males are, of course, in full nuptial plumage.

Millais (1913) says:

> The young male during May and June molts all signs of the brilliant spring plum-
> age, and passes into an eclipse similar to the adult male. It can, however, always
> be identified by the immature wing, which is brown and slate on all its upper parts,
> instead of being black with a large white area in the center, as in the adult male.
> During August, September, and October the general molt toward complete winter
> plumage is in progress, and the young male does not come into full dress until the
> end of November. It may then be considered adult at 17 months.

The fully adult plumage is worn during the winter and spring until
the molt into the eclipse begins; this sometimes begins in March and
proceeds very slowly, but more often it does not begin until late
spring or early summer; it is complete in August. Millais (1913)
thus describes a specimen in full eclipse plumage taken on August 20:

> Head, neck, and upper breast almost exactly similar to adult female, but with
> only a very short area of white on the chin; mantle and scapulars blackish brown,
> edged with gray; wings, which have just been renewed, as in winter; rump and
> lower back a mixture, brownish ash-gray feathers like the female, and white vermicu-
> lated with black (as in spring); flanks and sides of the chest brownish gray like the
> female. There are a few slate and brown vermiculated feathers at the sides of the
> vent. Under parts white, and soft parts as in spring, only not so bright.

The molt of the eclipse plumage begins early in September and
continues through October and November, or with some individuals
much longer; I have a specimen in my collection, taken November 7,
in which this molt is only fairly started; by January at the latest
most of the males are in full plumage again.

Of the immature females Millais (1913) says—

> in first plumage the young female is similar to the adult female, except for the less
> abundant crest and small area of black round the eye. Tail feathers are worn and
> wing markings less distinct. The scapular and mantle feathers, too, which remain
> unchanged until March are like nearly all immature female ducks pale and worn on
> their outer edges and generally gray or sandy and unlike the clean rich feathers of
> adults. By April it is difficult to distinguish between immature and adult females,
> except that the young never possess the large area of black round the eye nor the
> black feathers at the sides of the chin, and only the throat. The wings are as usual
> the main character in distinguishing age. I do not think these young birds breed
> nor are they adult until the following November.]

Food.—The red-breasted merganser is chiefly a fish eater, but it
does not disdain to gather up crustaceans and mollusks. In fresh
water it is fond of crawfish. Its long serrated bill with the teeth
pointing backward is well adapted to holding its slippery prey.
Nelson (1887) remarks that it feeds on sticklebacks, which abound
in the brackish ponds of Alaska. It delights in the rapids of rivers,
in tidal estuaries, and in the shallow places off sand beaches and at
the mouth of rivers, where small fish most do congregate. Strenuous
must be the life of the small fry in these regions when a large flock
of mergansers are diving together.

Behavior.—The flight of the shelldrake is lacking in the initial power shown by the black duck. Unlike the latter bird, it can not spring straight up into the air. Rising from the water or ground is indeed always a laborious process, but especially so in calm weather, when there is no wind to oppose its airplanes. There is a noisy flapping of the wings and a strenuous pushing away of the water or sand with the feet for some distance before the surface can be cleared. A pair that I disturbed from the beach on a calm day showed the marks of their feet for 29 yards before they succeeded in getting away from the sand. Once on the wing their flight is noiseless and is generally close to the water, differing in this way from that of the golden eye which frequents the same shores, but which usually rises to a considerable height. When flying in pairs in the spring, the female generally precedes. It is a rapid swimmer and perfectly at home in the roughest water. As a diver the bird is truly an expert, and it disappears under water with wings close to its sides, making use of its powerful feet alone except on rare occasions when its wings are also brought into play. At times it leaps clear of the surface, describes a graceful arc and enters the water like a curved arrow, while at other times it disappears with scarcely a sign of effort. It often swims with its head and neck stretched out in front, as if it were skimming the water and straining it with its serrated bill for food. Again it advances with the head, all but the crest, below the surface apparently on the lookout for fish, and, at such times, it is conantly diving. At the moment of diving the crest is flattened down; when the birds swim before a strong wind the crests often blow up and over the head.

On the land the red-breasted merganser is an awkward walker. It often rests flat on its belly or stands up with its body at an angle of 45°. Again, it stands with its body parallel with the ground like an ordinary duck.

The courtship note, or love song, has already been described. This may be heard not only in the spring but occasionally also in the autumn, as in the case of so many, if not all, birds, a phenomenon known as the "autumnal recrudescence of the amatory instinct." The rough croak of the female at this time has also been mentioned. A similar rough croak is emitted by these birds during the breeding season; I have heard it as they flew back and forth from their nests, and once on a small stream in Labrador, in early August, a female flew close to the water ahead of the canoe croaking hoarsely. She probably wished to entice me away from her young, which may have been concealed under the bushes.

Game.—Although very "fishy eating" the red-breasted merganser is assiduously hunted along the New England coast. It is a shy bird but comes in well to wooden decoys anchored off points, along the shore or in tidal estuaries.   The gunner takes his station near at hand in a blind made of brush or sea weed or sometimes of ice cakes, and is most successful in the early morning when the birds are coming in from their night's rest on the ocean.   Gunning punts covered with marsh grass are also used, but one must be a skillful sculler to be able to approach within gunshot of the wary birds.   Birds that are merely winged are almost impossible to recover, as they are wonderful divers and generally elude pursuit.   They often swim away with only the bill above water.

Winter.—In the latter part of September in New England, the species begins to arrive from the north and becomes exceedingly numerous during October and November.   In December the numbers diminish, but it is one of our most abundant waterfowl on the Massachusetts coast throughout the winter.   In the spring migration of March and April the numbers increase, but it is not until the last of May, or even the first of June that they have all left for the north. But the story of the migration of this bird is not so simple as the above statement would imply, for there is a sexual as well as an age difference to be considered.   The large flocks in the early fall appear to be all in brown dress, and this is the dress not only of the females and young but also of the adult males, who are then in the eclipse plumage.   In November this plumage is molted, and the males appear resplendent in their courtship dress, while the females and young of both sexes leave for the south, so that during the winter months the vast majority are in full male plumage.   Thus, one January day, out of 500 sheldrakes off Ipswich Beach I could count only 6 in the dull plumage.   Whether these were adult females or young or both I cannot say.   In March the females put in an appearance and courting begins, and by the last of April and in May the birds are largely paired, although flocks of either or both sexes are common as well as those of immature males who have not molted into full plumage are common.   Some at least of the immature males are slow in changing to adult plumage, and males in nearly complete immature dress with only a few greenish feathers about the head are often to be found in April and May.   On the other hand, I have seen a bird that was half molted into adult male plumage as early as the 16th of February; this was probably an adult changing from the eclipse plumage, the others immature birds.

The southern side of this picture, which rounds out and corroborates my northern observations has been given me by Mr. William Brewster, who says that in Florida, in winter, he has seen large flocks of female and immature red-breasted mergansers, and by Mr. Arthur T. Wayne (1910) who, says of this species:

From the time when these fish-eating ducks arrive until the first week in February, the adult drakes are seldom, if ever, seen, but toward the second week in February they make their appearance in large numbers.

It would seem, therefore, that some of the drakes go south to escort their partners back to the breeding home.

On the New England coast in winter this bird is to be found in largest numbers off the beaches and in the coves and harbors. It frequents also the tidal estuaries among the salt marshes into which it enters at dawn and from which it flies at sunset in order to sleep with more safety on the ocean; in this respect its habits are the opposite of those of the black duck. It is evident that the merganser is not as common of late years in tidal estuaries, as it is more apt to be disturbed by gunners and motor boats. It occasionally visits the fresh-water ponds and rivers during the migrations along the sea coast, but does not prefer them to salt water, as does its cousin the goosander. Its habits during the winter have been described above. Courting takes place all along the New England coast even that part far from the breeding range, and begins in good weather as early as February.

The long neck, head, and bill of the sheldrake, its flat body, and conspicuous white-marked wing makes its recognition in the air usually an easy one. The adult drake is easily distinguished by its reddish breast and by its crest from the goosander; the females and young can often be distinguished, even at a distance, from the very similar females and young of the goosander by the more clearly defined white throat of the latter bird. In the red-breasted species the white is less in extent and shades gradually into the brown of the neck. This is an important field mark and is often overlooked, for most authorities write that the female and young of these two species can only be distinguished in the hand by the position of the nostril, which is in the middle of the bill in the case of the goosander and nearer the base in the red-breasted species. The back of the female goosander is of pearl-blue color while that of the red-breasted species is dark ashy with a brownish tinge. These differences are also noticeable in the field.

DISTRIBUTION.

Breeding range.—Northern portions of the Northern Hemisphere. In North America, south to Newfoundland, Nova Scotia (Kings County), New Brunswick (Grand Manan), coast of Maine (Jericho Bay), northern New York (Adirondacks), southern Ontario (Parry Sound), central Michigan and Wisconsin (Green Bay), central Minnesota (near St. Paul), southern Manitoba (Lake Manitoba), central Alberta (Buffalo Lake), southeastern British Columbia (Columbia River), southern Alaska (Chichagof Island), and the Aleutian Islands. North to the Arctic coast of Alaska (Icy Cape), Mackenzie (Fort Anderson), southern Baffin Land (Cumberland Sound) and central Greenland (Upérnivik and Scoresby Sound). In the Eastern Hemisphere, the breeding range includes Iceland, Ireland, Scotland, Scandinavia, northern Russia, northern Siberia, and the Kurile Islands.

Winter range.—Mainly on the coasts of the United States. On the Atlantic coast from Maine to Florida, on the Gulf coast from Florida to Texas. On the Pacific coast from British Columbia to Lower California (La Paz). In the interior from the Great Lakes southward. In the Eastern Hemisphere it is generally distributed over Europe, the Mediterranean, north Africa, the Black and Caspian Seas, Persia, northwest India, China and Japan.

Spring migration.—Average dates of arrival: Quebec, Montreal, April 16 (earliest April 6); Prince Edward Island, North River, April 21 (earliest April 15); Ungava, Lake Mistassini, May 11; Minnesota, Heron Lake, April 3; Manitoba, Aweme, April 22; Alaska, Chilcat, May 8, St. Michael, May 24, and Kowak River, middle of June. Late dates of departure: Missouri, Kansas City, May 4; Ohio, Oberlin, May 22; Pennsylvania, Erie, May 30; Rhode Island, Newport, May 16; Massachusetts, Essex County, May 20; California, Monterey, May 25.

Fall migration.—Early dates of arrival: Massachusetts, Essex County, September 23; Pennsylvania, Erie, September 6; California, Monterey, October 9. Late dates of departure: Mackenzie River, latitude 63°, October 16; Quebec, Montreal, November 1.

Casual records.—Accidental in Cuba (Habana, December, 1891), Bermuda, and Hawaiian Islands.

Egg dates.—Labrador: Fourteen records, June 4 to July 16; seven records, June 26 to July 7. Magdalen Islands: Eleven records, June 17 to 26. Alaska: Five records, June 26 to July 9. Iceland: Five records, May 20 to June 23.

LOPHODYTES CUCULLATUS (Linnaeus).

HOODED MERGANSER.

HABITS.

In the overflowed, heavily wooded bottoms of our great interior rivers, where rising waters have half submerged and killed the forest trees, this pretty little timberland duck finds a congenial home among the half-sunken snags, stumps, and dead trees, which offer suitable nesting hollows and where its striking color pattern matches its surroundings so well that it is easily overlooked. It is a widely distributed species, found in suitable localities almost anywhere in the wooded portions of North America; it breeds more or less regularly throughout this range from Florida and Arkansas northward to northern Canada. Its center of abundance extends from the northern half of the Mississippi Valley into central Canada. The male, with his showy crest and neat color pattern, is one of the handsomest of our ducks, a fit companion for the gaudy wood duck with which it is often associated in the watery woodlands where it breeds.

Spring.—As some individuals are present both in winter and in summer over so much of its range, its migratory movements are not easily traced. The birds which have wintered just below the frost line begin to move northward before the ice has disappeared from our large lakes and streams, frequenting the smaller and swifter open streams; these birds move on as soon as conditions are favorable in their northern breeding grounds. Others come later and spread out over the country wherever they can find suitable breeding grounds.

Courtship.—The courtship of this species must be a beautiful performance. I have never seen it and can not find any account of it by American writers. Mr John G. Millais (1913) gives the following brief description of it:

> The courtship, according to my friend Mr. Francklyn, consists of a sudden rise of the body with depressed crest. On coming to the water again the crest is fully expanded. The males also stretch their necks forward with fully expanded crest.

Nesting.—The birds are probably mated when they arrive on their breeding grounds and soon begin the search for a suitable cavity for a nest, but they are not particular as to the size and shape of the cavity, the kind of a tree in which they find it, or the height from the ground; almost any hole or a hollow tree trunk will do, provided it is large enough to admit the bird and of the proper shape to hold and protect the eggs; even the open hollowed top of a stump or a fallen hollow log will do; and sometimes a hole in the ground is occupied.

Mr. Herbert Massey has sent me some notes regarding two sets of eggs in his collection. A set of 12 eggs, collected by Rev. P. B. Peabody, near Hallock, Minnesota, on May 9, 1899, was taken from a cavity in an elm tree about 100 feet from a wooded creek; the cavity was in a knot hole 15 or 20 feet from the ground and was 2 feet deep. The birds had used this tree for three years and had previously nested in an exactly similar hollow in an old elm stub half a mile below. The hole was so small that the bird could hardly squeeze into it. There was a scanty supply of trash at the bottom of the cavity, apparently brought in by squirrels, and there were a few of the breast feathers of the merganser mixed with the down; the eggs were nearly fresh. Mr. Edwin S. Bryant collected the other set of nine eggs, on May 28, 1899, near White Fish Lake, Montana; the nest of moss and down was in a hollow close to the top of a leaning tamarack stub 50 feet from the ground; the tree stood on a high ridge in a dense forest half a mile back from a small lake; the moss in the nest, apparently *Usnea*, Mr. Bryant thought had been brought in by flying squirrels. The female remained on the nest while he made the dangerous climb by nailing on cleats and he had to cut through from the upper side to pull her off the eggs.

Mr. J. Hooper Bowles has sent me the following interesting notes on his experience in inducing hooded mergansers to nest in boxes, near Tacoma, Washington:

I have never found a naturally located occupied nest of the hooded merganser, my rather limited experience being confined to nesting boxes that I put up for them. This was done through the kindness of Dr. G. D. Shaver, of Tacoma, Washington, who very kindly gave me entire use of his country estate near that city. The locality selected is a lake about half a mile in diameter, entirely surrounded by dense fir and deciduous woods, with a stream running in at one end and out again at the opposite end. At the head of the lake the stream runs through a large and heavily wooded swamp, in which I put up two of my boxes. A third was put up on a dead tree standing in the middle of the lake, a fourth on a tree at the outlet, a fifth on the side of the lake, and a sixth on a lone, giant fir tree that stands on a bare hillside some 300 yards from the water at the end of the lake. All are about 18 feet above the ground, or water, and seemed to cover as well as possible the nesting sites that might be suitable for these birds. Not to take up too much space, I will say that a set of 10 eggs was taken from one of the boxes in the swamp at the head of the lake, a brood being reared in the other box there. A set of 11 eggs was taken from the box on the tree in the lake, the bird using the box on the lone fir on the hillside for her second, and this time successful, attempt at rearing a brood for the season. The box on the side of the lake showed no signs of being visited, but down feathers on the entrance of the box at the outlet gave evidence that it had been thoroughly examined, although considered unsuitable for some reason. The birds are so exceedingly shy that I have never been able to see them enter their nests, but when leaving they come out at full flight, which would seem almost an impossibility under the circumstances. The eggs are just about the size, shape, and color of white billiard balls, and every bit as hard in their composition.

Mr. Glen Rinker (1899) describes two nests, found near Unionville, Missouri, as follows:

On the day mentioned I was sitting by the side of the lake watching a pair of females, when one of them raised and flew within 20 feet of my head. I was "all eyes" when she alighted on a snag about 50 yards back from me, and I noticed it looked down the hollow several times. I attempted to get closer, but she saw me and flew away. I then proceeded to examine the snag. It was about 2 feet in diameter and 10 feet high; the top was hollowed out to a depth of about 2 feet, and looked charred as though it had been burned. The nest was composed of leaves and some grass and a little moss, and had a complete lining of down. The eggs, six in number, were white, and were more round than most duck eggs.

June 13, 1899, found me near the lake again, but farther off in a thicket, watching a cardinal whose nest I knew was near. To my left was a tall bank where a lot of trees had fallen and which was overgrown with hazel bushes. I heard a whistle of wings, and looked up just in time to see a merganser settle down near on old stump. I waited about 5 or 10 minutes, and then walked quietly up to where I saw her light. When about 5 feet from the place, she jumped up with a quack, and started for the lake.

Now, I have several keys and other books, and they all say the hooded merganser nests in hollow trees and stumps, but this nest was on the ground under the roots of the stump, in a sort of a cave that was about 14 inches back under the stump. The nest was composed of about the same material as the other, but did not have as much down. There were only four eggs in the nest, so I left it until the 17th, when I collected them as only one more had been laid. On blowing them, incubation was just perceptible. The nest was in such a dark place that to photograph it was impossible without overexposing the outside. The down made the eggs hard to distinguish.

One of Major Bendire's correspondents, Mr. T. H. P. Lamb, writes that the Cree Indians of Saskatchewan call this bird the "beaver duck" and claim that it lays its eggs in deserted beaver houses, using the entrance under water, also occasionally in old muskrat houses. This seems hardly likely, however.

Where suitable nesting sites are scarce, the hooded merganser sometimes contends with other species of tree-nesting ducks for the possession of a coveted home and occasionally they share the home between them. Mr. George A. Boardman has been several times quoted as having witnessed such a contest between a wood duck and this species, which resulted in the two females laying in the same nest and occupying it by turns. Mr. George D. Peck (1896) writes:

I believe it is well known that the wood duck often drives the merganser from her nest, and in one nest I found 30 eggs of wood duck and 5 eggs of merganser. The hollow in the tree in which the nest was placed was not very large and the eggs were several layers deep.

In Maine, Mr. William Brewster (1900) says that several of the rounded, pure white, thick-shelled eggs of the hooded merganser are sometimes included in a set of the green, thin-shelled eggs of the whistler.

Eggs.—The hooded merganser is credited with laying anywhere from 6 to 18 eggs; probably from 10 to 12 would cover the usual numbers. The eggs are oval or subspherical in shape. The shell is thick and hard, smooth and usually quite glossy. The color is pure white, but they are often nest stained. The measurements of 116 eggs in various collections average 53.5 by 44.9 millimeters; the eggs showing the four extremes measure **57.5** by 45.2, 55.5 by **45.5**, **50** by 43, and 50.5 by **41.5** millimeters.

Mr. William Evans (1891) says that the period of incubation is 31 days: it is wholly performed by the female. The male is said by most observers, to desert the female as soon as the eggs are laid, but the following note by Mr. J. W. Preston (1892) is of interest in this connection:

While camping on Little Twin Lakes, northern Iowa, some years since, I noticed a male hooded merganser circling around a grove so often that it seemed certain that he was feeding his mate, which they do at incubating time. I concealed myself and watched for a long time, and finally was rewarded by seeing the fellow fly plump into a hollow in a gigantic oak. It would seem to be a piece of recklessness; certanly, if he had not aimed well he would have suffered for the error.

Young.—Several writers have written that the female conveys the young in her bill from the nest down into the water, soon after they are hatched, and Dr. P. L. Hatch (1892) says he has seen it done; he writes:

In one instance, a lady sharing my interest in birds and game, while rowing with me, noticed what we supposed to be a wood duck carrying her chick by the neck from a tree into the water. We waited in vain some time to see if the bird would not bring another young one. Reaching the middle of the small lake, we saw the duck, by the aid of the field glass, resume the loving task and discovered the bird to be a female of the species under consideration.

I suspect, however, that this instance was exceptional and that the usual method of precedure is for the mother to coax the young to climb up the edge of the cavity and then drop down into the water, or onto the soft ground, if circumstances are favorable, as is customary with most tree-nesting ducks. Their little bodies are so light and so elastic that the fall does not hurt them. Audubon (1840) says:

The affectionate mother leads her young among tall rank grasses which fill the shallow pools or the borders of creeks and teaches them to procure snails, tadpoles, and insects.

Mr. E. A. Samuels (1883) writes:

When the female is suddenly surprised, while with her young in a stream or pond, she gives a guttural, chattering cry, when the whole brood dives and swims off under the water to the shore, where they conceal themselves in the aquatic herbage. While they are thus retreating, the mother simulating lameness, almost exactly like some of the shore birds on the beach, flutters before the intruder, using every artifice to decoy him from the neighborhood of her young, when she takes wing and flies off. If, however, she has sufficient notice of the approach of a person before he reaches gunshot she swims rapidly off, with her whole brood paddling behind her, until she turns a point or neck in the pond or stream where she happens to be, when, silently creeping into shore, she, with her brood, hides herself in the herbage on the land until the danger is past. When about two-thirds grown, these young mergansers, like the young of most of the other fowls, are excellent eating. They are called "flappers" because of their habit of flapping their wings on the water to aid their escape from pursuers.

Plumages.—The downy young is thickly and warmly clothed with soft down in deep, rich shades of "bister" or "sepia" above, including the upper half of the head, the hind neck, and the flanks; the sides of the head, neck, and cheeks, up to the eyes, are "buff pink" or "light vinaceous cinnamon," the chin, throat, and under parts are pure white; and there is an obscure dusky band across the chest and an indistinct white spot on each side of scapular region and rump.

In the first plumage the sexes are alike and much resemble the adult female, but they are browner on the back and have undeveloped crests. Young males wear this immature plumage all through the first year, with only a slight change toward maturity during ths first spring and the following summer. The summer molt leaves them still in immature plumage and with but little change in the new wings, which still lack the pearl-gray lesser coverts and in which the greater coverts are only slightly white-tipped. In November and

December of this, their second, winter they begin to assume a plumage resembling that of the adult; the molt begins with the appearance of black feathers and white feathers in the head, spreading downward to the breast, flanks, and scapulars until by March or April a nearly adult plumage is assumed. In this plumage the colors are all duller than in old males; the crown, back, and rump are browner; the gray lesser wing-coverts are acquired, but the wings are otherwise immature. A partial eclipse plumage is assumed during the next summer, when the bird is 2 years old and late in the fall, November or December, the fully adult plumage is acquired. Young females can be distinguished from adults during the first year by their undeveloped crests and their duller and browner coloring everywhere; they become indistinguishable from the adults during the second winter.

Adult males have a semi-eclipse plumage in summer, in which the head and neck become largely mottled with brownish and the breast and flanks lose their brilliant colors and resemble those of the female. The double molt is probably not complete, though the whole plumage is changed at least once. The full plumage is assumed early in the fall, much earlier than in young birds, and is usually complete in October.

Food.—The hooded merganser lives and feeds almost exclusively on and in fresh water; I believe that some of its food is obtained on the surface, but it is an expert diver and finds much of its food on muddy or on stony bottoms. Its food is mostly animal, and consists largely of insects. Like other mergansers, it is expert at chasing and catching small fish, which probably constitute its chief supply; in muddy pools it finds frogs and tadpoles and snails, and other mullusks; on clear stony bottoms it obtains crawfish, caddis fly larvae, and dragon-fly nymphs; sand eels, small crustaceans, beetles, and various aquatic insects are also eaten. It is also known to eat some vegetable food, the roots of aquatic plants, seeds, and grain. Dr. F. Henry Yorke (1899) recognized among its vegetable food the following genera of water plants: *Limnobium, Myriophyllum, Callitriche,* and *Utricularia.*

Behavior.—Dr. D. G. Elliot (1898) writes of the flight of this species:

On the wing it is one of the swiftest ducks that fly, and it hurls itself through the air with almost the velocity of a bullet. Generally it proceeds in a direct line; but if it is alarmed at any object suddenly appearing before it, the course is changed with the swiftness of thought, and a detour made before again taking the first line of progression. Sometimes, without apparent reason, the course will be altered, and away it shoots at right angles to the first route; and again, it vacillates as though uncertain which way to take, or as if it was looking for a good feeding place. Usually five or six, but more frequently a pair, are seen flying together, and often, on dull days when the lookout in a blind is somewhat relaxed, and the sportsman is consoling himself for lack of birds with possibly a nap or the lunch basket, the first intimation of the presence of a hairy crown is given by one or more flashing close overhead with a startling whirr, and then as rapidly disappearing in the distance. It requires a steady hand and a correct eye to kill them on the wing, and the gunner must be ever mindful of the good old adage in duck shooting, "Hold well ahead." It rises from the water without any preliminary motions, and is on the wing at once, and in full flight, the pinions moving with a rapidity that almost creates a blur on either side of the body, the outline of the wing disappearing.

Dr. P. L. Hatch (1892) says:

Once in January, 1874, when the mercury had descended to 40° below zero while a north wind was blowing terrifically, I saw a flock of six of this species flying directly into the teeth of the blizzard at their ordinary velocity of not less than 90 miles an hour. The compactness of their flocks of half a dozen to 15 in their flight is characteristic, and their directness fully equal to that of the green-winged teal.

Mr. J. W. Preston (1892) observes:

A pleasing characteristic of the species is the manner of flying during nesting time. One may see them chasing round and round some wooded lake, speeding ever with a thrilling impetuosity; uttering a peculiar note as they glide along; then they have darted out into the forest, leaving the beholder pleased with the performance, and none the wiser as to the nest site. I timed one of this species, and it made its mile in less than one minute.

Audubon (1840) says: "When migrating, they fly at a great height, in small loose flocks, without any regard to order."

Of its swimming and diving habits, Doctor Elliot (1898) says:

The movements of this bird upon the water are quick and active, and it swims rapidly and dives with great celerity. It is a beautiful object, and few birds surpass the male in attractiveness as he swims lightly along, elevating and depressing his beautiful crest. If suspicious, this species will sink the body until the water is almost level with the back, and sometimes disappears beneath the surface, apparently without effort, as if some unseen hand was pulling it down. When wounded it is one of the most difficult birds to secure; and it dives with such quickness, remains under water so long, and skulks and hides with so much skill that it is very apt to make its escape, and always tries the patience of its pursuer, whether dog or man, to the utmost. Their progress under water is extremely rapid, and the wings as well as the feet are used as means of propulsion, perhaps more dependence being placed upon the wings, and they may be said to fly beneath the surface.

The same writer says of its voice: "It utters a hoarse croak like a small edition of the note of the red-breasted merganser."

Audubon (1840) writes:

Their notes consist of a kind of rough grunt, variously modulated, but by no means musical, and resembling the syllables "croo, croo, crooh." The female repeats it six or seven times in succession, when she sees her young in danger. The same noise is made by the male, either when courting on the water or as he passes on wing near the hole where the female is laying one of her eggs.

Fall.—A study of the migration records will show that the hooded merganser is not an early migrant in the fall, nor is it the very latest; the main flight comes along during the latter half of October and first half of November; the latest stragglers often linger until frozen out. Audubon (1840) gives an interesting account of its behavior at this season, which I quote, as follows:

At the approach of night, a person standing still on the banks of such a river as the Ohio first hears the well-known sound of wings whistling through the air, presently after, a different noise, as if produced by an eagle stooping on her prey, when gliding downward with the rapidity of an arrow, he dimly perceives the hooded mergansers sweeping past. Five or six, perhaps 10, there are; with quick beats of their pinions, they fly low over the waters in wide circles. Now they have spied the entrance of a creek; there they shoot into it, and in a few seconds you hear the rushing noise which they make as they alight on the bosom of the still pool. How often have I enjoyed such scenes, when enticed abroad by the clear light of the silvery moon, I have wan-- dered on the shores of la belle rivière to indulge in the contemplation of nature!

Up the creek the mergansers proceed, washing their bodies by short plunges, and splashing up the water about them. Then they plume themselves, and anoint their feathers, now and then emitting a low grunting note of pleasure. And now they dive in search of minnows, which they find in abundance, and which no doubt prove de- licious food to the hungry travelers. At length, having satisfied their appetite, they rise on wing, fly low over the creek with almost incredible velocity, return to the broad stream, rove along its margin until they meet with a clean sand beach, where they alight, and where, secure from danger, they repose until the return of day. A sly raccoon may, when in search of mussels, chance to meet with the sleeping birds, and surprise one of them; but this rarely happens, for they are as wary and vigilant as their enemy is cunning, and were the prowler to depend upon the hooded mergansers for food, he would be lean enough.

Game.—From the sportsman's standpoint this is not an important species. It is a difficult bird to hit on the wing, it is small and its flesh is not particularly attractive to eat; it is often very fat and when it has been feeding on grain or vegetable food its flavor is not bad. It is rather tame and unsuspicious, coming readily to decoys. It is known by a variety of names such as " wood sheldrake," "water pheasant," " hairy crown," etc.

Winter.—The hooded merganser is resident throughout the year over much of its range, wintering as far north as it can find open water in which it can obtain its food supply. Doctor Hatch (1892) says that, in Minnesota, " they stay as long as the ice will let them on the shores of the lakes, whence they go to open rapids, and late in November mostly drift more southward." Dr. Amos W. Butler (1897) writes, in regard to Indiana:

Throughout the State the hooded merganser may be found in winter, the more numerous the more open the winters, and always attracted to the open water, so that in the most severe winters they are most to be observed on the rapid streams of southern Indiana, where ripples and rapids are about the only places they can find at which to congregate.

Although a few migrate beyond our borders, the principal winter home of the species is in the States bordering on the Gulf of Mexico, where they frequent the inland waters, seldom if ever being seen on salt water.

DISTRIBUTION.

Breeding range.—Temperate North America, locally. East to western New Brunswick (St. Croix River), eastern New York (Adi- rondacks and Catskills), central Pennsylvania (Williamsport), and eastern South Carolina (Berkeley County). South to central Florida

(Titusville and Fort Myers), southern Tennessee (near Chattanooga), northeastern Arkansas (Big Lake), northern New Mexico, and northwestern Nevada (Truckee River). West to Oregon and northwestern Washington (near Tacoma). North to southeastern Alaska (Stikine River), central British Columbia (Cariboo district), southern Mackenzie (Great Slave Lake), northern Manitoba (Churchill), eastern Ontario (Algonquin Park), and perhaps the interior of Labrador.

Winter range.—Mainly in the Southern States. North to Massachusetts, Pennsylvania, Lake Michigan, Nebraska, Colorado, Utah, and southern British Columbia (Comox and Okanagan). South to Cuba and southern Mexico (Orizaba and Jalapa).

Spring migration.—Early dates of arrival: Iowa, central, March 5; Minnesota, Heron Lake, March 20; Ontario, Ottawa, March 21. Average dates of arrival: New York, western, March 20; Ontario, Ottawa, April 18; Michigan, southern, March 19; Iowa, central, March 22; Minnesota, Heron Lake, April 5.

Fall migration.—Average dates of arrival: New York, western, October 15; Virginia, Alexandria, October 26. Average dates of departure: Quebec, Montreal, October 29; Minnesota, southern, November 10; Iowa, central, November 26.

Casual records.—Accidental in Bermuda (January 10, 1849, and December 23, 1850), Great Britain (Wales, winter 1830–31), Ireland (County Cork, December, 1878, and County Kerry, January, 1881), and Alaska (St. Michael, October, 1865).

Egg dates.—Michigan: Four records, April 22 to May 19. Illinois: Three records, March 15, April 29, and May 5. Iowa: One record, June 5. Montana: Four records, April 27 to May 28. Washington: One record, April 21. Missouri: One record, June 13.

MERGELLUS ALBELLUS (LINNAEUS).

SMEW.

HABITS.

This is a Palaearctic species, of rare and doubtful occurrence as a straggler, on the North American continent. It is included in our check list on the strength of a female in the British Museum purchased from the Hudson's Bay Company, said to have been taken in Canada, but with no data as to the exact locality; there is also a record of a female, which Audubon (1840) claims to have taken in Louisiana in 1819, which is open to doubt. Evidently Wilson's (1832) references to the abundance of this species in New England were based on incorrect identifications.

On the Atlantic and Mediterranean coasts of Europe it is fairly common in winter and in the eastern Mediterranean quite abundant, whence it retreats northward in April to its breeding grounds in the northern portions of Europe and Asia.

Courtship.—Millais (1913) describes the courtship performance of the smew as follows:

The male swims slowly around the female, sometimes with the long scapulars slightly raised or expanded. The head and neck is often moved slowly forward in a pushing manner, and when about to make the act of display the neck is drawn back as far as possible between the scapulars. All this time the crest is raised and spread in a very peculiar fashion. It is separated into two parts, the front consisting of only a few feathers of the front of the crown. These stand quite clear away from the latter part of the crest, which is expanded above the nuchal patch of black. Often a single white feather stands out alone connecting the two sections of the crest. The nuchal patch lies flat, and the back of the head is not distended in any way.

The next act of show is to push farward the neck somewhat slowly and then back as far as possible, the crest on the crown being raised as already indicated, and the chin pointed upward, whilst there is a slight rise of the forepart of the body as it is lifted from the water. During this sedate movement the mating cry of the male is uttered. The throat is slightly swelled, and the note is a prolonged croak or grunt like the word "err-err-err-umph," the last sound being an exhalation to clear the lungs, and seeming to be an effort on the part of the bird. During this movement the bird is stationary, with the tail either lying under or on the surface of the water.

On the completion of the movement there is a quick forward dip of the head and bill, followed by a sudden rise of the forepart of the body out of the water, something like a "mallard and teal" show, but not nearly so upright. In fact, it is almost a forward movement. At the same time the feet are paddled vigorously to maintain equilibrium. The call is often made as the bird throws itself up and forward.

At the end of this movement the bird often drops to the water with neck outstretched and parallel to the water, and when in full show often makes a little rush forward.

Nesting.—For a long time the breeding habits of the smew remained a mystery, until Mr. John Wolley received some authentic eggs and established the fact that the species bred in holes in trees in Swedish Lapland; he published a full account of it in The Ibis in 1859, from which Yarrell (1871) and others have quoted extensively. Probably all statements to the effect that the smew nests on the ground are erroneous, as it is known to nest only in hollow trees and in nesting boxes put up by the Laps for ducks to nest in. It is not known to nest north of the tree limit.

The down in the nest is described by Millais (1913) as "small and grayish white, freely intermixed with fine white feathers. Fragments of rotten wood and moss may also be found mixed with the down at the bottom of the nest hole or nesting box."

Eggs.—He says of the eggs:

Usually 6 to 9 in number, but 10 have been recorded. They are creamy in color and smooth in texture. Average size of 107 eggs, 52.42 by 37.46 millimeters; maximum, 58 by 40.5; minimum, 47.7 by 34. They are smaller on the average than widgeons'; decidedly shorter as a rule, and not quite so broad; but the measurements of the species overlap. Full clutches may be taken in northern Europe from the last week of May to the middle of June.

Plumages.—Dresser's description of the downy young, as given by Millais (1913), is as follows:

Upper parts, including the sides of the head below the eye, but only the back of the neck, dark blackish brown, darkest on the crown and the lower part of the back; at the base of the wing joint a white spot, and another close to it, but rather lower down the back, and on each side of the rump another white spot; below the eye a very small white spot; under parts white; breast and flanks pale grayish or sooty brown. One young bird, which can only be 2 or 3 days old, has the bill so slightly serrated that the serrations can only be seen when very closely looked into; but another, which is a few days older, has the serrations very distinct.

The sequence of plumages to maturity is thus outlined by Millais (1913):

The young male in first plumage very closely resembles the adult female and young female, and until December it is very difficult to tell the sexes apart except by dissection. At the end of five months, however, the young male begins to turn much darker. The nape is now often changed to new black feathers and the upper wing has a larger area of white; the lores, too, show many dark feathers. The tail is often complete by December. So the advent of the male plumage continues to advance on the upper parts until April when the usual halt takes place, until an eclipse plumage closely resembling that of the adult male is assumed. The wings, which are always the key to identification, are not the same as the adult male, and always have more or less brown or blackish edges on the upper coverts instead of being the pure white of the adult male. The immature male passes through the same stages as the other mergansers and assumes its first complete plumage in late November—that is, at 17 months.

The same writer describes the molts and plumages of the adult as follows:

The adult male assumes its eclipse plumage in June. As Naumann points out, it closely resembles that of the adult female, though I fancy that the bird from which his description was taken was not yet in full eclipse, as it differs somewhat from those I have seen.

In July the adult male has gained a very rich red-brown crest, somewhat fuller than the female, and it can always be distinguished from the female by the rich coloring of the wing, the white irides, and the black patch round the front of the eyes; also by its larger size black edges to outer white scapulars, and a few vermiculated feathers above the thighs on the flanks. In other respects the whole of the rest of the plumage is like the adult female, except the mantle, which is nearly black. Wings as in winter. The autumn molt proceeds in the usual manner, and the adult male regains its winter plumage by the end of November. Sometimes a few eclipse plumage feathers remain in the plumage until the new year, but this is unusual.

Food.—The food of the smew consists chiefly of small fish, crustaceans, small frogs, water insects, mollusks, and sand eels, which it obtains by diving. It is an expert diver and exceedingly swift in its pursuit of fish. Naumann, as quoted by Millais (1913), gives a pleasing account of a flock of smews fishing in a river full of ice:

To watch a flock of smews at their fishing unseen affords a pleasant amusement. At one moment all are swimming together, and then in a flash all have vanished from the surface, the water is stirred by their paddling in it, and finally one after another appears on the top again, but scattered, and where there is room, often 30 to 50 paces from the original place; they assemble again, dive yet again, and to the surprise of the observer they appear this time perhaps quite close to him on the surface. It is very wonderful how they obtain their means of food only by diving often from such small opening in the ice of only a few square feet; and they conduct their fish chase then under the ice roof, but they always come up again to the open places to breathe and rest for a few moments; and this is a proof that their sight under water must reach to a considerable distance.   In places where the open water does not contain enough fish, or they have themselves caught or scared away a fish, they scour the bottom for insects or frogs taking their winter sleep in the mud, or for fish which have taken refuge and hidden there.

Behavior.—Millais (1913) says of the flight, swimming, and diving habits of the smew:

The flight is very rapid, and the neck held very stiff and straight.   When going at full speed they swing from side to side, and often shoot down suddenly close to water. On alighting on the water they often dive at once as a precautionary measure and on rising to the surface stop, preen, and bathe.   Like the other mergansers, they are constantly preening their feathers, whether on land or on the water.   In winter they seldom come ashore, but in summer they often emerge from the water and lie for hours asleep amongst the stones or on some sand spit or island.   Hennicke observed a flock of smews in Finland, in September, 1900, resting on tree trunks in the middle of the rapids of the Ulea River.

The swimming attitudes are the same as the red-breasted merganser, and they only "sink" the body in the water when alarmed.   When on feed they swim lower, and the tail trails, or is sometimes a little lower than the line of the water.

They dive with swiftness, and apparently more vertically than the other mergansers—this may be due to their feeding on slower-moving fish—but they do not seem to range over the same extent of ground as the larger species.   I have, however, seen a smew making long horizontal dives like a red-breasted merganser, and in this instance it was probably hunting for food or in pursuit of trout.   Certainly the few smews I have seen on feed did not change their ground much, but came up again near to the spot they had dived, and it may be true, as some authors have asserted, that this is their general habit.   I do not think that any of the mergansers use their wings under water as the eiders do.   They all seem capable of swimming distances under water without coming to the surface to breathe.   If the flock has separated, it soon swims together again before again diving.

Of the voice he says: "Smews very seldom make any cry, and in the winter only a harsh croaking note."

Winter.—The smew migrates to its winter home in southern Europe rather late in the fall, from the middle of October to the end of November, where it frequents the lakes and rivers until it is driven by the formation of ice in its favorite resorts to the estuaries, bays, and even the open seas, where it associates, on very intimate terms, with the golden eye.   It is at all times shy and difficult to approach.

Naumann, as quoted by Millais (1913), speaks of its haunts, as follows:

The smew does not seem to like the open sea, and it is seen almost always near land, in summer in deep narrow gulfs running far inland, in estuaries, or in land lakes near and on other pieces of open water, less often on salt than on fresh.   With us in the winter it most often keeps to the rivers and streams both in flat and hilly country, wooded or quite open country, and from there it visits other open places of the lakes, ponds, brooks, or even quite small springs.   Should the cold become more severe, and should therefore fewer places remain free from ice, then they go the round from one to the other and betake themselves as soon as they are disturbed to the next place and continue thus, doing this daily for weeks, and repeat this series of changes though not at regular intervals, until the cold weather either forces them farther southwest or the approach of milder weather opens again larger places for them on the rivers and permits them to remain there.   They can endure the most severe cold quite comfortably, and it is only the breaking up of the ice on the rivers which they hate, particularly if the so-called ground ice is driving hard; in that case they take refuge on the open places of quiet water in the neighborhood of the former and fly from one to another.   In time of need they do not despise an occasional stay on the smallest springs and brooks, and in our neighborhood often appear at such times quite close to the villages.

DISTRIBUTION.

Breeding range.—Northern Europe and Asia.   From northern Lapland and Finland eastward across northern Russia and Siberia to Bering sea.

Winter range.—On the eastern coasts from Norway to Morocco and inland as far south as the Swiss lakes, the Mediterranean, Black and Caspian Seas, Persia, Afghanistan, north India, China, Japan and the Commander Islands.

Casual records.—One reported taken by Audubon near New Orleans in winter of 1817.   Specimen in the British Museum purchased from the Hudson's Bay Company, and one in the Tristam collection, both supposed to have come from North America.

Egg dates.—Northern Europe: Twelve records, May 23 to June 26; six records, May 28 to June 14.

ANAS PLATYRHYNCHA Linnaeus.

MALLARD.

HABITS.

Spring.—With the first signs of the breaking up of winter, when the February sun, mounting higher in the heavens, exerts its genial power on winter's accumulations of ice and snow, and when the warm rains soften the fetters that have bound the lakes and streams of the middle west, the hardy mallards, the leaders in the migrating hordes of wild fowl, leave their winter homes in the Southern States and push northward whenever they can find water, about the margins of the ponds, in open spring holes, and among the floating ice of rivers and streams, flushed with the spring torrents from melting snow banks.   Because they follow so closely in the footsteps of retreating winter the earliest migrants have been termed "ice mallards" by the gunners.   The spring migration starts in the Central Mississippi Valley soon after the middle of February and advances north as fast as conditions will permit. By the second week in March the advance guard has reached the Northern States, and large flocks may be seen circling about over the lakes in search of open water or dropping into sheltered pond holes to feed on the first tadpoles and other small fry thawed out by the warm rays of the advancing sun. It is usually three weeks or a month later before they penetrate into central Canada and they do not reach the northern limits of their breeding range in the Mackenzie region until the first week in May, or in Alaska until the middle of May.

Throughout all the central portions of its range, in the Great Plains region of the Northern States and central Canada it is one of the most abundant and most widely distributed of the ducks, as well as the best known and most important of our game birds; eastward of the Prairie States it diminishes in abundance and is almost wholly replaced by its near relative, the black duck.

Courtship.—The plumage of the mallard drakes is at its highest stage of perfection before the end of winter, and the first warm days stimulate these vigorous birds to migrate to their northern homes. Many of them are already mated when they arrive and the flocks of mated birds soon break up into pairs and fly about in search of suitable nesting sites. Others are busy with their courtships, which are conducted largely on the wing. I have seen as many as three males in ardent pursuit of one female flying about, high in the air, circling over the marshes in rapid flight and quacking loudly; finally the duck flies up to the drake of her choice, touches him with her bill nd the two fly off together, leaving the unlucky suitors to seek other mates.

Dr. Charles W. Townsend (1916) describes the courtship of this species as follows:

When the mallard drake courts, he swims restlessly about following or sidling up to a duck. She may lead him quite a chase before she vouchsafes to acknowledge his presence, although he is continually bowing to her, bobbing his head up and down in nervous jerks so that the yellow bill dips into the water for a quarter of its length and comes up dripping. He also rears himself up in the water and from time to time displays his breast. She occasionally turns her head to one side and carelessly dabbles her bill in the water, but sooner or later, if all goes well, she begins to bow also, less vigorously at first—not touching the water at all—and to the empty space in front of her. Suddenly she turns and the pair bow to each other in the same energetic nervous jerks, and, unless a rival appears to spoil the situation, the drake has won his suit.

Mr. H. Wormald (1910) has given a detailed account of the courtship of the mallard, illustrated with excellent drawings, to which I refer the reader. He says:

The performance usually begins by four or five drakes swimming round a duck with their heads sunk, and their necks drawn back, and in this attitude they have the appearance of being most unconcerned. This I will call action No. 1. After swimming round in this fashion for some little time, the mallards will suddenly lower their bills so that the tips of them are under the surface, and as they do so they stand up in the water and then rapidly pass their bills up their breasts. This motion is performed with somewhat of a jerk, and if one observes very closely, a tiny jet of water will be seen to be thrown out in front by the bill being jerked from the water; this is interesting, as one also finds this jet of water in the spring "show" of the golden-eye, but in this case it is made by the drake kicking out a small jet of water with his foot while he quickly throws back his head.

The mallard while performing action No. 2 as I will designate it, utters a low note rather difficult to describe, but I think it may be said to be a low whistle with a suspicion of a groan in it, as though it caused the bird an effort to utter. Following this, the mallards lower their breasts and raise their tails two or three times in quick succession; and this, which we may call action No. 3 is often followed by a repetition of actions Nos. 1 and 2. A quick "throw up" of head and tail, with the feathers of the head puffed out, is action No. 4, and this is followed quickly by action No. 5 in which the drakes stretch out their necks with their throats just over the water and swim rapidly about in different directions, when, apparently by common consent, they all come back to action No. 1, and go through the whole performance over again.

Nesting.—In North Dakota I found the mallard breeding quite commonly, in 1909, about the lakes and sloughs of Nelson and Steele Counties, although it was outnumbered by at least three other species, the blue-winged teal, the pintail, and the shoveller. It begins laying in that region early in May, though fresh eggs were found as late as May 31. The locality there chosen for its nest is generally on or near the edges of a slough or lake, either among dry, dead flags where the ground is dry or only slightly marshy, or upon the higher land not far from the water and among thick dead reeds. It also nests on the open prairies and often at long distances from any water. Two of the nests we found were on an island in Stump Lake in the middle of a patch of tall, dry, reedlike grass, locally called "queen of the prairie" (*Phragmites*) which grows higher than a man's head. The nest is usually well hidden and consists of a hollow in the ground, well lined with broken dead reeds or flags, apparently picked up in the immediate vicinity, mixed with dark gray down and a few feathers from the bird's breast; the down is thickest around the edges of the nest and increases in quantity as incubation advances.

During my two seasons spent in southwestern Saskatchewan, 1905 and 1906, mallards were frequently seen flying about in pairs up to the middle of June, indicating that they had not all finished laying at that time. They were not as common as several other species of ducks, but were seen on many of the lakes and nearly all of the creeks. Only seven nests were found during the two seasons and five of these found on the great duck island in Crane Lake on June 17, 1905; these five nests contained 1, 2, 6, 8, and 9 eggs, respectively, showing that they breed later in that region than farther south, although these may have been exceptional cases.

While my own personal experiences with the nesting habits of the mallard undoubtedly illustrate its normal habits, certain departures from its customary manners of nesting are worth mentioning. Dr. Morris Gibbs (1885) mentions finding a nest "placed in a hollow stub, similiar to the wood duck's nest."

Mr. L. E. Wyman says of its nesting habits in the vicinity of Nampa, Idaho:

Breeds in the tules and swampy creek bottoms, and to some extent around the reservoir, where lack of that sort of vegetation essential to its breeding operations has led to its nesting in some cases in alfalfa fields a quarter of a mile away, a well-beaten path connecting nesting site and water.

Mr. J. Hooper Bowles (1909) describes the nesting habits of the mallard in Washington as follows:

West of the Cascades the nest is often built at a considerable distance from water, a nest found near Spanaway Lake serving for an example. It was situated 150 yards from the lake under a pile of brush on a bushy hillside. The duck, when flushed, tumbled along the ground, feigning a broken wing, but she soon flew quacking to the lake, where she was very shortly joined by the drake. Other nests are built in the heavy fir timber, being placed at the base of a giant tree in exactly the same manner as nests of the sooty grouse.

Mr. Robert B. Rockwell (1911) thus describes a rather unusual nest which he found in the Barr Lake region of Colorado:

On May 11, 1907, while wading out from shore through a sparse, burn'd-over growth of cat-tails, skirting a small lake, a female mallard flushed noisily from a large musk-rat house and revealed a beautiful set of 11 eggs deposited in a hollow, scraped in the dead cat-tails and débris forming the house, and well lined with down. The house was very conspicuous, standing over 2 feet above the surface of the water surrounding it, and the nest was an open one, as can plainly be seen from the accompanying illustration. There was no apparent attempt at concealment. The female flushed when we were fully 30 yards from the nest, and the male swam about well out of gunshot. A week later (on the 18th) we succeeded in approaching to within 10 feet of the brooding female, who was in plain sight even from a considerable distance. The nest was in much the same condition as on the preceding visit, but the downy lining was much less in evidence. On the 24th we found that the muskrats had been adding to the house, with the result that the mother bird, in order to keep her treasures from being buried, had been forced to move her nest over toward the edge of the pile. In fact four of the eggs were missing on this date, and we surmised that they had been pushed off into the water during the moving process. A week later (May 31) the house had been built up much higher, and the nest was on the ragged edge of the pile, with the eggs apparently far advanced in incubation. On June 8 the eggs had been hatched, and in our examination of the nest we were surprised to find the four missing eggs deeply buried in the débris at almost the exact spot where the nest was located when first found. A fascinating bit of the family history would have undoubtly been revealed had we been enabled to observe the attitude of the busy muskrats toward the brooding mother bird, and the process of moving the nest.

Mr. J. Hooper Bowles has sent me the following interesting notes:

In the vicinity of Takoma, Washington, the mallards have an extremely wide range of variation in their nesting habits, both as to date and locations for nesting sites. Many of them are paired by the middle of January, and the first eggs are usually deposited during the last week in February. Fresh eggs may be found from this date up to the middle of June, but the great majority are hatched by the latter part of April.

The early nests are nearly always, in my experience, placed either in trees or far back in the dense fir timber on the ground, in the latter case usually at the base of some huge fir, or under a fallen log among dense brush, often a quarter of a mile from the water. It has always been a mystery to me how a bird of the open water, like a mallard, can find its way back to the nest through timber and brush so thick that it requires all the ardor of the oologist. I well remember my first sight of mallards under these conditions, when I was hunting horned owls in some very heavy timber. It was a pair flying about ten feet from the ground and passing only a few feet from where I stood motionless. They were evidently hunting a favorable nesting site and they threaded their way swiftly, but surely, among the tree trunks, seeming as much at home as any grouse.

When building in trees the nests are never in those of the large tree-nesting birds, but are usually built in the fork of some large tree where an abundant growth of moss and tree ferns make the site both secure and well concealed. I have found such nests as high as 25 feet above the ground, the great majority of my observations being made on the estate of Dr. G. D. Shaver, who has made an especial study of these ducks and showed me all the nests that he could find.

As the season advances more open situations are often selected, sometimes at the base of a small oak on the dry prairie, at others among the rushes in a marsh over several feet of water, and again on a floating log in some small woodland pond. The mallards seem to lose much of their habitual shyness when the nesting season approaches, having little hesitation in building close to human habitations. However, they are very artful when leaving and returning to the nest, being experts at crawling and hiding, so that few people have any idea that there is such a thing as a duck within a mile of them.

The male is the most attentive to the female during the nesting season of any of our ducks, being seldom far from the nest at any time. I once saw a drake guiding a brood of downy young through a very brushy swamp, and was fortunate enough to have them pass directly under me as I was standing on a low, rustic bridge. The female was nowhere to be seen, which is so unusual under the circumstances that I believe she must have met with some accident.

The mallard occasionally lays its eggs in the nest of other ducks. I have found what were apparently mallard's eggs in nests with canvasbacks and redheads. Nearly all ducks when nesting in close proximity are more or less addicted to this habit though the mallard is less often guilty of it than several other species.

The nest of the mallard is generally well lined with large fluffy down, "bister" or "sepia" in color, with conspicuous white centers and faintly indicated whitish or light brown tips. Distinctly marked breast or flank feathers, with central brown streaks, or broadly banded with dusky and tipped with brown, are usually found in the nest, together with more or less rubbish. The nest and eggs somewhat resemble those of the pintail, but both the down and the eggs are larger and the feathers are distinctive.

Eggs.—Only one set of eggs is normally laid by the mallard which usually consists of from 8 to 12 eggs, sometimes 6 eggs constitute a full set and sometimes as many as 15 are laid. The eggs of the mallard might easily be mistaken for those of the pintail, but they average slightly larger, a little lighter in color and are not quite so much elongated. The female mallard when flushed may be readily distinguished from the pintail by its larger size, shorter neck, and by its blue speculum with conspicuous white borders. The eggs are elliptical ovate in shape and vary in color from a light greenish buff to a light grayish buff, or nearly white, with very little luster. The measurements of 93 eggs in various collections average 57.8 by 41.6 millimeters; the eggs showing the four extremes measure **64** by **41.5**, 63.5 by **45**, **52.5** by 39.5 and 53 by **38.5** millimeters.

Young.—Incubation, which is performed wholly by the female, lasts from 23 to 29 days, usually 26; it does not begin until after the last egg is laid, so that they all hatch out about the same time. As soon as the young have dried their downy coats and are strong enough to walk, they are led by their mother to the nearest water which is often a long distance away. The watchful mother is ever on the alert and at the approach of danger gives her note of alarm which sends the little ones scattering in all directions to hide in the underbrush or thick grass, while she diverts the attention of the intruder. She is very courageous in the defense of her young; I once surprised a female with her brood in a little pond hole in the timber; although the young were well hidden in the surrounding grass and bushes, the old bird was flapping about, within a few feet of me, splashing and quacking loudly, frequently rising and circling about me, then dropping into the pond again and showing every symptom of anxiety, totally regardless of her own safety; the young were too well concealed for me to find them and I left the anxious mother in peace. The drakes usually take no interest in family cares, after the eggs are laid, but gather in small flocks by themselves, molt into eclipse plumage and hide among the rushes in the sloughs where they spend the summer in seclusion. The female, according to Audubon (1840), cares for and rears the brood alone.

She leads them along the shallow edges of grassy ponds, and teaches them to seize the small insects that abound there, the flies, the mosquitoes, the giddy beetles that skim along the surface in circles and serpentine lines. At the sight of danger they run as it were on the water, make directly for the shore, or dive and disappear. In about six weeks those that have escaped from the ravenous fishes and turtles have attained a goodly size; the quills appear on their wings; their bodies are incased with feathers; but as yet none are able to fly. They now procure their food by partial immersions of the head and neck in the manner of the old bird.

Dr. Harold C. Bryant (1914) has noted that—

when diving to escape capture they would often cling to the weeds beneath the surface, and when finally forced to come to the top for air would expose to view the top of the bill only. They tried to escape by simply diving and clinging motionless to weeds more often than they attempted to swim long distances under water.

As soon as the young birds have acquired their first plumage, in September, they gather into flocks, old and young together, and feed in the grain fields, where they become very fat.

Plumages.—The downy young mallard, when first hatched, is richly colored; the upper parts, the crown and back, are "sepia" or "clove brown," darkest on the crown; the under parts, including the sides of the head and a broad superciliary stripe, are "napthalene yellow" more or less clouded, especially on the cheeks with "honey yellow" or intermediate shades; there is a loral and postocular stripe and an auricular spot of "clove brown"; four yellowish spots, two on the scapulars and two on the rump, relieve the color of the back. As the young birds increase in size the colors of the upper parts become duller and lighter and the yellows of the under parts fade out and are replaced by more buffy shades.

The juvenal plumage comes in first on the scapulars and flanks at an age of about 3 weeks, then a week later, on the rump and breast and finally on the head and neck, when the bird is nearly 2 months old; the tail begins to appear with the first plumage, but the last of the down has disappeared from the neck before the wings are even started; these are not completed until after the young bird is fully grown or about 10 weeks old. In this juvenal plumage the sexes are practically indistinguishable, though the male is slightly larger and has a larger bill. In this plumage the young birds resemble the adult female to a certain extent, but they are darker and more brownish, especially on the chest and back; the latter is "hazel" or even as bright as "burnt sienna" in young birds.

From this time on the sexes differentiate rapidly in their steady progress towards maturity; this is accomplished during the next two months by a continuous molt which is, perhaps, accompanied by some sympathetic change of color in the growing feather. The result is that the young birds have assumed by December, or when about 6 months old, a plumage which is practically the same as that of the adults, though the highest development of the plumage is not acquired until the following year.

The annual molts and plumages of the adult consist of a double molt of all the contour feathers, into the eclipse plumage in the summer and out of it again in the fall; the flight feathers are molted but once, while the drake is in the eclipse plumage, in August. Thus instead of a nuptial plumage, worn in the spring and summer, and a winter plumage, worn in the fall and winter, we have a full plumage, worn in the winter and spring, and an eclipse, or a concealing, plumage, worn for only a month in the summer, but with much time consumed in the two transitional molts. The same thing takes place, to a greater or a lesser extent, with nearly all of the ducks; the eclipse plumage is much more complete in the surface-feeding ducks than in the others, and it is more strikingly illustrated in the mallard than in any other species. It seems remarkable, indeed, that such a brilliant and conspicuous plumage, as that of the mallard drake, should disappear entirely and be completely replaced with an entirely different plumage, which only an expert can tell from that of the somber, mottled female; but such is the case; the wings and the larger scapulars, which are molted only once, are all that remain to distinguish the male. I have seen males molting into the eclipse plumage as early as May 10, but usually the molt does not begin until the latter part of that month. I have seen drakes in full eclipse plumage as early as July 20, but usually it is not complete until August. It is worn for about a month, the earliest birds beginning to molt out of it in August. Some birds regain their full plumage in October, but some not until November or even later. Mr. John G. Millais (1902), one of the greatest living authorities on ducks, has made a very thorough and exhaustive study of this subject and has written a particularly full and detailed account of the plumage changes of the mallard. Although we may not wholly agree with all of his interesting conclusions, regarding color changes without molt and control of the molt, we must accept them as probably correct until they are proven erroneous.

The tendency of several species of ducks to hybridize is well known and many interesting hybrids have been described. The mallard seems to be more inclined to hybridism than any other species, particularly with its near relative, the black duck. Numerous specimens of hybrids between these two species have been collected, showing various grades of mixed blood; they freely interbreed in captivity and their offspring are perfectly fertile. Specimens have been described showing first crosses of mallard blood with the muscovy duck, the green-winged teal, the baldpate, and the pintail. In connection with plumages it may be worth mentioning that many sportsmen throughout the West recognize two varieties of mallards, the yellow-legged variety, which is the earlier migrant in the spring and the later in the fall, and the red-legged variety, which is more of a warm-weather bird; the former is supposed to breed farther north and to frequent the prairies exclusively whereas the latter is more often found in the timbered swamps and streams. Probably the differences in the two varieties are due to age rather than geographical variation.

Food.—Mallards are essentially fresh-water ducks and find their principal feeding grounds in the sloughs, ponds, lakes, streams, and swamps of the interior, where their food is picked up on or above the surface or obtained by partial immersion in shallow water. In Alaska and on the Pacific coast they feed largely on dead salmon and salmon eggs, which they obtain in the pools in the rivers. On or near their breeding grounds in the prairie regions they feed largely on wheat, barley, and corn which they glean from the stubble fields. On their migrations in the central valleys they frequent the timbered ponds, everglades, and wooded swamps, alighting among the trees to feed on beechnuts and acorns or to pick up an occasional slug, snail, frog, or lizard. In the South they resort to the rice fields and savannas in large numbers, feeding both by day and night if not disturbed; where they are hunted persistently they become more nocturnal in their feeding habits.

Mr. W. L. McAtee (1918) has published an exhaustive report, based on the examination of 1,578 gizzards of the mallard by the Biological Survey, from which I quote as follows:

Approximately nine-tenths of the entire contents of the 1,578 mallard stomachs examined was derived from the vegetable kingdom. The largest proportion of the food drawn from any single family of plants came from the sedges and amounted to 21.62 per cent of the total. Grasses rank next in importance, supplying 13.39 per cent; then follow smartweeds, 9.83; pondweeds, 8.23; duckweeds, 6.01; coontail, 5.97; wild celery, and its allies, 4.26; water elm and hackberries, 4.11; wapato and its allies, 3.54; and acorns, 2.34 per cent. Numerous minor items make up the remainder. Some of the stomachs of the mallards were interesting on account of the large numbers of individual objects they contained. For instance, one collected at Hamburg, La., in February, revealed about 28,760 seeds of a bullrush, 8,700 of another sedge, 35,840 of primrose willow, and about 2,560 duckweeds as the principal items, a total of more than 75,200.

The animal food of the mallard duck though extremely varied may be classed in five main groups: Insects, which constitute 2.67 per cent of the total diet; crustaceans, 0.35; mollusks, 5.73; fishes, 0.47; and miscellaneous, 0.25 per cent.

Dr. Thomas S. Roberts (1919) has published the following interesting note, showing the useful work done by mallards in destroying mosquitoes.

The late Dr. Samuel G. Dixon, while health commissioner of Pennsylvania, published an article in the Journal of the American Medical Association for October 3, 1914, detailing results of experiments made by him along this line. Two dams were constructed on a stream so that the ponds would present exactly the same conditions. One was stocked with gold fish and in the other 20 mallard ducks were allowed to feed. After several months the duck pond was entirely free from mosquitoes while the fish pond "was swarming with young insects in different cycles of life." Ten well-fed mallards were then admitted to the infested pond. At first they were attracted by the tadpoles but "soon recognized the presence of larvae and pupae of the mosquito and immediately turned their attention to these, ravenously devouring them in preference to any other food present. At the end of 24 hours no pupae were to be found and in 48 hours only a few small larvae survived.

Mr. Edward H. Forbush (1909) says:

It sometimes attacks sprouting or ripened grain but like most fresh-water fowl it is undoubtedly of service in destroying such insects as the locusts and army worms which sometimes become serious pests. Professor Aughey found in the stomachs of ten mallards taken in Nebraska 244 locusts and 260 other insects, besides mollusks and other aquatic food.

Mr. J. H. Bowles (1908) records an interesting case of lead poisoning among mallards which had been feeding in a marsh that for many years had been a favorite shooting resort. The ground must have been thoroughly sprinkled with shot for the stomachs of the dead ducks were well filled with the pellets which had probably been picked up by mistake for gravel.

One stomach contained 19 shot, one 22, and the other 27. The large intestine was heavily leaded and seemed contracted, while the lining of the stomach could be easily scaled off in quite large crisp pieces. The gastric juices had evidently worked on the shot to some extent, as most of them were considerably worn and had taken various shapes.

Dr. Alexander Wetmore (1919) has published an interesting paper on this subject, based on investigations made near the mouth of Bear River, Utah, in 1915 and 1916, in which he shows that lead poisoning is a real cause of mortality among this and other species of ducks, where these birds have been feeding on grounds which have been shot over for many years. No practicable remedy has been suggested.

Doctor Wetmore (1915 and 1918) has published two other papers, based on his extensive investigations in Utah, from which it appears that the great mortality among waterfowl around Great Salt Lake is due largely, if not wholly to alkaline poisoning. Countless thousands of ducks and other waterfowl have perished within recent years in this and other similar localities, apparently from disease. He explains the cause very well as follows:

After June 15, as the spring waters in Bear River recede, great expanses of mud flat are laid bare in the sun. Surface evaporation and capillary attraction rapidly draw the salts held in solution in the mud to the surface and there concentrate them. As the mud becomes drier these concentrates are visible as a white deposit or scale (efflorescence). This in many cases is exposed only an inch or so above the surrounding water level. In the large bays strong winds bank up the water and blow it across these drying flats. As it advances it takes rapidly into solution the soluble salts, largely sodium chloride, but containing calcium and magnesium chloride also. This inflow of water carries with it quantities of seeds and myriads of beetles, bugs, and spiders, washed out of crevices and holes in the dried and cracking soil. The ducks come in eagerly to feed on this easily secured food and work rapidly along at the front of the advancing water, each bird hurrying to get his fill. Many individuals in this way secure a sufficient quantity of these poisons to render them helpless. As the water recedes again small pools are left in shallow depressions, and other ducks and shore birds feeding in these are affected.

The only remedy suggested is to supply the birds with a sufficient quantity of fresh water, under which treatment they recover.

Behavior.—The wild mallard is an active, wary bird, well worthy of the prominent place it holds among the game birds of the world. It springs from the water, at a single bound, straight up into the air for several yards and, when clear of all surrounding reeds, bushes or trees, flies directly away in a swift, strong and well-sustained flight. Several loud quacks are usually uttered as the bird springs into the air. The mallard, especially the female, is a noisy bird on its feeding grounds, the loud quacking notes, suggesting familiar barnyard sounds, give timely warning to the ardent hunter, as he seeks his quarry among the reedy sloughs. The mallard is not a diving duck and ordinarily does not go below the surface of the water; when wounded, however, it is skillful in avoiding capture by swimming under water or hiding among the rushes, with only its bill protruding; it has even been known to hide under a lily pad, lifting the leaf above the surface to enable it to breathe. Dr. Wilfred H. Osgood (1904) relates the following interesting incident illustrating the hiding ability of the mallard.

One foggy morning as we were slipping down the current of one of the narrow side channels a brace of mallards flew across a small peninsula to our left and alighted in a little cove, whence they hauled out on the muddy bank. Thinking to secure a good fat duck for dinner, we quickly swung the canoe into an eddy and paddled upstream toward the little cove. One of the birds flew while out of range, and at about the same time the other somehow disappeared, although there was but a small patch of grass for concealment. Expecting the bird to rise at any moment, we paddled on but were beginning to feel baffled, when just before the canoe touched the bank, we found our game giving a very pretty exhibition of its confidence in protective coloration. It was a female mallard, and lay on the brown mud bank, strewn with dead grass and decaying matter, which blended perfectly with the markings of its back. It was not merely crouching, but lay prostrated to the last degree, its wings closely folded, its neck stretched straight out in front of it with throat and under mandible laid out straight, and even its short tail pressed flatly into the mud. The only sign of life came from its bright little eyes, which nervously looked at us in a half hopeful, half desperate manner. When a paddle was lifted, with which it could almost be reached, the bird started up and was allowed to escape with its well-earned life.

Game.—Local fall flights of mallards begin before the end of summer, late in August or early in September, soon after the young birds are able to fly, but these are mainly wandering, drifting flights from their breeding grounds or summer hiding places in the sloughs, to favorite feeding grounds in the vicinity, where wild rice is ripening or where grain stubble offers a tempting food supply. The real fall migration does not begin in earnest until late in September, when the first early frosts, the brilliant hues of ripening leaves and the falling crop of acorns and beechnuts remind them of advancing autumn. But the waning of the harvest moon and the crisp, clear nights of early October also remind the hunters of the glorious sport of duck shooting; in the stillness of the night they push their flat skiffs out through the watery lanes among the acres of reeds and buckbrush to the shallow ponds, overgrown with smartweed and wild rice, where the ducks are wont to feed, their wooden decoys are anchored in some conspicuous open space and their skiffs are carefully concealed in blinds of thick reeds and grasses, where they patiently await the coming daylight, listen for the quacking notes of the awakening ducks and watch for the passing flocks on the way to their feeding grounds. If they have not been shot at too much mallards come readily to the decoys, but they become wary with experience; artificial duck calls are used to imitate their notes, which are quite effective when skillfully operated; line decoys, as they are called, are fastened to long lines run through fixed pulley blocks, so that they can be made to swim in towards the blind or out again, by pulling on the lines, to attract the attention of passing flocks. Large numbers of mallards are still killed in this way all through their main routes of migration, but they have decreased greatly in numbers owing to persistent shooting in both spring and fall and owing to the settlement and cultivation of their main breeding grounds in the northern prairie regions. The mallard is a splendid game bird and has always held the leading place among our wild fowl on account of its abundance, its wide distribution, and its excellent qualities as a table bird; in my estimation there is no duck quite equal to a fat, grain-fed mallard, not even the far-famed canvasback; unquestionably the mallard has always been our most important market duck and certainly more mallards have come into our markets than any other one species.

Winter.—The mallard is a hardy bird and its winter range is a wide one, reaching as far north as it can find open water. Hagerup (1891) found it " common the whole year round, but most numerous in winter, when they keep in small flocks along the shore, " in southern Greenland. In Alaska the mallard winters at several places at the outlets of lakes, in open streams near the seacoast and about the Aleutian Islands. Although essentially a fresh-water duck throughout its general range, the mallard is forced by circumstances in Greenland, Alaska, the northern Pacific Coast, New England, and other northern portions of its scattering winter range to resort to the mouths of rivers and bays where it can find open water. The main winter range, however, is in the lower half of the Mississippi Valley, south of the line of frozen ponds, and in the Gulf States from Texas to Florida. Here it lives and flourishes, mainly in fresh-water ponds, swamps, streams, everglades, and rice fields, fattening on the abundance of good food but still harassed by gunners and killed by market hunters and sportsmen in enormous numbers. " Big Lake, Arkansas, was and still is one of the favorite resorts, and during the winter of 1893–94 a single gunner sold 8,000 mallards, while the total number sent to market from this one place amounted to 120,000," writes Doctor Cooke (1906).

Mr. E. H. Forbush (1909) says:

In 1900 I visited a gunning preserve in Florida where northern sportsmen were shooting ducks by the hundred and giving them away to their friends and to settlers.

One of these gentlemen armed with repeating guns and supplied with a man to load and others to drive the birds to his decoys is said to have killed on a wager over 100 ducks in less than two hours. Even within the last two years reports of reliable observers on the Gulf coast aver that market hunters there have been killing 100 birds each per day.

The Houston (Texas) Post of January 29, 1908, asserted that during the previous week five citizens while hunting came upon a small lake into which the fowls were flocking in great numbers. Using their repeating guns and acting by a prearranged signal they flushed the game, emptied their guns, and gathered 107 killed not counting the wounded and missing. The birds were mainly mallards.

The foregoing quotation will serve to indicate the enormous slaughter which has been going on among our game birds, of which the mallard is merely a fair sample. This was due mainly to the increasing numbers of gunners and the improved effectiveness of firearms.

Owing to the prohibition of market hunting, the curtailing of the shooting season, and the establishment of breeding reservations and fall and winter sanctuaries, this rapid extermination has been checked and the birds are now holding their own and are even increasing in some places. The big reservations on the coast of Louisiana show the beneficial effect of protection. Here the mallards and other ducks gather in great numbers in the winter, feeding in the ponds or patches of open water in the marsh, or rising, when disturbed, in immense flocks with a mighty roar of thousands of wings.

DISTRIBUTION.

Breeding range.—Northern portions of the Northern Hemisphere. In North America mainly west of Hudson Bay and the Great Lakes. A few breed in Greenland, but these are considered subspecifically distinct *Anas platyrhyncha conboschas* Brehm, and are apparently resident. East sparingly to eastern Ontario, central New York (Cayuga County), northwestern Pennsylvania (Erie and formerly Williamsport), and central New Jersey (Passaic County and Burlington County). South to northern Virginia (upper James River) southern Ohio, southwestern Indiana (Knox County), southeastern Illinois (Wabash County), central Missouri (Johnson County), eastern Kansas (Johnson County), southern New Mexico, and northern Lower California (San Pedro Martir Mountains). West to the Pacific coasts of the United States, Canada, and Alaska, and west in the Aleutian Islands to Tanaga Island and probably farther. North to northern Alaska (Kotzebue Sound), the Arctic coast of Mackenzie (Mackenzie Delta and Anderson River), and the coast of Hudson Bay. In the Eastern Hemisphere it breeds in Iceland, throughout Europe (south of the Arctic Circle), in the Azores, and in northern Africa; in Asia from Turkestan to China, Japan, Chosen, the Kurile Islands, Kamchatka, and the Commander Islands.

Winter range.—Practically all of North America, south of Canada. East to the Atlantic coast, the Bahama Islands, and rarely to the Lesser Antilles (St. Vincent and Grenada). South to central Florida (Cape Canaveral), the Gulf coasts of Louisiana and Texas, and to southern Mexico (Jalapa and Colima). North along the Pacific coast to the Aleutian Islands; in the interior to central Montana (Fergus County), southern Wisconsin, and the Great Lakes; and on the Atlantic coast regularly to Virginia, irregularly to New York and New England, and casually to Nova Scotia.   In the Eastern Hemisphere it visits the Azores, Madeira, and the Canary Islands, and ranges south in Africa to the Tropic of Cancer and to India and Burma.

Spring migration.—Early dates of arrival: Manitoba, Aweme, March 24; Saskatchewan, Qu' Appelle, March 26; Mackenzie, Fort Resolution, May 7; Fort Providence, April 27; and Fort Simpson. May 3; Alaska, Kowak River, May 17.   Average dates of arrival: Pennsylvania, Erie, March 5; New York, central, March 23; Ontario, southern, March 24; Ottawa, March 27; Indiana, Frankfort, February 21; Missouri, central, February 26; Illinois, Chicago, March 19; Iowa, Keokuk, February 24, and Spirit Lake, March 10; Minnesota, Heron Lake, March 11; South Dakota, central, March 16; North Dakota, Larimore, March 28; Manitoba, Aweme, April 3; Saskatchewan, Qu' Appelle, April 10.   Late dates of departure: North Carolina, Raleigh, April 7; Mississippi, Shellmound, April 5; Missouri, central, March 28; Texas, northern, May 6.

Fall migration.—Average dates of arrival: Virginia, September 21; Illinois, Chicago, September 27; Iowa, Grinnell, September 17; Texas, northern, October 11; Panama, Miraflores, November 26. Average dates of departure: Quebec, Montreal, October 26; New Brunswick, Scotch Lake, November 7; Ontario, Ottawa, November 5; Manitoba, Aweme, November 12; Illinois, Chicago, November 13; Minnesota, southern, November 22; Iowa, central, November 15; Nebraska, central, November 18.   Late dates of departure: Quebec, Montreal, November 13; Ontario, Ottawa, November 14; Manitoba, Aweme, November 23; Minnesota, southern, December 11; Iowa, central, November 27; Nebraska, central, November 26.

Casual records.—Accidental in the Bahamas, Cuba, Jamaica, and Grenada; and the Hawaiian Islands.

Egg dates.—North Dakota, Minnesota, and Wisconsin: Thirty-one records, April 29 to July 6; sixteen records, May 17 to June 1. California and Utah: Twenty-nine records, March 25 to 27; fifteen records, April 27 to May 20.   Alberta and Saskatchewan: Thirteen records, May 15 to July 4; seven records, June 5 to 17.   Oregon and Washington: Twelve records, March 17 to July 2; six records, May 7 to 24.   Northern Alaska: Two records, June 9 and 19.

ANAS NOVIMEXICANA Huber.

NEW MEXICAN DUCK.

HABITS.

Contributed by Wharton Huber.

In the valley of the Rio Grande River from El Paso, Texas, north to Albuquerque, New Mexico, this northern form of the *diazi* group makes its home. Whether on the mud flats in the river, the numerous alkali ponds, or cat-tail swamps through the valley this duck is ever watchful and wary of man.

I have observed several New Mexican ducks about 3 miles north of the city of El Paso, Texas, hence they probably range down the river possibly as far as the Big Bend country in Texas. In June, 1915, I saw five individuals at Belen and two at Albuquerque, New Mexico, on the mud flats in the Rio Grande River.

Courtship.—During the months of April and early May, 1920, I watched the courtship of several pairs of these ducks along the Rio Grande River west of Las Cruces, New Mexico. In April, two, three, and sometimes five New Mexican ducks could be seen on the mud flats in the middle of the river, as often with flocks of mallards as alone. When with a flock of mallards they would stay together and not mix with the former. The male could be seen bowing to the female and occasionally pecking and pulling at her wing feathers. When in the water the male would swim close to the female he had chosen, generally behind her, swim close up and pull at her feathers quacking all the while. If another (presumably a female) came too close he would swim rapidly at the intruder until she was driven to a safe distance. Returning to his prospective mate he would bob his head up and down a number of times quacking contentedly. Early in May these ducks were evidently mated as they were always seen in pairs or single birds.

On May 7, 1920, while watching a pair of the ducks on a mud flat in the middle of the Rio Grande River west of Las Cruces, New Mexico, I witnessed a very interesting performance. Both ducks took flight simultaneously, rising in the air at an angle of about 30°. They were flying slowly, their wings seeming to raise higher than in ordinary flight, both quacking incessantly. They passed the point where I was concealed about 400 feet away and about 300 feet high, the male (as I afterward learned) directly above the female. Making a large circuit over the land the male all the while keeping his position directly above the female, they swung again over the river coming head up into the light wind, whereupon they set their wings and descended to the water, the female slightly in the lead. Immediately upon alighting copulation occurred.

Nesting.—The nest and eggs of the New Mexico duck, so far as I know still remain to be described. Although I hunted almost daily during the last half of May and the first half of June, I was not successful in locating a single nest of this species.

Young.—On July 20, 1920, in a cat-tail (*Typha latifolia*) swamp of about 7 acres extent, 4 miles southwest of Las Cruces, New Mexico, I flushed a female that evidently had young. She flew over the cat-tails in circles while I spent over an hour wading the swamp looking for the young, apparently not at all afraid of me, as she passed time and time again within a few feet of my head. I did not, however, find the young. On July 27, 1920, a young fully feathered male and an adult female were collected from a flock of 12 individuals that were feeding where the overflow from an irrigation ditch ran into the Rio Grande 5 miles southwest of Las Cruces, New Mexico. From this date on flocks of from 10 to 25 young accompanied by old females could be seen feeding along the river bank. Even at this age they were extremely wary, and one could get within range only by the greatest stealth and stalking.

Food.—The feeding habits of this species are similar to the mallard. They feed along the river banks, in the drainage canals, ponds, and cat-tail swamps. In the spring the flooded alfalfa fields are favorite grounds for food. Ever extremely wary, they pass much of the daytime on the mud flats in the middle of the river. At dusk they seek their favorite feeding grounds, a cat-tail swamp or flooded alfalfa field even though it lie close to a ranch house or small settlement. The food I found to consist of green shoots of alfalfa and cat-tail, grass roots, corn, wheat, and numerous small fresh-water shells together with the larger seeds of weeds and grasses.

Behavior.—The flight of the New Mexican duck is similiar to that of the mallard, but it is a stronger and somewhat faster flyer. It was during the very heavy wind storms lasting two or three days that occur in March in southwestern New Mexico that I noticed the greater strength of flight of this species over the mallard. One could easily distinguish an individual of this species in a flock of mallards by its darker color and conspicuous pyrite yellow bill.

While feeding in the ponds and flooded alfalfa fields it keeps a short distance away from the other ducks. Food is obtained in the deeper water by thrusting the head straight down and keeping the body nearly submerged by the use of the feet, the tail only standing straight up above water. I have never seen this duck dive even when wounded. Several times while hunting with decoys on some of the larger ponds, combined flocks of mallards and New Mexican ducks would alight a hundred or more yards beyond the decoys. Ever wary and suspicious the New Mexican ducks would feed by themselves and never venture nearer the decoys, while the unsuspecting mallards would soon be swimming in and out amongst the wooden ducks.

DISTRIBUTION.

Contributed by Wharton Huber.

Although little is yet known of the range of this species, we do know that it is most plentiful along the Rio Grande River from Albuquerque, New Mexico, south to El Paso, Texas. Wetmore in his paper on Birds of Lake Burford, New Mexico, 1920, speaks of seeing—

on May 25th (1918), a large very dark-colored duck in company with a mated pair of mallards. It had white bars on either side of the speculum and was much darker in color than the female mallard, resembling a black duck markedly. It is possible that this was a female mallard, but it seemed to have a clear olive green bill and was larger, thus resembling a male of the black duck group (possibly *A. dinzi*).

This evidently was an individual of the present species in the northwestern part of the State of New Mexico (Rio Arriba County). Probably the lakes and streams of Chihuahua, Mexico, will shortly be included in the known range of this duck.

[Author's note: A female, now in the Conover collection in the Field Museum in Chicago, was taken in Cherry County, Nebraska, on October 17, 1921.]

ANAS RUBRIPES TRISTIS Brewster.

BLACK DUCK.

HABITS.

The black duck, or dusky duck, as it was formerly and more properly called, for it is far from black, fills an even more important place among the wild fowl of eastern North America than does the far-famed mallard of the interior and western part of our continent. The black duck, by which name it is universally known among gunners, is decidedly *the* duck of the Eastern States, where it far outnumbers all other species of fresh water ducks. The West has many other species to divide the honors with the mallard, but in the East the black duck stands practically alone. It is the black duck more than any other that is suggested to my mind by those classic lines of William Cullen Bryant:

> Vainly the fowler's eye
> Might mark thy distant flight to do thee wrong,
> As, darkly lined upon the crimson sky,
> Thy figure floats along.

Spring.—When the gentle breath of spring calls him from his winter home on the New England seacoast the black duck seems to know in some mysterious way that the ice is going out of the lakes and streams far inland, perhaps he is impelled by the increasing warmth of the sunshine or by some impulse of returning love to leave behind him his fruitful feeding grounds in the salt marshes and the tidal estuaries; rising high in the air he sets his course toward his summer home in far-distant lakes and swamps; the sea knows him no more until the following autumn or winter. He is not the earliest of the migrants, nor yet the latest, but the latter part of March generally sees him well on his way. Black ducks migrate in pairs or in small flocks in the spring, usually at a great height; they are always extremely cautious, and before alighting in a woodland pond for the night, they usually circle around it several times and then scale down on stiff decurrent wings to alight in the open water far out from any dangerous cover; here they rest in peace and safety, but at the first blush of dawn their silver-lined wings are flashing over the tree tops and they are off for another day's journey.

Courtship.—While afield in early April in search of hawks' nests and other springtime treasures, I have often seen the spirited nuptial flight of this species. Near some woodland reservoir I have heard the loud quacking notes and looking up, have seen a pair, or perhaps, three, of these ducks flying over the tree tops at full speed; the courtship chase seems to be a test of speed and energy, a sort of aerial game of tag, as they sweep around again and again in a large circle or back and forth over the pond or swamp which they will probably choose for a summer home; finally the bride yields to the suitor of her choice and they fly off together or drop down into the the water. Mr. Edmund J. Sawyer (1909) describes a spectacular courtship performance of this species which I have never seen; he writes:

Most interesting were the actions of one pair that, from the time the flock came, constantly raced from end to end of the pond, one bird closely pursuing the other. Now and again the chase became too hot, and the leading bird in a thrilling swirl of water rose several feet into the air, followed immediately by the other. Toward the farther end of the pond they would splash into the water, soon to take wing again in the opposite direction. As, with necks stretched far out and downward, the pair flew half the length of the pond—2 or 3 rods—while the other ducks looked quietly on or went indifferently about their feeding, making the water dance till it seemed alive with ducks, the scene was really spectacular. Again and again I heard the pair of ducks break from the water, and the splash, splash, as they dropped into the pond again. Each time they rose, it seemed as though they must discover me, for at such times I was in open view, had they glanced in my direction.

Nesting.—The black duck nests in a variety of situations and does not seem to show any preference for any particular kind of surroundings provided it can find sufficient concealment. This makes it one of the hardest ducks' nests to find, for one never knows where or how to look for it and can only happen upon it by chance; I have spent many hours hunting for it in vain, around the edges of swamps or grassy meadows, along the shores of ponds, in thickets of under-brush or even in the borders of the woods near such places. The nest is generally placed in dry ground, but usually not very far from the water. The first nest I found was in the Magdalen Islands on June 21, 1904. It was in the center of a little islet or "nubble" in a small pond hole in the East Point marshes, a favorite breeding place of this and other ducks. The nest was prettily located and well concealed in a thick clump of tall dead grass; the hollow in the ground was lined with dry grass and only a little down, as the eight eggs that it contained were fresh; as with other ducks, more down would be added as incubation advanced. On another similar "nubble," two days later, we noticed a pathway leading through the grass to a clump of low bay-berry bushes, and on investigation we unearthed a black duck's nest with four eggs completely buried under the dry bayberry leaves and rubbish; the eggs were perfectly concealed under natural surround-ings and there was nothing to indicate a nest except the obscure path-way.

Audubon (1840) found nests in Labrador—

embedded in the deep moss, at the distance of a few feet or yards from the water. They were composed of a great quantity of dry grass and other vegetable substances; and the eggs were always placed directly on this bed without the intervention of the down and feathers, which, however, surrounded them, and which the bird always uses to cover them when she is about to leave the nest for a time.

Mr. M. A. Frazar (1887) reported the nests that he found, in the same region, as "being generally placed upon the outreaching branches of stunted spruces." Mr. John Macoun (1909) publishes an account of a nest, found by Rev. C. J. Young near Brockville, Ontario, on May 24, 1897, on the edge of a floating bog; he writes:

The place where the nest was made was not exactly wet, as there was a matted foundation of dry weeds among which it was well concealed, composed of dry grass and well lined with the down of the bird. Incubation had commenced about a week, which would make the time of commencing to lay about the first week in May in this case.

I have never succeeded in finding a nest in New England, but Mr. E. A. Samuels (1883) gives a satisfactory account of the nesting habits here, as follows:

The nest is built about the last week in April or the first in May. It is placed in a secluded locality in a tussock of grass, or beneath a thicket of briers or weeds; usually in a meadow, near a pond or stream, but sometimes in a swamp in which a small brook is the only water for miles around. This species sometimes follows these small brooks up to their sources; and I once found one with a nest on a low stump that overhung a small spring on the side of a hill, a mile from any other water. The nest of this species is constructed of pieces of grass and weeds, which are neatly arranged into a structure 18 inches in diameter on the outside, and 3 or 4 in depth. This is hollowed for perhaps an inch and a half or 2 inches, and lined with the down and feathers from the breast of the parent bird.

Mr. Robert T. Moore (1908) found a nest of this species in New Jersey on May 22, 1908, in a wooded point surrounded by meadows; he describes it very attractively, as follows:

The body of the nest filled the space between the roots of a large maple. Dark-green lichens spotted the tree forming a beautiful background, while light green was the color of the huckleberry bushes branching above and grouping on the left. The front and right were screened by a bunch of soft brown grasses, which converged above with the huckleberry bushes and made it impossible to thrust in a hand without breaking the grasses. The nest proper concaved about a depression 8 inches in diameter. It was filled with pine spills, bracken, and leaves of oak and maple, no down having yet been inserted. The eggs were packed closely, the leaves sticking up between them. In color they were cream buff, some of them having a slight greenish tinge. The whole interior of the nest was soft brown, leaves, spills, and eggs lending various shades, but all molding into each other. These browns harmonized with the greens above, and made a most attractive home. Four days later the nest contained 12 eggs, so full as to have the appearance of convexity. Three eggs had been laid in four days. Down was now present, having been inserted in little bunches over the inside of the nest, adding a touch of warmth.

The black duck has been known to nest in old deserted crow's and hawk's nests in trees. Mr. Edwin Beaupré (1906) records two such cases in Ontario, as follows:

The first instance occurred June 10, 1904, when, on a small island in the St. Lawrence River, a pair of these ducks had taken possession of an old crow's nest, and on the date of discovery had laid 10 eggs. The nest was saddled on a limb of a large elm 45 feet from the ground. With the exception of a liberal supply of down furnished by the bird the nest was in its original condition and so completely was it concealed by the foliage that the presence of the duck in her snug retreat would never have been suspected had she not been accidently observed flying to the tree. The difficulty I experienced in photographing the nest adds to the value of the excellent negative I secured.

April 29, 1905, I located the second nest; in this case, owing to the bareness of the trees, concealment was impossible. The duck had laid 10 eggs in a last year's nest of the red-shouldered hawk in a basswood tree 50 feet up, and the appearance of this large bird sitting on her nest among the naked branches was truly most unique.

The down in the black duck's nest much resembles that in the mallard's; it is large and fluffy in form, and "bister" or "olive brown" in color, with whitish centers, which are not so conspicuous as in the nest of the mallard. Mixed with the down a few characteristic breast or flank feathers are usually to be found; these dusky feathers with a central buffy streak or buffy edgings will serve to identify the nest.

Eggs.—The black duck lays from 6 to 12 eggs in a set, usually 8 or 10; it has been said to lay as many as 15, but anything beyond 12 is unusual. The eggs closely resemble those of the mallard and can not with certainty be distinguished. In shape they vary from elliptical ovate to nearly oval. The shell is smooth, but has very little luster. The color varies from dull white or creamy white to various pale greenish buffy shades, such as "pale olive buff" or "Marguerite yellow." The measurements of 82 eggs in various collections average 59.4 by 43.2 millimeters; the eggs showing the four extremes measure **64** by 43, 61.2 by **44.8, 55** by 42.5 and 58.5 by **41** millimeters.

Young.—Incubation lasts for 26 or 28 days and is performed by the female alone. The males usually desert the females as soon as the eggs are laid and flock by themselves, leaving their mates to hatch the eggs and care for the young. In this the duck proves to be a faithful and devoted mother; she sits close upon the eggs, particularly as the hatching time approaches. The process of hatching is described by Mr. Charles S. Allen (1893) in the following interesting detail:

The exact method adopted by the bird in freeing itself from the shell proved interesting. I will describe the procedure as it occurred in an egg that I took from the nest before the first crack had appeared. While examining it there was evidence of a strong muscular effort on the part of the bird inside, and a small disk of shell was chipped out and raised above the surface at about one-third of the distance from the end; then came a second or two of rest, followed by what felt like a scramble inside; then a second of quiet and the horny little knob on the end of the bill was driven through the shell one-eighth of an inch to the right of the first puncture. This routine was repeated over and over until some 25 or 30 punctures had been made, completely encircling one end of the egg, each being about one-eighth of an inch to the right of the preceding one. The efforts seemed stronger as it started around the same circle again, and the cap of the shell would be lifted a little each time, showing that it was attached by little more than the tough membrane beneath the shell. Before the second circle was half completed, it tore the cap loose so that it could be raised like the lid of a box, with 1 inch of the membrane acting as a hinge. In freeing itself from the shell the neck was stretched out and the little one breathed for the first time. Then the shoulders were pushed out into my hand, free of the shell, one wing after the other being freed, while the bird lay gasping and gaping widely with its bill. In half a minute more it was entirely free from the shell and lay weak and helpless in the sun, its wet, slimy skin absolutely bare, save here and there small dark hairs widely separated. As it began to dry it gained in strength and made feeble efforts to stand, resting on the whole length of the tarsus. In drying, the hairs no longer adhered to the skin. Soon each little pointed hair began to crack and split open, and from this protective casing there came a light fluff of down nearly as large as the end of one's finger. It was more surprising than the bursting of a grain of pop corn, though far less rapid. It took comparatively few of these yellow and brown fluffs to convert the naked weakling into a beautiful downy duckling that stood up boldly in my hand and began to notice what was going on about it, especially the calls of the parent bird close by. Each went through the same procedure, invariably breaking the shell from left to right. They showed no fear and would cuddle under one's hand very confidingly.

The young remain in the nest for a few hours after hatching sometimes not over an hour, until they have gained a little strength, become dry and freed the fluffy down from its wet sheaths. Then the careful mother leads them forth to introduce them to the world and its many dangers, teaching them how to escape from their various enemies, how to hide in the thickest grass, under the leaves or any other object that will cover them, how to crowd and "freeze" in any little protecting hollow, how to swim and dive in the water or scurry away to the nearest cover when they hear her warning call to hide. It is surprising how soon they learn the art of concealment, how quickly they obey the call, and how suddenly they vanish so completely that it is about useless to hunt for them. In the meantime the devoted mother, utterly regardless of self, uses every art known to her fertile brain to attract attention to herself and away from her young, flopping along the ground or water, as if hopelessly crippled, within a few yards, or even feet, of her giant enemy, returning again and again to throw herself at his feet beseechingly. Once I surprised a mother duck, far from land, swimming across a bay with a brood of little ones close at her heels; she would not desert them and my thoughtless boatman fired at her; fortunately he missed her and fortunately for him he did not shoot again or he would have measured his length overboard. The old duck sometimes makes long journeys over land on foot with her little brood. Judge J. N. Clark (1882) relates the following incident:

One of my neighbors, sitting by a window, had his attention called to a brood of young ducks running across the street. It was an old black duck and her young. He saw them enter a cow yard, and in one corner she called her brood under her wings and covered them. As he went near she flew some 15 rods and watched his movements, quacking her displeasure as he proceeded to capture her young ones. He secured 10 of them, all the brood but 2. After he had examined all he cared to he set them at liberty, and together they started on a run through Main street, continuing for 40 rods before they turned aside, a distance which they accomplished inside of five minutes; for the little things could run like squirrels.

I once found a little one that had come to grief on its overland journey; with one foot hopelessly entangled in some vines, it had fallen into a wagon rut; it was still alive, but had been deserted by its mother. I can imagine the consternation of the poor mother, who, after exerting every effort to free it from its predicament, was finally obliged to abandon it to save the rest of the brood.

Plumages.—The downy young black duck resembles the young mallard, but the color of the upper parts averages darker, much darker in many cases, and it extends farther down on the sides of the breast and flanks, often invading the belly; the under parts are less yellowish; and the dusky stripes on the head are darker, more pronounced, and more extensive. There is much individual variation in the latter character in the 17 specimens in my collection; in all there is a dusky stripe, of greater or less intensity, from the bill to the eye and from the eye to the occiput; in most of them there is a dusky rictal spot, and a dusky auricular spot, though in some the former is lacking; in some these spots are joined in a stripe; and in one very swarthy individual, in which even the lower parts are largely dusky, these two stripes are very broad and coalesce on the cheek.

The colors of the upper parts, including the crown down to the bill and the head stripes, vary from dark "mummy brown" to "bister" or "sepia." The sides of the head, including a broad superciliary stripe, are "buckthorn brown " or "honey yellow " becoming paler on the throat to "light buff" or "cream buff." Similar but duller shades appear on the under parts, from "Naples yellow" to "cream color," shading off to dull grayish white on the belly. The inner edge of the wing and the scapular and rump spots are pale yellowish buff.

The development of the young bird to maturity is practically the same as in the mallard, the sexes being indistinguishable and the wings being acquired last. The growth and development of the flight feathers in the young goes on simultaneously with the molt of the adults, so that both reach the flight stage together in September. During the first fall and perhaps for some time after that, I do not know how long, young black ducks can be distinguished from old birds, but during the first year, perhaps during the fall and early winter, they are rapidly becoming adult in appearance. Young birds during their first fall and winter may be recognized by the more striped appearance of the under parts, due to the fact that the feathers of the breast and belly are centrally black quite to the tip and broadly edged on the sides only with brown or buff; whereas in adults these feathers are very broadly dusky and only narrowly margined with buff, giving the under parts a much darker appearance; the lighter color of the neck is not so sharply separated from the dark colors of the body in the young as in the adult; and young birds have more conspicuous light edgings above and a partially immaculate chin and throat.

The age and seasonal changes in this species are not well marked or conspicuous, and one can not discuss them very far without becoming hopelessly involved in the much argued, sad case of the red-legged black duck, which has never been positively or even convincingly proven or disproven.

I have often been asked if the black duck has an eclipse plumage, with the double molt common to all the surface-feeding ducks. The eclipse plumage, if it had one would not be conspicuous and the double molt could be detected only by dissection or close inspection. It begins to molt very early in the summer and is in more or less continual molt for three months or more, but, as there is no necessity of an eclipse plumage for concealment, I doubt if there is an actual double molt. Lord William Percy, the British expert on ducks, tells me that none of the ducks in which the sexes are alike have an eclipse plumage; probably he is correct in this statement. The black duck then has, probably, only one annual molt, the postnuptial, which is prolonged and complete; the remiges are all molted at about the same time, so that the bird becomes practically flightless for a while.

The black duck crosses freely with the mallard and the two species are so closely related that the hybrids are fertile. A number of cases of first crosses have been recorded and specimens showing signs of mixed blood are rather common.

Food.—Black ducks are surface feeders or dabblers in shallow waters, where they can reach bottom by tipping up their tails and probe in the mud with their bills. In the shallow, muddy ponds and swamps where they spend the summer they feed largely on aquatic insects and their larvae, salamanders, tadpoles and small frogs, leeches, various worms, and small mollusks; many varieties of snails are found on the stems of sedges and grasses; small toads are not despised and even small mammals are eaten occasionally. With all this variety of animal food they mix a fair proportion of vegetable diet; seeds of aquatic and land plants are picked up and the succulent roots of many water plants are pulled up and eagerly devoured. Dr. F. Henry Yorke (1899) records the following genera of plants as recognized in the food of the black duck: *Limnobium, Zizania, Elymus, Danthonia, Piper, Myriophyllum, Callitriche,* and *Utricularia.*

Dr. Leonard C. Sanford (1903) writes:

In localities where blueberries grow near the water they are a favorite food. On the Magdalen Islands the writer has frequently seen black duck feeding high up on the hills among the blueberry bushes, in company with Hudsonian curlew.

In the fall, when the grains are ripened, they resort to the grain fields and feast on wheat, barley, buckwheat, and Indian corn. Later in the season they visit the timber where acorns and beechnuts are to be found in the vicinity of woodland ponds. The rice fields of the South are fruitful feeding grounds in winter where they grow fat and rich in flavor. On the seacoast in winter they resort mainly to the salt marshes to feed at night, returning to the open sea or to large bodies of water during the day; in the marshes and meadows they feed mainly on snails, bivalves and other small mollusks, crustaceans, and perhaps some vegetable food.

Dr. J. C. Phillips (1911) sent a lot of stomachs of ducks and geese, shot in Massachusetts in the fall of 1909, to Mr. W. L. McAtee for analysis; he quotes from Mr. McAtee's report as follows:

The contents of the black ducks' stomachs (29 in all, 4 empty) was 88.4 per cent vegetable, the principal items being seeds of bur reed (*Spanganium*), pondweed (*Potamogeton*), bullrush (*Scirpus*), eelgrass (*Zostera*) and mermaid weed (*Proserpinaca*), and buds, rootstocks, etc., of wild celery. The animal matter, amounting to 11.6 per cent, included, in the order of importance, snails, ants, chironomid larvae, bivalves, crustacea, and insects. The percentage of mineral matter of the gross contents was 36.5.

Mr. Ora W. Knight (1908) says:

I have known individuals to so gorge themselves with huckleberries in late August that they would go to sleep under the bushes near the water, and one which I started from under my feet in this condition when I too was after huckleberries was unable to fly, it was so gorged, but it managed to scramble into the water and swim away, disgorging itself until finally able to rise and fly away, all the time quacking incessantly.

He also speaks of two birds—

killed in winter on the Penobscot River [which were] literally crammed [with the fruit of] *Lepaigyraea canadensis* Nuttall, another shrub not known from this particular region.

Mr. Elon H. Eaton (1910) writes:

I shot a black duck from a flock of 75 birds, which were returning to Canandaigua Lake from a flooded cornfield. From its gullet and gizzard I took 23,704 weed seeds, which, together with a few pebbles, snail shells, and chaff, were the sole contents of its stomach. Of these seeds, 13,240 were pigweeds (*Chenopodium* and *Amaranthus*), 7,264 were knot grass (*Polygonum*), 2,624 were ragweed (*Ambrosia*), and 576 were dock (*Rumex*).

Behavior.—The black duck starts into flight, from land or water by a powerful upward spring, rising perpendicularly 8 to 10 feet into the air before it starts away in its swift and direct flight. When once under way its flight is strong and swift, usually high in the air, unless forced by strong adverse winds to fly low; its long neck is outstretched and its wings vibrate rapidly, the white underside of the wings flashing in the light and serving as a good field mark at a long distance. When descending from a height to alight in a pond the pointed wings are curved downward and rigidly held, as the smooth body glides through the air, tipping slightly from side to side, gradually dropping in a circle until near enough to check its momentum with a few vigorous flaps and drop into the water, feet first, with a gentle, gliding splash.

On land the black duck walks with ease and grace, running rapidly, if necessary, and holding its head high. It is ever on the alert and can seldom be surprised. It swims lightly and gracefully and with some speed. It does not ordinarily dive, but it can do so, if necessary, as every gunner knows who has wounded one and chased it. I have read that this duck can detect the presence of danger by the sense of smell, but I doubt it; it would not come so readily to well-concealed duck stands, where human beings are living constantly, if its nostrils were very keen. I should think it more likely that it depends on its sight and hearing, both of which are very acute and highly developed.

Dr. D. G. Elliot (1898) very aptly says:

Its note is so like the mallard's that it is difficult to distinguish them apart, and every few moments the quacks are shot forth in abrupt vociferations, as if the bird had just reached the limit of its power for suppressing them, and the voice had gained strength and sonorousness by long confinement.

The drake has only a low reedy quack, whereas the duck's note is a loud and resonant quack, in which she indulges freely; most of the noise is made by her. These ducks are generally very noisy while feeding and, as they are very alert and wary, their loud notes serve as timely warnings to other species on the approach of danger.

Fall.—Black ducks usually flock by themselves mainly because, in the regions where they are most numerous, there are comparatively few of the other surface-feeding ducks of similar habits. The early flights in September are often associated with blue-winged teal and later flights with a few of the other western ducks. The earliest flights consist mostly of young birds, often not fully feathered, and probably they are made up of family parties. The flocks are usually small, often less than 10 birds and seldom more than a dozen; large flocks are very rare except when congregated in winter quarters.

Mr. Walter H. Rich (1907) writes of the migration in Maine:

When the summer wanes and the young birds have become strong enough to journey, straggling ducks begin to make their appearance in the salt marshes, then in small bunches a few at a time; as cold weather approaches they gather at the sea into flocks ranging from 20 to 200 birds. Near my home they gather winter after winter at the mouth of a fresh-water river in a body of, at times, as many as 5,000 birds, coming in at night and spending their days on the salt water, except in bad weather, when they huddle on the ice at a safe distance from the shore. From the 1st of September such of their number as are not inclined to brave the rigors of a New England winter begin their longer journey to southern waters, and up to the middle of December the migrant birds continue to pass.

Dr. J. C. Philips says in his notes, published by Doctor Townsend (1905), referring to the fall migration at Wenham Lake, Massachusetts:

It has always seemed to me that there were three more or less distinct flights of black ducks observed here at the pond. The outside dates for these flights are about as follows: September 14 to October 5; October 1 to October 31; November 1 to November 20. These dates vary, of course, according to the season.

The first of the ducks are hastened along by an early frost or cool northwest weather, and their approach can be predicted almost to a certainty by a flight of ospreys, which precedes and accompanies them. The ospreys begin to come by in some numbers two or three days before the ducks arrive, and their flight seems to be at its height during the first day or two of the duck flight. Black ducks on this flight are very often accompanied by pintail and blue-winged teal.

The first and second flights sometimes merge into one another, but are commonly separated by an interval of some days to a week, or more, during which time few birds are observed. The second flight is scattered over a longer period and is accompanied by various other varieties of ducks. Widgeon and mallard are often seen with black duck at this time and sometimes pintail. The red-legged subspecies is common during the flight but rare among the early ducks. The second flight is much more pronounced during certain weather. Thus on the end of a stormy northwest wind or during brisk southwest weather, more birds are noted than at other times. At night, there are apparently many bunches which alight in the pond for a very short period of rest, and which leave of their own accord. These night flights are seen almost entirely during southwest winds and probably occur as often on dark as on moonlight nights.

The last flight is a more scattering and irregular affair and consists mostly of the red-legged variety. Some of these birds probably winter not far away. The red-legs average heavier and are a much wilder bird. They take to the larger ponds only and nearly always approach decoys with caution.

Prof. Lynds Jones (1909) reports this as "the commonest of the larger ducks, if, indeed, it is not the commonest of all ducks" in Ohio. He says:

Gunners report "millions" in the height of the gunning season. Such an estimate appears less extravagant when one realizes that the birds, almost crazed by the constant rattle of the guns, are flying back and forth and up and down, the same individuals reappearing many times in the course of an hour. I have seen many hundreds in a single day, but I doubt if more than a few thousands are even present on any day.

Game.—Whereas, this is only one of the many birds which interest ornithologists and bird protectionists, it is the bird of all others which interests the wild-fowl gunners of the Eastern States; it is the most important object of their pursuit, the most desirable as a game bird, one of the shyest, most sagacious, and most wary of ducks and the one on which their best efforts are centered. Therefore, I have always thought that it ought to be considered and treated more from a sportsman's standpoint than from any other and that any legislation for its protection ought to give due consideration to the rights of the sportsmen in the pursuit of such a noble game bird. To prohibit shooting it during January has always seemed to me unfair to many sportsmen on our seacoast, to whom it is not available during earlier months. The black duck has shown marked success in the struggle for existence; it is so sagacious, so wary, and so alert that it is one of the best equipped species to survive, even in a thickly settled region where it is constantly beset by hunters, but where, fortunately for its welfare, numerous safe refuges have been established. For these reasons it is hardly in need, as yet, of very stringent protective laws; therefore, I see no reason why sportsmen should not be allowed a reasonable amount of sport at its expense.

The methods employed for shooting black ducks are many and varied, but they all depend on the strategy and skill of the hunter in outwitting one of the keenest of game birds. They will not ordinarily come to wooden decoys, for their keen eyes readily detect the deception, but on the islands off the coast of Maine I have had fair sport over wooden decoys anchored just off the rocks where we lay concealed; the birds came in singly or in twos or threes, circling wide at first and then coming in to inspect the decoys; on discovering their mistake they would mount into the air and swerve off, but sometimes too late to escape the shot. In the winter when the ponds were frozen over, we used to find good shooting, without any decoys at all, where springs or small streams emptied into the salt water bays; here the ducks came in to drink or bathe in the only available fresh water under the cover of darkness; it is almost useless to attempt this kind of shooting except on moonlight nights and even then it is difficult and unsatisfactory.

Mr. Rich (1907) describes the method used in Maine, as follows:

Probably the most of these birds which fall a prey to the gunner's wiles are shot from "sinkboxes" and "blinds" in the reed-grown corners of fresh-water ponds, using live decoys to lure the birds on to their destruction. The successful duck shooter must be up betimes and be ready to endure much discomfort, for he must be at his position before daylight in order to get the cream of the shooting, and, where gunners are as numerous as in my section, a late comer is apt to find every stand occupied.

The decoys are placed before the blind, anchored, as a rule, so that one old drake is somewhat separated from the rest, and being dissatisfied and lonesome, he keeps up a continual remonstrant conversation with the rest of his flock. If a bunch of birds is passing, never fear but he will see them and find means to let the strangers know of his presence and whereabouts, and they, with a sudden turn from their course, with necks outstretched and wings stiffly set, come in at full speed. Now they turn away, careering around the pond two or three times because the foxy old fellow who leads them is not just suited with the appearance of things—some small matter of suspicion in his mind—but next time around a bird or two in the tail of the flock, more hungry than wise, drop out with slanting flight, then another and yet more, until finally the main body comes in like a flight of arrows. Splash! Splash! They have settled just outside the line of decoys and begin to swim in toward them. Now the gunner waits until they are bunched at a little distance from his "tolers," which, if old hands at the business, at once swim away from their visitors, and when his feathered assistants are surely safe the gunner pulls trigger where there is the greatest number of heads. The encore when the survivors rise like the scattered fragments of a bursting shell will hardly account for more than a pair, but usually the "pot shot" with the first barrel has done grand service toward thinning the game supply, and it is no common occurrence for one gun in experienced hands to gather in nearly all of the flock.

A modification of this method, more highly developed and modernized, is practiced in Massachusetts. On the shore of a pond frequented by migrating waterfowl, or on an island in it, a permanent camp is built, known as a "duck stand," at which one or more of the gunners live constantly all through the shooting season. This consists of a small house or shanty equipped with sleeping bunks for severa men, a stove for cooking and for heating it and shutters to prevent the lights showing through the windows at night. Along the shore is built a fence or stockade just high enough so that a man can shoot over it; there are portholes cut in the fence so that several men can shoot through it without being seen. The house and the fence are completely covered with branches of freshly cut pine and oak with the leaves on them, which renders the whole structure practically invisible from the lake. The stand is built where there is a beach or a point in front of it, or where a sandy beach can be artifically made. Various sets of wooden decoys or "blocks," as they are called, are anchored at some distance out in the lake. A large supply of live decoys, semidomesticated black ducks, mallards and Canada geese,

are kept in pens, inside or behind the enclosure, and a few are tethered on the beach, anchored in the water near it or allowed to roam
about. Sometimes a few are kept in elevated pens back of the stand,
so arranged that the pens can be opened by pulling a cord and
allowing the ducks or geese to fly out and meet the wild ones. With
all this elaborate equipment ready for action the gunners, I can
hardly call them sportsmen, spend their time inside the house, smok-
ing, talking, playing cards, or perhaps drinking, while one man
remains outside on the watch for ducks. Should a flock of wild ducks
alight in the pond, he calls the others and they all take their places
at the portholes, with heavy guns, ready for the slaughter. The
quacking of the decoys gradually tolls the wild birds in toward the
beach or perhaps the fliers are liberated at the critical moment.
Each gunner knows which section of the flock he is to shoot at and
waits in anticipation until the birds are near enough and properly
bunched, when the signal is given to fire. If the affair has been well
managed most of the flock have been killed or disabled on the water,
but, as the frightened survivors rise in hurried confusion, a second volley is poured into them and only a few escape. The wounded birds
are then chased with a boat and shot. There is no method of duck
shooting which is more effective and deadly; with gunners constantly
on the watch and decoys always ready to call a passing flock, very
few ducks get by without an attempt being made on their lives, and
often these attempts are only too successful. Probably before many
years this form of duck shooting will be prohibited by law, as too
destructive, and the more sportsmanlike method of shooting flying
birds from open blinds will give the ducks some chance for their lives.

Winter.—When the swamps, ponds, and lakes of the interior are
closed with ice the black ducks are driven to the seacoast to spend
the winter. They linger in the lakes, even after they are partially
frozen over, as long as an open water hole remains, resorting to the
spring holes and open streams, visiting the grain fields and marshes
or other places where they can find food and resting during the day in
large flocks on the ice, where they sleep for hours while some of their
number act as sentinels. On the coast their daily routine is to spend
the day at sea or on large open bays and to fly into the marshes,
meadows and mud flats to feed at night. At the first approach
of daylight, long before the rosy tints of sunrise have painted the sky,
black ducks may be seen, singly or in small scattered parties, winging their way out to sea, high in the air, their dark forms barely discernible against the first glow of daylight. At a safe distance from
land they rest on the tranquil bosom of the sea or sleep with their
bills tucked under their scapulars. It must be half-conscious sleep,
or perhaps their feet work automatically, for they never seem to drift
much. When the open sea is too rough their resting places are in

the lee of ledges in little coves or in the bays.   Often times they rest and sleep in large numbers on drifting ice, on sand bars or even on unfrequented beaches.   In very stormy weather they are often driven into the bays and harbors in enormous numbers.   During that memorable storm of November 27, 1898, I was out duck shooting all the morning at Plymouth, Massachusetts; the gale was so fierce that we could hardly walk against it and the driving snow and sleet was almost blinding; black ducks were driven inland in large numbers, the little pond holes in the woods were full of them and they could hardly fly against the storm; they even sought shelter in the orchards among the houses, and large numbers were killed.

DISTRIBUTION.

Breeding range.—Northeastern North America.   East to the Atlantic coast, from New Jersey northward.   South to eastern North Carolina (Pamlico and Currituck Sounds), northern Ohio (Lake County), northern Indiana (Lake County), northern Illinois (Calumet marshes), and northwestern Iowa (Spirit Lake).   West to central Minnesota (Kandiyohi County), eastern Manitoba (Lake Manitoba), and the west coast of Hudson Bay (Churchill).   Seen in summer at Fort Anderson. North perhaps to the latter point, to Ungava Bay, and northern Labrador (Okak).   Northern breeding birds are supposed to be the red-legged subspecies.

Winter range.—Eastern United States, mainly coastwise.   South to central Florida (Gainesville), the Gulf coasts of Alabama and Louisiana, and to south central Texas (San Antonio and Corpus Christi). West to eastern Nebraska (Lincoln), but rare west of the Mississippi Valley.   North to southern Wisconsin (Delavan), northern Ohio (coast of Lake Erie), northwestern Pennsylvania (Erie), sometimes the lake regions of central New York, on the coast of New England, and as far east as Nova Scotia (Chignecto Bay).   Casual farther west or north of above-named points and comparatively rare west of the Alleghenies.

Spring migration.—Early dates of arrival: Maine, southern, March 19; Quebec, Montreal, March 27; Quebec, Quebec, April 6; Prince Edward Island, April 5; Ontario, southern, March 16; Ontario, Ottawa, March 21.   Average dates of arrival: Maine, southern, April 7; Quebec, Montreal, April 14; Quebec, Quebec, April 18; Quebec, Godbout, April 21; Prince Edward Island, April 23; Ontario, southern, April 7; Ontario, Ottawa, April 14.   Late dates of departure: North Carolina, Raleigh, April 11; Florida, Wakulla County, May 2.

Fall migration.—Average dates of arrival: Virginia, Alexandria, September 30; South Carolina, Mount Pleasant, October 22 (earliest); Florida, Wakulla County, November 16.   Average dates of departure: Ontario, Ottawa, November 7; Quebec, Montreal, November 6; Prince Edward Island, November 13. Late dates of departure: Ontario, Ottawa, November 21; Quebec, Montreal, November 14; Prince Edward Island, December 8.

Casual records.—Accidental as far west as Saskatchewan (Davidson) and California (Willows, Glen County, February 1, 1911). Said to have occurred in Bermuda, Cuba, and Jamaica.

Egg dates.—Ontario, Quebec, and Nova Scotia: Thirty-six records, April 30 to June 28; eighteen records, May 20 to June 6. Massachusetts and Rhode Island: Seven records, April 23 to June 2. New York: Six records, April 18 to June 19. New Jersey: Eight records, April 25 to July 3. Virginia and Maryland: Several records, April 20 to May 10.

ANAS RUBRIPES RUBRIPES Brewster.

RED-LEGGED BLACK DUCK.

HABITS.

When our late lamented friend, William Brewster (1902) described the above subspecies, he started a controversy which has led to endless discussion and which has never yet been satisfactorily settled. A still further complication arose when the old, well-established name, *obscura*, was shown to be untenable; for this necessitated adopting Mr. Brewster's name, *rubripes*, for the species, to which he (1909) tacked on still another new name, *tristis*. The incident was sad enough to warrant the name, but our old friend was hardly recognizable after all the changes; fortunately we can still call him by the old familiar name, the black duck. Let us be thankful for the much-needed stability in the English names.

Sportsmen and others have long recognized the existence of two kinds of black ducks, the smaller birds with olive or brownish legs and olive colored bills, which appear early in the fall, and the larger birds with reddish or orange-colored legs and yellowish bills, which come later in the season and presumably from farther north. But whether these differences represent two geographical races and should be recognized in nomenclature, is another question.

It seems to me that the characters on which Mr. Brewster (1902) based his new form, *Anas obscura rubripes*, are the characters of the adult, while those which he leaves for *Anas obscura obscura* are those of immature birds. If we may reason by analogy from what takes place in the closely related mallard, we might expect to find in young black ducks a rapid approach toward maturity during the first winter, producing a plumage in the following spring which is practically, but not quite, adult. Then, if this theory is correct, the first winter plumage would be characterized by the olive bill, the dark pileum, the imperfectly spotted chin and throat, and the brown legs. The birds might be expected to breed in this plumage, as the mallards do.   At the first postnuptial molt, which is complete in August, it would then assume a plumage indistinguishable from adults, or nearly so, characterized by the yellow bill, the feathers of the pileum edged with grayish or fulvous, the throat and chin wholly spotted with blackish, and the red legs and toes.   All of these characters probably become more pronounced in very old birds and perhaps the many puzzling intermediates are birds of the second year.   There is another character which seems to be more pronounced in old birds, of the red-legged type, and that is the white tips of the greater wing coverts, forming a narrow white border of the speculum, which is conspicuous in older birds and either lacking or inconspicuous in birds of the first year.

As to the evidence in the case let us consider briefly a few salient points.   The strongest claim that the red-legged black duck has to recognition as a distinct subspecies is based on the well-established fact that nearly, if not quite, all the early migrants are brown-legged birds and that very few, if any, of the large, red-legged birds are seen or shot much before the 1st of October, the heavy flight coming after the middle of that month and presumably from farther north. This claim is somewhat weakened when we consider that the great bulk of the species nest far north of the points where observations have been made and records kept and that undoubtedly the younger and more tender birds migrate first and the older and hardier birds later, as is the case with some other species of ducks.   In this connection Dr. Charles W. Townsend (1905) writes:

Assuming, for the sake of argument, that *rubripes* is merely the adult male of *obscura*, it is interesting to note the similarity in seasonal distribution, between these two forms and the adult male red-breasted merganser as compared with the very differently plumaged females and immature.   In both cases the small, obscurely dressed birds come first during the early autumn, while the large showy birds come in late September and in October.   In both, these large birds are abundant in the winter, and the smaller ones are less common, while in both, the two forms appear again in the spring.   The remark of Doctor Phillips that "the first flight of black ducks consists mostly of young and often imperfectly feathered birds" is interesting in this connection.

In order to have any standing a subspecies must be shown to have a distinct breeding range, which has not been demonstrated in this case.   Mr. Brewster (1902) was able to find only four specimens of breeding ducks which he could unhesitatingly refer to the red-legged race, one from Ungava, northern Labrador, one from Moose Factory on James Bay, one from Cape Hope, Severn River, and one from Fort Churchill.   One of these seems doubtful, the Ungava bird, which the collector, Mr. Lucien M. Turner, describes in his original notes, as follows: "In the specimen procured by me the bill is of a dusky olive color; the nail black; the tarsus and toes deep orange red; webs, as well as under surface of toes and posterior portion of tarsus, blackish." The form *rubripes* is supposed to have a yellow bill. We have specimens of the old form, *tristis*, from southern and northern Labrador, Okak, and from Newfoundland; and I doubt if Mr. Brewster felt confident that all of the birds from the Hudson Bay localities, mentioned above, were *rubripes*. On the other hand we have some evidence to indicate that red-legged birds breed farther south. Dr. Jonathan Dwight (1909) had "a number of freshly killed birds" sent to him from Long Island, New York, "that scarcely needed dissection to prove them to be breeding birds. They were shot at various dates in April and all had red legs." Moreover, an adult male, killed on Long Island June 11, 1909, came fresh into his hands, which had the red legs and other characters supposed to belong to the northern race; it was "in full postnuptial molt, and evidently was recently mated." The only summer specimen I ever shot on Cape Cod had red legs. Mr. Horace W. Wright (1911) says of the birds seen by him, which were probably breeding near Jefferson, New Hampshire:

Most of those birds which have been seen on the ponds in the summer, near enough to distinguish whether they were of the type *rubripes* or *rubripes tristis*, have been of the latter type. Perhaps only two have been distinctly seen which were of the former type, namely, on July 30, 1908. These took wing so near to us on our approach that the red legs were clearly seen.

Mr. Edwin Beaupré writes to me from Kingston, Ontario, as follows:

Owing to the great number of black ducks in this vicinity this season (1920) the time was considered opportune for looking into the question of the subspecies. Between September 1 and November 4, 1920, 20 specimens were available for determination; of these five had red legs and were much larger than the brown-legged birds. The presence of these red-legged ducks in this locality September 1 is a reasonable indication of their having bred here.

Mr. P. A. Taverner has recently sent me some colored drawings of the bills and feet of black ducks, from which it appears that the breeding ducks of the Ottawa River region and of the Gaspé region are red-legged; also that what are evidently young birds show, at least a tendency toward red-legs.

It will be seen from the above remarks that the known facts regarding the distribution of the two forms are not conclusive either one way or the other, so we must turn to what little other evidence we have. Doctor Dwight (1909) says that the differences between the two forms—

are exactly the ones that distinguish old birds from young whether they occur in the United States or Canada. My evidence on this point is conclusive for I have skinned and dissected fully 50 specimens representing many localities, north and south, besides examining dozens of others shot by friends or found hanging in the markets.

We must admit that Doctor Dwight is an experienced expert in such matters and that his opinion ought to carry weight. Doctor

Townsend (1912) adds to our knowledge of the subject by recording the results of his observations on some black ducks hatched in Massachusetts and reared in confinement; he writes:

When 4 months old one of the females had a pure buffy throat, while the other female's throat had a few scattered spots on it. All three males had more or less fine spotting on a buffy ground. The bills of the females were dark greenish black, their tarsi brownish, while the bills of the males tended more to greenish yellow and their legs to orange. The next spring the bills of the males were slightly lighter in color, but by no means yellow, and their tarsi were possibly a little brighter orange. A study of the plumage showed, however, no suggestion of either an eclipse or a nuptial dress. In the third spring the appearance was essentially the same. The surviving male had a dark crown and nape, a buffy throat, fairly well, but not thickly spotted, a greenish yellow bill and orange feet—not by any means the coral red feet of *rubripes*. The female had a dark olive-green bill, dirty-yellow tarsi and an unspotted buffy throat. Their size was that of the smaller race.

This certainly proves that the bills of young black ducks grow yellower and the feet grow redder, as the birds grow older. We do not know how long it takes a black duck to acquire these evidences of age. We do know, however, that we have a similar case in the mallard, in which the hunters recognize a red-legged variety which migrates early in the fall and late in the spring, probably the younger birds, and a yellow-legged variety, which is the last to come in the fall and the first to appear in the spring; the latter is known as the "ice mallard" and is probably the very old bird. Mr. Fred H. Kennard (1913) thinks that he has settled the controversy by the discovery of a young bird with red legs. He says:

While at Monomoy Island, Massachusetts, during the last two weeks of October 1912, with a couple of friends, we shot a number of black ducks of the red-legged kind (there were no green legs), among which were several that were apparently young birds; and on October 25, there fell to one of our guns a female, which from its size, plumage, and general characteristics, was so evidently young that there could be no possible doubt about it. I personally skinned and sexed this specimen, which showed its immaturity in all those ways familiar to those who handle birds. It must have been one of a very late brood, for its upper mandible was a steel gray, and had not yet begun to show those shades of light olive green of the adult bird, and the "nail" at the end of the upper mandible was hardly darker than the rest of the bill, and nothing like the dark and glossy black of the adult bird. The lower mandible was pinkish and still quite soft and pliable, as in the case of very young ducks, and *the bird had red legs*.

Dr. John C. Phillips (1920) recognizes a distinct difference in habits between the two forms which he sums up as follows:

The habits that characterize the two forms as they appear in autumn in New England may be thus summed up: *Anas rubripes tristis*—Breeding locally and often migrating as early as, or before, mid-September, or at least "shifting ground" from inland nesting grounds to better feeding grounds near coast. Feeding in both ponds and salt meadows, but if in salt meadows, resorting to fresh water once or twice a day. Much less nocturnal in feeding habits than *rubripes*, because less shy, and much less inclined to spend day on open ocean. Prefers good fresh water and brackish water food, but spends the winters on the coast of New England in small numbers along with *rubripes*. Reaches great size at times. Largest male 3 pounds 10 ounces; largest female 2 pounds 15 ounces (Squibnocket, 1919). More difference in size between sexes than in *rubripes* ! Comes readily to live decoys, no matter how extreme the voice may be (too high or too low); and is more loquacious than the red-legged form.

A. rubripes rubripes.—Late migrant never becomes localized except near sea, and where marine food in the form of small mollusca is abundant. Very seldom resorts to small ponds or bogs, but likes large open sheets of fresh water near ocean, to which it often makes daily trips to drink and rest but not to feed. Is better able to sit offshore in rough seas; and in general appears a more rugged bird with heavier feathering and superior resistance to extreme cold. In winter, it does not depend on ponds for fresh water, but obtains a sufficient supply in small springs about salt meadows at low tide.

This is a much more wary bird, is more silent itself, and comes less easily to live decoys, toward which it manifests an instinctive fear, especially if they be loud or shrill callers. In the salt meadows the best gunners prefer seaweed bunches or canvas sacks, and find the live decoys useless, especially late in the season.

When a flock of *rubripes* alights on a pond near a shooting stand, they nearly always keep at a safe distance until perfectly satisfied of their surroundings. Then, more often than not, they will swim away from the stand and its live decoys. If they approach the stand, which they do with the utmost caution, and with necks erect, they are not apt to keep closely together as *tristis* does.

Extreme weights not much above that of *tristis*. Heaviest male noted by myself, 3 pounds 12 ounces. Average is a good deal heavier than *tristis*, females perhaps more nearly size of males than in *tristis*, but no figures at hand to bear out this point.

To sum up the evidence it does not seem to have been proven that a northern race, with a known breeding range, exists; but it does seem to have proven that the characters ascribed to it, are to be accounted for, at least partially if not wholly, by age variations. I am still prepared to believe that a northern race exists, but we need more evidence to prove it.

ANAS FULVIGULA FULVIGULA Ridgway.

FLORIDA DUCK.

HABITS.

Up to about 1874, when Mr. Ridgway described this species, the dusky ducks of eastern North America, from Texas to Labrador, were all regarded as one species. This well-marked southern species, characterized by its smaller size, lighter color, and particularly by its immaculate buffy throat, inhabits Florida and the other Gulf States. It is not known to intergrade with the northern black duck, and there is a considerable hiatus between the breeding ranges of the two species. The southern species has since been split into two subspecies, the Florida duck, restricted to Florida, and the mottled duck found in Louisiana and Texas; whether these two forms intergrade in the intervening States, or where they meet, does not seem to have been determined. Should a hiatus be found to occur between their breeding ranges it might be proper to regard them as distinct species, though all three forms are closely related and probably the intergrades have only recently disappeared.

In the central and southern portions of Florida this duck is an abundant resident bird. I have met with it frequently in the various portions of Florida that I have visited. On the islands in Indian River, where there were muddy ponds surrounded by marshes, we usually found a pair of these ducks, which were probably breeding there but had their nests too well concealed in the luxuriant growth of tall, thick grass for us to find them. We saw them occasionally in the inland lakes of southern Florida, but we found them most abundant in the extensive marshes of the upper St. Johns River; here they found ample feeding grounds and playgrounds among the dense tangles of vegetation, pond lilies, bonnets, water hyacinths, water lettuce, and other aquatic plants; the dense clumps of taller growth and the impenetrable saw-grass sloughs offered them concealment from their enemies; and they found safe sleeping and resting places in the centers of the larger bodies of water.

Nesting.—As I have not been fortunate enough to find one of their nests, I shall have to quote from the observations of others. Dr. D. G. Elliott (1898) says:

It breeds in April, and the nest, formed of grass and similar materials and lined with down and feathers, is placed upon the ground in the midst of matted grass, or under a palmetto, or some sheltering bush, near water.

The following account is published by Baird, Brewer, and Ridgway (1884) based on the excellent field notes of Mr. N. B. Moore:

This duck hatches in Florida from the first to the last of April, only one set of eggs being laid in a season, unless it fails in raising its first brood. The nest is always placed on the ground, and the number of eggs is usually 9 or 10. In one instance a nest was discovered which was nearly 300 yards from water, and other nests were met with still farther from water. The one first referred to was cautiously concealed in a thick mass of dead grass held upright by green palmettoes, about 2 feet high. Mr. Moore once noticed a pair of ducks fly from a pond, near which he was seated, and pass over the pine barrens. One of them dropped among the grass; the other returned to the water. Suspecting that the birds might have a nest, he visited the locality the next day, when the birds behaved as before. He soon made his way to the spot where the female alighted, and found her in a somewhat open space. On her return to the pond he soon discovered her nest. It was carefully screened from view on all sides, and so canopied by the standing grass that the eggs were not visible from above. There was a rim of soft down, from the mother's breast, around the eggs, partly covering those in the outer circle. On viewing the nest the next day this down was found to have been drawn over all the eggs. Mr. Moore took them and placed them under a hen; and six days after they were hatched. This was early in April. It would appear, therefore, that the statement that the male forsakes his mate during incubation is not well founded; for in this instance the male bird, about the twenty-fourth day of incubation, still kept in the vicinity of the nest. It is, however, the universal belief that he does not assist in rearing the young.

Mr. C. J. Maynard (1896) "found them breeding on Indian River, the nests being placed on the drier portions of the marshes, in grass which was about 18 inches high."

Eggs.—The Florida duck lays about 8 or 10 eggs which are similar to those of the black duck, but slightly smaller or shorter and rounder. In shape they are elliptical oval to oval. The shell is smooth and in some specimens slightly glossy. The color is creamy white or greenish white. The measurements of 52 eggs in various collections average 57 by 44.3 millimeters; the eggs showing the four extremes measure 62 by 46, 49.8 by 49, and 55 by 40.5 millimeters.

Young.—The period of incubation is probably the same as with the black duck, 26 to 28 days. It is performed wholly by the female, although the male does not entirely desert her. Mr. C. J. Maynard (1896) writes of the behavior of the mother and young:

The eggs were deposited during the first and second weeks of April; then about the 1st of May, I would frequently see flocks of little downy ducklings following the female, but unless I took care to conceal myself, I did not enjoy watching these little families long, for as soon as the parent became aware of my presence, she would emit a chuckling note, when away they would scamper, helter-skelter, into the nearest grass, where it was impossible, upon the most careful search, to discover a single young. I once surprised a brood, when they were some distance from any place of shelter, for they had ventured out upon the mud of a creek, at low tide, and I chanced to come out of the high grass, just in front of them. The old duck appeared to comprehend the situation at once, for she came directly toward me, driving her brood before her, hoping to engage my attention by a display of bravery, while the young escaped into the sheltering vegetation behind me; but placing my gun on the ground, I stooped down and grasped two of the little fellows, as they were running past. The diminutive ducklings uttered shrill cries when they were captured, which drove their parent nearly frantic, for regardless of possible consequences, she dashed about in front of me, with ruffled feathers and half-closed wings, often coming within a foot of me, at the same time, quacking loudly. This outcry attracted the attention of the drake, but he did not approach very near, merely circling about, some 50 yards distant, quacking softly. Leaving the old female to care for the remainder of the brood, I carried my captives into camp and placed them in a box, the sides of which were about a foot and a half high, but young as they were, they managed to escape.

Plumages.—As I have seen but few downy young of the Florida duck, as the series of immature birds available for study is very scanty and as the two subspecies are so much alike in these respects, I prefer to refer the reader to what I have written about the plumages of the mottled duck, which will probably fit this subspecies equally well.

Food.—According to Mr. W. L. McAtee (1918) the southern black ducks eat a larger proportion of animal food than their northern relatives. Based on the examination of 48 stomachs by the Biological Survey he found that 40.5 per cent of their food consisted of animal matter. Mollusks compose five-eighths of the animal food and snails as large as 1 inch in diameter are eaten. Insect food consists of dragon-fly nymphs (rarely adults), water bugs, caddis larvae, and a variety of beetles and flies, including horsefly larvae. Crawfish and small fishes are eaten in small quantities. Of the vegetable food he says:

Grasses are the most important element of the vegetable food of the southern black duck, forming almost half of it. Frequently the rootstocks are dug up and devoured, and some stems and leaves are eaten. Of the grass seeds consumed, cultivated rice is most important. Most of that found in the stomachs was waste, being taken in winter, and as it included red rice, some good was done by eating it. However, as the southern black duck spends the summer in the country where much rice is grown, it has the opportunity of feeding upon the crop in the younger and more appetizing stages. It is said to do this sometimes to a destructive extent. However, the game value of the duck makes it undesirable to take aggressive measures against it on behalf of the rice crop. A toll large enough, if not too large, is taken of the birds during the hunting season.

Next to grasses the seeds of smartweeds are preferred. They form almost a tenth (9.54 per cent) of the total diet. No fewer than 800 seeds of prickly smartweed (*Polygonum sagittatum*) were taken from a single stomach. The seeds and tubers of sedges compose the next largest item, namely, 6.34 per cent. Seeds of water lilies and coon tail make up 3.11 per cent, and seeds, stems, and foliage of pondweeds and widgeon grass, 1.6 per cent. Other items of vegetable food worth mentioning are bayberries and seeds of buttonbush.

Behavior.—I can not find much published on the habits of the Florida duck, in all of which it undoubtedly closely resembles the black duck. It is, of course, a surface feeder, but that it can dive, if hard pressed, I have learned to my sorrow in attempting to chase wounded birds; I have seen one dive and swim for several yards under water until it could find concealment among aquatic vegetation, where it remained hidden, probably with its bill protruding, and was never seen again. In flight, appearance, and behavior it is much like the black duck, the white lining of its wings being very conspicuous, but it is not nearly so shy as the northern species, perhaps because it is less hunted.

Game.—It is not an important factor as a game bird, because it is not migratory. It inhabits chiefly the less frequented and most inaccessible places in Florida, seldom visited by sportsmen. What few sportsmen visit its haunts usually come in the winter, when this species is widely scattered, or in the spring, when it is mated and breeding, and their time is usually fully occupied with hunting other, more numerous, species which offer better return for their trouble. For these reasons I have never heard of the Florida duck being systematically hunted and I doubt if its numbers are being seriously reduced except where its haunts are becoming thickly settled, cultivated, or drained. It is the same with them as with many of the western ducks, civilization and agriculture are killing them off faster than gunpowder.

Fall.—Mr. Moore says, in the notes referred to above—

that in August, September, and the first part of October parties of from 5 to 20 of this species leave the fresh ponds and fly across the bay to sand bars on the inner sides of the Keys, where they spend the night in the pools or coves near the mangroves and return at sunrise the next morning. Those at this time were all males; but in January, February, and March mated birds, flying in pairs, spend their nights in the same places.

DISTRIBUTION.

Breeding range.—Florida, mainly in the southern half. Said to be absent from northeastern Florida, but breeds on the eastern coast at least as far north as northern Brevard County and Orange County (Banana River and St. Johns River) and probably farther. Breeds along the northwestern coast of Florida and probably intergrades with *maculosa* between Florida and Louisiana.

Winter range.—Apparently the same as the breeding range, but perhaps some of the West Indies may be included.

Egg dates.—Florida: Fifteen records, February 28 to May 22; eight records, April 9 to 25.

ANAS FULVIGULA MACULOSA Sennett.

MOTTLED DUCK.

HABITS.

Mr. George B. Sennett (1889) first called attention to the characters which separated the ducks of the species *Anas fulvigula* which inhabit Louisiana and Texas from those found in Florida. He described the Texas bird as a new species and, as the two forms have not, apparently, been shown to intergrade, perhaps he was justified in doing so. In his description he sums up the characters, as follows:

The most marked differences between *A. maculosa* and *A. fulvigula* are that the cheeks of the former are streaked with brown, while those of the latter are plain buff; the speculum is purple instead of green; the general effect of the coloration, especially on the under sides, is mottled instead of streaked; the light color everywhere is a pale buff or isabella color instead of a rich, deep buff; and the tail markings also are different, as indicated.

Dr. D. G. Elliot (1898), in commenting on these characters, says:

The streaked cheeks are to be seen among some individuals of the Florida dusky duck, and the color of the speculum is at times merely a question of light, purple and green in metallic hues, being often interchangeable. An ornithologist might readily recognize to which form most of his specimens belonged, but the ordinary observer would probably have difficulty in distinguishing them.

Dr. John C. Phillips (1916), who has made a careful study of these ducks, has this to say on the subject:

In January, 1914, while paying a visit to Mr. E. A. McIlhenny, at Avery Island, Louisiana, I was able to collect a series of seven of the mottled ducks from the Vermilion Bay region. There are six adult males and one female. Taken as a whole, this Louisiana series is even darker than the Texas series; the breasts of the males are very dark, glossy chestnut, and the ground color of the cheeks and chin is distinctly more rufous than in the Texas series or in the Florida series. The cheeks are also quite heavily streaked, and this streaking extends in all cases far below the superciliary stripe; in the Florida ducks the streaking of the cheeks is finer and does not extend so far ventrally on to the chin, while the lores are plain buff and the chin itself is paler in all cases. The pileum of the mottled ducks from Louisiana is more solid black and less streaked black than is the case with the Florida birds; if anything it is darker than the Texas birds. On the upper surface of the Louisiana series and the Texas series the light edges of all the feathers (back, scapulars, rump, and tail) are darker and richer brown, but especially is this so in the Louisiana birds. The speculum character noticed by Sennett does not seem to me to hold good. It was said to be more green and less purple in *fulvigula* than in *maculosa*.

To sum up, I should say that the only character which seems important in distinguishing *A. f. maculosa* and *A. f. fulvigula*, aside from the generally darker tone of the former, is the coarser and more consistently striped head and neck of *A. maculosa*. In all cases the feathers bordering the sides of the culmen, the lores, are dotted with black in *maculosa* and plain buff in *fulvigula*. I believe the richer and more ruddy ground color of the head and neck of *A. f. maculosa* from Louisiana is partly due to the color of the water and mud in the Vermilion Bay region. These Vermilion Bay ducks are certainly more highly colored than ducks from the Brownsville region of Texas. The form *A. fulvigula maculosa*, therefore, will probably remain as a valid race.

The characters are slight, but fairly constant, and the new form, whether species or subspecies, seems to be distinct.

Nesting.—Audubon (1840) was the first to describe the nesting habits of this duck, although at the time he did not consider it as anything but a common black duck. He writes:

On the 30th of April, 1837, my son discovered a nest on Galveston Island, in Texas. It was formed of grass and feathers, the eggs eight in number, lying on the former, surrounded with the down and some feathers of the bird, to the height of about 3 inches. The internal diameter of the nest was about 6 inches, and its walls were nearly 3 in thickness. The female was sitting, but flew off in silence as he approached. The situation selected was a clump of tall slender grass, on a rather sandy ridge, more than a hundred yards from the nearest water, but surrounded by partially dried salt marshes.

Mr. George F. Simmons (1915) thus describes a nest found in a prairie pond near Houston, Texas:

As is the case with all ponds in this section of prairie, the whole with the exception of a small spot near the center was thickly covered with tall grass, rushes, water plants of various sorts, and sprinkled with a few bushes or reeds, locally known as "coffee-bean" or "senna."

The nest itself was placed about 8 inches up in thick marsh grass and rushes, over water 4 inches deep, and was neatly hidden by the tops of the grasses and rushes being drawn together over the nest. It was but 2 or 3 inches thick, a slightly concave saucer of dead, buffy rushes and marsh grass, supported by the thick grasses and by two small "coffee-bean" reeds. The lining was of smaller sections and fragments of the rushes and marsh grass, and a small quantity of cotton; and the 11 eggs were well, though not thickly surrounded by down and soft feathers evidently from the breast of the parent.

Mr. George B. Benners (1887) found three nests near Corpus Christi, Texas; "the nests were built on the edge of the river's bank and were so carefully concealed that if the birds had not flown up we would never have noticed them." Mr. James J. Carroll (1900) says that in Refugio County, Texas, it "breeds along the mainland near the beach and on the islands in April."

Eggs.—The eggs of the mottled duck are indistinguishable from those of the Florida duck, except that they seem to average a little smaller. The measurements of 75 eggs in various collections average 54.9 by 40.5 millimeters; the eggs showing the four extremes measure 60 by 40.2, 56.5 by 43, 51 by 41 and 54.5 by 38 millimeters.

Plumages.—The downy young of the mottled duck is similar to that of the black duck, but it is somewhat lighter colored and the dark markings on the head are much more restricted and paler. The upper parts are "mummy brown" varying to "Dresden brown," and to lighter on the forehead and flanks; the sides of the head, including a broad superciliary stripe, are "Isabella color" or "honey yellow" paling to "cream buff" or "cartridge buff" on the chin and throat; a dusky stripe extends from the bill to the eye and from the eye nearly, or quite, to the occiput; the under parts are "cream buff" or "cartridge buff"; the color of the back is relieved by scapular and rump spots of "cream buff" and the edge of the wing is the same color. The colors become paler with age. The progress toward maturity is apparently the same as in the black duck, the changes are not conspicuous and not easily traced beyond the earlier stages. The juvenal body plumage is worn for only a short time during the first fall; in this the broad edgings of the back and scapulars are "wood brown" or "avellaneous" and those of the lower parts are paler, varying from "avellaneous" to "vinaceous buff," the dusky markings on the breast are more longitudinal, less rounded, than in adults. The juvenal wing, characterized by its duller colors and by its incomplete speculum, is worn all through the first year until it is molted at the first complete postnuptial molt; the speculum in the young male is not only much duller in its metallic purple, but the color is much more restricted, occupying less area, and the black borders are narrower and lacking in velvety luster. During the late autumn and winter the progress toward maturity is rapid, until by spring the body plumage is practically adult and only the wings remain to distinguish the young bird. After the first postnuptial molt, when the bird is a little over a year old, the young bird is practically indistinguishable from the adult. The broad edgings are much more richly colored than in the young bird, varying from "tawny" on the back to "hazel" on the scapulars and from "hazel" to "amber brown" on the breast; the blackish markings on the under parts are more rounded and blacker; the dark colors of the breast are more sharply separated from the buff of the neck; and the speculum is now complete with its brilliant metallic purple, bordered with broad stripes of velvet black.   There is probably no recognizable eclipse plumage, but a complete annual molt in summer.

Behavior.—I have never seen this species in life and find practically nothing published on its habits, but there is no reason to suppose that it differs materially in its behavior from the closely related Florida duck.   It seems to be practically resident throughout its range.   In Louisiana it is called *canard noir d'été*, summer black duck, as the northern black duck is found there only in winter and is called *canard noir d'hiver*.   Messrs. Beyer, Allison, and Kopman (1907) say, of the status of *Anas fulvigula* (now restricted to *maculosa*) in Louisiana:

A regular resident on the coast, and especially on the islands, whence its local name, *canard des isles*.   Its numbers are greatly increased during the winter, and at that season it may be found on open lakes, even in the northern part of the State.

DISTRIBUTION.

Breeding range.—Mainly on the coasts of Louisiana and Texas, less common inland, up the Mississippi valley in Louisiana, and westward nearly to central Texas.   South to the mouth of the Rio Grande and perhaps into northern Mexico.

Winter range.—Approximately the same as the breeding range.

Casual records.—Has wandered to Colorado (near Loveland, March 15, 1889, and November 6, 1907); Kansas (Neosho Falls, March 11, 1876).

Egg dates.—Texas: Twelve records, April 18 to August 20; six records, May 3 to 16.   Louisiana: Four records, April 23 to June 1.

EUNETTA FALCATA (Georgi).

FALCATED TEAL.

HABITS.

This beautiful duck is a resident of eastern Asia, breeding abundantly in the southern half of eastern Siberia and migrating to its winter home in southeastern Asia.   It has occurred several times as a rare straggler in Europe, but has been recorded only once in North American territory.   Our reason for including it in our next check list is that Dr. G. Dallas Hanna has recently (1920) recorded the capture of a specimen in the Pribilof Islands, as follows:

A male of this beautiful crested teal was secured on St. George Island, April 18, 1917.   Its gorgeous coloration was admired by all who saw it.   The native hunters there do not readily distinguish the several species of ducks, and this was called by them "mallard," which name is applied to at least eight separate kinds.

As I knew nothing whatever about this duck and had no references to it in my index, I appealed to Dr. John C. Phillips, who is preparing an extensive monograph on the ducks of the world, and he very generously has sent to me his references and his unpublished manuscript on this species. With deep gratitude to him for his unselfish courtesy, I shall quote freely from his manuscript, merely selecting and arranging such parts as it seems best to use.

Spring.—Very little information and few dates are available for a study of the migration of these ducks. According to Dybowski (1868) they arrive in Dauria in April. Prjevalsky (1878) states that they appear at Lake Hanka from the middle of March to the middle of April, at which latter date Radde (1863) saw them arrive on the middle Amur. They appeared at Utskoi-Ostrog on May 3 (Middendorff, 1853) and at Nikolaievsk on May 18 (Schrenck, 1860). On the upper Amur they did not appear until early June.

The time of breeding, so far as one can judge, is not particularly early. They are said to nest early in June in Transbaikalia, and in east Siberia they begin to nest in late May (Taczanowski, 1873) continuing through June and perhaps into July (Baker, 1908).

Courtship.—The display as observed in captivity was first described by Finn (1915). He describes it as essentially like that of typical ducks, but the erection of the long crest made the head look enormous. He continues—"There was the same rear up, with the head bent down, followed by an upjerk of the hind parts; the long sickle-shaped tertials, so noticeable in this species, seemed little if at all expanded, and were not so prominent in the display as one would have expected from their abnormal character. But what especially attracted my attention, as I had noted the display of the male of this duck some time before, was that the females displayed simultaneously with the males, and with the same gestures."

Nesting.—The nest, so far as known, is always on the ground, built in swamps and along the low-lying banks of the larger rivers. It is rather well built, of leaves, grass, or rushes, compactly put together and lined with a very heavy complement of down. It is said to be not particularly well hidden, but hard to get at on account of the treacherous nature of the ground (Baker, 1908).

Eggs.—The eggs are six to nine in number, probably averaging eight. They are smaller than those of the mallard and are colored like those of the gadwall, although the yellow tinge is somewhat more pronounced (Taczanowski, 1873). The average of 21 eggs measured by Jourdain was 56.2 by 39.65 mm., the maximum being 58.5 by 39 and 55 by 41.5, the minimum 53 by 41 and 57 by 38 mm. (Hartert, 1920). The length of the iucubation period is not known. Baker (1908) seems to think that the drake assists, at least occasionally, in the duties of incubation, but I hesitate in attributing such habits to the males of any Palaearctic ducks. Baker also says that the male is seldom found far from the nest.

Food.—There are no detailed notes available, but the food seems to be of a vegetable nature (Stejneger, 1885; Radde, 1863).

Behavior.—The falcated teal lacks much of the elegance of the true teal or the mallard. It appears short, chunky, and large-headed for a surface-feeding duck. The long sickle-shaped tertials and short tail give the body a very stumpy appearance. Heinroth (1911) says that a male in the Berlin Gardens always kept his head and neck well drawn in, so that the mane lay on the upper part of his back. The writer never saw these crest feathers lifted, and the impression created was more like that of a diving duck.

There are no recorded observations as to the flight, except that it is said to be swift and teallike, which probably means that it is more erratic than that of the mallard. In Assam it appears singly or in pairs, more rarely in small parties. But in northern China, Prjevalsky (1878) speaks of their arriving on spring migration in large numbers and associating very commonly with other species of ducks.

The voice of the male is a short low trilling whistle (Walton, 1903), or, according to Prjevalsky (1878), a "tolerably loud and piercing whistle." Although I have never heard the note myself I gather from Heinroth's (1911) account that it is decidedly teallike. The note of the female is the typical mallardlike *quack*, said to be five times repeated (Finn, 1915).

Game.—Even to this day these birds are probably little disturbed over the greater part of the breeding area. But along the coasts of Japan and southern China they are undoubtedly hunted on an increasingly large scale. Great numbers were killed in the Pekin region over 40 years ago, especially in spring (David and Oustalet, 1877), and more recently a great many have been shipped from Hankow to the markets of Europe (Ghidini, 1911).

Fall.—In autumn they leave early, disappearing from the Amur region evidently in late September and early October. According to Dybowski (1868) some stay in Dauria till late December. It is an interesting fact that of the specimens taken in Burma and India a great majority are females (Finn, 1909).

DISTRIBUTION.

Breeding range.—Eastern Siberia. East to Kamchatka, probably the Commander Islands (Bering Island), the Kurile Islands and northern Japan (Yezzo). South on the mainland to the vicinity of Vladivostok and to approximately the northern border of Mongolia. West nearly, if not quite, to the upper Yenesei River. North to about 65° N., not quite to the Arctic Circle.

Winter range.—Southeastern Asia. East to Japan. South to the Japanese Archipelago, Formosa, southern China, Burma, and north central India (Delhi). The western and northern limits seem to be not well determined.

Casual records.—Rare straggler to Europe; specimens have been taken in Sweden, 1853, Hungary, 1839, and Bohemia. One taken on St. George Island, Bering Sea, on April 18, 1917.

CHAULELASMUS STREPERUS (Linnaeus).

GADWALL.

HABITS.

The arrival of the ducks on their breeding grounds in the great wildfowl nurseries of northwest Canada is a spectacular performance. I shall never forget the sights I saw, one cold, rainy day, June 13, 1905, as I walked down toward the great sloughs at the head of Crane Lake, Saskatchewan; hundreds of ducks arose from the wet meadows, from the sloughs, and from an island in the lake, flying around in great loose flocks; a great cloud of them rose, like a swarm of mosquitoes, from the mouth of Bear Creek; most of them were gadwalls, but there were also large numbers of canvasbacks, redheads, shovellers, and blue-winged teal, as well as lesser numbers of lesser scaups, mallards, baldpates, and ruddies, with a few Canada geese; the air seemed to be full of ducks, flying in all directions in bewildering clouds; I have never seen so many ducks before nor since. This was the center of their abundance in one of the greatest duck-breeding resorts I have ever seen. Probably all of the ducks had arrived on their breeding grounds at that time, but evidently many of them had not mated and others had not finished laying.

On June 17, 1905, Mr. H. K. Job and I made a careful census of the ducks breeding on the island, referred to above, by dragging a long rope over it as thoroughly as we could and by noting and record- ing the nests found by flushing the birds. The island was about 300 or 400 yards in length by about 100 yards in width, fairly high at one end and everywhere covered with a thick growth of grass, through which were scattered on the higher portion numerous small clumps and in some places large patches of rose bushes, offering ideal con- ditions as a breeding ground for ducks. There were several small ponds near the center of it lined with fringes of cat-tails and bull- rushes. On the lower portion of the island the grass was shorter, and where it extended out into a point the ground was bare. A colony of common terns occupied this point, which was also the favorite re- sort of a flock of white pelicans, which may have bred here later in the season. Marbled godwits, Wilson phalaropes, and spotted sand- pipers were breeding here, as well as western savanna sparrows.

A pair of crows had a nest in the only tree on the island, a small willow, and they must have fared sumptuously on stolen duck's eggs. A pair of short-eared owls had a nest on the island containing young in various stages of growth. We were unable to drag the whole island, as the rose bushes were too thick in many places, but in the course of two hours' work we recorded 61 nests, as follows: Mallard, 5 nests; gadwall, 23 nests; baldpate, 3 nests; green-winged teal, 2 nests; blue-winged teal, 10 nests; shoveller, 7 nests; pintail, 8 nests; and lesser scaup duck, 3 nests. The ducks were identified to the best of our abil- ity by eyesight; the female gadwalls and baldpates were very difficult to distinguish and there may have been more of the latter than we supposed, but certainly both the species were nesting there, as we saw a number of males in the small pondholes; the green-winged teals' nests were identified by seeing the female join a male of that species. We started a number of ducks, mostly pintails, where we failed to find nests, which probably meant broods of young and which were not counted. Most of the sets were incomplete or fresh, indicating that the ducks were only just beginning to lay; we therefore must have overlooked a great many nests, where the eggs were covered and no ducks flushed, as we found a number of such nests by accident. Considering these facts, making allowance for the unexplored parts of the island and judging from the immense numbers of ducks that were flying about or bedded out on the lake, I considered it fair to assume that at least 150 pairs of ducks were breeding or preparing to breed on this one island. In addition to the species above recorded, we saw on the island several American mergansers, a white-winged scoter and one cinnamon teal, making a total of 14 species of ducks which were probably breeding on the island or in sloughs around it. As may be imagined, it was with considerable interest and pleasant anticipation that I revisited this island in 1906, but I was most keenly disappointed to find it practically deserted. Instead of the immense flocks of ducks which I had seen rise from the sloughs like clouds of mosquitoes, only a few scattered flocks were seen. As we walked across the island expecting to see ducks flying up all about us, hardly a duck arose, and in place of the 60 odd nests that we expected to find only 3 nests were found. The mystery was soon solved by finding a nestful of broken eggs and bunches of yellowish hair clinging to the rose bushes. A coyote had been living on the island and had cleaned out all of the nests, and driven the ducks away. The destruction of the bird population of the island had been still further carried on by a family of minks and the entrance to their burrow was strewn with feathers. Whether the ducks will ever return to this island or not is an open question, but probably they have moved to some safer spot.

The prevailing impression which seems to exist in the minds of many writers that the gadwall is nowhere an abundant species should be dispelled by the foregoing account of its abundance in Saskatchewan, where it was at that time, and probably still is, the most abundant of all the ducks. It is undoubtedly steadily decreasing, as all the other ducks are, for advancing civilization and the demands of agriculture are usurping its breeding grounds. If a few such places, as I have just described, which are not particularly valuable for agricultural purposes, could be set apart as breeding reservations for waterfowl, this and many other species might be saved from extermination, which otherwise seems inevitable. Since the above was written I have learned from Mr. Hoyes Lloyd that much of the land around Crane Lake has been secured by the Canadian Government and that the locality described above will be included in an extensive bird reservation.

Courtship.—Dr. Alexander Wetmore (1920) has given us the following interesting account of the courtship of the gadwall:

The mating flight of the gadwall is always interesting and is seen constantly when the birds are on their breeding grounds. Here at Lake Burford opportunities for observing it were excellent. The flight was usually performed by two males and one female. In the beginning two males approached a female in the water, calling and bowing. She usually rose at once and flew with a slow flapping flight, mounting in the air with the males in pursuit, calling and whistling constantly. First one and then the other of the males swung in front of her, set his wings, inclined his body upward to show his handsome markings, and, after a few seconds, dropped back again to his former position.   Late in the season there was always one of the males who was favored and who displayed more often than the other, flying close to the female, so that in passing his wings often struck hers, making a rattling noise. After a short time the second male often left the pair and returned to the water. The birds frequently mounted until they were 300 yards or more in the air, and darted quickly from side to side, flying now rapidly and now slowly. When the flight was over the birds descended swiftly to the water again.   I was never able to ascertain whether there were some extra males about or not, as, though, there were usually two with the female in this flight I found them at other times always in pairs.

The female gadwall, like the mallards, also came out in the short grass of the shore and walked about with head down, quacking loudly, an action that I took for part of the mating display.

When the birds were in the shelter of the rushes they went through other mating actions of interest. The male swam toward the female bowing by extending his neck until the head was erect and then retracting it, bringing his bill down onto his breast. He then approached pressing his breast against the sides of the female and shoving her easily, first on one side and then on the other, biting her back and rump gently as he did so.   After a few seconds she lowered her body in the water and copulation took place with the female entirely submerged save for the crown of her head while half of the body of the male was under water. As the female emerged the male turned immediately to face her and bowed deeply, giving a deep reedy call as he did so.

Nesting.—In North Dakota, in 1901 we found the gadwall breeding quite commonly on the islands in the larger lakes, particularly on the islands in Stump Lake which are now set apart as a reservation and protected.   Baldpates and lesser scaup ducks were breeding abundantly on the same islands, far outnumbering the gadwalls; there was also a breeding colony of double-crested cormorants on one island and colonies of ring-billed gulls and common terns on two of them.   The gadwall's nests were usually well concealed in thick rank grass, tall reeds, dense clumps of wild rye, or patches of coarse weeds; they were always on dry ground and never very near the water.   The nests consisted of hollows scooped in the ground and well lined with strips or pieces of reeds, bits of dry grass, and weed stems, or whatever material could be most easily gathered in the vicinity, mixed with the down from the bird's breast; with incomplete sets or fresh eggs very little down is found, but as incubation advances the down is added until the eggs are surrounded and sometimes entirely covered with a profusion of dark gray down, which is usually mixed with bits of grass or straw.

Although the gadwall seems to prefer to nest on islands we found a number of nests in Saskatchewan in meadows or on the open prairie at long distances from water, where we flushed the birds from their nests as we drove along; such nests were well concealed in thick grass, which was often arched over them, or were hidden under small sage or rose bushes.   I have always found the gadwall a close sitter, flushed only when closely approached, but Mr. W. L. Dawson (1909) has noted variations in this respect, as follows:

The bird's behavior when surprised depends altogether upon the stage of incubation reached.   In general, the bird sits close until discovered; after that, if the eggs are fresh, the duck may flee upon sighting her enemy a hundred yards away; but if the eggs are near hatching, she will endeavor to lead the investigator astray by painfully dragging herself through the grass.   If too much harassed, however, she will desert her eggs outright rather than wait for what she regards as an inevitable doom, and the same remark will apply to almost any of the nesting ducks.

The down in the nest of the gadwall is smaller than that of the mallard, darker colored, and otherwise different in appearance.   In color it is dark "hair brown," almost "fuscous," with whitish centers and grayish tips.   The breast feathers mixed with the down are characteristic of the species, small, light colored, and with variable patterns of dusky markings in the center, but with light tips. It is difficult to distinguish, in the field, the nest of the gadwall from that of the baldpate, as the eggs of the two are indistinguishable, and the females are much alike.   But the gadwall has more white in the speculum, the bill is yellower, and the breast is spotted, all difficult points to see as the female flies from the nest.

Eggs.—The gadwall lays from 7 to 13 eggs, but the usual set consists of 10, 11, or 12 eggs.   I have occasionally seen one or two eggs of the lesser scaup duck in a gadwall's nest, and Mr. William Spreadborough, "on June 29, 1894, at Crane Lake, Saskatchewan, took a nest of this species containing 13 eggs, 7 of which were of the lesser scaup," according to Macoun (1909).   Undoubtedly the baldpate occasionally lays in the gadwall's nest, as the two species are often intimately associated, but the eggs are nearly indistinguishable.

The eggs of the gadwall are nearly oval in shape and are usually shorter and more rounded than those of the baldpate, but there is much individual variation in both species.   Their color is a dull creamy white, somewhat whiter than the baldpate's on the average. The measurements of 100 eggs in various collections average 55.3 by 39.7 millimeters; the eggs showing the four extremes measure **59.5** by 39.5, 57.5 by **43.5**, **49.5** by 38 and 51 by **34.5** millimeters.   The period of incubation, which is performed wholly by the female, is about 28 days.

Plumage.—The downy young of the gadwall is very much like that of the mallard, except that it is decidedly paler and less richly colored; the pale yellow of the under parts is more extensive on the sides and head extending nearly around the neck where it is separated by a narrow dark stripe on the nape, the light superciliary stripe is broader; the dark loral and postocular stripe is narrower and the uricular spot is hardly noticeable.   The upper parts are "bister," deepening on the crown to "bone brown"; the under parts are "cartridge buff," paler on the belly and deepening to "cream buff" or "Naples yellow" on the neck and sides of the head; the light patches on the scapulars and sides of the rump are buffy white.

The young birds become paler as they grow older. The plumage develops in the same sequence as in the mallard. Young birds gradually develop, during the first fall and winter, a plumage closely resembling that of the adult; by the month of March this first winter, or first nuptial, plumage is generally complete; there are usually a few spotted feathers scattered over the under parts, as signs of immaturity and the wings are much duller than those of adults, with little if any chestnut in the coverts. The molt into the eclipse plumage begins in June and during the transitions of this first double molt, young birds become indistinguishable from adults.

Adult males begin to molt into the eclipse plumage about the last of May or first of June and by the end of June many dark, brown-edged feathers, like those of the female are scattered through the breast and flanks. I have seen males in full eclipse as early as August 10 and as late as September 8; this plumage is an almost complete reproduction of the female's, or young male's, excepting, of course, the wings, which are molted only once in August. The molt out of the eclipse plumage consumes about two months; I have seen birds in this molt from September 8 to November 23, but I am inclined to think that old drakes usually attain their full plumage by November 1st or earlier. There is no winter or spring molt in old birds. Hybrids occur occasionally; Mr. William G. Smith (1887) mentions a beautiful male hybrid in which the color and size were about equally divided between the gadwall and the baldpate; he also "killed two specimens of gadwall with a distinct black ring about the neck. They were male and female and were together."

Food.—Like the mallard, the gadwall is a clean feeder, which makes its flesh desirable for the table. It consumes a great variety of food, most of which is obtained by tipping or dabbling about the edges of marshy ponds, sloughs, or grassy, sluggish streams; it can dive well for its food, however, when necessary. Its vegetable food consists of tender grasses, the blades, buds, seeds, leaves, and roots of various aquatic plants, nuts, and acorns; it visits the grain fields to some extent, where it picks up wheat, barley, buckwheat, and corn.

According to Mr. Douglas C. Mabbott (1920):

In habits the gadwall resembles the mallard, feeding either on dry land or in shallow water near the edges of ponds, lakes, and streams, where it gets its food by "tilting" or standing on its head in the water. The food of both the gadwall and the baldpate, however, is quite different in some respects from that of the mallard. These two feed to a very large extent upon the leaves and stems of water plants, paying less attention to the seeds, while the mallard feeds indiscriminately on both or even shows some preference for the seeds. In fact, in respect to the quantity of foliage taken, the gadwall and the baldpate are different from all other ducks thus far examined by the Biological Survey. They are also more purely vegetarian, their diet including a smaller percentage of animal matter than that of any of the other ducks.

As computed from the contents of 362 stomachs collected during the six months from September to March, 97.85 per cent of the food of the gadwall consists of vegetable matter. This is made up as follows: Pondweeds, 42.33 per cent; sedges, 19.91; algae, 10.41; coon tail, 7.82; grasses, 7.59; arrowheads, 3.25; rice and other cultivated grain, 1.31; duckweeds, 0.61; smartweeds, 0.59; wild celery and water weed, 0.53; water lilies, 0.52; madder family, 0.37; and miscellaneous, 2.61 per cent.

Considerably more animal food is taken in summer than in winter, owing, of course, to the fact that more is available at that time of the year. The percentage of animal food for the summer months is higher also because there are included in the averages analyses of numerous stomach contents of ducklings, which feed to a great extent upon insects. All of the 11 stomachs collected during the month of July (9 from North Dakota and 2 from Utah) were of young ducklings. A computation of the average contents of this series produced the following results: Water bugs, 56.18 per cent; beetles, 7.09; flies and their larvae, 2; nymphs of dragon flies and damsel flies, 0.27; other insects, 2; total animal food, 67.54 per cent; pondweeds, 12.55 per cent; grasses, 5.09; sedges, 2; water milfoils, 0.55; smartweeds, 0.09; miscellaneous, 12.18; total vegetable food, 32.46 per cent.

The animal food of adults includes small fishes, crustaceans, tadpoles, leeches, small mollusks, water beetles and other insects, larvae, and worms.

Behavior.—The gadwall can walk well on land, where it forages for oak mast in the woods and for grain in the open fields, often a long distance from water. It takes flight readily from either land or water, springing into the air and flying swiftly away in a straight line. When migrating, it flies in small flocks of about a dozen birds; in appearance and manner of flight it greatly resembles the baldpate, but the male can usually be distinguished from the latter by the white speculum and the brown wing coverts; a similar difference exists between the females, but only to a slight degree; practiced gunners claim to recognize other field marks, but they have proven too subtle for my eyes, and I have frequently mistaken one species for the other. The gadwall ought not to be mistaken for any other species, except the baldpate or the European widgeon, but it frequently is confused, by ignorant gunners, with the young males and females of the pintail, though its flight and general appearance are entirely different; the name "gray duck" has been applied to both the gadwall and the pintail, which has led to much confusion of records and to erroneous impressions as to the former abundance of the gadwall in New England, where, I believe, it has always been a rare bird.

Doctor Wetmore (1920) describes the notes of the gadwall as follows:

The call note of the female is a loud quack that is similar to that of the female mallard but is pitched slightly higher and is not quite so loud and raucous. Considerable experience is required, however, to distinguish with certainty the calls of the two birds. The male has a loud call like *kack kack*, a deep reedlike note resembling the syllable *whack*, and a shrill whistled call.

The gadwall associates freely with other species of similar habits and tastes, particularly with the baldpate and pintail, with which it seems to be on good terms.

Game.—There seems to be a difference of opinion among sportsmen as to the food value of the gadwall; some consider it a close second to the mallard and others say it is hardly fit to eat; probably this is due to the different kinds of food that it lives on in various localities.

Mr. Dwight W. Huntington (1903) writes of his experience in shooting it:

I found it fairly abundant in North Dakota and usually shot a few gadwalls with the other ducks. One day when shooting on a little pond quite near the Devils Lake, I shot a large number of ducks, and nearly all of them were gadwalls. They came quite rapidly toward evening, and standing in the tall rushes without much effort at concealment, I had some very rapid shooting. Far out on the lake the swans and geese were trumpeting and honking. Large flocks of snowgeese, or white brant, as they call them in Dakota, were always in the air; the mallard, sprigtails, teal, and all the ducks were flying everywhere; but the gadwalls were the only ducks which came to me in any numbers. Had I put out only gadwall decoys, there might have been a reason for this, but I had no decoys that day at all. In fact the ducks were always so abundant that I could kill far more than I could carry, without decoys, and an ambulance from the garrison came out to carry in the game.

Winter.—As the gadwall is one of the later migrants northward in the spring, not appearing usually until the ice is all out of the ponds, so it is also one of the earlier ducks to leave in the fall and start on its short flight to its winter home in the Southern States, principally in the lower Mississippi valley, and in Mexico. The gadwall is primarily a fresh water duck, breeding far in the interior and wintering principally in the inland ponds, marshy lakes, sloughs, and swamps, where it can find mild weather and plenty of food; but it frequents to some extent the brackish pools and estuaries along the coasts of Louisiana and Texas, where it is very common. Messrs. Beyer, Allison, and Kopman (1906) say of its winter movements in Louisiana:

As in the case of the mallard, the first came by the early or the middle part of October, and continue to increase decidedly until the middle of December, then remaining *in statu quo* or showing something of a decrease, according to the nature of the winter, until the middle of January. A strong northward movement begins at that time, and while it consists largely of individuals that have wintered in Louisiana, it is doubtless augmented also by the first passage of transients. This later movement continues more or less freely until about March 15, after which date, duck migration is restricted almost entirely to a few species, among which the gadwall is seldom if ever found.

DISTRIBUTION.

Breeding range.—Temperate regions of the Northern Hemisphere. In North America, east to Hudson Bay (Churchill), southeastern Manitoba (Shoal Lake), southern Wisconsin (Lake Koshkonong, formerly), and formerly in Ohio. South to central Minnesota (Becker County), northern Iowa (Kossuth County), southwestern Kansas (Meade County), southern Colorado (La Plata County and San Luis Valley), northwestern New Mexico (Lake Burford), southern California (San Jacinto Lake, Riverside County). West to the interior valleys of California (San Joaquin and Sacramento valleys), Oregon (Camp Harney), and Washington (Brook Lake). North to central Alberta (Lesser Slave Lake), and northern Saskatchewan (Athabasca Lake). Has been found breeding casually on Anticosti Island, Gulf of St. Lawrence. In the Eastern Hemisphere, Iceland and the temperate regions of Europe and Asia, from the British Isles, Denmark, Sweden, and Holland to Kamchatka; also southern Spain and northern Algeria.

Winter range.—Southern States and Mexico, east to the Atlantic coast from Maryland (Chesapeake Bay) to southern Florida. South to Jamaica, rarely, south central Mexico (Guadalajara), and southern Lower California (San José del Cabo). West to the Pacific coast. North rarely to British Columbia (Chilliwack) more commonly to the coasts of Washington (Puget Sound region), and Oregon, Utah, northeastern Colorado (Barr Lake), northern Arkansas (Big Lake), and southern Illinois (Mount Carmel). In the Eastern Hemisphere, the British Isles, the Mediterranean basin, northern Africa (to the Sudan and Abyssinia), northern India, China, and Japan.

Spring migration.—Early dates of arrival: Iowa, southern, March 10; Minnesota, Heron Lake, March 17; Montana, Terry, April 1; Manitoba, Aweme, April 23; Saskatchewan, Indian Head, April 18; Alberta, Edmonton, May 5. Late dates of departure: Lower California, Colnett, April 8; Oklahoma, Caddo, April 2.

Fall migration.—Early dates of arrival: Lower California, southern, September 27; Massachusetts, Essex County, October 2; Rhode Island, October 8. Late dates of departure: Ontario, Ottawa, October 29; Rhode Island, Point Judith, November 11; Long Island, Oakdale, December 13.

Casual records.—Accidental in Bermuda (December, 1849) and Alaska (St. Paul Island, November 13, 1911).

Egg dates.—North Dakota: Twenty-seven records, May 18 to July 16; fourteen records, June 7 to 19. Manitoba and Saskatchewan: Twenty records, June 6 to July 3; ten records, June 13 to 27. California and Utah: Sixteen records, April 16 to July 20; eight records, May 15 to June 17.

MARECA PENELOPE (Linnaeus).

EUROPEAN WIDGEON.

HABITS.

This is an old-world species which has occurred frequently as a straggler on both coasts of North Amercia, as well as in the interior. The Atlantic coast records are nearly all fall and winter records, but in the interior its occurrence seems to be wholly in the spring and on the Pacific coast in the winter. As I know nothing about the habits of this foreign species from personal experience with it and as comparatively little has been written about it in American bird books, I am quoting freely from Mr. J. G. Millais (1902) who has given a very satisfactory life history of the widgeon.

Spring.—As the spring approaches we see on fine days the flocks of widgeon splitting up into smaller parties and engaged in pairing. By the end of March many widgeon have paired, and proceed to their breeding grounds together; but in most cases the northern movement is undertaken in a series of small flocks, which gradually detach themselves from the main bodies. These small parties of from 25 to 30 birds follow one another in their migration, often stopping for a few days at some halting place, like the Shetlands or the Norwegian fiords, till, by the middle of April, none are left on our coast except a few stragglers.

Courtship.—The actual courtship of the widgeon differs somewhat from that of other surface feeders, and the display of the male bird is an interesting one. A female having shown herself desirous of selecting a mate, five or six males crowd closely round, hemming her in on every side and persecuting her with their attentions. If she swims away, they follow her in a close phalanx, every male raising his crest, stretching out his neck close over the water, and erecting the beautiful long feathers of the scapulars to show them off. He also depresses the shoulder joints downward, so as to elevate the primaries in the air. All the time the amorous males keep up a perfect babble of loud " Whee-ous, " and they are by far the noisiest of ducks in their courtship. Occasionally the cock birds fight and drive each other off, but ducks are not, broadly speaking, pugnacious birds, and success in winning the admiration of the female is rather a matter of persistent and active attention than physical force.

Nesting.—The nest of the female widgeon is generally placed at from 10 to 20 yards from the nearest water, and generally in coarse grass or heather. Sometimes, like the mallard, she will wander far in the tundra, and one of the only two nests I have found in Scotland I stumbled on by accident right in the middle of a grouse moor, and far from the lake near which I had been searching the whole morning. Generally from 7 to 10 cream-colored eggs are laid.

He also refers in a footnote to a nest he found at Scampston, Yorks, which was placed in nettles; I have found the nest of the American widgeon in a similar situation.

Eggs.—The eggs of the European widgeon are indistinguishable from those of the American widgeon or baldpate. The set usually consists of 7 or 8 eggs, but sometimes as many as 9 or 10 are laid. The measurements of 117 eggs, as given in Witherby's Handbook (1920), average 54.7 by 38.7; the eggs showing the four extremes measure 59.5 by 38.5, 58 by 41, and 49.9 by 35.2 millimeters.

Plumages.—The European bird is so closely related to our own, its downy young and its sequence of plumages are so similar, that I prefer to refer the reader to some of the leading British manuals rather than attempt to quote from them. Mr. Millais (1902) has treated the subject very fully and A Practical Handbook of British Birds, by H. F. Witherby and others, describes the plumages of this and other birds on the British list most exhaustively and satisfactorily.

Food.—Mr. Millais gives the following interesting account of the feeding habits of the widgeon:

In a regular feeding ground, generally some long open stretch of mud covered with *Zostera marina*, it is interesting to see the careful manner in which widgeon approach it. The first little pack will come flying up against the wind and alight on the water, at about two or three hundred yards from the shore, after having previously swung round once or twice to ascertain that no enemy is approaching. This generally takes place when the tide is half ebbed. Out on the water they remain packed close together and very quiet till the first green fronds of their favorite food are observed floating on the surface away inshore. Then the whole gathering begins slowly going shorewards, till at last one bird bolder than the rest swims in and commences picking at the floating weed. Even then they are subject to sudden fears, and, when about to follow their leader, will often suddenly put up their necks and swim rapidly out, the cocks whistling loudly. Once, however, they have reached the food, their taste for more generally asserts itself, and precautions against surprise are somewhat relaxed, as they one and all move in to still shallower water and commence to turn upside down so as to pull up the *Zostera* and eat the root, by far the most succulent part.

Sometimes widgeon, which are both conservative as to their beats and modes of life, will pay little attention to a vegetable diet, but live almost exclusively on animal food. Such I find to be the case with the birds living on the sandy coast near the town of Dornoch in Scotland, where all conditions are purely marine. The widgeon here feed by day and live entirely on small cockles. This renders their flesh poor, bitter, and quite uneatable. I have shot a good few of them there and found all to be the same, whilst birds from the other side of the same firth, and living on the *Zostera* beds to the west of Tain, were fat and as good as widgeon generally are. In spring widgeon are great grass eaters, and later on, like teal and garganey, they devour an enormous quantity of flies. One day in Iceland I observed with a telescope a small party of male widgeon whose wives were engaged in domestic affairs, paddling along the edge of a small lake near Myvatn, and picking the flies off the stones in hundreds. This particular insect, a sort of stinging house fly, is very nutritive and tastes like a piece of sugar. As you are obliged to eat plenty of them yourself, for they are always getting into your mouth, you soon get used to them, and swallow them with equanimity, and it is a common sight to see the Icelandic children of the Myvatn district picking these natural lollipops off their faces and eating them by dozens.

In certain northern firths, where widgeon and brent geese frequent the same ground, it is no uncommon sight to see widgeon in small parties of half a dozen "jackaling" the food which has been torn up by the large birds. The brent can reach far below the surface and tear up the *Zostera* and they themselves only eat the root and allow the fronds to drift away. These are eagerly devoured by the widgeon when they are hungry.

Behavior.—Macgillivray (1852) says of the behavior of widgeons:

They are frequently seen in very large flocks, but usually in small bodies, seldom intermingling with other species. They swim with great ease, and have a rapid direct flight, taking wing easily from the water, and producing a whistling sound as they fly. They are much addicted to garrulity, and at night especially emit a whistling cry, on account of which they have obtained the name of "whew-ducks."

Evidently the field marks of the widgeon are the same as those of our baldpate, but the two species can be readily distinguished by the reddish head of the adult male and the general ruddy tinge of plumage in the female and young male of the European bird; also the axillars in the baldpate are pure white in both sexes, whereas in the European bird they are freckled or clouded with gray.

Mr. Millais (1902) says:

The call of the male widgeon is a loud "whee-ou," a note both wild and musical, and dear to the heart of every gunner that has wandered on the coasts; it also makes a very peculiar "cheeping" note (rather like the call of the twite) when frightened. The female also has two calls, both somewhat similar yet quite distinct, both a sort of throaty croak one being used to attract the attention of others of her species; the other, somewhat harsher, is emitted in moments of fear.

Fall.—By the middle of August the old females and young begin to join together, and are generally the first to commence the southern migration. These are then followed, in September, by the stragglers and males with brown shoulders molting into white, and adult males still in nearly complete eclipse but showing the first signs of winter plumage in the upper scapulars. When all the males arrive they mix indiscriminately with other widgeon, and so the addition to the ranks is swelled gradually until November, when the large winter packs are formed.

Widgeon are more or less marine in their habits, and after arriving on our coasts, in September, they increase in numbers until December, when great packs are sometimes formed in estuaries suited to their tastes. They are the mainstay of the professional punt gunner, being numerous and always a marketable commodity, and it is interesting to note the appreciable change in the habits of the birds due to this enemy. By nature the widgeon is not necessarily a purely nocturnal feeder. In his summer home, where he is subject to little molestation, he feeds regularly in the early morning and late evening, resting only during the warm hours in the middle of the day. Now notice what happens when he arrives on the British coasts. At first the small packs continue to feed in daylight, as during summer, but a couple of raking shots in their midst, carrying death and destruction, tell them that this is too dangerous, so they become purely nocturnal feeders for the remainder of the season, and rest or fly about by day well out in the firths or open sea, according to the proportion of harassment. Where widgeon have been kept continually on the move; that is, after a series of gales sweeping over their resting grounds, as well as when several shots have been fired at them on the mud flats, they sometimes assemble in immense flocks, either on the principle of mutual protection or that "misery loves company". I have on more than one occasion seen the entire stock of widgeon frequenting a certain firth merged into one great gathering, which could not have contained less than five to seven thousand birds.

DISTRIBUTION.

Breeding range.—Northern parts of the Eastern Hemisphere. Iceland, the Faroes, Shetland and Orkney Islands, Scotland, and northern England. North in Europe and Asia to 70° N.; east to Kamchatka and perhaps to the Aleutian Islands.

Winter range.—The British Isles, the whole of southern Europe and northern Africa, south to Abyssinia; also southern Asia, to southern Japan.

Casual records.—North American records must be regarded as casuals until a definite breeding record for this continent can be established. Atlantic coast records are mostly in fall and winter, from October 20, 1899 (Halifax, Massachusetts) to March 25, 1899 (Keuka Lake, New York). Interior records are mostly in spring, from March 23, 1896 (English Lake, Indiana), to April 18, 1904 (Sandusky, Ohio). Greenland records fall between September 29, 1900, and December 17, 1900. The Pacific coast dates are mostly in December and February. The Alaska dates are, Unalaska, October 12, 1871, and Pribilof Islands, May 27, 1872 and April 30, 1911. Probably two migration routes reach the United States, one through Greenland to the Atlantic coast and one through the Aleutian Islands to the Pacific coast. Accidental in Spitsbergen, the Azores, Madeira, Canary and Marshall Islands.

Egg dates.—Iceland: Twenty records, May 12 to June 21; ten records, May 25 to June 15.

MARECA AMERICANA (Gmelin.)

BALDPATE.

HABITS.

I have always thought that the proper name for this species is the American widgeon, for it is certainly very closely related to and much resembles in many ways its European relative. The name widgeon is applied by gunners to various species of fresh-water ducks which they can not recognize, especially to the females; gadwalls, pintails, and the present species seem to be very confusing to sportsmen and are usually all lumped together as "widgeons." This name does well enough in the fall and winter, when associated with other species, but when seen in the spring, in the full glory of its nuptial plumage, with its glistening white crown, the name baldpate seems more appropriate; the name baldpate always suggests to my mind the mated pairs of the handsome ducks that I have so often seen swimming in these little ponds or streams of the western plains or springing into the air, if we drove too near, with a great display of their striking color patterns.

Spring.—The baldpate is not one of the earliest migrants; the ice has long since disappeared and spring is well under way before it starts, and many of the birds do not arrive in their breeding grounds in the Northern States until the latter part of May. Turner (1886) says of its arrival at St. Michael, Alaska:

It arrives about the 25th of May or even later. It is not at all gregarious, being found solitary or in pairs. It frequents the marshes, preferably those which are overflowed by the higher tides when it arrives. As soon as the season is advanced, the greater part of the snow is gone, and the little rivulets are full of muddy water, they resort to these places for food. They seem to delight in shoveling among the mud in search for their food. They plunge their heads at times completely under the soft soil to obtain a tender root or slug.

Mr. Aretas A. Saunders writes me, of its arrival in Montana, that it "arrives on its breeding grounds in the latter part of May. It is not mated before arrival, like the mallard and gadwall, but is seen more frequently in flocks of 5 to 15, during the first part of the spring migration."

Courtship.—Evidently the mating occurs after its arrival on its breeding grounds. I have never seen the courtship of this species, but it probably does not differ materially from that of the European widgeon, which is described under that species.

Dr. Alexander Wetmore (1920) describes the courtship flight of the baldpate, as follows:

The mating flight of this duck resembles that of the preceding species (gadwall), but is performed with more dash and speed. The birds fly swiftly and erratically. The males dart ahead of the female setting and decurving their wings and throwing their heads up, exhibiting their striking markings to the best advantage. The female calls *qua-awk, qua-awk* and the males whistle *whew whew* constantly during this performance. Occasionally as a pair swung in low over the water the male darted ahead and, with decurved wings and head thrown up, scaled down to the surface. Two males and a single female invariably took part in the display flight which began, as in the gadwall, by the males approaching the female, bowing and whistling and then following her as she rose in the air.

Nesting.—In North Dakota in 1901 we found the baldpate breeding abundantly, principally on the islands in the larger lakes. The baldpate is a late breeder, very few of the eggs being laid before June 1, and the majority of the sets are not completed until the second week in June or later. The greatest breeding grounds of this species were on the four small islands in the western end of Stump Lake, so graphically described by my companion Mr. Herbert K. Job (1898) under the appropriate title "The Enchanted Isles." These islands are now included in the Stump Lake Reservation. The islands were devoid of trees but supported a rank growth of grasses, tall coarse weeds, and various herbaceous plants, as well as several tall thick clumps of *Phragmites communis*, and patches of wild roses; they were high in the centers, sloping gradually down to gravelly beaches, with numerous loose rocks and bowlders scattered over them. Here, on June 15, 1901, we found no less than 15 nests of baldpates; probably there were more nests, which we did not find, as it was raining very hard when we explored the island where they were breeding most abundantly, so we made only a hurried search of about half an hour, finding 12 nests in this short time. We also found here numerous nests of other ducks, mallards, gadwalls, pintails, lesser scaup ducks, and white-winged scoters, besides a breeding colony of double-crested cormorants and large numbers of nesting ring-billed gulls and common terns. Though we were tramping around in a drenching downpour, the cloud of gulls and terns screaming overhead and the ducks flushing under our feet every few steps created enough excitement to make us forget our discomfort.

The nest of the baldpate is built on dry ground, often at a considerable distance from the water, in a slight hollow generally well lined with bits of dry grass and weed stems, with a plentiful supply of light-gray down surrounding the eggs, which increases in quantity as incubation advances. The bird frequently covers the eggs with the down when she leaves the nest, completely concealing them and making the nest almost invisible, even in an open situation, which is often selected. The nests which I found on the islands described above were located as follows: The first was well concealed in the center of a thick clump of goldenrod growing on the beach; it was lined with dried leaves and rubbish, with very little down around the eight fresh eggs. The second was in the center of a clump of nettles near the upper edge of a stony beach; it contained eight fresh eggs which were laid on the bare stones, one of them plainly visible in the center of the nest, and surrounded by a little down; it contained 10 eggs and a good supply of down two weeks later. The third nest was on higher ground, concealed in rather tall prairie grass; the 11 eggs in it were heavily incubated; it was profusely lined with down, mixed with bits of dry grass and weeds. The 12 nests found on June 15 were mostly under rose bushes, among the rocks, many of them in open situations; they contained from 9 to 11 eggs each. One of the nests contained a white-winged scoter's egg and one an egg of the lesser scaup duck, both of which were nesting on the island.

According to Baird, Brewer, and Ridgway (1884), Kennicott found several nests of the baldpate, on the Yukon, fully half a mile from the river:

He invariably found the nest among dry leaves, upon high, dry ground, either under large trees or in thick groves of small ones, frequently among thick spruces. The nest is rather small, simply a depression among the leaves, but thickly lined with down, with which, after incubation is begun, the eggs are covered when left by the parent. The nest is usually placed at the foot of a tree or bush, with generally no attempt at concealment. The female, when started from her nest, rises silently into the air, and usually flies to the nearest water, though sometimes she will alight on the ground a few rods distant.

The nest of the baldpate can only with difficulty be distinguished from that of the gadwall, as explained under the latter species. A careful study of the color patterns in the wings of the two females will help the collector to recognize the female as she flies from the nest. And the nest is distinguishable on careful comparison. The down in the baldpate's nest is lighter and smaller; it is "light drab" in color, with whitish centers and conspicuous whitish tips. The breast feathers in the nest are either pure white or with pale brownish or grayish centers.

Eggs.—From the writings of others I infer that the baldpate lays from 6 to 12 eggs, but, from my own experience, I should say that the usual full set consisted of from 9 to 11 eggs. The eggs are absolutely indistinguishable, with any degree of certainty, from those of the European widgeon or the gadwall, though, as a rule, the baldpate's eggs are slightly more elongated and of a purer, deeper cream color than those of the gadwall. They are creamy white in color, varying from deep cream to nearly white and are nearly elliptical ovate in shape. The shell is clear, smooth, rather thin and somewhat glossy, resembling in color and texture certain types of hen's eggs.

The measurements of 81 eggs in the United States National Museum and the author's collections average 53.9 by 38.3 millimeters; the eggs showing the four extremes measure 60 by 40, 58.2 by 40.2, 50.5 by 38 and 54 by 36 millimeters.

Young.—I can not find any definite data as to the period of incubation, but the European bird is said to incubate for 24 or 25 days, and our bird probably sits for the same period. This duty is performed by the female exclusively, though the male does not wholly desert her until the molting season arrives. The care of the young also rests with the female, and she guards them with jealous devotion. Nelson (1887) relates the following incident:

I once came suddenly upon a female widgeon, with her brood of 10 or a dozen little ducklings, in a small pond. As I approached the parent uttered several low, guttural notes and suddenly fluttered across the water and fell heavily at my feet, so close that I could almost touch her with my gun. Meanwhile the young swam to the opposite side of the pond and began to scramble out into the grass. Willing to observe the old bird's maneuvers, I continued to poke at her with the gun as she fluttered about my feet, but she always managed to elude my strokes until, just as the last of her brood climbed out of the water, she slyly edged away, and suddenly flew off to another pond some distance. I then ran as quickly as possible to the point where the ducks left the water, yet, though but a few moments had elapsed, the young had concealed themselves so thoroughly that, in spite of the fact that the grass was only 3 or 4 inches high and rather sparse, I spent half an hour in fruitless search.

By the last of August or the first of September the young are able to fly and are flocking with their parents for the autumnal flight. Baird, Brewer, and Ridgway (1884) quote Kennicott as saying:

The young, while unable to fly, are frequently found seeking the shelter of grassy lakes. As soon, however, as they can fly they return to their favorite river shores and open feeding places, where they obtain aquatic insects, a few small shells, and the seeds and roots of various plants. In the fall the broods often separate before leaving for the South; this they do about the middle of September.

Plumages.—Ridgway (1887) describes the downy young as follows:

Above, dark olive brown, relieved by a spot of greenish buff on posterior border of each wing, one on each side of back, and one on each side of rump; top of head and hind neck, dark olive, like back; rest of head and neck, with lower parts, pale olive buff or fulvous, the side of the head with a dusky streak, extending from bill, through eye, to occiput.

When about 4 or 5 weeks old, in August, the young baldpate assumes its first complete plumage, the wings being the last to reach full development. In this first mottled plumage the sexes are much alike, but in the male the gray feathers of the back begin to appear in September and the progress toward maturity proceeds rapidly; the brown mottled feathers of the back are replaced by the gray vermiculated feathers of the adult and the mottling in the breast disappears, leaving the clear vinaceous color of maturity; so that by December or January the most forward birds have acquired a plumage which closely resembles that of the old bird, except on the wings, which still show the gray mottling on the lesser wing coverts peculiar to young birds. In some precocious individuals the lesser wing coverts become nearly pure white before the first nuptial season, but in most cases the immature wing is retained until the first postnuptial molt, which is complete. With both old and young birds the molt into the eclipse plumage begins in June and the molt out of this into the adult winter dress is not completed until October or November. At this molt the white lesser wing coverts are assumed by the young, old and young birds becoming indistinguishable. The seasonal molts of the adult consist of the prolonged double molt of the body plumage, into the eclipse in June and July and out of the eclipse in September and October, and the single molt of the flight feathers in August. Old males in the eclipse plumage closely resemble females, except for the wings, which are always distinctive.

In the female the sequence of plumages is similar. During the first winter and spring, young birds make considerable progress toward maturity, but can be recognized by the immature wings. The fully adult plumage is acquired during the second fall and winter.

Food.—The baldpate feeds on or near the surface by dabbling in the mud or tipping up in shallow water. Where not disturbed it is liable to feed at any time during the day, though it is always more active in the early morning or toward night. But, as it seldom enjoys much security, it more often spends the day skulking in the reeds, dozing on some sunny bank or playing about on open water at a safe distance from land; then as dusk comes on it repairs in small flocks to its feeding grounds, where it can feed in safety during the greater part of the night. Its food is largely vegetable, consisting mainly of the seeds and roots of grasses and various water plants. Dr. John C. Phillips (1911) records the contents of stomachs of this species, taken in Massachusetts, as entirely vegetarian, consisting of "pond-weed, wild celery, water-lily seeds (*Brasenia*), burweed, and smart-weed seeds (*Polygonum hydropiper*), also "mineral matter 65 per cent." Dawson (1909) says that in Washington, "in late January and February, they confine their feeding largely to the water-soaked fields, digging up the young grass with their bills and eating roots and all."

Its well-known habit of robbing the canvasback on its feeding grounds in Chesapeake Bay has been often described; the baldpate, being a poor diver and yet extravagantly fond of the succulent roots of the, so-called, wild celery, has to be content with what small bits of this delicacy the canvasback lets drop or what it can steal from this expert diver on its return to the surface. In its winter home in the Southern States it feeds largely in the broken-down rice fields, where it finds an abundance of food and becomes very fat. Audu-bon (1840) says that it eats "beechnuts, small fry, and leeches." Warren (1890) found that two baldpates, taken in Pennsylvania, "had fed almost entirely on insects, chiefly beetles and crickets." Mr. F. C. Baker (1889), who dissected a large number, taken in Florida, found that their stomachs "contained shells of *Truncatella subcylindrica* (Say) and small seeds."

Mr. Douglas C. Mabbott (1920) says:

The vegetable food of the baldpate for the eight months from September to April averaged 93.23 per cent. This consisted of the following items in the order of their importance: Pondweeds, 42.82 per cent; grasses, 13.9; algae, 7.71; sedges, 7.41; wild celery and waterweed, 5.75; water milfoils, 3.48; duckweeds, 2.2; smartweeds, 1.47; arrow grass, 0.36; water lilies, 0.26; coontail, 0.24; and miscellaneous, 7.63 per cent.

Animal food amounted to 6.77 per cent of the contents of the 229 baldpate stomachs included in the computation. Even this figure is probably unduly large, because the greater part of the animal matter consisted of snails found in the gizzards of a series of ducks from southern Oregon, the only lot of birds found feeding almost exclusively upon such food. More than nine-tenths of the animal food (6.25 per cent of the total) consisted of mollusks, the remainder being made up of insects (0.42 per cent) and miscellaneous matter (0.1 per cent).

Behavior.—When alarmed the baldpate rises quickly from the water, almost perpendicularly, making a rattling sound with its wings, and flies rapidly away. Its flight is swift, strong, and direct; when migrating or when flying to or from its breeding grounds it flies in small flocks of irregular formation and at no great height from the ground or water. On its breeding grounds it is quite tame, but during the shooting season it becomes very shy. The drake is easily recognized by its striking color pattern, displaying so much white in the wings, the white crown, and the white belly. But the duck might easily be mistaken for the female gadwall, though it has a white unspotted breast and shows more white in the greater wing coverts, which is quite conspicuous as the duck flies away from its nest. It can readily be distinguished from the mallard duck by its smaller size and by the absence of the conspicuous white borders of the blue speculum. Doctor Townsend (1905) has called attention to the fact "that the under surface of the wings of the baldpate is gray, that of the mallard snowy white."

The ordinary call note of the male baldpate is a whistling *whew, whew, whew,* which is uttered on the wing or while feeding and swimming. Mr. J. H. Bowles (1909) has well described its vocal powers, as follows:

Their principal call is a lisping, throaty whistle, repeated three times in quick succession. It is surprisingly light in character for the size of the bird, and serves to confirm the bird's position on the list next to the teals. Although quite impossible to describe, the note is rather easily imitated when heard a few times, and frequently proves a valuable addition to the repertoire of the wild-fowl hunter. The only other note I have heard them utter is a low, short chattering, somewhat resembling that of the pintail, but greatly reduced in volume. Their quacks, or squawks, of alarm also express the limit of terror, but are still pathetically inadequate in comparison with those, say, of a hen mallard.

Doctor Yorke (1899) describes the cry as "a whistle like the last note of a Bartramian sandpiper." The female has a soft guttural note, which can hardly be called a "quack" and a louder cry, which Eaton (1910) says resemble "the syllables *kaow, kaow.*" Mr. Aretas A. Saunders writes to me in regard to the notes of this species:

They also rarely quack like the mallard and gadwall, but this note is less nasal than the mallard's and not so loud and sonorous as the gadwall's. The whistle differs in pitch with different individuals, and one may frequently hear whistles of two or three different pitches coming from the same flock of birds.

On their breeding grounds baldpates are associated on friendly terms with various other species, as has already been shown above. In their winter feeding resorts they associate with canvasbacks, redheads, and scaup ducks, stealing from them what bits of food they can grab. Neltje Blanchan (1898) says of this performance:

Such piracy keeps the ducks in a state of restless excitement, which is further induced by the whistling of the widgeons' wings in their confused manner of flight in and around the feeding grounds. Here they wheel about in the air; splash and splutter the water; stand up in it and work their wings, half run, half fly along the surface; and in many disturbing ways make themselves a nuisance to the hunter in ambush.

Doctor Townsend (1905) describes similar behavior with the American coot, as follows:

I have seen a flock of five baldpates eagerly following half a dozen American coots that were frequently diving in a pond and bringing up weeds from the bottom. The baldpates gathered about the coots as soon as they emerged on the surface and helped themselves to the spoils, tipping up occasionally to catch some sinking weed. They seemed even to be able to perceive the coot coming up through the water, for they would begin to swim toward the spot just before the coot emerged. The coots appeared to take the pilfering as a matter of course; in fact they pilfered from each other, and continued to work for themselves and the poachers.

Such behavior has earned for the baldpate the local name of "poacher."

Fall.—On the fall migration the baldpate starts rather early in September, well in advance of the heavy frosts.

On its migration in Montana, according to Mr. Aretas A. Saunders, it—

associates with many other species of ducks, most frequently with the shoveller. Flocks of these two species, mixed, are quite common in the spring migration. I have observed, with this species, on a small pond in the spring migration, the following other species: Gadwall, shoveller, blue-winged teal, pintail, lesser scaup, goldeneye, and buffle-head. In the large flocks of ducks that gather on the larger alkali ponds in the fall migration, this is one of the commonest species, and is associated commonly with the shoveller and lesser scaup.

Game.—As a game bird it will not rank in importance with several others, though its vegetable diet, especially when it has been feeding on the Chesapeake with the canvasbacks, makes its flesh very palatable and desirable. It is a favorite too with many sportsmen on account of its swiftness, its boldness, and its readiness to come to decoys. Blanchan (1898) says:

The gentlemen hidden behind "blinds" on the "duck shores" of Maryland and the sloughs of the interior and with a flock of wooden decoys floating near by, or the nefarious market gunner in his "sink boat" and with a dazzling reflector behind the naptha lamp on the front of his scow, bag by fair means and foul immense numbers of baldpates every season, yet so prolific is the bird, and so widely distributed over this continent, that there still remain widgeons to shoot. That is the fact one must marvel at when one gazes on the results of a single night's slaughtering in the Chesapeake country. The pothunter who uses a reflector to fascinate the flocks of ducks that, bedded for the night, swim blindly up to the sides of the boat, moving silently among them, often kills from 20 to 30 at a shot.

Winter.—After loitering along its way for several weeks in a most leisurely manner, as if waiting for the young birds to fatten and grow strong the baldpate finally reaches its winter home before cold weather sets in, spreading out from its inland breeding range to winter largely on the coasts, as well as in the lower Mississippi Valley. Its winter habits in the Chesapeake Bay, which marks the northern limit of its winter abundance on the Atlantic coast, have been referred to above and have been well described by others. It is common on the coast of Louisiana associating with mallards, gadwalls, pintails, and lesser scaup ducks. On the Pacific coast it winters abundantly as far north as Puget Sound, though according to Bowles (1909) it is not so common there as formerly; he says:

During fall, winter, and spring it is most numerous of all ducks in Washington, save possibly the bluebills and scoters. Large numbers of them congregate upon the tide flats of Puget Sound, and the bird is abundant also on the interior waters.

Constant persecution, however, has greatly reduced their ranks, as is the case with the entire duck family, and possibly for this reason their migratory habits have undergone a marked change. Eight or ten years ago they used to appear in enormous flocks during the first week in October, at which period I have seen on the Nisqually Flats, near Tacoma, what was estimated at about 500,000, all in the air at one time. For the past two or three years, however, no widgeon to speak of have appeared before November or December, and then in such greatly reduced numbers as to give rise to serious fear, not only as to the abundance, but as to the existence of future generations.

DISTRIBUTION.

Breeding range.—Northwestern North America. East to Hudson Bay, southeastern Manitoba (Shoal Lake), and formerly southern Wisconsin (Lake Koshkonong and Horicon marsh). South to northern Indiana (English Lake, rarely), perhaps northern Illinois, northern Nebraska (Cherry County), northern Colorado (Boulder County), northern Utah (Bear River), northwestern Nevada (Truckee Valley), and northeastern California (Modoc County). Seen in summer and probably breeding in northwestern New Mexico (Lake Burford) and northern Arizona (Mogollon Mountains). West to the interior of Oregon (Camp Harney) and Washington (Tacoma), central British Columbia (Fraser Valley), and central Alaska (Yukon River). North to northern Alaska (Kotzebue Sound) and northern Mackenzie (Franklin Bay).

Winter range.—All of North America south of the Northern States. East to the Atlantic coast, rarely from southern New England (Boston), and regularly from Maryland (Chesapeake Bay) southward. South to the Lesser Antilles (St. Thomas, Trinidad, Guadeloupe, St. Croix, etc.) and Costa Rica. West to the Pacific coast of Central America, Mexico, the United States, and southern British Columbia (Vancouver Island). North in the interior to southern Nevada (Pahrump Valley), central Utah (Provo), northeastern Colorado (Barr Lake), and southern Illinois (Ohio Valley).

Spring migration.—Average dates of arrival: Rhode Island, Newport, March 19; Ontario, Ottawa, April 20; New York, western, March 23; Pennsylvania, Erie, March 24; Ohio, Oberlin, March 17; Michigan, southern, March 25; Colorado, Loveland, March 10; Nebraska, central, March 17; Iowa, Keokuk, March 15; Minnesota, Heron Lake, March 29; Manitoba, southern, April 20; Saskatchewan, Indian Head, April 24; Alberta, Edmonton, April 17; Mackenzie, Fort Simpson, April 28; Alaska, Knik River, May 10, and Kowak River, May 22. Late dates of departure: North Carolina, Raleigh, April 26; Lower California, La Paz, April 1, and Colnett, April 1.

Fall migration.—Early dates of arrival: Pennsylvania, Beaver, August 30; Massachusetts, Marthas Vineyard, August 31; Maine, Merrymeeting Bay, September 20; Connecticut, East Hartford, September 29; Rhode Island, Middletown, September 20. Late dates of departure: Alaska, Kowak River, September 20, and St. Michael, October 1; Alberta, Edmonton, November 6; Ontario, Ottawa, November 6; Nova Scotia, Sable Island, November 7; Iowa, Keokuk, November 18.

Casual records.—Accidental in Bermuda (October, 1854, and October, 1874), Cuba, Jamaica, Porto Rico, and St. Thomas. Rare on migrations in Labrador (Hamilton Inlet, Natashquan, and Old Fort Bay, November 27, 1880) and New Brunswick (St. John, January, 1880). Accidental in Aleutian, Commander, and Hawaiian Islands, in the Azores, British Isles (six or more records) in France, and in Japan.

Egg dates.—Arctic America: Twenty-two records, June 5 to July 4; eleven records, June 16 to June 25. North and South Dakota: Twenty-one records, May 25 to July 13; eleven records, June 2 to 23. Alberta and Saskatchewan: Fourteen records, June 1 to 25; seven records, June 13 to 17. Utah: Nine records, May 5 to June 17; five records, May 10 to June 3.

NETTION CRECCA (Linnaeus).

EUROPEAN TEAL.

HABITS.

This well-known and widely distributed Palaearctic bird has always appeared on our check list as an occasional visitor or straggler with its name enclosed in brackets. And such I always believed it to be until our expedition visited the Aleutian Islands in 1911 and definitely established it, as a regular summer resident at least in North American territory. I stated in my report on the results of this expedition (1912) that:

The European bird is supposed to occur only rarely, or as a straggler, in the Aleutian Islands and the American bird is recorded by nearly all of the writers on Aleutian ornithology as the common breeding teal of the region. Teal of one of these species were common on all of the islands; we saw them frequently and found them breeding in nearly all suitable places along the small water courses and about small ponds. Doctor Wetmore found a nest containing 10 fresh eggs on June 7, near Unalaska, and shot the female; unfortunately the male was not secured. We naturally assumed that these were American green-winged teal and, therefore, made no special effort to shoot males on any of the eastern islands, but I now sorely regret that we did not collect at least a few males as the females of the two species are nearly indistinguishable. Among the western and central islands we collected quite a series of both sexes and every male taken proved to be an European teal; not a single male green-winged teal was collected or identified anywhere. On my return to Washington I looked through the National Museum collection for specimens from the Aleutian Islands and found only two males, No. 85615, collected by Lucien M. Turner on Atka Island, June 28, 1879, and No. 192391, collected by Dr. J. Hobart Egbert on Kiska Island, July 14, 1904; both of these proved to be typical European teal. Therefore, failing to find any positive evidence to prove that the green-winged teal breeds on the Aleutian Islands, we must assume for the present, on the strength of what evidence we have, that the European teal is the common breeding species of this region, where it is fairly abundant, and that the green-winged teal, which is so abundant on the main land of Alaska, occurs on the islands rarely, if at all.

Courtship.—Mr. John G. Millais (1902) has given us a beautiful colored illustration of the courtship of the teal in which a number of handsome males are seen displaying their plumage, sitting upright in the water around the different females or venturing nearer to offer their attentions. I quote from his description of it as follows:

It is a pretty sight, this spring display of the teal, all the more so as many take part in it, and the positions of the male birds are curious and extravagant. As if by mutual consent, several drakes raise their bodies from the water, erect the tail, arch the neck and pass their bills down the chest, at the same time they give voice to the low double whistle. During this movement the female sometimes permits one or even two drakes to approach her closely, whilst all the others are disposed in a circle or semicircle near at hand; but if any male that has not found favor in her eyes seeks to approach she will drive him off at once—an ignominious position which he seems to accept without question. It is only after some days of this volatile flirtation that the female eventually goes off with one male and remains strictly monogamous for the rest of the season, for after the end of April one never sees amongst teal the *tertium quid* arrangement so common with other ducks.

Nesting.—The same writer says of its nesting habits:

The nest is to be found in almost any sort of sheltered position near the water, but the female evinces a marked partiality for placing it in heather. In Scotland I have usually noticed it in open heaths, sometimes far from the lake or bog, but generally near to a burn that leads to them. The eggs number from 8 to 15, are of a creamy-white color, sometimes with a faint tinge of green, which fades soon after their contents are extracted: size 1.8 by 1.2 inches. None of the ducks show such an affection for their young as the female teal; when flushed with her young brood she will display greater bravery in their defence and evince more solicitude for their welfare than almost any bird. Teal drakes, on occasion, like the mallard and the shoveler, will sometimes even betray a very distinct alarm when their wives and families are threatened, for I once disturbed a teal duck with young on an open moor at Cawdor. The drake was with her, and he, much to my surprise, was almost as anxious as the female to lead me away, resorting several times to the broken-leg feints of his distressed partner.

The nest that we found at Unalaska, referred to above, was made of down, feathers, and bits of grass; it was well concealed in a thick clump of tall, coarse, dead grass, not over 10 feet from the bank of a swift and shallow stream, which flowed in a winding course through a broad alluvial plain back of Iliuliuk village. The plain was more or less gravelly in places and was partially covered with coarse grasses and scattered clumps of small willow bushes; it was surrounded by steep grassy hills, rising beyond to snow-capped mountains and narrowed at one end into deep valleys and gorges through which two mountain streams came tumbling down over the rocks to form the little river which had evidently formed the plain.

Similar picturesque valleys and flat alluvial plains were found on many of the Aleutian Islands; these were the favorite resorts of the teal, which were usually common and sometimes abundant among the western and central islands. With them we sometimes found red-breasted mergansers and a few mallards and scaup ducks, which were flushed from the streams or seen swimming on the little ponds.

The down in the nest of the European teal is very small and very dark colored, dark "hair brown" or "clove brown" with large conspicuous white centers. The breast feathers in the nest are small, with dusky centers and buff tips.

Eggs.—This teal has been known to lay as many as 16 eggs, but the usual numbers run from 8 to 12. In shape and color they are indistinguishable from eggs of the green-winged teal. The measurements of 100 eggs, given in Witherby's Handbook (1920), average 44.6 by 32.6 millimeters; the eggs showing the four extremes measure 49.5 by 34, 47.6 by 35.2, 41 by 32.9 and 42.2 by 31.2 millimeters.

Young.—The period of incubation is short, 22 days, and is performed by the female alone. The young teal have many enemies to contend with during their early existence, among which certain individuals of the brown-headed gull, which seem to develop murderous instincts, are most destructive, as the following striking instance related by Mr. Millais (1902) will illustrate:

About the year 1884, the brown-headed gulls, formerly represented by a couple of hundred pairs, began to increase on the bog at Murthly to an alarming extent. Their nests were everywhere in the reed tufts, and about this time the teal began to decrease. James Conacher, the keeper of the Moss, at once put it down to the gulls, who, he said, killed the ducklings as soon as their mothers brought them down to the bog, and said, moreover, that we should have no quantity of duck until a war of gull extermination had taken place. On talking the matter over with the head keeper, one James Keay, a very superior and observant man, he said that he had noticed that all the young teal that were killed lay dead near two places, and in an area of 30 yards square. This seemed plainly to point to the work of individuals, and on subsequently watching the places Keay saw a gull that had a nest close by actually seize a young teal, lift it into the air for a moment, and drop it dead. This gull and its partner were shot, and no more young ducks were found dead in that vicinity during the season; but the next year the gulls of certain nests were found to have again started the murders, and they were marked down and shot, after which no more ducks were killed for some time, and the teal increased greatly. All the young teal killed by the gulls were put to death in the same way, the skulls were nipped and crushed at the back, and they were not touched again. In June, 1890, another pair began duck killing, and near the nest of these birds Keay found the remains of 16 teal, 3 tufted ducks, and 2 mallard nestlings.

Plumages.—The downy young and the sequence of molts and plumages are so similar to those of our American bird that it seems unnecessary to repeat them here.

Food.—Bewick (1847), says of its food:

Buffon remarks that the young are seen in clusters on the pools, feeding on cresses, wild chervil, etc., and no doubt, as they grow up, they feed like other ducks, on the various seeds, grasses, and water plants, as well as upon the smaller animated beings with which all stagnant waters are so abundantly stored.

Macgillivray (1852) says:

Its food consists of seeds of grasses, slender rhizomata, which it pulls up from the mud, insects, mollusca, and worms.

Behavior.—Of its flight and vocal powers, Mr. Millais (1902) writes as follows:

During the day the teal is one of the most silent and inactive of birds. It will sit for hours motionless, apparently lost in a brown study or with the head buried in the scapulars. Out on the estuary a pack rests on the tidal heave without a sign of movement until night comes and with it the desire for food. In the daytime, during the early autumn, even in our much disturbed islands, teal are sometimes extremely tame, and will permit the approach of man within a few yards before flying away, and there are always certain holes in the large bogs where teal may be found and closely approached with certainty unless they have been previously disturbed. On being flushed they shoot up straight into the air, sometimes very rapidly, and often swaying slightly and rendering themselves a by no means easy mark—in fact, I once heard a friend, who had ineffectually expended 100 cartridges in one day, declare that *rising* teal were far more difficult to kill than snipe. Be that as it may, I can remember certain windy days when *driven* teal were wild and "dodgy," and were quite as difficult to bag as the snipe with whom they flew. Teal can suddenly turn in the midst of a straight forward flight and either dive downward, or, what is far more difficult for the gunner to accept, shoot straight upward, and only present as a target a practically invulnerable stern. It is a pretty sight on a sunny day to watch a flock of teal about to settle; they wheel and swing almost as much as flocks of dunlins, the dark backs and the light breasts alternately shining; and it is not until they have thoroughly surveyed their prospective resting place and its approaches that they come to a halt. Whilst on the wing one male occasionally utters his low double whistle, but teal are silent birds at all times, and the female rarely calls unless frightened, such as when the brood is threatened, when she emits a subdued little "quack."

Fall.—On the fall migration, teal are inclined to wander and, as most of our records have occurred during the late fall, winter, and early spring, they are probably stragglers from Palaearctic regions, or from the Aleutian Islands, that have strayed from their normal migration routes. Green-winged teal are found regularly in the Aleutian Islands in winter, but whether these are migrants from the mainland of Alaska, *Nettion carolinense*, or the resident breeding birds, *Nettion crecca*, I can not say. Probably most of the European teal that breed in the Aleutian Islands migrate in the fall down the Asiatic coast to Siam and India, with the birds from Siberia. Dr. John C. Phillips (1911a and 1912) relates an interesting incident which illustrates the tendency of this species to return each spring to the locality of its birth. A young European teal which was hatched and reared on his grounds in Wenham, Massachusetts, in 1910, returned to the same pond in 1911 and again in 1912.

DISTRIBUTION.

Breeding range.—Northern parts of the Eastern Hemisphere. Iceland, the British Isles, throughout Europe and Asia, north to 70° N.

and south in decreasing numbers to the Mediterranean, the Azores,
Turkestan, Mongolia, and the Amur Valley.   East to the Kurile and
Aleutian Islands, as far east as Unalaska.

Winter range.—South to the Canary Islands, Madeira, Abyssinia,
Sokotra, Persia, India, Ceylon, China, Japan, Formosa, and the Philippine Islands.   North as far as open water is to be found.   Apparently resident in the Aleutian Islands or migrating westward into
Asia.

Casual records.—Accidental in Spitsbergen, Greenland, Labrador
(Coues record, July 23, 1860, and Hamilton Inlet, no date given),
Nova Scotia and northeastern United States (Maine, Casco Bay, April
6, 1893; Massachusetts, Muskeget Island, March 16, 1890, and Sagamore, February 20, 1896; Connecticut, East Hartford, November 14,
1889; New York, Cayuga Lake, April 10, 1902 and Merrick, Long
Island, December 17, 1900; Virginia, Potomac River, 1885).   California records are indefinite.

Egg dates.—Great Britain: Nine records, May 3 to June 13.   Iceland: Thirteen records, May 1 to July 8; seven records, May 24 to
June 8.   Aleutian Islands: One record, June 8.

NETTION CAROLINENSE (Gmelin).

GREEN-WINGED TEAL.

HABITS.

Spring.—Following close on the heels of the pintail and the mallard, the hardy little green-winged teal is one of the earliest migrants
to start in the spring for its northern breeding grounds.   It begins
to leave its winter haunts in the lower Mississippi Valley in February,
proceeding slowly northward, and the first arrivals appear in its summer home in northern Alaska early in May.   Dr. F. Henry Yorke
(1899) says:

> The first issue arrives a day or two after the pintails and follows up the rivers, lakes,
> and sloughs, usually preferring the edges of muddy banks.   This issue stays only a
> short time and departs before the second arrives, usually about four or five days
> intervening; the second issue spreads over the country and is often joined by the
> third, staying for several weeks before they travel northward.   At times the third
> issue is delayed, probably, by overflowed lands in the south, where food is found in
> abundance; in such cases the third issue rushes by, or stays only a day or two late
> in the season.

Courtship.—Many of the birds are paired before the breeding
grounds are reached as there is ample time for courtship during the
leisurely migration; the warmth of returning spring stirs the amorous
instincts of the males and prompts them to strut before the females,
displaying their handsome colors in fantastic attitudes.   The performance is the same as that of the European teal, as described by
Millais (1902) an excellent account of which is given under that species.

Mr. George M. Sutton has sent me the following interesting notes on the courtship of the green-winged teal:

Suddenly, and apparently without any premeditation, two of the males started toward the center of the pond, one directly behind the other; the two birds in ridiculously similar attitudes, both with bills pointing somewhat upward, and head drawn back and down in a stiff and uncomfortable looking manner. Strange as it may seem, so similar were the birds in their every movement, that the feet, in swimming, seemed to stroke in perfect harmony, and the picture presented was one of unusual beauty. They swam deliberately, and in a direct line until they reached the center of the pond. It was not evident until now that a female bird had anything to do with the matter; but a sudden change in the attitude of the approaching males informed the observer that a very restless and inattentive female was the cause of the whole performance. Both males, still in perfect harmony of movement, were describing a circle about the female, swimming about 2 feet from each other, and at a tantalizingly deliberate speed. I could not help feeling that the atmosphere was growing tense, because the males seemed to be fairly quivering in their effort to curb spirit. The female, which had thus far been utterly unobservant, now became rather quiet and attentive, and the males, still in perfect accord, began a remarkable series of bobbings, opening their bills rather widely, and uttering a soft, not unmusical *pheep, pheep,* one call to every movement of the head. The call was given on the forward thrust of the head, and as the two beautiful birds wheeled about, in a circle possibly only 6 feet in diameter, it was only natural to call to mind two little boats emitting whistles at regular intervals, and indulging in quaint maneuvers, so totally unducklike the creatures seemed. Matters were even more complicated when it became evident that the males were now churning the water lustily with their feet, though their speed remained about the same. Again suddenly, the harmony of movement ceased; the female rushed at one savagely and seemingly without warrant, whereupon he, the favored one, stood up in the water, lifted his wings somewhat, and with rapidly churning feet made a most unusual noise, sounding like water thrown rapidly at some object in a fine stream, which in some manner, inexplainable thus far, must have been connected with a stream of water which seemed to pass from the bill to the rapidly treading feet. I could not get close enough to see clearly, and had no glasses, so the details of this very odd antic I have never been able to explain, but there seemed to be a fine stream of water shot out of the bird's bill, accompanied by the queer sound mentioned above. The sound was of a startling quality, and directly after its delivery the bird's feet quit their violent churning motion, and the bird sank to rest for a time. The other male, which had ceased operations for a momentary preening of feathers, would then "occupy the floor" and repeat the antic. Occasionally both males would do the stunt exactly at the same time. During the period of their greatest activity this act of standing in the water and treading was repeated about every 20 seconds. The part played by the female in these odd dramatics, was as far at least as the observer could see, a minor one. She was followed continually, but she did not follow in return. Her attitude was one of inattentiveness, save when one of the males came too near, or strange to say, on one occasion, when the performers lagged in their enthusiasm. At this time (observed only once) she tore madly across the pond and back again, in a manner indescribably nimble, past the males, whence her courters in steamboat formation, with the accompaniment of *pheep, pheep,* followed her.

The attitude of the males toward each other was one of dignified tolerance while the female was at hand. They apparently vied vigorously in matters of elegance of movement, but there was no sign of combat. Once, when the female rushed at the male, he surprised me by giving her a vicious jab in return, which seemed to subdue her for the time.

Nesting.—The green-winged teal is widely distributed during the nesting season, but throughout much of its breeding range, especially the eastern part of it, is only sparingly represented. We found a few scattering pairs in the Magdalen Islands, where it was undoubtedly breeding. Maynard (1896) found a nest here and gives the following good account of it:

On the southern side of Amherst Island, one of the Magdalen group, are several salt-water ponds which were formerly lagoons, but which the shifting sand of the beaches have cut off from the water of the gulf. These miniature lakes are surrounded by a thick growth of trees, composed mainly of spruce and hemlock, which have been so dwarfed by the severe climate that they rarely attain the height of 10 feet. I was making my way along the border of one of these ponds, on the 16th of June, in company with my friend, Mr. Gilman Brown, when a female green-winged teal rose within a yard of our feet, and stepping forward, we discovered a nest containing eight greenish eggs which were placed in a depression of the sandy soil on a few twigs, and surrounded with a ring of gray down, thus presenting a very pretty appearance. The spot was concealed by the overhanging branches of a little spruce, and had the bird remained quiet, we should have passed without discovering her treasures. The female was quite shy, and after circling about a few times disappeared.

Although the breeding range of the green-winged teal extends much farther north than that of the blue-winged teal, its center of abundance in the nesting season is in the vast prairie regions of the Northern States and western Canada. In both North Dakota and Saskatchewan we found a few pairs breeding with the other ducks in these great wild-fowl nurseries. Here the nests are usually concealed in the long grass near the borders of the lakes and sloughs or on the islands. The nest is generally well made in a hollow on dry ground and often at a considerable distance from the water. The hollow is first deeply lined with soft grasses and weeds, sometimes with a few fine twigs and leaves, on which is placed a thin layer of down from the bird's breast; more down is added as incubation advances, which, mixed with the loose dry grass, forms a convenient blanket to conceal and protect the eggs when the mother teal leaves them. Often the nests are placed in clumps of willows or under bushes on high land, a quarter of a mile or more from any water and occasionally a nest is found under a log.

Mr. R. C. McGregor (1906) records a nest found in the Krenitzin Islands, Alaska, which " was on the ground beneath the overhanging trunk of a twisted willow; it was thinly furnished with down about the top and the eggs rested on the ground. Inside diameter of nest about 5.5 inches; depth 3.5 inches." Henshaw (1875) reports a nest found in southern Colorado as follows:

A nest belonging to this species was found under a sagebush, perhaps 30 feet from the water's edge. A deep hollow had been scooped in the sand, and lined warmly with fine grasses and down, evidently taken from the bird's own breast, which was plucked nearly bare. The hen bird was sitting; in fact, so artfully was the nest placed that it was only when I had almost trodden upon it, and the old bird had shuffled out at my feet and made good her retreat behind some thick bushes, that I discovered it. Returning a couple of hours later, I found she had again taken possession of her treasures, nor did she leave till I had approached within 3 feet of her.

The down in the nest is exactly like that of the European teal, which is fully described under that species.

Eggs.—The green-winged teal lays from 6 to 18 eggs, the average number being from 10 to 12. The eggs are absolutely indistinguishable from those of the blue-winged teal; in shape they are ovate or elliptical ovate; in color they are dull white, cream color, or very pale olive buff. The measurements of 93 eggs in various collections average 45.8 by 34.2 millimeters; the eggs showing the four extremes measure 49 by 36, 48 by 37, 42 by 31.5 and 43 by 31 millimeters.

Young.—Incubation, which lasts 21 to 23 days, is performed by the female alone, as the male deserts her as soon as the eggs are laid. The entire care of the young also devolves on the mother teal, who performs her duty with exemplary devotion. The young all hatch within a few hours of each other and after a short rest the down becomes dry and they gain sufficient strength to make the perilous overland journey, which is often a long one, to the nearest water. Mr. Ernest Thompson Seton (1901) has drawn a very vivid picture of this momentous event in which he has portrayed some of the many dangers to which the little ducklings are exposed. Like other young ducks, they need no food for the first few hours but their mother soon teaches them to feed on the insects and other soft animal, as well as vegetable, food which they can pick up around the edges of the ponds and among the aquatic vegetation. They also learn to heed her warning cry when danger threatens, when to hide and how to escape their many enemies, but often they would not escape except for her bravery and zeal in their defense, even at the risk of her own life.

Plumages.—The downy young greenwing differs from the bluewing in having a smaller and shorter bill, with a hooked nail, and in its generally darker coloration. The upper parts are " mummy brown " or " Prout's brown," darkest on the crown and rump; the under parts shade from " buckthorn brown " or " clay color," on the sides of the head and throat, to " cinnamon buff" or " light buff," on the breast and belly; the side of the head is distinctly marked by a broad loral and postocular stripe of dark brown and a similar auricular stripe below it, from the eye to the occiput; a broad superciliary stripe of buff extends from the bill to the occiput, but it is interrupted by an extension of the dark crown nearly or quite down to the eye; the color of the back is relieved by buffy spots on the thighs, scapulars, and wings. I have never had any experience with hatching and raising this species, but presume that its plumage grows about as it does in the other surface-feeding ducks. The plumage appears first on the flanks and scapulars.

In the juvenal or first plumage the sexes are practically alike, except that in the young female the colors in the wing are somewhat duller, the pattern being the same in both sexes, and there is less spotting on the belly. But changes soon take place and the advance toward maturity is rapid. The young male becomes lighter below and the red plumage of the head appears in October; by December the young bird has become practically indistinguishable from the adult.

The adult male sometimes begins to molt into the eclipse plumage in June, usually in July, and in August this plumage is complete, all the contour feathers and scapulars having been molted; the flight feathers are renewed in August and the second complete molt of the contour feathers begins late in September and is completed in October or November. In the eclipse plumage old and young males and females look very much alike, but old males generally have fewer, more clearly defined, and well rounded spots below and old females are usually uniformly and thickly mottled on the under parts.

Food.—The green-winged teal enjoys a varied diet which it obtains in various ways in different parts of its habitat. In its summer home it loves to dabble in the shallow water about the edges of the sloughs, ponds, and creeks, with its body half immersed, its feet kicking in the air and its bill probing in the mud for aquatic insects or their larvae, worms, small mollusks and crustaceans, or even tadpoles. In such places it also feeds on the soft parts of various water plants and their seeds. In harvest time it wanders to the grain fields and picks up the fallen grains of corn, wheat, oats, barley, and buckwheat, where it also feeds on various other seeds, grasses, and vegetable matter. At this season and in the winter, when it lives in the southern rice fields feasting on the fallen harvest, it grows very fat and its flesh becomes very desirable for the table, equaling the finest of the ducks. It ordinarily feeds during the daytime, but in sections where it is much disturbed it is forced to become a night feeder. As it is active on land and can walk or run long distances, it often resorts to the dry uplands and woods to feed on berries, wild grapes, chestnuts, acorns, and other nuts, all of which help to improve the flavor of its flesh and make it a much sought game bird.

Neltje Blanchan (1898) says:

Nothing about its rankness of flavor when it has gorged on putrid salmon lying in the creeks in the northwest, or the maggots they contain, ever creeps into the books; and yet this dainty little exquisite of the southern rice fields has a voracious appetite worthy of the mallard around the salmon canneries of British Columbia, where the stench from a flock of teals passing overhead betrays a taste for high living no other gourmand can approve. When clean fed, however, there is no better table duck than a teal.

Mr. Douglas C. Mabbott (1920) says of its food:

Of the contents of 653 green-winged teal stomachs examined, more than nine-tenths (90.67 per cent) consisted of vegetable matter. By far the largest item of food contributed by any one family of plants came from the sedges, and this amounted to nearly two-fifths (38.82 per cent) of the total food. Next to the sedges, pondweeds are the favorite food supply, contributing 11.52 per cent, while grasses follow closely with 11; then smartweeds, 5.25; algae, 4.63; duckweeds, 1.9; water milfoils, 1.11; arrow grass, 0.91; and burreed, 0.85 per cent. The remaining 14.68 per cent is made up of a great number of smaller items.

Insects formed 4.57 per cent of the total food of the green-winged teal, the remainder of the animal food consisting of mollusks, 3.59 per cent; crustaceans, 0.92; and miscellaneous, 0.25; the total amounting to 9.33 per cent.

Behavior.—Nearly every writer on American ornithology has commented on the swiftness of flight of the green-winged teal, in which it certainly excels. In proportion to its size, and perhaps actually, it is the swiftest of the ducks, though its diminutive size might lead to an overestimate of its speed. It has been credited with a speed of 160 miles an hour, but this is undoubtedly an exaggeration. Mr. J. H. Bowles (1909) has well described its flight, as follows:

Moving at a rate of certainly not less than 100 miles an hour, the evolutions of a large flock of these birds are truly startling. They fly in such close order that one would think their wings must interfere, even on a straight course; yet of a sudden the whole flock will turn at a right angle, or wheel and twist as if it were one bird. The looker-on can only wonder what the signal may be which is given and obeyed to such perfection, for the least hesitation or mistake on the part of a single bird would result in death or a broken wing to a score.

On land this pretty little teal is quite at home; it walks gracefully and easily and it can run quite swiftly. It often travels long distances on foot in search of food or when moving from one pond to another; in making such overland journeys it sometimes moves in a compact flock, giving the pothunter a chance for a raking shot. In the water it swims easily and swiftly. Unlike most of the surface-feeding ducks it is an expert diver and can swim for a long distance under water to reach some needed shelter, where it can hide with only its head or its bill exposed. A wounded bird often escapes in this way and seems to have vanished. Mr. T. Gilbert Pearson (1919)—

recalls on one occasion seeing a wounded green-winged teal fall, which, on striking the water, instantly dived. After watching a few minutes, for it to reappear, he waded out to the point where it had disappeared and found the bird about 2 feet beneath the surface, clinging with its bill to a water plant.

The note of the male greenwing is a short mellow whistle or twittering call and that of the female a faint reproduction of the quack of the mallard. Mr. Aretas A. Saunders writes me that the note of the male—

is a high-pitched, short, staccato whistle, and is accompanied by a lower-pitched trilled note, uttered less frequently. The effect of this note, when repeated frequently, and heard from a distance is much like the peeping of spring hylas. It also somewhat suggests the piping noise made by a spring flock of evening grosbeaks.

The green-winged teal is associated on its breeding grounds with various other species of ducks and it flocks with other ducks, particularly the blue-winged teal, on its migrations. Still it can hardly be called a sociable species and seems to prefer to travel in large flocks of its own species. In the winter many kinds of ducks frequent the favorite breeding grounds together and usually live peaceably with each other.

Fall.—The fall migration begins with the first cold weather, often quite early in the season, but the birds linger on the way wherever they can find attractive feeding grounds in the wild rice patches or on cultivated lands; probably the early migrants are wanderers from near-by breeding grounds. The first snowstorms bring along the main late flight and the northern winter has set in before the last of the migrants are driven south by the ice and snow, together with the northern mallards, the last of the surface-feeding ducks.

Game.—From the sportsman's viewpoint the green-winged teal is an important member of the long list of American wild fowl. Its abundance assures him plenty of sport; its swift flight, with its sudden turnings and rapid twistings, tests his marksmanship to the limit; and its plump little body, fattened on the best of grains, nuts, and succulent herbs, provides a dainty morsel for the table. I quote two well-drawn pen pictures of this bird as a hunter sees it. The first, written by the illustrious Audubon (1840) tells of the advent of the first migrants, as follows:

Nothing can be more pleasing to an American sportsman than the arrival of this beautiful little duck in our Southern or Western States. There, in the month of September, just as the sun sinks beneath the horizon, you may find him standing on some mote or embankment of a rice field in Carolina, or a neck of land between two large ponds in Kentucky, his gun loaded with No. 4, and his dog lying at his feet. He sees advancing from afar, at a brisk rate, a small dark cloud, which he has some minutes ago marked and pronounced to be a flock of green-winged teals. Now he squats on his haunches, his dog lies close, and ere another minute has elapsed, right over his head, but too high to be shot at, pass the winged travelers. Some of them remember the place well, for there they have reposed and fed before. Now they wheel, dash irregularly through the air, sweep in a close body over the watery fields, and in their course pass near the fatal spot where the gunner anxiously awaits. Hark! two shots in rapid succession! The troop is in disorder, and the dog dashes through the water. Here and there lies a teal, with its legs quivering; there, one is whirling round in the agonies of death; some, which are only winged, quickly and in silence make their way toward a hiding place, while one, with a single pellet in his head, rises perpendicularly with uncertain beats, and falls with a splash on the water. The gunner has charged his tubes, his faithful follower has brought up all the game, and the frightened teals have dressed their ranks, and flying, now high, now low, seem curious to see the place where their companions have been left. Again they fly over the dangerous spot, and again receive the double shower of shot. Were it not that darkness has now set in, the carnage might continue until the sportsman should no longer consider the thinned flock worthy of his notice. In this manner, at the first arrival of the green-winged teal in the western country, I have seen upwards of six dozen shot by a single gunner in the course of one day.

And then, second, the pen of that keen sportsman, Dr. F. Henry Yorke (1891), describes the departure of the late flight, in the following words:

The last issue of bluewings had collected, circled high in the air, and, following their instinctive impulse, had traveled southward. The second issue of mallards had come and gone, after staying with us a short time. The pintails, widgeons, green-winged teal (first issue), redheads, canvasbacks, and bluebills had also departed, and Grass Lake was almost "duckless." Even the mudhens had almost disappeared, and only a few scattered individuals, or small flocks of belated widgeons or pintails could be seen. Once in a while a few mallards turned up, but they were old, wary birds, "not to be caught with chaff." The only chance we could get was when a "stranger" flock of mallards came in, drifting down from the last issue, just preceding the frosts.

A week like this about the end of October is not an unusual occurrence. The sun shines warm after the cold nights, and the hazy atmosphere of our "Indian summer" induces idleness to a very reprehensive degree. But there was nothing to do, and we waited for a blast from old Boreas to awaken the ducks and put new life into ourselves.

Suddenly the herald of winter was heard. A fierce storm of rain or snow swept down from the North, where the icy grip of winter already held the lakes, and all nature was awake again. The laggard ducks came streaming in, mallards, pintails, and widgeon. Bluebills rushed down the flyways, and the game little green-winged teal, whipping and pitching in all directions, made his second appearance. This time the ducks meant business. While the weather was more uncertain, they came and returned, loth to leave their happy nesting grounds in the far north; but now Jack Frost was after them, and they were bent on a long and inevitable journey although some of them dropping here and there, they would stay until they were absolutely frozen out before they betook themselves to the mild clime and the open waterways of the sunny South.

Winter.—This hardy little duck winters as far north as British Columbia and Montana in the west, in the central States of the prairie region, in southern New England and even in Nova Scotia, when it can find open water in the spring holes and the streams near the coast. But its main winter home is in the great wild-fowl resorts of the Southern States and Mexico, where it can find safe retreats and abundant feeding grounds. It prefers the rice fields of the interior and the inland sloughs and ponds, but it also visits the coastal estuaries and the mouths of streams occasionally.

DISTRIBUTION.

Breeding range.—Northern North America practically across the continent, but very sparingly in the east. South to the Gulf of St. Lawrence (Magdalen Islands), southern Quebec (Monacougan), casually in western New York (Niagara River and Montezuma marshes), rarely in southern Ontario (Toronto, Point au Pins, Oshawa, and

Gravenhurst) and northeastern Michigan (Neebish Island), formerly Wisconsin (Lake Koshkonong), formerly northeastern Illinois, southern Minnesota (Rice and Jackson Counties), formerly central western Iowa (Sac County), northern Nebraska (Cherry County), southern Colorado (San Luis River), northern New Mexico (San Miguel County), northern Utah (Bear River and Great Salt Lake), northwestern Nevada (Washoe Lake), and south central California (Tulare Lake and formerly Ventura County). North to the limit of trees in northern Alaska (Kotzebue Sound and Yukon River), northern Mackenzie (Fort Anderson), Great Slave Lake (Fort Rae), northern Manitoba (Churchill), and James Bay. Ungava and Labrador records doubtful. Replaced in Aleutian and perhaps Pribilof Islands by the European teal.

Winter range.—Southern North America, mainly in southwestern United States and Mexico. East to the Bahama Islands, Cuba, Jamaica, and the Lesser Antilles (Carriacoú, Grenada, Tobago, etc.). South to British Honduras (Belize River) and southern Mexico (Michoacan). North, more or less regularly, to southern British Columbia (Chilliwack and Okanagan), central Montana (Great Falls), northern Nebraska (Cherry County), northern Missouri (Kansas City), southern Illinois (Mount Carmel), Kentucky and the coast of Maryland (Chesapeake Bay); rarely or irregularly farther north to southern Alaska (Sitka), the Great Lakes, and southern New York (Long Island); and casually to Massachusetts (Boston) and Nova Scotia (Halifax).

Spring migration.—Average dates of arrival: Pennsylvania, southern, March 16; Connecticut, southern, April 6; Quebec, Montreal, April 27; Prince Edward Island, April 26; Missouri, central, February 26; Illinois, central March 7; Iowa, Keokuk, March 3; Minnesota, Heron Lake, March 24 (earliest March 6); South Dakota, central, March 20; North Dakota, northern, April 6; Manitoba, Aweme, April 16; Saskatchewan, southern, April 19; Alaska, Yukon River, May 3 (earliest). Late dates of departure: Florida, Wakulla County, April 11; North Carolina, Raleigh, April 13; Louisiana, Hester, April 6; Texas, northern, April 16; Iowa, Keokuk, April 30 (average April 7).

Fall migration.—Early dates of arrival: Pennsylvania, Erie, September 1; Long Island, Mastic, September 4; Virginia, Alexandria, September 22; Florida, Wakulla County, September 26. Average dates of arrival: Quebec, Hatley, October 11; Maine, Bangor, October 8; Pennsylvania, Erie, September 15; Virginia, Alexandria, September 29; Iowa, Keokuk, September 21; Kansas, central, September 12; Texas, central, September 22; California, central, September 17. Late dates of departure: Alaska, Taku River, September 26; Ontario, southern, November 7; Massachusetts, Essex County, December 2; Iowa, Keokuk, November 27.

Casual records.—Accidental in Bermuda (October 10, 1874, November, 1874, and fall of 1875), southern Greenland (Julianshaab, Godthaab, etc.), Great Britain (Hampshire about 1840, Yorkshire, November, 1851, and Devonshire, November 23, 1879), Hawaiiau Islands, and Japan.

Egg dates.—Alaska and Arctic America: Four records, June 4, 10, 18 and July 1. Saskatchewan and Alberta: Thirteen records, May 21 to June 21; seven records, May 25 to June 17. Colorado and Utah: Twenty-five records, May 6 to August 17; thirteen records, May 17 to June 22.

QUERQUEDULA DISCORS (Linnaeus).

BLUE-WINGED TEAL.

HABITS.

Spring.—Not until spring is well advanced and really hot weather has come in its winter haunts does this tender warm-weather bird decide to leave the sunny glades of Florida and the bayous of Louisiana, where it has spent the winter or early spring, dabbling in the shallow, muddy pools, and marshes. The early migrants are probably hardier individuals that have wintered farther north, but the later migrants linger in the Gulf States through April and even into May. Dr. F. Henry Yorke (1899) designates three distinct spring flights, as follows:

The first issue of this, our tenderest, duck arrives in latitude 37° from March 25 to April 1, staying about six or eight days. The second follows a few days after the first has departed northward, up to and past the boundary line. A short period elapses when they likewise travel north to the southern part of Minnesota and its parallel. The third soon follows, and stays an indefinite period, working up through Illinois, Indiana, Wisconsin, and eastward about the last week in April if the weathe permits, the Ohio, Missouri, and Mississippi, with their tributaries, furnishing the fly ways.

Dr. P. L. Hatch (1892) thus describes the arrival of this species in Minnesota:

No other species of the ducks is so cautious upon its arrival as the blue-winged teal, a trait by which the old hunter determines its identity at once. In parties of 8 to 10 or a dozen they will circle around, descending again and again only to rise again and go farther up or lower down the stream to repeat the same demonstrations of indecision, many times over, and just as unexpectedly they suddenly drop out of sight between the treeless banks. They are, as a general thing, several days later in their spring arrivals, and as much earlier than the greenwings in autumn. This is not true in every migration, for I have once or twice known them to come a little before the other, and several times simultaneously; but in my observations, extending over many years in succession, it has proved a noticeable characteristic in its migrations. They are seldom seen on the large clear lakes; but on small ponds, mud flats, and sluggish streams where various pondweeds and aquatic roots afford in abundance its favorite vegetable food.

Courtship.—The courtship of the blue-winged teal is largely performed on the wing much after the manner of the black duck, a nuptial chase as it were, of which Mr. Ernest E. Thompson (1890) says:

I have frequently remarked that during the breeding season this species may be seen coursing over and around the ponds in threes, and these when shot usually prove a male and two females. After dark they may be identified during these maneuvers by their swift flight and the peculiar chirping, almost a twittering, that they indulge in as they fly.

Nesting.—The breeding range of the blue-winged teal has been materially reduced in area during the past 50 years by the increasing settlement of the Middle West, the encroachments of agriculture on its breeding grounds, and by the constant persecution by gunners of an unsuspicious and desirable game bird. Although it formerly bred abundantly throughout all the Middle and Northern States east of the Rocky Mountains, it is now mainly restricted to the prairie regions of the northern United States and Canada, with only a few scattering pairs left in the eastern and southern portions of its breeding range. We found a few pairs breeding in the East Point marshes in the Magdalen Islands, and only a few are left in eastern Canada and south of the Great Lakes. In North Dakota it was still abundant in 1901; this, with the pintail and shoveller, were the three commonest ducks; almost every little pond hole, creek, or grassy slough contained one or more pairs of blue-winged teal, and we could see the pretty little ducks swimming in pairs, close at hand among the vegetation or springing into the air as we drove past.

Here their nests are generally well concealed in the long prairie grass growing around the borders of the sloughs and small pond holes, almost always on dry ground but not far from the water; they are sometimes located in moist meadows bordering such places, where the grass is long and thick enough to conceal them. I found one nest in an open place where the dead grass had been beaten down quite flat; it was beautifully concealed from view under the grass. They also nest sparingly with the baldpates and lesser scaup ducks on the islands. The nest of the blue-winged teal is well built; a hollow is made in the ground and filled with a thick soft lining of fine grass mixed with down, on which the eggs are laid, and the grass is arched over it for concealment; as incubation advances more down is added until a thick blanket is provided, which the female uses to cover the eggs when she leaves them. The nests are so well concealed that comparatively few are found, considering the abundance of the species.

In Saskatchewan in 1905 and 1906 the blue-winged teal was one of the most abundant of the ducks; we found 16 nests in all on dates ranging from June 13 to July 9; the nests were on the islands and in the meadows near the lakes, similar in location and construction to those we found in North Dakota. On that wonderful duck island in Crane Lake 10 out of the 61 ducks' nests found were of this species; only the gadwall, of which we found 23 nests, exceeded it in abundance.

Rev. Manley B. Townsend has sent me his notes on a nest which he found in a slough near Crystal Lake, in Nebraska, on June 10, 1910. He writes:

One June day we made a systematic search of the swamp for nests, and were rewarded in richest measure, finding numerous nests. As we picked our cautious way through the swamp we came to a small dry area, some 30 feet back from the open water. Out from under our feet burst a large bird with a startled "quack" and went hurtling off over the pond. It was a female blue-winged teal. There, beneath a tuft of grasses, in a hollow on the ground, was the nest, built of grasses and lined with dark-brown mottled down pulled from the mother's own breast. In the midst of the downy bedclothes rested 10 beautiful, cream-colored eggs—an exquisite casket of jewels destined to develop into living gems far lovelier than any rubies or diamonds ever dug from the earth. The beauty of such a spectacle can not be adequately described and must be seen to be appreciated. On leaving the nest, the bird is accustomed to nicely cover her treasures with the warm comforters to prevent too rapid evaporation of the heat. We had unexpectedly "jumped" her and she had left in too great a hurry to perform that customary function. Two weeks later we found the nest empty, but the whole family were out there on the pond, bobbing about as buoyant as corks, learning how to make a living and survive in a wonderful but dangerous world.

Several observers have reported nests in close proximity to railroad tracks, which seems to be a favorite location.

Mr. Robert B. Rockwell (1911) has made some extensive studies of the nesting habits of ducks in the Barr Lake region of Colorado; he writes:

By far the most abundant nesting duck throughout the Barr district was the pretty little blue-winged teal. No matter what type of ground our searches carried us over, we were sure to be startled by the occasional flutter of wings, as a dainty little gray-clad mother left her nest like a flash upon our too close approach. We found nests of these birds in the dense cat-tail growth along sloughs; on the soggy, spongy seepage ground under the big dykes; at the edge of beaten paths near the lake shore; by roadsides back from the water; among the dry weeds and sand of the prairie, far from the water's edge; amid the dense rank grass on a tiny island; in alfalfa fields, on grassy flats, and in cavities in and upon muskrat houses.

The nests exhibited a wide diversity in construction. The predominating type was a neat basketlike structure composed of fine soft dead grass, sometimes set well into a dense clump of rank grass on the surface of the ground, and sometimes sunken into a cavity until the top of the nest was flush with the surface of the ground. These nests were usually liberally lined with down; much thicker on the sides and rim of the nest than on the bottom. In fact several were examined which had no down whatever underneath the eggs. The quantity of down varied greatly in different nests, but apparently increased in quantity as incubation advanced.

A less common type of nest was made entirely of bits of dead cat-tail blades deepset into a cavity in the ground. This type of nest was usually found in marshy places, where this material was more available, and in these there was much less of the downy lining. The concealment of these nests was likewise less effective, and taken as a whole this type of nest was altogether inferior. We found a few built in wet places where the foundation of the nest was actually wet, but we did not find a single nest where the eggs were the least bit damp; and the large majority were in perfectly dry locations in close proximity to water.

The concealment of the better built nests, especially those in the center of a tussock of rank grass, was well-nigh perfect; in fact in most cases we were unable to see either the brooding bird or the eggs from a distance of 5 to 6 feet even when we knew the exact location of the nest. Upon leaving the nest during incubation the parent covered the eggs with the downy rim of the nest and the concealment thus afforded was remarkable.

Several radical departures from the characteristic habits were encountered. One bird had built her nest on a little flat amid some short blue grass which afforded her no concealment whatever. As she brooded her eggs she was plainly visible at a distance of 20 yards or more. She allowed me to approach to within 4 or 5 feet and set up my camera for an exposure; and then instead of springing lightly into the air as usual, she ambled awkwardly off the nest, waddled slowly between the legs of my tripod, uttering lazy little quacks of protest, and finally after walking a distance of 30 yards or more took flight.

While plowing our way through a dense cat-tail swamp in water above our knees we frightened a teal from a nest in a muskrat house. A careful search finally revealed the eggs fully a foot back from the entrance of a deep cavity in the side of the house. To our surprise the nest contained four eggs of the teal and five eggs of some big duck, all of which were incubated.

Another queer nest was found, which was a shallow depression on the side of a dilapidated muskrat house, which had been originally built between a fence post and its diagonal brace. The lower barbed wire of the fence prevented the top of the house from collapsing, while the side weathered away, leaving a cavity well protected by the overhanging top. In this cavity without a sign of lining or a bit of concealment lay the 10 conspicuous white eggs. They could be readily seen from a distance of 20 yards.

The down in the blue-winged teal's nest is larger and lighter colored than in that of the green-winged teal; it varies in color from "hair brown" to "drab," and it has large whitish centers.

Eggs.—The blue-winged teal lays from 6 to 15 eggs, but the numbers most commonly found in full sets are 10, 11, and 12. All ducks are more or less careless about laying in each other's nests. This seems to occur less frequently with the teals than with the larger species, but the nest mentioned above by Mr. Rockwell (1911), containing "four eggs of the teal and five eggs of some big duck," shows that the little teal is sometimes imposed upon.

The eggs of the blue-winged teal vary in shape from ovate to elliptical ovate; the shell is very smooth, but only slightly glossy. In color they are dull white, light-cream color, creamy white, or pale olive white. They are not distinguishable from those of other teals; but if the female is flushed from the nest, she can be distinguished from the green-winged teal by the blue wing-coverts, but not so easily from the cinnamon teal.

The measurements of 93 eggs in various collections average 46.6 by 33.4 millimeters; the eggs showing the four extremes measure **49.5** by 35, 47.2 by **36.2**, **43.5** by 32, and 45.6 by **31.3** millimeters.

Young.—As the male deserts the female soon after the eggs are laid, incubation is performed solely by her. Incubation does not begin until after the last egg is laid, one egg having been laid each day until the set is complete. The period of incubation is from 21 to 23 days. The young hatch almost simultaneously, or at least within a few hours; they remain in the nest until they have dried off and are strong enough to walk, when they are led to the nearest water and taught by their devoted mother to feed. Their food at this age consists mainly of soft insects, worms, and other small, tender, animal food, but they soon learn to forage for themselves and pick up a variety of vegetable foods as well. The young are guarded with tender care by one of the most devoted of mothers; when surprised with her brood of young she resorts to all the arts and strategies known to anxious bird mothers to draw the intruder away from her brood or to distract his attention, utterly regardless of her own safety, while the young have time to hide or escape to a place of safety. The young are experts at hiding, even in open situations, where they squat flat on the ground and vanish; but they usually run or swim in among tall grass or reeds, where it is almost useless to look for them. All through the remainder of the summer, until they are able to fly, she remains with them teaching them where to find the choicest foods and how to escape from their numerous enemies; they learn to know her warning calls, when to run and when to hide, and by the end of the summer they are ready to gather into flocks for the fall migration.

Plumages.—In the downy young the colors of the upper parts vary from "mummy brown" to "Dresden brown," darker on the crown and rump, lighter elsewhere, the down being much darker basally; the under parts are "maize yellow," shaded locally with "buff yellow," due to the darker tips of the down; the sides of the head are "yellow ocher" or pale "buckthorn brown" in young birds, but these colors soon fade and all the colors grow paler as the young bird increases in size. The color pattern of the head consists of a dark-brown central crown bordered on each side by a broad superciliary stripe of yellow ocher, below which is a narrow postocular stripe, a loral patch, and an auricular spot of dusky. On the back the brown is broken by four large spots of yellowish, one on each side of the rump and one on each scapular region. Young blue-wing teal closely resemble young shovellers, but the latter are paler colored, with all the brown areas more extensive, with less of the rich buff and yellow tints and with longer and more broadly tipped bills.

The young develop more rapidly than those of the larger ducks, as they are late breeders and early fall migrants. The first feathers to appear on the downy young are the mottled feathers of the sides, below and above the wings; these come when the young bird is hardly one-third grown, sometimes by the end of June.   The growth of feathers spreads over the breast first, then over the back and head, the down disappearing late on the rump and last on the hind neck; by the end of July the young teal is nearly fully grown and the whole of the spotted juvenal plumage has been acquired except the wing quills which are still in their sheaths.   During August the wings and and tail are acquired and before the end of that month the young birds can fly.   Before the wings are grown the sexes are practically indistinguishable and both resemble the adult female except that they are lighter colored below and often nearly immaculate white on the belly.

During the fall and winter the young teal makes slow progess toward maturity; the blue lesser wing coverts and the green speculum are acquired as soon as the wings are grown, but they are duller than in adults; other changes come slowly until spring, when the first nuptial plumage is assumed, hardly distinguishable from the adult nuptial plumage, but the colors are all duller and the long blue-edged scapulars are not yet developed.

The first eclipse plumage is assumed in July and August; and at this first complete postnuptial molt the young bird becomes indistinguishable from the adult, when about 14 months old.

The eclipse plumage in the adult involves the change of all the contour feathers and the scapulars; it does not begin until July, is complete in August, when the flight feathers are molted, and lasts through September.   In this plumage the male closely resembles the female, but can always be recognized by the wings, in which no marked seasonable change takes place.   Adults are slow in shedding the eclipse plumage, individuals varying greatly in this respect.   The full body plumage is seldom acquired before the middle of winter and sometimes not until March, so that the gradual changes taking place might be regarded as a prolonged prenuptial molt.

Hybrids among the teals are not common, but Mr. William G. Smith (1887) records a specimen, which he took in Colorado, "the whole body color of the cinnamon teal, with the head the color, and snow-white cheek marks distinctly, of the bluewing."

Mr. Frederic H. Kennard (1919) has described, under the subspecific name *albinucha*, a supposed southern race of the blue-winged teal, the sole distinguishing character being a continuation of the white crescents over the eyes in thin superciliary lines down to the nape, where they join to form a white nuchal patch.   It does not seem to have been proven that *all* southern breeding teal are so marked, and I have seen several northern breeding teal partially so marked.   Mr. Stanley C. Arthur (1920) records a case where a bird in captivity lost this marking after molting into a new spring plumage.   This marking may prove to be merely a high stage of plumage, assumed by the most vigorous birds. Mr. Arthur's bird died soon after assuming the normal spring plumage, which may mean that waning vitality was the cause of its losing its white adornment.

Food.—The blue-winged teal is decidely a surface feeder; it feeds in shallow, muddy pond holes overgrown with aquatic vegetation, about the reedy shores of lakes and sloughs, and even in wet meadows, particularly along the banks of grassy ditches and creeks, where it is usually concealed from view; its food is usually obtained on the surface or within reach of its submerged head and neck, but occasionally its tail is tipped up and its body half immersed. Its food consists largely of tender aquatic plants.

In the fall it visits the grain fields occasionally and eats some wheat and barley. It eats wild rice wherever it can find it and, on its winter feeding grounds, it lives and feasts in the extensive rice fields. Its animal food includes tadpoles, worms, snails, and other small mollusks, water insects, and larvae. Dr. J. C. Phillips (1911) found that the stomachs of birds shot in Massachusetts contained "many young snails, various insects, and seeds of burreed, pondweeds, smartweed, and various sedges and grasses. Animal matter, 88 per cent; vegetable, 12 per cent; mineral, 8 per cent."

Mr. Douglas C. Mabbott (1920) sums up the food of the blue-winged teal as follows:

About seven-tenths (70.53 per cent) of the blue-winged teal's food consists of vegetable matter. Of this about three-fourths is included in four families of plants. Sedges (Cyperaceae), with 18.79 per cent; pondweeds (Naiadaceae), 12.6; grasses (Gramineae), 12.26; and the smartweeds (Polygonaceae), 8.22. The remainder of the plant food is made up of algae, 2.95 per cent; water lilies (Nymphaeaceae), 1.37; rice and corn, 0.98; water milfoils (Haloragidaceae), 0.71; bur reeds (Sparganiaceae), 0.38; madder family (Rubiaceae), 0.35; and miscellaneous 11.92 per cent.

Animal matter constitutes 29.47 per cent of the total food of the blue-winged teal, which is more than three times the percentage of animal food eaten by the green-wing. Over half of this (16.82 per cent) is mollusks, the remainder being made up of insects, 10.41 per cent, crustaceans, 1.93, and miscellaneous, 0.31 per cent.

Behavior.—From the water the blue-winged teal springs into the air with surprising agility, and when under way is one of the swiftest of the ducks in flight; it has been credited with attaining a speed of 90, 100, or even 130 miles an hour, but probably these speeds are all overestimated, as there is very little accurate data on which to base an estimate. Doctor Yorke (1899) says: "They travel at the rate of about 130 miles an hour, exceeded only by the green-winged teal." This seems incredible.

Audubon (1840) says:

The flight of the blue-winged teal is extremely rapid and well sustained. Indeed, I have thought that, when traveling, it passes through the air with a speed equal to that of the passenger pigeon. When flying in flocks in clear sunny weather, the blue of their wings glistens like polished steel, so as to give them the most lively appearance, and while they are wheeling over the places in which they intend to alight, their wings being alternately thrown in the shade and exposed to the bright light, the glowing and varied luster thus produced, at whatever distance they may be, draws your eyes involuntarily toward them. When advancing against a stiff breeze, they alternately show their upper and lower surfaces, and you are struck by the vivid steel blue of their mantle, which resembles the dancing light of a piece of glass suddenly reflected on a distant object. I have never observed them traveling in company with other ducks, but I have seen them at times passing over the sea at a considerable distance from land. Before alighting, and almost under any circumstances, and in any locality, these teals pass and repass several times over the place, as if to assure themselves of the absence of danger, or, should there be cause of apprehension, to watch until it is over. They swim buoyantly, and generally in a close body, at times nearly touching each other.

Nuttall (1834) says that "when they alight," they "drop down suddenly among the reeds in the manner of the snipe or woodcock."

About the vocal powers of this teal there is very little to be said. Dawson (1903) has covered the ground very well in the following words:

In addition to the whistling of the wings, the teals have a soft lisping note, only remotely related to the typical anatidine *quack*, and is uttered either in apprehension or encouragement.

While feeding and at other times these teal are usually silent; the lisping or peeping of the male are more often heard when the birds are in flight than at other times and are probably used as signals, as to dangers or the presence of food. The female has a faint quacking note.

On their breeding grounds blue-winged teal are associated with various other species, notably shovellers, pintails, gadwalls, and mallards. On their migrations they usually fly in flocks by themselves, but often resort to the same feeding grounds as other surface-feeding ducks. Doctor Yorke (1899) says:

They mix a great deal with the coots, eagerly devouring the seeds of the teal moss, which the former by diving tear up by the roots, and the long sprays covered with seeds float upon the surface of the water.

In Florida and Louisiana they seem to associate with the larger shore birds, feeding with them in the shallow lagoons. They are always gentle and harmless towards other species. Their only enemies are the predatory birds and animals, among which the human hunter is most destructive.

Fall.—As soon as the young are able to fly, or even before that, they begin gathering into flocks preparing for the fall migration, which begins with the first early frosts in August and is mainly accomplished during September, for these delicate birds are very sensitive to the approach of autumn and are the earliest ducks to migrate. Doctor Yorke (1899) has described this movement very well; he writes:

> About the early part of August the local ducks of each State begin to work north-ward; during September they flock together and form the first flight, passing over the same grounds. The collecting or flocking together of the local birds, which form the first fall issue, presents an interesting sight. For nearly two days the ducks will be noticed as getting very uneasy, whipping about without the regularity which had hitherto been customary upon their feeding, playing, and roosting grounds. On the day of their departure, after feeding, they will flock to some large common play-ground; where, instead of quietly resting, as usual, they assume a stage of activity. About 3 in the afternoon, instead of drifting back to their feeding grounds as usual in little flocks, singles, and pairs, they form flocks and sweep up and around the open water and alight again. The flocks soon increase in size and after two or three circles around the open water, each time rising higher and higher, they proceed south in well-defined and distinct flocks, each under a leader, and soon vanish in the distance, never returning that fall. Three or four days of no shooting occurs, except upon those which were too weak and incapacitated for a long flight, before the second issue arrives, which stays a few days. A cold snap brings down the third, the weather determining the length of their stay. The second and third depart at night or late in the evening, but evince no disposition to assemble as the first. They are the second of our warm-weather birds to leave, closely following the wood ducks.

Game.—The little blue-winged teal is a favorite with the sportsmen; it comes at the beginning of the season, when he is eager to try his skill at one of the swiftest of ducks; it decoys readily, especially to live decoys; it flies in large, compact flocks, which offer tempting shots as they twist and turn or swing and wheel in unison; it is unsuspicious of its hidden foe, is easily killed with small shot and makes a fine table bird. We used to look for it about the full of the moon in September and could always count on finding plenty of birds in the shallow ponds, marshes, and grassy creeks; but, unfortunately, it has been steadily decreasing since the early eighties and is now quite scarce in Massachusetts. In the good old days, when these birds were abundant, they were an easy mark for the youthful gunner, as they huddled together in a compact flock on the water, and a large number could be killed at a single discharge of the old muzzle-loader.

Dr. L. C. Sanford (1903) writes of shooting blue-winged teal as follows:

> In late August we find them fully fledged, frequenting the marshes of the West where the wild rice grows. They are relentlessly hunted from time of first arrival. During the hours that are sacred to the duck marsh, the time after dawn and toward dusk, they are found. At first many are killed by pushing through the grass as they jump up in front of the skiff or on their line of flight between the ponds. At the approach of evening the first line appears over the tops of the rush grass, flying low and with a speed possessed only by a teal. Another minute and they have passed; the rush of their wings told how closely they came; but no one but an old hand could have stopped one. The next flock follow, the gunner rises in time, and they sheer off, crowding together in an attempt to turn; but a well-placed shot drops several birds, So they come on until dark, when the soft whistling overhead tells of ducks still looking for a spot to feed and spend the night in peace.

Mr. Dwight W. Huntington (1903) pays the following tribute to their speed:

After some days' shooting at the sharp-tailed grouse, I went one day to a famous duck pass in North Dakota, when the teal were flying from the Devils Lake to a smaller one to breakfast. As soon as I had made my blind, they began to come singly and in pairs, sometimes three or four together or a small flock, and although they came in quick succession and the shooting was fast enough to heat the gun, I believe it was an hour or more before I killed a bird. I was almost in despair, when I fired at a passing flock, holding the gun a yard or more before the leading birds, and at the report a single teal, some distance behind the others, fell dead upon the beach. I at once began shooting long distances ahead of the passing ducks, and before long I had a large bag of birds.

A few days afterwards an officer from the garrison near by, a good shot in the upland fields and woods, went with me to my duck pass to shoot at teal. We made our blinds some two gun shots apart and soon began to shoot. The birds came rapidly as before, and my friend gave them two barrels as they passed, but was entirely out of ammunition before he killed a bird. His orderly came to my blind for shells, and with them I sent a message to shoot three times as far ahead as he had been doing, and he was soon killing birds.

Winter.—They are still abundant in some parts of the South, where they make their winter home in the great rice fields and extensive marshes, feeding on the ripened grains that fall upon the water, feasting and growing fat. Here they are safe enough as long as they paddle about and remain hidden in the innermost recesses of the rice fields and inaccessible swampy pools; but the sportsmen soon learn their haunts and habits, build their blinds near their favorite feeding grounds or fly ways and shoot them as they fly about in search of food and shelter. Constant persecution has thus materially reduced their numbers, but since such extensive sanctuaries have been established in Louisiana, it is to be hoped that they will have a safe haven of rest, in the fall at least; this may also result in larger numbers sojourning there for the winter, rather than passing on farther south, as the majority of this species now does.

DISTRIBUTION.

Breeding range.—Mainly central North America, more rarely toward the east and west coasts. East rarely or casually to Gulf of St. Lawrence (Magdalen Islands) and New Brunswick (St. John County). South casually to southeastern Maine (Washington County), southern Rhode Island (Sakonnet), and southern West Virginia (Brooke County); more recently to northern Ohio (Ottawa and Sandusky Counties), southwestern Indiana (Gibson County), southern Illinois (Union County), central Missouri (Missouri River valley), central Kansas (Emporia and Wichita), northern New Mexico (Lake Burford), central Utah (Fairfield), and northern Nevada (Truckee valley and Washoe Lake). West only to the Sierra Nevada and Cascade Mountains. North to central British Columbia (Lac la Hache and Cariboo), southern Mackenzie (Great Slave Lake), northern Saskatchewan (58°N), central Manitoba (Lake Winnipegosis), and probably sparingly in the interior of Ontario and Quebec. Has bred in Louisiana (Marsh Island), Oklahoma (Fort Reno), and Texas (San Antonio). Birds which breed south of United States are probably subspecifically distinct.

Winter range.—Southern North America and northern South America. East to the Atlantic coast of the United States from Maryland southward, the Bahamas, the Greater and Lesser Antilles and the coasts of Venezuela, French Guiana, and Brazil. South to central Chile (Ovalle). West to the Pacific coasts of Chile, Peru, Ecuador, Colombia, Central America, Mexico, and the United States. North irregularly to southern California (Santa Barbara and Los Angeles Counties), southern Illinois and Indiana, and eastern Maryland; but not common in winter north of Mexico, Texas, Louisiana, and South Carolina.

Spring migration.—Early dates of arrival: North Carolina, Raleigh, March 23; Pennsylvania, Erie, March 27; Massachusetts, Templeton, April 1; Prince Edward Island, April 20; Iowa, central, March 18; Minnesota, Heron Lake, April 7; North Dakota, central, April 12; Manitoba, Aweme, April 27; Alberta, Edmonton, May 1. Late dates of departure: Panama, February 7; Texas, San Antonio, May 14; Louisiana, New Orleans, May 21; California, Santa Barbara, May 7; Florida, Gainesville, April 29; North Carolina, Raleigh, May 6; Maryland, Baltimore, May 7.

Fall migration.—Early dates of arrival: Nova Scotia, Sable Island, August 19; Pennsylvania, Philadelphia, August 24; Virginia, Alexandria, August 18; Florida, Wakulla County, September 2; Alabama, Alabama River, September 20; California, Santa Barbara, August 25; Panama, October 14. Average dates of arrival: Virginia, Alexandria, August 31; Kansas, central, September 12; Mississippi, southern, September 16. Late date of departure: Nova Scotia, Sable Island, November 1; Prince Edward Island, October 8; Maine, Lewiston, November 7; New Jersey, Cape May, December 5; North Carolina, Raleigh, December 7; Ontario, Ottawa, October 27; Manitoba, Aweme, October 30; Illinois, Chicago, October 22; Iowa, southern, November 4; Missouri, central, November 13.

Casual records.—Occasional in Bermuda (October 22, 1854, April 30, 1875, etc.). Accidental in the British Isles (Dumfriesshire, 1858, Cheshire, about 1860, Anglesey, 1919, and County Cork, September, 1910) and in Denmark.

Egg dates.—Colorado and Utah: Twenty records, May 10 to July 21; ten records, May 31 to June 24. Manitoba and Saskatchewan: Nineteen records, June 4 to July 26; ten records, June 17 to July 4. Minnesota and North Dakota: Thirty-three records, May 8 to July 23; seventeen records, May 31 to June 13.

QUERQUEDULA CYANOPTERA (Vieillot).

CINNAMON TEAL.

HABITS.

The "western champion," as Dawson (1909) has aptly called this species, holds a unique position among American ducks, for it is the only member of the family that is confined to the western part of the continent with its center of abundance west of the Rocky Mountains and the only member of the family which has a regular breeding range in South America separated from that in North America by a wide gap of about 2,000 miles. The history of its discovery is also interesting. Coues (1874) says:

It has not often occurred that an abundant bird of North America has been first made generally known from the extreme point of South America, and for a long time recognized only as an inhabitant of that continent. Yet this species furnishes such a case, having been early named by King *Anas rafflesi*, from a specimen taken in the Straights of Magellan. It is, moreover, a singular fact, that it was first discovered in the United States in a locality where it is of very unusual and probably only accidental occurrence.

Subsequent to its discovery in Louisiana in 1849, it was afterwards rediscovered, as a North American bird, and found to be one of the most abundant species west of the Rocky Mountains, by the various survey expeditions to the Pacific coast during the next 20 years.

Spring.—The spring migration of the cinnamon teal is not a long flight, for its winter and summer ranges overlap and it is absent in winter from only the northern portion of its breeding range. The northward movement begins in March and continues through April. Dr. J. C. Merrill (1888) noted that, at Klamath, Oregon, "early in May several flocks of this beautiful teal arrived, and before the end of the month it was common in the marsh, mostly paired and not at all shy."

Courtship.—Mr. W. Leon Dawson has sent me the following notes on the courtship of this species:

Upon a little pond entirely surrounded by reeds I watched six or eight cinnamon teals disporting themselves and indulging in courting antics. A male would follow about very closely after his intended, and bob his head by alternately extending and withdrawing his neck in a lively fashion. Now and then the female would make some slight acknowledgment in the same kind. In at least one instance I think I appeared in the decisive moment, for from pretended indifferences a duck responded to long bobs of inquiry with emphatic bobs of approval given face to face, and immediately thereafter joined her favored suitor in chasing away discredited rivals. The males were repeatedly charging upon each other with open beaks, but it is hard to think that they could or would do each other bodily harm.

The teals, by the way, of both kinds, associate closely, so that the females of the two species are sometimes confused by the observer, and the males exhibit some jealousy toward each other, as though really fearing confusion of brides. A favorite play on the part of these teals is leap-frog. A bird will vault into the air and pass over another's head and down again with a great splash, and the other as likely as not will repeat the same trick, especially two males of two pairs playing together.

Dr. Alexander Wetmore (1920) says:

These single males persisted in paying attention to females already mated, much to the disgust of the paired drakes, who drove them away, bowing at them and chattering angrily. On one occasion six were seen making demonstration toward one female who paid no attention to them, but followed her mate. He swam first at one and then another after each chase returning to his mate and bowing rapidly, while occasionally she bowed to him in return. After a few minutes another mated pair of teal flew by and four of the males flew off in pursuit of them, leaving the first males only two to combat.

Nesting.—Mr. Dawson has also sent me more or less data on some two dozen nests of this species found in Washington and about a dozen found in California, from which I have made a few selections to illustrate the variations in nesting habits. A nest containing nine eggs, found at Stratford, Washington, on June 8, 1906, was located while dragging a rope in a pasture. The nest was a deep depression in the ground in a "loose clump of rye grass, lined sparsely with bits of grass and copiously with down. The down arches up at the hinder end and makes a little rear wall above the ground. Depth 5 inches; width 5 inside." On the same day he flushed a bird from a nest of 11 eggs in a "thick clump of yellow dock and mint. The rope gave a vicious tug at the clump else she never would have flown." On his return later to photograph the nest, he peered down into the vegetation and surprised the teal at home; she struggled wildly to escape and left the usual deluge of fresh excrement on the eggs, as evidence of her fright. The nest was "a shallow depression scantily lined with broken grass and trash, and heavily with dark down"; it measured "6 inches across and 3 deep inside." All of the other Washington nests were apparently on dry ground, concealed in tall grass or rank herbage, often on high land and many of them were from 75 to 200 feet away from the nearest water. The California nests were in more varied situations. On May 13, 1911, in Nigger Slough, near Los Angeles, he flushed a bird at close quarters in heavy saw grass;" the nest was "built up above damp earth" and contained 11 fresh eggs. On May 24, 1912, at Los Banos, he found two nests "buried in the heart of cat-tails built up to a height of some 6 inches out of a foot of water"; the "nests were really woven baskets placed in the depths of the reeds, an unusual situation for cinnamon teals."

One of these nests originally held eight eggs of the teal; but two eggs of the mallard had been added and three of the teal's eggs had been thrown out into the water; this nest "was built up of dried cat-tail and sedges, 5 inches high in the center and 9 at the edges, with a free way to the water after the manner of coots. It was about 7 inches across," and was wet and bulky.

Mr. Harry H. Sheldon (1907) refers to three nests which he "found in a grain field" near Eagle Lake, in the Sierra Nevada Mountains. Mr. Fred A. Schneider (1893) describes a nest which he found in a marsh near College Park, California, as "very neatly constructed an inch or two above the water and firmly fastened to the round marsh grass, which grew about 30 inches high and almost concealed the nest from view." It "was made entirely of marsh grass and lined profusely with gray down, especially around the edges. By cutting off the grass which supported the nest it could easily have been removed without danger of its falling apart."

Mr. Robert B. Rockwell (1911) found a number of cinnamon teal breeding in the Barr Lake region of Colorado, but positively identified only four nests as belonging to this species, in which he was—

unable to detect any radical departures from the habits already attributed to the bluewings except that two of the four nests were in very wet locations, where the eggs were in constant danger of becoming damp. These two nests were practically devoid of the downy lining while the other two nests, which were built in perfectly dry locations were warmly lined with down. One of the nests was on a dry prairie fully 100 feet back from the shore of the lake amid a fairly thick growth of weeds and grass.

The down in the nest of the cinnamon teal is much like that of the blue-winged teal, but lighter than that of the green-winged teal. It is "hair brown" to "drab" in color, with large conspicuous white centers. Two types of breast feathers are found in the nests, dusky with buff edges and tips, or dusky with whitish central markings.

Eggs.—The cinnamon teal lays from 6 to 14 eggs, the usual set being from 10 to 12. In shape they are ovate, elliptical ovate, elliptical oval or almost oval. The shell is smooth and only slightly glossy. The color varies from "pale pinkish buff" or "cartridge buff" to almost pure white.

The measurements of 90 eggs in various collections average 47.5 by 34.5 millimeters; the eggs showing the four extremes measure 53 by 35, 48 by 37 and 44 by 30 millimeters.

Young.—Although the male does not wholly desert the female during the nesting season, the duties of incubation seem to be wholly performed by her. The period of incubation does not seem to have been accurately determined, but it is probably not very different from that of closely related species. Mr. John G. Tyler writes me:

I have observed that the male of this species departs from the usual rule among the ducks and very often assists the female in caring for her brood of young. It is rather unusual to find young cinnamon teal that are not accompanied by both parents and the solicitude of the male bird increases with the age of the ducklings; in fact, the male is often far more demonstrative than his mate. In one instance I observed three males and a single female accompanied by 10 downy young, the males showing unmistakable evidence of their great distress at the near presence of a man while the female swam about near her family in a most unconcerned manner.

On the authority of Mr. A. M. Shields, of Los Angeles, Mr. Fred A. Schneider (1893) has published the following interesting account of the behavior of the young:

After being hatched, the mother duck (joined by her mate) escorts the young brood to the nearest body of water and manifests the greatest solicitude for the welfare of the little fellows, giving a signal upon the slightest approach of danger, which is followed by the almost instant disappearance of the entire brood, as if by magic. If on the shore they disappear in the grass; if in the water, they dive, and that is generally the last seen of them, for the time being at least, as they swim under water for great distances until reaching the edge of the stream or pond, when they imperceptibly secrete themselves among the water moss or grass. I once watched a little fellow as he made his way under the clear water. He went straight for a little bunch of floating moss, and by gazing intently I could just distinguish the least possible little swelling of the moss; a small hump, as it were, about the size of a marble. He had come to the surface (as intended) under the patch of moss, and his head and bill were responsible for the little hump in the moss.

Possibly one thing more than anything else helps the little fellows to disappear in such marvelously quick time and before you can realize it. The old duck flutters and falls around you just out of your reach and most successfully imitates a fowl badly winged, hardly able to rise from the ground. Her actions are bound to more or less avert your attention for a moment at least, and it is just that moment that the little fellows disappear, as the mother duck undoubtedly intended. After a short time, when the little ones are all securely hidden, the mother, feeling no further anxiety, gracefully recovers from her crippled condition, flies off a few hundred yards, and there awaits your departure, when she returns to her family, who soon gather around her one by one till they are all assembled and everything goes on as though nothing had happened—until the next intruder appears, when "Presto! change!" and the same actions are repeated.

Plumages.—The downy young of the cinnamon teal is "mummy brown" above, darkest on the crown, and the tips of the down are "buffy citrine," producing a golden olivaceous appearance on the back; the forehead, the sides of the head, including a broad superciliary stripe, and the under parts vary from "mustard yellow" on the head to "amber yellow" on the breast and "naphthaline yellow" on the belly; there is a narrow stripe of dark brown on the side of the head; and the color of the back is relieved by a yellowish spot on each side of the rump, scapular region, and edge of the wing.

The first feathers appear on the scapulars and flanks; these are brownish black, edged with "cinnamon brown." When the young bird is about half grown the tail appears and the under parts become feathered; the chest and flanks appear to be lustrous "Sanford's brown" and the belly silvery whitish, both mottled with dusky, each feather being centrally dusky. The bird is fully grown before it is fully feathered, the down disappearing last on the hind neck and rump; and the wings are the last to appear. A young bird nearly two-thirds grown is only partially feathered on the head; the back is wholly covered with glossy down, varying from "bister" to "sepia" and darkest on the rump; and the wing quills have not yet burst their sheaths.

In the full juvenal plumage, which in California is complete in July, the young male closely resembles the female, except that the wings are more like those of the adult male; the wings are duller colored and less complete than those of the adult male; the tertials and the scapulars are dusky, edged with "cinnamon brown," the former with a greenish sheen. During the winter and first spring the young male makes steady progress toward maturity; the "mahogany red" plumage comes in on the head, neck, breast, and flanks; the adult barred plumage appears on the upper back; and some of the gaily colored scapulars, blue on the outer web and having a buffy median stripe, are acquired. The young bird then in its first spring closely resembles the adult male, except that the belly still remains more or less dull brown, the colors are everywhere less brilliant and the wings and scapulars are less perfect.

Both old and young males then molt into an eclipse plumage. Beginning in June the head and neck become mottled with new buffy feathers, centrally dusky, which gradually replace the red; the red of the chest and flanks is gradually replaced by handsome feathers, centrally dusky but broadly edged and barred with rich shades of buff and brown in a variety of patterns; the faded brown plumage of the breast and belly are then invaded and gradually replaced by a new growth of buff, whitish-tipped feathers, each with two large spots or central areas of dusky; when absolutely fresh the long white tips of these new feathers give the under parts a silvery white appearance, but the tips soon wear off, leaving these parts as in the female. While this eclipse plumage is at its height, in August, the wings are molted, the secondaries first, with the greater and lesser coverts, and then the primaries; there is much individual variation in the time at which the showy tertials and scapulars are molted; the large, blue-tipped tertials are sometimes renewed before the eclipse plumage is complete and sometimes not until after it is shed; the long, pointed, white-striped scapulars are usually the last to be acquired. The tail is molted in August with the wings and the back plumage is renewed by a double molt simultaneously with that of the under parts; the eclipse feathers of the back are dusky, narrowly edged with buff. In September a new growth of "mahogany red" or "burnt sienna" feathers begins to replace the eclipse plumage on the breast and the renewal of the fully adult plumage spreads over the rest of the body, neck, and head, until, sometime in October or November, the full plumage is complete.

Food.—Mr. Tyler writes me that:

This duck seems to prefer, at all times, the shallow ponds and overflowed areas rather than deep canals and sloughs. The feeding operations are carried on entirely above the water and for the most part along the margin of the ponds or even out on the banks. I have never known them to dive in search of food and in fact believe that the female seldom, if ever, dives for any purpose whatever. The males, however, occasionally, but not often, plunge below the surface of the water during the mating season; this feat usually being accomplished in the presence of a rival.

Mr. Douglas C. Mabbott (1920) says:

Like the greenwing and the bluewing, the cinnamon teal lives mainly upon vegetable food, this comprising about four-fifths (79.86 per cent) of the total contents of the stomachs examined. And, like the other teals, its two principal and most constant items of food are the seeds and other parts of sedges (Cyperaceae) and pondweeds (Naiadaceae). These two families of plants furnished 34.27 and 27.12 per cent, respectively, of the bird's entire diet. The grasses (Gramineae) amounted to 7.75 per cent; smartweeds (Polygonaceae), to 3.22; mallows (Malvaceae), 1.87; goosefoot family (Chenopodiaceae), 0.75; water milfoils (Haloragidaceae), 0.37; and miscellaneous, 4.51.

The 41 cinnamon teals examined had made of animal matter 20.14 per cent of their food. This consisted of insects, 10.19 per cent; mollusks, 8.69 per cent; and a few small miscellaneous items, 1.26 per cent.

Behavior.—Mr. Tyler writes me:

Cinnamon teal are seldom found associated in large flocks but are most often encountered in pairs before the breeding season and in small family groups during the fall. So far as my observations go, the male is quite silent at all times and the only note that I have ever heard the female give is a very matter-of-fact "quack" which serves as an alarm note and is heard just as the bird takes wing.

Doctor Wetmore (1920) says:

The only note that I have ever heard from the male cinnamon teal is a low rattling, chattering note that can be heard only for a short distance.

I have had only limited opportunities of observing this beautiful species in life, but, judging from what I have seen and from what I have read about it, I should say that it differs very little in behavior from the blue-winged teal, to which it is closely related. In the shallow tule-bordered lakes and marshes of the far West, where this handsome little duck makes its summer home, it finds abundant shelter in the thick growth of tules and other luxuriant vegetation, in which to escape from its many enemies, prowling beasts and birds of prey. It is a prolific and persistent breeder and seems to maintain its abundance in spite of the frequent raids upon its eggs and young by predatory animals. Mr. Dawson's notes contain many references to raided nests, of which the following is a fair sample:

As I was returning at 2 p. m. from examination of a gadwall's nest I came upon two broken eggshells of a cinnamon teal. A little search revealed the nest about 6 feet from the nearest egg, and a glance showed the tragedy which had been enacted last night. The grass tussock gaped open and the dark down was scattered. A befouled and broken egg bore sad testimony to the mortal fright of the mother, although none of the remaining six were broken. A runt egg lay a foot or so from the nest, and I think the mother bird must have dropped it there long before the fatal night. A bit of blood on the down showed that it was the bird rather than the eggs the miscreant was after, and I found her lying dead upon her back only 6 feet away. There was a sharp deep wound over the heart—no other mark of violence—and dissection showed that although the heart itself had not been pierced, the neighboring blood vessels had and the blood was practically withdrawn.

This species, like many others, has always been able to cope successfully with its natural enemies, but against its chief enemy, man, it is powerless. The encroachments of civilization and agriculture have driven it from many of its former haunts by draining, cultivating, or destroying its breeding grounds, its shelters, and its feeding places. Many nests are destroyed and some birds are killed by mowing the fields in which it breeds. In the San Joaquin Valley, in 1914, I was disappointed to find that during dry season the land company, which controls vast areas, had drawn off the water for irrigation purposes and left its wonderful sloughs dry and almost duckless. But the worst enemy of all ducks is the unrestrained market hunter, of which Mr. Vernon Bailey (1902) says:

The young are protected in the tule cover until old enough to fly, but they have many enemies. The prowling coyote dines with equal relish on a nest full of eggs or an unwary duck, and there are hawks by day and owls by night. The teals could hold their own against these old time enemies, however, but a new danger has come to them in the form of the unrestrained market hunter. He goes to the breeding ground just before the young can fly and while the old ducks are molting and equally helpless, and day after day loads his wagon with them for the train. This wholesale slaughter has gone on until some of the breeding grounds have been woefully thinned not only of teal, but of other ducks. Without speedy and strenuous efforts to procure and enforce protective laws, many species of ducks that breed principally within our limits will soon be exterminated.

Fall.—As the cinnamon teal winters as far north as southern California and central New Mexico, the fall migration is short and merely means withdrawal from the northern part of its breeding range, during September and the first half of October. During the short southward flight, it flocks in large numbers into all suitable sloughs and lakes, where it is eagerly sought by the sportsmen and is fully as popular as its eastern relative, the bluewing, which it closely resembles in all its habits. I am tempted to quote in full the attractive and vivid picture which Doctor Coues (1874) has drawn of this bird in its fall and winter haunts. He writes:

I have in mind a picture of the headwaters of the Rio Verde, in November, just before winter had fairly set in, although frosts had already touched the foliage and dressed every tree and bush in gorgeous colors. The atmosphere showed a faint yellow haze, and was heavy with odors—souvenirs of departing flowers. The sap of the trees coursed sluggishly, no longer lending elastic vigor to the limbs, that now cracked and broke when forced apart; the leaves loosened their hold, for want of the same mysterious tie, and fell in showers where the quail rustled over their withering forms. Woodpeckers rattled with exultation against the resounding bark, and seemed to know of the greater store for them now in the nerveless, drowsy trees, that resisted the chisel less stoutly than when they were full of juicy life. Ground squirrels worked hard, gathering the last seeds and nuts to increase their winter's store, and cold-blooded reptiles dragged their stiffening joints to bask in sunny spots, and stimulate the slow current of circulation, before they should withdraw and sink into torpor. Wild fowl came flocking from their northern breeding places, among them thousands of teal, hurtling overhead and splashing in the waters they were to enliven and adorn all winter.

The upper parts of both forks of the Verde are filled with beavers, that have dammed the stream at short intervals, and transformed them, in some places, into a succession of pools, where the teal swim in still water. Other wild fowl join them, such as mallards, pintails, and greenwings, disporting together. The approach to the open waters is difficult in most places, from the rank growths, first of shrubbery, and next of reeds, that fringe the open banks; in other places, where the stream narrows in precipitous gorges, from the almost inaccessible rocks. But these difficulties overcome, it is a pleasant sight to see the birds before us—perhaps within a few paces, if we have very carefully crawled through the rushes to the verge—fancying themselves perfectly secure. Some may be quietly paddling in and out of the sedge on the other side, daintily picking up the floating seeds that were shaken down when the wind rustled through, stretching up to gather those still hanging, or to pick off little creatures from the seared stalks. Perhaps a flock is floating idly in midstream, some asleep, with the head resting close on the back and the bill buried in the plumage. Some others swim vigorously along, with breasts deeply immersed, tasting the water as they go, straining it through their bills, to net minute insects, and gabbling to each other their sense of perfect enjoyment. But let them appear never so careless, they are quick to catch the sound of coming danger and take alarm; they are alert in an instant; the next incautious movement, or snapping of a twig, startles them; a chorus of quacks, a splashing of feet, a whistling of wings, and the whole company is off. He is a good sportsman who stops them then, for the stream twists about, the reeds confuse, and the birds are out of sight almost as soon as seen.

DISTRIBUTION.

Breeding range.—Western North America and southern South America. In North America east to western Montana (Missoula County), eastern Wyoming (Lake Como), southwestern Kansas (Meade County), and south central Texas (Bexar County). South to southwestern Texas (Marathon), northern Mexico (Chihuahua), and northern Lower California (San Rafael Valley). West to practically all the central valleys of California, central Oregon (Paulina Marsh), and northwestern Washington (Tacoma). North to southern British Columbia (Revelstoke, Okanogan and Chilliwack). In South America, from central Argentina (Buenos Aires) south to the Falkland Islands, and from the Straits of Magellan north in the Andes to central Peru (Santa Luzia).

Winter range.—Southwestern North America and central South America. In North America east to southern Texas (Brownsville). South to south central Mexico (Jalisco and Puebla) and perhaps farther; has occurred in Costa Rica. North to central California (Stockton), southern Arizona (Tucson), central New Mexico, and probably southwestern Texas. In South America south to central Patagonia (Senger River) and southern Chile (Chiloe Island). North to southern Brazil (Rio Grande de Sul), southern Paraguay, Bolivia (Lake Titicaca), Peru (Corillos), and rarely to Ecuador (Quito) and

Colombia (Bogota and Santa Marta). These latter records may have been stragglers from North America.

Spring migration.—Early dates of arrival: Nevada, Ash Meadows, March 18; Idaho, Grangeville, April 11; British Columbia, Chilliwack, April 22; Colorado, Beloit, March 23, Loveland, April 13, and Lay, April 20; Missouri, Lake City, April 15; Nebraska, Omaha, April 10; Wyoming, Lake Como, May 5. Late date of departure: Lower California, Colnett, April 8.

Fall migration.—Withdrawal from the northern portions of the breeding range begins in September and is completed by the middle of October. A late northern record is, North Dakota, Mandan, October 10.

Casual records.—Has wandered on migrations as far east as Alberta (Edmonton, May 12, 1917), Manitoba (Oak Lake), Wisconsin (Lake Koshkonong, October 18, 1879, and October 9, 1891), Ohio (Licking County Reservoir, April 4, 1895), New York (Seneca Lake, about April 15, 1886), South Carolina (a somewhat doubtful record), Florida (Lake Iamonia and Key West), and Louisiana (Lake Pontchartrain).

Egg dates.—California: Thirty-seven records, April 18 to July 14; nineteen records, May 14 to June 17. Colorado and Utah: Forty-two records, May 3 to July 8; twenty-one records, May 15 to June 3. Oregon and Washington: Thirteen records, May 8 to June 13; seven records, May 26 to June 2.

CASARCA FERRUGINEA (Pallas).

RUDDY SHELDRAKE.

HABITS.

The fact that this Old World species has been taken several times as a straggler in Greenland constitutes its slim claim to be included in the list of North American birds. Its center of abundance seems to be in eastern Europe and Asia.

Nesting.—Yarrell (1871) says of its breeding habits:

The ruddy sheld duck makes its nest in a hole; sometimes in the middle of a cornfield or in a marmot's burrow on the plains; at others, in clefts of precipitous rocks, as in Algeria and in Palestine, where Canon Tristram, found nests amongst those of griffon vultures, etc. In southern Russia hollow trees are said to be selected, the male bird keeping watch on a branch while the female is sitting; felled hollow logs and deserted nests of birds of prey are also utilized; and, according to Colonel Prjevalsky, the female sometimes lays her eggs in the fireplaces of villages abandoned by the Mongols, becoming almost black with soot while sitting.

Eggs.—The ruddy sheldrake is said to lay from 8 to 16 eggs, but probably the smaller numbers are commoner. The color is described as white, creamy white or tinged with yellowish. A set of eight eggs in my collection is nearly pure white in color; they vary in shape between oval and elliptical oval; and the shell is smooth, with very little luster. The measurements of 71 eggs, given in Witherby's Handbook (1920) average 67 by 47 millimeters; the eggs showing the four extremes measure 72 by 49, 68.8 by 49.5, 61.5 by 45.6 and 65 by 45 millimeters.

Young.—The period of incubation is said to be from 29 to 30 days. Yarrell (1871) says:

The male does not share the task of incubation, but afterwards he is very assiduous in his attentions to the young. The female is said to carry the nestlings to the water.

Plumages.—The same writer says on this subject:

A nestling from the Volga, in the collection of Mr. E. Bidwell, is dull white on the forehead, cheeks, and entire under parts; the crown of the head to the eye, nape, and back, brown, with broad streaks of white on the inner side of each pinion and on each side of the center of the rump. The young of the year are like the female, but rather duller in color; the inner secondaries and scapulars are brown, marked with rufous; and the wing coverts are grayish white.

Food.—Morris (1903) says of the food of this species:

They feed early in the morning, and again toward nightfall, in corn and stubble fields, resorting thither from the marshes, which they otherwise inhabit. Their food, water plants, water insects and their larvæ, worms, and the roe and young fry of fish.

Behavior.—Referring to its habits he writes:

These birds assemble in flocks, except when paired in the summer. They seem not to associate with other species. They are difficult to be tamed, but have been kept for ornament, and have even been known to breed in confinement, on being provided with burrows in the earth for the purpose. The male and female seem much attached to each other. They are very shy and restless birds.

Yarrell (1871) says:

The call note, when uttered on the wing, is described by Pallas as resembling a clarionetlike *a-oung*, whence the name of *Aangir* given to the bird by the Mongols, who hold it sacred; and *Ahngoot*, by the natives of the vicinity of Lake Van, in Armenia. According to a Hindoo legend, as given by Jerdon, the birds represent two lovers talking to each other across a stream at night—"Chakwa, shall I come? No, Chakwi. Chakwi, shall I come? No, Chakwa." In confinement the note is a sort of *kape* or *ka*, several times repeated. In its manner of walking this species resembles a goose, and it feeds in a similiar manner, grazing in the fields of young corn and picking up seeds of grass, grain, etc. In summer the birds go in pairs, but at other times they are gregarious, and Jerdon says that on the Chilka Lake he has seen thousands in one flock in April.

DISTRIBUTION.

Breeding range.—Mainly in southeastern Europe and central Asia East to Manchuria and China. South to the plateau of Tibet, Persia, and rarely to Algeria and northern Morocco. West rarely to southern Spain; more regularly to the Adriatic Sea. North to Roumania, Bulgaria, Macedonia, southern Russia and Siberia, Lake Baikal, and Mongolia.

Winter range.—Resident over much of its breeding range. East in winter to Japan. South to Formosa, Ceylon, India, southern Arabia, Egypt, Abyssinia, Sahara, Algeria and Morocco.

Casual records.—Wanders to Scandinavia, Great Britain, Iceland, and Greenland.

Egg dates.—Southern Russia: Eight records, May 7 to June 1.

TADORNA TADORNA (Linnaeus.)

SHELD DUCK.

HABITS.

Here we have the latest addition to the American list of ducks, the common sheld duck of Europe, which has recently been taken on the coast of Massachusetts.   Mr. Albert P. Morse (1921) has recorded the important event, as follows:

An example of the common sheld duck, a female, was killed October 5, 1921, by Capt. Howard H. Tobey, of Gloucester, in Ipswich Bay off Annisquam, not far from the mouth of the Essex River.   Through the kind efforts of Mr. Carl E. Grant, game warden at Gloucester, the specimen was secured for the Peabody Museum of Salem, and identified by State Ornithologist Forbush, who has reported its occurrence to the Auk.   It has been mounted by J. W. Goodridge, of South Hamilton, and now adds interest to the Essex County collection of the Peabody Museum.   The bird was described as being extremely wild, and its plumage showed no signs of the wear and tear or soilure indicative of captivity, so that this specimen can properly be regarded as a wanderer from the Old World.

Nesting.—Yarrell (1871) refers to the nesting habits of this species as follows:

The sheld duck breeds, as already stated, in some kind of burrow, which often describes an imperfect circle, the nest being sometimes 10 or 12 feet from the entrance. It is composed of bents of grass and is gradually lined, during the progress of laying, with fine soft down, little inferior to that of the eider duck and collected in some places for its commercial value.   The eggs are of a smooth, shining white, and measure about 2.75 by 1.9 inches.   The nest may sometimes be discovered by the print of the owner's feet on the sand, but the wary bird will often fly straight into the entrance without alighting outside.   The old bird is sometimes taken by a snare set at the mouth of the burrow, and the eggs being hatched under domestic hens, the birds thus obtained are kept as an ornament on ponds.

On the North Frisian Islands, according to Mr. Durnford, the natives make artificial burrows in the sand hillocks, and cut a hole in the turf over the passage, covering it with a sod, so as to disclose the nest when eggs are required.   There are sometimes as many as a dozen or 15 nests in one hillock within the compass of 8 or 9 yards.   The eggs are taken up to the 18th of June, after which the birds are allowed to incubate: but the nest is never robbed of all the eggs.   Naumann, who had already given a similar account of the way in which these birds are farmed in the island of Sylt, states that if no eggs are taken the same bird never lays more than 16; but if the first 6 eggs are left, and all those subsequently laid are taken, she will continue laying up to 30.   Some German authorities state that nests have been found in the "earths" of the fox and the badger.

Eggs.—Macgillivray (1852) describes the eggs as follows:

The eggs, from 8 to 12, are of an oval form, rather pointed at one end, smooth glossy, and thin shelled, of a white color, slightly tinged with reddish, their length from $2\frac{11}{12}$ inches to $2\frac{8}{12}$ inches and their breadth an inch and ten or eleven twelfths. The male continues in the neighborhood of the nest during incubation, and is said occasionally to take the place of the female.

Witherby's Handbook (1920) gives the number of eggs as normally 8 to 15, but as many as 16, 20, 28, and even 32 have been recorded. The measurements of 100 eggs, therein recorded, average 65.7 by 47.3 millimeters; the eggs showing the four extreme measure **71** by 48.8, 69 by **50**, **60** by 44, and 62.8 by **43.3** millimeters.

Young.—The period of incubation is given by various writers as from 24 to 30 days or about 4 weeks. It is said to be performed mainly by the female, but apparently partially by the male as well. Bewick (1847) writes:

During this time the male, who is very attentive to his charge, keeps watch in the daytime on some adjoining hillock, where he can see all around him, and which he quits only, when impelled by hunger, to procure subsistence. The female also leaves the nest for the same purpose in the mornings and evenings, at which times the male takes his turn and supplies her place. As soon as the young are hatched, or are able to waddle along, they are conducted, and sometimes carried in the bill, by the parents to the full tide, upon which they launch without fear, and are not seen afterwards out of tide mark until they are well able to fly; lulled by the roarings of the flood, they find themselves at home amidst an ample store of their natural food, which consists of sand hoppers, sea worms, etc., or small shellfish, and the innumerable shoals of the little fry which have not yet ventured out into the great deep but are left on the beach or tossed to the surface of the water by the restless surge.

If this family, in their progress from the nest to the sea happen to be interrupted by any person, the young ones, it is said, seek the first shelter, and squat close down, and the parent birds fly off, then commences that truly curious scene, dictated by an instinct analogous to reason, the same as in the wild duck and the partridge; the tender mother drops, at no great distance from her helpless brood, trails herself along the ground, flaps it with her wings, and appears to struggle as if she were wounded, in order to attract attention, and tempt a pursuit after her. Should these wily schemes, in which she is also aided by her mate, succeed, they both return when the danger is over, to their terrified motionless little offspring, to renew the tender offices of cherishing and protecting them.

Food.—Mr. John Cordeaux (1898) says of its feeding habits:

As far as my own observation goes, on the Lincolnshire coast, the sheld duck appears to live exclusively on various mollusca and crustaceans; the stomach is remarkable for its very thick and strong muscular coat, capable of digesting any tough morsel. In the stomach of one I found some sand and many small shells of the genus *Buccinum*. The late Mr. Thompson opened the stomachs of 10 shot in Belfast Bay and took from one of them 9,000 specimens of *Skenea depressa* and *Montacuta purpurea*, and about 11,000 others, making a total of 20,000 shells *in the crop and stomach of a single sheld duck*. Mr. St. John says: "Its food appears to consist almost wholly of small shellfish, and more especially of cockles, which it swallows whole. It extracts these latter from the sand by paddling or stamping with both its feet; this brings the cockle quickly to the surface. I have often seen the tame birds of this species do the same in the poultry yard when impatient for or waiting for their food."

Witherby's Handbook (1920) gives the following list of food:

Chiefly mollusca (*Buccinum, Paludina, May, Skenea, Tellina, etc.*) crustacea (shrimps, prawns, and small crabs), with a small quantity of vegetable matter (algae and fragments of gramineae) and occasionally insects (*Carabus* and larvae of diptera.)

Behavior.—Macgillivray (1852) writes of the habits of the sheld duck, as follows:

It seems to continue in pairs all the year round, although frequently in winter and spring large flocks may be seen in which the families are intermingled. I have never met with it inland, or in fresh water near the coast; but have seen it feeding in wet pastures near the sea, although more frequently on wet sands, and am unable, from my own observation, to say of what its food consists. Various authors allege that it feeds on shellfish and marine plants; but this, judging from the structure of its bill and its general appearance, I felt inclined to doubt until I met with Mr. Thompson's statement. It walks with ease, in the manner of the wild geese, but with quicker steps, and flies with speed, in the manner of the mallard and other ducks, with more rapid beats of the wings than the geese. In spring and the early part of summer it has a habit of erecting itself, thrusting forward its neck, and shaking its head, as if endeavouring to swallow or get rid of something too wide for its gullet; but this appears to be merely an act of attention to the female. Being shy and vigilant, and frequenting open places, it is not easily approached unless when breeding.

Mr. Cordeaux (1898) quotes Mr. G. H. Caton Haigh as saying:

It is an extremely common bird on the coast of Merionethshire both as a winter visitor and a breeding species. In the former season it appears in flocks about the latter end of November, the numbers are very variable, but in severe weather is sometimes present in immense quantities. At such times it frequents the open sands, particularly in the estuaries, in company with widgeon and mallard. It is (excepting geese) the most wary of all the fowl, and will frequently not allow a punt to approach within 300 yards. In February another large increase takes place, when the breeding birds return to their summer haunts, and from thence to September they are one of the most numerous birds on the shore. From the middle of October to the end of November the sheld duck is entirely absent from the coast. The first clutches of young generally appear about the end of May or early in June, and heavy weather at this time produces great mortality amongst them. The old remain with the young for a very short time, and young broods are often to be seen alone, or with 40 to 50 young and one pair of old birds.

During winter the sheld duck feeds at night, but in summer it feeds at low water both during the day and night. Large numbers of nonbreeding birds spend the summer on the coast. They are very noisy birds, and the harsh quack or laugh of the female, and whistle of the male, is heard both day and night in spring, and there is much fighting amongst the males at this season. It is a poor diver, and rarely goes under water, even when wounded.

He writes further in regard to it:

The sheld duck is heavier and stands higher than the mallard, and it is much more a goose in manner than a duck, having an erect carriage and light active step, instead of waddle; their flight too, more resembles that of geese and swans. The young are so active that it is almost impossible to catch them. In winter, not unfrequently, great numbers visit the Lincolnshire coast, particularly in those seasons when a grain ship is wrecked and broken up on some of the outlying sand banks, at which time ducks congregate in large numbers from all parts to the feast. I have, at this season, known flocks of two to three hundred sheld ducks to be seen off the coast.

With us the sheld duck is in all seasons of the year inseparably connected with one of its most favorite haunts, the dreary flat coast of Lincolnshire, where the sea, at the ebb of spring tides, recedes for miles, and is scarcely visible from the dune except by a far-away glimmer along the horizon, or, if there is any *breeze*, by that long checkered line of black and white, like the squares of a chessboard, rising and falling alternately, in almost rhythmical pulsations, as the breakers on the sand banks flash into light or recoil into deep shadows.

DISTRIBUTION.

Breeding range.—Temperate portions of Europe and Asia. East to eastern Siberia. South to Mongolia, southern Siberia, Turkestan, Caspian and Black Seas, France, and Spain. West to the British Isles. North to 70° N. in Norway and 51° N. in the Ural Mountains.

Winter range.—Southern Europe and Asia. East to Japan. South to Formosa, China, Burma, northern India, Egypt, and northern Africa to the Tropic of Cancer. West to the British Isles. North to the Mediterranean basin and the Black and Caspian Seas.

Casual records.—A straggler in the Faeroes and Iceland. One record for North America (Ipswich Bay, Massachusetts, October 5, 1921).

SPATULA CLYPEATA (Linnaeus).

SHOVELLER.

HABITS.

The little shoveller is one of the best known and the most widely distributed ducks in the world; by its peculiar spatulate bill and by the striking color pattern of the drake it is easily recognized; it is universally common over nearly all of the continents of North America, Europe, and Asia, wandering south in winter to northern South America and Africa and even to Australia. It is essentially a fresh-water duck at all seasons, never resorting to the seacoasts except when forced to by stress of weather; it is a bog-loving species, fond of inland sloughs, marshes, streams, and ponds, where it can dabble in the shallows like a veritable mud lark. It is always associated in my mind with the shallow pond holes and sluggish creeks which are so characteristic of the wet, grassy meadows of the prairie region, where pairs of these handsome birds are so frequently seen jumping into the air, surprised by a passing train or wagon.

Spring.—The shoveller is not a hardy bird and is therefore not an early migrant in the spring; it comes along with the gadwall and the baldpate after the ice has entirely left the sloughs. The migration in the south is well under way before the end of March, but they do not wholly disappear from Louisiana until early in May and the first arrivals do not reach northern Alaska until about the middle of May. On the spring migration the birds are in small flocks, frequenting the ponds and rivers, usually not associating much with other species. Soon after their arrival on their breeding grounds they spread out among the sloughs, creeks, and marshes, breaking up into pairs or small parties of three or four.

Courtship.—The courtship of the shoveller does not amount to very much as a spectacular performance; Millais (1902) describes it, as follows:

The spring courtship on the part of the male shoveler is both quiet and undemonstrative, nor does his ladylove betray any particular emotion. He swims slowly up to her, uttering a low guttural croak, like the words konk, konk, and at the same time elevating his head and neck and jerking his bill upwards. The female then bows in recognition, and both proceed to swim slowly round in circles, one behind the other, with the water running through their bills.

A somewhat unusual circumstance in the matrimonial arrangements of this duck is the prevalence of polyandry where circumstances seem to call for it, and the amiability with which it is accepted by the united drakes. As a rule, where the sexes are equal in a breeding haunt the male and female pair and keep together in the usual way; but where there is a preponderance of males it is quite common to see a female with two males constantly in attendance, and these two husbands will remain with her, apparently in complete amity, until she has commenced to sit. The custom is, of course, quite common in the case of mallards, but with them there is a certain amount of jealousy on the part of the males, either of whom will drive off and, if possible, keep away altogether, his marital partner. Somewhat remarkable, too, is the fact that after two adult shovelers have paired, the additional male is generally a bird of the previous year whose plumage is only partially complete. Possibly this may be due to the misfortune of the young Lothario, who, finding that most of the young females of the previous year have gone off by themselves and will not pair, must content himself with such favor as he may find with an older and already mated bird. Certainly, on Loch Spynie, in the month of May, I have seen quite as many trios as pairs of shovelers, and in nearly every case the third bird was in immature plumage.

It also indulges in spirited courtship flights, in which two males often pursue a single female in an aerial love chase, exhibiting their wonderful powers of flight with swift dashes and rapid turnings until one of the males finds himself outclassed.

Nesting.—In North Dakota in 1901 we found the shoveller evenly distributed everywhere, one of the commonest ducks, frequenting the same localities as the blue-winged teal and equally tame. We saw them frequently flying about in pairs, up to the middle of June, from which I inferred that their sets were not complete until about that time. In that region the nesting ground of the shoveller was the broad expanse of virgin prairie, often far away from the nearest water, sometimes on high dry ground and sometimes in moist meadow land or near a slough or pond. The first nest that we found was in the center of a hollow in the prairie between two knolls, where the ground was moist but not actually wet, and where the grass grew thick and luxuriantly.   The nest was well hidden in the thick, green grass, so that we never should have found it if we had not flushed the bird within 10 feet of us.   It was merely a depression in the ground, well lined with dry grasses, and sparingly lined with gray down around the eggs; more down would probably have been added as incubation advanced. The 10 eggs which it contained were perfectly fresh when collected on June 3.

The second nest was found on June 7 while driving across the prairie in Nelson County.   We had stopped to explore an extensive tract of low "badger brush," looking for the nest of a pair of short-eared owls which were flying about, as if interested in the locality. We were apparently a long distance from any water, and while returning to our wagon over a high dry knoll, flushed the duck from her nest, which was only partially concealed in the short prairie grass. The slight hollow in the ground was lined with dead grasses and a plentiful supply of down.   It contained 11 eggs which were too far advanced in incubation to save.   Although the shoveller frequently breeds in open and exposed situations at a long distance from water, I think it prefers to nest in the rank grass around the boggy edges of a slough or pond.

In southwestern Saskatchewan in 1905 and 1906 we found shovellers everywhere abundant, breeding on the islands, on the meadows near the lakes, and on the prairies.   On that wonderful duck island in Crane Lake, on June 17, 1905, we found 7 nests of the shoveller—2 with 8 eggs, 1 with 9, 2 with 10, and 2 with 11; the nests were located in the long grass and under rosebushes, scattered indiscriminately among the nests of mallards, gadwalls, baldpates, green-winged and blue-winged teals, pintails, and lesser scaup ducks; this island has been more fully described under the gadwall.   The nests were very much like those of the other ducks, hollows scooped out in the ground, sparingly lined with dry grass and weeds and surrounded by a rim of down; as incubation advances the supply of down increases until there is enough to cover the eggs when the duck leaves the nest.

I believe that the above-described nests illustrate the normal nesting habits of the shoveller, but Mr. Edward Arnold (1894) records a nest which "was built in a heavy patch of scrub poplars," in Manitoba.   Mr. W. Otto Emerson (1901) thus describes a nest which he found in California in an exceedingly exposed situation in a salt marsh:

After working over the marsh for several hours I started back and when half way across I again saw a pair of ducks headed inland, but thought nothing of it until a single duck started up 10 feet from me and 300 yards from the mainland. On going to the spot there lay a nest in open sight on the bare ground among the saltweed. It was not over 4 inches off the ground and contained 14 eggs. The nest was composed of dry stems of the saltweed, lined with down and a few feathers from the parent bird, and measured 14 inches across the top with a depth of 5 inches.

The down in the shoveller's nest is larger than that of the teals, but smaller and darker than that of the pintail; it varies in color from dark "drab" to light "hair brown," with large grayish-white centers. The breast feathers in the nest are quite distinctive; they have large rounded gray centers, with broad buff and white tips and margins.

Eggs.—The shoveller is said to lay from 6 to 14 eggs, but the set usually consists of from 10 to 12 eggs. Only one brood is normally raised. In color and texture the eggs are strikingly like those of the mallard and pintail; I have never been able to detect any constant difference between the three in these respects, the individual variations in all three overlapping; but the shoveller's eggs are, of course, smaller and usually more elongated. In shape they are nearly elliptical ovate or elliptical oval. The color varies from a very pale olive buff to a very pale greenish gray. The shell is thin and smooth, with very little luster.

The measurements of 177 eggs in various collections average 52.2 by 37 millimeters; the eggs showing the four extremes measure 58 by 38.5, 54.5 by 39, 48 by 37, and 50.5 by 34.5 millimeters.

Young.—Morris (1903) gives the period of incubation as "three weeks"; others give it as from 21 to 23 days. Incubation is performed entirely by the female, though the male does not wholly desert her during the first part, at least, of the process and is often quite solicitous if the nest is disturbed. But before the broods are hatched the males congregate in small flocks in the sloughs and ponds, leaving the care of the young to their mates. The young are led to the nearest water by the female, carefully guarded and taught to feed on insects and soft animal and vegetable food. The young are expert divers; we had considerable difficulty in catching what specimens of grown young we needed. By the time that the young are fully fledged, the molting season of the adults is over, and the old and young birds are joined together in flocks.

Plumages.—Even when first hatched the young shoveller's bill is decidedly longer and more spatulate than that of the young mallard, and it grows amazingly fast, so that when two weeks old there is no difficulty in identifying the species. The color of the downy young above varies from "olive brown," or "sepia," to "buffy brown," darker on the crown, which is "clove brown" or "olive brown"; the color of the back extends far down onto the sides of the chest and on the flanks. The under parts vary from "maize yellow" or "cream buff" to "cartridge buff" or "ivory yellow"; this color deepens to "chamois" on the cheeks. There is a stripe of "olive brown" through the eye, including the loral and postocular region, also an auricular spot of the same. There is a light buffy spot on each side of the back, behind the wings, and one on each side of the rump. The buffy or chamois colored stripes above the eyes are well marked and often confluent on the forehead. All of these colors fade out to paler and grayer shades as the bird grows older.

The flank feathers are the first to appear, then the mottled feathers of the breast and belly, together with the scapular and head plumage, then the tail and lastly the wings. Birds in my collection, as large as blue-winged teal, collected July 17 and 18 in Manitoba, are still downy on the back of the neck and rump, with the wing quills just bursting the sheaths; they evidently would not be able to fly until fully grown in August. In this first plumage the sexes are alike, but the male is slightly larger.

Millais (1902) gives the following full account of the progress toward maturity:

By the middle of September we see the molt beginning, and from this date till the following February there is no surface-feeding duck whose plumage change progresses so slowly. In its ordinary course there is little difference between September and January, but toward the end of the latter month a big flush of new feathers takes place, either on the whole of the breast down to the vent, or amongst the feathers of the lower neck, where a few pure white feathers appear. In very advanced birds the molt extends over the whole of the lower neck and breast. By the middle of March, numbers of the dark-green feathers begin to show themselves on the cheeks, and in April there is an accession of white feathers on the scapulars. In May and June the whole plumage continues to trend toward maturity, and many new feathers which have come in the plumage on the scapulars and sides of the neck are changing color all the time, from a half compromise with the old first plumage to that of the adult bird. Nevertheless, the whole bird can not be said to be anything like complete, and still undergoes feather recoloration and molt until the full and complete molt of the eclipse takes place at the beginning of July.

The young drake then molts the wings for the first time in August, and, passing through the usual autumnal color change and molt, arrives at a plumage dull and incomplete, yet resembling that of the adult male. Thus we see that in gaining adult dress, this bird takes the same time as the widgeon, namely, about 17 months. His plumage, however, so far as my experience goes, is never absolutely perfect until the third season. In that year his full breeding dress seems to attain perfection earlier than at any previous season. Amongst those that I have kept in confinement from immaturity the bill seemed blacker, and all the colors of the plumage more brilliant, when they reached this age. Male shovelers of 21 months old generally have a number of arrowhead-brown bars on the sides of the white breast shield and upper scapulars. The presence of these broad-arrow marks on the white chest must, however, not be taken as indisputable evidence of immaturity, for many perfectly adult males retain year after year one or two of these markings, whilst others have a wholly white shield. It will nevertheless be found that these markings, together with a sandy-edged breast, are constant signs of difference between the young and the old males; for in the first spring the immatures of all the surface feeders, except the mallard, whose appearance is largely due to condition and feeding, always lack the color, size, and finish of the perfectly adult drake.

Similar changes take place in the young female, a complete new dress being acquired, except on the wings, by January, in which young birds can be distinguished from old birds by their dark shoulders and wings; the fully adult dress is not acquired until the following October or at the age of 17 months. Millais (1902) also says that the immature females do not breed during their first spring.

The midsummer eclipse plumage of the male is quite complete, and closely resembles the female plumage, except for the wings, which, of course, are molted only once in August, and for the breast and belly, which remains largely brown. The molt into the eclipse begins about the 1st of July and the change is very rapid. The molt out of the eclipse in the fall is more protracted; it sometimes does not begin until the middle of October and is not complete until December or later. Adult males can always be recognized by the wings.

Food.—In feeding the shoveller uses its highly specialized bill to advantage. All the surface-feeding ducks have the edges of the upper and lower mandibles more or less well supplied with rows of comblike teeth or lamellae through which the water and mud is sifted to obtain food; in some species these are somewhat rudimentary, but in the shoveller they reach their highest development because the shoveller is more essentially a surface feeder than any other duck, dabbling along the surface to sift out what small particles of food it can find, shovelling in the soft muddy shallows and straining out its food much after the manner of a right whale. The tongue, the roof of the mouth, and the soft edges of the broad bill are all well supplied with sensitive nerves of touch and taste, which helps the bird to retain what it wants to eat and to reject worthless material. The shoveller seldom tips up to feed by semi-immersion, but paddles quickly along, skimming the surface, with its head half submerged so that whatever is found is taken into the mouth, tasted by the sensitive tongue, and sifted out through the pectinated bristles of the bill if not wanted.

Millais (1902) relates the following incident to illustrate the activity of the shoveller in feeding:

To the observer who sees the shoveler casually by day he appears to be somewhat of a lethargic nature; but, when he cares to do so, he can move faster on the water than any of the fresh-water ducks. I have watched with pleasure the wonderful sight, calculation, and quickness of a male shoveler that I once kept in confinement on a small marshy pond at Fort George. About the last week in April a certain water insect, whose name I do not know, would "rise" from the mud below to the surface of the pool only to be captured by the shoveler, who, rushing at full speed along the water, snapped up the beetle the moment it came to the surface. How it could see the insect in the act of rising I could never make out, for it was invisible to me standing on the bank above, and I could only just catch a glimpse of it as the shoveler reached his prey and dexterously caught the beetle as it darted away again. After each capture the duck retired to the side of the pool again and there awaited the next rise—commonly about 25 feet away. While thus occupied he seemed to be in a high state of tension; the feathers are closely drawn up and he kept his neck working backwards and forwards, in preparation, as it were, for the next spring, exactly like a cat "getting up steam" for the final rush on a victim.   Sometimes he seemed to get into a frantic state of excitement, darting here and there as if he saw beetles rising in every direction.   I noticed also that while devouring his prey the pupils of his eyes were unusually contracted, and the golden circlets seemed to shine more brilliantly than usual.

The food of the shoveller consists of grasses, the buds and young shoots of rushes, and other water plants, small fishes, small frogs, tadpoles, shrimps, leeches, aquatic worms, crustaceans, small mollusks, particularly snails, water insects, and other insects, as well as their larvae and pupae.

Doctor Yorke (1899) adds the following to the list: "Teal moss (*Limnobium*), various water lilies, flags, duck-weeds, and pondweeds."

The shoveller is an exceedingly active flyer; it rises quickly from the water, mounting straight up into the air, and darting off with a swift though somewhat erratic flight.   Its flight is somewhat like that of the teals and, like them, it frequently makes sudden downward plunges.   It is not shy and shows a tendency to return to the spot where it was flushed.   On migrations it flies in small flocks by itself, though in the fall it is often associated with the gadwall, baldpate, or lesser scaup duck.   During the mating season it is usually seen flying in pairs, with the male leading, or in trios, with a female leading two males.   The shoveller is easily recognized in flight; the striking colors of the drake can not be mistaken; and the females and young can easily be identified by the long slender necks and conspicuously large bills; I have seldom been in doubt when flushing a female shoveller from her nest.

The shoveller has a small throat and a weak voice.   It is usually silent, but the female sometimes indulges in a few feeble quacks and the male makes a low guttural sound like the syllables *woh, woh, woh,* or *took, took, took;* this sound has been likened by some writers to the sound made by turning a watchman's rattle very slowly.

Mr. Robert B. Rockwell writes me:

From a good many years of observation as a duck hunter I am of the opinion that the shoveller is one of the most sociable species of wild duck.   Single shovellers are very frequently seen in flocks of other species, especially teal, and the ease with which individuals and even good-sized flocks of these birds are decoyed is in itself good evidence that they are of a sociable disposition.

Throughout our Barr work the drake shovellers during the nesting season were seen in considerable numbers but were seldom seen swimming about alone, nearly always being in company with other species of ducks; nor did they seem to prefer the company of males of their own species particularly.

Fall.—The shoveller is one of the earliest migrants in the fall; the first autumnal frosts, late in August or early in September, are enough to start it drifting along with the blue-winged teal; the migration is well under way by the middle of September, and a month later it is practically over.

Game.—Mr. T. Gilbert Pearson (1916) says:

Shovellers feed mostly at night, especially in places where they are much pursued by gunners. I have often seen dozens of flocks come from the marshes at sunrise and fly out to the open water, far from any place where a gunner might hide. There, if the weather is fair and not too windy, they will often remain until the shades of night and the pangs of hunger again call them back to the tempting marshes. They do not gather in enormous flocks like some other ducks. I have never seen over 40 in one company, and very often they pass by in twos and threes. In hunting them the fowler usually conceals himself in a bunch of tall grass or rushes, on or near the margin of an open pond, and, after anchoring near-by 20 or 30 wooden duck dummies called decoys, sits down to wait the coming of the birds. Sometimes the ducks fly by at a distance of several hundred yards. It is then that the hunter begins to lure them by means of his artificial duck call. *Quack-quack, quack-quack*, comes his invitation from the rushes. The passing birds, unless too intent on their journey to heed the cry, see what they suppose to be a company of mallards and other ducks evidently profiting by a good feeding place, and, turning, come flying in to settle among the decoys. It is just at this moment, with headway checked and dangling feet, that they present an easy mark for the concealed gunner.

Audubon (1840) says: "No sportsman who is a judge will ever pass a shoveller to shoot a canvasback." I can not quite agree with this view for the shoveller never seems to get very fat and, to my mind, its flesh is inferior to that of several others. It lives largely on animal food which does not add to its flavor. Perhaps under favorable circumstances it may become fatter and more palatable.

Winter.—Its main winter range is in the Southern States and Mexico, where it frequents shallow inland waters and rarely is it driven to the coast by severe weather.

DISTRIBUTION.

Breeding range.—Temperate regions in the Northern Hemisphere. In North America east more or less regularly to the west coast of Hudson Bay and the eastern boundary of Manitoba. Casually east to west central New York (Cayuga County). South to northwestern Indiana (Lake County) and northern Illinois formerly; more recently to western Iowa (Sac County), central western Nebraska (Garden County), Kansas (probably locally), northwestern New Mexico (Lake Burford), central Arizona (Mogollon Mountains), and southern California (Los Angeles County); rarely and locally in Texas (Bexar County and East Bernard), and perhaps in northern Mexico. West to the central valleys of California, central Oregon (Tule Lake and Malheur Lake), northwestern Washington (Lake Washington), and central British Columbia (Fraser Valley and Cariboo District). North regularly to central Alberta (Edmonton) and the valley of the Saskatchewan River; irregularly farther north to the Bering Sea coast of Alaska (Kuskokwim River to Kotzebue Sound), the Anderson River region, and Great Slave Lake. In the Eastern Hemisphere it breeds from southern Europe and central Asia northward nearly or quite to the Arctic Circle; and from Great Britain east to Kamchatka and the Commander Islands.

Winter range.—Milder portions of both hemispheres.   In America east to the Atlantic coast of southern United States, the Greater (Cuba, Jamaica, Porto Rico) and the Lesser Antilles (St. Thomas, Barbados, Trinidad, etc.).   South to northern South America (Colombia).   West to the Pacific coast of Central America, Mexico, and United States.   North to coast of southern British Columbia (Vancouver and Puget Sound region); in the interior north to central California (Fresno), Arizona, New Mexico, eastern Texas (Galveston), the lower Mississippi Valley, rarely to southern Illinois (Cairo and Mount Carmel), and the coast of Virginia (Cobb Island); has occurred in winter at Lanesboro, Minnesota, and Atlantic City, New Jersey, but is not common north of South Carolina.   Winters in Hawaiian Islands.   In the Eastern Hemisphere winters south to the Canary Islands, Senegambia, Somaliland, Arabia, India, Ceylon, Borneo, southern China, Formosa, the Philippine Islands, and Australia.

Spring migration.—Early dates of arrival: Alberta, Edmonton, May 1; Mackenzie, Fort Chipewyan, May 7, and Fort Resolution, May 18.   Average dates of arrival: Illinois, central, March 23; Iowa, central, March 23; Minnesota, Heron Lake, March 26; North Dakota, central, April 13; Manitoba, southern, April 21.   Late dates of departure: Lower California, Colnett, April 8; Rhode Island, Point Judith, April 29.

Fall migration.—Early dates of arrival: Ontario, Beamsville, September 19; Rhode Island, Point Judith, September 24; Pennsylvania, Erie, September 6; Lower California, southern, October 18; Panama, October 16.   Late dates of departure: Ontario, Rockland, November 2; New York, Branchport, November 12; Rhode Island, Point Judith, November 7

Casual records.—Accidental in Bermuda (December, 1844) and Labrador (Cartwright, September, 1901).   Rare on migrations as far east as Maine.

Egg dates.—Minnesota and North Dakota: Forty records, May 9 to July 3; twenty records, May 31 to June 17.   Manitoba and Saskatchewan: Eighteen records, June 1 to July 5; nine records, June 5 to 11.   California and Utah: Eighteen records, March 28 to July 11; nine records, May 3 to 21.

DAFILA ACUTA TZITZIHOA (Vieillot).

AMERICAN PINTAIL.

HABITS.

Spring.—Northward, ever northward, clearly indicated on the distant sky, points the long slim figure of the pintail, in the vanguard of the spring migration, wending its way toward remote and still frozen shores. Vying with the mallard to be the first of the surface-feeding ducks to push northward on the heels of retreating winter, this hardy pioneer extends its migration to the Arctic coast of the continent and occupies the widest breeding range of any North American duck, throughout most of which it is universally abundant and well known.

Prof. George E. Beyer (1906) says that, in Louisiana, "winter visitant individuals, as with similar individuals of the mallard, move northward very early, probably never later than the middle of January," whereas the spring transients in that State "are the latest of all the ducks except the teals and the shoveller." This accounts for the two distinct flights of pintails with which gunners are familiar. Dr. F. Henry Yorke (1899) recognizes three distinct flights; he says:

The spring migration above the frost line commences with the first breaking up of winter; the ducks follow the open pools of water to be found in sloughs, lakes, and rivers, and with the yellow-leg mallard are the first of the nondivers to start for their northern nesting grounds. They arrive in three distinct issues, the first leaving, in bulk, at least, before the second arrives; these stay about a week before they proceed northward. An absence of pintails, for three or four days, generally follows before the third issue puts in an appearance, which stay a week or 10 days, according to the weather, then travel northward, breeding chiefly south of the Canadian line.

Mr. Edmonde S. Currier (1902) says of its arrival in Iowa:

If the great break-up of the ice comes late in the season, as the first week in March, which often happens after a severe winter, we find the eager sprigtails (*Dafila acuta*), and the first flight of mallards coming up, and then there is a bird life worth seeing. Although the number of ducks that pass here is rapidly falling off, still thousands are left.

The first flight of pintails is, with us, the greatest, and they always appear while the ice is running. Several days before the ice gives way an occasional flock will come up and circle around over the frozen river as if taking observations, and then disappear to the south. If a rain comes before the ice goes out, and forms pools in the bottom-land corn fields, they will settle in these until the rivers open, or a cold wave strikes us.

The pintail reaches its breeding grounds in northern Alaska early in May and sometimes before the end of April, while winter conditions are still prevailing. Dr. E. W. Nelson (1887) says:

One spring a small party was found about a small spring hole in the ice on the seashore the first of May, while a foot of snow still covered the ground and the temperature ranged only a few degrees above zero. As snow and ice disappear they become more and more numerous, until they are found about the border of almost every pool on the broad flats from the mouth of the Kuskoquim River north to the coast of Kotzebue Sound.

Courtship.—The courtship display of the shy pintail is not often seen, for even on their remote northern breeding grounds the males are ever alert and are not easily approached. The performance resembles that of the teals, where several drakes may be seen crowding their attention on a single duck, each standing erect on the water proudly displaying his snowy breast, with his long neck doubled in graceful curves until his bill rested upon his swelling chest and with his long tail pointed upwards; thus he displays his charms and in soft mewing notes he woos his apparently indifferent lady love until she expresses her approval with an occasional low quack.

A more striking form of courtship, and one more often seen, is the marvelous nuptial flight, which Doctor Nelson (1887) has so well described as follows:

Once, on May 17, while sitting overlooking a series of small ponds, a pair of pintails arose and started off, the male in full chase after the female. Back and forth they passed at a marvelously swift rate of speed, with frequent quick turns and evolutions. At one moment they were almost out of view high overhead and the next saw them skimming along the ground in an involved course very difficult to follow with the eye. Ere long a second male joined in the chase, then a third, and so on until six males vied with each other in the pursuit. The original pursuer appeared to be the only one capable of keeping close to the coy female, and owing to her dextrous turns and curves he was able to draw near only at intervals. Whenever he did succeed he always passed under the female, and kept so close to her that their wings clattered together with a noise like a watchman's rattle, and audible a long distance. This chase lasted half an hour, and after five of the pursuers had dropped off one by one the pair remaining (and I think the male was the same that originated the pursuit) settled in one of the ponds.

Nesting.—Mr. F. Seymour Hersey says in his notes on this species in northern Alaska:

There is probably no place within the breeding range of this widely distributed duck where it is more abundant than on the stretch of tundra bordering the Bering Sea coast of western Alaska. Almost every little tundra pond will contain a few birds—perhaps a pair or a female and two or three males—and parties of two to five or six are constantly flying from one pond to another.

The pintail very often makes its nest farther from water than any other of the northern breeding ducks, although the greater number nest near the shores of ponds. Before the set is complete, the eggs are covered with down, intermingled with leaves, sticks, dead grass, and mosses, and the female spends the day at a considerable distance from the nest. Incubation begins only when the set is complete. Early in June, 1914, while walking over the tundra some miles back from St. Michael I noticed a few pieces of down clinging to the base of some dwarf willow bushes. It aroused my suspicions and searching among the accumulated dead leaves and moss at the roots of the bush I soon disclosed an incomplete set of pintail's eggs. They were thoroughly concealed and had it not been for the few telltale bits of down would have remained undiscovered. The female later completed this set, and on June 10 the nest held nine eggs. This nest was at least a half mile from the nearest water.

At the mouth of the Yukon on June 17, 1914, two nests were found in the center of some clumps of willows in a marsh. The bushes were growing in a few inches of water through which a heavy growth of coarse grass protruded. About the base of the willows the dead grass of previous years was matted and in this dead grass the nests were made. This was the wettest situation that I ever knew this species to select in the north.

As might be expected of an early migrant, the pintail is one of the earliest breeders; in North Dakota it begins to lay by the 1st of May or earlier and we found that many of the broods were hatched by the first week in June. The nest is placed almost anywhere on dry ground, sometimes near the edge of a slough or pond, sometimes on an island in a lake, but more often on the prairie and sometimes a half a mile or more from the nearest water; it is generally poorly concealed and is often in plain sight. Once, while crossing a tract of burned prairie, I saw a dark object fully half a mile away, which on closer inspection proved to be a pintail sitting on a nest full of half roasted eggs; this was a beautiful illustration of parental devotion and showed that the bird was not dependent on concealment. A deep hollow is scooped out in the ground, which is sparingly lined with bits of straw and stubble, and a scanty lining of down is increased in quantity as incubation advances.

My North Dakota notes describe four nests of this species. The first nest, found on May 31, 1901, was concealed in rather tall prairie grass on the highest part of a small island in one of the larger lakes. On June 15 we found another nest in an open situation among rather sparse but tall prairie grass, which was in plain sight, the eggs being beautifully concealed by a thick covering of down. Another nest was shown to us by some farmers who were plowing up an extensive tract of prairie and had flushed the bird as they passed within a few feet of the nest; they left a narrow strip containing the nest unplowed, but something destroyed the eggs a few days afterwards; this nest was fully half a mile from the nearest water. The fourth nest was on the edge of a cultivated wheat field, near the crest of a steep embankment sloping down into a large slough; the nest was a deep hollow in the bottom of a furrow, 7 inches wide by 4 deep lined with bits of straw and weed stubble, with a moderate supply of down surrounding the eggs; it was very poorly concealed by the scanty growth of weeds around it; the eight eggs, which it contained on June 10, proved to be heavily incubated.

In Saskatchewan, in 1905 and 1906, we recorded 11 nests of pintails, 8 of which were found on one small island on one day, where this species was breeding with large numbers of gadwalls, blue-winged and green-winged teals, shovellers, mallards, baldpates, and lesser scaup ducks. One pintail's nest was prettily located under a wild rosebush among the sand hills near Crane Lake, 1 mile from the nearest creek and 2 miles from the lake.

Mr. Robert B. Rockwell (1911) found two nests of this species, in the Barr Lake region of Colorado, in decidedly exposed situations, which he describes as follows:

The first nest, found May 11, 1907, was probably the most unusually located nest of the pintail on record. It was just a trifle less than 18 feet from the rails of the main line of the Burlington route, over which a dozen or more heavy trains thundered every day, and well within the railroad right of way, where section hands and pedestrians passed back and forth continually. The mother bird had found a cavity in the ground, about 8 inches in diameter and 8 inches deep, and had lined it with grass; and the two fresh eggs which it contained on this date were deposited without any downy lining whatever. The female flushed as we passed along the track about 20 feet distant, thus attracting our attention. A week later (on the 18th) the nest was fairly well lined with down and contained nine eggs, one egg having apparently been deposited each day. On May 24 the nest contained 11 eggs and the parent was much tamer than on the two preceding visits, allowing us to approach to within 15 feet of her, and alighting within 20 yards of us upon being flushed.

Another peculiar nest was found May 30, 1908, containing 11 eggs which hatched during the first week in June. This nest was a depression in a perfectly bare sandy flat without a particle of concealment of any kind. The cavity was located in the most exposed position within hundreds of yards, and was fairly well lined with weed stems, grass, etc. and well rimmed with down. The brooding female was very conspicuous against the background of bare sand, and could be readily seen from a distance of 50 feet or more. This bird was rather wild and flushed while we were yet some distance from the nest.

Mr. Eugene S. Rolfe (1898) records, what I have never seen, a pintail's nest in a wet situation, which is very unusual; he says:

The nesting of the pintail differs little generally from other ducks that select high dry spots among the prairie grass, badger brush, or old stubble; but a young farmer this year piloted me to a clump of thick green bulrushes covering a space as large as a dining table in the midst of a springy bog, and in the center of this, built up 6 inches out of water (18 inches deep) on a foundation of coarse dried rushes, exactly after the manner of the redhead, canvasback, or ruddy, and lined with down, was a veritable nest of the pintail. The female was at home, and permitted approach within 6 feet; and I stood some moments watching her curiously and regretting the absence of my camera before I realized that this was the pintail in a very unusual situation.

The down in the pintail's nest most closely resembles that of the shoveller, but it is larger and darker. It varies in color from "hair brown" to "fuscous" or "clove brown" with whitish centers. The breast feathers mixed with the down are either of the characteristic banded pattern or are grayish brown with a broad white tip.

Eggs.—Only one brood is raised in a season and the number of eggs in the set averages less than with other surface feeding ducks. The set varies from 6 to 12 eggs, but it is usually less than 10. It is unusual to find the eggs of other ducks in a pintail's nest, but as the eggs closely resemble those of some other species, it may be a commoner occurrence than it is supposed to be. Mr. Edward Arnold (1894) records the finding of a golden eye's egg in a pintail's nest in

Manitoba. The eggs closely resemble, in color and general appearance, those of the mallard and the shoveller, but they average smaller than the former and slightly larger than the latter, the measurements overlapping in both cases. In shape they are usually elliptical ovate and the color varies from very pale olive green to very pale olive buff, which fades out to a mere tint.

Although the eggs of the pintail can not be separated with certainty from those of the above two species the nests of all three can usually be identified if a clear view of the female is obtained as she flies from the nest; the female pintail can be distinguished from female mallard by the absence of the purple speculum with its conspicuous white borders and by its long slender form; she can be distinguished from the shoveller by her larger size and her small bill; the female shoveller has a long neck, but a conspicuously large bill; the wing pattern is different, but the difference is difficult to detect in the rapidily moving wings of a flying duck.

The measurements of 102 eggs, in various collections, average 54.9 by 38.2 millimeters; the eggs showing the four extremes measure **60** by 38.5, 58.5 by **40.5, 50.5** by 37.2 and 53 by **35** millimeters.

Young.—The period of incubation is about 22 or 23 days and the incubation is performed wholly by the female; she is a very close sitter and is often nearly trodden upon before she will leave the nest; I have heard of one being knocked over with a stick or a plowman's whip as she fluttered off, and it is not a difficult matter to photograph one on her nest. The male does not, I believe, wholly desert the female during the process of incubation and he assists somewhat in the care of the young, though he is not as bold in their defense. The young remain in the nest for a day or so after they are hatched or until the down is thoroughly dried. The whole brood usually hatches within a few hours, for, although only one egg is laid each day, incubation does not begin until the set is complete. As soon as the young are strong enough to walk they are led by their mother to the nearest water, which is often a long distance away, and taught to feed on soft insect and aquatic animal food. I have seen some remarkable demonstrations of parental solicitude by female pintails; they are certainly the most courageous of any of the ducks in the defense of their young. Once in North Dakota as we waded out into a marsh a female pintail flew towards us, dropped into the water near us, and began splashing about in a state of great excitement. The young ducks were probably well hidden among the reeds, though we could not see or hear them. During all the time, for an hour or more, that we were wading around the little slough that pintail watched us and followed us closely, flying about our heads and back and forth over the slough, frequently splashing down into the water near us in the most reckless manner, swimming about in small circles or splashing along the surface of the water, as if wounded, and often near enough for us to have hit her with a stick, quacking excitedly all the time. I never saw a finer exhibition of parental devotion than was shown by her total disregard of her own safety, which did not cease until we left the locality entirely. I have had several similar experiences elsewhere. If alarmed, when swimming in the sloughs, the young seldom attempt to dive though they can do so, if necessary; they more often swim into the reeds and hide while the mother bird attracts the attention of the intruder. Doctor Coues (1874) says that during July in Montana—

the young were just beginning to fly, in most instances, while the old birds were for the most part deprived of flight by molting of the quills. Many of the former were killed with sticks, or captured by hand, and afforded welcome variation of our hard fare. On invasion of the grassy or reedy pools where the ducks were, they generally crawled shyly out upon the prairie around, and there squatted to hide; so that we procured more from the dry grass surrounding than in the pools themselves. I have sometimes stumbled thus upon several together, crouching as close as possible, and caught them all in my hands.

Dr. Harold C. Bryant (1914) relates the following incident:

On May 21 a pintail with 10 downy young was discovered on the bank of a pond. When first disturbed she was brooding her young on dry ground about 10 feet from the water. The moment she flew the downy young assumed rigidly the same poses they had variously held beneath the mother. Some were standing nearly erect whereas others were crouching, but all were huddled close together. They remained perfectly motionless while, leaving Kendall to watch, I went for the camera. I had gone over a hundred yards before they moved. By the time I returned they had wandered off about 10 yards. They marched in single file and every now and then huddled close together posing motionless for a few moments.

Plumages.—The downy young is grayer and browner than other young surface-feeding ducks and thus easily recognized. The crown is dark, rich "clove brown"; a broad superciliary stripe of grayish white extends from the lores to the occiput; below this the side of the head is mainly grayish white, fading to pure white on the throat and chin, with a narrow postocular stripe of "clove brown" and a paler and broader stripe of the same below it. The back is "clove brown," darkest on the rump, with grayish or buffy tips on the down of the upper back; the rump and scapular spots are white, the latter sometimes elongated into stripes. The lower parts are grayish white, palest in the center. The chest, and sometimes the sides of the head, are suffused with pinkish buff, but never with yellow. The colors become duller and paler as the bird grows older. When the young bird is about 3 weeks old the first feathers appear on the flanks and scapulars and the tail becomes noticeable; about a week later feathers begin to show on the rump, breast, head, and neck, and the bird is fully grown before its contour plumage is complete; the flight feathers are the last to be acquired. The length of time required to complete the first plumage varies greatly in different individuals, but the sequence in which it appears is uniform.

Mr. J. G. Millais (1902) says of the sequence of plumages to maturity:

When in first plumage the young male and female are exceedingly like one another, especially at the commencement of this period; they also resemble the mother to a certain extent, but from her they can be easily distinguished by the small spots which cover the breast and belly, and the narrow brown edge of the feathers on the back and scapulars. The young male pintail, however, like the young mallard drake, almost as soon as he has assumed his first dress commences to color change in the back and scapulars. A gray tinge suffuses the brown plumage and slight reticulations appear on the feathers themselves, rendering it easy to notice the difference between him and the young female. He is also somewhat larger. By the middle of September the usual molt and the more advanced feather changes commence, and sometimes, in birds in a high state of condition, advance so rapidly, that young drakes of the year may attain the full plumage of the adult drake by the beginning of December. Most of them, however, retain a considerable proportion of the brown plumage until February, when the spring flush finishes off the dress. Even then young pintail drakes are not nearly so brilliant as 2 or 3 year old birds, and often show their youthfulness by their shorter tail, dull coloring on the head, and reticulated black bars traversing the white stripes on either side of the neck.

There is considerable individual variation in the length of time required by young birds to throw off the last signs of immaturity, but old and young birds become practically indistinguishable before the first eclipse plumage is assumed and entirely so after it is discarded. Some male pintails begin to show the first spotted feathers of the eclipse plumage early in June and during July the molt progresses rapidly and uniformly over the whole body, head, and neck until the full eclipse is complete in August, and the males are indistinguishable from females except by the wings and the difference in size. The wings are molted only once, of course, in August; and, after the flight feathers are fully grown, early in September, the second molt into the adult winter begins; this molt is usually not completed until November or December, the time varying with different individuals. I have never detected any signs of a spring molt in male pintails, but Mr. Millais calls attention to the fact that females which have pure white breasts in the winter become more or less spotted during the nesting season.

Food.—The pintail is a surface feeder, dipping below the surface only with the fore part of its body, with its tail in the air, maintaining its balance by paddling with its feet, while its long neck is reaching for its food. Here it feeds on the bulbous roots and tender shoots of a great variety of water plants, as well as their seeds; it also finds some animal food such as minnows, crawfish, tadpoles, leeches, worms, snails, insects, and larvae. Dr. F. Henry Yorke (1899) states that it feeds on wheat, barley, buckwheat, and Indian corn. Audubon (1840) says of its animal food:

It feeds on tadpoles in spring and leeches in autumn, while, during winter, a dead mouse, should it come in its way, is swallowed with as much avidity as by a mallard. To these articles of food it adds insects of all kinds, and, in fact, it is by no means an inexpert flycatcher.

Dr. P. L. Hatch (1892) says that, in Minnesota, the pintails may be found in spring "along the recently opened streams, and in the woodlands where they spend much of their time in search of acorns, insects, snails, and larvae of different kinds, which are under the wet leaves and on the old decaying logs with which the forests abound." Mr. Edward A. Preble (1908) found it feeding on small mollusks (*Lymnaea palustris*) in northern Canada, and Mr. F. C. Baker (1889) dissected 15 stomachs in Florida, all of which contained "shells of *Truncatella subcylindrica* (Say)." Mr. Douglas C. Mabbott (1920) sums up the food of the pintail as follows:

Vegetable matter constitutes about seven-eighths (87.15 per cent) of the total food of the pintail. This is made up of the following items: Pondweeds, 28.04 per cent; sedges, 21.78; grasses, 9.64; smartweeds and docks, 4.74; arrow grass, 4.52; musk grass and other algae, 3.44; arrowhead and water plantain, 2.84; goosefoot family, 2.58; water lily family, 2.57; duckweeds, 0.8; water milfoils, 0.21; and miscellaneous vegetable food, 5.99 per cent.

The animal portion, 12.85 per cent, of the food of the pintail was made up of mollusks, 5.81 per cent; crustaceans, 3.79 per cent; insects, 2.85 per cent; and miscellaneous, 0.4 per cent.

Behavior.—The pintail is built on graceful, clipper lines and is well fitted to cleave the air at a high rate of speed; it has been credited by gunners with ability to make 90 miles an hour; this may be rather a high estimate of its speed, but it is certainly very fleet of wing and surpassed by few if any of the ducks. Mr. Walter H. Rich (1907) says:

The pintails flight will at once remind the bay gunner of that of the "old squaw," so well known along the Atlantic coast. The same chain lightning speed and darting and wheeling evolutions are common to both species.

Dr. E. W. Nelson (1887) who had good opportunities for studying this species in Alaska, gives the following graphic account of one of its remarkable flight performances:

During the mating season they have a habit of descending from a great altitude at an angle of about 45,° with their wings stiffly outspread and slightly decurved downward. They are frequently so high that I have heard the noise produced by their passage through the air from 15 to 20 seconds before the bird came in sight. They descend with meteorlike swiftness until within a few yards of the ground, when a slight change in the position of the wings sends the birds gliding away close to the ground from 100 to 300 yards without a single wing stroke. The sound produced by this swift passage through the air can only be compared to the rushing of a gale through tree tops. At first it is like a murmur, then rising to a hiss, and then almost assuming the proportions of a roar as the bird sweeps by.

The pintail can generally be distinguished in flight by its long, slim neck and slender build, which is conspicuous in both sexes; the tail is also more pointed than in other species, even without the long tail feathers of the full plumaged male. The pintail springs upward from the water, much like a teal, and gets under way at once; a flock of pintails flushed suddenly will often bunch together so closely as to give the gunner a chance for a destructive shot.

The pintail is a graceful swimmer, riding lightly on the surface, with its tail pointing upward, its general attitude suggestive of a swan and with its long neck stretched up, alert to every danger, the first to give the alarm and always the first of the shy waterfowl to spring into flight. The hunter must be very cautious if he would stalk this wary bird. Though not a diver from choice, the pintail can dive when necessity requires it. It often escapes by diving while in the flightless stage of eclipse plumage.

Mr. Hersey's notes on this species in Alaska record the following interesting observation:

While the pintail is not a diving duck it can dive readily if wounded and in other emergencies. On one occasion a female followed by two males flew past and I shot the female. She dropped into a nearby pond but when I reached the shore had crawled into the grass and hidden. Circling the pond, which was but 30 or 40 feet in width by about the same number of yards in length, I soon reached my bird. Without hesitation she dove and crossed to the other side under water. The water was fairly clear and not more than 30 inches deep and the bird's movements could be plainly watched. The body was held at an angle, with the neck extended but not straight and the head slightly raised. The wings were partly opened but were not used and the feet struck out alternately as in running rather than with a swimming motion. The bird reminded me of a frightened chicken crossing the road in front of an automobile but the speed was much slower through the water than in the case of the chicken. The bird did not run on the bottom of the pond but was perhaps 6 or 7 inches from the bottom. On reaching the opposite shore she came up directly into the concealment of the grass. This proceeding was repeated in exactly the same manner several times before I secured the bird.

The following incident, described by Mr. Frank T. Noble (1906) will illustrate a strange habit which this and nearly all ducks have of disappearing beneath the surface when wounded; he had shot two pintails, one being—

killed outright, the other, a big drake, being hard hit and with one wing broken. Before the latter could be shot over, he made a dive with considerable difficulty and disappeared from view. We waited perhaps half a minute for him to appear again, but not doing so we paddled to the spot, where we found the water thereabouts to be scarcely 3 feet deep, and the bottom to be thickly covered with various kinds of lily pads and grasses. A few moments of careful search and the duck was discovered on the bottom, grasping with its bill the tough stem of a cowslip. The body of the bird floated upward posteriorly, somewhat higher than the position of the head, and the long tail feathers were a foot or more nearer the surface than the former. The bird's feet were outstretched, but he was motionless until molested, then he kicked and fluttered vigorously, all the time retaining his hold upon the bottom, and it required considerable force to break him away from his queer anchorage.

Mr. J. G. Millais (1902) says that:

The nuptial call of the drake is identical with that of the teal. The female only occasionally utters a low quack, but she sometimes makes a call something like the growling croak of the female widgeon. The notes of both sexes are always quite distinct.

The ordinary note of the male pintail is a low mellow whistle, and I doubt if it ever utters the quacking note which should be attributed to the female; the rolling note, similar to that of the lesser scaup duck, may be common to both sexes; Dr. E. W. Nelson (1887) says that this note " may be imitated by rolling the end of the tongue with the mouth ready to utter the sound of *k.*"

The pintail associates freely on its breeding grounds with various species of ducks, particularly with the mallard, gadwall, blue-winged teal, baldpate, shoveller, and lesser scaup duck. It usually flocks by itself, however, on migrations. Its most formidable enemy is man; for with the sportsman the pintail is a favorite. Its eggs are also sought for food, in some localities quite regularly, for the nests are easily found and the eggs are very palatable. Mr. Robert B. Rockwell (1911) has published a photograph of a bull snake robbing a pintail's nest in Colorado. I have seen nests in Saskatchewan which showed signs of having been robbed by coyotes.

Fall.—Although the pintail is one of our earliest migrants in the spring, it seems much less hardy in the fall and is one of the first of the ducks to seek the sunny South as soon as the first frosty nights proclaim the approach of autumn. Doctor Yorke (1899) says of the fall migration:

In the fall migration they differ from other cold-weather birds of the nondivers in returning south before the cold weather sets in; in fact, the first frost finds those which bred in the United States rapidly wending their way toward the frost line. The first issue to come down in the fall usually leaves the northern part of Minnesota and North Dakota about the end of August. They associate a good deal with the baldpates and gadwalls, using the same feeding, roosting, and playgrounds in the fall, not associating with them in the spring owing to their having gone north several weeks before them, and feeding to a large extent upon grain and corn fields. The second fall issue generally overtakes the first before they reach the frost line. They collect in some quiet piece of water, migrate at night and never return that fall. They do not assume their full plumage north of the frost line.

Game.—As a game bird the pintail ranks about third among the surface-feeding ducks, next in importance to the mallard and black duck; its wariness and its swiftness on the wing test the cunning and skill of the sportsman; its wide distribution, its abundance and its excellent table qualities give it a prominent place as a food bird. Late winter and early spring shooting was popular in the Middle West before the laws prohibited it, where the birds arrived early, as soon as the ice began to break up in the marshes and sloughs; here the birds were shot on their morning and evening flights to and from their feeding grounds from blinds or boats concealed in their fly ways, no decoys being necessary. Pintails will come readily to live mallard decoys during the daytime on their feeding grounds and they will respond to duck calls if skillfully handled, offering very fine sport where they are not shot at too much.

Dr. Leonard C. Sanford (1903) says:

In portions of the West where they frequent the ponds and smaller lakes they are much more easily killed than on larger bodies of water. The pintail arrives on the coast of North Carolina late in October, and are found in numbers through the brackish sounds. Decoys attract them occasionally, but never in as large numbers as the other ducks, for they are always wary and quick to suspect danger. These birds can be distinguished afar. The white under parts of the male and their long necks mark them at once. The flight is high in lines abreast, but almost before the flock is seen they are by and out of sight. When about to decoy no bird is more graceful; they often drop from a height far out of range and circle about the stool, watching carefully for the slightest motion; finally they swing within range and plunge among the wooden ducks. After realizing the mistake, they spring up all together, and are out of shot almost before you realize the chance is gone.

Winter.—Like many other fresh-water ducks of the interior the pintail winters largely on the warm seacoasts of the Southern States, though it is also abundant among the inland ponds and marshes below the frost line. It is particularly abundant in Florida, as the following account by Mr. C. J. Maynard (1896) will show:

On one occasion, while I was making my way down Indian River, numbers of these ducks were passing over my head southward. They flew in straggling flocks, consisting of from twenty to some hundreds of specimens, and one company followed another so closely that there was an almost unbroken line. They continued to move in this manner all the morning; thus many thousands of individuals must have passed us. Shortly after noon they began to alight along the beaches in such numbers that they fairly covered the ground, and were so unsuspicious that my assistant, who had left the boat some time previous, walked within a few yards of them, and killed three or four with a single discharge of a light gun which was merely loaded with a small charge of dust shot. This occurred in early March and the birds were evidently gathering, preparatory to migrating northward, for in a few days they had all disappeared.

While wintering on the seacoast, especially where it is much molested, the pintail often spends the day well out on the ocean, flying in at night to feed in the shallow tidal estuaries on the beds of *Zostera* or on the mud and sand flats where it finds plenty of small mollusks.

DISTRIBUTION.

Breeding range.—The species is circumpolar. The North American form breeds east to the west coast of Hudson Bay, and James Bay (both coasts), and rarely east of Lake Michigan. It has been known to breed in New Brunswick (Tobique River, 1879) and in southern Ontario (Rondeau, Lake Erie) and southeastern Michigan (St. Clair Flats). South to northern Illinois (formerly, but now scarce even in Wisconsin), central Iowa (Hamilton and Sac Counties), central western Nebraska (Garden and Morrill Counties), northern Colorado (Larimer County and Barr Lake region), northern Utah (Bear River marshes), and southern California (Riverside County).   West to the central valleys of California (Los Angeles, Kern, Merced, Sutter, and Butte Counties), central Oregon (Klamath and Malheur Lakes), western Washington (Pierce County), central British Columbia (Cariboo), and the Bering Sea coast of Alaska.   North to the Arctic coast of Alaska (Point Barrow), northern Mackenzie (Fort Anderson), and the Arctic coast west of Hudson Bay.   Replaced in northern Europe and Asia by a closely allied subspecies.

Winter range.—East to the Atlantic coast of the United States, the Bahamas, Cuba, and Porto Rico, and rarely to the Lesser Antilles (Guadeloupe, Martinique, and Antigua).   South to Jamaica and Panama.   West to the Pacific coast of Central America, Mexico, and the United States.   North along the Pacific slope to southern British Columbia (Chilliwack and Okanagan Lake); in the interior north to northeastern Colorado (Barr Lake), Oklahoma, central Missouri (Missouri River), southern Illinois (Mount Carmel), southern Ohio (Ohio River), Maryland (Chesapeake Bay), and eastern Virginia (Cobb Island).   Said to winter regularly in southern Wisconsin and casually as far north as southeastern Nebraska (Lincoln) and southeastern Maine (Calais).   Winters in Hawaiian Islands.

Spring migration.—Early dates of arrival: Pennsylvania, Erie, February 23; New York, northwestern, February 25; Newfoundland, Grand Lake, April 20;   Illinois, Chicago, March 12; North Dakota, Larimore, March 20; Manitoba, Raeburn, April 5; Mackenzie, Fort Simpson, April 28; Alaska, Kowak River, May 14; and Demarcation Point, May 24.   Average dates of arrival: Illinois, southern, February 26; Missouri, central, February 26; Iowa, Keokuk, February 18; Illinois, Chicago, March 20; Minnesota, southern, March 9; Minnesota, northern, April 8; North Dakota, Larimore, April 3; Saskatchewan, Qu' Appelle, April 10; Manitoba, Raeburn, April 8; Mackenzie, Great Slave Lake, May 1; Alaska, St. Michael, about May 1.

Fall migration.—Early dates of arrival: Quebec, Montreal, September 3; Long Island, Mastic, August 21; Massachusetts, eastern, September 11; Pennsylvania, Erie, September 6; Virginia, Alexandria, September 13; Florida, Wakulla County, September 11; Texas, Corpus Christi, August 18; California, Santa Barbara, August 25; Lower California, southern, August 29.   Late dates of departure: Alaska, Point Barrow, September 7; Kowak River, September 14; and St. Michael, October 10; Mackenzie, Fort Franklin, September 27; Long Island, East Rockaway, December 24.

Casual records.—Has occurred in Porto Rico (Cartagena Lagoon, April 8, 1921), Bermuda (winter 1847–48 and October 26, 1875),

Greenland (Godthaab and "northern"), and Labrador (Hopedale, Davis Inlet, etc.). Recorded from Laysan Island.

Egg dates.—Alaska and Arctic America: Fifty-five records, May 23, to July 16; twenty-eight records, June 10 to 24. California, Colorado, and Utah: Twenty-two records, April 30 to June 29; eleven records, May 15 to 30. Manitoba and Saskatchewan: Twenty records, May 16 to July 3: ten records, June 4 to 14. North Dakota: Twenty-three records, May 11 to June 27; twelve records, May 23 to June 10.

POECILONETTA BAHAMENSIS (Linnaeus).

BAHAMA PINTAIL.

HABITS.

This beautiful duck has been recorded only once in North America. Mr. W. Sprague Brooks (1913) reported the capture of a specimen by Mr. Gardner Perry at Cape Canaveral, Florida, in March, 1912. Mr. Perry generously presented the specimen to the Museum of Comparative Zoology at Cambridge.

The bird was in company with a small flock of green-winged teal, and the wind at the time was southeast. It seems a strange fact that this bird has not been recorded from Florida before, a region that has so long received the attentions of sportsmen and naturalists.

The Bahama pintail, or Bahama duck, as it is also called, has long been known as a wide ranging species, from the Bahama Islands to southern South America. Mr. W. H. Hudson (1920) refers to it in his Argentine Ornithology under the name of "white-faced pintail"; he seems to object to the use of the name "Bahama pintail." He says that it is one of the commonest ducks in Brazil; he also says:

The brown pintail is our most abundant species in Argentina, and I have noticed in flocks of great size, sometimes of many thousands, of that duck, that a single white-faced duck in the flock could be detected at a long distance by means of that same snowy whiteness of the face.

Mr. Outram Bangs (1918) has recently shown that there are two recognizable subspecies, of which he says:

Specimens from the Guianas and the lower Amazon are quite like West Indian examples, and are true *Poecilonetta bahamensis* (Linn.). Those from southern South America—southern Brazil, Paraguay, Argentina, etc.—though little different in color, are much larger, and represent a recognizable subspecies for which there are several names. I have seen no intergrades, but doubtless these occur in middle Brazil or Bolivia.

Very little seems to have been published on the habits of the Bahama pintail and I have been able to learn only a few meager facts about it. Dr. Glover M. Allen (1905) says of its haunts in the Bahama Islands:

On the south side of Great Abaco, stretching for many miles east and west, is a tidewater region locally known as "the Marls." Long reaches of shallow water alternate with clayey flats a few inches above the tide level.   These flats are thinly covered with a growth of small mangroves, grasses, and a few other halophytes, while here and there are little pools surrounded by taller mangrove bushes.   In this sort of country we found a good number of these handsome ducks.   Most of those seen were in pairs, but one flock of 15 birds was started from a small pond among the mangroves, July 6.

Nesting.—Mr. Charles B. Cory (1880) writes:

This pretty little species was quite abundant at Inagua, frequenting the large salt ponds of the interior.   On May 27, while shooting on a small island in the lake back of Mathewstown, I observed a number of these birds, and shot several, all of which were in full breeding dress.   While passing through a small marsh I discovered the nest of this species, the old bird flying away as I approached.   It was simply a mat of grass placed on the ground, and contained nine eggs of a pale brown color,   Another nest, taken a few days later, contained eight eggs, slightly darker than the first set.

Young.—Dr. Alexander Wetmore (1916) was fortunate enough to find a brood of young in Porto Rico, of which he writes:

May 26 the birds were common at the Laguna de Guanica, where they would flush singly or in pairs from a growth of water plants covering a large area of the lagoon and, after circling over the open water, return to the same cover.   Once in the short grass of a marsh a female flew out, but almost immediately fell back as though with a broken wing, repeating the performance several times.   At the same time the low *peep, peep* of young birds was heard and two about 5 days old were caught.   A third promptly dived and apparently never came up, while the others rapidly scattered to safety through the grass.   The down of these little birds was not at all soft, but had a peculiar stiff bristly feeling.

Plumages.—Mr. W. E. Clyde Todd (1911) says that a young bird, collected on Watling Island on March 23,—

is assuming the juvenal dress, and already resembles the adult below.   In the downy stage the general color is dull brown, with a white stripe on the flanks and an illy defined pale superciliary stripe.   The throat and cheeks are white also, as in the adult.

Food.—Doctor Wetmore (1916) says of the food of this species:

Stomachs of eight adults and two downy young which were collected were examined by W. L. McAtee, of the Biological Survey.   The adults had eaten nothing but vegetable matter.   Seeds of ditch grass (*Ruppia maritima*) were found in every stomach and formed 16.25 per cent of the total bulk the largest amounts being 180 and 125, seeds, respectively.   Foliage and antheridia of algae (*Chara, sp.*) made up 83.75 per cent and formed the great bulk in all the stomachs.   The two downy young had eaten animal matter (amounting to 3.5 per cent), composed of remains of a water boatman (*Corixa, sp.*), bits of a water creeper (*Pelocoris, sp.*), and young snails.   Grass seeds, foxtail grass (*Chaetochloa, sp.*), barnyard grass (*Echinochloa crus-galli*), and a species of guinea grass (*Panicum, sp.*) formed 94 per cent of the food of these ducklings, and a few other seeds 2.5 per cent.

He seems to think that they need protection, for he says:

These birds were much disturbed by egg hunters who were continually searching the marshes, and many were shot by gunners during the breeding season.   They should be free from molestation from March 1 to December 1 at least.   In a few years their range will be even more restricted than at present, because of the draining and clearing of swamps and marshes, and unless protected they will disappear entirely.

Breeding range.—The Bahama Islands (Abaco, Andros, the Caicos, the Inaguas, Long Island, etc.), Porto Rico, some of the Lesser Antilles, the Guianas, and northern Brazil. The southern limit of the northern race is not determined. Replaced farther south by a larger race. Some form of this species breeds on the Galapagos Islands.

Winter range.—Same as above, apparently not migratory.

Casual record.—Accidental in Florida (Cape Canaveral, March, 1912).

AIX SPONSA (Linnaeus).

WOOD DUCK.

HABITS.

Spring.—While wandering through the dim cathedral aisles of a big cypress swamp in Florida, where the great trunks of the stately trees towered straight upward for a hundred feet or more until the branches interlaced above so thickly that the sunlight could not penetrate, we seemed to be lost in the gloom of a strange tropical forest and far removed from the familiar sights and sounds of the outside world. Only the frequent cries of the omnipresent Florida red-shouldered hawk and an occasional glimpse of a familiar fly-catcher or vireo, migrating northward reminded us of home. But at last the light seemed to break through the gloom, as we approached a little sunlit pond, and there we saw some familiar friends, the center of interest in a pretty picture, framed in the surroundings of their winter home, warmed by the genial April sun and perhaps preparing to leave for their northern summer home. The sunlight filtering through the tops of the tall cypresses which surrounded the pool shone full upon the snowy forms of 50 or more white ibises, feeding on the muddy shores, dozing on the fallen logs, or perched upon the dead stumps or surrounding trees; the air seemed full of them as they rose and flew away. But with this dazzling cloud of whiteness there arose from the still waters of the pool a little flock of wood ducks, brilliant in their full nuptial plumage, their gaudy colors flashing in the sunshine, as they went whirring off through the tree tops. What a beautiful creature is this Beau Brummel among birds and what an exquisite touch of color he adds to the scene among the water hyacinths of Florida or among the pond lilies of New England!

The wood duck is a strictly North American species and principally a bird of the United States, for its summer range extends but a short distance north of our borders, except in the warmer, central portions of Canada, and even in winter it does not migrate far south of us. It is one of the most widely distributed species, breeding throughout most of its range and wintering more or less regularly over much of its habitat in the United States. For these reasons its migrations are not easily traced except in the Northern States and Provinces. It is a moderately early migrant, coming after the ice has left the woodland ponds and timbered sloughs. Dr. F. Henry Yorke (1899) says:

They arrive in three distinct issues, after sunset and through the night, suddenly appearing in the morning upon their accustomed haunts. The first stays but a brief period, and departs for the north to breed; the second puts in an appearance a few days later, but soon leaves to nest in the northern parts of the United States; the third arrives directly after the second leaves and scatters over the Middle States to nest. This issue forms the local ducks of each State it breeds in.

Dr. P. L. Hatch (1892) writes:

Arriving simultaneously with the other earlier species, none other braves the last rigors of the departing winter in the closing days of a Minnesota March with greater spirit. And when they come, like the rains of the Tropics, they pour in until every pool in the woodlands has been deluged with them.

Courtship.—Audubon's (1840) account of the courtship is very attractive; he writes:

When March has again returned, and the dogwood expands its pure blossoms to the sun, the cranes soar away on their broad wings, bidding our country adieu for a season, flocks of waterfowl are pursuing their early migrations, the frogs issue from their muddy beds to pipe a few notes of languid joy, the swallow has just arrived, and the bluebird has returned to his box. The wood duck almost alone remains on the pool, as if to afford us an opportunity of studying the habits of its tribe. Here they are, a whole flock of beautiful birds, the males chasing their rivals, the females coquetting with their chosen beaux. Observe that fine drake, how gracefully he raises his head and curves his neck! As he bows before the object of his love, he raises for a moment his silken crest. His throat is swelled, and from it there issues a guttural sound, which to his beloved is as sweet as the song of the wood thrush to its gentle mate. The female, as if not unwilling to manifest the desire to please which she really feels, swims close by his side, now and then caresses him by touching his feathers with her bill, and shows displeasure toward any other of her sex that may come near. Soon the happy pair separate from the rest, repeat every now and then their caresses, and at length, having sealed the conjugal compact, fly off to the woods to search for a large woodpecker's hole. Occasionally the males fight with each other, but their combats are not of long duration, nor is the field ever stained with blood, the loss of a few feathers or a sharp tug on the head being generally enough to decide the contest. Although the wood ducks always form their nests in the hollow of a tree, their caresses are performed exclusively on the water, to which they resort for the purpose, even when their loves have been first proved far above the ground on a branch of some tall sycamore. While the female is depositing her eggs, the male is seen to fly swiftly past the hole in which she is hidden, erecting his crest, and sending forth his love notes, to which she never fails to respond

Nesting.—The wood duck has earned the common name of "summer duck" on account of its breeding and spending the summer so far south; it has also been called the "tree duck" from its habit of nesting in trees.   Its favorite nesting site is in a fairly large natural cavity in the trunk or large branch of a tree; it has no special pref- erence for any particular kind of tree and not much choice as to its location; it probably would prefer to find a suitable hollow tree near some body of water, but it is often forced to select a tree at a long distance away from it and sometimes very near the habitations of man.   The size and depth of the cavity selected vary greatly, and its height from the ground may be anywhere from 3 or 4 feet to 40 or 50.   If it can not find a natural cavity that suits its taste, the wood duck occasionally occupies the deserted nesting hole of one of the larger woodpeckers, such as the ivory-billed or pileated wood- pecker, or even the flicker; sometimes the former home of a fox squirrel or other large squirrel is selected, in which case the old nest- ing material, dry leaves and soft rubbish, is left in the cavity and mixed with the down of the duck.   Such material is often found in the nest of the wood duck, but I doubt if it is ever brought in by the bird.

A few quotations from the writings of others will give an idea of the variety of nesting sites chosen.   Audubon (1840) gives the best general idea of the nesting habits of the wood duck as follows:

The wood duck breeds in the Middle States about the beginning of April, in Massa chusetts a month later, and in Nova Scotia or on northern lakes, seldom before the first days of June.   In Louisiana and Kentucky, where I have had better oppor- tunities of studying their habits in this respect, they generally pair about the 1st of March, sometimes a fortnight earlier.   I never knew one of these birds to form a nest on the ground, or on the branches of a tree.   They appear at all times to prefer the hollow broken portion of some large branch, the hole of our large woodpecker (*Picus principalis*), or the deserted retreat of the fox squirrel, and I have frequently been surprised to see them go in and out of a hole of any one of these, when their bodies while on wing seemed to be nearly half as large again as the aperture within which they had deposited their eggs.   Once only I found a nest (with 10 eggs) in the fissure of a rock on the Kentucky River a few miles below Frankfort.   Generally, however, the holes to which they betake themselves are either over deep swamps, above cane- brakes, or on broken branches of high sycamores, seldom more than 40 or 50 feet from the water.   They are much attached to their breeding places, and for three succes- sive years I found a pair near Henderson, in Kentucky, with eggs in the beginning of April, in the abandoned nest of an ivory-billed woodpecker.   The eggs, which are from 6 to 15, according to the age of the bird, are placed on dry plants, feathers, and a scanty portion of down, which I believe is mostly plucked from the breast of the female.

Wilson (1832) describes a nest which he found, as follows:

On the 18th of May I visited a tree containing the nest of a summer duck, on the banks of Tuckahoe River, New Jersey.   In was an old grotesque white oak, whose top had been torn off by a storm.   It stood on the declivity of the bank, about 20 yards from the water.   In this hollow and broken top, and about 6 feet down, on the soft decayed wood, lay 13 eggs, snugly covered with down, doubtless taken from the breast of the bird.   This tree had been occupied, probably by the same pair, for four successive years.

Mr. William B. Crispin gave me his notes on a nest which he found near Salem, New Jersey, on April 25, 1908; it was in a natural cavity in a sour gum tree 40 feet from the ground; the 16 eggs were 3 feet below the opening in a nest of down mixed with dry leaves, which were probably taken there by squirrels the previous season; two gray squirrels were living just a few inches below the nest.

Mr. Henry R. Buck (1893) describes a nest found in a hole in a large apple tree near Hartford, Connecticut, as follows:

This tree was hardly 5 rods from an occupied house, and perhaps three times as far from a well-traveled road leading to the city. There was nothing to hide it from the road, and only a few trees in the immediate neighborhood. The trunk was hollow and had a wide split in one side from a height of 6 feet nearly to the ground.

I have a set of 14 eggs in my collection, taken in Norton, Massachusetts, on May 8, 1892, from a hollow apple tree; the cavity was 3 or 4 feet deep and the eggs lay in their bed of down 3 feet below the opening and only 2 feet above the ground. I found a nest in Taunton, Massachusetts, on May 19, 1917, containing 9 eggs, about 40 feet from the ground in a dead pine tree in a grove of tall trees near a house; the tree was so rotten that the cavity, which had once been a flicker's nest, had broken open and much of the down had fallen out and was scattered around the grove; a few feet below the duck's nest was a gray squirrel's nest in a cavity, with several half grown young in it. I was shown another nest, near Taunton, in a natural cavity in a large elm, about 30 feet from the ground; the tree stood close to a much-traveled road and in the front yard of a farm house. Mr. R. S. Wheeler found a nest in a barn near the Sacramento River, California; the birds entered through a hole in the boards and built a nest in the hay. Mr. Herbert K. Job found a nest similarly located in a barn located near Kent, Connecticut. Mr. Arthur T. Wayne (1910) found a nest in South Carolina on April 25, 1906. "The eight eggs were nearly hatched, and were laid in a sleeping hole of the pileated woodpecker, in a living sweet gum tree, 40 feet above the ground and more than a mile from the nearest reservoir." Mr. T. G. Pearson (1891) found a nest in Florida, on April 13, containing 13 fresh eggs. "The nest was in a hollow stump 30 feet from the ground. The entrance had been made by a yellow-shafted flicker, and it really seemed impossible for a duck to pass in and out of a hole of such small size. The nest was lined with a thick layer of downy feathers from the breast of the old bird." Mr. Walter B. Sampson (1901) records a nest, which he found in California on April 29, 1900, "in a deserted home of a red-shafted flicker and placed about 25 feet up in a white oak tree"; this nest contained the remarkable number of 21 eggs.

The down in the wood duck's nest is grayish white or "pallid mouse gray," with nearly pure white centers. More or less rubbish from the cavity is mixed with it and the breast feathers found in it are pure white.

Eggs.—The wood duck raises but one brood in a season in any part of its wide range. The set usually consists of from 10 to 15 eggs, but sometimes only 6 or 8 eggs are laid and occasionally much larger sets have been found, ranging from 18 to 29 eggs. Mr. George D. Peck (1911) mentions a remarkable set that he found in Iowa, containing 31 eggs of the wood duck and 5 eggs of the hooded merganser. There are other cases on record where these two species have contended for the use of the same hole or have occupied it jointly, as mentioned under the latter species. The eggs are nearly oval in shape, with a slight tendency toward ovate. The shell is smooth, hard, and somewhat glossy. The color is dull white or creamy white, perhaps pale buffy white in some cases or a color resembling old ivory white.

The measurements of 99 eggs in various collections average 51.1 by 38.8 millimeters; the eggs showing the four extremes measure 55.5 by 41, 53.5 by 42, 48 by 38.5 and 50.5 by 37.3 millimeters.

Young.—The period of incubation is from 28 to 30 days. This duty is performed wholly by the female, but the male is more or less in attendance on her during this period and returns to help her care for the young. The young are provided with sharp claws which they use in climbing from the nest up to the entrance of the cavity, a distance of often 3 to 4 feet and sometimes as much as 6 or 8 feet. Much has been written about how the female conveys the young from the nest to the water in her bill, between her feet or even on her back, and several writers claim to have seen the first method employed. I am inclined to think that this method of conveyance is used only when circumstances make it necessary; if the nest cavity is not too high, or if it overhangs the water, or if there is soft open ground below it, I believe that the young are usually coaxed or urged to jump or flutter down and are then led by the old bird to the nearest water; certainly such is often the case.

Mr. J. H. Langille (1884) describes it very well as follows:

When the young are about 24 hours old, if the limb containing the nest be over the water, they may find their way severally to the edge, and dropping into their favorite element, begin life's perilous career. If the nest be a little distant from the water, as is generally the case, the mother may seize them by the wing or neck, and convey them to it, or, landing them thus on the ground, may lead them thither in a flock. More commonly, however, the mother having thoroughly reconnoitered the place for some time, and now uttering her soft cooing call at the doorway, the little ones scramble up from the nest with the aid of their sharp toenails, and huddle around the mother a few minutes. The mother, now descending to the ground, calls again to the young, and they drop one by one on to the soft moss or dried leaves, their tiny bodies so enveloped in long down, falling scarcely harder than a leaf or a feather. Again they huddle around the mother bird; and, as the distance of the nest from the water is sometimes as much as 60 or 70 rods, and generally more or less on an elevation, they need the maternal guidance to their favorite element.

Audubon (1840) says:

If the nest is placed immediately over the water, the young, the moment they are hatched, scramble to the mouth of the hole, launch into the air with their little wings and feet spread out, and drop into their favorite element; but whenever their birthplace is at some distance from it, the mother carries them to it one by one in her bill, holding them so as not to injure their yet tender frame. On several occasions, however, when the hole was 30, 40, or more yards from a bayou or other piece of water, I observed that the mother suffered the young to fall on the grasses and dried leaves beneath the trees, and afterwards led them directly to the nearest edge of the next pool or creek. At this early age, the young answer to their parents' call with mellow *pee, pee, pee*, often and rapidly repeated. The call of the mother at such times is low, soft, and prolonged, resembling the syllables *pe-ee, pe-ee*.

The young are carefully led along the shallow and grassy shores, and taught to obtain their food, which at this early period consists of small aquatic insects, flies, mosquitoes, and seeds. As they grow up, you now and then see the whole flock run as if it were along the surface of the sluggish stream in chase of a dragon fly, or to pick up a grasshopper or locust that has accidentally dropped upon it. They are excellent divers, and when frightened, instantly disappear, disperse below the surface, and make for the nearest shore, on attaining which they run for the woods, squat in any convenient place, and thus elude pursuit.

Mr. E. G. Kingsford (1917) has seen the wood duck carry its young to the water and thus relates his personal experience:

Early in July, 1898, while tented on the bank of the Michigamme River, township 43, north range 32 west, section 1, Iron County, Michigan, I had the good fortune to see it done. The nest was in a hollow pine that stood directly back of the tent and about 200 feet from the water, and the hole where the old duck went in, was 50 or 60 feet from the ground. After seeing the old duck fly by the tent, to and from her feeding grounds up the river many times during the time of incubation, one morning before sunrise she flew by from the tree to the river with a little duck in her beak which she left in an eddy a short distance upstream. She then made 10 or 12 trips to the nest and each time took a little duck in her beak by the neck to the water, where they all huddled in a little bunch. It was all done in a few minutes, and she evidently took them to the water very soon after they hatched, as they were only little balls of down. In going to and from work, we passed the little bunch many times. On our approach the old duck would fly away and leave the little ones huddled in a bunch near the shore where the water was quiet.

Mr. E. F. Pope in a letter to Mr. Edward H. Forbush says:

Once while fishing on the Nueces River in southeastern Texas, I observed a female wood duck bringing part of her brood of 10 ducklings down from a white-oak stub 28 feet above the water. There were three or four of the young already in the water when I appeared on the scene. She emerged from the cavity in the stub with a young duck on her back and simply dropped straight down into the water, using her wings to check the speed of her descent. When she arrived within a foot or two of the surface she suddenly assumed a vertical position which caused the duckling to slide from her back into the water. She rose quickly, circled a time or two, reentered the stub, and at once repeated the performance until the whole brood of 10 were on the water.

Mr. W. S. Cochrane, State game warden of Arkansas, also in a letter to Mr. Forbush, describes a similiar performance; after watching for three hours, he saw the female carry down the young on her back, as follows:

She visited the nest several times and after circling around the woods returned and rested on the edge of the nest which was in a hollow stub of the oak. After resting there about 10 minutes she flew down toward the water with her wings slightly elevated, and when about 10 feet from the water she began flying in an upward position, allowing one of the young which she was carrying on her back to slide off over her tail into the water. She went through this performance 14 times.

Mr. A. B. Eastman (1915) gives us the following account of the behavior of the young:

One day a friend and I were out on a little camping and canoe trip and on rounding a sudden bend in the creek above the pond, we came upon a mother duck and about seven little ones. A sudden note from the mother caused a prompt disappearance of the ducklings into the depths below. The courageous mother, however, instead of beating a hasty retreat, as one would most naturally expect, came flying toward the canoe and flopped down just in front of us, beating the water with her wings and trying by every means to make us believe that a crippled duck was just within our grasp. Seeing no signs of the little ones we started to follow the mother as if intending to catch her. She skillfully decoyed us up by the creek until around another bend when we were, in her estimation, a safe distance from her little brood. She then suddenly and miraculously recovered and quickly disappeared among the heavy growth of hardwood timber which clothes the banks of the creek. We promptly returned to the scene of the first encounter. The little ones had evidently recovered from their fright as we saw three of them swimming around. On seeing us, two of them dove, while the other made slowly for the bank, half submerged like a grebe. As soon as it landed we made a dash for the spot and the little fellow led us a merry chase through fallen timber, across ditches and through thicket and tangle. We finally corralled him, however, and made him pose as a photograph, much against his will. After taking a good look at the youngster, we set him down near the creek bank, and by the way he took to the water, we could imagine him congratulating himself on his fortunate escape from his terrible captors.

Mr. Manly Hardy, in his manuscript notes sent to Major Bendire, relates the following incident:

I once came suddenly upon a female with six half-grown young. As I approached the young ran into the tall grass while the mother flew away. I captured one while they were trying to escape to a bend in the stream above. An hour or more after, while approaching the stream above by a road through the woods from which I could see and not be seen, I saw the old one who had evidently been below looking for the missing one, flying high in the air until she was nearly opposite me, when dropping into the water she uttered a sharp call note upon which three young came out from the bushes on the right-hand bank and swam toward her—this evidently not pleasing her, she uttered a different note when they turned and swam back. She then, without moving, gave the first call note again, when two swam out from the left bank and came to her. Taking these with her she swam up abreast of where the others had disappeared, called them out and swam upstream with the united family. It was plain that she could count enough to know if one was missing, also that she had different notes by which she called her young or sent them away from her.

Plumages.—The downy young wood duck is much darker above
and paler below than the young mallard; the lower mandible and
the smaller tip of the upper mandible are of a rich yellowish shade,
which will serve to distinguish it from other ducks.   The crown is a
very deep rich "seal brown" or "bone brown," or halfway between
these colors and black; a stripe of the same color extends from the
eye to the dark color of the occiput and there is a lighter auricular
spot; the back shades from "bister" anteriorly to the same color as
the crown posteriorly; the hind neck is of a darker shade of "bister";
the sides of the head and neck, including a superciliary stripe and
the lores are "cream color" shaded locally with "Naples yellow";
the throat and under parts are "ivory yellow" to "Marguerite yellow," the colors of the upper and under parts mingling on the sides;
there is a pale yellowish spot on each wing and on each side of the
rump.

The plumage appears first on the scapulars and flanks, then on the
tail, breast, and belly, then on the back and head, the last of the
down showing on the hind neck and rump when the bird is nearly
fully grown; the wing feathers are the last to grow.   In this juvenal
plumage the back varies from "argus brown" to "raw amber" with
a metallic luster of purple, bronze, or green; the wings are similar to
those of the adult female; the under parts are whitish, mottled with
dull brown and tinged with bright brown or buff on the chest and
flanks.   The sexes look very much alike, but the wing of the male is
more brilliant than the female's and the head pattern is different in
the two sexes, each being a suggestion of the adult pattern; the
crown is "clove brown" in both sexes but in the male it has a greenish luster; the white around the eye is more conspicuous in the
female; the sides of the head are dull gray and the throat is white
in both sexes, but in the male the white extends up into the cheek
and side of the neck, as in the adult.   The sexes soon begin to differentiate and the progress toward maturity is rapid.   In the young
male the mottled belly is replaced by white during September and
October; the rich chestnut brown comes in on the chest and the
vermiculated flank feathers are acquired.   During October the adult
color pattern of the head is assumed, and many of the brilliant,
bronze, green, blue, and purple feathers appear in the back, scapulars,
and tail, so that by November the young male has assumed a plumage which is practically adult, though the full brilliancy and perfection of plumage is not acquired until the following year.

The adult male begins to molt into the eclipse plumage in June or
July, and the wings are molted in July or August, while the eclipse
plumage is at its height.   This plumage much resembles that of
the young male, except that the belly of the adult is nearly pure
white, instead of mottled as in the young, and the back retains

nearly as much of the metallic colors as in the full plumage. The wings are molted only once and are always distinctive; also the brilliant colors of the eyes, feet, and bill are retained during the eclipse stage, though they lose a little of their brilliancy. The molt out of the eclipse occurs in August and September; I have seen an adult male in full plumage again as early as September 12 and another that had not finished the molt on October 16.

Food.—The wood duck obtains most of its food on or above the surface of the water, though it can tip up to feed on shallow bottoms if necessary, and it feeds largely on land. A large part of its food consists of insects which it finds on the surface of the water or on the leaves and stems of aquatic plants, such as beetles, mayflies, locusts, and various creeping insects. Here it also obtains small fish, minnows, frogs, tadpoles, snails, and small salamanders. Nuttall (1834) says:

I have seen a fine male whose stomach was wholly filled with a mass of the small coleoptera, called *Donatias*, which are seen so nimbly flying over or resting on the leaves of the pond lily. These birds are therefore very alert in quest of their prey, or they never could capture these wary insects.

Probably the greater part of the food of the wood duck, during the fall and winter particularly, is vegetable, of which a great variety is consumed. The bulbs of *Sagittaria* and other water plants, as well as the seeds and leaves of many varieties, are taken with the animal food in summer. Later in the season the wild rice marshes are visited and many wild fruits such as grapes and berries are found on dry land. The grain fields are apparently never visited, but the southern rice fields are favorite feeding grounds in fall and winter. The wood duck is particularly fond of acorns, chestnuts, and beechnuts, which it picks up on the ground in the woods, turning over the fallen leaves to find them. Messrs. Beyer, Allison, and Kopman (1909) state that, in Louisiana, "an undoubted factor in determining the abundance of the wood duck is the presence of the water chinquapin (*Nelumbium luteum*). As a food of the wood duck the seeds of this plant are extremely important."

Mr. Douglas C. Mabbot (1920) says of the food of this duck:

More than nine-tenths (90.19 per cent) of the food of the wood duck consists of vegetable matter. This high proportion of vegetable food is very similar to that taken by the mallard. With the wood duck it is quite evenly distributed among a large number of small items, chief among which are the following: Duckweeds, 10.35 per cent; cypress cones and galls, 9.25; sedge seeds and tubers, 9.14; grasses and grass seeds, 8.17; pondweeds and their seeds, 6.53; acorns and beechnuts, 6.28; seeds of water lilies and leaves of water shield, 5.95; seeds of water elm and its allies 4.75; of smartweeds and docks, 4.74; of coontail 2.86; of arrow arum and skunk cabbage, 2.42; of bur marigold and other composites, 2.38; of buttonbush and allied plants, 2.25; of bur reed, 1.96; wild celery and frogbit, 1.31; nuts of bitter pecan, 0.91; grape seeds, 0.82; and seeds of swamp privet and ash, 0.72 per cent. The remaining 9.4 per cent was made up of a large number of minor items.

The wood duck's animal food, which amounted to 9.81 per cent of the total consisted chiefly of the following items: Dragon flies and damsel flies and their nymphs,
2.54 per cent; bugs, 1.56; beetles, 1.02; grasshoppers and crickets, 0.23; flies and
ants, bees, and wasps, 0.07; miscellaneous insects, 0.97; spiders and mites, 0.63;
crustaceans, 0.08; and miscellaneous animal matter, 2.71 per cent. Thus, nearly
two-thirds of the animal food consisted of insects.

Behavior.—No duck is so expert as the wood duck in threading its
way through the interlacing branches of the forest, at which its skill
has been compared with that of the passenger pigeon. I have stood
on the shore of a woodland pond in the darkening twilight of a summer evening and watched these ducks come in to roost; on swift and
silent wings they would glide like meteors through the tree tops,
twisting, turning, and dodging, until it was almost too dark for me
to see them. Ordinarily its flight is swift and direct, usually high in
the air. The short neck and white breast are good field marks for
the female and the color pattern of the male is conspicuous at a long
distance; it is said to resemble the baldpate in flight. When migrating it flies in small flocks, probably family parties.

The wood duck is a swift and agile swimmer and can dive if necessary. Audubon (1840) says of its movements:

On the ground the wood duck runs nimbly and with more grace than most other
birds of its tribe. On reaching the shore of a pond or stream, it immediately shakes
its tail sidewise, looks around, and proceeds in search of food. It moves on the
larger branches of trees with the same apparent ease; and, while looking at 30 or 40
of these birds perched on a single sycamore on the bank of a secluded bayou, I have
conceived the sight as pleasing as any that I have ever enjoyed. They always
reminded me of the Muscovy duck, of which they look as if a highly finished and
flattering miniature. They frequently prefer walking on an inclined log or the fallen
trunk of a tree, one end of which lies in the water, while the other rests on the steep
bank, to betaking themselves to flight at the sight of an approaching enemy. In this
manner I have seen a whole flock walk from the water into the woods, as a steamer
was approaching them in the eddies of the Ohio or Mississippi. They swim and
dive well, when wounded and closely pursued, often stopping at the edge of the
water with nothing above it but the bill, but at other times running to a considerable
distance into the woods, or hiding in a canebrake beside a log. In such places I
have often found them, having been led to their place of concealment by my dog.
When frightened, they rise by a single spring from the water, and are as apt to make
directly for the woods as to follow the stream. When they discover an enemy while
under the covert of shrubs or other plants on a pond, instead of taking to wing, they
swim off in silence among the thickest weeds, so as generally to elude your search
by landing and running over a narrow piece of ground to another pond. In autumn,
a whole covey may often be seen standing or sitting on a floating log, pluming and
cleaning themselves for hours. On such occasions the knowing sportsman commits
great havoc among them, killing half a dozen or more at a shot.

Mr. P. A. Taverner has contributed the following on the notes of
a captive bird:

Its only notes seem to be little whistles. One of its most peculiar notes is uttered
when it is disturbed and consists of a series of little *chick, chick, chick's* low and hardly
discernible at a distance of 30 feet. Accompanying these little monosyllables is a

low thump that seems to be uttered immediately before the *chick* but seeming to be made by different organs than are used vocally.   It has the peculiar intensity of the sound made by the springing in and out of the bottom of a tin or other can.   It may be made during the utterance of the *chick*, for though quite loud positively it is so illusive that it is hard to tell exactly just when it is made.   It does seem however to be made quite independently of the other sounds, though it is never heard alone.

Another note he gives when he is quiet and usually when quite alone.   I have heard it several times in the dead of night.   It is comparatively loud and consists of a series of from half a dozen to a dozen whistles like *H-o-o-w-c-e-e-t*.   They follow each other rather rapidly and are without accent, the *H-o-o* gliding smoothly into the *w-e-e-e-t* without change in inflection.   The whole having much the timbre of the sound made by drawing the finger nail sharply over and across the grain of heavily shot silk.   Another note is made when he seems to be talking to himself and is something like *Chick a wangh*, the *angh* being rather drawn out, and the first syllable short. It is not loud either, in fact none of the notes it makes seem fitted for any more than the most private conversation.   The only other note that I have heard it utter is a little short *cheep, cheep*.

Mr. Elon H. Eaton (1910) describes the note as follows:

The call of the drake is a mellow *peet, peet*, but when frightened it utters a harsher note which is usually written *hoo eek, hoo eek*.   The note of the duck, when startled, is a sharp *cr-r-e-ek, cr-r-e-ek, cr-r-e-ek*, somewhat like the drake's alarm note.

The intimacy of the wood duck with the hooded merganser on its breeding grounds has been already referred to above, as well as under the latter species.   It also associates with the hooded merganser somewhat at other seasons, as similar haunts are congenial to both species.   On migrations it usually flocks by itself and is not much given to frequenting the open resorts of other ducks.   It is more essentially a bird of the wooded bottoms, narrow sluggish streams, heavily timbered reservoirs, and forest swamps.

Young wood ducks have many natural enemies to contend with, such as large pickerel, pike, and snapping turtles, which attack them from below and drag them under water to drown them.   I quote again from Audubon's (1840) matchless biography of this species:

Their sense of hearing is exceedingly acute, and by means of it they often save themselves from their wily enemies the mink, the polecat, and the raccoon.   The vile snake that creeps into their nest and destroys their eggs, is their most pernicious enemy on land.   The young, when on the water, have to guard against the snapping turtle, the garfish, and the eel and, in the Southern Districts, against the lashing tail and the tremendous jaws of the alligator.

The wood duck has always been able to hold its own against its natural enemies, but it has yielded to the causes of destruction brought about by the hand of man and by the encroachments of civilization. The wholesale cutting down of forests and draining of swampy woodlands has destroyed its nesting sites and made its favorite haunts untenable.   Its beautiful plumage has always made it an attractive mark for gunners, collectors, and taxidermists, and its feathers have been in demand for making artificial trout flies.   Almost anyone who has found a wood duck's nest has been tempted to take the eggs home to hatch them, as these ducks are easily domesticated and make attractive pets. It is so tame and unsuspicious that it is easily shot in large numbers and it has been extensively caught in traps. From the great abundance, noted by all the earlier writers, its numbers have been reduced to a small fraction of what they were; in many places, where it was once abundant, it is now unknown or very rare; and it has everywhere been verging towards extinction. Fortunately our attention was called to these facts by Dr. A. K. Fisher (1901) and Mr. William Dutcher (1907) before it was too late, and now that suitable laws have been enacted for its protection in many States, it has been saved from extinction and is even on the increase in some places.

Fall.—The fall migration starts early. Doctor Yorke (1899) says of it:

The first fall issue consists of local ducks, which migrate during the early part of the month of September. The second comes down from the Northern States about the end of September, while the last comes down in the early part of October. The second and third do not stay nearly so long as the first issue, which is the largest and collects in quantities on favorite grounds. The second and third collect in a different manner; they drop into willows, buck brush and on rivers and timber-clad ponds, in singles, pairs, or little flocks, about nightfall, and depart before morning; these places are used by them nightly during their migrations, until all have gone south, and appear to be regular stopping places. The ducks of the third issue are full fledged upon their arrival.

Game.—As a game bird the wood duck has always been popular, as it is a clean feeder, often very fat, and a delicious table bird. It will come readily to live decoys or even to well-made wooden decoys, if properly handled; it is such a swift flier and so clever in avoiding places that it has found to be dangerous that considerable skill and strategy is necessary to hunt it successfully. One of the best methods of hunting it is to lie in wait for it, properly concealed, on one of its fly ways between its feeding grounds and its roosting places, but to succeed in this the hunter must make a thorough study of its movements and learn all he can about the nature of the country in which it lives. Wood ducks usually roost for the night in small open pools in the woods, where they are sheltered and secure. About an hour before sunrise, or as soon as it begins to be light, they leave these pools and fly to their feeding grounds in the wild rice marshes, in sluggish streams and ponds filled with aquatic vegetation or along the wooded banks where they can pick up seeds, nuts, and acorns. If necessary, they will rise and fly over the tops of the forest trees, but they prefer to fly along the open lanes, streams or passageways which are usually found connecting the ponds in the regions they frequent. Here they fly low in regular flight lines and if the gunner places his blind in some narrow passageway between the trees in such a fly way, he is practically sure of good sport for about three hours in the morning and again for an hour or two on the return flight at sunset.

Mr. Dwight W. Huntington (1903) describes another method of hunting them:

At English Lake I shot them from a light boat, jumping them in the wild rice. The punter pushed the boat (which contained a revolving office chair for the gunner) rapidly. The birds often arose at short range and presented easy marks. They were very abundant on the Kankakee at certain bends in the river, where they fed on acorns which dropped from the oaks into the water. A friend one day killed over 70 of these birds over decoys, and I often made fairly good scores shooting from a blind, but my fondness for moving about and exploring the marshes and ponds for other ducks and a change of scene always prevented my making very large bags.

Winter.—Long before the autumn frosts have begun to close the northern ponds the tender "summer duck" has moved southward toward its winter home in the rice fields of the Southern States, the wooded sloughs and timbered ponds of Louisiana, and the cypress swamps of Florida, mingling with the summer birds of these congenial climes. A few hardier individuals winter farther north, where they can find sheltered ponds and streams with an abundant food supply. They do not, like many other ducks, frequent the seacoast in winter; if found near the coast at all, they are in the fresh-water ponds and streams, protected from the winter winds.

DISTRIBUTION.

Breeding range.—United States and southern Canada, entirely across the continent. Breeds locally in almost every State and southern Province, where suitable conditions exist. South to Cuba, the Gulf of Mexico, south central Texas (San Antonio), probably Colorado, Utah, and Nevada, and in southern California (Ventura County). North to southern British Columbia (lower Fraser Valley and Okanogan Lake), northwestern Montana (Flathead Lake), rarely Great Slave Lake (Fort Providence), southern Manitoba (Lake Winnipeg), southeastern Ontario (Parry Sound and Muskoka districts) and central eastern Labrador (Hamilton Inlet).

Winter range.—Mainly in southern United States. South to Jamaica (rarely) and central Mexico (valley of Mexico and Mazatlan). North to southern British Columbia (Chilliwack), central Missouri (Missouri River) southern Illinois (Mount Carmel), and southern Virginia (Petersburg). Winters casually north to Michigan (Kalamazoo County), and Massachusetts.

Spring migration.—Early dates of arrival: New York, central, March 16; Ohio, northern, March 10; Ontario, Ottawa, March 26; Iowa, central, March 7; Minnesota, Heron Lake, March 24; Manitoba, southern, April 2. Average dates of arrival: New York, central,

March 25; Massachusetts, eastern, March 24; Quebec, Montreal, April 24; Iowa, central, March 20; Ohio, northern, April 1; Michigan, Petersburg, March 15; Ontario, southern, April 17, and Ottawa, April 22: Minnesota, Heron Lake, April 4; Manitoba, southern, April 15.

Fall migration.—Average dates of departure: Ontario, Ottawa, October 27; Quebec, Montreal, November 1; Maine, southern, October 27; Massachusetts, Essex County, December 16; Iowa, southern, November 9. Late dates of departure: Ontario, Ottawa, November 7; Maine, southern, November 2; Massachusetts, Charles River, December 28; Iowa, southern, November 21; Ohio, Loraine Reservoir, December 3.

Casual records.—Accidental in Bermuda (December 16, 1846).

Egg dates.—New England and New York: Eighteen records, May 4 to June 17; nine records, May 13 to 22. New Jersey: Four records, April 17 to May 16. Florida: Four records, April 8 to May 14. Illinois and Iowa: Seven records, April 17 to June 4. Minnesota, Michigan and Wisconsin: Seven records, May 10 to 30.

NETTA RUFINA (Pallas).

RUFOUS-CRESTED DUCK.

HABITS.

This beautiful European duck has but a slight claim to a place on our list. About all we know of it, as an American bird, is contained in the following statement by Mr. Robert Ridgway (1881):

About nine years since (February 2, 1872), Mr. George A. Boardman, of Calais, Maine, sent to the Smithsonian Institution a mounted specimen of a duck obtained in Fulton Market, New York City, and supposed to have been shot on Long Island Sound, which he was unable to determine satisfactorily, but which he supposed to be a hybrid between the redhead (*Aethyia americana*) and some other species. The specimen was in immature plumage, with the feathers of the first livery much worn, while those of the new molt, which were generally interspersed, indicated a very different garb when the molt should have been completed. At the time the specimen was received at the Smithsonian, I (also supposing it to be a hybrid) made comparisons with nearly, if not quite, all the American species of ducks, but was unable to get the slightest clue to its parentage. It was then put back in the case and not again thought of until a few days ago, when in removing the specimens with a view to their rearrangement I happened to take the one in question in one hand and an adult female of the European rufous-crested duck (*Fuligula rufina*) in the other; and having the two thus in a very favorable position for comparison, I at once perceived a striking similarity in general appearance and in the form of the bill, which induced me to extend the examination to an adult male, the result being that no question remained of the bird in question being an immature male of *F. rufina*, a species hitherto not detected in North America.

Yarrell (1871) observes that "it may be doubted if the presence of this solitary individual in the United States was due to natural causes"; it seems likely that the specimen may have come over in some shipment of foreign game or may have escaped from some private preserve.

As the bird is entirely unknown in this country I shall have to cull its life history from the writings of European authors. Mr. John G. Millais (1913) writes:

Essentially a southern species, the red-crested pochard comes north to Germany or to England in October and November before the frost and snow and leaves for the south on the first signs of Arctic conditions, whilst a few come north in March and April and wander about in small parties before seeking their breeding places in May. In Europe they do not appear to be very gregarious, as they are in India, where they arrive in flocks of thousands in late October and November. Hume mentions finding them in "flocks of many thousands and acres of water paved with them," whilst Reid says: "One morning in December I came across countless numbers in a jheel in the Fyzabad district, closely packed and covering the whole surface of the water, with their red heads moving independently, while the breeze kept their crests in motion; a distant spectator might have mistaken them for a vast expanse of beautiful aquatic flowers."

The red-crested pochard is essentially a duck of the fresh water and is never found upon the open sea. The ponds and lakes they like to frequent are reedy, sedge-lined sheets of water with a considerable area of deep water in the centre.

Courtship.—The red-crested pochards arrive at their breeding places at the end of March or early in April, but the females do not begin making their nests till the end of the latter month. The courtship of the male is somewhat showy but not very varied. It throws up the body from the water, depressing the bill to the fore part of the neck, and at the same time displaying, i. e., erecting and spreading the whole of the beautiful feathers of the crest, the body raised to about an angle of 75°. During this sudden act of show the bird utters a low squeaking whistle, and as the body falls to the water again the crest resumes its normal position, and, releasing the air in the chest, it utters a low grunt or groan. Sometimes when in full show the male will frequently swim round the female with depressed bill and expanded crest, but beyond this I have seen no other efforts at display. The female resorts to attitudes similar to the other diving species, such as swimming round the male with lowered body and extended head and neck held out along the water. She also frequently utters her harsh guttural cry at this season.

Nesting.—Dr. Baldmus, who took 10 nests in 1866–1870 in central Germany, states that—"The nest is always placed in the rushes or flags, usually on a small island in a pond or on the flags, and, like all ducks' nests, it has a foundation of rotten stems of rushes and dead leaves, on which a warm bed of down is placed, this down being plucked from the breast of the female. When the female leaves the nest quietly, she covers her eggs, as do all the ducks, even our common tame species. During the time the female is sitting the males are to be seen on the water with those of *ferina*, *leucopthalmus*, and *clypeata*, but generally somewhat apart from them."

Mr. W. Eagle Clarke (1895) describes a nest of this species, which he found on an island in a shallow *etang* in the southwestern Camarque, as—

placed in the center of a thick tangled mass of purslane (*Atriplex portulacoides*) so dense that it was reached by a covered way, 2 feet in length, worked in the shrub where it rested on the soil; the nest was on the ground and consisted of a broad rim of down, with a few short dry tamarisk twigs, and contained 10 fresh eggs. A few yards farther on another duck of this species was disturbed—this time from under an immense shrub of seablite, quite 4 feet in height and as many in diameter. The nest in all respects resembled the last, and contained 17 eggs of two distinct types, and probably the production of different females. The eggs of one set were white and were all singularly malformed. The normal eggs are of clear pea green and a trifle smaller than those of the pochard. The down in the nest closely resembles that of the eider duck in tint. Both nests were about 6 yards from the water, and the birds wriggled off at our feet.

Eggs.—Mr. Millais (1913) says that the usual number of eggs is from 7 to 10, but that 14, in one case 17, eggs have been found in a nest. The—

eggs are decidedly lighter and more thin shelled than those of the common pochard. When fresh, the eggs are a clear green stone-color with a gloss, but lose their bright tints and gloss after being blown, then becoming a dull grayish olive or greenish gray. The texture is smooth, fine, and clear, but somewhat fragile for a duck's egg. In form they are a broad oval with both ends the same size.

Rev. F. C. R. Jourdain furnishes the measurements of 74 eggs, which average 58.1 by 41.8 millimeters; the eggs showing the four extremes measure 61 by 42, 56.5 by 43.5, and 53.5 by 39.6 millimeters.

Plumages.—Mr. Millais (1913) describes the downy young as:

Upper parts, dull olive gray; under parts, buff or yellowish gray; a buff spot on either shoulder; a yellowish-gray stripe passes over each eye, and in front of and behind the eye runs a dark stripe which divides behind the eye; irides, dark brown; bill reddish brown, with the nail white; feet, ash-gray with a green tinge; webs and toes narrowly edged with yellowish white.

Of the young male he says:

Somewhat similar to the female, only darker and with an indication of a crest. The center of the feathers of the under parts are brown instead of gray, and the back and front of the breast is a much darker brown. The young male and female are easily recognized by the usual immature feathers on the lower breast, vent, and tail coverts, and frayed tail. The principal molt commences in November with a few black feathers on the lower parts and scapulars, and proceeds rapidly in February and March.

By April the young male has gained the whole of the adult plumage, although it is not nearly so rich or bright as that of a 2-year-old male. By the beginning of May the only sign of immaturity is a dark brown line as broad as a pencil on the upper surface of the bill, but this mark disappears as soon as the young male molts into full eclipse dress at the end of May, when the bird may be said to be adult at 10 months. Young males bred by Mr. St. Quintin in June, 1910, were just losing the last sign of immaturity on May 1, 1911, when I visited Scampston. The irides are brown or reddish brown, becoming red in March; the feet and legs, at first olivaceous orange, also become orange red in spring.

According to his colored plate, the male has a well-marked eclipse plumage, of which he writes:

If we do not accept the summer plumage of the long-tailed duck as an eclipse dress for reasons to be explained later, the red-crested pochard and the gadwall are the earliest species to change from spring into the eclipse dress. A male in my possession began to dress the first brownish-gray feathers on the flank as early as May 10 and another in the Scampston collection was in full molt on May 20. The eclipse dress of the male is very like the plumage of the female, but they may be at once distinguished by the wings, and the brighter color of the eye, eyelids, bill, and feet, and by the darker color of the under parts. The crest also is much longer and more pronounced.

Food.—Regarding the food of the rufous-crested duck, he quotes Naumann, as follows:

These ducks like to feed on tender roots, buds, shoots, the tips of leaves, flowers, and seeds of various kinds of plants growing rampant at the bottom of the water—thus on any kinds of *Potamogeton* of *Myriophyllum*, and *Ceratophyllum*. As the last named grow in a considerable depth of water, shooting up high toward the surface, and often form thick green plantations under the water, such places in the pool are the favorite haunt of these ducks. They are continually diving down in search of such undergrowth, and occasionally, in addition to the vegetable food, they catch the living creatures to be found on them. In places where this undergrowth approaches nearer to the surface, they attempt to get at it by merely tipping up the hinder part of the body and reaching for it by stretching the neck down vertically. They also fish for much which they enjoy when merely swimming on the surface, but they employ the last two methods less often than that of diving under completely for their food. For this reason they like deep water, and come extremely seldom to the bank for the sake of getting food. Along with the above-mentioned substances their stomachs always contain a quantity of sand and small pebbles the size of peas.

Behavior.—The same writer says:

The red-crested pochard frequently comes ashore on lakes where they are seldom disturbed; but if much harassed, they keep to the deep water the whole day. On land they stand and walk in a manner quite different from other diving ducks, and seem to be able to walk and run with less roll and greater ease than other species. At such times the neck is very much drawn up, with the bill depressed, and when moving fast it takes the form of the letter S, whilst the body is held more or less horizontal. If they approach anything suspicious or are suddenly frightened, the body is suddenly held up. They seldom leave the banks of a lake except during the nesting season. In swimming, or when about to dive for food, the body is held low in the water, the tail trailing on the surface, the neck is stiff and almost upright, and the bill held depressed. The bird at such times has an air of intent alertness, as if minutely searching the depths below. Although skillful divers, they do not stay below the surface as long as other species, 30 seconds being a long dive. Unlike other diving ducks they show a distinct preference for shallows at certain seasons, and especially in places where they are undisturbed. Here they may be seen paddling for hours round the edge of a lake, frequently tipping up the hinder parts after the fashion of mallard or pintail, and reaching for delicacies with their long necks. Their flight is similar to other diving species, and it is accompanied by a faint whistling sound, and is strong and well sustained. They have some difficulty in rising if there is no wind.

Mr. Millais (1913) says further:

The usual call generally uttered by the female is a harsh *kurr*, and it is not often emitted except in moments of excitement. Hume says the male utters a "sharp sibilant note—a sort of whistle," but does not state at what season he has heard it. This note is commonly uttered by the male in courtship, but I have never heard it at other times.

Game.—Those who have had experience in studying these ducks are of opinion that they are shy and difficult to approach when in large flocks, but as easily killed as other diving ducks when found on small pieces of water. Mr. Stuart Baker, who has had many opportunities of studying the species, says:

"From a sporting point of view, the red-crested pochard is all that can be desired. About as smart as they make them, he seems to have special aptitude for judging the length of range of different guns; and a flock may be caught once but seldom twice, whatever the distance the gun may reach. They swim so fast that they can by this means generally escape, and they are often very loath to rise when they can thus get out of shot."

As a table bird the red-crested pochard resembles the common pochard and the widgeon in its flesh. That is to say, when it feeds on fish and shellfish it is rank and uneatable, and when it eats vegetable matter it is excellent. "On account of their great timidity," says Naumann, "you can only creep up to them to shoot them unseen and against the wind, if they are swimming near enough to the bank; but as they almost always choose the open center of larger pieces of water as their places of sojourn, there is in this case no other method than to approach them openly in a boat, which can certainly only succeed with solitary specimens if they have not yet suffered any pursuit at that place, and then not always, whilst larger flocks generally take to flight when within a hundred paces of you. Occasionally when flying round afterwards they get near enough to the boat for a lucky shot. In the morning and evening twilight they are sometimes by chance brought down when flying over. It is easy to creep up to solitary specimens which have wandered off to a small pond if some care is exercised, but they can seldom endure to be shot at by a gun approaching them openly. Birds which have been lamed by a shot are generally lost to the pursuer on larger pieces of water, even with the help of a good water dog, as they do not easily tire of diving under, and, if they can reach some sedge, are very clever at hiding themselves in it, and in so doing only keep the head as far as the eye above the surface of the water. They can easily be caught in large decoy nets placed at their favorite places in the water."

DISTRIBUTION.

Breeding range.—Portions of Europe, Asia, and Africa. From southern Germany and Spain eastward through southern Russia to northern Persia and eastern Turkestan, and southward into northern Africa.

Winter range.—The basins of the Mediterranean, Black, and Caspian Seas, the Persian Gulf, India, Burma, and Ceylon.

Casual records.—Wanders to the British Isles, France, Belgium, Holland, Denmark, Germany, and China. One record for North America (Fulton Market, New York, 1872).

Egg dates.—Southern Russia: Eight records, April 26 to June 12.

NYROCA AMERICANA (Eyton).

REDHEAD.

HABITS.

The redhead or American pochard ranks as one of our most important game birds, for it is well known and widely distributed; from its main breeding grounds in central Canada and the northern Central States it spreads out its migrations to both coasts and appears, at some season of the year, in nearly every State.

Spring.—Dr. F. Henry Yorke (1899) says of the spring migration:

The first spring flight of this well-known duck passes the frost line whilst the ice still remains upon our lakes, water only existing in open holes or channels; the birds follow closely after the canvasback and like that bird appear in good-sized flocks. They stay but a short time, working rapidly toward the north and going to the far end of the British possessions. The second issue arrives about a week after the first has departed; if abundance of food be present, they stay until the advent of the third issue, then travel north also beyond the boundary line. The third begins to pair upon reaching latitude 44° and spreads all over the country up to Manitoba.

Courtship.—Dr. Alexander Wetmore (1920) gives the following interesting account of the courtship of the redhead:

The peculiar mating display of these birds seen on several occasions was observed to advantage on June 4. A party of four males and three females were swimming in open water, two of the birds apparently being mated. Suddenly one of the females began to display, approaching one of the males with her head held high, sometimes jerking it up and down and again holding it erect, and at intervals calling *quek que-e-ek*, the last a peculiar rattling note. The male chosen extended his neck, holding his head erect, frequently whirling quickly to show the female his back, or again sank down with his head drawn in while the female bowed before him. At short intervals she opened her mouth and bit at him gently or, if he was swimming, sprang quickly in front of him with her head erect and back partly submerged. She transferred her attentions from one male to another in turn, even approaching the one who apparently was mated. The males showed considerable jealousy over these favors and drove each other about in fierce rushes. At intervals they called, the note being a curious drawn-out groaning call, resembling the syllables *whee ough* given in a high tone. As it was given the male sometimes raised his breast, elevated his head, and erected his crest. Again he threw his head straight back so that it touched his dorsum above the rump, with the throat up and the bill pointing toward the tail. The bill was then thrown up and head brought again to the erect position as the call was made. The curious actions of the male in calling continued after he was mated, and the strange call note was heard often. Mated males were seen driving savagely at their mates and biting at them while they escaped by diving.

Nesting.—My first experience with the nesting habits of the redhead was gained in North Dakota in 1901 where we found it breeding abundantly in all of the larger sloughs where there was plenty of deep open water in the center, surrounded by extensive areas of cat-tail flags (*Typha latifolia*), bullrushes (*Scirpus lacustris*), and tall reeds (*Phragmites communis*); its nest was most often found among the flags or bullrushes, growing in water a foot or more deep, and least often among the *Phragmites* which usually grew in shallower or drier places. I quote from my own published notes (1902) as follows:

We first met with it on June 3 in a large slough in Nelson County, where the water was not over knee-deep, except in a few scattered open spaces, and where the reeds and flags were somewhat scattered and open. A pair of Canada geese nested in this slough and two pairs of marsh hawks, but it was chiefly tenanted by yellow-headed blackbirds, coots, and long-billed marsh wrens. The blackbirds fairly swarmed in this slough, and the constant din of their voices was almost bewildering, especially whenever one of the marsh hawks sailed over the slough, which sent them all up into the air at once, cackling and squeaking, hovering and circling about for a few moments, and then settling down into the reeds again. Redheads were flying back and forth across the slough, killdeers, willets, and Wilson phalaropes were flying about the shores, and long-billed marsh wrens were singing among the flags on all sides. While wading along a shallow ditch through a small patch of last year's flags, a big brown duck sprang into the air from a clump of tall reeds, and, after a short search, I found my first nest of the redhead, well concealed among the reeds. It was a handsome nest, well made of dead reeds, deeply hollowed and lined with broken pieces of the reeds mingled with considerable white down, especially around the upper rim; it measured 16 inches in diameter outside and 8 inches inside, the upper part of the rim being about 10 inches above the water; it rested on a bulky mass of dead reeds built up out of the shallow water, the whole structure being firmly held in place by the live growing reeds about it. It held 11 handsome eggs, in which incubation had just begun. I could not photograph this nest, as it was raining hard, but I collected the nest and eggs, which are now in my cabinet.

We found the redheads breeding in two large, deep sloughs in Steele County. One of these, in which we found four nests of the redhead, is illustrated in the photograph. In the open part of this slough, shown in the foreground, the water was too deep to wade, but, in the southern end of the slough, shown in the background, the water was seldom deeper than the tops of our hip boots, and in many places quite shallow. The principal growth was the tall slough reeds, quite thick in some places, and often as high as our heads, with numerous thick patches of tall cat-tail flags and several patches of the "queen of the prairie" reeds growing in the drier portions. The redheads' nests were all located in the shallower parts of the slough where the reeds and flags were growing less thickly.

The redheads' nests found here on June 10 contained 6, 10, 14, and 16 eggs, respectively, none of which were collected. The latter of these is shown in the photograph, it was located in the center of a tangled mass of broken-down dead flags, in a nearly dry, open space, near the edge of the slough, well concealed from view by the arching over of the dead flags above it. The bird proved to be a close sitter, as we twice flushed her from the nest. We tested one of the eggs and found it far advanced in incubation.

Mr. J. H. Bowles (1909) gives the following attractive account of the nesting habits of the redhead in Washington:

They are essentially lovers of shoal bodies of fresh water, and in summer resort in considerable numbers to the larger lakes of central Washington for the purpose of rearing their young. One of their favorite breeding grounds may be found at Moses Lake, a beautiful body of water situated in the north central part of the State. At this place, in the summer of 1906, it is certain that at least 150 pairs remained to nest. Paddling our canoe along the margin of the lake, close to its heavy fringe of cat-tails, we would flush a pair or two at intervals of every hundred feet. As is customary with all waterfowl during the nesting season, they were remarkably tame, allowing such a close approach as to give an excellent view of the handsome nuptial plumage of the male.

Leaving the canoe and plunging at random into the sea of rushes, fortune may favor us sufficiently to permit of our happening upon one of their nests. This is a heavy, deep basket of rushes placed in the thickest of the growth, either upon a small muddy island left by the receding water, or built up amongst the flags upon the matted dead stems which cover the surface of the lake in these places. It is a structure of such beauty as to cause the bird student to pause almost breathless upon its discovery.

The mother duck has heard his noisy approach long since and departed, first carefully spreading over the eggs a heavy blanket taken from the lining of the nest. This consists entirely of down of the most delicate shade of white faintly tinged with gray, which the duck plucks from her own breast. A faint glimpse only can be obtained of the 12 or 14 greenish-drab eggs which seem completely to fill the nest, but let the sun be shining brightly with the dense green rushes for a background, and be sure that fatigue, soaked clothing, mosquitoes, and a dozen other discomforts will instantly vanish from remembrance at the sight.

Mr. Robert B. Rockwell (1911) writes of the nesting habits of this species in the Barr Lake region of Colorado:

The redheads' nests, like those of the teal, exhibited a wide variation in structure and location. The first two nests were found June 10, 1906. These, containing five fresh eggs and nine incubated eggs, respectively, were within 2 feet of each other, in burrows in the top of a large muskrat house at the edge of a small lake in a sparse growth of cat-tails. The birds had burrowed in about 18 inches, lined the cavity with down, and deposited the eggs at the end of the cavity. A careful examination of all the muskrat houses seen (and they were so conspicuous that in all probability none was overlooked) during the balance of 1906 and the full nesting seasons of 1907 and 1908, failed to reveal any other similarly located nests of this species.

On May 31, 1907, we found a beautiful set of 11 fresh eggs in a large, bulky nest somewhat resembling an overgrown nest of the coot; but much less compact and not so neatly cupped or lined as the average coot's nest. There was little or no downy lining in the nest which was built in an average growth of cat-tails over about 18 inches of water, and some 20 yards from the open water of the lake. There was no apparent attempt at concealment, and it was very conspicuous owing to its large size. The female flushed widely, with a good deal of noise, when we were fully 40 yards from the nest, thus attracting our attention to it. Eight of these eggs hatched on or about June 20, the remaining three being addled.

The finest nest of this species which came to our attention was found June 15, 1907, in a dense cat-tail swamp between two small rush-encircled lakes. It was a beautifully built structure of dead cat-tail blades, mostly broken into small pieces, well built up above the surface of the water (which at this spot was only a few inches deep), deeply cupped, plentifully lined with down, and well concealed in the dense cat-tail growth.

Eggs.—The redhead incubates on a large set of eggs; my notes record various numbers from 6 to 22, but many of the largest sets contain eggs of other species; probably the redhead itself usually lays from 10 to 15 eggs. The redhead also seems to be careless about laying its eggs in other ducks' nests. In North Dakota we found one of its eggs in a ruddy duck's nest and in three cases we found three to four of its eggs in the nests of the canvasback, on which the latter duck was incubating. These two species seem to have a peculiar habit of building nests in which large numbers of eggs are laid, by both species, but are apparently not incubated; we found two such nests in Saskatchewan, one of which contained 19 eggs; this set is now in my collection and apparently contains eggs of the redhead, canvasback, and mallard; it was evidently a canvasback's nest originally. Messrs. Willett and Jay (1911) mention a nest found at San Jacinto Lake, California, which contained 27 eggs and which "was undoubtedly the product of at least two females, as there were 17 eggs of one type and 10 of another. In fact the 10 eggs may not be redheads' at all, as they resemble very much the eggs of the pintail."

The eggs of the redhead can generally be distinguished from those of other species by their color, size, and texture, but I have seen eggs that were puzzling; the nest, however, is always distinctive; it is built like that of the canvasback, but the down in it, which is usually mixed with the reeds or flags, is *whiter* than that of the canvasback. Although the down is practically white, certain portions of it have a slight grayish tinge. The down in the nests of this and all other species of diving ducks is more closely matted or in less well-defined, fluffy pieces than the down in the nests of the surface feeding ducks.

The shell of the egg is extremely hard and tough, with a smooth, glossy surface; it will dull the cutting edges of an egg drill in a short time. The color varies from "pale olive buff," matching almost exactly certain types of mallard's eggs, to a pale "cream buff" or "cartridge buff." The eggs are larger than mallard's eggs and more glossy and they are very different in color from canvasback's eggs. Taking into account the nest, the down, and the size, color, and texture of the eggs, there should never be any difficulty in recognizing a redhead's nest, even if the bird were not clearly seen. In shape the eggs vary from a somewhat rounded to a considerably elongated elliptical ovate; they are sometimes nearly oval. The measurements of 79 eggs in various collections average 61.2 by 43.4 millimeters; the eggs showing the four extremes measure **66.8** by 43.5, 66.2 by **45.5, 58** by 41.8 and 61.5 by **41.2** millimeters. Incubation is performed by the female alone and lasts for a period of 22, 23, or 24 days.

Plumages.—The downy young is quite different from other ducklings, being more uniformly colored with less contrast between the light and dark areas. The upper parts, including the crown, back, rump, and tail are "light brownish olive," but the deep color of the basal portion of the down is much concealed by the light yellowish tips; the side of the head and neck, including the forehead and a broad stripe above the eye, are "olive-ocher" paling to "colonial buff" on the throat and chin; the remainder of the under parts is "colonial buff" with deeper shadings; there are shadings of "chamois" on the sides of the head and neck, but no conspicuous dark markings; in some specimens there are suffusions of brighter yellow in all of the lighter-colored parts, such as "amber yellow" or "citron yellow"; there is a yellowish spot on each of the scapulars and on each side of the rump. All of the colors become paler and duller as the duckling increases in size.

The plumage develops in the young redhead in the same sequence as in the young canvasback and when 7 or 8 weeks old it is fully feathered, except the wings, and is a little more than half grown.

The scapulars and back are dark gray, edged with brownish, the breast reddish brown, the belly mottled with brown and white, and the head is reddish brown. This is the juvenal plumage in which the sexes are alike and somewhat resemble the adult female; young birds, however, are more mottled, with less clear brown above and less clear white below. The contour feathers are fully acquired and the young bird is nearly fully grown before the wings are fairly started. Young males are generally browner and darker than young females, particularly on the breast and head. By November the black feathers begin to appear on the breast and neck of the young male, each black feather being tipped with brown, which wears off later; in December the red feathers appear in the head and neck, and the gray vermiculated feathers in the back, scapulars, and flanks are assumed; and by January, or February at the latest, the plumage is practically adult, though the full perfection of the adult plumage is not acquired for at least another year. The progress toward maturity in the young female is practically the same, though the change is not so conspicuous. Probably young birds breed during their first spring.

The adult male has a partial eclipse plumage, involving a double molt of much of its plumage; the molt into this plumage begins early in August, the flight feathers are shed about the middle or last of August, and the full winter plumage is complete again in October or November. In the eclipse plumage the head and neck become browner, the breast and under parts become mottled, as in the breeding female; there are many brown feathers in the back, the rump is largely brownish, and the crissum is veiled with light edgings. The adult female assumes during the nesting season and the summer a more mottled plumage than is worn in the winter; the clear dark brown of the upper parts is veiled with lighter edgings, and the clear white of the under parts is mottled with brownish.

Food.—The favorite feeding grounds of the redhead during the summer are in the open lakes of the interior where it dives in deep water or in shallower places to obtain the roots and bulbs of aquatic plants or almost any green shoots which it can find; it is not at all particular about its food and is a gluttonous feeder. It also dabbles with the surface-feeding ducks in the muddy shallows where it finds insects, frogs, tadpoles, and even small fishes and water lizards. Audubon (1840) says that "on several occasions" he has "found pretty large acorns and beechnuts in their throats, as well as snails, entire or broken, and fragments of the shells of various small unios, together with much gravel."

Dr. D. G. Elliot (1898) writes:

Redheads feed much at night, especially if the moon is shining, and at such times are exceedingly busy, and the splashing of diving birds the coming and going of others, and the incessant utterings of their hoarse note, are heard from dark to daylight. They also feed by day, if the weather has been stormy, but on quiet, pleasant days they rarely move about much, but remain quietly out in the open water, sleeping, or dressing their feathers, or occasionally taking a turn beneath the surface as though more in an exploring mood, than for the purpose of seeking food.

Among the vegetable food of the redhead, Dr. F. Henry Yorke (1899) has recognized in its food the following genera of plants: *Vallisneria*, *Limnobium*, *Zizania*, *Iris*, *Nymphaea*, *Nuphar*, *Myriophyllum*, *Callitriche*, and *Utricularia*.

In its winter home on or near the seacoast it frequents the tidal estuaries, as well as the ponds, and feeds in company with the canvasback, the scaup ducks, and the baldpate, diving in deep water for the roots, as well as the stems and buds of the wild celery (*Vallisneria*), on which it becomes very fat and its flesh assumes a flavor almost indistinguishable from that of the canvasback. But it does not wholly confine itself to this food, feeding largely on other aquatic plants and on marine animal life, which detracts from the flavor of its flesh.

Behavior.—Prof. Walter B. Barrows (1912) says of the flight of the redhead:

It travels in V-shaped flocks like geese, and flies with great rapidity, but the common statement that its speed reaches 100 miles per hour is certainly a gross exaggeration. It is safe to say that no species of duck when migrating flies more than 50 or 60 miles per hour—most species hardly more than 40 miles.

Doctor Elliot (1898) writes:

The flocks rarely alight at first, even when there may be numbers of ducks congregated on the water, but traverse the length of the sound or lake as if reconnoitering the entire expanse and trying to select the best feeding ground. After having passed and repassed over the route a few times, the flock begins to lower, and gradually descending, at length the wings are set and the birds sail gradually up to the chosen spot, usually where other ducks are feeding, and drop in their midst with many splashings. But while this is the usual method adopted by newcomers, sometimes the program is changed and the birds, attracted by a large concourse of their relatives, particularly if the day be calm and the sun shining with considerable heat, will suddenly drop from out the sky with a rapid zigzag course, as if one wing of each duck had been broken, and they cross and recross each other in the rapid descent, their fall accompanied by a loud whirring sound, as the air is forced between the primaries. On such occasions the flock is mixed all up together in a most bewildering manner, until, arriving a few feet above the water, the wings become motionless and the birds glide up to and alight by the side of their desired companions.

Early in the morning, and again late in the afternoon, the redhead regularly takes a "constitutional." The flocks that have been massed together during the night or the middle of the day, rise from the water, not all together but in companies of several dozen, and stringing themselves out in long, irregular lines, each bird a little behind and to one side of its leader, fly rapidly up and down, at a considerable height over the water. Sometimes these morning and evening promenades are performed at a great elevation, so that the movement of the wings is hardly perceptible. On such occasions they appear like a dark ribbon against the sky, and the comparison is strengthened by the fact that every movement of the leader elevat-

ing or depressing his course is imitated exactly by all those which follow, and so the
line has frequent wavy motions like currents passing through it, as when a ribbon is
held in the fingers and a flip given to it which causes it to undulate along its whole
length.

Doctor Elliot (1898) has well described the note of this species as a
"hoarse guttural rolling sound, as if the letter R was uttered in
the throat with a vibration of the tongue at the same time. It is
easily imitated, and the bird readily responds to the call of its
supposed relative." Rev. J. H. Langille (1884) gives an entirely
different impression of it; he writes:

Not infrequently the males are quite noisy, loudly uttering their deep-toned *me-ow*,
which is the precise imitation of the voice of a large cat. The female, especially if
rising from her nest or out of the water, has a loud, clear *squak*, on a higher tone than
that of the mallard or dusky duck, and so peculiar as to be readily identified by the
ear, even if the bird is not in sight.

Doctor Yorke (1899) confirms this impression, saying: "The
redheads' cry whilst floating about in compact bunches resembles the
mewing or cry of a cat, but their call is a very modest quack."

Fall.—The fall migration of the redhead follows soon after that
of the canvasback and spreads out over much the same route; from
its main breeding grounds in the central part of the continent, the
prairie regions of southern Canada, and the Northern States, it migrates almost east, through the region of the Great Lakes to the coasts
of southern New England, southeast to the Chesapeake Bay region,
and south through the Mississippi Valley to the Gulf coast; there is
also probably a southwestward migration to the Pacific coast and a
southward one to Mexico. Redheads migrate in large flocks by
themselves or late in the season they often mingle with scaup ducks.
They become very abundant in the fall along the southern coast of
New England, especially in the large fresh or brackish ponds on
Marthas Vineyard, where several thousand of them are reported as
congregating every fall; some of the ponds, which are controlled by
sportsmen, are planted with *Vallisneria, Potamogeton,* and other duck
foods which have attracted an increased number of redheads and
scaup ducks. A party of four men are said to have killed 110 of
these two species in five hours' shooting.

Game.—Redheads are abundant on the Chesapeake, where they
are shot in large numbers with the canvasbacks from the batteries;
when feeding on wild celery their flesh is of fine flavor. They are
very popular as game birds on the lakes and sloughs of the Mississippi
Valley; they travel about in large flocks and are easily decoyed to
wooden decoys set near the hunter's well-concealed blind or sink box.
A net set on poles around the gunner's boat or duck float may be
rendered quite inconspicuous by weaving branches or grass into it so
that it will match its surroundings; the ducks do not seem to notice

it and very good shooting may be had from such a blind. Doctor Yorke (1899) writes:

Their playgrounds are in open waters upon large lakes, or some distance from the shore on the coasts, where they float about in rafts or flocks. They are easily lured to shore by tolling, either by a red handkerchief raised and lowered, or by some odd moving object, for they are most inquisitive birds; sometimes a dog is trained to run along the shore and bark at the water's edge, the gunner lying concealed close by; even after being shot at, they soon seem to forget the occurrence and gradually work in again to the object which had previously attracted them. Should, however, a few baldpates be mixed up with them, these soon spoil the game; being more suspicious, the baldpates will keep turning and swimming back without approaching within shot, drawing the redheads with them. Even upon a flight, the baldpates lead many flocks of redheads away out of shot by their shying away from any object which they distrust and which the redheads would have unhesitatingly approached.

Winter.—The redhead winters as far north as it can find open water; Mr. Thomas McIlwraith (1894) states that for—

two seasons a flock of 100 or 150 remained in Lake Ontario all winter, about half a mile from shore, opposite the village of Burlington. The birds spent most of their time at one particular place, sometimes diving, sometimes sitting at rest on the water, and always close together, as if for greater warmth. When the weather moderated in March they shifted about for a few days, and then went off to the northwest, the direction taken by most waterfowl when leaving this part of Ontario in the spring

Occasionally they linger too long in freezing lakes and some of them perish, but they are usually more hardy and better able to take care of themselves than the canvasbacks. Even in its winter haunts on the seacoasts the redhead prefers to feed in fresh-water ponds, associating with baldpates, scaup ducks, mallards, and shovellers; it also frequents brackish ponds and salt-water estuaries in company with the canvasbacks. It must venture out onto the ocean at times, for it is known to winter in the Bahamas, occurring there in large flocks.

On the coasts of Virginia and North Carolina the redhead is abundant in winter. I saw many large flocks in Back Bay and Currituck Sound, usually flying high in the air. The practiced eye of the experienced gunner can recognize them at a distance by their flight; they seem, to me, to move their wings more rapidly than canvasbacks; they look darker and shorter; and they fly in more irregular formations and more erratically. On pleasant smooth days, especially if they have been shot at in the morning, they may be seen flying out to sea in large flocks to spend the day in safety; they return again toward night to the fresh-water bays to feed on the roots of foxtail grass and wild celery.

Mr. J. A. Munro (1917) says that the redhead is "the commonest duck on Okanogan Lake," British Columbia—

in winter. Late in January, when their feeding grounds at the south end of the lake become frozen, they congregate in enormous flocks in the vicinity of Okanagan Landing. The prevailing winds are southerly and serve to keep the shallow water here free of ice. Several specimens of pondweeds (*Potamogeton*) afford an abundant food supply. By February 15, the flocks have reached their maximum and number several thousand. They remain in these large bands until March, when they move north. A small number remain and breed. Males outnumber females in the proportion of 15 to 1. Courtship commences about the last week in February. This is interesting in view of the fact that they are one of the last ducks to breed.

DISTRIBUTION.

Breeding range.—Central and western North America. Probably breeds in Newfoundland (Sandy River) and has been found breeding in southeastern Maine (Calais). Otherwise east to southeastern Michigan (St. Clair Flats). South to southern Wisconsin (Lake Koshkonong), southern Minnesota (Heron Lake), central western Nebraska (Garden and Morrill Counties), southern Colorado (San Luis Valley), northwestern New Mexico (Lake Burford), southwestern Utah (Rush Lake), central Nevada (Ruby Lake), and southern California (Riverside and Los Angeles Counties). West nearly to the coast in southern California (Ventura County), to the inland valleys farther north (San Joaquin and Sacramento Valleys), central Oregon (Klamath and Malheur Lakes), central Washington (east of the Cascade Mountains), and central southern British Columbia (Swan Lake). North to central British Columbia (Lac la Hache), central Alberta (Edmonton), Great Slave Lake (Fort Resolution rarely), central Saskatchewan (Saskatchewan River), and south central Manitoba (Lake Winnipegosis).

Winter range.—Mainly in the southern United States. East to the Atlantic coast and to the Bahamas. South to the West Indies (Cuba and Jamaica), the Gulf of Mexico, and central western Mexico (Manzanillo). West to the Pacific coast of Mexico and the United States. North to southern British Columbia (Okanogan Lake), southeastern Arizona (San Pedro River), northeastern Colorado (Barr Lake), northern Arkansas (Big Lake), probably southern Illinois, and eastern Maryland (Chesapeake Bay). More rarely north to Lake Erie and Ontario and southern New England.

Spring migration.—Early dates of arrival: Indiana, central, March 6; Ontario, southern, March 14; Iowa, central, March 8; Wisconsin, southern, March 10; Manitoba, southern, April 12; Maine, Scarboro, March 27. Average dates of arrival: Ohio, Oberlin, March 10; Ontario, southern, March 24; Iowa, Keokuk, March 7; Minnesota, Heron Lake, March 26; Manitoba, southern, April 21.

Fall migration.—Early dates of arrival: Ontario, southern, September 10; Virginia, Alexandria, October 5; Iowa, Iowa City, October 6; Missouri, St. Louis, October 16; Texas, San Angelo, October 1. Average dates of arrival: Ontario, southern, September 19; Pennsylvania, Erie, October 7; Virginia, Alexandria, October 12.

Casual records.—Has wandered on migrations northwest to southern Alaska (Kodiak Island).

Egg dates.—California, Colorado, and Utah: Twenty-seven records, April 23 to July 7; fourteen records, May 24 to June 9.   Minnesota and North Dakota: Eighteen records, May 18 to June 28; nine records, June 3 to 17.   Manitoba and Saskatchewan: Nine records, June 1 to July 6.

AITHYIA FERINA (Linnaeus).

EUROPEAN POCHARD.

HABITS.

The common pochard of the Old World is closely related to our redhead; authorities differ as to whether it is a distinct species or only a subspecies.   The American bird is larger, more intensely colored and has black edges on the wing coverts which the European bird lacks; our bird also lacks the black base of the bill, which is conspicuous in the pochard.   Audubon evidently regarded the two birds as identical, and Wilson, although expressing some doubt, apparently agreed with him.   Nuttall followed their lead.

Dr. Barton W. Evermann (1913) recorded the capture of a specimen of the European pochard on St. Paul Island, in the Pribilof group, on May 4, 1912, which constitutes the first and, so far as I know, the only record of the occurrence of this species in North America.   It was probably a straggler from its Asiatic range; it is widely distributed in central Asia, as far east as Lake Baikal in southern Siberia, and perhaps farther east.

In compiling the life history of this species, which is entirely unknown to me, I can not do better than to quote from the excellent and very full account of it written by Mr. John G. Millais (1913). Referring to the haunts of this pochard, he writes:

The home of this pochard is large, fresh-water lakes, or big reed-inclosed swamps with deep water pools in the center, where they can dive for food and remain beyond the reach of the gun.   They are not adverse to still tidal estuaries, generally of brackish water, but seem to regard the sea itself merely as a place of refuge when driven from their true homes.   Where pochards are most at home are large open stretches of fresh water that contain wide areas that are not of too great a depth.   They seem to like lakes with rather muddy bottoms, where vegetation grows on pure sand, in which there is an abundance of water insects and much molluscae.   From such a center they travel out at night to smaller ponds, and return at daybreak to their sanctuary. This proves that the pochard is intelligent, and, like all diving ducks, first considers its safety and then its food supply.   In migration time, single birds or a few together may be found in quite small pools, but they never stay long in such places, but pass on until they find safety in numbers.   As a rule, pochards keep well to the center of a lake or offshore during the day, and are only to be seen diving near reed beds or close to the banks of sluggish rivers, where they receive continuous protection.   They are at all times suspicious of man, and at once swim for deep water on the least alarm.   Even during gales they like to keep just out of shot of shore on the edge, as it were, of rough water, and take just as much advantage of bank shelter as is compatible with safety. This sense of caution is also evinced in their methods of going ashore to sleep and preen, for they generally chose some gentle shallow or low sloping island over which some members of the flock can see at all times, and on which the rest of the flock can rest at midday. On smaller pools they show an affection for those small green islands round which the muddy bottom produces an abundance of plant growth. Where constantly protected, it is common to see them in close proximity to the rushy banks where alders and willows grow and keep off the winds. Like all ducks, they seem to dislike a draft, and avoid wind-swept areas of water.

Spring.—The pochards that intend to nest within a certain area follow the general rule of all diving ducks and arrive in one flock, generally on the largest sheet of open fresh water in the neigborhood from the 10th to the 15th of March, or even later if the weather is still inclement. The curious groaning wheeze of the male may now be frequently heard, and courtship commences. The finest colored males being those of 2 years or over, are always the first to pair, and drive off the young males which, at a distance, may appear to be adult. The latter remain in a flock apart and seem to be easily discouraged from paying attention to the females. If, however, there is not a preponderance of males, as there usually is in the case of this duck, these young males will often pair with the females, who are quite ready to make love to them.

Courtship.—At the commencement of courtship, generally on the first warm day, several males are to be seen showing off before one duck. In most birds, pairing is generally due to the disposition on the part of the female to accept attentions, and you will usually notice that some particular female is in advance of the rest of her sex in this respect. As I have shown in my drawing, which is done direct from life, four or five males are crowding round one female who, in turn circles round some male, dipping her bill in the water stretching her neck low on the water, and occasionally uttering her coarse cry of *kurr-kurr-kurr*. The males continuously keep up their curious groan, which is somewhat like a man affected with asthma and being told by the doctor to "take a deep breath." In addition to this call, they also utter a soft low whistle, which the spectator must be close at hand to hear. The first attitude of the male consists in throwing the head and neck back until the back of the head touches a point between the shoulders. This is repeated constantly at the commencement of courtship. The more common display is to blow the neck out with air, with the head raised horizontally, and utter the groan as the air is released. During this show a distinct "kink" is to be observed in the lower part of the neck, whilst the center is unusually swollen. The fullest display is usually performed as the male approaches the female. The male then lies very flat on the water and stretches the head and neck to the fullest extent, at the same time blowing out the neck and frequently turning the head on one side so to display its full beauty. Two or three males may thus often be seen together laying themselves out to attract the female's attention, and the effect is somewhat striking. During these moments of intense excitement the pupil of the eye of the male nearly disappears, and the eye itself seems to blaze a very rich lacquer red.

Nesting.—In the breeding season pochards seem to prefer small lakes whose sides are overgrown with dense vegetation or even large reed-beds. Small islands are also very attractive to them, but, if absent, they will seek out nesting sites that run into meadows of sedge and grass, from which flow channels connected with the main pools. They are not at this season averse to the close proximity of man, and the pair of birds keep very close together until the female commences to sit. The nest is usually built just above the level of the water on the edge of a clump of reeds where the soil is firm, or in the center of a small island. As a rule, it is entirely covered with undergrowth and well lined with down. The female usually deposits from 7 to 9 eggs. Leverkühn records one nest of 10 eggs and Saunders and Naumann one each of 13 eggs, whilst Professor Newton had a clutch of 14 eggs sent from Yorkshire, probably the result of two females laying in the same nest. Full clutches are usually to be found in England in the first or second week in May, and the second week in May in Germany, and third week in May in Scotland.

"The female shows great devotion," says Naumann, "during the time of sitting. She approaches the nest with caution, flies past it accompanied by the male without, however, circling round it, lowers herself with the male on to the water at some distance away from it, and both sit there motionless for some time, with very erect necks, until finally the female, swimming in an attitude of diving, or running, huries back to it. The male meanwhile remains on the open water close by and warns her of the approach of any danger with a loud gabbling cry, but is always the first to take to flight, and later on, when the sitting is over, troubles himself no more about her, stays in the daytime far away from her on the open water near, and only comes back to her in the evening if she leaves the nest for a rest."

The female keeps adding down, plucked from her own breast, to her nest as incubation proceeds, until there is a considerable quantity deposited, and with this she covers the eggs carefully if she leaves the nest.

Eggs.—The eggs are a somewhat broad oval with the shell waxy and smooth but not glossy. In color a pale greenish gray, generally tinged with yellow. After being blown they often assume a dull brownish drab color. Average size of 100 eggs, 61.4 by 43.6 millimeters. Maximum, 68 by 45.5 and 64 by 46.5; minimum 57.2 by 43 and 61 by 39.2 (or in inches, 2.42 by 1.72) (F. C. R. J.).

Young.—Observers seem to be agreed that the young do not leave the nest until the day after they are hatched, and they are then tended with the most assiduous care by the mother. At first she keeps them close to the edge of the reeds, especially if there is any wind, and dives for food, which she breaks up and offers to them. Very soon they learn to catch flies and pick up floating seeds, and they may be seen diving of their own accord when only a day or two old. The cry of the young is a gentle *peep*, which they emit until fully fledged and able to fly. From early days the young are expert divers, and soon learn to escape by that method if threatened with danger, but on first alarm they pack closely together, as if for mutual protection.

Before reaching full powers of flight, pochards, as well as other ducks which nest in central Europe, have many enemies to contend with. No doubt large pike kill them in numbers. Rats and others account for a certain number, whilst hen and (on the Continent) marsh harriers account for a few. Magpies, carrion and hooded crows search out the nests and destroy the eggs.

Food.—The principal food in summer and autumn is vegetable and fresh-water mollusks. They eat large quantities of the roots, seeds, leaves, and flowers of aquatic plants, which they take and swallow at the bottom. They are especially fond of the seeds of *Polygonum amphibium*, and, in the autumn, of the seeds of *Potamogeton marinus* and *P. pectinatus*, also the tender parts of *Myriophyllum*. In confinement they refuse many hard foods such as acorns, etc., which surface-feeding ducks will eat with avidity. In summer the young birds eat quantities of floating insects, but the old birds seem to take few of these, although they catch numbers of water beetles, small fish, tadpoles, and small frogs. With their liking for seeds of all kinds, it is not difficult to get pochards to feed on any sort of grain or bird seeds. Like other diving ducks, they swallow a considerable quantity of sand or small stones, to assist digestion. Pochards seldom go on land to feed unless upon some mound of mud and water reeds which drought or a falling lake has exposed. They also seldom tip up the hind part of the body to reach food with the bill. They are not averse, however, to taking floating seeds and insects off the surface of the water.

Behavior.—Generally busy feeding at night, they like to rest and sleep a great part of the day with bill tucked into the shoulder feathers. In this attitude they remain for hours half asleep, but not so soundly that they avoid using their feet to maintain their position in the same spot.

It has often struck me, in watching a flock of pochards, that there is always an unusual preponderance of males, and a party can usually be recognized at a considerable distance by the redheads and shining lead-blue bills of the males. Females and young are always more difficult to distinguish from other ducks owing to their more uniform color. With their feet so far to the rear they walk with a decided roll, keeping the body in a fairly vertical position. But when standing still or taking alarm ashore, they raise the breast and assume a somewhat upright attitude. They never stay long on land, on which they appear to be little at home, but on the water they are expert swimmers and quick in all their movements. They swim deep, with the tail trailing in the water, and when engaged in diving further sink the body, depress the tail under water, and even allow the water to wash over the mantle.

In diving, their leg push is powerful and creates a considerable swirl after the bird passes out of sight. The bird swims rapidly to the bottom and probes in every direction for food, staying under as long as a minute, and then floating quickly to the surface with legs stationary on either side. Generally they come to the top in very nearly the same place at which they have dived. Nearly all their food is swallowed where it is found, but I have seen them bring fish to the surface, where it is passed across the bill several times until rendered soft enough to swallow whole. Certain roots are also treated in the same fashion. Naumann states that pochards can remain under water for "nearly three minutes." This may be possible, but I have never timed one, even in confinement, to stay so long beneath the water.

Their flight is rapid and "scurrying." The wings, not being large, have to be beaten quickly to bear the weight of the body, and the pace is not very swift. It is accompanied by a rushing sound; the birds fly very close together in a somewhat compact mass. When high in the air they often assume a V-formation, as if desirous of being led by some experienced individual, and the whole flock sometimes indulge in a remarkable "header," or plunge from the sky down to some sheet of water where they wish to alight. They can not rise easily from the water unless there is a considerable breeze, and sometimes scurry along the surface for some distance before getting under way. They also alight on the water somewhat clumsily. In the air they are readily recognized by the large head, body, and feet, short stumpy tail, and short wings. Although this duck may be said to be cautious on large sheets of water, it is not a difficult bird to approach even in large flocks, especially in a small sailing boat, and this may be due to its disinclination to fly, especially as it must come *upwind* toward the point of disturbance. I have sailed right in amongst pochards and scaup in October before putting them to flight. On small ponds they show even greater tameness, and, if undisturbed, will often consort with pinioned birds and tame species, and soon become as tame as domestic ducks. There are many instances of wild pochards joining domesticated ducks, and remaining with them for months. I have never found pochards on the sea in Scotland except during hard frosts. A few days of 10° below freezing point and I was certain to find pochards on the Moray Firth, where I shot with the big gun for three seasons, and if the frost continued for more than 10 days the birds left for the winter, most probably for the open water of the southwest, not returning until the lakes were open in March.

Game.—When found on small ponds pochards are by no means shy, and will generally allow a gunner to walk within gunshot if simple precautions are taken, but it is a mistake to shoot these birds in such places if there is a desire on the part of the landowner to establish the species as a resident, for all ducks soon learn the spots where they are protected, and will not tolerate much molestation. If specimens are required, or the needs of the pot are pressing, it is much better to attack the birds on large sheets of water or on the estuaries, which they are not easily made to forsake. In the autumn these large flocks are easily approached by a small sailing boat to within gunshot of an 8-bore, or even a full choke 12-bore, but if numbers are wanted the punt gun will do great execution in their serried ranks.   I have seldom fired at pochards on the sea, but one frosty morning in February, 1891, when returning from an unsuccessful raid on the widgeon in Castle Stuart Bay, Moray Firth, I spied a small but dense flock of duck in Campbeltown Bay, not far from the village.   These were about 60 pochards driven to the sea by stress of weather from the various Nairnshire lochs. Knowing that they would be tame and had doubtless never seen a punt, I reserved fire until I was within 80 yards, and cut a clear lane right through the flock, killing dead 20 birds, and afterwards recovering 2 winged ones.   On the east coast of Scotland such a shot with the big gun is rare, but I have seen occasions on Loch Leven (where, Heaven forbid, a punt gun should ever be used) and the Loch of Strathbeg when a very much larger number of birds could easily have been killed.   There are sometimes good opportunities of getting a shot at these ducks at flight, when they leave the estuaries or large lakes, and pass out to feed on smaller sheets of water at dusk.   I was once waiting at a point on the Island of Mugdrum, Tay Estuary, when, hearing a rush of wings, I looked up, and had just time to snap two barrels into a flock of duck that passed on my left; the result was six pochards down, but I lost two in the darkness.   If it is desired to shoot pochards on a small lake, it is much better to drive them off it, and station the gun or guns away from the water, as this form of shooting does not seem to terrify them nearly so much as stalking them from the shore.   They are not more or less difficult to kill than other diving ducks, but require to be hit well forward, as winged birds may give much trouble.

DISTRIBUTION.

Breeding range.—Sub-Arctic portions of Europe and Asia. East to southern Siberia (Lake Baikal).   South to eastern Persia, the Caspian Sea, northern Algeria, and southern Spain.   West to the British Isles.   North to the Sub-Arctic portions of Scandinavia, Finland, and Russia.

Winter range.—From the Mediterranean Basin (Morocco to Egypt) to India, China, and Japan.

Casual records.—Wanders to Iceland, the Faroes, Azores, and Canary Islands.   Accidental in the Commander Islands (Bering Island, May 13, 1911) and the Pribilof Islands (St. Paul Island, May 4, 1912).

ARISTONETTA VALISINERIA (Wilson).

CANVASBACK.

HABITS.

The lordly canvasback, the most famous American game bird, from the standpoint of the epicure, is distinctly a Nearctic species and was discovered or, at least, first described by Alexander Wilson. It must have been taken by earlier sportsmen, but it was apparently not recognized as different from its near relative the European pochard, which it superficially resembles.

Spring.—It is a hardy species wintering just below the frost line, and one of our earliest migrants.   The first spring flight appears above the frost line before the ice disappears from the ponds, lingers but a short time and passes on northward as fast as the ice breaks up ahead of it.   The dates vary greatly in different seasons depending on the breaking up of winter conditions, but the migration often begins in February and is generally well under way by early March. The general direction is northwestward over the Great Lakes, for the birds wintering on the Atlantic coast, northward from the Gulf of Mexico through the Mississippi Valley and northward and eastward from Mexico and the Pacific coast, in converging lines toward its main breeding grounds in the prairie and plains region of central Canada.

Courtship.—All through the spring immense flocks of canvasbacks congregate on the larger lakes on or near their breeding grounds, floating in dense masses far out from shore, playing, feeding, or resting until the time arrives to break up into pairs for the breeding season.   This usually occurs before the middle of May, but I have seen them in large flocks as late as the last week in May in southern Saskatchewan.   I have never seen their courtship performances and can not find any description of them in print.   But Dr. Arthur A. Allen has sent me the following interesting notes on what he has observed under somewhat artificial conditions.

Upon several occasions prior to 1917 I had observed small groups of canvasbacks on Cayuga Lake behaving in a manner which I took to be their courtship performance.   Several females would draw together holding their heads up and their necks stiff until they were almost touching breast to breast, when about an equal number of males would swim rapidly around them.   Occasionally the males were seen to throw their heads back toward their tails, or one of the females would dart out at a male that approached more closely.   These performances took place at some distance from shore, however, and many of the details were missed.

During February of 1917, however, several pairs of canvasbacks were captured and placed with clipped wings on a small pond within 100 feet of my windows where they could easily be observed.   They became quite tame in a remarkably short time and before the summer was over would eat from one's hand.   About the middle of April they were first observed going through their courtship performances, and, inasmuch as they paid scant attention to one on the shore of the pond less than 20 feet away, every detail could be watched.   First signs of excitement were evidenced by the males which began to call.   As the canvasback is normally a very quiet duck this immediately attracted my attention.   The call consists of three syllables *ick, ick, cooo,* with a little interval between the second and third.   When the first two syllables are being produced the bird opens his bill slightly and then with considerable force appears to inhale quickly, jerking his bill as he does so.   It appears as though this sudden inhalation abruptly closes the glottis so as to produce the two rather high-pitched, sharp, quick, *ick, ick* notes.   Accompanying these notes the back of the neck swells and the feathers rise as though a gulp of air were being swallowed. Immediately, however, it seems as though exhalation occurred with the bill closed, accompanied by a low *cooo* like a muffled bark or distant moo of a cow and not so very different from the ordinary grunting note of the male bird when alarmed. Accompanying this note the chin swells out for an instant with a curious swelling about the size of an ordinary marble.

Very frequently this note was accompanied by the head-throwing performance, already referred to, the *ick, ick* notes being given when the head was thrown back, and the *cooo* when the head was brought forward again, the swelling on the chin being noticeable as the head assumed the normal position. This head-throwing performance was practically the same as has been described by Doctor Townsend for the golden-eye and has been observed by me frequently while watching redheads and scaup ducks as well.

The calls of the males were answered by the females with a low, guttural *cuk cuk*. The four females then drew together until their breasts nearly touched, jerking their heads and holding their necks stiff and straight as they did so. The males then began swimming about them in circles, sometimes with their heads close to the water after the fashion of the mallards, sometimes calling as already described, and frequently jerking their heads so that the occiput struck the back. Occasionally one of the males would approach a little closer to the females and then one of the females would lower her head and chase him away, returning to her stand in the middle of the circle. This performance was observed many times but there were no further developments, and the birds never paired or selected mates on this pond so far as I could observe.

Nesting.—In the summer of 1901 we found the canvasbacks breeding quite abundantly in Steele County, North Dakota. Even then their breeding grounds were being rapidly encroached upon by advancing civilization which was gradually draining and cultivating the sloughs in which this species nests. Since that time they have largely, if not wholly disappeared from that region, as breeding birds, and their entire breeding range is becoming more and more restricted every year, as the great northwestern plains are being settled and cultivated for wheat and other agricultural products. This and other species of ducks are being driven farther and farther north and must ultimately become exterminated unless large tracts of suitable land can be set apart as breeding reservations, where the birds can find congenial surroundings. As my experience with the nesting habits of the canvasback in North Dakota will serve to illustrate its normal methods, I can not do better than to quote from what I (1902) have already published on the subject, as follows:

The principal object of our visit to the sloughs in Steele County was to study the breeding habits of the canvasbacks; so, soon after our arrival here, late in the afternoon of June 7, we put on our hip-boots and started in to explore the northern end of the big slough shown in the photograph. In the large area of open water we could see several male canvasbacks and a few redheads swimming about, well out of gun range. Wading out through the narrow strip of reeds surrounding the open water, and working along the outer edge of these, we explored first the small isolated patches of reeds shown in the foreground of the picture. The water here was more than knee-deep, and in some places we had to be extremely careful not to go in over the tops of our boots so that progress was quite slow. We had hardly been wading over 10 minutes when, as I approached one of these reed patches, I heard a great splashing, and out rushed a large, light-brown duck which, as she circled past me, showed very plainly the long sloping head and pointed bill of the canvasback.

A short search in the thick clump of tall reeds soon revealed the nest with its 11 eggs, 8 large, dark-colored eggs of the canvasback and 3 smaller and lighter eggs of the redhead. It was a large nest built upon a bulky mass of wet dead reeds, measuring 18 inches by 20 inches in outside diameter, the rim being built up 6 inches above the water, the inner cavity being about 8 inches across by 4 inches deep. It was lined with smaller pieces of dead reeds and a little gray down. The small patch of reeds was completely surrounded by open water about knee-deep, and the nest was so well concealed in the center of it as to be invisible from the outside. The eggs were also collected on that day, and proved to be very much advanced in incubation.

The other nests of the canvasback that we found were located in another slough, about half a mile distant, which was really an arm of a small lake separated from the main body of the lake by an artificial dyke or roadway with a narrow strip of reeds and flags on either side of it. In the large area thus inclosed the water was not much more than knee-deep, except in a few open spaces where it was too deep to wade.

Here among open, scattered reeds, the pied-billed grebes were breeding abundantly. A few pairs of ruddy ducks had their nests well concealed among the tall thick reeds. Coots and yellow-headed blackbirds were there in almost countless numbers. Long-billed marsh wrens were constantly heard among the tall thick flags. Red-winged blackbirds, soras, and Virginia rails were nesting abundantly in the short grass around the edges. Marbled godwits and western willets were frequently seen flying back and forth over the marshes acting as if their nests were not far away and clamorously protesting at our intrusion. Killdeers and Wilson phalaropes hovered about us along the shores. Such is the home of the canvasback, an ornithological paradise; a rich field indeed for the naturalist, fairly teeming with bird life. Our time was well occupied during our visit to this interesting locality, and the days were only too short and too few to study the many interesting phases of bird life before us, but we devoted considerable time to the canvasback, and, after much tiresome wading, succeeded in finding three more nests in this slough. The first of these was found on June 8, while wading through a thick patch of very tall flags, higher than our heads; we flushed the female from her nest and had a good look at her head as she flew out across a little open space. The nest was well concealed among the flags, but not far from the edge. It was well built of dead flags and reeds in water not quite knee-deep, and was sparingly lined with gray down. This nest contained 11 eggs, 7 of the canvasback and 4 of the redhead, which were collected on June 13 and found to be on the point of hatching.

Another nest, found on June 8, was located in a small, isolated clump of reeds, surrounded by water over knee-deep, on the edge of a large pondlike opening in the center of the slough, as is admirably illustrated in the photograph kindly loaned me by Mr. Job. The nest was beautifully made of dead and green reeds firmly interwoven, held in place by the growing reeds about it, and sparingly lined with gray down. It was built up out of the water, and was about 5 inches above the surface of the water; the external diameter was about 14 inches and the inner cavity measured 7 inches across by 4 inches deep. The nest and eggs, now in my collection, were taken on June 11, at which time incubation was only just begun; it contained eight eggs of the canvasback and one of the ruddy duck. All the canvasbacks' nests that we found contained one or more eggs of the ruddy duck or redhead, but we never found the eggs of the canvasback in the nest of any other species. The canvasbacks are close sitters, generally flushing within 10 feet of us, so that we had no difficulty in identifying them by the peculiar shape of the head; in general appearance they resemble the redheads very closely, except that the female canvasback is lighter colored above. The gray down in the nest will also serve to distinguish it from the redhead's nest, which is generally more profusely lined with white down.

In the extensive marshes near the southern end of Lake Winnipegosis and about the Waterhen River in Manitoba we found canvasbacks breeding abundantly in 1913, where we had ample opportunities for studying their nesting habits and the development of the young in captivity, in connection with Mr. Herbert K. Job's extensive experiments in hatching and rearing young ducks. On June 5 we examined seven nests of this species scattered over a wide area of marshy prairie; five of these nests contained 8 eggs each, one held 9 and one held 10 eggs, in various stages of incubation, but mostly well advanced. Most of the nests were in typical situations, more or less well concealed in thick clumps of bulrushes (*Scirpus lacustris*) or flags (*Typha latifolia*), but several were located in open places among short sedges (*Scirpus campestris*) where they were in plain sight. As we approached a small pond hole surrounded by a wide border of these sedges, the brown dead growth of the previous season, our guide pointed out a nest, about halfway from the shore to the open water, on which we could plainly see the duck sitting, only slightly concealed by the low scanty vegetation. The nest was one of the handsomest I have ever seen, a large, well-built structure of dead reeds, flags, and sedges, placed in shallow water and built up 9 inches above it; it measured 18 inches in outside diameter with an inner cavity 4 inches deep and 8 inches in diameter; it was profusely lined with the characteristic gray down which covered the whole interior and upper part of the nest, as if more warmth were necessary in such an exposed situation. In this, and in other similar cases, where incubation was advanced the ducks sat very closely and allowed us to walk up to within a few feet before leaving the nest.

All of the slough-nesting ducks seem to be very careless about laying their eggs in the nests of other species, which may be due to inability to find, or lack of time to reach, their own nests. Occasionally nests are found which are used as common dumping places for several species, where eggs are deposited and perhaps never incubated; we found such a nest at Crane Lake, Saskatchewan, on June 7, 1905, which contained 19 eggs, of at least three different species—canvasback, redhead, and mallard, and possibly others; the nest was partially broken down on one side and some of the eggs had rolled out into the water; it was originally a canvasback's nest, but had apparently been deserted.

The down in the canvasback's nest is large and soft in texture, but not so fluffy as in the surface-feeding ducks. It varies in color from "hair brown" to "drab." The breast feathers in the nest are whitish, but not pure white.

Eggs.—The canvasback usually lays from seven to nine eggs, but the set is often increased, if not usually so, by the addition of several eggs of the redhead, ruddy duck, or other species. The eggs when fresh can be readily distinguished by their color, which is a rich grayish olive or greenish drab of a darker shade than that usually seen in the eggs of other species. They vary in shape from ovate to elliptical ovate and have much less luster than the eggs of the redhead.

The measurements of 88 eggs in various collections average 62.2 by 43.7 millimeters; the eggs showing the four extremes measure 66.8 by 43.2, 63 by 45.8, 56.5 by 40.7, and 57 by 38.8 millimeters.

Incubation lasts for 28 days and is performed entirely by the female. The males desert the females as soon as the eggs are laid and gather into large flocks in the lakes and large open spaces in the sloughs.

Plumages.—The downy young show their aristocratic parentage as soon as they are hatched in the peculiar wedged-shaped bill and head. The color of the upper parts—crown, hind neck, and back—varies from "sepia" to "buffy olive." The under parts are yellowish, deepening to "amber yellow" on the cheeks and lores, brightening to "citron yellow" on the breast, fading out to "naphthalene yellow" on the belly and to almost white on the throat. The markings on the side of the head are but faintly indicated; below the broad yellow superciliary stripe is a narrow brown postocular stripe and below that an indistinct auricular stripe of light brown. The yellow scapular patches are quite conspicuous, but the rump spots are hardly noticeable. The colors become duller and browner as the young bird increases in size.

Before the young bird is half grown, or when about 5 weeks old, the first feathers begin to appear on the flanks and scapulars; at about the same time small "russet" feathers appear on the face, and the head soon becomes fully feathered; the breast plumage comes next, then the tail; and the last of the down is replaced by feathers on the neck and rump before the wings are even started. The young bird is fully grown before the wings appear and is 10 or 12 weeks old before it can fly. The sexes are nearly indistinguishable up to this age, but the young male is more clearly "russet" brown on the head than the female; both have light throats and brown backs. The young male, however, makes rapid progress toward maturity and soon begins to acquire the red head and the vermiculated black and white feathers of the back; by November he has assumed a plumage much like the adult, except that all the colors are duller or mixed with juvenal feathers and the back is darker, about the color of an adult male redhead. By the following spring only a few vestiges of the immature plumage are left, a few brown feathers in the back, light edgings in the breast, and less perfection in the wings.

The canvasback has a partial eclipse plumage which it wears for a short time only. The head and neck become mottled with dusky and dull brown; the black chest is mixed with brown and gray feathers; and the belly is more or less mottled. Dr. Arthur A. Allen tells me that molting begins from the first to the middle of August, possibly somewhat earlier, as it is inconspicuous at first. By September 1 they are in full eclipse, such as it is. Breeding plumage begins to show in October and they are in full plumage again by November 1.

Food.—The principal food of the canvasback, or at least the food which has made it most famous as a table delicacy, is the so-called "wild celery" (*Vallisneria spiralis*); it is in no way related to our garden celery and is more commonly known as "eelgrass," "tape grass" or "channel weed"; it grows most abundantly in the Chesapeake Bay region and is supposed to be the chief attraction for the vast number of canvasbacks and other ducks which resort to these waters in winter; but it also grows abundantly all along the Atlantic coast in estuaries and tidal streams, where the current is not too swift, the long slender, ribbonlike leaves floating in or out with the tide in dense masses, often so thick as to impede the progress of boats or seriously interfere with the use of oars. The canvasback prefers to feed on the root of the plant only, which is white and delicate in flavor and said to resemble young celery; it is obtained by diving and uprooting the plant; the roots are bitten off and eaten and the leaves or stems are left to float away in tangled masses. While feeding on *Vallisneria* the canvasback is often accompanied by other species of ducks which appreciate the same food, such as the redhead, baldpate, and scaup duck; the redhead and scaup can dive almost as well as the canvasback and so succeed in pulling up the roots for themselves; but the baldpate has to be content with the parts discarded by the canvasback or with what it can steal by force; the baldpate frequently lies in wait for the canvasback and, as soon as it appears on the surface with a bill full of choice roots, attacks it and attempts to steal what it can; the American coot also persecutes the canvasback in the same way. Audubon (1840) says, writing of its food in Chesapeake Bay, that the *Vallisneria*—

is at times so reduced in quantity that this duck, and several other species which are equally fond of it, are obliged to have recourse to fishes, tadpoles, water lizards, leeches, snails, and mollusca, as well as such seeds as they can meet with, all of which have been in greater or less quantity found in their stomachs.

On the inland lakes, streams, and marshy ponds, along its migration routes and on its breeding grounds, the canvasback lives on a variety of food both vegetable and animal, such as aquatic plants of various kinds, wild oats, water-lily and lotus seeds, small fishes, crustaceans, mollusks, insects and their larvae. Dr. F. Henry Yorke (1899) has added the following list of plants eaten by the canvasback: Teal moss (*Limnobium*), blue flag (*Iris versicolor*), water chinquapin (*Nymphaea lutea*), tuber-bearing water lily (*Nymphaea tuberosa*), yellow pond lily (*Nuphar Kalamanum*), water milfoil (*Myriophyllum*), water starwort (*Callitriche*), bladderwort (*Utricularia*) and a number of other water plants. Grinnell, Bryant, and Storer (1918) say:

In California the canvasback partakes of more animal food, for wild celery does not grow in this State. On the shallow water of the tidelands and marshes it feeds extensively on crustaceans and shellfish, thereby acquiring a "fishy" taste and thus becoming undesirable as a table bird. The stomachs of some canvasbacks collected on San Pablo Bay contained clams (*Mya arenaria*), and snails (*Odostomia*, species); one stomach from Tia Juana Slough, near San Diego, contained periwinkles (*Cerithidea californica*), and another from the same place contained grass blades, stems, and roots. A stomach from Guadalupe, San Luis Obispo County, was filled with barley, there being 22 whole kernels and many hulls; but there is a possibility that this was bait put out by hunters.

In connection with the feeding habits of the canvasback it may be well to call attention to an interesting case of lead poisoning in this species, resulting from feeding on grounds which have been shot over considerably.

Mr. W. L. McAtee (1908) published the following account of it in The Auk:

Conditions similar to those described by Mr. J. H. Bowles for the Nisqually Flats, Puget Sound, exist at Lake Surprise, Texas. To the latter locality canvasbacks resort from November to March. About the 1st of January, each year, many of these ducks are found among the rushes along the shore in various stages of sickness. Some can dive, but can not fly, and all become emaciated. A part of these of course are cripples, but most of them, although free from wounds, are plainly diseased, and according to the belief of those who have had most experience with them, the cause is lead poison from shot in the gizzards. No fewer than 40 shot have been taken from a single gizzard and the shot generally bear evidence of more or less attrition. As the season advances, the diseased ducks gradually disappear; the greater part die, but some it is thought recover. According to the information at hand no other species than the canvasback is thus affected at Lake Surprise.

Ducks secure a great deal of their food by sifting mud through their bills; if shot are abundant in mud, it is not hard to understand how the birds may collect a considerable number in a day. Resisting digestion to a marked degree, as shot do, the quantity in the gizzard is added to day by day, the ducks continuing to feed over the same grounds, until finally the gizzard is clogged with shot, and malnutrition, if not actual poisoning, ensues. Epidemics, such as we now have evidence of on Puget Sound and at Lake Surprise, in all probability will increase in number, adding another to the almost overwhelming array of unfavorable conditions against which our ducks must more and more hopelessly struggle.

Behavior.—The flight of the canvasback, though apparently labored, is really quite rapid, strong, and well sustained. When migrating or when flying to and from their feeding grounds they fly in wedge-like flocks, usually at a considerable height and with more velocity than is apparent. When on the wing the canvasback can be recognised by the long, slender neck and head, carried in a downward curve, by the long pointed bill and by the sharp-pointed wings; it is a longer and more slender bird than the redhead; when sitting on the water it can be distinguished from the redhead or the scaups, almost as far as it can be seen, by the extreme whiteness of the back.

The canvasback is essentially a diving duck and one of the most expert at it; it swims low in the water like a grebe and dives quickly, swimming for long distances under water, using its wings for this purpose; if pursued it comes to the surface only for an instant, diving again promptly and swimming away so far and so swiftly as to distance its pursuer; it hardly pays gunners to chase the crippled birds, as they are tough and hard to kill, as well as skillful divers; well-trained retrievers have been taught that it is useless to attempt to catch them. The canvasback can dive to great depths and is said to be able to obtain its food at a depth of from 20 to 25 feet.

Mr. Thomas McIlwraith (1894) noted a peculiarity in its diving habits, which is decidedly grebelike:

> Before going under water it throws itself upward and forward, describing a curve as if seeking to gain impetus in the descent, just as boys sometimes do when taking a header off a point not much above the water level.

The vocal performances of this species are not elaborate nor are they frequently heard. The male has a harsh, guttural croak or "a peeping or growling note. The female canvasback can quack almost as well as the black duck, and also gives voice to screaming *currow* when startled," according to Eaton (1910).

Fall.—The fall migration route of the canvasback from its main breeding grounds on the central plains of Canada is peculiar and interesting, as it has shown some marked changes within recent years; it has always been somewhat fan-shaped, spreading out in three directions; the two main flights have been, in a general way, southeastward to the Atlantic coast from Delaware southward, and southward through the Mississippi Valley to the Gulf of Mexico; a third line of flight of less importance takes a more southwesterly course to Mexico and the Pacific coast. There is also a southward flight along the Pacific coast of birds which have bred in British Columbia and Alaska. During recent years canvasbacks have been increasing in abundance, during the fall migration, in the vicinity of the Great Lakes, in New York and in southern New England, indicating a more northerly range or a more directly eastward migration route to the Atlantic coast. Previous to 1895 records of this species in Massachusetts were exceedingly scarce and it was regarded as very rare or a mere straggler; during the next few years records became more frequent and since 1899 there have been records of canvasbacks taken every year, with increasing frequency, until now the bird has become a regular, if not a common, visitor in certain localities. For a full account of this interesting change in habits, I refer the reader to Mr. S. Prescott Fay's (1910) excellent paper on the subject in The Auk. Such a marked change in a migration route is not easily accounted for, though several causes may have had their effect in bringing it about. I believe that the principal cause has been the increased population of the Mississippi Valley and the Central West, which has brought about the draining and cultivation of many of its former feeding grounds and resting places; this, with the increased persecution by gunners throughout its former migration route, has driven the birds farther northward to a migration route along the Great Lakes. The species seems to be declining in abundance on the Gulf coast, which would seem to support this theory, though it may mean a reduction in the numerical strength of the species as a whole. Its breeding grounds have become more restricted to more northerly localities, which has also tended to give it a more northerly migration route eastward. The theory has been advanced that the wild celery now grows more abundantly farther north than formerly, though I doubt if this can be proven, or if it has had as much effect as the other two causes.

Prof. Walter B. Barrows (1912) says of its fall migration in Michigan:

This duck is seen almost invariably in flocks, these gathering often into large companies of many hundred individuals. Like the redhead this species in Michigan is more common along the Great Lakes than on the ponds and streams of the interior, yet it occurs sparingly in the latter situations.

In the fall it reappears in October and in places where food conditions are favorable may remain until late December. Its favorite food, the "eelgrass," or so-called wild celery (*Vallisneria spiralis*) has been planted in several places during recent years and attracts many kinds of ducks.

Game.—On account of its world-wide fame as a table bird and its prominence as a game bird, it seems worth while to devote some space to the consideration of the canvasback from the standpoint of the sportsman and to give some account of the methods of hunting it. Professor Barrows (1912) says of the methods employed during its migration through Michigan:

Formerly the birds were slaughtered by all sorts of abominable devices, including night floating, punt guns, sail boats, and steam launches, * * * as well as by more legitimate methods of decoys. At present they are sometimes obtained by "sneaking" or drifting down upon flocks in the open water in a boat more or less concealed by rushes, bushes, and similar disguises, but the greater number are shot from blinds or hiding places over painted wooden decoys.

Good shooting used to be found on the inland lakes, on the early spring migration, which occurs while the lakes are still partially covered with ice. The gunner selects a small open water hole, which the ducks have been seen to frequent, where he anchors his decoys in the water, pulls his skiff up onto the ice and builds a blind around it of ice cakes, where he can lie concealed within easy gunshot of the water holes; a decoy, which can be made to dive by pulling a cord, will help to attract passing flocks which are looking for a feeding place. New arrivals will usually decoy readily to such places, but birds which have spent some time in the vicinity soon learn to avoid such dangerous water holes and frequent the places where they can feed in safety.

The coast region of Virginia and North Carolina with its numerous estuaries and tributary streams has always been the most famous winter resorts of canvasbacks, and many other species of wild fowl, in North America. Vast hordes of canvasbacks, redheads, scaup ducks, as well as geese and swans formerly frequented these waters, attracted by the mild climate and the abundance of food. Several generations of gunners, by persistent and constant warfare, have seriously reduced the numbers of these hosts of wildfowl, but the birds are still sufficiently plentiful to attract sportsmen in large numbers and to keep alive the various gunning clubs which now control nearly all of the best shooting grounds. Some of the more destructive methods of killing ducks, such as night shooting and wholesale slaughter with swivel guns, have been prohibited by law. Netting ducks in gill nets sunken a short distance below the surface proved very destructive, but was abandoned as the ducks caught in this way became water soaked and of inferior flavor.

One of the oldest and most sportsmanlike methods of shooting ducks on Chesapeake Bay is known as point shooting. The sportsman lies concealed in a blind, with a retriever to pick up his birds, and waits for passing flocks to come near enough for a shot. The best flight is early in the morning, between dawn and sunrise when the ducks are flying to their feeding grounds; they usually fly around the points rather than over them; but if the wind is favorable, they often come within gunshot. This kind of shooting requires considerable practice and hard shooting guns, for the canvasbacks fly swiftly, often high in the air and are hard to kill, all of which makes it attractive to the true sportsman. Similar shooting is obtained on narrow sand bars where the ducks fly directly overhead; this is even more difficult. Canvasbacks are also shot over decoys at the points, from blinds on the flats, and from water holes in the ice on the rivers.

An interesting ancient method of shooting canvasbacks was by tolling them in with a small dog, especially trained for the purpose. Some quiet place was selected where a large flock of canvasbacks was bedded a short distance offshore and where the hunters could conceal themselves in some suitable ambush near the water. A small dog was kept running up and down the beach after sticks or stones, with a white or red handkerchief fluttering from some part of his body, which would so arouse the curiosity of the ducks that they would raise their heads and swim in toward shore to study the cause of such peculiar actions. Often their discovery of the hidden danger came too late, for as they turned to swim away they would receive a broadside from a battery of guns and large numbers would be killed. Tolling is now prohibited in many places.

The old-fashioned dugout, in which the hunter lay concealed with his boat covered with celgrass has been entirely replaced by the modern surface boat or battery, an ingenious contrivance from which more canvasbacks are shot than by any other method. It consists of a stout wooden box, just long enough and deep enough to effectually conceal a man while lying down, surrounded by a broad wooden platform, attached to its upper edge; the platform is also surrounded with frames covered with canvas; it is so constructed and ballasted that the platform floats flush with the surface of the water and the box is entirely below it; the platform is constantly awash, but the water is kept out of the box by projecting flanges. The battery is towed out to the shooting grounds and anchored with 200 or more wooden decoys anchored around it. The gunner is entirely out of sight, except from overhead, as he lies flat in the bottom of the box until the birds are near enough, when he rises and shoots. An assistant is needed with a sailboat, launch, or skiff to pick up the birds.

When the canvasbacks first come in the fall, they gather in large numbers in the salt waters of Chesapeake Bay. During November they come down into the fresh waters of Back Bay, Virginia, and Currituck Sound, North Carolina, their favorite winter resorts. Here they feed on the roots and seeds of the foxtail grass which grows abundantly in these bays, but will not grow in salt water. The growth of this excellent duck food, on which the numerous duck clubs largely depend for their good shooting, is being much injured by carp and by the increasing abundance of swans; both of these species root up or trample down this grass so extensively that the feeding grounds for ducks are seriously injured. An open season on swans might reduce their numbers and improve the duck shooting. The canvasbacks, like the redheads, will feed in the bays all day, if not disturbed, but usually large flocks, or flocks of flocks, may be seen flying out to sea in the morning and back again at night.

Winter.—The canvasback is a late migrant and often lingers in the vicinity of the Great Lakes until driven farther south by the freezing of its favorite lakes and ponds, which sometimes proves disastrous. Mr. Elon H. Eaton (1910) says, of its occurrence in the central lake region of New York:

The winters of 1897–98 and the three following winters were remarkable for the large flocks of canvasbacks which appeared about the 1st of December on these waters and remained until early in March. On Canandaigua Lake a flock of nearly 1,000 canvasbacks passed a large part of the winter, and on Keuka Lake flocks of 200 birds were frequently seen. In February, 1899, many of these ducks were killed on Canandaigua Lake about the air holes which remained open. Most of those killed were in poor flesh and some were picked up on the ice in a starving condition.

The freezing of Cayuga Lake in February, 1912, caused the death of many canvasbacks and other ducks by starvation; I quote from Mr. Alvin R. Cahn's (1912) interesting paper on the subject as follows:

These ducks suffered, to all appearances, as much as any species on the lake. A flock of 22 was approached to within 30 feet one afternoon before they gave any heed, but finally they rose heavily and flew low over the ice a distance of 60 yards, where they lit, and immediately assumed a resting posture. Two of these ducks were captured alive, both being taken almost as easily as one would take an apple from the ground. The first made one feeble flight when approached, but that was all. He was followed and picked up off the ice without a struggle. The second was taken from the ice without having made any attempt to fly. The condition of both of these birds was pitiful, to say the least. Hardly able to stand erect, and too feeble to mind what was going on around them, they sat on the ice in a more or less dazed condition. The feathers were unpreened, and those of the breast and belly were yellow and matted with grease. Both of these birds were found on the ice of Fall Creek. There are records of 22 canvasbacks that were found dead within this area.

DISTRIBUTION.

Breeding range.—Western North America. East to the eastern edge of the prairie region in central Manitoba (Lake Winnipegosis, Lake Manitoba, and Shoal Lake), rarely in southern Minnesota (Heron Lake), and casually in southern Wisconsin (Lake Koshkonong). South to central western Nebraska (Garden and Morrill Counties), northern New Mexico (Cimarron), northern Utah (Box Elder and Davis Counties), and western Nevada (Pyramid Lake). West probably to eastern or central Oregon and Washington and to southern British Columbia (Lumby and Grand Forks), and central British Columbia (Lac la Hache). North to central Alaska (Fort Yukon), northern Mackenzie (Anderson River), and Great Slave Lake (Fort Rae and Fort Resolution).

Winter range.—Southern North America. East to the Atlantic coast of United States. South to Florida, the Gulf coasts of Louisiana and Texas, central Mexico (valley of Mexico and Mazatlan); rarely to Cuba and Guatemala. West to the Pacific coasts of northern Mexico and United States. North to southern British Columbia (Puget Sound region and Okanogan Lake), northwestern Montana (Flathead Lake, until frozen), northern Colorado (sparingly), northeastern Arkansas (Big Lake), southern Illinois, and eastern Maryland (Chesapeake Bay); rarely as far north as Lakes Erie and Ontario, and eastern Massachusetts (Boston).

Spring migration.—Average dates of arrival: Iowa, Keokuk, March 12; Minnesota, Heron Lake, March 28; Nebraska, central, March 14; North Dakota, northern, April 18; Manitoba, southern, April 21; Pennsylvania, Erie, March 13 to 26; Ohio, Oberlin, March 17; New York, Cayuga Lake, April 1.

Fall migration.—Early dates of arrival: Maine, Pittston, about October 8; Long Island, Mastic, October 11; Virginia, Alexandria, October 15; California, southern, October 20. Late dates of departure: Maine, Falmouth, November 14; Rhode Island, Middletown,

November 18; Minnesota, Heron Lake, November 27; Pennsylvania, Erie, December 21.

Casual records.—Accidental in Bermuda (October 30, 1851). Rare or accidental on migrations east to New Brunswick and Nova Scotia.

Egg dates.—Manitoba, Saskatchewan, and Alberta: Eighteen records, May 26 to 27; nine records, June 1 to 11. Minnesota and North Dakota: Twelve records, May 9 to June 25; six records, May 31 to June 11. Colorado and Utah: Four records, May 23 to June 20.

FULIGULA FULIGULA (Linnaeus).

TUFTED DUCK.

HABITS.

This widely distributed Palaearctic species is closely related to our ring-necked duck and might be said to replace it throughout its extensive breeding range from western Europe to extreme eastern Asia. Audubon (1840) says, referring to the ring-necked duck:

We are indebted for the discovery of this species to my friend the Prince of Musignano, who first pointed out the difference between it and the tufted duck of Europe. The distinctions that exist in the two species he ascertained about the time of my first acquaintance with him at Philadelphia in 1824, when he was much pleased on seeing my drawing of a male and a female, which I had made at Louisville, in Kentucky, previous to Wilson's visit to me there. Wilson supposed it identical with the European species.

Mr. Ned Hollister (1919) has also referred to this relationship.

There is, so far as I know, but one record of the capture of a tufted duck in North American territory, for which we are indebted to Dr. Barton W. Evermann (1913) who reported the capture of a female on St. Paul Island, Alaska, on May 9, 1911. "The bird was accompanied by the male which escaped."

I have never seen this species in life, but fortunately Mr. J. G. Millais (1913) has written a very full and satisfactory life history of it from which I shall quote, as follows:

Throughout its range the tufted duck is essentially an inhabitant of open sheets of fresh water, preferring those of moderate size that have a considerable depth in the center, and whose shallows are overgrown with reeds and other aquatic plants. They also like lakes with numerous islands and backwater, not too narrow, where they can sit and preen in the shallows in non-feeding hours, and whose vegetation gives them protection from the wind. In fact, all ducks that frequent open lakes of fresh water dislike drafts and take full advantage of the cover that grows along the banks, either sitting under the lee, or resting and diving at such a distance from shore that some protection is afforded. It is only in still weather or moderate breezes that they assemble in numbers on the open and deep parts of a lake, or when subject to frequent disturbance.

Spring.—On large lakes, like Loch Leven, where tufteds intend to breed, most of the adult birds are paired off by the end of March, and keep closely together during the early part of the breeding season. There are, however, many small lakes and ponds where tufteds breed, which are not frequented by the birds in winter, owing probably to the fact that they have been frozen. On these the tufteds arrive in one small flock late in February or early in March, and at once commence courtship and pairing. As soon as they are paired they become very tame, and it adds much to the charm of a day's spring fishing on Loch Leven to see these charming birds, with hosts of other ducks, circling round the boat, and taking but little notice of intruders in the sanctuary.

Courtship.—Early in March the large flocks of tufted ducks split up into smaller companies; and if the weather is fine, and they are observed with the glass, it will be seen that a constant commotion is taking place amongst their ranks. Two or three males are sometimes to be seen "showing off" before a duck, and vice versa, some drakes seem to have a decided attraction for the females, which swim rapidly round and alongside them, dipping their bills frequently, and uttering their harsh call. The courtship of the male tufted duck is probably the most undemonstrative of any of the *Anatidae.* I myself, and such good observers as Mr. Gerald Legge and Mr. Hugh Wormald, who have these birds constantly under notice both in a wild and domesticated condition, have never seen any show on the part of the male except the following: The male swims rapidly past the female but without turning his head in her direction, and extends the neck to its full length. At the same time the bill is raised to an angle of 45°, and retained in this position for some seconds, whilst it utters frequently a low gentle whistle something like the word *hoi,* and well-nigh impossible to express onomatopoetically. In many cases in which male birds are furnished with ornaments of exceptional beauty, we notice that these parts are displayed in courtship, but in the case of the tufted drake, the bird seems to be incapable of displaying his long crest in any fashion, for at the period of courtship it hangs limp at the back of the head as at other seasons. In moments of excitement the pupil of the eye almost disappears, as it does in so many birds, and the golden iris seems to blaze with unusual fire.

Nesting.—Considering the fact that tufted ducks pair early, it is somewhat curious that they are not by any means early breeders. It is not long before they seek out a suitable nesting site, but it is generally well into May before the females think of nesting. The site chosen is generally only a few yards from the water, often amid dense herbage or the top of a sloping bank on some island, tongue of land, or embankment. At Patshull 8 or 10 nests are annually placed on a low dike separating two small lakes. The distance of each nest from the water would be 2 to 5 yards and the site hidden in rushes and coarse grass where a few stunted willows grow. I have found them with little covering but a few grass blades, and at other times, some 20 yards from the water, in a thicket of willows, Scots fir, bramble, and reeds. A favorite position is in center of a tuft of rushes, only slightly raised above the level of the lake. Naumann says they will travel as far as 80 to 100 paces from the water to make the nest in a clump of sedge or osier, rushes or tufts of grass, in places once wet and now dry.

Eggs.—Eggs rather coarse in texture, with some gloss; color yellowish brown. Sometimes with greenish tinge. Shape frequently a much elongated ellipse or long oval. Average size of 150 eggs, 59.0 by 40.9 millimeters; maximum, 65.9 by 46.3 and 63.9 by 47.2; minimum, 53 by 38 (or in inches, 2.32 by 1.61). (F. C. R. J.)

The number of eggs in a clutch usually ranges from 8 or 9 to 10, but at times much larger numbers are found. R. J. Ussher has recorded a nest with 14 from Ireland, and in May, 1899, Mr. Malloch, of Perth, sent me a photo of a nest high up on the old castle at Loch Leven which also contained 14 eggs. The Rev. F. C. R. Jourdain has met with clutches of 11, 12, 15, 16, and 18, but the last seemed certainly to be the produce of two ducks. The late T. E. Buckley found clutches of 16 and 17 in Caithness. Newton in the *Ootheca* mentions 21 eggs as found in one nest, and Jourdain found a duck sitting on a pile of 28 eggs at Osmaston, Derbyshire, which, of course, she was quite unable to cover, but in this case about five ducks were laying in one nest. Stuart Baker speaks of 40 eggs as found in one nest, but gives no details.

Young.—The incubation period is somewhat variable, lasting from 23 to 28 days. A female sits very close, and only deserts her nest in presence of urgent danger. She plucks her breast of the dark-gray down, and surrounds her eggs with it, as well as covering them with it when necessity compels her to obtain some food. When the young escape from the eggs, they follow the mother at once to the water, and crowd very closely round her as she swims. If disturbed by man, she will fly a short distance and dive, when the young, even if very small, at once imitate her movements. In a very few days the young are expert divers. During the first days of life the young are largely fed by the mother, or, to speak more correctly, have food placed before them by the parent, who obtains it from the bottom and then breaks it up, when it is at once swallowed by the the hungry brood. All the time she is so engaged the latter are busy catching flies and *diptera* on the surface as they swim along.

Young tufted ducks begin to dive very soon after they enter the water. Mr. Wormald allows his young birds to enter a pond and seek for food as soon as they are hatched. As instancing their lack of knowledge in the art of diving and their quick acceptance of this method of gaining their food, Mr. J. Whitaker tells me the following interesting fact, which he noticed at Rainworth in the summer of 1912. A female tufted duck led her bunch of young ones which had just been hatched, to the middle of the pond. She then dived immediately; the young rushed in every direction on the surface of the water, evidently under the impression that they had lost their mother. She reappeared in a minute, however and all the brood hurried to her side.

At the next dive they did not appear to be so frightened, but looked about waiting for her reappearance. The third time she dived two of the young ones copied her movements, and in a very short period the whole of the family were diving with their mother in quite professional fashion. This little incident shows how quickly education may be completed in birds whose instincts naturally trend in certain directions.

Food.—When diving for its food the tufted duck makes a full semicircle with the head and neck, and, giving a vigorous kick, passes quickly out of sight, leaving a boil on the troubled waters. It remains below the water from a few seconds to half a minute, and finds most of its food on the bottom. Like most of the fresh-water diving ducks, it will take quantities of food on the surface such as flies, *diptera*, and duckweed, of which it is especially fond. Even when quietly preening on shore I have seen a tufted duck dash at and swallow a small frog that incautiously sprang into a shallow beside it. Most authorities speak of the food as being entirely animal, but this is not the case. Dresser, however, does not make this mistake, and correctly states that it will eat roots, seeds, and the buds of aquatic plants. I have never seen the tufted duck actually feed on land, for we must not regard habits developed in confinement as natural. Its chief food consists of aquatic animals of various kinds, fresh-water mussels and snails, insects, frogs, and tadpoles. Various tufted ducks that I have kept in confinement caught quantities of flies, water beetles, small fish, and ate large quantities of pondweed. They can, however, be easily "fed off" on to grain. "In the stomachs of some killed in Bavaria," says Naumann, "Jäckel found fish spawn, a grass frog (*Rana esculenta*), mussels (*Pisidum fontinale*), the larvae of *Phryganea* and *Ephemera*, and the seeds of *Polygonum amphibium*, *persicaria* and *Lapathifolium*, *Rumex*, and *Potamogeton*." The stomachs of tufted ducks generally contain a quantity of sand, fine shell, or small stones.

Behavior.—Unless the sun is shining, when the snow-white flanks of the males appear bright and glistening, the appearance of this duck is very black. It swims low in the water, with the head well sunk between the shoulders. The tail is usually carried just above the water, but when alarmed, wounded, or bent on feeding, it can sink the body and depress the tail below, or even just under the water. At a short distance the golden eye and blue bill are very noticeable, and in the spring the eye of the male is very bright, the pupil being almost indistinguishable, especially when courtship is proceeding. If alarmed near the shore, the tufted is very quick to apprehend danger. It raises the head, stiffens the neck, sinks the body slightly, and at once commences to swim to deep water at a considerable pace. Should it consider that it is not possible to gain a point beyond gun range by swimming, it rises at once with considerable splashing and some noise, especially if the day is calm or the wind offshore, and then quickly rising with rapid beating wings, it passes away. Before leaving a lake tufted ducks always circle over the water many times sometimes rising to a height of 20 or 30 yards, and sometimes diving through the air toward the water again, which they always seem loath to abandon. The flight is rapid and very straight once the birds have decided on their course. They have a very black-and-white appearance in the air, and if the sun is upon them, even a glistening or "twinkling," which can be recognized from a great distance.

During the day the companies of tufted ducks spend most of the time in resting, preening, and feeding, but as evening comes on they become restive and keep much on the wing. Like many other ducks, most of their journeys are performed at night, which fact is proved by their frequent disappearance from certain lakes and appearance in the morning on others. When traveling over short distances the flight is generally performed within gunshot of the land or water, but when making longer journeys they mount to a considerable height in the air like the golden-eye. They generally fly in very close irregular companies in a swift arrowlike manner, swinging and swaying to take advantage of any wind breaks, hills, woods, etc. In summer single pairs of birds will resort to any pond that is quiet and undisturbed, preferring those that are well lined with sedge, rushes, grassy banks, embankments, and heather islands. In autumn the immatures may be found even in pools in fields, wide drains, and large sewage tanks. I have killed several in an unsavory bog right in the heart of the town of Glasgow known as the Postle Marsh, but they do not seem partial to swift-flowing rivers and if found there it is certain that they are only on passage. As a rule they come ashore on long low tongues of land or small islands from which a good view may be obtained, and are very quick to take alarm given by the cries of other birds or the use of their own eyes. During gales of wind they are very clever to take advantage of the shelter of islands or headlands, and yet remain on the water just out of shot of any spot that may hide a gunner. Resting on the water they appear to be asleep, yet their little feet are in motion all the time so as to prevent the wind from drifting them too far into rough water. Thus they will maintain one position for hours at a time.

On shore they walk slowly and clumsily, with a decided roll. On the water they are expert divers and, when feeding, keep in close companies. When feeding they dive all together or very quickly one after the other, remaining below from a few seconds to a minute (generally 50 seconds). They are very buoyant and rise to the surface with a "jump" at different points, when they at once reassemble and commence diving again. In this manner they spend a great part of the day. When at the bottom, in clear water, they probe the mud, sand, or pebbles in search of food, and, like the golden-eye, I have seen them turn over stones of considerable size with the bill. The food is swallowed under water as a rule, but if a fish, frog, or large piece of succulent root or vegetable matter is found it is brought to the surface and crushed or broken up before being swallowed. The usual cry, uttered by both sexes, but somewhat louder and harsher in the case of the female, is *korr, korr, korr*, or *ka-ka-ka, karr*. They emit this when rising, quarreling, or suddenly alighting, or on being scared. The call of the male in spring is a low gentle whistle, and the onlooker must be at close range to hear it at all.

Game.—On the whole the tufted duck is not very easy to shoot on large sheets of water. But even in such places they may be stalked from behind banks or through woods, and watched when swimming within shot of the shore. When the flock is found on feed the gunner can then run in and obtain his chance as the birds rise to the surface. When little disturbed it is possible to sail within gunshot of a flock on the open water, but the old birds are usually difficult to obtain in this way unless they are "cornered" in some backwater or arm of the lake, when they will not fly overhead but pass within shot to the open waters of the lake. I have killed many by lying hidden on small islands in Loch Leven. There they will pass at close range on stormy days, but always keep well out of shot of the larger islands. Winged birds shot from the shore are seldom recovered unless shot again at once before they commence to dive, but from a boat winged birds may be tired out and killed more easily than pochard or scaup, since they neither possess the constitution nor vitality of these ducks. On small lakes or ponds tufted ducks are easily shot, as there is always some corner or point of land where the gunner can stand in bushes and hide himself to intercept them as they leave the place. It is merely necessary to find this spot and send a man round to drive the birds and they will come straight to the gunner. Moreover, in leaving small sheets of water tufted ducks do not rise high, and so offer an easy mark.

Winter.—Speaking of the winter habits of the species in Germany, Naumann says: "Although they seem fairly unsusceptible to cold, as long as ice does not entirely close the pieces of water to them, yet for all colder lands they remain birds of passage. From September or the beginning of October onward they assemble in small companies on larger sheets of water, and these flocks grow bigger in proportion as the year advances until finally in November or December they have become flocks of many thousands; at the approach of frosts they endeavor to prevent the complete freezing of certain places on the water by continued movement, and all at first start on their journey together if they can no longer succeed in doing this and the water is altogether covered with ice. They wander off in great flocks in search [of water] from which only a few occasionally through some mishap become separated, for afterwards on still open places on the rivers you seldom come across heron-duck (tufteds), and these will soon follow after, so that in the middle of the winter (unless it is quite a mild one) there are none to be seen in our country. Whilst those assembled in the north and east of Germany desert us in order, some of them winter in southern lands in Switzerland, Italy, and Hungary, on large inland lakes, or on the sea coasts."

Some remain in the sea or the north and east coast of Germany, but generally about the tidal estuaries. Their appearance on the open sea Naumann very rightly regards as exceptional.

DISTRIBUTION.

Breeding range.—Palaearctic region. From the Faroes, the British Isles, and Norway entirely across Europe and Asia to eastern Siberia and Kamchatka. North to about 70° N. and south to about 50° N.

Winter range.—Southern Europe, northern Africa to Abyssinia and southern Asia (India, China, and Japan), and Formosa.

Casual records.—Wanders to Madeira, Liberia, the Seychelle, Pelew, Marianne and Philippine Islands, and Borneo; also the Kurile and Pribilof Islands (St. Paul Island, May 9, 1911).

FULIX MARILA NEARCTICA (Stejneger).

AMERICAN SCAUP DUCK.

HABITS.

The scaup duck of Europe, which is closely related to or perhaps identical with our own bird, was so named, according to some of the earlier writers, on account of its habit of feeding on the beds of broken shellfish which are locally called scaup; but it is equally fair to assume that its name may have been chosen from its resemblance to one of its characteristic notes. The two American species of scaup ducks resemble each other in general appearance and almost intergrade in size and color, so much so that they have often been confused; still intelligent gunners have long recognized two species of "bluebills," one larger and one smaller. The subject of this sketch is known to the gunners as the "big bluebill," "big blackhead," and a variety of other names. It is very distinct from the lesser scaup in its distribution and habits; it breeds much farther north over a much wider area, which is practically circumpolar; its migration routes are quite different; and its winter home is mainly on our more northern seacoasts, where it is more of a salt-water duck than its smaller relative.

Spring.—From its principal winter home on the Atlantic coast the spring migration is decidedly northwestward, through the Great Lake region to the interior of Canada and Alaska; there is also a northward migration up the Mississippi Valley and another northward, and perhaps northeastward, from the Pacific coast. The species breeds abundantly in northern Alaska, but we do not know positively whether all of these birds have migrated from Pacific coast winter resorts or not. Dr. F. Henry Yorke (1899) says of the spring migration in the central valleys:

The first issue stays but a short time, soon passing northward as fast as the ice disappears, for they rarely leave the frost line until the ice has departed, working up in the interior, through the lakes and overflowed bottoms below St. Louis, following behind the ringbills. Some years they arrive in great numbers, while at other seasons they are very few. They prefer still to running water; naturally, large ponds and lakes, bayous, bays, and inlets are their favorite resorts.

Courtship.—The courtship of the scaup duck is described by Mr. John G. Millais (1913) as follows:

The male scaup anxious to pair approaches the female with head and neck held up to their fullest extent, the bill being raised in the air to an angle of 50° to 60°. If the female responds to this she also lifts the neck stiffly, at the same time uttering a crooning sort of note like the words *Tuc-tuc-turra-tuc*. If alarmed, or pretending to be so, she swims away quickly with powerful strokes, uttering her quacking cry, *Scaar-scaar*. When paired the female often comes up to the male and bows her head gently several times. The actual show of the male is a quick throw up of the head and neck, which is greatly swollen with air as it extends. At the summit of extension the bird utters a gentle cry like the words *Pa-whoo*, only uttered once. As he makes this show, the female sometimes swims round him, lowering the head and dipping the bill in the surface of the water and making a gentle call, *Chup-chup*, or *Chup-chup-cherr-err*. Quite as frequently the cry of the male is uttered after the head is raised and slightly lowered. The male also utters a very low whistle. Except the harsh loud cry of the female, all these calls of pairing scaup are very low in tone, and the spectator must be within a few yards of the birds to hear them.

Nesting.—The best known, and probably the most populous, breeding grounds of the greater scaup duck are in northern Alaska. Dr. Joseph Grinnell (1900) describes three nests, which he found in the Kotzebue Sound region, as follows:

In the Kowak Delta this species was quite common in June, and on the 14th of that month I took a set of 11 fresh eggs, also securing the female as she flushed from the nest. This nest was on a high, dry hummock, about 10 yards from the edge of a lake. It was almost hidden from view by tall, dead grass of the previous year's growth. The eggs rested on a bed of finely broken grass stems, while the rim of the nest was indicated by a narrow margin of down. A second set of 10 fresh eggs was taken on the same day and the nest was similar in construction, but was out on the tundra between two lakes, and fully a quarter of a mile from either. A set of seven fresh eggs taken on the 15th was quite differently situated. The nest was almost without feathers or down, and consisted of a neat saucer of matted dry grass blades, supported among standing marsh grass and about 4 inches above the water. It was in a broad, marshy swale about 30 feet from a small pond of open water. The swale was drained into the main river channel by a slough, so that in this case there was little danger of a rise in the water of more than an inch or two.

Mr. Hersey collected four sets for me in the vicinity of St. Michael in 1915. Three of the nests were more or less concealed in tufts of grass close to the shores of small ponds; the nest cavities were lined with fine, dry grass and in one case a well-formed nest of this material was made; no down was found in the newest nests containing fresh eggs, but, as incubation increased, considerable down became mixed with the grass. One nest, found June 19, was in a clump of dead flags in a pond 3 feet out from the shore and surrounded by water; the nest was made of bits of broken flags mixed with dark gray down and a few white breast feathers of the duck; it contained eight eggs.

Mr. Chase Littlejohn (1899) has published the following notes on a nesting colony of this species which he found on an island near the end of the Alaska Peninsula. He writes:

The island contains about 4 acres, one-half of which is about 50 feet above sea level; but on both the east and west ends there is quite an area only a few feet above water. These gravel points are covered for the most part with a species of salt weed less than 1 foot in height, common to the seashore of that country. Among these weeds on the west end there is a colony of about 50 pairs of scaups which have, to my knowledge, bred there for several years; while on the east end not a single nest can be found, although the conditions are practically the same. Furthermore, there is quite an area on the west end well suited to their wants; but they prefer to occupy a narrow strip along the edge of the weeds and place their nests close together, some of them not over 2 feet apart, others 10 at the most, showing that they prefer to be neighbors, I can not remember one isolated nest of *Fuligula marila*, and I have found many.

At the eastern extremity of its American breeding range the scaup duck has been found breeding, at least twice, in the Magdalen Islands, Quebec. Mr. Herbert K. Job found a nest, on June 29, 1900, in a small grassy islet, one of a series of small islets known as the "egg nubbles," in the great pond near East Cape; the nest was a bed of down in the thick grass and held nine fresh eggs. I have explored this pond several times since, but have never succeeded in even seeing a scaup duck. Rev. C. J. Young also found them breeding here in 1897 and sent Prof. John Macoun (1909) the following note, received from one of his correspondents:

I found a bluebill's nest in a strange place, after you left me. It was in a bunch of rushes at the head of the bay, growing in water that took me up to my middle to reach them.

The greater scaup may breed in North Dakota, Manitoba, and Saskatchewan, but during our various explorations in these regions we found no positive evidence to prove it. There is, however, a positive nesting record of the species farther south. Mr. W. H. Collins (1880) reported finding a nest at St. Clair Flats, Michigan, in 1879, which he identified by shooting the female.

The nest was built in a tuft of flags and composed of rushes and wild rice lined with some down and feathers. It was situated similarly to the redheads' nest resting in the water, and being held in place by the tuft of flags in which it was built.

The down in the nest of the scaup duck is small, soft, and compact in texture and "clove brown" or "bone brown" in color, with small inconspicuous, lighter centers. The breast feathers mixed with it are small and white or grayish white.

Eggs.—The scaup duck lays ordinarily from 7 to 10 eggs; sometimes only 5 or 6 constitute a full set and as many as 19 and 22 have been reported; probably these larger sets are the product of two females. The eggs can usually be recognized by their size and color. The color is about the same as in eggs of the lesser scaup and ringnecked ducks, a much darker olive buff than in other ducks' eggs.

It varies from "deep olive buff" or "olive buff" to "yellowish glaucous." The shell is smooth, but not glossy when fresh. The shape is usually elliptical ovate. The measurements of 180 eggs in various collections average 62.4 by 43.7 millimeters; the eggs showing the four extremes measure **68.5** by 44, 59 by **48**, **54.5** by 41.5 and 66.3 by **40.7** millimeters.

Young.—The period of incubation is said to be about four weeks, but probably it is nearer three and one-half weeks. This duty is performed by the female alone, as she is deserted by her mate as soon as incubation begins. Mr. Hersey's Alaska notes state that "there is little doubt that the males of this species go out to sea as soon as the females have laid their eggs and there molt into the eclipse plumage. I never saw any about the tundra ponds after incubation had begun." The female evidently assumes full care of the young also, leading them about in the ponds and marshes and teaching them to catch flies and other insects. Mr. Hersey came upon a female with a brood of nine young in a large pond out on the tundra. She did not fly or dive, but, calling her young about her, swam to the farther side of the pond. As he walked around the shore she kept at a distance and would not allow him to come nearer. When he withdrew she came ashore with her brood and led them away.

Plumages.—The downy young scaup duck is a swarthy duckling, deeply and richly colored with dark brown on the upper parts. The crown, hind neck, and entire back are a deep rich "raw umber," darker than any color in Ridgway's standards, with glossy reflections of bright "argus brown"; this color invades the lores and cheeks and shades off gradually on the neck and sides into the color of the under parts; the sides of the head and neck are "old gold" or "olive ocher," shading off to "colonial buff" on the throat and to "cream buff" and "cartridge buff" on the belly; an area of darker color, approaching that of the upper parts, encircles the lower neck and fore breast and invades the posterior under parts, restricting the light-colored belly. There are no light-colored spots on the scapulars and rump, as seen in the surface-feeding ducks. All the colors become duller with increasing age. The white plumage of the breast and belly is the first to develop, then the brown scapulars, the tail, the head and the back; the young bird is fully grown before the last of the faded down disappears from the neck; and the wings are the last of all to be developed. This flapper stage lasts all through August and into September, while the adults are also flightless and in the partial eclipse plumage.

In the first fall plumage in September young birds of both sexes are much alike and resemble the adult female superficially, but the white face is confined to the lores and chin, instead of including the forehead, as in the adult female, and it is more or less mottled with brown; the head, neck, and chest are paler brown than in the old female. At this age males can generally be distinguished from females by having the lesser wing coverts somewhat vermiculated with grayish white. In October young birds begin to assume a plumage more like the adults in both sexes and a steady progress toward maturity continues through the winter and spring. During October the greenish-black feathers begin to appear in the head and neck; the brown feathers of the back are replaced gradually by gray vermiculated feathers; and the first white feathers vermiculated with black appear in the scapulars. In November the first black feathers appear in the chest. By February the head is practically adult, and the remainder of the plumage closely resembles that of the adult, before summer. Young birds of both sexes do not breed the first spring but remain in flocks by themselves completing the molt.

A complete molt of both old and young birds occurs in summer, but it produces only a partial eclipse plumage, and after this molt young birds become practically indistinguishable from adults, although the full perfection of plumage is not acquired until a year later. Mr. Millais (1913) says of the eclipse plumage:

The adult male is somewhat late in assuming its eclipse dress, and seems to require to be in good health to attain it, for both pochards and scaup which I have kept in confinement have not fully changed as the wild birds do. About the middle or end of July the adult male passes into a fairly complete eclipse. The whole of the wings, scapulars, back, rump, tail and chest are at once molted direct to the winter dress, a feature of the chest feathers being a broad band of white on the edge of every feather. But an intermediate or temporary plumage for July, August, and September is furnished in a large number of eclipse feathers for parts of the head, neck, mantle, and flanks. The head becomes a dull brownish black, showing light gray on the cheeks (due to the old winter feathers reaching the extremity of their length). A few white feathers come into the lores (showing a distinct affinity to female plumage), the neck assumes a gray collar, and the nape and mantle, instead of being black, are filled with new gray and black vermiculated feathers similar to those on the back. The flanks instead of being white as in spring and winter, are now filled with white feathers finely vermiculated with brown. All of these new eclipse feathers are again molted gradually. From the end of September, when the bird is still in eclipse dress, till the end of October new winter feathers are constantly coming in and displacing the old ones; and the full winter plumage is not assumed until November.

Dr. Arthur A. Allen tells me that in both of the scaup ducks molting begins about mid-August and the birds are in full eclipse by mid-September. Breeding plumage begins to show again in mid-October, but the full plumage may not be attained until the following April, though some birds, probably the oldest, are practically in full plumage by December 1st.

Food.—The feeding grounds of the scaup duck are mainly in fairly deep water at a safe distance from the shore where their food is obtained by diving; they are expert at this and can remain under water for 50 or 60 seconds. Where food is plentiful they often feed in large companies, diving separately, indiscriminately, or all in unison; they show no particular system in their manner of diving and are not very careful about posting sentinels to watch for dangers; sometimes the whole flock will be below the surface at the same time, so that an approach is fairly easy. In their summer homes in fresh-water lakes and ponds they more often feed on or near the surface, where they live on fish fry, tadpoles, small fishes, small snails and other mollusks, flies, and water insects; they also eat some vegetable food, such as the buds, stems, roots, and seeds of floating and submerged water plants. Dr. F. Henry Yorke (1899) has identified the following genera of water plants in the food of this duck: *Vallisneria, Lymnobium, Zizania, Piper, Elymus, Iris, Nuphar, Nymphaea, Myriophyllum, Callitriche,* and *Utricularia.*

During the winter on the seacoast its food consists of surface-swimming crustaceans, crabs, starfish, and various mollusks; small mussels, obtained by diving in the mussel beds, form the principal part of its animal food at this season; but it also eats considerable vegetable food, such as the buds and root-stocks of wild celery (*Vallisneria*), and the seeds and succulent shoots of *Zostera marina.* In the Chesapeake Bay region the scaup ducks feed on the roots of the wild celery with the canvasbacks and redheads, where they are quite as expert as any of the diving ducks in obtaining these succulent roots; consequently they become very fat and their flesh, which is ordinarily undesirable, acquires an excellent flavor.

Mr. Arthur H. Norton (1909) found the stomach of a scaup duck, killed on the coast of Maine in winter, filled with shells of *Macoma balthica.* Dr. J. C. Phillips (1911) reported that the stomachs of scaup ducks, killed on Wenham Lake, Massachusetts, in the fall, "held animal and vegetable matter in equal proportions, the items being bur reed, pondweed, and bivalves (*Gemma gemma*)."

Behavior.—Mr. Millais (1913) gives the best description of the flight of this species that I have seen; I can not do better than to quote his words, as follows:

In flight they proceed at a rapid pace in a somewhat compact formation. The birds fly very close together, and the sound produced by their wings is somewhat loud and rustling. On rising to fly the neck is straightened out, and the bird runs along the surface of the water with considerable splashing for a few yards, but the distance traveled on the surface of the water is coincidental with the amount of head wind. In calm weather, if not much disturbed, they are always liable to take to wing, and if the boat does not press them they will swim away for a long time before turning around and facing up wind. When sitting on the sea, scaup often keep in one long unbroken line parallel to the coast, and when rising the first bird at one end takes wing and is followed in order right across the flock. When flying they keep at a moderate elevation, but if the wind is offshore and they are desirous of coming in to some estuary, they nearly always strike the sands or part of the coast line which they desire to cross at exactly the same spot every day and at a considerable height. As they approach the waters of the estuary and feeding grounds the leading birds then often make a dive downward, their movements being followed in line by the rest of the flock, so that if the line of birds is a long one it often has a curious *waving* appearance. Doubtless this rising high as they approach the coast line is dictated by common sense, for it is on the sands and rocky shore they are most often shot at, and they learn caution from bitter experience. When on migration by day I have seen scaup circling at a great height, but when leaving the sea or open water for the feeding grounds at night scaup as a rule do not fly much above 30 feet above the land or water. I have, when waiting for duck on the mussel beds at dawn and sunset, occasionally obtained shots at flight at scaup, and the sound of their rushing wings has often foretold their approach, when, if they could be seen in time, I have occasionally made successful shots. When in small parties scaup may sometimes be seen flying in oblique formation like other ducks, but when in large companies they generally hold together in a solid phalanx, or in one long unbroken line massed in several places.

The scaup duck is a bold, strong swimmer, making the best of speed even in rough weather; it is a hardy sea duck, unexcelled in its powers of swimming and diving. It is not particularly shy and can usually be approached with a little caution; but it must be hard hit to be secured, as it is tough, has a thick coat of feathers, and is such a powerful swimmer and diver that it is useless to pursue a wounded bird unless it is shot over at once. It dives quickly and swims rapidly away under water with its wings tightly closed, as many of the best divers do. I have seen scaup ducks, which I had dropped as if killed, sit up and shake themselves, dive before I could shoot them over, and never show themselves again; if the sea is at all rough, they can easily escape without showing enough to be seen. Mr. Charles E. Alford (1920) has published some interesting notes on the diving habits of this species, which seems to dive with extreme regularity for definite periods; the dives varied in duration from 25 to 29 seconds and the periods between the dives varied from 11 to 19 seconds.

Except during the mating season, as described above, scaup ducks are usually silent. Their most characteristic note is a harsh, discordant "scaup, scaup," from which their name may have been derived. They also occasionally utter soft guttural or purring sounds.

Fall.—The fall migration is the reverse of the spring route, southeastward through the Great Lakes to the Atlantic seacoast and southward through the Mississippi Valley. Professor Cooke (1906) says that these two routes are clearly revealed in the fall, "when this species scarcely occurs in Indiana, though common both to the east and west of that State." The first flights come fairly early in the fall, with the first frosts, probably made up of the more tender birds which have bred farther south and hatched out earlier. The later flights consist of hardier birds from the far north, which come rushing down ahead of the wintry storms and cold weather, probably driven out by ice and snow. They frequent the lakes, larger ponds, and rivers, feeding and resting on open water, even in rough weather; they often gather in large flocks, which has given them the names, "raft duck" and "flocking fowl"; a dense pack of these unsuspicious birds resting on a sand bank in a river or floating on the surface of a pond often offers a tempting shot to the unscrupulous gunner.

Game.—The true sportsman, however, finds excellent sport in shooting these swift-winged ducks over decoys. They decoy readily to the painted wooden decoys used by the bay men of Long Island and the Chesapeake and large numbers are killed from the floating batteries, such as are used for shooting canvasbacks and redheads.

This method is well described by Mr. Dwight W. Huntington (1903) as follows:

Just before daybreak we reached the place determined upon and found it unoccupied. The battery was placed in the water, the decoys were arranged about it within close range, and my gunner sailed away to leave me lying below the surface of the bay in the box with its wide rim floating on the water. As the first light came in the east I could see the ducks, mostly scaups and redheads, flying swiftly across the dim gray light. Soon there was a rush of wings quite close to my head as a flock of blackheads swung in to the decoys. Sitting up I fired two barrels at the shadowy forms, but nothing struck the water, and the noisy whistling of wings was soon lost in the darkness. As the sun came up the ducks came rapidly, sometimes one or two, more often a flock. I shot at every one, with but poor success. The cramped position, the hasty shot from a sitting position, were new to me and strange, and it was some time before I began to kill the ducks. A single bird coming head on was about to settle to the decoys, when I fired at him at close range, and he struck the water dead. Shortly afterwards I made a double from a flock, and with growing confidence my shooting improved. I soon had a goodly lot of scaups showing black and white upon the waves as they drifted with the breeze. Meanwhile the bay man, who had been cruising far enough away not to alarm the ducks, approached and gathered in the slain.

Mr. Walter H. Rich (1907) says that on the coast of Maine—

most of the bluebills are killed from the "gunning float," the gunner clad in a white suit and the little craft itself "dressed down" to the water's edge with snow and ice to represent a floating ice cake. It is no wonder that the poor victims are "deluded" for it needs sharp eyes and close attention to make out anything dangerous in an object so harmless in appearance. There is commonly little trouble in approaching within easy range of a flock if the gunner is skilled in handling his craft, but to get within shot reach is not all, for any duck which can last out the New England winter will carry off a good load of shot, as the bird must have an abundance of vitality and an extra-heavy suit of underwear to endure the climate. Both of these our hero has.

Winter.—On the Pacific coast there is a southward migration route from the Alaskan breeding grounds and probably a southwestward flight from the interior. Mr. W. L. Dawson (1909) writes of their arrival on the Washington coast:

At Semiahmoo Spit, upon our northern boundary, the bluebills begin to arrive from the north about the 20th of September, and their numbers are augmented for at least a month thereafter. The earlier arrivals come in small flocks of from a dozen to 25 individuals, borne upon the wings of a northwest breeze, and as they pass the narrow promontory of sand, the waiting gunners exact toll of those which enter the harbor. Upon the waters of the inner bay, Drayton Harbor, the incoming birds assemble in a great raft, five or ten thousand strong, and if undisturbed, deploy to dive in shallow water, feeding not only upon the eelgrass itself, but upon the varied forms of life which shelter in its green fastnesses.

About half an hour before sunset, as though by some preconcerted signal, a grand exodus takes place. Flock joins flock as the birds rise steadily against the wind. Mindful of their former experience, the ducks attain a height of two or three times that at which they entered the harbor and, strong in the added confidence of numbers, the serried host, some 40 companies abreast, sweeps over the spit in unison—a beautiful and impressive sight. Some five minutes later a second movement of a similar nature is organized by half as many birds remaining; while a third wave, containing only a hundred or so of laggards, leaves the harbor destitute of scaups.

On the way to their winter homes on the seacoast these ducks often linger in the lakes until driven out by the ice and often many perish in the freezing lakes. Mr. Alvin R. Cahn (1912) describes such a catastrophe on Cayuga Lake, New York, as follows:

The largest flock seen was just off Portland Point. This flock was discovered at rest upon the ice, and so close together were they, and so numerous, that the birds gave the appearance of a solid black line, and it was not until one had approached to within 100 yards of them that one could be sure that it was indeed a flock of ducks. The birds were quite indifferent to being approached, and it was not until one was within 200 feet of them that they showed any signs of uneasiness. When within 100 feet, they rose slowly and flew some little distance down the lake, where they settled once more into their compact formation. It was not until they rose that one realized that there were easily over 400 ducks in the flock. It was all but impossible for these birds to rise clear of the ice. The indifference shown toward unguarded approach, the reluctance with which they rose, the short distance which they flew, in fact, their every action bespoke exhaustion and weakness. In a small piece of open, rapidly flowing water in Fall Creek, a female of this species was caught by hand without difficulty. The bird, too exhausted even to try to fly, could make no headway against the current, and was therefore easily captured. It was too weak to eat, and died within 24 hours. Two peculiar incidents with regard to bluebills have been brought to my notice. One specimen was found while still alive, in which over half the webbing of both feet had been frozen and dropped off. Another was found frozen in a cake of ice, nothing but the head and about half the neck protruding from the mass. The duck, still alive, was chopped out, when it was found that the ice had in some way frozen over the duck, leaving water next to the body. This was undoubtedly kept from freezing by the action of the legs and the body heat. The bird was uninjured, and after being fed, seemed little the worse for its experience.

Large numbers of scaup ducks spend the winter on the New England coast and they are especially abundant in the Vineyard Sound region, south of Cape Cod, and on the ocean side of Long Island. Here they may be seen in large flocks, sometimes numbering several hundred, riding at ease on the rough or choppy sea. Their movements are largely governed by the condition of the mussel beds on which they feed. From Chesapeake Bay to Currituck Sound, North Carolina, they are also abundant and are regarded as one of the desirable species of game birds. On the coast of Louisiana, according to Beyer, Allison, and Kopman (1906), "the occurrence of this species is confined chiefly to the colder parts of the winter. This species is seldom found away from the coast, and occurs more frequently on the open Gulf waters than any other species."

DISTRIBUTION.

Breeding range.—The North American form breeds east to the west coast of Hudson Bay (Churchill), southwestern Ungava (Great Whale River), and casually to the Gulf of St. Lawrence (Magda-

len Islands and northern New Brunswick).   South to southeastern
Michigan (St. Clair Flats, casually), formerly northern Iowa (Clear
Lake), rarely, if at all, now in Minnesota or North Dakota, but
probably still in southern or central Manitoba (Lake Winnipeg),
central Saskatchewan (Prince Albert), central Alberta (Buffalo Lake),
and central British Columbia (east of the Cascades).   West to the
Aleutian Islands (Atka and Agattu) and the Bering Sea coast of Alaska.
North to the Arctic coasts of Alaska and Canada.   In the eastern and
southern portions of its breeding range it is rare or casual.   The
European form breeds in Iceland, the Faroe Islands and northern
Europe and Asia, from Scotland to Bering Sea, and from about 70°
north latitude southward.

Winter range.—North America mainly on the seacoasts of the
United States.   On the Atlantic coast from Maine to Florida, most
commonly from southern New England and Long Island to North
Carolina.   On the Gulf coasts of Louisiana and Texas nearly to the
Mexican boundary.   On the Pacific coast from the Aleutian Islands
to southern California (San Diego).   A few winter in the Great Lakes,
and a few in the southwestern interior (Colorado, Utah, Nevada,
Arizona, and New Mexico).   The European form winters south to
the Mediterranean Sea, northern Africa (Algeria, Tunis and Egypt),
the Black and Caspian Seas, the Persian Gulf, northern India (rarely),
China, Japan, and Formosa (Taiwan).

Spring migration.—Early dates of arrival: Indiana, central, March
1; Ohio, Oberlin, March 9; Illinois, northern, March 6; Manitoba,
southern, March 31; Yukon, Fort Reliance, May 1; Alaska, St. Michael, May 8, and Kowak River, June 1.   Average dates of arrival:
Illinois, northern, March 23; Ohio, Oberlin, March 24; Ontario,
southern, March 30; Iowa, central, March 16; Minnesota, Heron Lake,
April 2; Manitoba, southern, April 16; Mackenzie, Fort Simpson, May
24.   Late dates of departure: Florida, Pinellas County, March 4;
Long Island, Mastic, May 30; Massachusetts, Nantucket, May 1.

Fall migration.—Early dates of arrival: Labrador, Ticoralak, October 11; New York, Long Island, September 26; Virginia, Alexandria,
October 18; South Carolina, Mount Pleasant, October 31.   Late
dates of departure: Alaska, St. Michael, October 15; Quebec, Montreal, November 14; Minnesota, Heron Lake, November 27.

Casual records.—Rare or casual on both coasts of Greenland
(Neanortalik, Godhavn, and Stormkap, June 21, 1907), eastern Labrador and Newfoundland.

Egg dates.—Alaska and Arctic America: Eleven records, June 14 to
July 5; six records, June 15 to 20.   Manitoba, Saskatchewan, and
Alberta: Twelve records, May 25 to July 6; six records, June 12 to
19.   Iceland: Eight records, May 30 to July 10.

FULIX AFFINIS (Eyton).

LESSER SCAUP DUCK.

HABITS.

Unlike the larger scaup duck, this species is distinctly an American duck, but of wider distribution on this continent. It is more essentially an inland species, showing a decided preference for the smaller lakes, ponds, marshes, and streams, whereas its larger relative seems to prefer the larger lakes in the interior and the seacoast in winter. Its breeding range is more extensive and its center of abundance during the breeding season is much farther south, its chief breeding grounds being in the prairie regions of central Canada and the Northern States. Though differing in distribution and in their haunts, the two species are closely related and much alike in appearance, so much so that so good an observer as Audubon failed to distinguish them; nearly all that he wrote about them evidently referred to the lesser scaup, with which he was most familiar, and he criticised Wilson for some of his remarks which evidently referred to the greater scaup. Adult males of the two species are, of course, easily recognized, but the females and young birds are so much alike and vary so much in size that they are often confused. Rev. W. F. Henninger writes me that a series of *Fulix affinis* which he has examined measure up to the minimum measurements given for *Fulix marila* and that the males show both purple and green reflections on the head; this suggests the possibility of intergradation between the two species.

Spring.—The lesser scaup duck is not one of the earliest migrants, but it begins to move northward from its winter home soon after the melting ice and snow begin to indicate the coming of spring. On its migration it follows the courses of the larger streams and rivers, but when it settles down to feed it soon spreads out into the sloughs, marshes and shallow ponds. Prof. Lynds Jones (1909) says that, in Ohio, "it literally swarms in the marshes during late March and the most of April, where feeding companies cover large areas of the open waters of the marshes." Where spring shooting is allowed it flies wildly about, seeking refuge on the open lakes beyond range, but on certain reservoirs where it is not molested it appreciates the security and becomes very tame. In such places a few birds linger well into the summer and some apparently remain to breed.

Courtship.—Very little has been published about the courtship of this species, but Audubon (1840) makes the following brief reference to it:

At the approach of spring the drakes pay their addresses to the females, before they set out on their journey. At that period the males become more active and lively, bowing their heads, opening their broad bills, and uttering a kind of quack, which to the listener seems produced by wind in their stomach, but notwithstanding appears to delight their chosen females.

Dr. Alexander Wetmore (1920) gives the following account of it:

A pair rested in open water in front of me when suddenly the female began to swim back and forth with the head erect, frequently jerking the tip of her bill up while the male drew his head in on his breast and lowered his crest, giving his crown a curious flattened appearance. The female turned alternately toward and away from the male, sometimes biting gently at him, while occasionally he responded by nipping at her with open mouth. At short intervals she dove toward him, barely sliding under his breast, and emerged at once only a few feet away, or at times advanced toward him brushing against him and then turning away. A second male that tried to approach was driven away by quick rushes though the female paid no attention to him. She continued her diving and finally at intervals the male began to dive with her, both emerging at once. As the display continued he joined her under the water more and more frequently and finally both remained below the surface for over 30 seconds where copulation apparently took place. When they emerged the female swam away for a short distance with the male following her. Frequently during these displays the female gave a peculiar rattling, purring call like *kwuh-h-h-h* while the males whistled in a low tone.

Nesting.—Although they arrive on their breeding grounds fairly early, they are very deliberate about nesting preparations and are among the later breeders. All through the extensive western prairies these little ducks may be seen, throughout May and the first half of June, swimming about in pairs in the little marshy creeks, sloughs, and small ponds; they are apparently mated when they arrive and seem to enjoy a protracted honeymoon. In the Devils Lake region in North Dakota we found the lesser scaup duck nesting abundantly in 1901 and examined a large number of nests. On the small islands in Stump Lake, now set apart as a reservation, we found 16 nests of this species in one day, June 15, and all of the eggs proved to be fresh or nearly so. The nests were almost invariably concealed in the taller prairie grass, but some nests were located under small rosebushes and one was placed against the side of a small rock surrounded by tall grass, but in a rather open situation. The nest consisted of a hollow scooped in the ground, profusely lined with very dark down mingled with a little dry grass and occasionally a white feather from the breast of the bird. The females seemed to be very close sitters; we always flushed the bird within 10 feet of us or less; but when once flushed they seemed to show no further interest in our proceedings. The males apparently desert the females after incubation has begun and flock by themselves in the sloughs or small ponds. Lesser scaup ducks occasionally lay in other duck's nests; we found one of their eggs in a gadwall's nest and one in a white-winged scoter's nest; but we found no evidence that other ducks ever lay in the scaup's nests.

In southwestern Saskatchewan the lesser scaup duck was not so abundant as in North Dakota, but still quite common; we found 6 nests in situations similar to those described above; three of these were on that wonderful island in Crane Lake, more fully described under the gadwall. In Manitoba, about Lake Winnipegosis, we found a few nests one of which was in a different situation from any other we had seen; it was built like a canvasback's nest in the water near the edge of a clump of bulrushes (*Scirpus lacustris*), but it contained the dark down and the characteristic eggs of the lesser scaup. Nests have been reported by other observers in such situations, but the nest is usually placed on dry ground. MacFarlane (1891) found over a dozen nests of this species near the northern limit of the wooded country on the east side of the Anderson River, of which he says:

They were usually found in the midst of a swamp—a mere hole or depression in the center of a tuft of turf or tussock of grass, lined with more or less down, feathers, and hay.

Dr. Joseph Grinnell (1909) refers to a nest found by Mr. Littlejohn on an island in Glacier Bay, Alaska; it was at the edge of a small pond "placed within a heavy growth of grass about a foot from the water's edge, and consisted of grass stems lined with a little down from the parent's breast."

The down in the lesser scaup duck's nest is indistinguishable from that of its largest relative, "clove brown" or "bone brown" in color, with inconspicuous lighter centers. The small breast feathers in it are white or grayish white.

Eggs.—The lesser scaup duck lays from 6 to 15 eggs, but the commonest numbers run from 9 to 12. The eggs are like those of the larger scaup duck but they are decidedly smaller. The shape varies from elliptical ovate to nearly oval. The shell is smooth and slightly glossy. The color varies from "ecru olive" or "dark olive buff" in the darkest eggs to "deep olive buff" in the lightest eggs. When seen in the field the deep *café au lait* color of all the scaup duck's eggs is distinctive and unmistakable, but in cabinet sets it has usually faded more or less and is not so conspicuous. It is always much easier to identify ducks' eggs in the field than in collections, for there is usually something about the eggs, the nest, or the bird which is distinctive. The measurements of 88 eggs, in the United States National Museum and the writer's collections, average 57.1 by 39.7 millimeters; the eggs showing the four extremes measure **61.5** by 38, 59 by **42.5**, and **50** by **35.5** millimeters.

Young.—Incubation is performed by the female alone and probably lasts from three to four weeks. When the young are hatched she leads them to the nearest water, which is usually not far distant, and teaches them how to escape from their numerous enemies and how to catch their insect food. While engaged in rearing and studying young ducks in Manitoba we employed Indians to catch the small young of this and some other species which we did not succeed in hatching in the incubators. Mr. Hersey's notes describe their methods as follows:

A brood of lesser scaup found on a small pond acted very differently from young golden-eyes. Instead of separating they drew close together and swam back and forth a few feet. The Indians plunge into the pond, clothes and all and drive the brood toward our end. They swim along quietly and as they near the end of the pond the Indians close in until they are within a few feet of the birds. Then suddenly the birds begin to dive, each one swimming under water past the men and coming up well out toward the middle of the pond. If the water is clear the Indians will watch the young bird swimming and catch them under water, but if muddy, they all get safely by and then the whole performance is repeated.

It often happens when a brood dives in this way, that one or more birds get separated from the rest. The single birds are picked out and captured first, while the rest of the brood wait at the other end of the pond. It is no easy matter to catch one of these youngsters. When he realizes he is being chased he makes every effort to get back to his brothers and sisters, pattering along the surface much faster than a man can move through the water. However, they usually head him off and he then returns to diving. After a while he gets tired and diving once more swims under water until close to the shore when he crawls into the grass. Once on land he loses no time but pushes his way rapidly through the grass. Unless his pursuer is quick he will yet make his escape, but the Indians aware of this habit watch the tops of the grass closely, following his movements by the slight waving and soon overtake him.

Plumages.—The downy young is darkly and richly colored. The upper parts are dark, lustrous "mummy brown" or "sepia," shaded with "brownish olive"; these colors are darkest and most lustrous on the posterior half of the back and lightest on the shoulders; the dark colors cover the upper half of the head and neck, the back and the flanks, fading off gradually into a dusky band around the lower neck and encroaching on the ventral region posteriorly. The color of the under parts, which covers the lower half of the head, throat, breast, and belly, varies in different individuals; in some it runs from "olive ocher" to "primrose yellow," but in most specimens from "chamois" to "cream buff"; these colors are brightest and richest on the cheeks and on the breast. The markings on the head are usually indistinct, but a superciliary buff stripe, a loral dusky stripe and a postocular dusky stripe are discernible in the majority of a series of 11 specimens in my collection. There is also an indistinct yellowish spot on each scapular region, but none on the rump. The colors become duller and lighter as the duckling grows older.

So far as I can judge from the study of available material, the sequence of plumages to maturity and the seasonal molts of adults are practically the same as in the greater scaup duck. Young birds do not breed during their first spring and become practically adult in plumage after their first complete summer molt, or when from 14 to 16 months old. The eclipse plumage of the adult male is only partial and not conspicuous. The adult female seems to have a distinct breeding plumage, which is much browner than the winter plumage and in which the white face wholly or partially disappears.

Food.—The feeding habits of the lesser scaup are much like those of the greater scaup, except that the smaller species is confined almost wholly to fresh water. Mr. Vernon Bailey (1902) writes:

Like all of the genus, the lesser scaups are great divers and keep much in the open lakes, often in large flocks, where they dive for food, or sleep and rest on the water in comparative safety. They can not resist the temptation of the rice lakes, however, and swarm into them by thousands to fatten on the delicious grain, which they glean from the mud bottoms after it has been threshed out by the wind and the wings of myriads of coots and rails. While they eat, the hunters lie hidden in the tall rice and on the ridges which they must pass in going from lake to lake, and in spite of their bullet-like flight the sadly thinned flocks show the penalty they have paid for leaving the open water.

Their animal food consists of small fry and fish spawn, tadpoles, pond snails and other small mollusks, worms, crawfish, water insects, and larvae. They also consume a variety of vegetable food among which Dr. F. Henry Yorke (1899) has identified all the plants mentioned under the preceding species. The stomachs of this species, taken by Dr. J. C. Phillips (1911) in Massachusetts, contained "seeds of burreed, bayberry, and saw grass (*Cladium effusum*), and snails (*Lunatia heros*) and ants."

Behavior.—The lesser scaup like its larger relative, is an expert diver and can remain under water for a long time, grubbing on the bottom for its food. Like many of the best divers, its large and powerful feet enable it to swim rapidly beneath the surface without the use of its wings, which are held tightly closed. It swims away so rapidly under water when wounded that it is useless to pursue it; it is said by gunners to cling to the weeds or rocks on the bottom until dead; it seems more likely that in most cases it swims away to some place where it can hide or that it skulks away with only its bill above water; Mr. W. E. Clyde Todd (1904), however has published the following note from Mr. Samuel E. Bacon:

I once wounded a duck of this species in shallow water and, wading out to where I saw it last, I found it holding to a strong weed by its bill, 2 or 3 feet below the surface, stone dead.

Audubon (1840) writes:

The scaup duck seems to float less lightly than it really does, its body being comparatively flat. It moves fast, frequently sipping the water, as if to ascertain whether its favorite food be in it. Then turning its head and glancing on either side to assure itself of security, down it dives with all the agility of a merganser, and remains a considerable time below. On emerging, it shakes its head, raises the hind part of its body, opens its short and rather curved wings, after a few flaps replaces them, and again dives in search of food. Should any person appear when it emerges, it swims off a considerable distance, watches every movement of the intruder, and finally either returns to its former place or flies away.

On the wing, as well as on the water, the lesser scaup duck is a very lively, nervous, and restless bird; its flight is very swift and often erratic with frequent unexpected twists and turns, which make it a difficult bird for the sportsman to hit; but it often flies in large flocks, closely bunched, or with a broad front of many birds abreast, which gives the gunner an opportunity for an effective raking shot. When much disturbed by shooting these ducks fly about from one lake to another high in the air twisting and turning in a most erratic manner and finally darting down almost vertically, making the air whistle with their wings. Audubon (1840) says:

When these birds are traveling, their flight is steady, rather laborious, but greatly protracted. The whistling of their wings is heard at a considerable distance when they are passing over head. At this time they usually move in a broad front, sometimes in a continuous line. When disturbed, they fly straight forward for a while, with less velocity than when traveling, and, if within proper distance, are easily shot. At times their notes are shrill, but at others hoarse and guttural. They are, however, rarely heard during the day, and indeed like many other species, these birds are partly nocturnal.

Fall.—The fall migration starts rather late with this species, as it is one of the last to leave its northern breeding grounds, and it proceeds southward in a leisurely manner in advance of the frost line. The migration route is practically a reversal of the route traversed in the spring, mainly in the interior, over the sloughs, marshs, lakes, and rivers most frequented by gunners. Constant persecution by sportsmen keeps these little ducks on the move and they have little time to rest and feed, except at night on the larger lakes. They decoy readily and many are shot over live or wooden decoys from blinds made in the rushes near their feeding grounds; they are killed by ambushed gunners on their fly ways between the marshes and the lakes where they roost; and they are hunted out of the cover where they feed in the sloughs of the North and the rice fields of the South. They are safe only in the center of some large body of water.

Mr. Todd (1904) quotes another interesting note from Mr. Bacon, describing the departure of these ducks from Lake Erie as follows:

On one occasion I saw, as I believed, all the lesser scaups in this neighborhood start for the south. The bay had frozen over a few nights before, and on this particular afternoon a large flock of these ducks kept circling over the lake, sometimes high in the air, again dropping swiftly to the surface and skimming along for a mile or so. Finally having evidently gathered into one flock all the birds of the vicinity, they rose to a great height and, starting southward, were soon lost to view.

Winter.—They are very abundant all winter throughout the southern half of the United States, where they find some safe havens of rest. Large numbers winter on the Indian River in Florida and on the lakes in the interior of that State; on Lake Worth they are very abundant and so tame that they have learned to feed almost out of the hands of the winter tourists. On the Louisiana coast they are the commonest ducks and they soon learn to appreciate the security which they find on the protected reservations. It must be a relief to them to find such a wild fowl paradise after running the gauntlet of shooting grounds and sportsmen's clubs.

DISTRIBUTION.

Breeding range.—Northern interior of North America. East to the west coast of Hudson Bay (Churchill) and southeastern Ontario (Lake Temiskaming). South to northern Ohio (Lake, Lorain, and Sandusky Counties), southern Wisconsin (Lake Koshkonong), southeastern Iowa (Keokuk), possibly northern Nebraska (Cherry County), and northeastern Colorado (Barr Lake, few). West to northwestern Montana (Teton County), central British Columbia (Quesnelle Lake and Lac la Hache), and the coast of southern Alaska (Glacier Bay). Has bred casually near San Francisco, California. North to central Alaska (Yukon River) and the northern limit of timber in northern Canada (Mackenzie and Anderson River regions). Breeding records east of Hudson Bay probably refer to *marila*, and perhaps some of the northern records do.

Winter range.—Southern North and Central America. East to the Atlantic coast of United States, the Bahamas, and the Lesser Antilles (St. Thomas, St. Lucia, Trinidad, etc.). South to Panama. West to the Pacific coast of Central America and United States. North to southern British Columbia (Vancouver and Okanogan Lake), southeastern Arizona (San Pedro River), northeastern Colorado (Barr Lake), northeastern Arkansas (Big Lake), southern Illinois, and eastern Maryland (Chesapeake Bay); rarely as far north as Long Island and Massachusetts (Boston).

Spring migration.—Early dates of arrival: Iowa, Keokuk, February 21; Minnesota, Heron Lake, March 5; Michigan, southern, March 11; Alberta, Stony Plain, April 19; Mackenzie, Fort Simpson, May 24. Average dates of arrival: Colorado, Loveland, March 12; Iowa, central, March 21; Minnesota, Heron Lake, March 22; Ohio, Oberlin, March 24; New York, Cayuga Lake, April 1; Illinois, Chicago, April 6; Ontario, Ottawa, April 26; Manitoba, Raeburn, April 9. Late dates of departure: Panama, March 25; Lower California, San Martin, April 23: Porto Rico, Culebra Island, April 21; Florida, Wakulla County, May 23; New York, Cayuga Lake, June 24.

Fall migration.—Early dates of arrival: Ontario, Ottawa, October 12; New York, Cayuga Lake, October 1; Virginia, Alexandria, September 25; Florida, Wakulla County, October 18; Panama, November 25. Average dates of departure: Ontario, Ottawa, November 11; New York, Cayuga Lake, November 15; Manitoba, southern, November 18; Minnesota, southern, November 13; Iowa, Keokuk, December 2. Late dates of departure: Quebec, Montreal, November 12; Ontario, Ottawa, November 21; Illinois, Chicago, December 22.

Casual records.—Accidental in Bermuda (December 19, 1846, January 8, 1849, and February 25, 1876). Rare in migration to Newfoundland and Nova Scotia. Accidental in Greenland (Egedesminde).

Egg dates.—Alaska and Arctic America: Eighteen records, June 17 to July 18; nine records, June 22 to July 5. Manitoba, Saskatchewan and Alberta: Thirteen records, May 20 to July 14; seven records, June 10 to July 3. Minnesota and North Dakota; Eighteen records, May 1 to July 10; nine records, June 12 to 25.

PERISSONETTA COLLARIS (Donovan).

RING-NECKED DUCK.

HABITS.

Although usually classed with the scaup ducks and resembling them in general appearance, this species seems to be more closely related to the European tufted duck than to any American species. Wilson figured and described it under the name, "tufted duck," supposing it to be identical with that species. Its gray speculum separates it from the scaups and its black head and conspicuous crest make it seem very distinct from the redhead, though female ringnecks and redheads look very much alike. I am interested to note that, since I wrote the above, Mr. Ned Hollister (1919) has very ably advanced a similar theory. Its distribution is similar to that of the lesser scaup. It is essentially a fresh-water duck of the interior. It prefers the marshes and sloughs to the open lakes and streams and is less gregarious than the scaups.

Spring.—It is not an especially early migrant in the spring but usually appears soon after the breaking up of the ice, coming along with the scaup ducks and frequenting much the same resorts, but flocking by itself in small scattered groups around the marshy edges of the ponds and in the sloughs.

Courtship.—Audubon (1840) refers briefly to the courtship of this species as follows:

They have an almost constant practice of raising the head in a curved manner, partially erecting the occipital feathers, and emitting a note resembling the sound produced by a person blowing through a tube. At the approach of spring the males are observed repeating this action every now and then while near the females, none of which seem to pay the least attention to their civilities.

Nesting.—The first account we have of the breeding habits of the ring-necked duck was funished by Dr. T. S. Roberts (1880); he found a nest on May 27, 1876, near Minneapolis, Minnesota, and on June 1 he shot the female and collected the eggs. He described the nest, as follows:

The situation chosen for the nest was in a narrow strip of marsh bordering a large shallow pond or slough. About halfway between the shore and the edge of the open water was a mass of sunken débris, probably the remnants of an old muskrat house, which reached nearly or quite to the surface of the water, here about 8 inches deep. On this foundation was the nest, a rather compact, bulky structure, built mainly of fine grass with a little moss intermingled. Outside, the grass is long and circularly disposed, while the bottom, inside, is composed of short broken pieces and the inside rim of fine grass bent and loosely tangled together with considerable down among it. Measurements were not taken before removing the nest, but in its present condition the walls and base are 2½ inches thick, the diameter inside 6 inches, and the depth of the cavity 3 inches. The clutch was nine eggs, which contained small embryos.

My own experiences with the nesting habits of this species have been rather unsatisfactory, but I will give them for what they are worth. On June 12, 1901, while exploring some extensive wet meadows about the sources of a branch of the Goose River in Steele County, North Dakota, I flushed a strange duck from her nest; she circled past me two or three times within gunshot, so that I had a fairly good look at her, but I had no gun with me at the time; I judged from her appearance and gait that she was a scaup, but she lacked the white speculum of the other two species. I made two subsequent visits to the nest alone and on the following day Doctor Bishop and Mr. Job went with me; she proved too shy for us to shoot, but we all concluded that she was a ring-necked duck, as the eggs were unmistakably scaup's and if she had been one of the two other species we would certainly have seen the conspicuous white speculum. The nest was well concealed in thick grass in a rather open place in the meadow about 10 yards from the river; it was made of bits of dry grass and thickly lined with very dark gray down; it contained 10 eggs, nearly fresh. This set is now in the collection of Herbert Massey, Esq., in England.

I found another doubtful nest in the Crane Lake slough in Saskatchewan on June 23, 1906; while hunting through the bullrushes (*Scirpus lacustris*) for canvasback's nests, I flushed a small duck from her nest and shot at her as she went fluttering off over the water, but lost her in the bullrushes; the eggs were evidently scaup ducks' and I felt certain that she had a gray speculum. The nest was in a thick clump of dead bullrushes, made of dry bullrushes and lined with very dark down; it measured 10 by 12 inches in diameter, the inner cavity was 7 inches across and 3 inches deep; the rim was built up about 3 inches above the water, and the eggs were wet and partly in the water; there were eight eggs, one of which was a redhead's.

Mr. Herbert K. Job (1899) found a nest in the Turtle Mountain region of North Dakota, on June 14, 1898, which he felt sure was a nest of the ring-neck duck. He writes:

It was in a reedy, boggy bayou, or arm of a lake, which was full of bitterns, black terns, and bronzed, red-winged and yellow-headed blackbirds. I was on my way out to photograph a bittern's nest already found, and was struggling along more than up to my knees in mud and water, when a smallish duck flushed almost at my feet from some thick, dead rushes, disclosing 12 buffy eggs, nearly fresh. The clear view within a yard of the pearly gray speculum and the total absence of white on the wing told the story. She alighted near by in open water, and gave me and my companion such fine opportunity to study her with the glass and note every detail of her plumage, both as she sat and as she flew back and forth before us, that it was not necessary to sacrifice her for identification. Nothing was seen of the male.

Maj. Allan Brooks (1903) records a nest which he found in the Cariboo District of British Columbia on June 27, as follows:

The nest was in a tussock of grass, in eight inches of water: it was composed of coarse green grass and arched over with the drooping blades of the tussock. The nine eggs contained small embryos.

From this and the foregoing records it would seem that the ringnecked duck habitually builds its nest in wet situations and not on dry ground, as is usually the case with the lesser scaup duck. The down in the ring-necked duck's nest is smaller and a little lighter in color than that of the lesser scaup duck; it is "warm sepia" or "bister," with lighter centers; the breast feathers in it are pure white or pale grayish, tipped with white.

Eggs.—The set seems to consist of from 8 to 12 eggs, which are practically indistinguishable from those of the lesser scaup; the shape, texture of shell, and color are all the same; further description would be useless repetition. The measurements of 75 eggs, in various collections, average 57.5 by 39.8 millimeters; the eggs showing the four extremes measure 60.5 by 41.9, 58 by 42.2, 53.5 by 38.5 and 54.9 by 38 millimeters.

Young.—I have no data on the period of incubation. The female alone performs this duty, as the males desert the females during this period and do not assist in the care of the young. I have never seen a brood of young ringnecks and can not find anything in print about their behavior or their development.

Plumages.—I have never seen a small downy young of this species, which was positively identified, but Maj. Allan Brooks (1903) says:

The young in down are very light colored, resembling the young of the canvasback and redhead, and quite different from the dusky, unspotted young of the lesser scaup.

His excellent plate shows this to advantage. A larger downy young bird, measuring 8 inches long in the skin, collected by Major Brooks and now in the United States National Museum, I should describe as follows: The whole head, except the posterior half of the crown, is yellowish, shading from "chamois" or "cream buff" on the cheeks and auriculars to "colonial buff" on the throat; the posterior half of the crown and the occiput are "bister," nearly separated by points of yellow from a broad band of "bister" which extends down the hind neck to the back; narrow dusky postocular streaks are faintly suggested; the dark color of the back changes gradually from "sepia" anteriorly to "bister" posteriorly; the under parts are "ivory yellow" tinged with "cream buff;" there are two large scapular patches, two narrow wing stripes and two small rump patches of "cream buff"; there is also a narrow streak of the same color in the center of the upper back. All of these colors would probably be richer and brighter in a younger bird.

In the juvenal plumage, during the early fall the two sexes are very much alike. The upper parts are dull, dark brown, or blackish brown, with lighter edgings; the under parts are mottled with dull, light brown, and whitish; the wings are similar to those of the adult female, the secondaries in the speculum being dull gray, subterminally dusky and only very narrowly, if at all, tipped with white; the sides of the head and neck are mottled with brown and whitish; the crown is deep brownish black, mottled with brown; and the chin is broadly white.

During September and October the sexes differentiate rapidly. New black feathers appear in the head and neck of the young male; new black feathers with a greenish gloss gradually replace the brown feathers of the mantle; and the under parts become whiter, with white vermiculated feathers appearing among the brown feathers of the flanks. By the last of December the young male is in nearly full plumage with the two rings on the bill in evidence with only a few brown feathers left in the back; the brown neck ring is hardly noticeable, the wing is still immature and all the colors are duller. Further progress is made toward maturity during the winter and spring, but it is not until after the new wings are acquired, at the complete molt the next summer, that young birds become indistinguishable from adults, when about 14 months old.

I have never seen the eclipse plumage of the ring-necked duck but it probably has a partial eclipse plumage, or a prolonged double molt in August, very much like what takes place in the tufted duck, to which it is closely related.

Food.—Dr. F. Henry Yorke (1899) says:

The feeding grounds are more inshore than those of the bluebills, and they feed more upon seeds such as frog bit, duck and pond weed, being very fond of bulbs of the nonscented water lily, upon which they will gorge themselves and get exceedingly fat; at that time they are counted a delicacy for the table. The playgrounds are in open pieces of water surrounded by weeds and lily pads, in buck brush, willows, and wild rice. The roosting grounds are in buck brush, the edges of timber, down smartweed, and flags.

In his food chart for the ring-necked duck he gives the same list of foods as given for the scaup duck. It is also said to feed on minnows, small frogs, tadpoles, crawfish, snails, insects, aquatic roots, various seeds, and even grains. Audubon (1840) says:

Whilst in ponds, they feed by diving and dabbling with their bills in the mud amongst the roots of grasses, of which they eat the seeds also. as well as snails and all kinds of aquatic insects. When on rivers, their usual food consists of small fish and crays, the latter of which they procure at the bottom. A male which I shot near Louisville, in the beginning of May, exhibited a protuberance of the neck so very remarkable as to induce me to cut the skin, when I found a frog, the body of which was nearly 2 inches long, and which had almost choked the bird, as it allowed me to go up within a dozen or 15 paces before I took aim.

Mr. Arthur H. Howell (1911) writes:

The food of the ringneck consists mainly of the seeds and stems of pond weed, hornwort, and other aquatic plants, with many nymphs and larvae of water insects.

Behavior.—Although the ring-necked duck feeds largely in the shallow water of the marshes, it is nevertheless a good diver and can, if necessary, dive in deep water. Its feet are large and powerful, it dives with its wings tightly closed and swims below the surface very rapidly by the use of feet alone. It swims lightly and rapidly on the surface and rises readily from the water, making a whistling sound as it does so. Its flight is swift and vigorous and it is as lively as the other scaup ducks in all its movements. It flies mostly in small flocks of open formation, rather than in close bunches or lines, so that it does not offer such tempting shots as the other bluebills. While on its feeding grounds it is also usually more scattered and more often flushed singly or in pairs. It should be easily recognized in flight by its general resemblance to the scaups and by the absence of the white speculum; the males are conspicuously marked and can be easily recognized by the black back and crested head and by the ringed bill, if near enough; the small white chin does not seem to be very conspicuous in life. Mr. Horace W. Wright (1910) has called attention to another good field mark; he says:

A conspicuous feature of his plumage as he sits on the water, even at some distance, is a white band on the side of the breast in front of the wing when closed, having the appearance of a bar, but continuous with the white under the wing when the wing is spread. With closed wing as the bird sits on the water the upper portion of this white bar lies between the black of the breast and the black of the wing; the lower portion between the black of the breast and the finely barred side.

The female is not so easily recognized, as it closely resembles the female redhead, but, if near enough, the white cheeks, faint white eye-ring and ringed bill may be seen.

Fall.—The fall migrations of these ducks come along slightly in advance of the scaup ducks, southward through the Mississippi valley and southeastward to the South Atlantic States. They frequent the marshes and small ponds on the way and become very abundant in the rice fields and bayous of the Southern States, where they remain all winter and furnish excellent sport for the gunners. They are generally very fat at that season, when they have been feeding on vegetable food, seeds, and grain, and their flesh becomes excellent in flavor.

Game.—The methods employed for shooting the "ringbills" as they are called, are the same as for the "bluebills." Blinds are set in their fly ways or passes, to and from their feeding grounds, where they decoy well to wooden decoys and where large numbers are killed. Although not so universally abundant as some other species and not so well known, this is one of the most abundant ducks of the South Atlantic and Gulf States in winter. On the coast of Louisiana these ducks spend the night out on the Gulf, but come into the ponds to feed at daybreak. They come in small flocks of from 3 or 4 to 10 or 12, flying with great speed, and drop at once without circling, into the pond they have selected. They seem to have certain favorite feeding ponds, for while one pond will yield excellent sport, the gunner in an adjoining pond may not get a shot. They are naturally not shy and are not easily driven from their favorite feeding grounds. Mr. Arthur H. Howell (1911) writes that on Big Lake, Arkansas, "in November and December it is often the most abundant duck, and gunners there frequently kill as many as 50 birds in a few hours. A few remain all winter."

DISTRIBUTION.

Breeding range.—Central North America. East to northern Saskatchewan (Athabaska Lake region), western Ontario (Lac la Seul), and southeastern Wisconsin (Lakes Koshkonong and Pewaukee). Has been known to breed in southeastern Maine (Calais). South to northern Illinois (formerly at least), northern Iowa (Clear Lake), northern Nebraska (Cherry County), and northern Utah (Salt Lake County). West to northeastern California (Lassen County), central southern Oregon (Klamath Lake), and central southern British Columbia (Chilliwack and Cariboo district). North to the central Mackenzie Valley (Fort Simpson) and Athabasca Lake (Fort Chipewyan). Breeding records from farther north are open to question.

Winter range.—Southern North America. East to the Atlantic coast of United States, the Bahama Islands and rarely to Porto Rico and Cuba. South throughout Mexico to Guatemala. West to the Pacific coast of Mexico and United States. North to southern British Columbia (Okanogan Lake), probably Nevada, New Mexico, and northern Texas, to northeastern Arkansas (Big Lake), southern Illinois (Ohio Valley), and eastern Maryland (Chesapeake Bay). Casual in winter as far north as eastern Massachusetts (Boston).

Spring migration.—Early dates of arrivals: Pennsylvania, Erie, March 15; New York, Niagara Falls, March 10; Massachusetts,

Essex County, April 7; Indiana, English Lake, February 27; Iowa, Keokuk, March 4; Minnesota, Heron Lake, March 15; Alberta, Stony Plain, April 19.   Average dates of arrival: Pennsylvania, Erie, April 16, Indiana, English Lake, March 11; Iowa, Keokuk, March 14; Minnesota, Heron Lake, March 27.   Late dates of departure: Florida, Leon County, March 24; Indiana, northern, May 11; Kansas, May 24.

Fall migration.—Early dates of arrival: Louisiana, Gulf coast, about September 15; Valley of Mexico, September 28; Virginia, Alexandria, October 6.   Late dates of departure: Ontario, Ottawa, November 21; Massachusetts, November 23; New York, Brockport, December 10; Pennsylvania, Erie, December 3; Michigan, Hillsdale, November 26; Indiana, English Lake, November 22.

Casual records.—Accidental in Bermuda (November 13, 1850). Only record for Great Britain is questioned by latest authorities. Has wandered east to Nova Scotia (Sable Island, 1901).

Egg dates.—Manitoba, Saskatchewan, and Alberta: Thirteen records, May 31 to July 6; seven records, June 7 to 19.   Minnesota and North Dakota: Five records, June 1 to 18.

REFERENCES TO BIBLIOGRAPHY.

ALFORD, CHARLES E.
   1920—Some Notes on Diving Ducks. British Birds, vol. 14, pp. 106–110.
ALLEN, CHARLES SLOVER.
   1893—The Nesting of the Black Duck on Plum Island. The Auk, vol. 10, pp. 53–59.
ALLEN, GLOVER MORRILL.
   1905—Summer Birds in the Bahamas. The Auk, vol. 22, pp. 113–133.
ANDRUS, FRED H.
   1896—Unusual Nesting of American Merganser. The Nidiologist, vol. 3, pp. 72–73.
ARNOLD, EDWARD.
   1894—My '94 Outing Trip in Northwest Canada. Nidiologist, vol. 1, p. 168; vol. 2, pp. 11–13 and 23–25.
ARTHUR, STANLEY CLISBY.
   1920—A note on the "Southern Teal." The Auk, vol. 37, pp. 126–127.
AUDUBON, JOHN JAMES.
   1840—The Birds of America, 1840–44.
BAILEY, VERNON.
   1902—Notes in Handbook of Birds of the Western United States, by Florence Merriam Bailey.
BAIRD, SPENCER FULLERTON; BREWER, THOMAS MAYO; and RIDGWAY, ROBERT.
   1884—The Water Birds of North America.
BAKER, EDWARD CHARLES STUART.
   1908—The Indian Ducks and Their Allies.
BAKER, FRANK COLLINS.
   1889—Contents of the Stomachs of Certain Birds Collected in Brevard County Florida, Between Jan. 5 and April 15, 1889. Ornithologist and Oologist, vol. 14, pp. 139–140.
BANGS, OUTRAM.
   1918—Notes on the Species and Subspecies of Poecilonetta Eyton. Proceedings of the New England Zoological Club, vol. 6, pp. 87–89.
BARROWS, WALTER BRADFORD.
   1912—Michigan Bird Life.
BEAUPRÉ, EDWIN.
   1906—Unusual Nesting Site of the Black Duck (*Anas obscura*). The Auk, vol. 23, pp. 218–219.
BENNERS, GEORGE B.
   1887—A Collecting Trip in Texas. Ornithologist and Oologist, vol. 12, pp. 49–52, 65–69, and 81–84.
BENT, ARTHUR CLEVELAND.
   1902—Nesting Habits of the Anatidae in North Dakota. The Auk, vol. 18, pp. 328–336, vol. 19, pp. 1–12 and 165–174.
   1912—Notes on Birds Observed During a Brief Visit to the Aleutian Islands and Bering Sea in 1911. Smithsonian Miscellaneous Collections, vol. 56, No. 32.

BEWICK, THOMAS.
    1847—A History of British Birds.
BEYER, GEORGE EUGENE; ALLISON, ANDREW; and KOPMAN, HENRY HAZLITT.
    1906—List of the Birds of Louisiana. The Auk, vol. 23, pp. 1–15, and 275–282;
        vol. 24, pp. 314–321; vol. 25, pp. 173–180 and 439–448.
BLANCHAN, NELTJE.
    1898–1908—Birds that Hunt and are Hunted.
BOWLES, JOHN HOOPER.
    1908—Lead Poisoning in Ducks. The Auk, vol. 25, pp. 312–313.
    ·1909—The Birds of Washington.
BREWSTER, WILLIAM.
    1900—Notes on the Breeding Habits of the American Golden-eyed Duck or
        Whistler. The Auk, vol. 17, pp. 207–216.
    1902—An undescribed form of the Black Duck (*Anas obscura*). The Auk, vol.
        19, pp. 183–188.
    1909—Something More about Black Ducks. The Auk, vol. 26, pp. 175–179.
BROOKS, ALLAN.
    1903—Notes on the Birds of the Cariboo District, British Columbia. The Auk,
        vol. 20, pp. 277–284.
BROOKS, WINTHROP SPRAGUE.
    1913—An addition to the A. O. U. Check List. The Auk, vol. 30, pp. 110–111.
BRYANT, HAROLD CHILD.
    1914—A Survey of the Breeding Grounds of Ducks in California in 1914. The
        Condor, vol. 16, pp. 217–239.
BUCK, HENRY ROBERT.
    1893—Wood Ducks and Bobwhite. The Nidiologist, vol. 1, p. 54.
BUTLER, AMOS WILLIAM.
    1897—The Birds of Indiana. Department of Geology and Natural Resources.
        Twenty-second Annual Report.
CAHN, ALVIN R.
    1912—The Freezing of Cayuga Lake in its Relation to Bird Life. The Auk, vol.
        29, pp. 437–444.
CALL, AUBREY BRENDON.
    1894—An American Merganser's Nest. The Nidiologist, vol. 1, p. 101.
CARROLL, JAMES JUDSON.
    1900—Notes on the Birds of Refugio County, Texas. The Auk, vol. 17, pp.
        337–348.
CLARK, JOHN NATHANIEL.
    1882—Woodcock and Black Duck. Ornithologist and Oologist, vol. 7. p. 144.
CLARKE, WILLIAM EAGLE.
    1895—On the Ornithology of the Delta of the Rhone. The Ibis, 1895, pp.
        173–211.
COLLINS, WILLIAM H.
    1880—Notes on the Breeding Habits of Some of the Water-Birds of St. Clair
        Flats, Michigan. Bulletin of the Nuttall Ornithological Club, vol. 5,
        pp. 61–62.
COOKE, WELLS WOODBRIDGE.
    1906—Distribution and Migration of North American Ducks, Geese, and Swans.
        United States Department of Agriculture, Biological Survey, Bulletin
        No. 26.
CORDEAUX, JOHN.
    1898—British Birds with Their Nests and Eggs. Order Anseres, vol. 4, pp.
        52–203.

CORY, CHARLES BARNEY.
  1880—Birds of the Bahama Islands.
COUES, ELLIOTT.
  1874—Birds of the North-West.
CURRIER, EDMONDE SAMUEL.
  1902—Winter Water Fowl of the Des Moines Rapids. The Osprey, vol. 6, pp.
        71–75.
DAVID, ARMAND, and OUSTALET, EMILE.
  1877—Les Oiseaux de la Chine.
DAWSON, WILLIAM LEON.
  1903—The Birds of Ohio.
  1909—The Birds of Washington.
DUTCHER, WILLIAM.
  1907—The Wood Duck. Bird-Lore, vol. 9, p. 189-193.
DWIGHT, JONATHAN, Jr.
  1909—The Singular Case of the Black Duck of North America. The Auk, vol.
        26, pp. 422–426.
DYBOWSKI, BENEDICT NALENTSCH, and PARREX, A.
  1868—Verzeichniss der wahrend der Jahre 1866 und 1867 im Gebiete der Miner-
        alwasser von Darasun in Daurien beobachteten Vögel. Journal für
        Ornithologie, vol. 16, pp. 330–339.
EASTMAN, A. B.
  1915—The Wood Duck. The Oologist, vol. 32, p. 95.
EATON, ELON HOWARD.
  1910—Birds of New York.
ELLIOT, DANIEL GIRAUD.
  1898—The Wild Fowl of North America.
EMERSON, WILLIAM OTTO.
  1901—Nesting of *Spatula clypeata*. The Condor, vol. 3, p. 116.
EVANS, WILLIAM.
  1891—On the Periods Occupied by Birds in the Incubation of Their Eggs. The
        Ibis, 1891, pp. 52–93.
EVERMANN, BARTON WARREN.
  1913—Eighteen Species of Birds New to the Pribilof Islands, Including Four New
        to North America. The Auk, vol. 30, pp. 15–18.
FAY, SAMUEL PRESCOTT.
  1910—The Canvasback in Massachusetts. The Auk, vol. 27, pp. 369–381.
FINN, FRANK.
  1909—The Waterfowl of India and Asia.
  1915—Display of Female *Eunetta falcata*. Zoologist, series 4, vol. 19, p. 36.
FISHER, ALBERT KENRICK.
  1901—Two Vanishing Game Birds: The Woodcock and the Wood Duck. Year-
        book of Department of Agriculture for 1901, pp. 447–458.
FORBUSH, EDWARD HOWE.
  1909—The Mallard. Bird-Lore, vol. 11, pp. 40–47.
FRAZAR, MARTIN ABBOTT.
  1887—An Ornithologist's Summer in Labrador. Ornithologist and Oologist, vol.
        12, pp. 1–3, 17–20, and 33–35.
GHIDINI, ANGELO.
  1911—Les canards du Yang-tsze en Europe. Revue Française d'Ornithologie
        vol. 2, p. 78.
GIBBS, MORRIS.
  1885—Catalogue of the Birds of Kalamazoo County, Michigan. Ornithologist
        and Oologist, vol. 10, pp. 166–167.

GRINNELL, JOSEPH.
    1900—Birds of the Kotzebue Sound Region. Pacific Coast Avifauna, No. 1.
    1909—Birds and Mammals of the 1907 Alexander Expedition to Southeastern
        Alaska. University of California, Publications in Zoology, vol. 5, pp.
        171–264.
GRINNELL, JOSEPH; BRYANT, HAROLD CHILD; and STORER, TRACY IRWIN.
    1918—The Game Birds of California.
HAGERUP, ANDREAS THOMSEN.
    1891—The Birds of Greenland.
HANNA, G. DALLAS.
    1916—Records of Birds New to the Pribilof Islands Including Two New to North
        America. The Auk, vol. 33, pp. 400–403.
    1920—Additions to the Avifauna of the Pribilof Islands, Alaska, Including Four
        Species New to North America. The Auk, vol 37, pp. 248–254.
HARTERT, ERNST JOHANN OTTO.
    1920—Die Vögel der Paläarktischen Fauna.
HATCH, PHILO LUOIS.
    1892—Notes on the Birds of Minnesota.
HEINROTH, OTTO.
    1911—Beiträge zur Biologie, namentlich Ethologie und Psychologie der Anati-
        den. Verhandl. 5th Intern. Ornith. Kongr. Berlin, 1910, p. 589–702.
HENSHAW, HENRY WETHERBEE.
    1875—Report upon the Ornithological Collections made in Portions of Nevada,
        Utah, California, Colorado, New Mexico, and Arizona during the years
        1871, 1872, 1873, and 1874. Report upon Geographical and Geological
        Explorations and Surveys West of the One Hundredth Meridian.
HOLLISTER, NED.
    1919—The Systematic Position of the Ring-necked Duck. The Auk, vol. 36,
        pp. 460–463.
HOPWOOD, CYRIL.
    1912—A List of Birds from Arakan. Journ. Bombay Nat. Hist. Soc., vol. 21,
        pp. 1196–1221. Anseres, p. 1220.
HOWELL, ARTHUR HOLMES.
    1911—Birds of Arkansas. United States Department of Agriculture, Biological
        Survey, Bulletin No. 38.
HUDSON, WILLIAM HENRY.
    1920—Birds of La Plata.
HUNTINGTON, DWIGHT WILLIAMS.
    1903—Our Feathered Game.
JOB, HERBERT KEIGHTLEY.
    1898—The Enchanted Isles. The Osprey, vol. 3, pp. 37–41.
    1899—Some Observations on the Anatidae of North Dakota. The Auk, vol. 16,
        pp. 161–165.
JONES, LYNDS.
    1909—The Birds of Cedar Point and Vicinity. The Wilson Bulletin, No. 67,
        vol. 21, pp. 55–76, 115–131, and 187–204; vol. 22, pp. 25–41, 97–115,
        and 172–182.
KENNARD, FREDERIC HEDGE.
    1913—The Black Duck Controversy Again. The Auk, vol. 30, p. 106.
    1919—Notes on a New Subspecies of Blue-winged Teal. The Auk, vol. 36, pp.
        455–460.

KINGSFORD, E. G.
  1917—Wood Duck Removing Young from the Nest. The Auk, vol. 34, pp. 335–336.
KNIGHT, ORA WILLIS.
  1908—The Birds of Maine.
LANGILLE, JAMES HIBBERT.
  1884—Our Birds and Their Haunts.
LITTLEJOHN, CHASE.
  1899—On the Nesting of Ducks. The Osprey, vol. 3, p. 78–79.
MABBOTT, DOUGLAS CLIFFORD.
  1920—Food Habits of Seven Species of American Shoal-water Ducks. United States Department of Agriculture, Bulletin, No. 862.
MACFARLANE, RODERICK ROSS.
  1891—Notes on and List of Birds and Eggs Collected in Arctic America, 1861–1866. Proceedings of the United States National Museum, vol. 14, pp. 413–446.
  1908—List of Birds and Eggs Observed and Collected in the Northwest Territories of Canada, between 1880 and 1894. In Through the Mackenzie Basin by Charles Mair.
MACGILLIVRAY, WILLIAM.
  1852—A History of British Birds.
MACOUN, JOHN.
  1909—Catalogue of Canadian Birds. Second Edition.
MAYNARD, CHARLES JOHNSON.
  1896—The Birds of Eastern North America.
MCATEE, WALDO LEE.
  1908—Lead poisoning in Ducks. The Auk, vol. 25, p. 472.
  1918—Food Habits of the Mallard Ducks of the United States. United States Department of Agriculture, Bulletin No. 720.
MCGREGOR, RICHARD CRITTENDEN.
  1906—Birds Observed in the Krenitzin Islands, Alaska. The Condor, vol. 8, pp. 114–122.
MCILWRAITH, THOMAS.
  1894—The Birds of Ontario.
MERRILL, JAMES CUSHING.
  1888—Notes on the Birds of Fort Klamath, Oregon. The Auk, vol. 5, pp. 139–146.
MIDDENDORFF, ALEXANDER THEODOROVICH VON.
  1853—Reise in den Aussersten Norden und Osten Sibiriens wahrend der Jahre 1843 und 1844 mit Allerhochster Genehmigung auf Veranstaltung der Kaiserlichen Akademie der Wissenschaften zu St. Petersburg ausgeführt und in Verbindung mit vielen Gehehrten herausgegeben. Vol. 2, Zoologie, pt. 2, Wirbelthiere.
MILLAIS, JOHN GUILLE.
  1902—The Natural History of the British Surface-Feeding Ducks.
  1913—British Diving Ducks.
MOORE, ROBERT THOMAS.
  1908—Three Finds in South Jersey. Cassinia, Proceedings of the Delaware Valley Ornithological Club, No. 12, pp. 29–40.
MORRIS, FRANCIS ORPEN.
  1903—A History of British Birds. Fifth edition.

MORSE, ALBERT PITTS.
    1921—A Sheld Duck (Tadorna tadorna L.) from Essex County, Mass. Bulletin
        of the Essex County Ornithological Club of Massachusetts, December
        1921, p. 68.
MUNRO, JAMES ALEXANDER.
    1917—Notes on the Winter Birds of the Okanogan Valley. The Ottawa Nat-
        uralist, vol. 31, pp. 81–89.
NELSON, EDWARD WILLIAM.
    1887—Report upon Natural History Collections Made in Alaska.
NOBLE, FRANK T.
    1906—Why Wounded Ducks Disappear. The Journal of the Maine Ornithological
        Society, vol. 8, pp. 60–61.
NORTON, ARTHUR HERBERT.
    1909—The Food of Several Maine Water-Birds. The Auk, vol. 26, pp. 438–440.
NUTTALL, THOMAS.
    1834—A Manual of the Ornithology of the United States and Canada, Water Birds.
OSGOOD, WILFRED HUDSON.
    1904—A Biological Reconnaisance of the Base of the Alaska Peninsula. North
        American Fauna, No. 24.
PEARSON, THOMAS GILBERT.
    1891—The Wood Duck. Ornithologist and Oologist, vol. 16, pp. 134–135.
    1916—The Shoveller. Bird-Lore, vol. 18, pp. 56–59.
PEARSON, THOMAS GILBERT; BRIMLEY, CLEMENT SAMUEL; and BRIMLEY, HERBERT
        HUTCHINSON.
    1919—Birds of North Carolina. North Carolina Geological and Economic Survey,
        vol. 4.
PECK, GEORGE DELRANE.
    1896—Melanism in Eggs of the Hooded Merganser. The Oregon Naturalist, vol.
        3, p. 84.
    1911—Reminiscences of the Wood Duck. The Oologist, vol. 28, pp. 35–36.
PHILLIPS, JOHN CHARLES.
    1911—Ten Years of Observation on the Migration of Anatidae at Wenham Lake,
        Massachusetts. The Auk, vol. 28, pp. 188–200.
    1911a—A case of the Migration and Return of the European Teal in Massachu-
        setts. The Auk, vol. 28, pp. 366–367.
    1912—The European Teal (*Nettion crecca*) again returning to Wenham, Mass.
        The Auk, vol. 29, p. 535.
    1916—A Note on the Mottled Duck. The Auk, vol. 33, pp. 432–433.
    1920—Habits of the Two Black Ducks, *Anas rubripes rubripes* and *Anas rubripes
        tristis*. The Auk, vol. 37, pp. 289–291.
POST, WILLIAM S.
    1914—Nesting of the Merganser (*Mergus americanus*) in 1913. The Oriole, vol.
        2, pp. 18–23.
PREBLE, EDWARD ALEXANDER.
    1908—A Biological Investigation of the Athabaska-Mackenzie Region. North
        American Fauna, No. 27.
PRESTON, JUNIUS WALLACE.
    1892—Notes on Bird Flight. Ornithologist and Oologist, vol. 17, pp. 41–42.
PRJEVALSKY, NICOLAS MICHAELOVICH.
    1878—The Birds of Mongolia, the Tangut Country, and the Solitudes of Northern
        Thibet. Rowley's Ornith. Miscell., vol. 3, pp. 87–110, 145–162.
RADDE, GUSTAV FERDINAND RICHARD VON.
    1863—Reisen im Süden von Ost–Sibirien, vol. 2, Die Festlands–Ornis des
        Südöstlichen Sibiriens.

RICH, WALTER HERBERT.
    1907—Feathered Game of the Northeast.
RIDGWAY, ROBERT.
    1881—On a Duck New to the North American Fauna. Proceedings of United
        States National Museum, vol. 4, pp. 22–24.
    1887—A Manual of North American Birds.
RINKER, GLEN.
    1899—Peculiar Nesting of the Hooded Merganser. The Osprey, vol. 4, p. 19–20.
ROBERTS, THOMAS SADLER.
    1880—Breeding of Fuligula Collaris in Southeastern Minnesota, and a Description
        of Its Nest and Eggs. Bulletin of the Nuttall Ornithological Club, vol.
        5, p. 61.
    1919—Water Birds of Minnesota Past and Present. Biennial Report of the State
        Game and Fish Commission of Minnesota, for the Biennal Period Ending
        July 31, 1918.
ROCKWELL, ROBERT BLANCHARD.
    1911—Nesting Notes on the Ducks of the Barr Lake Region, Colorado. The
        Condor, vol. 13, pp. 121–128 and 186–195.
ROLFE, EUGENE STRONG.
    1898—Notes from the Devils Lake Region. The Osprey, vol. 2, pp. 125–128.
SAGE, JOHN HALL.
    1881—Notes from Moosehead Lake, Me. Ornithologist and Oologist, vol. 6
        pp. 50–51.
SAMPSON, WALTER BEHRNARD.
    1901—An Exceptional Set of Eggs of the Wood Duck. The Condor, vol. 3, p. 95.
SAMUELS, EDWARD AUGUSTUS.
    1883—Our Northern and Eastern Birds.
SANFORD, LEONARD CUTLER; BISHOP, LOUIS BENNETT; and VAN DYKE, THEODORE
        STRONG.
    1903—The Waterfowl Family.
SAWYER, EDMUND JOSEPH.
    1909—The Courtship of Black Ducks. Bird-Lore, vol. 11, pp. 195–196.
SCHNEIDER, FREDERICK ALEXANDER, JR.
    1893—Nesting of the Cinnamon Teal. The Nidiologist, vol. 1, pp. 20–22.
SCHRENCK, LEOPOLD VON.
    1860—Reisen und Forschungen im Amur-lande in den Jahren 1854–1856, vol. 1,
        pt. 2, Vögel des Amur-Landes.
SENNETT, GEORGE BURRITT.
    1889—A New Species of Duck from Texas. The Auk, vol. 6, pp. 263–265.
SHELDON, HARRY HARGRAVE.
    1907—A Collecting Trip by Wagon to Eagle Lake, Sierra Nevada Mountains.
        The Condor, vol. 9, pp. 185–191.
SIMMONS, GEORGE FINLAY.
    1915—On the Nesting of Certain Birds in Texas. The Auk, vol. 32, pp. 317–331
SMITH, WILLIAM G.
    1887—Hybrid Ducks. Ornithologist and Oologist, vol. 12, p. 169.
STEJNEGER, LEONHARD.
    1885—Results of Ornithological Explorations in the Commander Islands and in
        Kamtschatka. Bulletin of the United States National Museum, No. 29.
STRONG, REUBEN MYRON.
    1912—Some Observations on the Life History of the Red-breasted Merganser.
        The Auk, vol. 29, pp. 479–488.

SWARTH, HARRY SCHELWALDT.
    1911—Birds and Mammals of the 1909 Alexander Alaska Expedition. University of California Publications in Zoology, vol. 7, pp. 9–172.
TACZANOWSKI, LADISLAS.
    1873—Bericht über die ornithologischen Untersuchungen des Dr. Dybowski in Ost–Sibirien. Journal für Ornithologie, vol. 21, pp. 81–119.
THOMPSON, ERNEST EVAN.
    1890—The Birds of Manitoba. Proceedings of the United States National Museum, vol. 13, pp. 457–643.
THOMPSON, ERNEST SETON.
    1901—The Mother Teal and the Overland Route. Lives of the Hunted, pp. 195–209.
TODD, WALTER EDMOND CLYDE.
    1904—The Birds of Erie and Presque Isle, Erie County, Pennsylvania. Annals of the Carnegie Museum, vol. 2, pp. 481–596.
    1911—A Contribution to the Ornithology of the Bahama Islands. Annals of the Carnegie Museum, vol. 7, pp. 388–464.
TOWNSEND, CHARLES WENDELL.
    1905—The Birds of Essex County, Massachusetts. Memoirs of the Nuttall Ornithological Club, No. 3.
    1909—The Use of the Wings and Feet by Diving Birds. The Auk, vol. 26, pp. 234–248.
    1911—The Courtship and Migration of the Red-breasted Merganser (Mergus serrator). The Auk, vol. 28, pp. 341–345.
    1912—The Validity of the Red-legged Subspecies of Black Duck. The Auk. vol. 29, pp. 176–179.
    1916—The Courtship of the Merganser, Mallard, Black Duck, Baldpate, Wood Duck, and Bufflehead. The Auk, vol. 33, pp. 9–17.
TURNER, LUCIEN MCSHAN.
    1886—Contributions to the Natural History of Alaska.
VAN KAMMEN, I. T.
    1915—Odd Nesting of the American Merganser. The Oologist, vol. 32, pp 166–168.
WALTON, HERBERT JAMES.
    1903—Notes on the Birds of Peking. The Ibis, 1903, pp. 19–35.
WARREN, BENJAMIN HARRY.
    1890—Report on the Birds of Pennsylvania.
WAYNE, ARTHUR TREZEVANT.
    1910—Birds of South Carolina. Contributions from the Charleston Museum, No. 1.
WETMORE, ALEXANDER.
    1915—Mortality among Waterfowl around Great Salt Lake, Utah. United States Department of Agriculture, Bulletin No. 217.
    1916—Birds of Porto Rico. United States Department of Agriculture, Bulletin No. 326.
    1918—The Duck Sickness in Utah. United States Department of Agriculture, Bulletin No. 672.
    1919—Lead Poisoning in Waterfowl. United States Department of Agriculture, Bulletin No. 793.
    1920—Observations on the Habits of Birds at Lake Burford, New Mexico. The Auk, vol. 37, pp. 221–247 and 393–412.
WILLETT, GEORGE, and JAY, ANTONIN.
    1911—May Notes from San Jacinto Lake. The Condor, vol. 13, pp. 156–160.

WILSON, ALEXANDER.
  1832—American Ornithology.
WITHERBY, HARRY FORBES, and OTHERS.
  1920—A Practical Handbook of British Birds.
WORMALD, HUGH.
  1910—The Courtship of the Mallard and Other Ducks. British Birds, vol. 4,
      pp. 2–7.
WRIGHT, HORACE WINSLOW.
  1910—Some Rare Wild Ducks Wintering at Boston, Massachusetts, 1909–1910.
      The Auk, vol. 27, pp. 390–408.
  1911—The Birds of the Jefferson Region in the White Mountains New Hamp-
      shire. Proceedings of the Manchester Institute of Arts and Sciences,
      vol. 5, pt. 1.
YARRELL, WILLIAM.
  1871—History of British Birds. Fourth Edition, 1871–85. Revised and enlarged
      by Alfred Newton and Howard Saunders.
YORKE, F. HENRY.
  1891—Green-Wing Teal Shooting. The American Field, vol. 35, No. 22, pp.
      533–535.
  1899—Our Ducks.

INDEX.

Page.

acuta Dafila tzitzihoa 144
affinis, Fulix 217
Aithyia ferina 185
Aix sponsa................................... 158
albellus, Mergellus 30
Allen, Arthur A., on canvasback 190
Allen, Charles S., on black duck 54
Allen, Glover M., on Bahama pintail 156
American merganser 1
   pintail 144
   scaup duck 207
americana, Mareca 89
   Nyroca 175
americanus, Mergus merganser 1
Anas fulvigula fulvigula.................... 68
   maculosa............................... 72
   novimexicana........................... 48
   platyrhyncha 34
   rubripes rubripes...................... 64
   rubripes tristis....................... 50
Andrus, Fred H., on American merganser .. 4
Aristonetta valisineria 189
Audubon, J. J.—
   on American merganser 4, 9
   on black duck.......................... 52
   on blue-winged teal 117
   on canvasback.......................... 195
   on green-winged teal 108
   on hooded merganser................... 26, 28
   on lesser scaup duck 217, 221, 222
   on mottled duck 73
   on pintail 150
   on ring-necked duck 224, 228
   on tufted duck 202
   on wood duck 159, 160, 163, 167, 168
Bacon, Samuel E., on lesser scaup duck... 221, 222
Bahama pintail 156
bahamensis, Poecilonetta.................... 156
Bailey, Vernon—
   on cinnamon teal 128
   on lesser scaup duck 221
Baird, Brewer, and Ridgway—
   on baldpate 91, 92
   on Florida duck........................ 69, 72
baldpate 89
Barrows, Walter B.—
   on canvasback 198
   on redhead 181
Bangs, Outram, on Bahama pintail 156
Beaupré, Edwin—
   on black duck.......................... 53
   on red-legged black duck 66

Bent, A. C.—
   on canvasback 191
   on redhead 176
   on red-breasted merganser............. 17
Bewick, Thomas—
   on European teal....................... 100
   on sheld duck 133
Beyer, Allison, and Kopman—
   on gadwall 84
   on mottled duck........................ 75
black duck 50
   red-legged 64
Blanchan, Neltje—
   on baldpate 95, 96
   on green-winged teal 106
blue-winged teal 111
Bowles, J. H.—
   on baldpate 95, 96
   on green-winged teal 107
   on hooded merganser.................... 24
   on mallard 37, 43
   on redhead 177
Brooks, Allan, on ring-necked duck 226
Bryant, Harold C.—
   on mallard 39
   on pintail 149
Buck, Henry R., on wood duck.............. 161
Butler, Amos, on hooded merganser 29
Cahn, Alvin R.—
   on American scaup duck................ 215
   on canvasback 200
canvasback 189
carolinense, Nettion........................ 102
Casarca ferruginea 130
Chaulelasmus streperus 77
cinnamon teal 122
Clark, John N., on black duck 55
Clarke, W. Eagle, on rufous-crested duck .. 172
clypeata, Spatula 135
Cochrane, W. S., on wood duck 164
collaris, Perissonetta....................... 224
Collins, W. H., on American scaup duck.... 209
Cordeaux, John, on sheld duck............. 133, 134
Cory, Charles B., on Bahama pintail........ 157
Coues, Elliott—
   on cinnamon teal 122, 128
   on pintail 149
crecca, Nettion............................. 98
cucullatus, Lophodytes 22
Currier, Ed. S., on pintail................. 144
cyanoptera, Querquedula..................... 122
Dafila acuta tzitzihoa....................... 144

241

Dawson, W. L.—   **Page.**
    on American merganser.................   4
    on American scaup duck.................   214
    on blue-winged teal.................   118
    on cinnamon teal.................   122, 127
    on gadwall.................   81
    on mallard.................   37
discors, Querquedula.................   111
duck, American scaup.................   207
    black.................   50
    Florida.................   68
    lesser scaup   217
    mottled   72
    New Mexican   48
    red-legged black.................   64
    ring-necked   224
    rufous-crested   171
    sheld   132
    tufted   202
Dwight, on red-legged black duck.................   66
Eastman, A. B., on wood duck.................   164
Eaton, Elon H.—
    on black duck.................   58
    on canvasback.................   200
    on wood duck.................   168
Elliot, D. G.—
    on black duck.................   58
    on Florida duck.................   69
    on hooded merganser.................   27
    on mottled duck   72
    on redhead.................   180, 181, 182
Emerson, W. Otto, on shoveller   137
Eunetta falcata   75
European pochard   185
    teal   98
    widgeon.................   86
falcata, Eunetta.................   75
falcated teal.................   75
ferina, Aithyia   185
ferruginea, Casarca   130
Florida duck   68
Forbush, Edward H., on mallard................. 42, 45
Frazar, M. A., on black duck.................   52
Fuligula fuligula.................   202
Fulvigula, Anas fulvigula.................   68
    maculosa.................   72
Fulix affinis.................   217
    marila nearctica.................   207
gadwall   77
green-winged teal.................   102
Grinnell, Bryant, and Storer, on canvasback   195
Grinnell, Joseph, on American scaup duck..   208
Haigh, G. H. Caton, on sheld duck.................   134
Hanna, G. Dallas, on falcated teal.................   75
Hardy, Manly—
    on American merganser.................   9
    on wood duck.................   164
Hatch, P. L.—
    on blue-winged teal.................   111
    on hooded merganser.................   26, 28
    on pintail.................   151
    on red-breasted merganser.................   16
    on wood duck.................   159
Henshaw, H. W., on green-winged teal......   104
Hersey, F. Seymour—
    on lesser scaup duck   220
    on pintail.................   145, 152

                                                                  Page
Honecker, Joseph W., on wood duck........   164
Hooded merganser.................   22
Howell, Arthur H., on ring-necked duck....   228
Huber, Wharton, on New Mexican duck....   48
Hudson, W. H., on Bahama pintail.........   156
Huntington, Dwight W.—
    on American scaup duck.................   214
    on blue-winged teal.................   120
    on gadwall   84
    on wood duck.................   170
Job, Herbert K., on ring-necked duck.......   225
Jones, Lynds, on black duck.................   60
Kennard, Fred H., on red-legged black duck   67
Kingsford, E. G., on wood duck   163
Knight, Ora W.—
    on American merganser.................   9
    on black duck.................   57
Langille, J. H., on wood duck.................   162
Lesser scaup duck.................   217
Littlejohn, Chase, on American scaup duck..   208
Lophodytes cucullatus.................   22
Mabbott, Douglas C.—
    on baldpate.................   94
    on blue-winged teal.................   117
    on cinnamon teal.................   127
    on gadwall.................   82
    on green-winged teal   107
    on pintail   151
    on wood duck.................   166
MacFarlane, Roderick, on lesser scaup duck..   219
Macgillivray, William—
    on European teal.................   101
    on European widgeon.................   87
    on sheld duck.................   133, 134
Macoun, John, on American scaup duck   209
maculosa, Anas fulvigula.................   72
mallard   34
Mareca americana.................   89
    penelope   86
marila, Fulix nearctica.................   207
Maynard, C. J.—
    on Florida duck.................   70
    on green-winged teal.................   104
    on pintail.................   154
McAtee, W. L.—
    on canvasback.................   196
    on Florida duck.................   71
    on mallard.................   42
McIlwraith, Thomas—
    on canvasback.................   197
    on redhead.................   183
merganser, American.................   1
    hooded.................   22
    red-breasted.................   13
    Mergus americanus   1
Mergellus albellus   30
Mergus merganser americanus.................   1
    serrator   13
Millais, John G.—
    on American merganser................. 7, 8, 11
    on American scaup duck......... 207, 211, 212
    on European pochard.................   185
    on European teal.................   99, 100, 101
    on European widgeon.................   86, 87, 88
    on hooded merganser.................   23
    on pintail.................   150, 153

Millais, John G.—Continued. **Page.**
  on red-breasted merganser.............. 17, 18
  on rufous-crested duck............. 172, 173, 174
  on shoveller........................ 136, 139, 140
  on smew............................ 31, 32, 33
  on tufted duck............................ 202
Moore, Robert T., on black duck............. 53
Morris, F. P., on ruddy shelldrake.......... 131
Morse, Albert P., on sheld duck............. 132
Mottled duck.................................. 72
Munro, J. A., on redhead.................... 183
Nelson, E. W.—
  on baldpate............................ 92
  on pintail......................... 144, 145, 151
Netta rufina................................. 171
Nettion carolinense.......................... 102
  crecca.................................. 98
New Mexican duck............................ 48
Noble, Frank T., on pintail................. 152
novimexicana, Anas.......................... 48
Nuttall, Thomas, on wood duck............. 166
Nyroca americana............................ 175
Osgood, Wilfred H., on mallard............. 44
Pearson, T. Gilbert—
  on green-winged teal.................... 107
  on shoveller 142
Peck, George D., on hooded merganser...... 25
penelope, Mareca........................... 86
Perissonetta collaris....................... 224
Perry, Gardner, on Bahama pintail.......... 156
Phillips, J. C.—
  on black duck.......................... 57, 59
  on falcated teal........................ 76
  on mottled duck........................ 72
  on red-legged black duck............... 67
pintail, American........................... 144
  Bahama 156
platyrhyncha, Anas.......................... 34
pochard, European.......................... 185
Poecilonetta bahamensis..................... 156
Pope, E. F., on wood duck.................. 163
Post, William S., on American merganser.. 6
Preston, J. W., on hooded merganser........ 25, 28
Querquedula cyanoptera..................... 122
  discors 111
red-breasted merganser..................... 13
redhead..................................... 175
red-legged black duck...................... 64
Rich, Walter H.—
  on American merganser.................. 11
  on American scaup duck................. 214
  on black duck.......................... 59, 61
  on pintail............................. 151
Ridgway, Robert—
  on baldpate............................ 93
  on rufous-crested duck................. 171
ring-necked duck............................ 224
Rinker, Glen, on hooded merganser......... 24
Roberts, Thomas S.—
  on mallard..... 42
  on ring-necked duck.................... 224
Rockwell, Robert B.—
  on blue-winged teal.................... 113
  on cinnamon teal....................... 124
  on mallard............................. 37

Rockwell, Robert B.—Continued. **Page.**
  on pintail............................. 147
  on redhead............................. 178
  on shoveller........................... 141
Rolfe, Eugene S., on pintail............... 147
rubripes, Anas rubripes..................... 64
  Anas tristis 50
ruddy shelldrake............................ 130
rufina, Netta............................... 171
rufous-crested duck......................... 171
Sage, John H., on American merganser...... 3
Samuels, E. A.—
  on black duck.......................... 52
  on hooded merganser.................... 26
Sanford, Leonard C.—
  on black duck.......................... 57
  on blue-winged teal.................... 119
  on pintail............................. 154
Saunders, Aretas A.—
  on baldpate............................ 95, 96
  on green-winged teal................... 107
Sawyer, Edmund J., on black duck.......... 51
scaup duck, American........................ 207
  Lesser 217
Schneider, Fred A., on cinnamon teal....... 125
Sennett, George B., on mottled duck........ 72
serrator, Mergus............................ 13
Shaw, Fred A., on American merganser... 3, 6, 12
sheld duck.................................. 132
shelldrake, Ruddy.......................... 130
shoveller................................... 135
Simmons, George F., on mottled duck....... 73
Smew....................................... 30
Spatula clypeata........................... 135
sponsa, Aix................................. 158
streperus, Chaulelasmus.................... 77
Sutton, George M., on green-winged teal.... 103
Swarth, Harry S., on American merganser.. 9, 10
Tadorna tadorna............................ 132
Taverner, P. A., on wood duck............. 167
teal, blue-winged 111
  cinnamon............................... 122
  European............................... 98
  Falcated 75
  green-winged........................... 102
Thompson, Ernest E., on blue-winged teal.. 112
Todd, W. E. Clyde, on Bahama pintail..... 157
Townsend, Charles W.—
  on American merganser.................. 1
  on baldpate............................ 95
  on mallard............................. 35
  on red-breasted merganser............. 13
  on red-legged black duck............... 65, 67
Townsend, Manley B.—
  on American merganser.................. 12
  on blue-winged teal.................... 113
  on red-breasted merganser............. 17
tristis, Anas rubripes...................... 50
tufted duck................................. 202
Turner, Lucien M., on baldpate............. 89
Tyler, John G., on cinnamon teal..... 124, 126, 127
tzitzihoa, Dafila acuta..................... 144
valisineria, Aristonetta.................... 189
Wayne, Arthur T., on red-breasted merganser.................................... 20

Wetmore, Alexander—   Page.
    on Bahama pintail........................ 157
    on baldpate.............................. 90
    on cinnamon teal....................... 123,127
    on gadwall............................... 79,83
    on lesser scaup duck.................... 218
    on mallard............................... 43
    on New Mexican duck.................. 50
    on redhead.............................. 176
widgeon, European........................... 86
Wilson, Alexander, on wood duck...... ... 160
Witherby's Handbook on sheld duck....... 134
wood duck.................................. 158
Wormald, H., on mallard................... 35
Wright, Horace W.—
    on red-legged black duck................ 66
    on ring-necked duck.................... 228

                                          Page.
Wyman, L. E., on mallard................. 37
Yarrell, William—
    on ruddy shelldrake.................. 130,131
    on rufous-crested duck................. 171
    on sheld duck.......................... 132
Yorke, F. Henry—
    on American scaup duck................ 207
    on blue-winged teal............... 111,118,119
    on green-winged teal................. 102,109
    on pintail............................ 144,153
    on redhead 176,183
    on ring-necked duck.................... 227
    on wood duck......................... 159,169

PLATES

PLATE 1. PINTAIL. A flock of pintails on the Ward-McIlhenny Reservation, Louisiana, January 1, 1910, presented by Mr. Herbert K. Job.

PLATE 2. AMERICAN MERGANSER. *Upper:* Nesting site of American mergansers, Lake Winnipegosis, Manitoba, June 19, 1913, referred to on page 3. *Lower:* Nest and eggs in above locality, rocks removed to expose it, June 16, 1903, presented by Mr. Walter Raine.

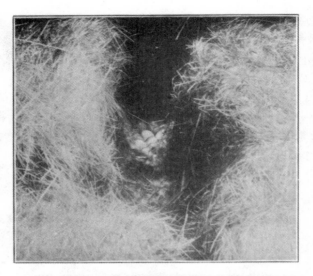

PLATE 3. AMERICAN MERGANSER. *Upper:* Nest and eggs of American merganser, among bales of hay in an old ice house, Lake Winnipegosis, Manitoba, June 18, 1913, bales removed to expose the nest, referred to on page 4. *Lower:* Nesting stub of American merganser, Grand Lake, Maine, June 3, 1920, presented by Mr. Frederic H. Kennard.

PLATE 4. AMERICAN MERGANSER. *Upper:* Female American merganser on her nest, Four Brothers Islands, Lake Champlain, New York, July 8, 1910, presented by Mr. Francis Harper. *Lower:* Young American mergansers, Eagle Lake, California, May 27, 1921, presented by Mr. Jules Labarthe, Sr., and Mr. Milton S. Ray.

PLATE 5. RED-BREASTED MERGANSER. *Upper:* Nest and eggs of red-breasted merganser, under balsam firs, branches cut away to expose the nest, Magdalen Islands, Quebec, June 21, 1904, referred to on page 15. *Lower:* Another nest of same in above locality, in thick grass, June 20, 1904, referred to on page 15.

PLATE 6. HOODED MERGANSER. Nesting box occupied by hooded merganser, near Tacoma, Washington, April 21, 1907, presented by Mr. J. Hooper Bowles, referred to on page 24.

PLATE 7. MALLARD. *Upper:* Nest and eggs of mallard, among "niggerheads," St. Michael, Alaska, June 9, 1915, from a negative taken by Mr. F. Seymour Hersey for the author. *Lower:* Nest and eggs of mallard, in a clump of reeds, North Dakota, presented by Mr. Herbert K. Job.

PLATE 8. MALLARD. *Left:* Mallard on her nest, 10 feet up on the limb of a maple, among ferns, near Tacoma, Washington, March 17, 1913, presented by Mr. J. Hooper Bowles, referred to on page 37. *Right:* Nest and eggs of mallard, under a rosebush, Crane Lake, Saskatchewan, June 21, 1905, presented by Mr. Herbert K. Job.

PLATE 9. MALLARD. *Upper:* Immature male mallard assuming first winter plumage, in captivity at Ithaca, New York, presented by Dr. Arthur A. Allen. *Lower:* Young mallard, 5 weeks old, Lake Winnepegosis, Manitoba, August 1, 1913, presented by Mr. Herbert K. Job.

PLATE 10. MALLARD. *Upper:* Adult male mallard in full plumage in September. *Lower:* Adult male mallard in eclipse plumage. Both photographs of birds in captivity, Ithaca, New York, presented by Dr. Arthur A. Allen.

PLATE 11. NEW MEXICAN DUCK. New Mexican duck, young male, Las Cruces, New Mexico, July 27, 1920, presented by Mr. Wharton Huber.

PLATE 12. BLACK DUCK. *Upper:* Nesting site of black duck, Magdalen Islands, Quebec, June 21, 1904, referred to on page 52. *Lower:* Nest and eggs of the same in above locality.

PLATE 13. BLACK DUCK. *Upper:* Nest and eggs of black duck, Magdalen Islands, Quebec, presented by Mr. Herbert K. Job. *Lower:* Black duck on her nest, a photograph purchased from Mr. Bonnycastle Dale.

PLATE 14. GADWALL. *Upper:* Nest and eggs of gadwall, Teton County, Montana, May 30, 1918, presented by Mr. A. D. DuBois. *Lower:* Nest and eggs of gadwall, in a clump of reeds, Stump Lake, North Dakota, June 15, 1901, referred to on page 80.

PLATE 15. GADWALL. Nest and eggs of gadwall, San Luis Valley, Colorado, presented by the Colorado Museum of Natural History.

PLATE 16. GADWALL. *Upper:* Young gadwall, 2 weeks old, Lake Winnipegosis, Manitoba, July 28, 1913, presented by Mr. Herbert K. Job. *Lower:* Nest and eggs of gadwall, Shoal Lake, Manitoba, June 28, 1912, presented by Mr. Herbert K. Job.

PLATE 17. BALDPATE. *Upper:* Nest and eggs of baldpate, in a clump of nettles, Stump Lake, North Dakota, May 31, 1901. *Lower:* Another nest of same, in thick, tall grass, same locality and date. Both referred to on page 90.

PLATE 18. EUROPEAN TEAL. *Upper:* Nesting site of European teal, Unalaska, Alaska, June 8, 1911, referred to on page 99. *Lower:* Nest and eggs of same, above locality and date.

PLATE 19. GREEN-WINGED TEAL. *Upper:* Nest and eggs of green-winged teal, Crane Lake, Saskatchewan, June 21, 1905, presented by Mr. Herbert K. Job. *Lower:* Another nest of same, Alberta, June 16, 1906, presented by Mr. Walter Raine.

PLATE 20. GREEN-WINGED TEAL. Nest and eggs of green-winged
teal, Alberta, a photograph purchased from Mr. S. S. S. Stansell.

PLATE 21. GREEN-WINGED TEAL. *Upper:* Green-winged teal in full plumage, adult male. *Lower:* Adult male of same in nearly full eclipse plumage. Both photographs of captive birds, Ithaca, New York, presented by Dr. Arthur A. Allen.

PLATE 22. BLUE-WINGED TEAL. *Upper:* Nest of blue-winged teal, covered, Cherry County, Nebraska, July 25, 1911. *Lower:* Same nest, uncovered to show the eggs. Both photographs presented by Mr. Frank H. Shoemaker.

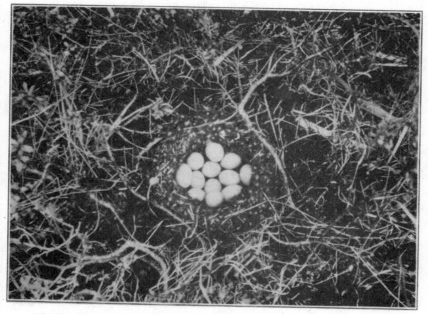

PLATE 23. BLUE-WINGED TEAL. *Upper:* Brood of young blue-winged teal, a few days old. *Lower:* Nest and eggs of blue-winged teal, Magdalen Islands, Quebec, June 16, 1900. Both photographs presented by Mr. Herbert K. Job.

PLATE 24. CINNAMON TEAL. Nest and eggs of cinnamon teal, Barr Lake, Colorado, presented by the Colorado Museum of Natural History.

PLATE 25. CINNAMON TEAL. *Upper:* Nest of cinnamon teal, concealed, Barr Lake, Colorado. *Lower:* Same nest, uncovered to show the eggs. Both photographs presented by Mr. Robert B. Rockwell.

PLATE 26. SHOVELLER. *Upper:* Nest and eggs of shoveller, Nelson County, North Dakota, June 7, 1901, referred to on page 137. *Lower:* Nest and eggs of shoveller, Crane Lake, Saskatchewan, June 5, 1905.

PLATE 27. SHOVELLER. *Upper:* Young shovellers, 1 and 2 weeks old, Lake Winnipegosis, Manitoba, July 28, 1913. *Lower:* Young shovellers, nearly fully grown, St. Marks, Manitoba, July, 1912. Both photographs presented by Mr. Herbert K. Job.

PLATE 28. PINTAIL. *Upper:* Nest and eggs of pintail, under a rose bush, Crane Lake, Saskatchewan, June 4, 1905, referred to on page 146. *Lower:* Nest and eggs of pintail, on edge of a cultivated field, Steele County, North Dakota, June 10, 1901, referred to on page 146.

PLATE 29. PINTAIL. *Upper:* Nest and eggs of pintail, Crane Lake, Saskatchewan, June 2, 1905. *Lower:* Nest and eggs of pintail, Lake Manitoba, Manitoba, July 3, 1912. Both photographs presented by Mr. Herbert K. Job.

PLATE 30. PINTAIL. *Upper:* Female pintail, in captivity, Ithaca, New York, presented by Dr. Arthur A. Allen. *Lower:* Young pintail, Klamath River, Oregon, presented by Mr. Wm. L. Finley and Mr. H. T. Bohlman.

PLATE 31. PINTAIL. *Upper:* Adult male pintail in full plumage. *Lower:* Adult male pintail in partial eclipse plumage. Both photographs of birds in captivity, Ithaca, New York, presented by Dr. Arthur A. Allen.

PLATE 32. WOOD DUCK. *Left:* Nesting site of wood duck, in a dead elm stub, about 30 feet up, nest contained 23 eggs, Yates County, New York, May 12, 1907. *Right:* Nesting site of wood duck, in a living elm, about 50 feet up, May 13, 1906, Yates County, New York. Both photographs presented by Mr. Clarence F. Stone.

PLATE 33. WOOD DUCK. *Upper:* Nesting site of wood duck, in a low stub, Yates County, New York, presented by Mr. Clarence F. Stone. *Lower:* Brood of young wood ducks, with mallard foster mother, Amston, Connecticut, July 23, 1920, presented by Mr. Herbert K. Job.

PLATE 34. WOOD DUCK. *Upper:* Adult male wood duck, in full plumage. *Lower:* Adult male wood duck, in eclipse plumage. Both photographs of captive birds, Ithaca, New York, presented by **Dr. Arthur A. Allen.**

PLATE 35. REDHEAD. *Upper:* Nest and eggs of redhead, Steele County, North Dakota, June 10, 1901, presented by Mr. Herbert K. Job. *Lower:* Nearer view of same nest, referred to on page 177.

PLATE 36. REDHEAD. *Left*: Nest and eggs of redhead, San Luis Valley, Colorado. *Right*: Nearer view of same nest. Both photographs presented by the Colorado Museum of Natural History.

PLATE 37. REDHEAD. *Upper:* Nest and eggs of redhead, Sweetwater Lake, North Dakota, July 15, 1915, presented by Mr. Frank M. Woodruff. *Lower:* Young redheads, St. Marks, Manitoba, July, 1912, presented by Mr. Herbert K. Job.

PLATE 38. CANVASBACK. *Upper:* Nesting site of canvasbacks, Steele County, North Dakota, June 10, 1901, referred to on pages 177 and 191. *Lower:* Nest and eggs of canvasback, above locality and date.

PLATE 39. CANVASBACK. *Upper:* Nest and eggs of canvasback, Steele County, North Dakota, June 11, 1901, referred to on page 192. *Lower:* Nest and eggs of canvasback, in open situation in low sedges, Lake Winnipegosis, Manitoba, June 9, 1913, referred to on page 193. Both photographs presented by Mr. Herbert K. Job.

PLATE 40. CANVASBACK. *Upper:* Young canvasbacks, presented by Mr. Herbert K. Job. *Lower:* Male canvasbacks, in different stages of eclipse plumage, captive birds, Ithaca, New York, presented by Dr. Arthur A. Allen.

PLATE 41. SCAUP DUCK. *Upper:* Nest and eggs of scaup duck, St. Michael, Alaska, June 5, 1915, referred to on page 208. *Lower:* Nearer view of same nest. Both photographs from negatives taken by Mr. F. Seymour Hersey for the author.

PLATE 42. SCAUP DUCK. *Upper:* Nesting site of scaup duck, Magdalen Islands, Quebec. *Lower:* Nest and eggs of scaup duck, in above locality, referred to on page 209. Both photographs presented by Mr. Herbert K. Job.

PLATE 43. LESSER SCAUP DUCK. *Upper:* Nest and eggs of lesser scaup duck, Crane Lake, Saskatchewan, June 17, 1905. *Lower:* Another nest of same, Stump Lake, North Dakota, June 15, 1901, referred to on page 218.

PLATE 44. LESSER SCAUP DUCK. *Upper:* Nest and eggs of lesser scaup duck, Lake Winnipegosis, Manitoba, June, 1913, referred to on page 219. *Lower:* Another nest of same, Lake Manitoba, Manitoba, July 3, 1912. Both photographs presented by Mr. Herbert K. Job.

PLATE 45. LESSER SCAUP DUCK. *Upper:* Young lesser scaup duck, 1 month old, Lake Winnipegosis, Manitoba, August, 1913, presented by Mr. Herbert K. Job. *Lower:* Adult male lesser scaup duck in eclipse plumage, captive bird, Ithaca, New York, presented by Dr. Arthur A. Allen.

PLATE 46. RING-NECKED DUCK. *Upper:* Nest and eggs of ring-necked duck, Carver County, Minnesota, June 16, 1898, presented by Dr. Thomas S. Roberts. *Lower:* Nest and eggs of ring-necked duck, Steele County, North Dakota, June 13, 1901, referred to on page 225.

PART II

INTRODUCTION

The same general plan has been followed and the same sources of information have been utilized. Nearly all those who contributed material for former volumes have rendered similar service in this case. In addition to those whose contributions have been previously acknowledged our thanks are due to the following new contributors:

Photographs have been contributed by Charles Barrett, W. J. Erichsen, Audrey Gordon, W. E. Hastings, A. B. Klugh, G. M. McNeil, C. W. Michael, J. A. Munro, J. R. Pemberton, J. K. Potter, M. P. Skinner, and F. W. Walker.

Notes and data have been contributed by H. P. Attwater, A. C. Bagg, D. B. Burrows, K. Christofferson, H. B. Conover, M. S. Crosby, S. T. Danforth, A. D. Henderson, R. W. Jackson, J. W. Jacobs, W. DeW. Miller, Catharine A. Mitchell, J. A. Munro, J. R. Pemberton, F. J. Pierce, R. D. Camp, A. J. van Rossem, William Rowan, M. P. Skinner, T. C. Stephens, W. A. Strong, and C. L. Whittle.

THE AUTHOR.

TABLE OF CONTENTS

	Page
Family Anatidae	1
Glaucionetta clangula americana	1
American goldeneye	1
Habits	1
Distribution	13
Glaucionetta islandica	14
Barrow goldeneye	14
Habits	14
Distribution	23
Charitonetta albeola	24
Bufflehead	24
Habits	24
Distribution	31
Clangula hyemalis	32
Oldsquaw	32
Habits	32
Distribution	49
Histrionicus histrionicus histrionicus	50
Atlantic harlequin duck	50
Habits	50
Distribution	57
Histrionicus histrionicus pacificus	58
Pacific harlequin duck	58
Habits	58
Distribution	61
Camptorhynchus labradorius	62
Labrador duck	62
Habits	62
Distribution	67
Polysticta stelleri	67
Steller eider	67
Habits	67
Distribution	73
Arctonetta fischeri	74
Spectacled eider	74
Habits	74
Distribution	78
Somateria mollissima borealis	79
Northern eider	79
Habits	79
Distribution	93
Somateria mollissima dresseri	94
American eider	94
Habits	94
Distribution	102
Somateria v-nigra	102

	Page
Family Anatidae—Continued.	
Pacific eider	102
Habits	102
Distribution	107
Somateria spectabilis	107
King eider	107
Habits	107
Distribution	118
Oidemia americana	119
American scoter	119
Habits	119
Distribution	127
Melanitta fusca	128
Velvet scoter	128
Habits	128
Distribution	131
Melanitta deglandi	131
White-winged scoter	131
Habits	131
Distribution	142
Melanitta perspicillata	143
Surf scoter	143
Habits	143
Distribution	151
Erismatura jamaicensis	152
Ruddy duck	152
Habits	152
Distribution	160
Nomonyx dominicus	161
Masked duck	161
Habits	161
Distribution	163
Chen hyperborea hyperborea	164
Snow goose	164
Habits	164
Distribution	170
Chen hyperborea nivalis	173
Greater snow goose	173
Habits	173
Distribution	178
Chen caerulescens	178
Blue goose	178
Habits	178
Distribution	184
Exanthemops rossi	185
Ross goose	185
Habits	185
Distribution	188
Anser albifrons albifrons	188
White-fronted goose	188
Habits	188
Distribution	195
Anser albifrons gambelli	196

Family Anatidae—Continued.

Page
Tule goose _____ 196
    Habits _____ 196
    Distribution_____ 198
Anser fabalis_____ 198
Bean goose_____ 198
    Habits _____ 198
    Distribution_____ 200
Anser brachyrhynchus_____ 200
Pink-footed goose_____ 200
    Habits _____ 200
    Distribution _____ 203
Branta canadensis canadensis _____ 204
Canada goose_____ 204
    Habits _____ 204
    Distribution_____ 222
Branta canadensis hutchinsi_____ 223
Hutchins goose _____ 223
    Habits _____ 223
    Distribution_____ 226
Branta canadensis occidentalis_____ 227
White-cheeked goose _____ 227
    Habits _____ 227
    Distribution_____ 230
Branta canadensis minima _____ 231
Cackling goose _____ 231
    Habits _____ 231
    Distribution_____ 236
Branta bernicla bernicla_____ 237
Brant_____ 237
    Habits _____ 237
    Distribution_____ 248
Branta bernicla nigricans _____ 249
Black brant _____ 249
    Habits _____ 249
    Distribution_____ 257
Branta leucopsis_____ 258
Barnacle goose _____ 258
    Habits _____ 258
    Distribution_____ 262
Philacte canagica _____ 263
Emperor goose_____ 263
    Habits _____ 263
    Distribution_____ 268
Dendrocygna autumnalis _____ 269
Black-bellied tree-duck_____ 269
    Habits _____ 269
    Distribution_____ 272
Dendrocygna bicolor _____ 272
Fulvous tree-duck _____ 272
    Habits _____ 272
    Distribution_____ 277
Cygnus cygnus_____ 278

Family Anatidae—Continued.   Page
    Whooping swan _____ 278
        Habits _____ 278
        Distribution_____ 280
    Cygnus columbianus_____ 281
    Whistling swan _____ 281
        Habits _____ 281
        Distribution_____ 292
    Cygnus buccinator_____ 293
    Trumpeter swan_____ 293
        Habits _____ 293
        Distribution_____ 300
References to bibliography_____ 302
Index_____ _____ 311

LIFE HISTORIES OF NORTH AMERICAN WILD FOWL ORDER ANSERES (PART)

By Arthur Cleveland Bent
of *Taunton, Massachusetts*

Family ANATIDAE, Ducks, Geese, and Swans

GLAUCIONETTA CLANGULA AMERICANA (Bonaparte)

AMERICAN GOLDENEYE

HABITS

Spring.—With the breaking up of winter in Massachusetts, when the February sun has loosened the icy fetters of our rivers and the ice cakes are floating out of our harbors, the genial warmth of advancing spring arouses amorous instincts in the breasts of the warm-blooded goldeneyes. The plumage of the drakes has reached its highest stage of perfection; their heads fairly glisten with metallic green luster, in sharp contrast with their spotless white under parts; and their feet glow with brilliant orange hues. They must seem handsome indeed to their more somber companions of the opposite sex, as they chase each other about over the water, making the spray fly in ardent combat. They are strenuous, active suitors, and their courtships are well worth watching.

Courtship.—This interesting performance, the most spectacular courtship of any of the ducks, has been fully described in detail by Mr. William Brewster (1911). Rather than attempt to quote from such an exhaustive account, I would refer the reader to this excellent article, which is well illustrated and worthy of careful study. I prefer to quote Dr. Charles W. Townsend's (1910) account of it, which is more concise and yet quite complete; he writes:

One or more males swim restlessly back and forth and around a female. The feathers of the cheeks and crest of the male are so erected that the head looks large and round, the neck correspondingly small. As he swims along, the head is thrust out in front close to the water, occasionally dabbling at it. Suddenly he springs forward, elevating his breast, and at the same time he enters on the most typical and essential part of the performance. The neck is stretched straight up, and the bill, pointing to the zenith, is opened to emit a harsh, rasping double note, *zzee-at*, vibratory and searching in character. The head is then quickly snapped back until the occiput touches the rump, whence it is brought forward again with a jerk to the normal position. As the head is returned to its place the bird often springs forward kicking the water in a spurt out behind, and displaying like a flash of flame the orange-colored legs.

As these courtships begin on warm days in February and last through March, probably many pairs are mated before they migrate to their breeding grounds in April. Doctor Townsend writes me that he saw a pair copulating at Barnstable, Massachusetts, on March 28. Mr. Charles E. Alford (1921) writes:

Though the habit of lying more or less prone upon the water is common to most females of the Anatidae when they desire to pair, the duck goldeneye carries this performance beyond all normal bounds; her behavior on such occasions being, indeed, scarcely less amazing than that of the drake. With neck outstretched and her body quite limp and apparently lifeless, she allows herself to drift upon the surface exactly after the manner of a dead bird. When first I witnessed this maneuver I was completely deceived, for she remained thus drifting toward the shore, and with the male swimming round her for fully 15 minutes before actual pairing took place. This occurred on February 2, 1920, a beautiful springlike day, the whole of that month being unusually mild and sunny.

Nesting.—The American goldeneye, so far as I know, invariably places its nest in a cavity in a tree, preferably in a large natural cavity and often entirely open at the top. Considerable variation is shown in the selection of a suitable nesting site, which depends on the presence of hollow trees. Near Eskimo Point, on the south coast of the Labrador Peninsula, I found a nest on June 10, 1909, in a white birch stub on the bare crest of a gravel cliff over 100 feet above the beach. The stub, which stood in an entirely open place, was 6 feet in circumference and about 18 feet high, broken and open at the top down to about 12 feet from the ground. A female goldeneye flew out of the large cavity, in which were 15 handsome, green eggs on a soft bed of rotten chips and white down. The nest was about a foot below the front edge of the cavity. I have never seen another nest in such an open and exposed situation.

Mr. Brewster (1900) found this species breeding abundantly at Lake Umbagog, in Maine, in 1907, and made some valuable and interesting observations on its breeding habits. About the location of its nest, he says:

All the whistlers' nests which I have examined have been placed over water at heights varying from 6 or 8 to 50 or 60 feet and in cavities in the trunks of large hardwood trees such as elms, maples, and yellow or canoe birches. As the supply of such cavities is limited, even where dead or decaying trees abound, and as the birds have no means of enlarging or otherwise improving them; they are not fastidious in their choice, but readily make use of any opening which can be made to serve their purpose. Thus it happens that the nest is sometimes placed at the bottom of a hollow trunk, 6, 10, or even 15 feet below the hole at which the bird enters, at others on a level with and scarce a foot back from the entrance, which is usually rounded, and from 6 to 15 inches in diameter, but occasionally is so small and irregular that the whistler must have difficulty in forcing its bulky body through. I remember one nest to which the only access was by means of a vertical slit so narrow and jagged that it would barely admit my flattened hand.

In North Dakota, in 1901, we found goldeneyes nesting commonly in the timber belts around the shores of the lakes and along the streams in the Stump Lake region.

The goldeneyes choose for their nesting sites the numerous natural cavities which occur in many of the larger trees. They seem to show no preference as to the kind of tree and not much preference as to the size of the cavity, any cavity which is large enough to conceal them being satisfactory.

The occupied cavity can usually be easily recognized by the presence of one or two pieces of white down clinging to its edges; sometimes considerable of the down is also scattered about on the nearest branches. The first nest that we found, on May 30, was in an exceedingly small cavity in a dead branch of a small elm, about 10 feet from the ground. We heard a great scrambling and scratching going on inside, as the duck climbed up to the small opening, through which she wriggled out with some difficulty and flew away. I measured the opening carefully and found it only 3 inches wide by 4½ inches high; the cavity was about 3 feet deep and measured 6 inches by 7 inches at the bottom. The fresh eggs which it contained were lying on the bare chips at the bottom of the cavity, surrounded by a little white down.

On June 1 we explored a large tract of heavy timber on a promontory extending out into the lake for about half a mile, where we located five nests of the American goldeneye. The first nest was about 20 feet up in a cavity in the trunk of a large swamp oak and contained 4 eggs, apparently fresh. The second was in the trunk of a large elm and held only 1 egg, evidently a last year's egg. The third, which held 5 eggs, was in an open cavity in an elm stub about 12 feet from the ground. None of these eggs were taken and doubtless the sets were incomplete. While climbing to a Krider hawk's nest I noticed an elm stub nearby with a large open cavity in the top, which on closer investigation was found to contain a goldeneye's nest with 10 eggs buried in a mass of white down. The stub was about 10 feet high and the cavity about 2 feet deep; the bird was not on the nest, but the eggs proved to have been incubated about one week. A pair of western house wrens also had a nest in the dead branch above the cavity.

The fifth and last nest was found while walking along the shore, by seeing the goldeneye fly out over our heads from a small swamp oak on the edge of the woods. I could almost reach the large open cavity from the ground; the opening was well decorated with the tell-tale down, and at the bottom of the cavity, 2 feet deep, was a set of 14 eggs, in which incubation had begun, and one addled last year's egg, completely buried in a profusion of white down, so well matted together that it could be lifted from the eggs without falling apart, like a soft warm blanket.

In the Lake Winnipegosis region in Manitoba, where large hollow trees are scarce, we found the goldeneyes making the best of rather poor accommodations. We examined four nests all of which were in small, hollow burr oaks (*Quercus macrocarpa*) which were about the only trees in which suitable hollows could be found; the entrances to all of these nests were not over 5 feet from the ground; in some cases the trees were so badly split that the eggs were partially exposed to wind and rain and much of the down from the nests had been blown out onto surrounding trees and bushes; two such nests, found on June 2, with incomplete sets, were at the bottoms of large cavities, practically on a level with the ground in old stubs so badly cracked that the eggs were plainly visible. We were told that the "wood ducks," as they are called, would desert their nests if the eggs were handled, which proved to be true in the only two instances where we tried it.

According to Mr. John Macoun (1909) a nest was found by Mr. William Spreadborough "in a hollow cottonwood log on the ground," near Indian Head, Saskatchewan. He also quotes Mr. G. R. White as saying that the "nest is composed of grass, leaves, and moss and lined with feathers." I have never seen anything but rotten chips and down in a goldeneye's nest, and I doubt if any outside material is ever brought in. Probably the duck does not always take the trouble to clean out a cavity, but lays its eggs on whatever accumulation of rubbish happens to be there. The down is added as incubation advances until a thick warm blanket is provided to cover the eggs, when necessary, during the absence of the bird. I have a beautiful nest of this species in my collection, taken in 1901, with a thickly matted down quilt over the eggs which, though repeatedly handled, has retained its shape and consistency up to the present time.

According to Rev. F. C. R. Jourdain the goldeneye has been frequently induced to nest in nesting boxes in Germany. Mr. A. D. Henderson tells me that he has tried the experiment successfully near Belvedere, Alberta.

The down in the goldeneye's nest is large, light and fluffy; it is practically pure white in color. The breast feathers in it are pure white.

Eggs.—The goldeneye ordinarily lays from 8 to 12 eggs; 5 or 6 eggs sometimes complete the set; I have found as many as 15 and

Mr. Brewster has found 19. Mr. Brewster (1900) thinks that two females sometimes lay in the same nest, and says "several of the rounded, pure white, thick shelled eggs of the hooded merganser are somtimes included in a set of the green, thin-shelled eggs of the whistler."

The eggs of the goldeneye are handsome and easily distinguished from those of any other North American duck except its near relative, the Barrow goldeneye. In shape they vary from elliptical oval to elliptical ovate; a few specimens before me are almost ovate. The shell is thin, with a dull luster. The color is usually a clear, pale "malachite green," varying in the darker specimens to a more olivaceous or "pale chromium green"; various shades of color often occur in the same set. The measurements of 84 eggs, in various collections, average 59.7 by 43.4 millimeters; the eggs showing the four extremes measure 65 by 44, 59 by 45.5, 48.8 by 43.5, and 59 by 41.2 millimeters.

Young.—Incubation is performed entirely by the female and lasts for a period of about 20 days. Only one brood is raised in a season. The young remain in the nest for a day of two, until they are strong enough to make the perilous descent to the ground or water. Many of the earlier writers have asserted that this, and other species of tree-nesting ducks, carry the young to the nearest water in their bills, but their observations seem to be based largely on hearsay or on insufficient evidence. Mr. Brewster's (1900) study of this species has given us positive evidence to the contrary. Although he personally missed the opportunity of seeing the performance, his trustworthy assistant, R. A. Gilbert, gave the following graphic account of what he saw, when the young were ready to leave the nest:

At 6.45 the old duck appeared at the entrance to the nest, where she sat for five minutes moving her head continually and looking about in every direction included within her field of vision; then she sank back out of sight, reappearing at the end of a minute and looking about as before for another five minutes. At the end of this second period of observation she flew down to the water and swam round the stub three times, clucking and calling. On completing the third round she stopped directly under the hole and gave a single loud cluck or call, when the ducklings began scrambling up to the entrance and dropping down to the water in such quick succession as to fall on top of one another. They literally *poured* out of the nest much as shot would fall from one's hand. One or two hesitated or paused for an instant on reaching the mouth of the hole, but the greater number toppled out over the edge as soon as they appeared. All used their tiny wings freely, beating them continuously as they descended. They did not seem to strike the water with much force.

While this was going on the old duck sat motionless on the water looking up at the nest. When the last duckling dropped at her side she at once swam off at the head of the brood, quickly disappearing in a flooded thicket a few rods away.

Dr. W. N. Macartney (1918) observed a similar performance near Dundee, Quebec; he writes:

On the afternoon of July 7 the old duck was seen at the foot of the tree, standing on the ground. She gave several low quacks or calls, and out of the hole in the tree overhead promptly tumbled about a baker's dozen of fledgling ducks. They were unable to fly, but were sufficiently grown to be able to ease their fall to the earth, and not unlike a flock of butterflies, they came down pell-mell, fluttering and tumbling, some of them heels over head, until they reached the ground, unharmed. The tree was nearly but not quite perpendicular, so they were unable to scramble down. The old bird gathered them in a bunch and piloted them along the fence for some 3 or 4 rods to the river. Down the rocky shore they went and into the water. The old duck then sank low in the water and the ducklings gathered over her back in a compact clump. She took them across the bay to a bed of rushes, some 10 rods distant, where they disappeared from sight.

Very little seems to be known about the food of the young, but probably they are fed largely on insects and soft animal food. Dr. Charles W. Townsend (1913) gives the following account of the behavior of a mother goldeneye and her young on a Labrador stream:

The old bird crouched low in the water, her golden eyes shining very prominently, and uttered hoarse rasping croaks. The young, whose eyes were gray-blue and inconspicuous, at once scattered, diving repeatedly, and disappeared in the bushes, while the mother kept prominently in view within 20 yards of the canoe leading us downstream. After repeatedly swimming and flying short distances ahead of the canoe for half a mile or so, croaking all the time, she disappeared around a bend and undoubtedly flew back to the young. Near at hand the young made no sound, but at a distance a loud beseeching peep was uttered.

Plumages.—The downy young goldeneye is quite distinctively colored and marked; it also has a carriage all its own, for it walks in a more upright position than other young ducks and it carries its head in a more loftly and perky attitude, which gives it a very smart appearance. The upper part of the head, down to a line running straight back from the commissure to the nape, is deep, rich, glossy "bone brown"; the throat and cheeks are pure white, the white spaces nearly meeting on the hind neck; the upper parts vary from pale "clove brown" on the upper back to deep "bone brown" on the rump; these colors shade off to "hair brown" on the sides and form a ring of the same around the neck; the posterior edges of the wings are white, and there is a white spot on each scapular region and one on each side of the rump; the belly is white. The colors become paler with age.

The first feathers appear on the flanks and scapulars and then in the tail while the bird is very small. According to Millais (1913):

Three nestlings hatched by Mr. Blaauw, at Gooilust, in Holland, on June 20, 1908. began to show feathers on the scapulars on July 18th. On August

8 they were completely feathered except for the flight feathers, which were just beginning to grow. At this date the irides were chocolate brown and the legs and toes yellowish. On August 25 the young birds were able to fly.

Early in the fall, as soon as the young birds have attained their full growth, the first winter plumage begins to develop. This plumage in the male is entirely different from the adult plumage and closely resembles that of the female. The young male may be distinguished from the female by its decidedly larger size; it also has less gray on the breast (which decreases toward spring), the back is darker gray, the head is darker and more or less mottled with dusky, and there is a more or less distinct suggestion of the white loral spot, which increases toward spring. This plumage is worn all through the first winter and spring, with slight and gradual changes toward maturity by a limited growth of new feathers; the head becomes darker and greener, the loral spot whiter, and the scapulars are changed. Individuals vary greatly in the time and extent of these changes. I have a young male in my collection, taken on May 27, which is still in the first winter plumage. In July the young male passes into the eclipse plumage, in which it can be distinguished from the adult by the wings, which are not molted until later. The change from the eclipse into the adult winter plumage is very slow in young birds, lasting well into the winter, and it is not until this molt is completed that old and young birds become indistinguishable.

The adult male assumes a semieclipse plumage late in July or in August, involving principally the head and neck, which becomes brown and mottled like that of the young male; the white loral spot partially disappears; the scapulars resemble those of the young male, and there are brownish feathers in the flanks. This is followed by a complete molt into the winter plumage, which is sometimes prolonged until late in the fall, but not so late as in the young bird.

The molts and plumages of the female are parallel with those of the male, but old and young birds are not so easily recognized. I believe that specimens showing the orange zone in the bill and the well-marked black band across the white space in the wing are old birds. The white neck of the adult female is acquired during the first spring.

Food.—While with us on the coast the goldeneye feeds largely on small mussels and other mollusks, which it obtains by diving in deep water or by dabbling in the shallows near the shore, it feeds to some extent also on the seeds of eel grass (*Zostera marina*). The stomach of a bird taken by Dr. John C. Phillips (1911) in a lake in Massachusetts "contained seeds of pondweed, water lily, bayberry, and burr reed, buds and roots of wild celery, and bits of water boatmen, and dragonfly nymphs."

On the Pacific coast Mr. W. L. Dawson (1909) found it feeding on mussels, crabs, marine worms, and on the remains of decayed salmon. On inland streams it may often be seen in the rapids chasing young trout fry or other small fish; tadpoles, fish spawn, and the larvae of insects are also eaten. Audubon discovered it hunting for cray-fish in the clay banks of our inland rivers. Throughout the interior, in fresh-water lakes and streams, it lives largely on vegetable food; it feeds on a great variety of aquatic plants, such as teal moss (*Limnobium*), flags (*Iris*), duckweed, pondweed, water plantain, and bladderwort, according to Doctor Yorke (1899).

Behavior.—The flight of the goldeneye is exceedingly swift and strong. About its breeding grounds among the lakes and streams of eastern Canada it is very active on the wing, circling high in the air about the lakes or flying up and down the streams above the tree tops, singly or in pairs, the female usually leading; it seems to show some curiosity or anxiety as to the intentions of the intruder, for it often repeats its flight again and again over the same course. The vibrant whistling of its wings in flight is audible at a long distance and has earned for it the popular name of "whistler" or "whistle-wing."

Mr. W. L. Dawson (1909) has thus graphically described it:

Of all wing music, from the droning of the rufous hummer to the startling whirr of the ruffed grouse, I know of none so thrilling sweet as the whistling wing note of the goldeneye. A pair of the birds have been frightened from the water, and as they rise in rapid circles to gain a view of some distant goal they sow the air with vibrant whistling sounds. Owing to a difference in wing beats between male and female, the brief moment when the wings strike in unison with the effect of a single bird is followed by an ever-changing syncopation which challenges the waiting ear to tell if it does not hear a dozen birds instead of only two. Again, in the dim twilight of early morning, while the birds are moving from a remote and secure lodging place to feed in some favorite stretch of wild water, one guesses at their early industry from the sound of multitudinous wings above, contending with the cold ether.

When migrating, goldeneyes travel in small flocks usually high in the air. When rising from a pond they usually circle about for a few times, gradually climbing upward, and fly off at a considerable height; even on the seashore they are seldom seen flying for any distance close to the water. They can usually be recognized by their short necks, large heads, and stout bodies, as well as by the large amount of white in their plumage. This latter character has given them the name of "pied duck" or "pie bird" among the natives of the eastern Provinces.

The goldeneye is an expert diver; and although at times it uses both wings and feet under water, its method of diving, with wings pressed close to the sides, shows that it generally uses its feet alone. Dr. Arthur A. Allen writes to me that he has "seen goldeneyes using their wings, half spread, when feeding normally." When undisturbed it dives with great ease; the bill is pointed forward until it touches the water, when the bird slips out of sight without an effort, causing hardly a ripple. But when alarmed it plunges forward and downward with great vigor, cleaving the water as it does so.

Mr. F. S. Hersey timed a goldeneye diving and found that it dove with great regularity, remaining under for 21 seconds and on the surface for 13 seconds between dives. Although it usually feeds in rather shallow water, it can dive to great depths in search of shellfish if necessary; for this reason it is called "le plongeur" by the French residents of southern Labrador.

J. G. Millais (1913) narrates the following interesting incident, illustrating its power as a plunger:

No ducks are more bold in the "headers," they will take from the clouds when pursued by a raptorial bird. I was collecting birds one day in February, 1882, on Loch Leven, the Inverness-shire sea loch, when I heard the sound of goldeneye, accompanied by a peculiar hum of something passing through the air. On looking up I was just in time to see the interesting spectacle of a peregrine making a stoop at three goldeneyes. The ducks at this moment were high, I should say 80 yards in the air, and closed their wings as they heard or saw the peregrine coming, and dropped as if shot to the surface of the water. On striking the water there was no pause, they just passed out of sight, rising nearly 100 yards away, and flying low over the water. The peregrine, after its unsuccessful "stoop," did not pursue them. Like the long-tailed duck, but scarcely with the same skill in starting, the goldeneye has the power of opening its wings immediately on reaching the surface of the water, and commencing to fly. I have seen other ducks act in a similar manner when chased by peregrines, but none displayed such promptitude or fell from such a height as did these goldeneyes.

He says further:

In clear water it is easy to note the powerful strokes of the legs of these ducks, which seem to beat with great rapidity under water and much power. The stroke is more or less parallel to the wings; the head is held out straight in front. I have watched for hours the male goldeneye that lived for three years on the island below Perth bridge, and used to find his food at the bottom of the river in some 8 to 10 feet of water. In summer this water was as clear as crystal, and from the bridge above the observer could note every movement on the part of the bird. It always proceeded to a depth of 8 to 10 feet of water, and began to dive. On reaching the bottom, it at once commenced to turn the stones over with the bill, and from under these various water insects were found or caught as they attempted to escape. Sometimes it would find a small batch of young fresh-water mussels, and these it would devour very quickly one after the other, like a duck taking grain out of a pan. It never stayed under water more than a minute, even when finding food abundant in one spot, but came up, rested a moment or two on the surface, and dived again. All food was swallowed where it was found, and small pebbles and fairly large stones were pushed over in the search. Several times I saw the bird just move a flat stone. It would go all around it and try it from every point. If unsuccessful it would come to the surface and rest awhile, and then go down again for another effort. In a lake the goldeneye will dive in perpendicular position, but in flowing water it dives in a slant against the stream or tideway. Their bodies are very light, and bounce up to the surface like a cork immediately they cease to push downward with the feet. In still water the goldeneye often dives in circles to get to the bottom.

The goldeneye is not much given to vocal performances. The courtship note of the male has been described by Doctor Townsend (1910) as "a harsh, rasping, double note, *zzee-at*, vibratory and searching in character." Elon H. Eaton (1910) says that the male when startled or lost has a sharp *cur-r-rew*. Edward H. Forbush (1912) credits the female with "a single whistling peep." And Ora W. Knight (1908) has "heard the parents utter a low-pitched quack to call their young." M. P. Skinner says that "the quack of this duck seems harsher than the mallard's."

Game.—During the four years that I lived on the coast our most interesting winter sport was whistler shooting. Long before daylight we braved the winter's cold and pushed out our skiff to our blind among the ice cakes. We wore white nightgowns over our clothes, white caps and gloves, and sometimes had our gun barrels whitewashed, for the goldeneyes are very wary birds and it is necessary to remain motionless and invisible to be successful. The wooden decoys are placed, as soon as it is light enough to see, in some convenient open space, preferably off the mouth of some fresh-water creek. The blind is made of ice cakes or snow, high enough to conceal the gunners. With the coming of the daylight birds begin to move; large gray gulls are seen flapping slowly up the bay to feed on the mud flats; a flock of black ducks flies out from an open spring hole where it has been feeding all night. The winter sunrise is beautiful, as the rosy dawn creeps up from the cold, gray sea and sends a warm glow of color over floating ice and banks of snow. Our eyes are trained seaward to catch the first glimpses of incoming whistlers. At last a black speck is dimly discerned in the distance against a pink cloud; on it comes straight toward the blind, and we recognize it as an old cock whistler, the advance guard of the morning flight; he circles, sets his wings and scales down over the decoys; in our eagerness we betray ourselves by a sudden movement; he sees us and scrambles upward into the air to escape, but it is too late, the guns speak and the first kill is scored. Soon a small flock of five birds comes in, the shrill whistling of their wings sending a thrill of pleasure through our chilled veins; they scale down toward the decoys, but see the blind, wheel, and fly off without offering us a shot; they settle in the water away off among the floating ice and it is useless to stalk them. We have been too conspicuous to the keen eyes of the birds and must conceal ourselves better; so we pile up more ice around the blind and keep more quiet. Better luck follows in consequence, for the ducks decoy well, if their suspicions are not aroused, and during the next two hours we have good sport. By the time the early morning flight is over, an hour or two after sunrise, we have had enough of it and are glad to return home with a small bag of the keen-witted goldeneyes.

Winter.—To the residents of New England the hardy goldeneye, or " whistler " as it is more often called, is known chiefly as a winter resident or an early spring and late fall migrant, mainly along the seacoast now, though formerly, when less persecuted by gunners, it was often seen in inland ponds, where it is now seldom seen. It is an exceedingly wary and sagacious bird, soon learning to desert dangerous localities, but frequenting freely and regularly such places as the Back Bay basin in the city of Boston, where it is free from molestation.

On the coast, goldeneyes spend their days playing or feeding off the beaches, just beyond the breakers, swimming about among the ice cakes or flying into the tidal estuaries to feed. At night they usually fly off shore, where they can sleep in safety, bedded on the open ocean. They leave the marshes or ponds near the sea at, or within a few minutes of, sunset.

Goldeneyes linger to spend the winter as far north as they can find open water, in the interior as well as on the coast. In the swift rapids and open air holes of our large rivers they find congenial resorts as far north as Iowa, where they congregate in thousands. E. S. Currier (1902) says of the winter habits of the goldeneye on the Mississippi River:

The goldeneyes are very playful and, as spring approaches, noisy. The swift current is constantly forcing them toward the ice at the lower end of the pool, so that they are obliged to take wing and go to the other end of the air hole frequently. They rise on rapidly beating wings, the clear whistling ringing across the dark water and white ice fields, and scurrying upstream in irregular groups, drop in again with a noisy splash. This drifting down and flying back again seems to be enjoyed as much by the ducks as is coasting by the children.

Each group of arrivals is received with many bows and much flapping of wings by the ones on the water, and the penetrating cry of the drakes " *speer* " " *speer* " reaches to a great distance. It is a scene of great activity from daylight until darkness sets in, and makes winter less dreary to the birds of this locality.

The greatest movements take place about sundown when they all head for a favorite air hole (usually the largest) on whirring wings. Here they settle in with much bustle and confusion, playing and feeding until darkness sets in. They spend a great part of the night on thin, new ice at the edge of the open water. As a rule, unless migration is on or the ice is running, there is little movement during the night; but frequently you hear the noisy whistling of the wings of some belated or disturbed bird, soon followed by the distant splash as it strikes the water again.

As winter abates and the increasing warmth causes the ice to give way, followed by the great break-up as the ice goes out, the duck is at its best. The moving ice fields then keep them on the watch, and as the open water they are in narrows, they spring up and fly over the grinding, churning mass, drop into the next clear space upstream.

The instant they hit the water they go to playing, chasing each other, and diving to great distances. At times a part of the flock will rise and depart for some distant open water, soon followed by others, and then perhaps by the remainder, and that particular place will be deserted by them for the time being. Again they will congregate in an open space with the ice rumbling and roaring around them on all sides, seemingly loath to leave, but when another change takes place in the ice and a block sweeps toward them they are forced to leave.

Goldeneyes are often common on the larger northern lakes as long as they remain unfrozen; sometimes they are caught in the ice or perish through inability to find open water; but they are so hardy and such strong fliers that they do not suffer so much in this way as some other species.

M. P. Skinner has sent me the following notes on the winter habits of the goldeneye in the Yellowstone National Park:

The goldeneye is a winter visitor in the proportion of one male to three females. Usually these ducks frequent the larger lakes and streams, but I once found some in a pool of Pelican Creek under the lee of a high bank, and frequently on the reservoir near Mammoth where they dive for their food. Once I flushed a single bird from an irrigation ditch 6 feet wide. In winter, the only time they are at all common, they frequent the streams (Gardiner, Firehole, and Gibbon Rivers) kept open by hot water from hot springs and geysers. They are seldom seen on shore or standing on stones, although I have seen them on the edge of the ice along the Lamar River.

These birds are wilder than the more common Barrow goldeneye; they are here so short a time that they remain exceptions to the general rule that the wildfowl become extremely tame under the absolute protection afforded. Whenever they see me approaching they will swim together in a dense flock. They like swift water and are experts at shooting down the rapids. They are at times associated with buffleheads and mallard; sometimes this goldeneye and the Barrows are together, but more often the two species keep apart. Possibly rivalry of males extends to their cousins, but this is a weak explanation, for the Barrow males are often amicable among themselves when in small flocks containing both sexes.

The European goldeneye, which is supposed to be subspecifically distinct from our bird, may be added to our list on the strength of the capture of a female, supposed to be of the European race, on St. Paul Island, Alaska, on November 27, 1914, reported by Dr. G. Dallas Hanna (1916). He says of this specimen:

It is the same size as specimens from the Commander Islands and China; and while these are somewhat larger than birds from the Atlantic coast region of Europe, they are smaller than those from continental North America.

DISTRIBUTION

Breeding range.—The North American form breeds mainly north of the United States, entirely across the continent. South to Newfoundland (Humber and Sandy Rivers), northern New Brunswick (Northumberland County), central Maine (Washington to Oxford Counties), New Hampshire (Umbagog Lake and Jefferson region), northern Vermont (St. Johnsbury), northern New York (Adirondacks), northern Michigan (Neebish Island, Sault Ste. Marie), northern Minnesota (Lake County); northern North Dakota (Devils Lake), northwestern Montana (Flathead Lake and Glacier National Park), and the interior of British Columbia.

North to the limits of heavy timber in central Alaska (Yukon Valley), southern Mackenzie (Fort Rae, Great Slave Lake), the southwest coast of Hudson Bay (York Factory), and the northeast coast of Labrador (near Nain). Replaced in northern Europe and Asia by a closely allied race.

Winter range.—Cold coasts and large lakes south of frozen areas. On the Atlantic coast commonly from Maine to South Carolina; more rarely north to the Gulf of St. Lawrence and Newfoundland and south to northern Florida (Wakulla County). Rarely to the Gulf coasts of Mississippi, Louisiana, and Texas. On the Pacific coast from the Commander and Aleutian Islands to southern California (San Diego) and casually to central western Mexico (Mazatlan). On the Great Lakes (Michigan, Erie, and Ontario). Irregularly north in the interior to southern British Columbia (Okanogan Lake), northwestern Montana (Teton County), and the valleys of the Missouri and Mississippi Rivers, as far as Nebraska and Iowa; and south to Colorado (Beasley Lake and Barr Lake) and Arkansas (Big Lake) and occasionally to Arizona (Tucson) and Texas (Galveston and Corpus Christi).

Spring migration.—Northward and northwestward and away from the coasts. Early dates of arrival: Southern Maine, inland, March 27; Quebec, Montreal, March 19; Ontario, Ottawa, February 14; Minnesota, Heron Lake, March 14; Manitoba, southern, March 29; Alberta, Edmonton, April 6; Montana, Great Falls, March 9; Mackenzie, Fort Resolution, May 7, and Fort Simpson, April 28; Alaska, Nulato, May 3.

Average dates of arrival: Southern Maine, inland, April 5; Quebec, Montreal, April 4, and Lake Mistassini, May 3; Ontario, Ottawa, April 12; Minnesota, Heron Lake, March 25; northern North Dakota, April 20; southern Manitoba, April 21. Leaves the Massachusetts coast by May 1 or earlier.

Fall migration.—Southward and southeastward and toward the coasts.

Early dates of arrival: Massachusetts, October 8; Virginia, Alexandria, October 8. Average dates of arrival: Massachusetts, Woods Hole, November 15; Virginia, Alexandria, October 26; Iowa, Keokuk, November 24. Late dates of departure: Quebec, Montreal, November 7; Manitoba, Aweme, November 10.

Casual records.—Four records for Bermuda (April 10, 1854; December 29, 1874; February 5, 1875; and January 22, 1876). Two records for Pribilof Islands (May 6, 1917, and January 1, 1918). Accidental in Cuba and Barbados.

Egg dates.—North Dakota: Nineteen records, May 10 to June 11; 10 records, May 21 to June 1. Manitoba: Five records, June 2 to July 5. Labrador Peninsula: Three records, May 3 to June 30.

GLAUCIONETTA ISLANDICA (Gmelin)

BARROW GOLDENEYE

HABITS

This species has been well named, the Rocky Mountain goldeneye, for outside of the vicinity of the Continental Divide in the northern States and in southern Canada it is nowhere in this country an abundant species at any season. It is so rare throughout most of its American range that few ornithologists have ever seen it in life.

For this reason it is not strange that it was overlooked by some of the earlier writers and that until recently its distribution was so poorly understood. Wilson makes no mention of the species, and it was entirely overlooked by Audubon, who may have regarded it as a summer plumage of the common species. Even Coues (1874) refers to it as "the most northerly species of the genus, having apparently a circumpolar distribution, breeding only (?) in high latitudes, and penetrating but a limited distance south in interior"; the question mark is his and it is interesting to note that his doubt was removed by finding it breeding in the Rocky Mountains of Montana. It is now known to breed in these mountains as far south as Colorado, east in Canada to the north shore of the St. Lawrence, in Greenland, and in Iceland; but it is far from being circumpolar, for it occurs on the Old World continent only as a straggler; and it is not known to breed north of the Arctic Circle.

Courtship.—J. A. Munro (1918) has given us an interesting account of this species, in British Columbia, from which I quote as follows:

The birds first begin to appear on Okanogan Lake early in March, but are not plentiful until the small mountain lakes are free of ice, early in April. The lakes selected for courtship, and later for the rearing of the young, are usually quite open and free of tules; hence the goldeneyes are always conspicuous and much easier to study than ducks that breed in the sloughs and hide their young in the thick vegetation. Generally by the 15th of April each little lake has its flock of courting goldeneyes, often 30 or 40 on a sheet of water of 50 acres extent or less. In these flocks adults and immatures are present in about equal numbers. The young of either sex do not breed until the second year, and do not assume their breeding dress until the second fall after they are hatched ; that is, when they are over a year old.

The courtship display is witnessed in the flocks just prior to their splitting up into pairs. It is attended by much solemn bowing on the part of the drake, with a frequent backward kick, sufficiently strong to send a jet of water several feet into the air. His violet head is puffed out to the greatest possible extent, and altogether he is a handsome bird as, in a frenzy of sexual excitement, he swims up to the soberly attired duck. Sometimes the entire flock will commence to feed as if at a given signal, and again all the birds will simultaneously take wing and circle about the lake several times before once more splashing down to resume their courtship.

He also contributes the following note :

Two mated pairs in a small lake in the hills were under observation for two hours. The males acted as if extremely jealous of each other and on several occasions left their mates and engaged in spirited encounters. They rushed together over the surface with much splashing, and when about to meet rose upright and buffeted each other with their wings. A female, whose mate had been killed on an adjacent pond, flew into this lake and immediately one of the mated drakes left his mate and dropped in beside her, when he began bowing, but the strange female did not respond. The male then dove several times trying to rise beneath her, at which she flew some distance away and the drake then rejoined his mate.

M. P. Skinner contributes the following :

Early in the winter the ducks outnumber the drakes; but as spring approaches the proportion becomes more equalized. By February 1 the tendency of the flocks to pair off becomes noticeable; courting begins about the same time and lasts until June in some cases. Almost all the flocks are broken up by April 1. While the drakes do most of the " chasing " and " dancing," the females sometimes go through similar movements. The drake swims across the water with jerky motions, not necessarily toward the duck, occasionally an extra kick raises the breast above the surface and at the same time the bill is pointed up and opened and shut twice. Then the neck is stretched backward until the head rests on the lower back, then forward to the normal position, ending with a kick backwards that throws up a little spurt of water. The duck is frequently chased by the drake, with his head and neck stretched out horizontally in front and almost on the water surface.

Nesting.—Dr. T. M. Brewer (1879) published an interesting paper on this species which added greatly to our knowledge of it at that time. Edwin Carter, " who was probably the first to actually secure the nest and eggs of this species within the limits of the United States," sent to Doctor Brewer considerable information about the breeding habits of the Barrow goldeneye in Colorado. He says:

They nest in hollow trees, and it is surprising to see to what small cavi-

(1877) I have examined a great many trees, and every one that had a suitable opening either contained an occupant or indicated recent nesting by eggshells and other marks.

Maj. Allan Brooks (1903) found the Barrow goldeneye breeding quite commonly in La Hache Valley, in the Cariboo district of British Columbia. He says:

One set of eggs was taken from a hole in a dead Douglas fir, 50 feet from the ground, probably the deserted nest of a flying squirrel. The tree stood about 400 yards from the nearest water. The eggs (7) at this date (17th June) contained large embryos. I saw another nesting hole but was unable to reach it. The female brought 14 young ones out from this.

Mr Munro (1918) says of the nesting habits of this species:

By May 1 all breeding birds are mated and scattered over the country, seldom more than one or two pairs on a lake. The Barrow goldeneye shows a marked predilection for lakes that are strongly alkaline, even if they are poor in aquatic vegetation and in the midst of an open country with the nearest timber a half mile or more away. Such lakes are rich in small crustaceans, the chief food of this duck, and no doubt the lakes are occupied on account of the food provided, without reference to the availability of nesting sites.

An abandoned flicker's hole is usually selected for the nest, frequently in a dead yellow pine, for in this tree decay is rapid, and the hole soon becomes much enlarged. One can generally tell if the hole is occupied, by the fragments of down adhering to the rough bark at the entrance. The tree is often so much decayed that a single tug at the bark near the hole will remove the whole adjacent surface, exposing the gray-green eggs where they lie in the clinging soft down. It is rather hard to locate the nest when the tree selected by the bird is in heavy timber a half mile or more from the lake, but when the female is sitting it may be done by making an early morning trip to the lake, remaining under cover, and waiting for her to come to the lake to feed. She generally arrives between 9 and 11 and immediately joins the drake. After splashing and preening her feathers, she feeds most industriously for perhaps an hour and then flies directly back to the nest. I include here data for three nests taken in the Okanogan region.

Okanogan, British Columbia, May 12, 1916. A nest containing 11 fresh eggs was found in the hayloft of a deserted log barn, on the shore of a lake. The eggs were placed in a hollow scooped in the straw under a heavy beam which rested on the piled-up straw. The loft was well lighted through the spaces between the logs and by a large opening at one end. This situation is of course, most unusual, but it had apparently been used some years before the nest was found. I had seen broods of young on this lake in previous years, when I was not able to find the nest. The birds would generally alight on top of a chimney in an unused house close by before flying into the barn.

Farneys Lake, Okanogan, May 31, 1912. A nest with seven partly incubated eggs was placed in a large cavity in a yellow-pine stump, standing in 8 inches of water on the shore of the lake. The cavity containing the eggs was 18 inches above the water, and the eggs were in plain view of a person standing several feet away.

Rollings Lake, May 26, 1917. A nest containing seven fresh eggs was found in an old fir stub standing in 18 inches of water near the shore of the lake. The top of the stub had rotted out to a depth of 2 feet and the eggs were at the bottom of this cavity. Down could be seen protruding through a small hole in the stub, a few inches above the eggs.

John G. Millais (1913) says of the breeding habits of this species in Iceland:

Barrow's goldeneye arrive at their breeding places about the end of March, in flocks, and at once proceed to pair. I have been unable to discover any ornithologist who has seen the courtship display of this species, but I have little doubt that when we are able to procure specimens alive from Iceland, and keep them in good health, we shall find that it is much the same as that of the common goldeneye. The nest is usually placed in a hole in the bank of a stream flowing into a lake, in a hole in the lava rocks close to the water, or on some low island under bushes of dwarf willow, dwarf birch, amongst coarse grass or low scrub, such as *Empetrum nigrum* or *Azalea procumbens*. I found two nests just tucked in under large stones, and not 2 feet above the level of the stream. They are also said to nest in the turf walls of the sheep shelters.

He also quotes Riemschneider as saying:

The nest was always placed in more or less of a hollow, in natural hollows of the rocks, in covered-over cracks in the lava, or, as already mentioned, in the outer walls of peat shelters, erected for sheep, where a few blocks of peat have been taken out to form a nesting place, and even, and that not seldom, inside the shelter, in which case the food rack or a place like it would serve as a nesting place; as exit for flight the door of the shelter would in such a case be used. Such customs have given rise to the Iceland names for the species. In the natural hollows, holes in the rocks, fissures, etc., the nest is placed now in the foreground, now so far inside that you could not reach to it from the entrance opening, but were obliged to lift off the stones covering it for this purpose. Whilst as a rule the position of the nest is to be found approaching the level of the surface of the ground, I saw a nest in the Kalvastrond which was built in a hollow in the lava at more than twice a man's height. In the nest trough, which was formed to begin with in the food racks of the stalls, by pulling together dry grass stalks and other remnants of food round the nest, there was a very ample, delicate lining of whitish down, which had a very small admixture of fine, dry parts of plants. The eggs, 12 to 15 in number, and only exceptionally more, are distinguished from other ducks' eggs by their pure, blue-green color, are rather bulgy in shape, and have a smooth, not very shining shell.

From the above accounts it will be seen that the Barrow goldeneye prefers to nest in hollows; the absence of suitable trees in Iceland forces it to select other cavities; but in this country it seems to nest in situations similar to those chosen by the common goldeneye and, like that species, it lines the nest cavity with pure white down, scantily at first, but more profusely as incubation advances; probably no other material is brought into the cavity, but undoubtedly whatever material it finds there is not wholly removed. The down in the nest is indistinguishable from that of the common goldeneye.

Eggs.—The set consists of anywhere from 6 to 15 eggs, but probably the usual number is in the neighborhood of 10. The eggs

are practically indistinguishable from those of the common goldeneye, though they may average slightly larger. The shape varies
from elliptical ovate or elliptical oval to nearly oval. The color
varies from "deep lichen green" to "pale olivine" or "pale glass
green"; when freshly laid some of the darkest eggs may approach a
pale shade of "malachite green." The measurement of 79 eggs,
in various collections, average 61.3 by 44 millimeters; the eggs showing the four extremes measure **66.6** by 42, 61 by **47.2**, **57.3** by 42, and
61.9 by **41.4** millimeters.

Rev. F. C. R. Jourdain, who has studied the Barrow goldeneye in
Iceland, writes me that incubation is performed by the female alone
and that it is said to last for four weeks; he says that the female sits
very closely and at times has to be removed by force, if one wants to
see the eggs. The male remains close at hand during incubation.

Mr. Munro, however (1918), writes:

Immature males leave the country with the adult males in May, soon after
the females have begun to brood their eggs. I have never seen an adult male
at this season. Mr. Allan Brooks is of the opinion that the males go directly
to the coast at this time.

Young.—He says of the young:

May 22 is the earliest date on which I have seen the young, and by August 1
they are full grown. At this time they are remarkably tame, allowing an
approach to within a few yards and then, if alarmed, swimming to the middle
of the lake, rather than taking wing. This fearlessness is characteristic until
the shooting season opens in September, when they soon become wary. At
this time, the birds rise from the water as one approaches, but almost invariably circle about the lake several times and then fly toward anyone standing on the shore, thus affording an easy shot. By the last week in October,
when the common goldeneye, redhead, and scaups are returning from the
north, the last of the Barrow goldeneyes have left.

Plumages.—The downy young of the Barrow goldeneye is very
much like that of the common goldeneye. The upper half of the
head, from below the eyes, and the hind neck are deep "bone brown"
or "seal brown"; the upper parts are "bone brown," relieved by
white on the edge of the wing and by scapular and rump spots of
white; the lower half of the head and the under parts are white;
there is a brownish gray band around the lower neck.

The plumage changes are similar to those of the common goldeneye. Of the development of the plumage in the young male, Mr.
Millais (1913) says:

In November the new inner scapulars appear, and these at once give a character to the identification of the species. The black portion of the inner
scapulars is much extended in Barrow's goldeneye, whereas in the common
goldeneye it is confined to the margin of the feathers. At this date, too, the
first white feathers come in between the bill and the eye. These increase in
number throughout the winter, whilst numbers of pure white feathers come

on the chest until the brown of immaturity disappears. Thus the advance of plumage continues to take place until March, when the young male has gained a considerable portion of its first spring dress, which is more or less similar to the adult male, except that the black and white scapulars are never fully attained, nor are the hind neck or flanks complete. The wings and tail still show the bird to be immature until the latter part of June or early July, when the usual complete molt takes place, the whole of the bird going into a partial eclipse similar to the adult male. In September the eclipse is shed, and all traces of immaturity have disappeared, so that in the following month, or, more correctly speaking, November, the bird is adult, at about 16 months.

The same writer describes the semieclipse plumage of the male, as follows:

At the beginning of July the adult male undergoes a fairly complete change to an eclipse plumage, although the white feathers in front of the eye are never completely lost. In this month the head and neck become a somewhat dirty gray brown, very light in the throat; the flanks, hind neck, and upper mantle, also portion of the lower neck and chest are brown with gray edgings; mantle, scapulars, brown, with light brown or gray edgings or tips; the whole bird now resembles a somewhat dirty-looking female, but its sex can easily be recognized by its superior size, small white feathers on the head, and by the wings, which always remain the same, which, with the tail and part of the back and tail coverts, are only molted once in the season. The adult male has scarcely assumed its eclipse dress before it again commences to molt into winter plumage, and in the case of all these ducks the process of change at this season may be said to be practically continuous.

The female undergoes the same sequence of plumage to maturity as the female goldeneye, attaining full maturity at an age of about 15 months. The females of these two species are very difficult to distinguish at any age. Mr. Millais (1913) says:

The characters of the female Barrow's goldeneye, apart from superior size, are the black back and tail, blackish head and longer crest, and general difference of a more intensified black and white. The yellow bill spot is also more extensive.

William Brewster (1909a) has made an exhaustive study of this subject, and I would refer the reader to his excellent paper on it. I would refer the reader also to a paper on this subject by H. F. Witherby (1913) and a still more exhaustive treatise by Maj. Allan Brooks (1920).

Food.—The food of the Barrow goldeneye seems to be the same as that of the common species. Dr. F. Henry Yorke (1899) records it as feeding on minnows and small fishes, slugs, snails, and mussels, frogs, and tadpoles, in the way of animal food; he has also found in its food considerable vegetable matter, such as teal moss, blue flag, duckweed, water plantain, pouchweed, water milfoil, water starwort, bladderwort, and pickerel weed. Mr. Munro (1918) says:

The feeding habits of the two species of goldeneye are identical. Both species are greatly attracted by the small crawfish lurking under large stones in shallow water. While hunting these shellfish, the ducks work rapidly along the shore, diving every few minutes, to probe under the edges of the large stones. They invariably try to submerge even if the water is not deep enough to cover their backs, and I have never seen them dipping as redheads and scaups frequently do. One can follow the goldeneye's movement as it encircles the large stones, by the commotion on the surface and by frequent glimpses of the duck's back. In shallow water, the birds remain below from 15 to 20 seconds, the crawfish being brought to the surface to be swallowed. By the end of winter the feathers on the forehead are generally worn off, through much rubbing against stones in this manner of foraging. When feeding in deep water, over the beds of *Potamogeton*, they stay in the same place until satisfied. In such places the small snails and crustacea that attach themselves to the stems of *Potamogeton* form their chief food, but little vegetable matter being taken beyond what is eaten with the shells. The small shellfish are swallowed while the birds are below the surface of the water, unlike the procedure followed with the larger crawfish. Their stay under water is of fairly uniform duration, ranging from 50 to 55 seconds. At the beginning of the dive the tail is raised and spread to its full extent.

Behavior.—He writes of its habits:

As far as I have been able to observe, there is no difference in the flight of the two species of goldeneye. Both have the same clumsy way of rising, and of flying close to the surface before attaining any speed; once under way they travel swiftly, and one's attention is held by the distinctive, musical whistle of their wings. Both the Barrow goldeneye and the American goldeneye are less gregarious than others of our ducks with the exception of the mergansers. I have never seen the Barrow goldeneye in large flocks except in the mating season. When feeding, two or three birds together are the rule, and five or six the maximum number noted.

Dr. D. G. Elliott (1898) writes of its behavior:

I have found it at times quite numerous on the St. Lawrence near Ogdensburg, and have killed a goodly number there over decoys, and some specimens, procured on these occasions, are now in the Museum of Natural History in New York. The two species were associated together on the river, and I never knew which one would come to the decoys, but I do not remember that both never came together, unless it might be the females, for, as I have said, it was difficult to distinguish them without an examination.

The birds would fly up and down the river, doubtless coming from, and going to, Lake Erie, stopping occasionally in the coves to feed, and floating down with the current for a considerable distance, when they would rise and fly upstream again. My decoys were always placed in some cove or bend of the stream where the current was least strong, for I noticed the birds rarely settled on the water where it was running swiftly. This duck decoys readily in such situations, and will come right in, and if permitted, settle among the wooden counterfeits. They sit lightly upon the water and rise at once without effort or much splashing. The flight is very rapid, and is accompanied with the same whistling of the wings so noticeable in the common goldeneye. In stormy weather this bird keeps close to the banks, seeking shelter from the winds. It dives as expertly as its relative, and frequently remains under water for a considerable time. The flesh of those killed upon the river was tender and of good flavor, fish evidently not having figured much as an article of their diet.

Maj. Allan Brooks writes that "the note is a hoarse croak. They have also a peculiar mewing cry, made only by the males in the mating season."

Mr. Millais (1913), who studied this species extensively in Iceland, writes of its behavior there as follows:

On the water the male of this species looks a larger, clumsier, and blacker bird than the common goldeneye. It seemed to me that it sits higher on the water, and was a bird that commanded instant attention. In summer the males, which, when the ducks have begun to sit, consort in small parties of two to six, or more, are exceptionally tame, and will permit an approach to within a few paces, if the observer moves slowly to the banks of the river where they are feeding or resting. In rising to fly they are somewhat clumsy, and run along the surface with considerable splashing, but they did not seem to me to make nearly so much noise in flight as the common species. The "singing" or "ringing" note is heard, but it is neither so loud nor so metallic. On June 27 the males were still in their breeding dress. A few seem to keep on the river near the nesting females, as if for form's sake, but the majority were resorting to the great lake of Myvatn, where the parties seemed to increase in size day by day. Females, with young, often floated past me while I was trout fishing, and once I had to draw in my line to prevent hooking a too confiding mother. Whilst watching males on feed, it struck me that they were less expert than the common goldeneye, and had more difficulty in getting under water. There was more noise and splash to get under, but once below the surface they seemed to be skilled performers of the highest order. I saw them more than once, from the high bank where my tent was pitched, feeding in exactly the same manner as the common species, turning over all the small stones, and probing beneath all large ones, and into holes. They stay less time under water in shallows than in the deep water of the lake, the time occupied being a half to one minute. On the river they reappeared again and again at the same spot, only pausing for a moment's rest and splash down again, whereas on the lake they would often keep moving forward in their dives, and take up a fresh position every time. They will stay and fish in very rough streams, edging into the current and out again as soon as they rise, but do not like such wild places as the harlequin.

In Iceland their enemies seem to be Richardson's skua, *Stercorarius parasiticus* L., which regularly attacks the females of all diving ducks and seizes their young, and the Iceland falcon, *Falco rusticolus islandicus*, which kills a few of the adults. There was hardly a morning or evening when I stayed at Myvatn, in June-July, 1889, that we did not see one or other of these two species harrying the ducks. Sitting in the tent to escape the awful plague of flies, a sudden roar of startled ducks would be heard, and on my going to investigate there was the falcon, with perhaps two young birds in attendance, bearing off some victims of its prowess. None of the ducks seemed to be unusually scared when the falcons passed by, as they often did, by day and night. They crouched on the water or rushed with their broods under the banks and hid as well as possible. It was only after the stoop and kill, when the bird of prey came on to their own level, that there was a general stampede of these ducks in the immediate vicinity of the murder.

Mr. Lucien M. Turner, in his unpublished notes, says:

These goldeneyes are common along the entire coast of Labrador and occur in scattered flocks of two or three to rarely more than a dozen in number. I have never found the nest or eggs of this species and am not positive that it breeds on the coast; although it occurs during the summer season, arriving by the 1st of June, and remains until early November. During the latter part of its stay it frequents the places of swift tide currents where it dives with wondrous celerity to procure its food from the bottom of soundings. Numbers of these birds were seen in a pocket some 2 miles from the mouth of the Koksoak River and on the left band. This place is locally known as Partridge's fishing place. I was camped there while delayed by stormy weather, and early each morning great numbers of these birds frequented the inner portion of the cove. Strange to say, these birds never made the same noise with their wings when they flew into the cove that they did when they flew out. The tempestuous weather and great distance prevented me from securing any specimens in that locality. This was late in September, and these birds congregated in large numbers, for some of the flocks certainly contained 200 individuals and were doubtless preparing to journey to the southward. None were seen after the last of September. I observe that these ducks are nocturnal in their habits and especially noisy toward the approach of day. They search for fresh feeding grounds from daylight to sunrise and appear to be very quiet, unless disturbed, during the midday hours.

Mr. Skinner says, in his notes:

I usually find these ducks by ones and twos and small groups, but once I found a flock of 85 swimming in a compact group off the shore of Yellowstone Lake. When in pairs, it is the female that takes alarm and flushes first. They take great delight in "shooting the rapids"; nothing in the Gardiner River, at least, being too rough for them. They drop down over a fall 3 feet high, and at the bottom go out of sight in the foam and spray, but nevertheless keep right on swimming along. Should they tire of this boisterous sport, they are quick to take advantage of any eddy, or rest behind a bowlder. As a rule these are the tamest of our ducks; on the reservoir and other roadside waters they are unalarmed even while the big autos go thundering past. If I approach a flock too closely, the Barrows swim away, or go coasting down the rapids, instead of flushing as the mallards do. But if they do flush, they go only a little way, come back, and drop down again into the water without hesitation or fear.

I do not believe the Barrows seek the society of other ducks, but common tastes bring them to many other ducks, mostly deep-water ducks, such as mallards, mergansers, buffleheads, ruddy ducks, bluebills, and American goldeneyes. Sometimes the last named and the Barrows are together, but more often the two species keep apart, possibly due to the rivalry of the males.

Flight is low and labored at first, as they rise against the wind, and they are often compelled to kick the water for the first 20 or more wing strokes. I have seen them start and later strike the water again where the average pitch of the rapids was 6 per cent or less. Rising against a strong head wind, they do much better, and then they may fly at a greater height than in calm weather, say of 30 or 40 feet. Once I was passing up a narrow stream with the wind behind me when I found a half dozen Barrows before me. They could not fly up into my face and the canyon was too high and narrow to fly out sideways, so the ducks were obliged to swim down past me and rise behind my back. Apparently they can not jump up as the mallard does so frequently. But once under way, flight is swift and powerful, giving rise to a distinct whistling sound.

These ducks bathe by standing almost erect on the water and rapidly flapping their wings so as to throw the water forward and over them; later by plunging under and shaking themselves at the same time. They usually dress their feathers while on the water, turning far over, first on one side, then on the other, to get at places ordinarily under the surface. Once I found a Barrow preening on a half submerged bowlder.

Winter.—The winter home of the Barrow goldeneye is not far south of its summer range, and its migration is not much more than a movement off its nesting grounds to more satisfactory feeding grounds. It seems to be fairly common on the Gulf of St. Lawrence in winter, where it frequents about the same resorts as the common goldeneye, but farther south on the Atlantic coast it is rare. It winters on some of the large lakes and rivers of the interior, as well as on the Pacific coast.

J. A. Munro (1918) says that "throughout the winter months it is found on the seacoast, in the many sheltered estuaries from Puget Sound to Hecate Strait and Dixon Inlet." He also writes to me "that a few birds winter on the Okanogan River below Okanogan Falls in a rapid stretch of water with strong bottom, where crawfish are very abundant. They are usually in company with the common goldeneye."

Mr. Skinner writes to me:

While the majority migrate on the freezing of the waters, a few remain along the Gardiner and Yellowstone Rivers all winter, and become even tamer than usual, entitling them to be rated as resident (in Montana) at all seasons. Barrows that had wintered along the Gardiner in 1920–21 began leaving about February 25, or about the time that waters elsewhere were beginning to open. First to go were the males, then the females and immatures; until only one was left on March 1, and that one went next day. But cold, freezing temperature brought them back, a female on the 7th and six drakes and five females on the 12th; then they decreased again. By the 24th they were abundant at the outlet of Yellowstone Lake at 1,000 feet higher altitude or just over 7,700 feet above sea level.

DISTRIBUTION

Breeding range.—In North America, a few breed on the Labrador Peninsula from the Gulf of St. Lawrence (Point des Monts) to northern Labrador (Davis Inlet). But the main breeding range is in the vicinity of the Rocky Mountains. East to western Alberta (Banff), northwestern Montana (Glacier National Park) and central northern Colorado (Boulder County). South to southwestern Colorado (Dolores County). West to southwestern Oregon (Crook County and Douglas County), central British Columbia (Okanogan and La Hache Valleys), to the coast of southern Alaska (Chilkat and Sitka), and south central Alaska (Lake Clark). North to northern Mackenzie (Fort Anderson rarely) and Great Slave Lake

(Fort Rae and Providence). Breeds abundantly in Iceland and in Greenland up to 69° or 70° N.

Winter range.—From the Gulf of St. Lawrence southward along the coast regularly to eastern Maine (Washington County), rarely to southern New England and as a straggler beyond. On the Pacific coast from southern Alaska (Wrangell and Portage Bay) to central California (San Francisco Bay). Rarely and irregularly in the interior, south to southern Colorado (La Plata River), and north to southern British Columbia (Okanogan Lake) and northern Montana (Great Falls).

Spring migration.—Dates of arrival: Quebec City, April 14 to 16; Mackenzie, Fort Anderson, June 14. Late dates: Ontario, Toronto, April 18, 1885; North Carolina, near Asheville, May 6, 1893.

Fall migration.—Dates of arrival: Quebec, Montreal, October 23; Connecticut, East Haven, November 14; Massachusetts, Wareham, November 27; District of Columbia, November 22, 1889; Wisconsin, Lake Koshkonong, November 14, 1896.

Casual records.—All records east of the Rocky Mountain region and south of New England must be regarded as casual. Most of these records are based on females, incorrectly identified. The records given above, under migrations, are believed to be authentic, as are also the following: Michigan, Ottawa County, 1907, and Detroit River, April 1, 1905.

Egg dates.—Iceland: Fourteen records, May 19 to June 30; seven records, June 2 to 17. British Columbia: Five records, May 12 to 31. Alberta: Two records, May 28 and 30.

CHARITONETTA ALBEOLA (Linnaeus)

BUFFLEHEAD

HABITS

The propriety of applying the name " spirit duck " to this sprightly little duck will be appreciated by anyone who has watched it in its natural surroundings, floating buoyantly, like a beautiful apparition, on the smooth surface of some pond or quiet stream, with its striking contrast of black and white in its body plumage and with the glistening metallic tints in its soft fluffy head, relieved by a broad splash of the purest white; it seems indeed a spirit of the waters, as it plunges, quickly beneath the surface and bursts out again in full flight, disappearing in the distance with a blur of whirring wings.

Spring.—Although a hardy species and generally regarded as a cold-weather bird, the bufflehead is rather slow in making its spring migration; it follows gradually the retreat of winter, but lingers on the way. Dr. F. Henry Yorke (1899) says:

The first issue of these birds appears in the interior above the frost line late in the spring, a short time before the bluewinged teals arrive; and with the ruddy ducks are the last of the divers to travel northward. They soon depart to the far north, where they are followed by the second and third issues, which scatter over the country before they also follow the advanced flight.

Courtship.—Although the bufflehead lingers in some of our ponds until quite late in the spring and during some seasons is fairly common, I have not been particularly successful in studying its courtship on account of its shyness. On bright, warm days during the latter part of April or early in May the courtship of this species may be studied with some hope of success, though long and patient watching through powerful glasses may be necessary. The males are quite quarrelsome at this season and fight viciously among themselves for the possession of the females. The male is certainly a handsome creature as he swims in and out among the somber females, his bill pointing upward, his neck extended, and his beautiful head puffed out to twice its natural size and glistening in the sunlight. Standing erect he struts about, as if supported by his feet and tail, with his bill drawn in upon his swelling bosom, a picture of pride and vanity, which is doubtless appreciated by his would-be mate. Suddenly he dives beneath her and on coming up immediately deserts her and flies over to another female to repeat the process. He seems fickle or flirtatious in thus dividing his attentions, but perhaps they have not been graciously received or he has been rebuffed. Sometimes he becomes coy and swims away until she shows interest enough to follow him. Eventually he finds the one best suited to him and the conjugal pact is sealed.

Dr. Charles W. Townsend (1916) describes the courtship of the bufflehead as follows:

A group of 35 or 40 of these birds, with sexes about equally divided, may have been actively feeding, swimming together in a compact flock all pointing the same way. They dive within a few seconds of each other and stay under water 14 to 20 seconds, and repeat the diving at frequent intervals. Suddenly a male swims vigorously at another with flapping wings, making the water boil, and soon each male is ardently courting. He spreads and cocks his tail, puffs out the feathers of his head and cheeks, extends his bill straight out in front close to the water and every now and then throws it back with a bob in a sort of reversed bow. All the time he swims rapidly, and, whereas in feeding the group were all swimming the same way in an orderly manner, the drakes are now nervously swimming back and forth and in and out through the crowd. Every now and then there is a commotion in the water as one or more drakes dive, with a splashing of water, only to come up again in pursuit or retreat. As the excitement grows a drake flaps his wings frequently and then jumps from the water and flies low with outstretched neck toward a duck who has listlessly strayed from the group. He alights beside her precipitately, sliding along on his tail, his breast and head elevated to their utmost extent and held erect. He bobs nervously. And so it goes.

Nesting.—The center of abundance of the bufflehead in the breeding season seems to be in the wooded regions of Canada lying west and north of the Great Plains, where it is well distributed and in some places quite common. Sidney S. S. Stansell (1909) says that in central Alberta it is "about as common as the mallard; nearly every small pond has its pair, and some of them two pairs, of this beautiful little duck. When two or more pairs occupy a single pond, the males are usually very pugnacious, often quarreling and trying to drive each other off the pond for hours at a time." A set of 12 eggs in my collection collected by Mr. Stansell, near Carvel, Alberta, on June 11, 1912, was taken from an old flicker's nesting hole, 20 feet from the ground; as the eggs were nearly fresh, there was no lining in the nest except the chips left by the previous occupant.

Herbert Massey has sent me some data regarding a set of 10 eggs in his collection, taken by Mr. W. H. Bingaman, at Island Lake, Saskatchewan, 50 miles west of Prince Albert, on May 28, 1905. The nest was in an enlarged flicker excavation 15 feet from the ground and 2 feet from the broken-off top of a dead poplar tree; the eggs lay 15 inches below the very irregular opening, among rotten wood dust, flicker feathers, and light-colored down of the duck; the tree was 10 yards from the shore of the lake; the female was sitting and was secured. The collector says:

I found this species nowhere abundant in Saskatchewan, and two sets are the complete result of my season's work among this species. I took one other set at Montreal Lake, 95 miles northeast of Island Lake, and the nesting site was almost a duplicate of this one; it also contained 10 eggs.

Maj. Allan Brooks (1903) thus describes the breeding habits of the bufflehead in the Cariboo district of British Columbia:

Almost every lake has one or more pairs of these charming little ducks. Unlike Barrow's goldeneye, the nests were always in trees close to or but a short distance away from water. These nests were invariably the deserted nesting holes of flickers, and in most cases had been used several years in succession by the ducks. The holes were in aspen trees, from 5 to 20 feet from the ground, and the entrance was not more than 3¼ inches in diameter. The number of eggs ranged from 2 to 9, 8 being the average; in color they resemble old ivory, without any tinge of green. I have several times seen the eggs of this duck described as "dusky green," but these have evidently been the eggs of some species of teal. The female bufflehead is a very close sitter, never leaving the nest until the hole was sawed out, and in most cases I had to lift the bird and throw her up in the air, when she would make a bee line for the nearest lake, where her mate would be slowly swimming up and down unconscious of the violation of his home. In many cases the eggs had fine cracks, evidently made by the compression of the bird's body when entering the small aperture.

J. A. Munro found a nest—

in an old pileated woodpecker's hole near the top of a yellow pine stub, without bark or branches and broken off 40 feet from the ground. It stood among young Murray pines and poplars 20 yards from the shore of the lake. Down adhering to the entrance of the hole identified the nest as belonging to the bufflehead. The nest had been used the previous year by buffleheads and during the following winter by flying squirrels. This was indicated by a quantity of old bufflehead down, with fragments of eggshell adhering, lying at the bottom of the tree. To this down the flying squirrels had added a quantity of moss. Apparently the female bufflehead had removed the mixture of moss and down before commencing to lay.

Where trees are scarce, as in certain parts of Saskatchewan, the bufflehead is said to lay its eggs in a hole in a bank, after the manner of the belted kingfisher, using for this purpose the deserted burrow of a gopher near some small lake. Such cases must be exceptional, however. The down in the nest is small, light, and flimsy; it is " pallid purplish gray " in color, with small white centers. The breast feathers in it are pure white.

Eggs.—The bufflehead lays from 6 to 14 eggs, but 10 or 12 seems to be the usual number. M. P. Skinner writes to me that he " encountered a female on Yellowstone River with 16 well-grown young, and, as I could not find another parent, I have always assigned this extraordinary brood to the one mother."

The shape is bluntly ovate, elliptical ovate, or nearly oval. The shell is smooth and slightly glossy. The color varies from " ivory yellow " to " marguerite yellow " or "pale olive buff." The measurements of 86 eggs in various collections, average 48.5 by 34.7 millimeters; the eggs showing the four extremes measure **55** by 37, 53.5 by **38**, and **40** by **26** millimeters.

Plumages.—As might be expected, the downy young bufflehead closely resembles the young goldeneye in color pattern. The upper parts, including the upper half of the head from below the lores and eyes, the hind neck, the back and the rump, are deep rich " bone brown," with a lighter gloss on the forehead and mantle; the inner edge of the wing is pure white; there is a large white spot on each side of the scapular region and on each side of the rump; and an indistinct whitish spot on each flank. The under parts, including the chin, throat, cheeks, breast, and belly are pure white, shading off gradually into the darker color on the sides of the body and with an indistinct brownish collar around the lower neck.

In the juvenal plumage the sexes are much alike and resemble the adult female, except that the colors are duller and browner and the white cheek patches smaller than in the adult. The young male soon begins to differentiate from the young female, by increasing faster in size and by the development of the head, with a more conspicuous white patch. The progress toward maturity is very slow, and even in May the young male has only partially assumed the adult plumage; the tail and much of the body plumage has been renewed, the wings are still immature, and the head has acquired large white patches, but only a few of the purple feathers of the adult. A complete summer molt occurs in July and August, after which the adult plumage is gradually assumed and is completed in November and December. The young male thus becomes adult at an age of 17 or 18 months. The young female makes practically the same progress toward maturity.

I have never seen the eclipse plumage of the bufflehead, but according to Mr. Millais (1913) both old and young males assume " a fairly complete eclipse, resembling a similar stage of plumage in the goldeneye."

Food.—The bufflehead obtains its food by diving, usually feeding in small companies so that one or more remain on the surface to watch for approaching dangers while the others are below; sometimes only one remains above, but it is only rarely that all go below at once; should the sentinel become alarmed it communicates in some way with the others which come to the surface and all swim or fly away to a safe distance.

Neltje Blanchan (1898) describes its feeding habits very neatly, as follows:

A bufflehead overtakes and eats little fish under water or equally nimble insects on the surface, probes the muddy bottom of the lake for small shellfish, nibbles the seawrack and other vegetable growth of the salt-water inlets, all the while toughening its flesh by constant exercise and making it rank by a fishy diet, until none but the hungriest of sportsmen care to bag it.

Audubon (1840) says:

Their food is much varied according to situation. On the seacoast, or in estuaries, they dive after shrimps, small fry, and bivalve shells; and in fresh water they feed on small crayfish, leeches, and snails, and even grasses.

Ora W. Knight (1908) says that in the inland regions of Maine "they feed on chubs, shiners, small trout fry, and other small fish. Along the coast their diet is very similar." Other writers include in their food various small mollusks, crustaceans, beetles, locusts, grasshoppers, and other insects.

Dr. F. Henry Yorke (1899) lists the following genera of plants among the food of the bufflehead: *Limnobium, Myriophyllum, Callitriche, Utricularia,* and *Pontederia.* Vegetable matter seems to form only a small part of the food of this species and is eaten mainly during the summer.

Behavior.—The flight of the bufflehead is exceedingly swift and direct, generally at no very great elevation above the water, and is performed with steady and very rapid beats of its strong little wings. It rises neatly and quickly from the surface of the water and sometimes from below it, bursting into the air at full speed. When alighting on the water it strikes with a splash and slides along the surface. It generally travels in small irregular flocks made up largely of females and young males, with two or three old drakes.

It is one of the best of divers, disappearing with the suddenness of a grebe, with the plumage of its head compressed and its wings closely pressed to its sides. It can often succeed in diving at the flash of a gun and thus escape being shot. Under water it can swim with closed wings swiftly enough to catch the small fish on which it feeds so largely; but I believe that it often uses its wings under water for extra speed. It can also dive to considerable depths to secure its food from the bottom. Charles E. Alford (1920) says that it seldom or never dives to a greater depth than 2 fathoms. He timed a large number of dives and found that the period of immersion varied from 15 to 23 seconds, usually it was about 20, and the interval between dives varied from 4 to 8 seconds.

The following incident, related by Mr. Samuel Hubbard, jr. (1893), shows that its diving powers are sometimes taxed to the limit:

A broad, sandy bay made in from the harbor, the upper end of which terminated in a shallow slough about 18 inches deep. I waded across and was proceeding toward the beach, when my attention was attracted by a small bufflehead duck (*Charitonetta albeola*) commonly called butterball. He was swimming around in the slough and obtaining his food in the way common to his kind, by diving and picking up that which came his way. With an admiring glance at his beautiful plumage, I was about to pass on, when one of those pirates of the air, a duck hawk (*Falco peregrinus anatum*) came in sight. Without hesitating an instant, he made straight for my little friend and swooped at him. His long talons came down with a clutch, but they closed on nothing, for the duck was under the water. Undaunted the hawk hovered overhead, and as the water was clear and shallow, he could follow every movement of his prey. Again the duck came up; the hawk swooped to seize him, each move being repeated in quick succession and each dive becoming shorter and shorter. It was evident that the poor little hunted creature was getting desperate, for the next move he made was to come out of the water flying. The hawk promptly gave chase. There was some clever dodging in the air, but the duck, frightened and tired, soon saw that his swift pursuer was getting the best of it, so he closed his wings tight against his body and dropped like a stone into the water and plunged out of sight. Now comes the beginning of the end. While he was under water he either saw the hawk hovering over him or else he became bewildered, for he came again out of the water flying. Like lightning the hawk struck; there was a muffled "squawk," and the tragedy was ended.

Dr. J. G. Cooper (1860) writes:

I once saw a male that I had just wounded dive in clear water, and, seizing hold, by its bill, of a root growing under water, remain voluntarily submerged for almost five minutes, until he supposed all danger past, when, again ascending to the surface, he paddled off with great rapidity.

I cannot remember that I have ever heard its note, but Dr. D. G. Elliot (1898) says that "it utters at times a single guttural note, which sounds like a small edition of the hoarse roll of the canvasback and other large diving ducks."

L. R. Dice (1920) says of its notes:

As a rule they are silent; only on a few occasions were any calls heard. Once while driving a pair in front of a blind to take pictures, the male and female became separated. Then the male gave a squeaky call, which the female answered with a hoarse *quack*, *quack*, and the male immediately flew to her side. At another time a female alighted in an eddy of the river and gave a low call, *quk*, *quk*, *quk*, *quk*, *quk*, *quk*, *quk*, slowly, and the male in a few minutes appeared and alighted beside her.

Fall.—In the fall this species is one of the later migrants, coming along with the hardier winter ducks. It is not of much account as a game bird; its body is small and its flesh is not particularly desirable, as it feeds so largely on animal food. It is, however, often very fat, from which it has derived the name of "butterball." It is apparently not regularly hunted or sought for by gunners, but is often shot while hunting other species.

Winter.—W. L. Dawson (1909) says of the habits of this species on the coast of Washington:

Buffleheads are among our most abundant ducks in fall and winter throughout the State. They are found alike in swift rivers and on placid mill ponds. Brackish pools and tide channels, tide flats, and tossing billows, all are alike to these happy and hardy little souls. Perhaps the greatest number, however, are found upon the bays and shallower waters of Puget Sound. They associate chiefly in little flocks of from half a dozen to 50 individuals, and they venture inshore, as often as they dare, to feed on the rising tide. When they reach us in October they are fat as butter (whence, of course, "butterball"), but they have gained their flesh on the cleaner feeding grounds of the northern interior. On a fare of fish and marine worms, which they obtain in salt water almost entirely by diving, their flesh soon becomes rank and unprofitable.

M. P. Skinner has sent me the following notes on the habits of buffleheads in Yellowstone Park:

As a rule these ducks are on the larger waters such as Yellowstone Lake and Yellowstone River, resorting to smaller lakes and ponds at very infrequent intervals. In stormy times, they are driven to quieter waters, but even then prefer to find a calm spot near shore of Yellowstone Lake or a back water on the river. When on streams, they do not care for the swifter water. They are fond of sitting on sand bars, gravel bars, mud points, and on the beaches about Yellowstone Lake. Many of these birds are to be seen all winter in openings in the ice on the lake, and on the river where kept ice-free by the current, along the Firehole River kept open by hot geyser water, and on the Gardiner River below the mouth of warm Boiling River. They are social and keep together in small, compact flocks. Similar food habits bring them in close contact with some ducks and the limited open water in winter with others. In these ways, they are often with mergansers, Barrow goldeneye, American goldeneye, canvasbacks, redheads, bluebills, coot, grebes, mallard, green-winged teal, baldpate, shovellers, ruddy ducks, geese, and swans. On the sandy beaches, they are often near spotted sandpipers, or pelican, if not actually with them.

From the above it will be inferred that the bufflehead winters as far north as it can find open water in the interior. On the coasts it is found as far north as New England and British Columbia. It seems to prefer to be on or near the frost line and does not go much south of the United States in winter.

Dr. Leonard C. Sanford (1903) writes:

The butterball is common on both coasts, and is fond of shallow, sandy bays, frequenting the tide rips and mouths of rivers, remaining through the coldest weather. A few years ago this bird was common all along the New England shore. Large numbers wintered on the sound between New Haven and Stratford, where the coast is shallow and sandy, early in the morning leaving the outer flats and feeding up the rivers. It was a simple matter to shoot them on their flight, as they came over the bars, low down and usually in the same course. Recently the butterball seem to have largely disappeared from the New England coast, though still common on bays farther south.

DISTRIBUTION

Breeding range.—Mainly in the interior of Canada. East to northern Ontario (probably), said to breed in New Brunswick and recorded once as breeding in southeastern Maine (Washington County). Has been recorded as breeding formerly, and probably only casually, south to southeastern Wisconsin (Pewaukee Lake), northern Iowa (Clear Lake, etc.), and Wyoming (Meeteetse Creek); but it evidently does not breed now anywhere south of the Canadian border except in northern Montana (Milk River, Flathead Lake, and Meagher County). West to central British Columbia (Sumas and southern Okanogan). There is a recent breeding record for California (Eagle Lake). North to west central Alaska (Kuskokwim River and the Yukon Valley), northern Mackenzie (nearly to the mouth of that river), Great Slave Lake (Forts Rae and Resolution) and the southwestern coasts of Hudson Bay and James Bay.

Winter range.—Mainly in the United States, entirely across the continent. South casually to Cuba; commonly to South Carolina, northern Florida (Leon County), the Gulf coasts of Louisiana and Texas; and less commonly or rarely to central Mexico and Lower California (San Quintin). North to the Aleutian and Commander Islands, the Alaska Peninsula, southern British Columbia (Okanogan Lake), northwestern Montana (Tetlow County), the Great Lakes (Michigan, Huron, and Ontario) and the coast of Maine.

Spring migration.—Northward and inland. Early dates of arrival: Pennsylvania, Renovo, February 29; Massachusetts, March 11; Ontario, Ottawa, March 26; Illinois, Shawneetown, February

27; Iowa, southern, March 1; Minnesota, Heron Lake, March 6; Alberta, Alix, April 24; Alaska, Cross Sound, April 13, and Craig, May 9; Pribilof Islands, May 19. Average dates of arrival: Pennsylvania, Renovo, March 18; Massachusetts, March 11; New Brunswick and Nova Scotia, March 22; Indiana, central, March 2; Illinois, northern, March 21; Michigan, southern, March 31; Ontario, southern, April 7, and Ottawa, April 24; Nebraska, Omaha, March 15; Iowa, southern, March 22; Minnesota, Heron Lake, March 26; South Dakota, central, April 8; Manitoba, southern, April 25; Saskatchewan, Osler, May 2; Mackenzie, Fort Simpson, May 11. Late dates of departure: North Carolina, Smith's Island, April 15; Massachusetts, Taunton, May 2; California, Los Angeles County, April 22.

Fall migration.—Gradual southward movement, mainly inland. Dates of arrival: Ontario, Ottawa, October 26; Nova Scotia, Sable Island, November 7; Massachusetts, October 8; Rhode Island, October 13; Pennsylvania, November 10. Late dates of departure: Alaska, Fort Reliance, October 7; Quebec, Montreal, November 1; Ontario, Ottawa, November 8.

Casual records.—Accidental in southern Greenland (Godhaven, 1827, and Frederikshaab, 1891). Two records for Bermuda (November, 1875, and December, 1845). Accidental in Cuba, Porto Rico, and Hawaiian Islands (Maui).

Egg dates.—British Columbia: Six records, May 15 to June 4. Alberta, Saskatchewan, and Manitoba: Five records, May 31 to June 11. Alaska: Two records, June 6 and 12.

CLANGULA HYEMALIS (Linnaeus)

OLDSQUAW

HABITS

Spring.—Oldsquaws, or long-tailed ducks, as I should prefer to have them called, are lively, restless, happy-go-lucky little ducks, known to most of us as hardy and cheery visitors to our winter seacoasts, associated in our minds with cold, gray skies, snow squalls, and turbulent wintry waves. Though happy and gay enough during the winter, the height of their merriment is seen in the spring or when the first signs of the breaking up of winter announce the coming of the nuptial season and arouse the sexual ardor of these warmhearted little ducks. Early in the spring they become more restless than ever, as they gather in merry flocks in the bays and harbors of the New England coasts; the males, in various stages of budding nuptial plumage and fired with the enthusiasm of returning passion, gather in little groups about some favored female in fantastic postures, rushing, flying, quarreling, and filling the air with their musical love notes. If noisy at other times, they are still more so now, vieing with each other to make themselves seen and heard; it is a lively scene, full of the springtime spirit of joy, love, and life.

The increasing warmth of the April sun and the stimulus of the courtship activities start the restless birds on their spring migration by various routes to their summer homes on Arctic shores. While cruising along the north shore of the Gulf of St. Lawrence on May 23, 1909, we saw what was probably the last of the spring migration on the south coast of Labrador; between the Moisie River and Seven Islands we saw numerous large flocks of from 50 to 200 birds each, perhaps 1,000 or 1,500 birds in all. They were noisy and very active, on the water and flying about high in the air, and many seemed to be in summer plumage or changing into it. They were evidently preparing for their overland flight to Hudson Bay; we saw none farther east along the coast, and, from what we could learn from the natives, we inferred that very few migrate around the eastern coast of Labrador and that the bulk of the flight passes overland northwestward to Hudson Bay. Oldsquaws no longer breed on the south coast of Labrador, where Audubon found them, and probably very few still breed on the northeast coast; I saw none during the summer of 1913 even as far north as Cape Mugford, but I obtained a skin of a male in full breeding plumage from an Eskimo at Okak and saw a set of eggs in Rev. W. W. Perrett's collection, taken at Ramah. Lucien M. Turner's unpublished notes state that "they arrive at the mouth of the Koksoak River as soon as the ice breaks up; this being a variable date, of course influences the time from the 20th of May to the 10th of June. Their first appearance is usually in the smaller fresh-water ponds and lakes from which the ice earlier disappears, long before the sea ice in the coves and bays begins to move out." Probably these birds reach this portion of Ungava by the Hudson Bay route rather than by an outside route and through Hudson Straits, which are badly icebound at this season.

There is an extensive northward migration through the interior. E. A. Preble (1908) writes:

In the spring of 1904 I first saw this species at Fort Simpson May 10, from which date it was common. The birds, usually in small flocks, floated down with the current among the ice floes, occasionally rising and winging their way swiftly upstream to regain lost ground. The males played about on the water, chasing each other and uttering their loud, clear notes, which soon became associated in the mind with the long, cool evenings of the Arctic spring, with the sun hanging low in the northwestern horizon. When they are lightly swimming about, the long tails are elevated at an angle of about 45°, and with their striking color pattern the birds present a very jaunty appearance. They are usually rather tame, sometimes rising and coming to meet the canoe, and actually becoming less wild if shot at. When slightly wounded they are among the most expert of divers and are difficult to secure. The males played together considerably before the females arrived, but after that important event their gymnastic and vocal performances knew no bounds.

Dr. E. W. Nelson (1887) says that this is the first of the ducks to reach high northern latitudes in Alaska.

The seal hunters find them in the open spaces in the ice off St. Michaels from the 1st to the 20th of April, and the first open water in shore is sure to attract them. After their arrival it is no uncommon occurrence for the temperature to fall to 25° or 30° below zero, and for furious storms of wind and snow to rage for days, so the first comers must be hardy and vigorous to withstand the exposure.

W. Elmer Ekblaw has sent me the following attractive account of the arrival of the oldsquaws in northern Greenland:

The distinctive resonant call of the oldsquaw announces the arrival of real spring to the far Arctic shores. The earlier herald, the snow bunting, comes while yet the land is covered with snow, while still the ice lies solid and unbroken throughout the wind-swept fjords, and while yet the midnight sun is new and even the noonday is chill; the oldsquaw comes when the snow is gone from the valleys and the slopes, and the first saxifrage and willow have burst into blossom, when great dark leads and pools of open water break the white expanse of fjord ice, and when the sun at midsummer height is warm at midnight as at noon. When the challenging clarion of the oldsquaw rings out over the great north, spring has come.

The first few oldsquaws come winging noisily in along the open leads the first week in June. The males predominate in the first flocks, but by mid-June, when the immigration is at its height, the females appear to be as numerous as the males. Until the inland ponds and lakes are open, the oldsquaws frequent the leads and open pools in the fjord ice; they are most numerous along the shore where the tidal crack opens up the ice, and where the warmer fresh water coming down the slopes and hills melts away the ice foot from the shore. In this along-shore water they apparently find more food, or food more to their liking—generally crustacea and small fish.

From mid-June to the 1st of July the ice on the inland lakes melts away rapidly. Just as soon as the belts of open water show along the banks, the oldsquaws begin to leave the sea and enter the fresh-water lakes. In flight the female always leads, distinguishable by her plumper, dull-colored body and shorter tail; in swimming the male usually leads. Every lakelet has its pair or two of oldsquaws. Some of the pairs seems to be mated when they arrive in the northland, but many mate after their arrival. In the last two weeks of June the local mating season is at its height. Because the males are the more numerous, the rivalry for the females is very keen, and the fighting continuous. During this time, the lake-dotted plains and valleys in the flats about North Star Bay resound with the clamor and din of mating oldsquaws, and the birds may be seen flying swiftly from pool to pool, from point to point. The Eskimo consider them the swiftest flying birds of the northland.

Courtship.—The season of courtship is much prolonged or very variable with this species. This is one of the few ducks that have a spring molt and nuptial plumage; the time and extent of the molt varies greatly in different individuals; and the flush of sexual ardor is probably contemporary with the change of plumage. Consequently some individuals molt and mate before they start on the spring migration and others not until after they have reached their breeding grounds. Many males apparently do not acquire a full nuptial plumage during the whole summer and probably do not mate that season; I have seen males in Alaska in midsummer in practically full winter plumage and in various stages between that and full nuptial plumage; the full development of the latter seems to be rather rare.

John G. Millais (1913) writes:

As previously stated, the actual courtship of the male is generally aroused and brought about by the sexual desire of the female, and amongst ducks the females are very irregular as to the time of their coming into season. Thus only one or perhaps two females in a large flock may be well advanced in their summer plumage and their breeding instincts, and these are the special objects of desire of all the males. I have noticed a bunch of 8 or 10 females swimming apart and not a male going near them, whilst 10 or 15 males will crowd round some particular female and lavish upon her all their arts of charm. The most common attitude of the male in courtship is to erect the tail, stiffen the neck to its fullest extent, and then lower it toward the female with a sudden bow, the bill being held outward and upward. As the head curves down, the call is emitted. Sometimes the head is held out along the water before the female, who herself often adopts this attitude, or makes a " guttering " note of appreciation with head held in close to the body. Another common attitude of the male is to throw the head right back till it almost touches the scapulars, the bill pointing to the heavens. As the bird throws the head forward again the call is emitted. Many males will closely crowd round a female, all going through the same performance. It is not long before a fight starts amongst the males, so that the lady of the tourney is in the midst of a struggling clamorous mass of squabbling knights, each endeavoring to show his qualifications to love by his extravagant gestures or strength. To add to the confusion, any male long-tails in the neighborhood are sure to hear the noise and come flying in all haste to take part in the jousts. Even males still in full winter plumage will come and be almost, if not quite, as active as the rest. They advance with all haste, swaying from side to side, their sharp-pointed wings being only arrested when almost above the contest. Then they close the wings in mid-air and dash into the fray with all their ardour. So impetuous and gallant are males of this species that they will chase each other for long distances, falling often in the sea and sending the spray flying; down they go under the water and emerge almost together on the surface to continue the chase in mid-air. I have twice seen a male when flying seize another by the nape and both come tumbling head over heels into the sea in mad confusion.

In Mr. Hersey's notes, made at the mouth of the Yukon, I find the following account of the later courtship, observed on June 19, 1914, which shows that the birds are not all paired when they arrive on their breeding grounds.

To-day I watched the courtship of a pair of this species. A male and two females were swimming about in a small pond. As the male began calling another female joined the party. The male, however, paid all his attentions to one of the females and did not notice either of the others. As this favored bird swam slowly about her admirer followed, his head drawn in close to his shoulders and the bill pointing downward, the tip not more than an inch or two from the surface of the water. When within 6 or 7 feet of the female he would raise his head till it pointed straight upward and give a succession of deep notes not unlike the baying of hounds heard at a distance. These notes were usually in series of four or five, and with each the head was thrown still farther back. The long tail was carried straight out horizontally as a general thing, or depressed slightly, but at times was elevated to an angle of about 45°. After calling, the bird dropped his head to its former position close to the water. All this time the female kept up a low quacking. After several of these sallies she would face her suitor, extend the neck and head flat upon the water and swim toward him, turning when within a foot or two, and pass him whereupon he turned and the performance began all over again. After about an hour of this the female took flight closely followed by the male, and after circling the pond several times both birds returned to the water. The other two females had retired to the other end of the pond where they had been quietly feeding, but the male now chased both of these birds out of the pond and then returned to the remaining bird. I have several times seen a female flying closely pursued by two males, all three twisting and turning so that it was difficult for the eye to follow them, but the female always kept in the lead.

Mr. Ekblaw, in his notes, writes:

On July 1, 1914, near the little Eskimo village, Umanak, on North Star Bay, I was able to study the mating antics of the oldsquaw at close range. The day was ideally calm, clear, and mild, and the birds were unusually stirred by the "cosmic urge." Just across the steep ridge southeast of the house lies the broad, terraced, flood plain of a creek which now is a mere remnant of a stream unquestionably much larger in the past. The lowest terrace of this plain is one of such imperfect drainage that ponds and swales are numerous. About the shallow ponds and wet swales grasses and sedges grow in abundance. The ponds teem with tiny animal life. Here the oldsquaws breed and nest in numbers. It is one of their favorite haunts. I was concealed among the rocks of a ledge some 50 yards from a rather large, comparatively deep pond, where the ice was melted along the edges. In the open water, on the edge of the ice, and along the grass-covered banks, seven pairs of oldsquaws were distributed, and two males were struggling strenuously for an unmated female. The paired birds were swimming contentedly about the pool, busily preening their feathers on the ice, or sleeping cosily on the banks; the unmated female and the two males were strenuously sweeping the water or chasing over the pond in swift zigzag flight. Whenever one of the males attempted to mate with the female, the other invariably attacked, much to the evident displeasure of the female, who would then take quick wing, noisily protesting, and pursued by both males. Settled in the pool the males fought fiercely, splashing and churning the water. Neither seemed able to vanquish the other, and when I left my hiding place they were still struggling.

Nesting.—Audubon's (1840) historic account of finding the oldsquaw breeding on the southern coast of Labrador is now ancient history, but it is worth quoting as a record of conditions which no longer exist. He writes:

In the course of one of my rambles along the borders of a large freshwater lake, near Bras-d'Or, in Labrador, on the 28th of July, 1833, I was delighted by the sight of several young broods of this species of duck, all carefully attended to by their anxious and watchful mothers. Not a male bird was on the lake, which was fully 2 miles from the sea, and I concluded that in this species, as in many others, the males abandon the females after incubation has commenced. I watched their motions a good while, searching at the same time for nests, one of which I was not long in discovering. Although it was quite destitute of anything bearing the appearance of life, it still contained the down which the mother had plucked from herself for the purpose of keeping her eggs warm. It was placed under an alder bush, among rank weeds, not more than 8 or 9 feet from the edge of the water, and was formed of rather coarse grass, with an upper layer of finer weeds, which were neatly arranged, while the down filled the bottom of the cavity, now apparently flattened by the long sitting of the bird. The number of young broods in sight induced me to search for more nests, and in about an hour I discovered six more, in one of which I was delighted to find two rotten eggs.

The following extracts from Mr. L. M. Turner's notes will illustrate the nesting habits of this species in Ungava, where it probably still breeds regularly:

To the freshwater ponds, around whose margins high grasses and sedges grow, the oldsquaws resort to build their nests. The nest is composed of grass stalks and weeds to a depth of 2 or 3 inches, in which the first egg is deposited. This is covered with down plucked from the bird, and to it a greater quantity is added as the number of eggs increases. The eggs, in the clutch, vary from 5 to 17; 9 to 13 being the usual number. The distance of the nest from salt water varies greatly, for I have seen a nest, on a small, low island, not more than a yard from the edge of the water, and again I have found one that was more than half a mile, where a large lake on the level of the higher land was connected by a swampy tract with the head of a long and deep but narrow gulch through which a small stream coursed.

A few pairs breed on the Pribilof Islands. I saw a pair on the village pond on St. Paul Island, but did not have time to hunt for its nest. Mr. William Palmer (1899) found a nest and nine eggs about 40 feet from this pond on June 12.

It was placed on a little hillock on the killing ground. When flushed, about 10 feet off, the bird flew directly to its mate in the pond. Leaving the eggs, I returned soon, to find that she had been back, had covered them completely with down and dry, short grass, and returned to the pond.

The main breeding grounds of the oldsquaw, in North America, extend from the mouth of the Yukon all around the coast of northern Alaska and all along the Arctic coast of the continent and the northern islands to Greenland. Throughout the whole of this region it is one of the most abundant ducks. The nests are widely scattered over the tundra, but are more often found near the shores of the small ponds or on little islands in them; the nest is usually well concealed in thick grass or under small bushes, but it is often found in open situations. The female is a close sitter, and when she leaves the nest she covers it so skillfully with the dark sooty brown down, grass, and rubbish that it matches its surroundings and is about invisible. It is well that she does so for she has many enemies, wandering natives, roving dogs and foxes, jaegers, gulls, and other nest robbers that are always on the lookout for eggs. Mr. Hersey found a nest near St. Michael on July 5, 1915, containing six eggs; it was in an open situation in short grass 20 feet from the shore of a small pond, and while going for his camera, only a short distance away, some short-billed and glaucous gulls found the nest and destroyed the eggs.

Mr. Ekblaw, in his notes, says:

The nests are built in small-cup-like hollows, sometimes in the grass near the pools, but more frequently among the rocks at considerable distances from any water. The sites are selected with a view to concealment. The nest is well lined with mottled brown down from the female's breast. When the eggs are covered with the down in the absence of the bird, or when she is brooding them, the nest is well-nigh impossible of detection. The female is not readily frightened from her nest; when she is driven off she simulates injury and distress to draw away the intruder, in the manner common to so many birds. The foxes take toll of the oldsquaw eggs as of the eggs of all the birds.

The down in the oldsquaw's nest is very small; it varies in color from "bister" to "sepia," and has small but conspicuous whitish centers.

Eggs.—The oldsquaw is said to lay as many as 17 eggs, but the set usually consists of from 5 to 7. Only one brood is raised in a season. In shape the eggs are ovate, elliptical ovate, elongate ovate, or even cylindrical ovate; they are often more pointed than ducks' eggs usually are. The surface is smooth, but not very glossy. The color varies from "deep olive buff" to "olive buff" or from "water green" to "yellowish glaucous." The measurements of 139 eggs, in the United States National Museum collection, average 53 by 37 millimeters; the eggs showing the four extremes measure 60 by 39, 58 by 40, 48 by 37.5, and 51.5 by 35.5 millimeters.

Young.—The period of incubation is said to be about three and a half weeks. It is performed by the female alone, but the male does not wholly desert her, remaining in the nearest pond and encouraging her with demonstrations of affection. About the time that the young are ready to hatch he flies away and joins others of his kind on the seacoast. As soon as the eggs are hatched and the young are strong enough to walk, the mother leads them over the perilous journey to the nearest water. Mr. Turner watched a mother bird conducting her brood of 13 young for more than half a mile from a swampy tract through a long and deep but narrow gulch, through which a small stream flowed, down to a cove into which it opened. His notes state:

The old bird was much disturbed when I came upon her and she pretended to be wounded. She fluttered and waddled about in a frantic manner, but while chasing her I saw the young and could then have easily taken the old bird in my hand, as she actually fluttered at my feet, so intent was she to withdraw my attention from her young. I retired, and with peculiar call she gathered the young ones and began her march. I followed them to the salt water where the mother seemed frantic with joy, as she flopped around like a tame duck at the approach of rain. The young were not more than two days old and had awaited until they had sufficient strength to undertake the long journey. They took to the water as though they had been accustomed to it for weeks. I must confess that I felt pleased that I did not molest them for I have seldom seen anything that afforded me greater satisfaction than to witness the pleasure evinced by the old bird when she had her young on the bosom of the sea where she felt so secure.

There are so many enemies to be contended with at this critical period that it is a wonder that any of these ducks ever succeed in raising a brood. It is only by good luck in many cases that the nest is not discovered and robbed; and only eternal vigilance and a constant struggle on the part of the devoted mother serves to protect the little ones from their enemies. In the instance just related several occupied fox dens were within a short distance of the nest, yet the eggs were hatched and the young were conducted away in safety.

The following incident is related by Mr. Millais (1913):

I watched a newly hatched brood of long-tailed ducks one day for a long time and noticed that they took very little food for themselves. They caught a few flies, but most of their food was obtained by the mother diving incessantly and bringing up substances from the bottom and placing it before her brood. When she appeared they all kept up a gentle "peeping" sound and kept close together in a bunch, seldom running to catch flies as other young ducks do. After watching these birds for some time I wandered up the river to the Lake of Myvatn to look at a scoter's nest, and on returning witnessed the attack of two Richardson's skuas, a black and a white bellied one, on the same brood of long-tailed duck. The method of attack was exactly the same as I have seen employed by carrion crows in Hyde Park. One skua swooped down and distracted the mother's attention to one side by hovering over the water. The anxious parent opened her bill and gave a series of grating calls. As the marauder came to the level of the water the long-tailed duck with raised crest made a fierce rush of a few yards at it and in this short space of time the second skua swooped down, picked up a nestling, and swallowed it alive, head first. The frantic mother then darted in the other direction when the skua that had first attacked nimbly picked up a duckling and swallowed it whilst mounting into the air. These skuas, which are plentiful at Myvatn, must commit considerable havoc amongst the very young ducks and doubtless constitute their chief enemies. Mr. Manniche, whom I had the pleasure of meeting in Denmark in 1911, tells me that the glaucous gull is equally mischievous in destroying the young of long-tails and king eiders in East Greenland and probably Buffon's skua is another successful pirate.

The young are taught to dive at an early age, but at first they are not very successful. Mr. Hersey's notes state that on July 5, 1915, a female and eight recently hatched young were "seen on a small pond. The female did not fly but swam around the young calling softly to them. At an apparent signal from the mother all would dive, but the young were unable to stay below the surface more than four or five seconds. The parent would then come to the surface and again try to coax them to follow her below. She did not attempt to lead them to the shore." When the young are fully grown and able to fly they all leave the small ponds and sheltered places where they have been living and move off to the shore. This often occurs quite late in the season, for small downy young are often to be found up to the middle of August or later; the hatching date is very variable, as the eggs are so often disturbed and a second or third laying made necessary. The lateness of the fall migration gives a long breeding season and plenty of time to make several attempts at raising a brood.

Mr. Ekblaw's notes state that:

While the females are brooding the eggs the males and the sterile females fly and swim about the ponds in promiscuous flocks. These sterile females are restless and active, quite different from the mated females during the mating season. In the mating season the female of a pair usually rests quietly on the bank of the pond, apparently heavy with eggs, while her mate swims about near her. The sterile females are noisy and uneasy.

These sterile females and the males leave the land and the environs of the shore about the 20th of July and seek the outer skerries and open water. The nesting females take their little ducklings down to the salt water as soon as they can toddle along, and from then until they hie themselves away to the southland they spend all their time along the rocky shores in the pleasant coastal bays and fjords or about the icebergs and floes. Very frequently two mother birds join their flocks, and then, when swimming about in the open sea, one mother leads the flock while the other brings up the rear.

The young birds grow fast and quickly develop strength for swimming far and fast. They can dive as well as they can swim. They soon lose their first down and take on a juvenal dark-brown downy covering, into which the feathers gradually come. It is not until they are fully grown, about the last week in August or first week in September, that they are able to fly, and then, fat and plump and strong, they start southward by easy stages, developing wing power as they go. Long before the elders begin leaving, the oldsquaws are gone from the coast, and then winter soon sets in.

Plumages.—The downy young oldsquaw is very dark-colored above, very deep, rich "clove brown," becoming almost black on the crown and rump, and paler "clove brown" in a band across the chest. This dark color covers more than half of the head, including the crown, hind neck, and cheeks; it is relieved, however, by a large spot below the eye and a smaller one above it of whitish, also an indistinct loral spot and postocular streak of the same. The throat is white and the sides of the neck and auricular region are grayish white. The belly is white. Both the dark and the light brown areas become duller and grayer with age.

The plumage appears first on the under parts; the breast and belly are fully feathered first, then the flanks and scapulars; the plumage covers the back, head and neck before the wings are grown, in September. All this takes place while the old birds are molting their wings and are flightless. Both old and young birds are able to fly by October and are then ready to start on their migrations.

Mr. Millais (1913) describes the juvenal plumage, as follows:

In first plumage, in September, the young male has the crown dark brown; the back of the neck is grayish-brown till it meets the mantle, which, with the wings, back, and tail, are black, with a dark-gray suffusion. A dark band of grayish-black also crosses the upper part of the chest, and these feathers, as well as the gray and spotted ones on the sides of the chest, are edged with light sandy-brown; the scapulars blackish-brown, edged with light sandy-brown; flanks gray, tinged with sandy-brown; thighs gray; breast, belly, and vent white. In many specimens only the center tail feathers are black, the rest being brown, edged with white, whilst some have a few sandy edged feathers on the upper tail coverts. Round the eye and lores whitish-gray; cheeks, throat, and chin brown-gray. In many specimens the secondaries are brown, and the breast spotted with brownish-gray. In this month the young male is no larger than the female, but by the end of October it has grown to nearly the full size of the adult male. By the end of this month, and during November, new feathers are rapidly coming in, and the immature feathers of the head are being replaced by others resembling those of the adult.

From this time on during the winter and spring there is a slow but steady progress toward maturity of plumage by a practically continuous molt. The crown, throat, and neck become gradually whiter, the brownish-black cheek patches develop and brownish-black feathers appear in the chest; the gray face begins to show, the back becomes blacker and the grayish-white scapulars and flank feathers appear. By the end of March the young male begins to look like the winter adult, but the colors are not so pure or so intense. In April the molt into the first nuptial plumage begins, in which the young bird can be distinguished from the adult by the faded and worn wings, the imperfect and mottled appearance of the breast, and the absence of the long tail feathers. During August and September a complete molt occurs, at which the wings and tail are renewed, the long tail feathers are acquired and the adult winter plumage is assumed; by the end of November, at the latest, this plumage is complete and the young bird may be said to be adult at seventeen months of age.

The seasonal changes of plumage in the adult male oldsquaw are unique, striking, and very interesting; it is one of the few ducks in the world to assume a distinctly nuptial plumage. The molt into this plumage begins in April and in the oldest and most vigorous birds it is completed in May; but in the younger birds and less vigorous individuals, the molt is prolonged into the summer and is often incomplete. Some birds acquire the full nuptial dress (in which the face is " smoky gray," with a white space around and behind the eye, the feathers of the upper back and scapulars are broadly edged with "sayal brown" and the rest of the head, neck, breast, back and wings are deep, rich "seal brown," nearly black on the upper surfaces) before they migrate north in the spring; I have seen birds in the full perfection of this plumage as early as May 10; but most birds reach their breeding grounds in various stages of transition, showing more or less white or gray feathers in the dark areas. There is no real eclipse plumage in the oldsquaw, but Mr. Millais (1913) says:

During August the male long-tailed duck completely changes the wing, tail, back, and black portion of the mantle and black breast band, these parts being replaced by the new winter plumage. The head, neck, and upper mantle, showing worn and faded plumage feathers, remain until shed at the end of September. The elongated scapulars are shed and not renewed until late September, but in late July a considerable number of new blackish and brown feathers come into the upper scapulars and mix with the old worn summer plumage feathers, whilst a number of new dark-gray feathers, similar to those worn by the scaup, tufted duck, and goldeneye male in eclipse, come unto the flanks and remain until shed again in early October. The reason of this, I take it, is that since Nature abhors sudden changes of color from dark to light, whilst the landscape is still under the warm colors of summer and autumn, the male long-tail only renews those parts of its plumage to the full winter dress which are directly in harmony with its surroundings, adding, however, temporary feathers, as it were, to carry it over the three temperate months when it hides in the shadows of banks or rocky inlets. Thus all the dark parts of its plumage are renewed once, and once only, and the light parts which would be noticeable are delayed by a temporary makeshift until such a time as concealment is no longer necessary.

Of the plumage changes of the female he says:

In first plumage the immature female closely resembles the young male, except that the color is somewhat paler. They are also easily recognized by October by the incoming feathers of the respective sexes. In the case of the young female the advance of plumage is somewhat slower than that of the male, and she only obtains a few of the winter dress feathers. In April the greater part of the adult summer plumage is assumed, but there is little or no change on the back, breast, and lower parts, whilst the wings and tail are not shed at all until the principal molt in July and August. The young female then gradually assumes her winter dress, which is complete in October. She is thus adult at 16 months, and will pair and breed the following summer.

Young females may be recognized during their first year by their imperfect and more or less mottled head pattern and by the broad, gray edgings of the upper back and scapulars. Adult females in winter have the feathers of the back, scapulars, and wing coverts broadly edged with "tawny" or "cinnamon brown," and the upper chest and flanks are suffused with lighter shades of the same. The partial prenuptial molt occurs in April, leaving the wings worn and faded; the head becomes largely brownish black, with whitish spaces before and behind the eye, and the upper parts are nearly uniform brownish black. In August and September a complete molt produces the winter plumage.

Food.—Most of the oldsquaw's food is obtained by diving in water of moderate depths to the beds of mussels (*Mytelis edulis*) and other bivalve and univalve mollusks, but many of these are picked up in shallow water, as the rising tide covers the ledges; as the mussels open their shells to procure food they are picked out by the ducks. Much food is also picked up along the beaches, such as shrimps, sand fleas, small mollusks, crustaceans, beetles, and marine insects, together with some seaweeds and a quantity of sand. On their breeding grounds the food consists largely of the roots, leaves, buds, and seeds of various aquatic plants; the young live largely on insects, larvae, and soft animal food which abounds in the tundra pools. Dr. F. Henry Yorke (1899) includes in their vegetable food teal moss (*Limnobium*), blue flag (*Iris*), duckweed, water plantain, pondweed, and pickerel weed.

George H. Mackay (1892), writing of the habits of this bird on the Massachusetts coast, says:

Oldsquaws do not seem to be at all particular in regard to their food, eating quite a variety, among which are the following: A little shellfish, very small, resembling a diminutive quahog (*Venus mercenaria*), but not one; sand fleas; short razor shells (*Siliqua costata*); fresh-water clams; small white perch; small catfish; penny shells (*Astarte castanea*); red whale bait (brit); shrimps; mussels; small blue-claw crabs; and pond grass. It was during the early part of the severe winter of 1888 that many oldsquaws sought the land. Alighting on the uplands adjacent to the north shore of the island, they came in flocks of a hundred or less, in order that they might obtain and eat the dried fine top grass (*Anthoxanthum odoratum*) which grows wild there; when engaged in plucking it their movements while on the ground were far from awkward, in fact rather graceful, as they ran quickly about gathering the grass, some of which was still in their mouths when shot.

William B. Haynes (1901) observes:

Most authorities agree that the oldsquaw is unedible when killed on the Great Lakes, but here (Ohio) they vary their diet with worms and are far better eating than scaup or goldeneye. I have found the common angleworm and a large green worm resembling a cutworm in their throats.

Edwin D. Hull (1914) says that in Jackson Park, Chicago, in winter:

The plants, rocks, and piers constitute a very favorable habitat for immense swarms of silvery minnows (*Notropis atherinoides*), which seem to be almost if not entirely the sole source of food for the old squaw in this locality. The stomach of an adult female found floating in a lagoon April 1, 1912, contained approximately 140 of these minnows, all entire, besides many fragments of the same fish, but no other food. The fish averaged about 2 inches in length.

Behavior.—When migrating, old squaws fly high in the air in irregular flocks or in Indian file, but at other times they fly close to the water or a few feet above it, but almost never in a straight line; they twist and turn suddenly, showing the breast and belly alternately like shore birds, swinging in broad circles most unexpectedly. Their flight is so swift and so erratic that it is very difficult to shoot them, but they are often very tame or stupid and are quite as likely to swing in toward a gunner's boat as away from it; then in turning they often bunch together so closely that a tempting shot is offered; I have seen as many as nine dropped out of such a bunch at one shot. I have seen them, when shot at, dive out of the air into the water, swim for a long distance under water, and then come out of the crest of a wave flying at full speed, as if they had never broken their flight. They can rise readily off the surface of even smooth water, and when alighting on it often drop in abruptly with an awkward splash. If there is a strong wind blowing they are more inclined to circle into the wind, glide down gently against it on set wings and alight with a sliding splash. Old squaws can generally be recognized at a long distance by their peculiar method of flight and by their striking color pattern, the white head and neck and the short, sharp-pointed, black wings being very conspicuous.

Toward spring they are particularly restless and active on the wing and often indulge in aerial evolutions, such as Mr. Mackay (1892) describes, as follows:

These ducks have a habit of towering both in the spring and in the autumn, usually in the afternoon, collecting in mild weather in large flocks if undisturbed, and going up in circles so high as to be scarcely discernible, often coming down with a rush and great velocity, a portion of the flock scattering and coming down in a zigzag course similar to the scoters when whistled down. The noise of their wings can be heard for a great distance under such conditions. In one such instance, at Ipswich Bay, Mass., a flock of several hundred went up twice within an hour.

The old squaw swims low in the water, but makes rapid progress even in rough water; it rides easily over the ordinary waves, but dives under the crest of a breaker with good judgment and precision. It is one of the most expert of the diving ducks and will often dodge under at the flash of a gun; in diving the wings are partially opened as if they were to be used under water; probably they generally are so used, but not always. It can dive to great depths if necessary. Prof. W. B. Barrows (1912) says:

Several observers mention the fact that it is often caught in the gill nets set in deep water for lake trout and whitefish (in the Great Lakes.) One fisherman at St. Joseph told me most positively that he had seen it caught repeatedly in net set at a depth of 30 fathoms (180 feet).

Dr. A. W. Butler (1897) and Mr. E. H. Eaton (1910) both make similar statements, and the latter says that " at Dunkirk, N. Y., between five and seven thousand have been taken at one haul "; this seems almost incredible.

When feeding in flocks their diving tactics are interesting to watch. L. M. Turner (1886) writes:

When searching for food they string out in a long line and swim abreast. At a signal one at the extreme end goes down, the rest follow in regular time, never all at once, and rarely more than two or three at a time. The last one goes down in his turn with the regularity of clockwork. As they dive they seem to go over so far as to throw the long tail feathers until they touch water on the other side. They remain under water a long time and usually come up near each other.

His notes state that they " remain under water for periods varying from 40 to 92 seconds." This last figure seems as if it might be an error, for the following observations by Mr. Seton Gordon (1920) seem to indicate great regularity in the diving periods of this species; he says:

On one occasion, December 16, I timed a drake during six dives, as follows: 37, 37, 37, 30, 37, 37 seconds. As will be seen, his periods of submersion were extremely regular. On December 18 I watched for some time a pair diving energetically. The drake kept under longer than the duck, half a dozen of his dives being as follows: 37, 42, 36, 35, 33, 32 seconds, and those of the duck, 33, 37, 35, 33, 33, 32 seconds. On emerging, the duck seemed to shoot up more buoyantly than the drake. In the afternoon I timed the drake for four dives, as follows: 42, 40, 42, 45 seconds. The periods during which the birds were above water between the dives I timed as follows: 10, 8, 6, 8, 7, 11 seconds. On December 21 I timed a pair diving and emerging almost simultaneously, as follows: 34, 32, 37, 38, 40, 43, 36 seconds. Before the two longest of these dives, the birds swam for some time on the surface of the water.

If there is any one thing for which the old squaw is justly notorious it is for its voice. It certainly is a noisy and garrulous species at all seasons, for which it has received various appropriate names, such as old squaw, old injun, old wife, noisy duck, hound, etc. The names south-southerly, cockawee, quandy, coal and candle light, as well as a variety of Indian and Eskimo names have been applied to it as suggesting its well-known notes; all of these are more or less crude imitations of its notes, which are difficult to describe satisfactorily, but when once heard are afterwards easily recognized, for they are loud, clearly uttered, and very distinctive. Mr. Francis H. Allen has given me the best description of it as " *ow-owdle-ow* and *ow-ow-owdle-ow* with a Philadelphia twang; that is, with a short *a* sound in the *ow*. The last syllable is higher pitched than the rest and is emphasized."

Rev. J. H. Langille (1884) describes it very well in the following words:

To my ear it does not recall the common name "south-southerly" given it on the Atlantic coast, but is well expressed by an epithet given it by the Germans about Niagara River, who call it the "ow-owly." *Ow-ow-ly, ow-owly, ow-owly,* frequently repeated in succession, the first two notes considerably mouthed, and the last syllable in a high, shrill, clarion tone, may suggest the queer notes to anyone whose ear is familiar with them. Not infrequently the last syllable is left out of the ditty, the bird seeming somewhat in a hurry, or the note becomes a mere nasal, *ah, ah, ah,* rapidly uttered.

Doctor Nelson (1887), referring to the notes heard on their breeding grounds, writes:

During all the spring season until the young begin to hatch, the males have a rich musical note, imperfectly represented by the syllables *A-léedle-a, a-léedle-a,* frequently repeated in deep, reedlike tones. Amid the general hoarse chorus of waterfowl at this season, the notes of the old squaw are so harmonious that the fur traders of the Upper Yukon have christened it the " organ duck," a well-merited name. I have frequently stopped and listened with deep pleasure to these harmonious tones, while traversing the broad marshes in the dim twilight at midnight, and while passing a lonely month on the dreary banks of the Yukon delta I lay in my blankets many hours at night and listened to these rhythmical sounds, which with a few exceptions were the only ones to break the silence. These notes are somewhat less common during the day.

Mr. Ekblaw, in the notes, describes them as follows:

The call is a loud, ringing *ong, ong-onk* that carries far and clear. The call is given with a quick hard recoil of the head with the emission of each syllable, as if requiring considerable force. The vibrant resonance of the call is undoubtedly due to the peculiar development of the voice box. At the base of the trachea, just at the junction of the bronchial tubes, is a coiled enlargement resembling a mellophone, with a tightly stretched membrane along one side, probably the mechanism by which the volume and quality of the call are produced.

Oldsquaws fly in flocks by themselves, but in their winter haunts they are associated more or less with red-breasted mergansers, scoters, eiders, and goldeneyes, frequenting similar feeding grounds. They are said to show a decided antipathy to cormorants and to leave their feeding grounds when these birds visit them. Mr. Millais (1913) says:

The principal enemies of the species are the cowardly white-tailed eagles, who kill numbers of half-grown young and wounded birds, the Greenland and Iceland falcons, the three long-tailed skuas, and the great blackback and glaucous gulls. Arctic foxes and polar bears also account for a good many before they can fly.

Fall.—By the time that the young birds are strong on the wing, during the early part of the fall, both old and young leave their breeding grounds in the north and begin to gather in large flocks on the Arctic coast. John Murdoch (1885) says, of the beginning of the migration at Point Barrow:

Through July and August they vary in abundance, some days being very plenty, while for two or three days at a time none at all are to be seen. At this season they fly up and down not far from the shore and light in the sea. Toward the end of August they are apt to form large " beds " near the station, and this habit continues in September whenever there is sufficient open water.

Many come from the east in September and cross the isthmus at Pergniak and continue on down the coast to the southwest. We noticed them going southwest past Point Franklin, August 31, 1883, in very large flocks. After October 1 they grow scarcer, but some are always to be seen as late as there is any open water.

In northern Labrador similar movements take place; "from the last of August to the middle of October immense numbers of these birds assemble in Hudson Straits," according to Mr. Turner's notes; he says that they disappear from Fort Chimo about the middle of November.

On the New England coast the first cold storm of late October brings a few scattering flocks of oldsquaws, but it is not until late in the fall or when early winter conditions are almost here that the heavy flight comes along; driven like snowflakes ahead of a howling norther, flock after flock of these hardy little sea fowl sweep and whirl over the cold gray waves; or high in the air they twist and turn, twinkling like black and white stars against the leaden sky. The shore birds' whistles are no longer heard; they have passed on to warmer climes; but like the cries of a distant pack of hounds the merry notes of the oldsquaws cheer the gunner's heart as he sits in his anchored boat behind a string of wooden decoys waiting for a shot at passing "coots." The main flight of scoters has passed, an occasional V-shaped flock of geese passes overhead, honking its warning of approaching winter, and soon long lines of brant will be looked for winging their apparently slow and heavy flight close to the water. As Walter H. Rich (1907) puts it:

Winter is close at hand. There is a sting in the wind, a nip in the air, and the fingers are numb and blue as they hold the gun barrels. But out on the water, careless of wind or wave, rides a flock of "squaws" making always a merry clatter. Ever and anon some of their number rise against the breeze to dart off at lightning speed, apparently in the mere enjoyment of flight, for, circling a half a mile about, they plump down again among their comrades, all the time noisily calling to each other. We might almost say they are the only song birds among the ducks, for really their notes are very pleasant to hear and quite musical in comparison with the usual vocal production of the family.

Game.—Oldsquaws are not held in much esteem as game birds; their flesh is rank, fishy, and tough; but there are gunners that will eat them. Many are shot, however, every fall by gunners who are out after scoters; later in the season large flocks of oldsquaws frequently pass over or along the line of boats anchored in their path. They decoy well to the wooden blocks used for this kind of shooting, and are often quite tame or full of curiosity. They often offer tempting shots, and their flight is so swift and erratic that it requires considerable skill and practice to hit a single bird; when they are flying before the wind one must hold well ahead of them. They are so tough that only a small portion of the birds shot down are killed, and it is almost useless to pursue the wounded ones, as they are more than a match for the gunner in rough water.

Winter.—Oldsquaws are common in winter as far north as southern Greenland and the Diomede Islands in Bering Straits, where they can find open water among the ice, but they are more abundant below the regions of frozen seas. Even on the New England coast they sometimes encounter ice conditions too severe for them. Mr. Mackay (1892) writes:

Although, as their Latin name expresses, they are particularly a cold-weather bird, it is a matter of interest that ducks with such Arctic proclivities should find the effects of the climate so rigorous at times on the New England coast that they are unable to sustain life and are in consequence obliged to succumb. Yet such is the case. It was during the winter of 1888, when, standing on the high land of Nantucket Island and looking seaward in any direction, nothing but ice was visible; for a month the harbor was closed and there was sleighing on it. There was no open water in sight except an occasional crack in the ice caused by the change of tides; most of the sea fowl had left this locality during the early stage of the severely cold weather. Many oldsquaws remained, however, until they were incapacitated through lack of food and consequent loss of strength from doing so. As a result it was a common occurrence to find them lying around dead or dying on the shore. Those that were alive were so weak they could not fly, and on examination proved to be nothing literally but skin and bone, others apparently had starved to death.

Referring to their habits here, he says:

Off the south side of Nantucket Island the oldsquaws collect in countless myriads. On February 19, 1891, I saw a flock of oldsquaws estimated to contain 2,000 birds off the south shore of Nantucket about 5 miles from the island, and I know of no better place to observe them in numbers. They arrive about the third to the last week in October, according to the weather, and remain until the latter part of November; most of them then move farther south. The height of their abundance is the first half of November. They congregate on " Old Man's Rip" and on " Miacomet Rip," shoal ground 2 to 3 miles from the south shore of the island, the water there being 3 to 4 fathoms deep. Here they live in security, with an abundance of food, during the day. About 3 o'clock p. m. they commence to leave this place for the Sound (the movement continuing until after dark) where they regularly roost, flying around that part of the island which affords them at the time the greatest shelter from the wind, returning on the following morning to their feeding ground by which ever route is the most favorable. An examination of the stomachs of some of those oldsquaws which I shot in the early morning coming from the Sound, showed them to be empty. I think occasionally on clear calm nights they remain on their feeding grounds, and do not go into the Sound to roost. They apparently prefer to feed in water not more than 3 to 4 fathoms deep, or shallower, unless compelled in order to obtain food. I have noticed north of Cape Cod during the winter months that some oldsquaws will feed and remain just back of the line of breakers on the beaches, and also around the rocks, but generally they are in small and detached groups of but few individuals.

Many oldsquaws spend the winter in the Great Lakes and in other large bodies of water in the interior, but it is decidedly a maritime species by preference. For a study of the habits of this species on Lake Michigan in winter, I would refer the reader to an excellent paper on this subject by Edwin D. Hull (1914) based on observations for three seasons at Chicago. I can not afford the space to quote from it as freely as it deserves. Severe winter conditions sometimes drive a few birds as far as the southern borders of the United States. Messrs. Beyer, Allison, and Kopman (1907) record the capture of one in Louisiana on February 13, 1899. "At the time of the capture of this specimen a severe blizzard was sweeping the South. Zero temperatures were reported at points near the Louisiana coast."

DISTRIBUTION

Breeding range.—Arctic coasts of both hemispheres. On the Labrador Peninsula south, in Audubon's time, to the southeastern coast of the peninsula (Bras d'Or), but now probably not much south of northern Labrador (Okak and Nain). Ungava Bay and the lower Koksoak River (Fort Chimo) and down the eastern shore of Hudson Bay, perhaps as far as Cape Jones. On Southampton Island and other lands north of Hudson Bay, and on the west coast of the bay at least as far south as Cape Fullerton and perhaps as far as Churchill. Along the entire Arctic coasts and barren grounds of Canada and Alaska. South on the Alaskan and Siberian coasts of Bering Sea to the Aleutian and Commander Islands and on all the islands in that sea. Along the Arctic coasts and barren grounds of Asia and Europe, south in Scandinavia to about 60° north. On the Faroe Islands, on Iceland, and on both coasts of Greenland. North on practically all Arctic lands as far as they have been explored up to 82° north.

Winter range.—In North America south on the Atlantic coast abundantly to southern New England, commonly to Chesapeake Bay and North Carolina, more rarely to South Carolina, Florida (Brevard and Leon Counties) and occasionally to the Gulf coast of Louisiana; north, when open water is to be found, to the Gulf of St. Lawrence and sometimes southern Greenland. On the Pacific coast south regularly to Washington, less commonly to California, as far south as San Diego; north to the Aleutian Islands, and sometimes to the Diomede Islands. In the interior it winters abundantly on the Great Lakes and more rarely or irregularly on other large bodies of water west and south to Nebraska (Omaha), Colorado (Barr Lake), and Texas (Lake Surprise). In southern Europe south to about 40° north, on the Black and Caspian Seas; and in Asia, south to Lake Baikal, China, and Japan.

Spring migration.—Mainly coastwise, but also overland to northern coasts. Dates of arrival: New Brunswick, Grand Manan, March 9; Ontario, Ottawa, April 2; Mackenzie, Fort Simpson, May 10; northern Greenland, Etah, May 20; Boothia Felix, latitude 70°, June 12; Winter Harbor, latitude 75°, June 22; Cape Sabine, latitude 78°, June 1; Fort Conger, latitude 81°, June 6. Dates of arrival in Alaska: Chilcat, March 11; Admiralty Island, April 17; St. Michael, April 1; Cape Prince of Wales, April 22; Kowak River, May 22; Humphrey Point, May 20; Point Barrow, May 15.

Late dates of departure: Rhode Island, May 4; Massachusetts, May 22; Maine, May 21; Gulf of St. Lawrence, May 23; Pennsylvania, Erie, May 18; Alberta, Fort McMurray, May 15; southern Alaska, May 19.

Fall migration.—Reversal of spring routes. Early dates of arrival: Great Bear Lake, August 28; Pennsylvania, Erie, September 13; Massachusetts, September 30; New York, Long Island, October 8 (average October 16). Late dates of departure: Northern Greenland, latitude 82°, September 16; Alaska, Point Barrow, December 9, and St. Michael, October 20.

Egg dates.—Arctic Canada: Fifty-three records, June 7 to July 18; 27 records, June 19 to July 4. Alaska: Sixteen records, May 22 to July 28; eight records, June 16 to July 9. Labrador: Three records, June 16, 17, and 27.

HISTRIONICUS HISTRIONICUS HISTRIONICUS (Linnaeus)

ATLANTIC HARLEQUIN DUCK

HABITS

The harlequin duck is a rare bird on the Atlantic coast of North America, where its chief summer home is in Labrador and Ungava. Comparatively little is known about it even there, as very little thorough ornithological work has been done in that largely unexplored region. But in western North America the species is widely distributed and in some sections of Alaska, notably the Aleutian Islands, it is very abundant. W. Sprague Brooks (1915) has recently separated the western bird, as a distinct subspecies, under the name *pacificus*. As this seems to be a well-marked form with a distinctly separate range, I have compiled a separate life history for it. Except for the descriptions of the eggs and plumages, which are the same for both forms, the following remarks refer mainly to the Atlantic form.

Spring.—Mr. Lucien M. Turner's notes state that—

They arrive at Fort Chimo by the 25th of May and then frequent the smaller fresh-water ponds and lakes. They retire to the seashore by the 5th of June, or even earlier if the ice has cleared from the beach. The outlying islets are favorite places in the earlier days after their arrival; but when the water is mostly clear of ice they prefer the rugged shores of the larger islands and shores of the mainland where the reefs and jagged, sunken rocks are to be found; these birds are rarely to be seen along shingly beaches unless they may be merely passing from one point to another.

He says of their behavior:

The males are extremely pugnacious and quickly resent the approach of another male toward their mates. They flop through the water with surprising speed toward the intruder with open mouth, uttering a hissing sound, and seize the offender by the body and quickly pluck out a beakful of feathers if the pursued bird does not dive or flutter away.

Nesting.—Audubon (1840) claims to have found them breeding on islands in the Bay of Fundy; he writes:

There they place their nests under the bushes or amid the grass, at the distance of 20 to 30 yards from the water. Farther north, in Newfoundland and Labrador, for example, they remove from the sea, and betake themselves to small lakes a mile or so in the interior, on the margins of which they form their nests beneath the bushes next to the water. The nest is composed of dry plants of various kinds, arranged in a circular manner to the height of 2 or 3 inches, and lined with finer grasses. The eggs are five or six, rarely more, measure $2\frac{1}{8}$ by $1\frac{7}{8}$ inches, and are of a plain greenish-yellow color. After the eggs are laid, the female plucks the down from the lower parts of her body and places it beneath and around them, in the same manner as the eider duck and other species of this tribe.

Dr. C. Hart Merriam (1883) contributes the following:

While in Newfoundland last winter I learned that these birds, which are here called "lords and ladies," are common summer residents on the island, breeding along the little-frequented watercourses of the interior. I was also informed, by many different people, that their nests were built in hollow trees, like the wood duck's with us. Mr. James P. Howley, geologist of Newfoundland, has favored me with the following response to a letter addressed to him on this subject: "I received your note inquiring about the harlequin duck, but delayed answering it till the arrival of one of our Indians. It is quite true the birds nest in hollow stumps of trees, usually on islets in the lakes or tarns of the interior. They usually frequent the larger lakes and rivers far from the seacoast, but are also found scattered all over the country."

Most of the eggs of the harlequin duck in collections came from Iceland, where the species breeds abundantly and where many nests have been found. John G. Millais (1913) gives the following attractive quotation from Reimschneider, illustrating the behavior and nesting habits of this species in Iceland:

This is the finest of all the species here. Their movements both on land and water are quick, skillful, and graceful; they run swiftly on dry land, and their gait reminds one very little of the waddling of other ducks, but in walking the small head with its beautiful beak is stretched rather forward, and the long tail pointing downward, with the proportionately slender body and the peculiar coloring, all give this bird a rather foreign appearance, though certainly not an unlovely one. The plumage of this small duck charmed

me particularly when I saw it swimming upstream with unparalleled swiftness through the frothing foam of the Laxa, winding about through the
eddies of the strongest breakers, and making use of the quieter places in the
most skillful way. I then always had in mind the other much less common
Icelandic name *Brindufa* (breaker dove). I have never seen the harlequin
duck make an even temporary stay on the lake, but they always keep to the
swiftly flowing rivers of the neighborhood; e. g., on the Laxa, where I visited
a small breeding colony near the Helluvad farm. When I came to this place
on June 24 I was several times obliged, in order to reach the nests, to ride
through the water of the river to a series of small heath-overgrown rock
islands upon which the ducks breed. Here I found, in addition to several nests
of the *Fuligula marila*, four nests of the *F. histrionica;* it is certain that
there were still more nests to be found close to. I put the number of pairs
nesting at this place at from 10 to 12. The first nest, standing under a thick
clump of heath, had a sort of bank of dry heath around the shallow hollow of
the site of the nest. This hollowed-out basin contained the first half-finished
lining of gray down mingled with fine dry grass. In the nest lay five eggs,
which I took away, and which proved not to have been sat on at all. This
nest had been hitherto untouched by human beings, but not so the others
which I saw, and which had already lost some of their eggs. The next nest
showed exactly the same construction, and in this the down lining was still
altogether wanting. This one contained only two eggs. While the two first
nests we have just described were some paces from the edge of the island,
the next, unprotected by heath growth, was placed on a small piece of rock
jutting out over the river. The basin contained a complete lining of gray
down mixed with grass, and the loose edge of this was carefully pulled down
over three eggs which were in the nest. The duck flew away from the fourth
nest which I visited as soon as I was quite close to it, and this one again was
placed more in the middle of the island under a clump of heath, and was very
plentifully lined with down with an unusually small admixture of parts of
plants; it contained three eggs.

The down in the harlequin duck's nest is " olive brown " or " drab,"
with rather large, but not very conspicuous, whitish centers. Small
whitish breast feathers, with a pale brownish central spot and pale
brownish tip, are usually found in the down.

Eggs.—The harlequin duck lays from 5 to 10 eggs, usually about
6. The shape varies from bluntly ovate to elongate ovate, and some
eggs are quite pointed. The shell is smooth and slightly glossy.
The color varies from " light buff " or " cream color " to paler tints
of the same. The measurements of 90 eggs, in various collections,
average 57.5 by 41.5 millimeters; the eggs showing the four extremes
measure **61** by 42.5, 59 by **44, 52** by 39, and 56.2 by **37.5** millimeters.

Young.—Incubation is performed entirely by the female, who
also assumes full care of the young. Audubon (1840) writes:

The male leaves her to perform the arduous but, no doubt to her, pleasant
task of hatching and rearing the brood, and, joining his idle companions,
returns to the seashore, where he molts in July and August. The little ones
leave the nest a few hours after they burst the shell, and follow their mother
to the water, where she leads them about with the greatest care and anxiety.
When about a week old she walks with them to the sea, where they continue,

in the same manner as the eiders. When discovered in one of these small inland lakes, the mother emits a lisping note of admonition, on which she and the young dive at once, and the latter make for the shores, where they conceal themselves, while the former rises at a good distance, and immediately taking to wing, leaves the place for awhile. On searching along the shores for the young, we observed that, on being approached, they ran to the water and dived toward the opposite side, continuing their endeavors thus to escape, until so fatigued that we caught four out of six. When at sea, they are as difficult to be caught as the young eiders.

Mr. Millais (1913) says that the period of incubation is said to be three and one-half weeks.

It is presumed that the young are at first fed by the old bird direct from the bill, as newly hatched young always hold their bills upward to the beak of the foster parent, and will not at first pick up food for themselves. At first the food is principally the larvae of *Ephemerae*. The down period of the young is said by Faber to be about 40 days.

Mr. O. J. Murie has sent me the following interesting notes on the behavior of young harlequin ducks:

The harlequins acquire their love for rough water early, for the young are brought up among the rapids of northern rivers. Several broods of these ducklings were found on the Swampy Bay River, in northern Ungava. I saw the first family one day when we had paddled across the swift current above a rapid, to hunt for a portage. As we floated into a sheltered eddy near shore, a band of ducklings swam quietly out past our canoe. They appeared singularly unconcerned and unafraid. At first I did not recognize them as harlequins and they all looked the same size to me. But one of the Indians declared one of them was the mother. They swam around the base of a huge bowlder and headed deliberately into the swift water. In astonishment I watched them go bouncing down the rapid, around the bend out of sight.

A few days later I witnessed a still better exhibition. We stopped to camp at the head of a rapid which culminated in an abrupt fall of 20 or 30 feet. Here we found some more harlequins. I got two young and the mother between me and the fall and attempted to corner them for a photograph. There was but a narrow lane of comparatively quiet water near shore. As I neared the little group the mother flew upstream, and the little ones spattered up over the water, actually entering the edge of the swift current in order to get by me. Upon repeating the performance several times, I had an opportunity to perceive their wonderful knowledge of currents and their skill in navigating them. Finally, when pressing them close for a near approach, they again entered the swift water. At the same time the mother came flying low and passed downstream. This time the youngsters were evidently caught, for the current carried them out of sight over the falls. With a feeling of remorse I looked below. I had not intended to be the means of their destruction. At first I could distinguish nothing among the ripples and the foam-flecked current below. Then I saw them floating along, rising to shake the water from their down, then quietly preening themselves. Although they had clearly endeavored to avoid the falls, they were none the worse for the accident when it did happen.

Plumages.—The downy young is " bister " or " Prout's brown " above, including the top of the head down to the level of the eyes, the lores, hind neck, back and rump; the under parts, including the cheeks up to the eyes, are pure white; there is a white spot above and in front of the eye and an indistinct whitish streak on each scapular region; the front of the wing is margined with white. The juvenal plumage comes in first on the flanks and scapulars; the former are, at first, "olive brown" with white tips and the latter are "warm sepia."

In the juvenal plumage in the fall the young male resembles the adult female, but can be recognized by the looser texture of the plumage, the worn tail, the gray instead of brown flanks, and by having less white on the breast. J. G. Millais (1913) says:

Toward the end of November the young male begins to assume the adult dress rapidly; the tail and tail coverts are replaced by adult feathers; a tinge of burnt sienna appears on the long flank feathers; the wing coverts, the scapulars, mantle, and the whole of the adult feathers on head and neck come in, so that by the end of January a young male in my possession is almost like an adult, except for the smaller black and white bars on the sides of the chest, a brown rump and bill, mottled and immature under parts, and immature wings.

The change then proceeds very slowly. From specimens in Mr. Schioler's collection it is clear that the male harlequin follows the same course of plumage as the long-tailed duck and the goldeneye. A greater or lesser part of the immature under parts are shed between the months of March and June, and the last signs of immaturity in the shape of the wings are not shed until late July or August, when the young male goes into an eclipse similar to the adult male. By September the new wings are obtained and the portions that were assumed as eclipse are being shed, so that it is not until November—that is, at 14 months—that the young male stands in full dress. It will breed in the following spring.

This does not agree with what specimens I have seen, which indicate that the young male makes but little progress toward maturity during his first year. Among the large flocks of immature males which we saw in the Aleutians in June very few birds showed anything approaching the adult plumage, and most of them could hardly be distinguished from females, except at very short range. Most of the specimens seen and collected were in worn immature plumage, dull brown above, with lighter edgings, wholly mottled below, and with varying amounts of the slaty feathers and the white markings of the adult on the head. Perhaps these were especially backward birds, and others, which we took to be adults, were normal or advanced young birds; but the latter were certainly in a very small minority.

The young female requires about the same time to reach maturity—about 16 months. Mr. Millais (1913) says:

There seems to be less difference between the young and adult female harlequin than almost any of the diving ducks. Yet the immature female, prior to February, when the new tail is assumed, can always be recognized by the worn ends and lighter colors of the tail and under parts. The under parts are not nearly so broadly speckled as the adult, and there is a greater area of white. The flanks are grayer, and have a sandy tinge. Also the white spaces about the eye are always more heavily edged with slaty-brown.

I should add to this that in the young female the head is usually duller brown and the feathers of the back show more light edgings.

Of the eclipse plumage Mr. Millais (1913) says:

The whole plumage of the adult male in eclipse is a uniform dark slate gray, the head and neck being somewhat darker, as well as the rump, under and upper tail coverts, which are almost black; the single white ear covert spot is retained, and the white space in front of the eye is dull white, both these parts being edged with black; long scapulars, lower neck, upper and lower flanks, sooty brown; about the end of August the wings and tail are shed (as usual only once). Like all the diving ducks, the male harlequin is practically in a state of molt from July 1 until it reaches the full winter plumage early in October.

Food.—Most of the harlequin duck's food is obtained by diving, but much of it is picked up along the shores or about the rocky ledges. On the inland streams where it breeds it consists largely of water insects and their larvae, among which the caddis fly is prominent; it also includes fish spawn, small fishes, small frogs, tadpoles, small fresh-water crustaceans and mollusks, and some aquatic plants. On the seacoast it feeds on similar kinds of marine animal life which it picks up on the kelp-covered rocks at low tide or obtains by diving in the surf along the shore or over the ledges; it apparently does not often dive for its food in deep water. The common black mussel (*Mytelus edulis*) is one of its main food supplies; these mollusks grow in immense beds on shallow ledges and are easily obtained; occasionally a large mussel has been known to trap the duck and cause its death by drowning. Small crustaceans, such as sand fleas and small gasteropods, are also picked up.

R. P. Whitfield (1894) gives the following account of the contents of a bird's stomach, taken on Long Island:

In December, 1893, Mr. William Dutcher brought to me the stomach contents of a harlequin duck (*Histrionicus histrionicus*) shot at Montauk Point, Long Island, about the 3d of the month. An examination of the material showed what an industrious collector the bird must have been, for it had in its crop remains of no less than three individuals of the small mud crab of our coast, *Panopeus depressa* Smith, one carapace being almost entire; besides remains of some other forms of Crustaceans. Of the little shell *Columbella lunata* (*Astyris lunata* of the Fish Commission Reports), there were no less than 39 individuals represented, besides several small Littorinas. This shell is seldom more than one-sixth of an inch long, and is usually quite rare on our shores. It could only have been obtained in such numbers by a sort of sifting of the bottom mud of the bays by the duck, and indicates how carefully the process had been carried on in order to obtain so small an article of food.

Behavior.—Mr. Millais (1913) describes the flight of this species as follows:

The beautiful markings of the male of this species are only noticeable when the observer is close at hand, so that they are not the easiest duck to identify except when in flight. The flight, at first somewhat laborious, is very rapid. The short, pointed wings are beaten swiftly, and the bird constantly swings from side to side, even more frequently than the long-tailed duck. The elevation is moderately high, performed at an altitude similar to the goldeneye, but when passing up or down stream it zigzags and turns, to accommodate its line to every bend of the stream, however slight. The harlequin never thinks of cutting off corners, and it would seem that it imagines its life depends on keeping exactly over the water, however much it bends or twists. I have seen harlequins fly religiously above a bend in a stream that formed almost a complete circle in its course, and yet the birds did not cut across it to shorten their route.

I have watched harlequin ducks in flight many times and have shot quite a few of them, but I never noticed any swinging from side to side, as referred to above, and several writers have referred to their flight as straight. They usually fly close to the water and often in such compact flocks that a large number may be killed at a single shot. They also swim in close formation, sometimes with their bodies almost touching.

Walter H. Rich (1907) says:

If a shot is fired at a flock on the wing they will sometimes plunge from the air into the water and after swimming below the surface again take wing, coming up a hundred yards away—seeming, the instant they reappear, to dash from the depths into the air at full speed, leaving the gunner inexperienced in their ways, and who perhaps had thought that by some miraculous chance he had killed the entire flock, to find that he doesn't care for that kind of duck after all. I passed through just such an experience once, and remember yet how disgusted and surprised I was when after steaming up to where the whole flock should have been dead—no duck—and what may have been their ghosts rising from their watery graves 60 yards away.

Harlequin ducks are fond of feeding in rough water along rocky shores or in the surf just off the beaches, where they ride the waves lightly and dive through the breakers easily and skillfully. They dive so quickly that they often escape at the flash of a gun. In diving the wings are usually half opened as if they intended to use the wings in flight under water, which they probably do.

The peculiar whistling note of this duck has been likened to the cry of a mouse, whence it has been called the " sea-mouse " on the coast of Maine. Mr. Bretherton (1896) describes it as "a shrill whistle descending in cadence from a high to a lower note, commencing with two long notes and running off in a long trill." Mr. Millais (1913) writes:

When first arriving at the breeding grounds in flocks in early May they are very restless, constantly flying to and fro, whilst the females utter their usual call of "*Ek-ek-ek-ek*," to which the males respond with a low or hoarse "*Hu*" or "*Heh-heh*." These calls they also frequently make in winter, and I have heard single females uttering their cry constantly when flying, as if they had lost their companions and were seeking them. When they are paired both sexes utter a different note, "*Gi-ak*," and this note is used at all times when the pair meet, until the males leave the females at the end of June.

Mr. Aretas A. Saunders writes me:

I heard these birds call several times. The call note is usually uttered when on the wing. It sounded to me like "*oy-oy-oy-oy*" rapidly repeated, usually seven or eight times. I never heard the note from any but the males, and it was usually uttered when in pursuit of one of the females.

Winter.—The winter home of the harlequin duck is on the sea-coast. On the Atlantic coast they are not common south of Maine and not abundant even there. They are often seen about the rocky bays of the eastern Provinces in winter, but more often they frequent the outlying rocky islands and ledges. In spite of the brilliant coloring of the males they are surprisingly inconspicuous among the kelp-covered rocks and the wet, shiny seaweeds of varied hues. On the Atlantic coast they are widely known as "lords and ladies," and by the French inhabitants of Quebec they are called "canards des roches" or "rock ducks." They usually flock by themselves in small flocks, but are frequently associated with oldsquaws.

DISTRIBUTION

Breeding range.—Iceland, southern Greenland (north on the east coast to Scoresby Sound and on the west coast to Upernavik), the Labrador Peninsula (Nain, Lance au Loup, Fort Chimo, etc.), and Newfoundland (Hawks Bay, etc.). Birds said to breed in the Ural Mountains and the Yaroslav Government may be of this subspecies, but the breeding birds of eastern Siberia are probably referable to *pacificus*.

Winter range.—The Atlantic coast of North America, south regularly to the Bay of Fundy and the coast of Maine, more rarely to Long Island Sound and casually farther south. Resident in Iceland.

Spring migration.—Atlantic coast birds retire northward in February and some reach Greenland in March. Arrive at Fort Chimo, Ungava, May 25. Seen in the Gulf of St. Lawrence as late as May 29.

Fall migration.—Early dates of arrival: Maine, October 19; Massachusetts, November 1; Rhode Island, November 28.

Casual records.—Rare or casual on Lake Ontario (Toronto. October 20, 1894, and December 4, 1920). Accidental as far south as South Carolina (Mount Pleasant, January 14–16, 1918) and Florida

(Pensacola, March 20, 1886).   Rare or casual in Scandinavia, Russia, Germany, Switzerland, Italy, and Great Britain.

Egg dates.—Iceland: Twenty-three records, May 20 to July 9; twelve records, June 6 to 30.   Labrador: Two records, June 3 and 10.   Greenland: One record, June 24.

HISTRIONICUS HISTRIONICUS PACIFICUS Brooks

PACIFIC HARLEQUIN DUCK

HABITS

I had always supposed that the harlequin duck was a comparatively rare and somewhat solitary species until I visited the Aleutian Islands in the summer of 1911; here we found this subspecies to be one of the commonest and most widely distributed of the ducks; we saw them in large or small flocks about all of the islands wherever they could find the rocky shores that they love to frequent.   I saw more harlequin ducks here in one day than I have ever seen elsewhere in my whole life.   Most of the birds were in large flocks, some of them in immense flocks, but they were also frequently seen in pairs, feeding about the kelp-covered rocks at low tide, among which they were surprisingly inconspicuous and were easily approached.   Even the large flocks were not wild or shy, and we had no difficulty in shooting all we wanted.   The large flocks were made up almost wholly of females and immature males, but they were usually led by two or three adult males.   The presence of mated pairs and some small flocks of adult males led us to suppose that they were breeding there, perhaps back in the interior in the rocky canyons of the mountain streams, but we found no signs of nests around the shores. Similar gatherings of harlequin ducks are found all summer about the Pribilof Islands and all along the southern coasts of Alaska and British Columbia, as far south as Puget Sound.   Nearly all, if not all, of these birds are probably immature birds which are not yet ready to breed, or unmated or barren birds, mainly the former. Some may be birds which have bred early, have lost their broods or their mates, and have returned to join their fellows in these summer-flocking resorts, which are practically the same as the winter resorts. The migrations of this species do not amount to much more than a brief withdrawal into the interior during the nesting season.

Courtship.—The best account that I have seen of the courtship of this species is by B. J. Bretherton (1896), as follows:

The writer has often watched the males in spring, calling, and the actions of these birds may justly be said to resemble the crowing of a rooster.   In giving forth their call the head is thrown far back with the bill pointed directly upward and widely open; then with a jerk the head is thrown forward and downward as the cry is uttered, and at the same time the wings are slightly expanded and drooped.   Afterwards they will rise in the water and flap their wings.

Charles W. Michael (1922), who has had exceptional opportunities to study the behavior of harlequin ducks at short range, describes another courtship performance, as follows:

When the birds appeared in front of camp on the morning of April 12 they were acting strangely. Apparently they were making love. They were bobbing and bowing to one another, swirling around, touching their bills together, and uttering little chatty sounds. One of the moves on the female's part was to slowly submerge her body until just her head and neck appeared above the surface of the water—a bold invitation on her part for attention. In spite of the wanton actions of the female, the love-making failed to reach the climax.

Nesting.—I have never found the nest of the harlequin duck, and I infer that few others have succeeded in doing so in North America, for surprisingly little is to be found in print about the nesting habits of this species. None of the well-known Alaskan explorers speak of finding nests, except Turner (1886), who says:

The nest and eggs were not procured, and the only nest I ever saw was near Iliuliuk village, on Unalaska Island. Two immense blocks of rock had become detached from the cliff above, and when they fell their edges formed a hollow place beneath. In under this I discovered a deserted nest, which the native who was with me asserted was that of a bird of this species. The form was similar to that of the nest of *C. hyemalis,* and in fact so closely resembled it that I persisted in it being of this bird until the native asked me if I did not know that the oldsquaw did not build in such places.

Major Bendire wrote to Dr. D. G. Elliot (1898):

The harlequin duck undoubtedly nests both in our mountain ranges in the interior—Rockies and Sierra Nevadas—as well as on many of the treeless islands of the Alaskan Peninsula and the Kurile Islands, and I have not the least doubt that it breeds both in hollow trees, where such are available, and either on the ground or in holes made by puffins where it can find such, not far from water.

Dr. E. W. Nelson (1887) writes of the breeding haunts of this species:

Among the host of waterfowl which flock to the distant breeding grounds of Alaska in spring, this elegantly marked bird is the most graceful and handsomely colored. As if conscious of its beauty, the harlequin duck leaves the commonplace haunts sought by the crowd of less noble fowls, and along the courses of the clear mountain streams, flowing in a series of rapids into the larger rivers, they consort with the water ouzel, Swainson's thrush, and such other shy spirits as delight in the wildest nooks, even in the remote wilderness of the far north. Dark lichen-covered rocks, affording temporary shelter to the broad-finned northern grayling or the richly colored salmon trout as they dart from rapid to rapid, steep banks overhung by willows and alders, with an occasional spruce, forming a black silhouette against the sky, and a stillness broken only by the voices of the wind and water, unite to render the summer home of these birds, along the Yukon, spots devoted to nature alone, whose solitude is rarely broken, and then only by the soft footsteps of the savage in pursuit of game.

Mr. D. E. Brown has sent me the following note:

On May 7, 1924, a fisherman flushed a female western harlequin duck from a set of seven eggs. This nest was near Port Angeles, Clallam County, Washington, and was on a rocky point of a swift running mountain stream.

Eggs.—Eggs of the Pacific harlequin duck are scarce in collections, and I have no measurements available for comparison, but they probably do not differ essentially in color, shape, or size from those of the Atlantic bird.

Plumages.—The sequence of molts and plumages of this western subspecies are apparently the same as those of its eastern relative.

Behavior.—Aretas A. Saunders writes me from Montana that:

While fishing they sit in midstream, facing the current, often where it is swiftest, paddling just enough to keep themselves stationary. Whenever they see a fish, they dive for it, and usually appear again, a considerable distance downstream with the fish. They dive down into the middle of swift rapids, in places where one would expect them to be dashed in pieces against the rocks, yet they always emerge again, unharmed. Whenever the birds go downstream they usually swim down, and from what I have observed, do this largely under water. As soon as they come to the surface they generally turn and face the current. I have never seen them swim upstream, even where the water is not swift, and believe that when they wish to go upstream they nearly always rise and fly. One afternoon I watched a male bird fishing at the edge of a large pool where the water was not swift. He took up a position to watch at the edge of the pool, standing with his feet and under parts in the water but his head and breast out. From this position he dove after fish whenever he saw them, but I could not make out that he was always successful in catching the fish.

Mr. Michael (1922) says:

Harlequins are expert swimmers and divers. They dive and swim under water with all the ease of a grebe, besides possessing the ability of the water ouzel to walk about on the river bed against the swift currents. When feeding, so far as we were able to observe, they show no preference as to depth of water. When working upstream along the shore they wade in the shallow water, prying among the stones. Where the water is deeper they tip up in the manner of mallard ducks, and where the water is still deeper they dive. They dive in water a foot deep and they dive in water 6 feet deep, always going down where there is a gravelly bottom. Most often they stay under water not more than 15 seconds. Often they stay down 20 seconds, and occasionally they remain under the water as long as 25 seconds. To leave the surface of the water they use their wiry tails as a spring to make the plunge and as they go down both wings and feet are used as a medium of propulsion. When once on the gravelly bottom the wings are closed, the head is held low, and the progress is made against the current, as they walk along poking amongst the stones. When coming to the surface they float up like bubbles, without movement of wings or feet. Their bills break the water and their bodies pop suddenly onto the surface where they rest a moment. While poising on the surface between plunges their bodies float high. When earnestly feeding, seldom more than 10 seconds elapse between plunges. The birds seldom dive simultaneously. The female usually acts first.

At times the harlequins choose the swiftest riffles, and when feeding there their method is the same as when in the less joyous waters. They apparently dive from any position with equal ease, but always as they go down they turn upstream, and even in the swiftest currents they come up in about the same spot at which they went down. When feeding in these racing waters they merely hesitate on the surface, and four or five dives are made in rapid succession. Such work as this is strenuous, but the birds are quite at home in the swiftest currents, and when tired from their exertions they swing into an eddy behind some snag or bowlder and rest as they bob about on the surface.

M. P. Skinner writes to me that they have been observed coasting down on the Yellowstone River almost to the brink of the Lower Falls, 308 feet high, and then, when it seemed as if they would surely go over, they would fly upstream again and repeat the performance.

Game.—As a game bird the harlequin duck is of little importance. It is a comparatively rare bird, or entirely unknown, in most of the regions frequented by gunners; and even where it is fairly common its haunts are rather inaccessible. Moreover, it lives so largely on animal food that its flesh is not particularly palatable. Among the natives of the Aleutian Islands and other parts of Alaska, however, large numbers are killed for food. Mr. Bretherton (1896) describes the method of hunting employed by the natives of Kodiak Island, as follows:

When first the writer went to Kodiak he tried hunting with a boat, relying on wing shooting to get his birds, but without much success; and seeing that the natives always got more birds, he changed his plan and took to the natives' method, as follows: When a band of ducks was seen feeding, a landing was made and the beach approached from the land, the hunter being careful not to be seen. By watching the flock it would be seen that they all dived about the same time, and the time they remained down was about the same length each time. When the last duck dives, the hunter runs toward them, dropping in the grass or behind a rock about the time he calculates the first duck should be coming up again. In this manner he can approach close to the flock, that nearly always feed in the shallow water along the shore. When the last run is made, the hunter, if an old hand, stands on the edge of the water, the gun at "ready," and a couple of extra shells in the hollow of his right hand, the flock all being down. The first duck that comes up gets it, and the second one gets the second barrel, and in this way, by sharp practice, it is often possible to bag six or seven out of one flock.

DISTRIBUTION

Breeding range.—Western North America and northeastern Asia. East in northwestern Canada probably to the Mackenzie Valley and Great Slave Lake, but nowhere else east of the Rocky Mountain region. South in the Rocky Mountain region to Montana (Glacier National Park, Chief Mountain Lake, etc.), Wyoming (Shoshone River), and Colorado (Blue River near Breckenridge). West to central California (west slope of Sierra Nevada Mountains) and Washington (Cascade and Selkirk Mountains) and the mountain regions of British Columbia, and Alaska (Sitka region, Sanakh Island, etc.). Westward throughout the Aleutian, Commander, and Kurile Islands. Probably on St. Matthew and St. Lawrence Islands. West in Siberia to Lake Baikal and the Lena River and east to Kamchatka and northeastern Siberia (Providence Bay, Marcova, etc.). North in summer and probably breeding to the Arctic coasts of Alaska (Barter Island) and Canada (Mackenzie Bay).

Winter range.—Mainly on the seacoasts, but also on inland waters, not far from the southern parts of its breeding range. Winters sparingly in its Rocky Mountain breeding range; other interior records are regarded as casuals. On the Pacific coast south to central California (Monterey Bay) and north to the Aleutian and Pribilof Islands. On the Asiatic side from the Commander Islands south to Japan.

Spring migration.—First arrivals reached Fort Simpson, Mackenzie, on May 25, 1904. Usually arrives at the mouth of the Yukon, Alaska, about June 1. A late date for Pierce County, Washington is June 5, 1915.

Fall migration.—Early dates of arrival: Washington, Kitsap County, September 10; California, San Louis Obispo County, October 8.

Casual records.—Rare or accidental in the interior as far south as Nebraska (Omaha, September 16, 1893 and 19, 1895) and Missouri (St. Louis, October 29, and Montgomery County, March 21, 1897).

Egg dates.—Alaska: Four records, June 13 to July 1. Mackenzie Bay: One record, June 20. Montana: One record, June 10. Washington: One record, May 7.

CAMPTORHYNCHUS LABRADORIUS (Gmelin)

LABRADOR DUCK

HABITS

What little there is known about the life history of this extinct species has already been published and repeatedly quoted by various writers. Probably nothing more of importance will ever be learned about its former abundance or its habits. It is doubtful if any more specimens will ever be brought to light. Therefore, in writing this obituary notice, it is necessary only to compile what has already been written in order to make its life history as nearly complete as possible.

Nesting.—It is supposed to have bred, formerly, from the south coast of Labrador northward, but there is very little positive evidence on which to substantiate even this indefinite statement and much less evidence on which to elaborate it. We might infer from what Coues (1861) says that the Labrador duck bred farther north and passed through Labrador on its migrations; he says:

I was informed that though it was rarely seen in summer, it is not an uncommon bird in Labrador during the fall.

William Dutcher (1894) undertook to obtain some further information regarding the occurrence of the species in Greenland, through Mr. Langdon Gibson, who accompanied the Peary expedition to that region in 1891, acting as ornithologist of the party. Although Mr. Gibson made numerous inquiries and showed pictures of the bird to various people along the coast, he could find no evidence to indicate that the Labrador duck had ever been seen there. A portion of his report is worth quoting in full:

In August, 1892 (the latter part, I believe), on our way home we touched at Godthaab, the largest town in Greenland. Here we were entertained by Herr Anderson, the Danish inspector of South Greenland, an accomplished naturalist, and at his house I had the pleasure of inspecting one of the finest collections of Arctic birds I had ever seen. I showed him my little pamphlet on the Labrador duck, and also presented it to him on my departure. He told me that his collection represented 20 years' work, and all the hunters in South Greenland (some 500 men) had instructions to bring to him any strange birds that they might get. In this way he has added to his collection from time to time many rare birds and eggs. In all this time he claims to have heard nothing of the Labrador duck, which I consider is substantial proof that within the last 20 years the Labrador duck has not visited Greenland. From Godthaab we came directly home to Philadelphia, and this ended my ineffectual attempts at learning something more definite regarding this species.

Audubon (1840) did not see a living specimen of this duck in Labrador, where it was supposed to be breeding commonly. It hardly seems likely that he could have overlooked it, if it had been there. Therefore, his brief account of its breeding habits must be considered unsatisfactory and unreliable. He says:

Although no birds of this species occurred to me when I was in Labrador, my son, John Woodhouse, and the young friends who accompanied him on the 28th of July, 1833, to Blanc Sablon, found, placed on the top of the low tangled fir bushes, several deserted nests, which from the report of the English clerk of the fishing establishment there, we learned to belong to the pied duck. They had much the appearance of those of the eider duck, being very large, formed externally of fir twigs, internally of dried grass, and lined with down. It would thus seem that the pied duck breeds earlier than most of its tribe.

Professor Newton (1896) writes:

This bird, the *Anas labradoria* of the older ornithologists, was nearly allied to the eider duck, and like that species used to breed on rocky islets, where it was safe from the depredations of foxes and other carnivorous quadrupeds. This safety was, however, unavailing when man began yearly to visit its breeding haunts, and, not content with plundering its nests, mercilessly to shoot the birds. Most of such islets are, of course, easily ransacked and depopulated. Having no asylum to turn to, for the shores of the mainland were infested by the four-footed enemies just mentioned, and (unlike some of its congeners) it had not a high northern range, its fate is easily understood.

Maj. W. Ross King (1866), who spent three years shooting in and about the Gulf of St. Lawrence, previous to 1866, says: "The pied duck or Labrador duck is common in the Gulf of St. Lawrence, and breeds on its northern shore, a short distance inland." The foregoing quotations, though meager and unsatisfactory, contain about all we know about the breeding habits of the Labrador duck.

Food.—Very little seems to have been recorded about its food and feeding habits. Audubon (1840) says:

A bird stuffer whom I knew at Camden had many fine specimens, all of which he had procured by baiting fishhooks with the common mussel, on a trot-line sunk a few feet beneath the surface, but on which he never found one alive, on account of the manner in which these ducks dive and flounder when securely hooked. It procures its food by diving amidst the rolling surf over sand or mud bars; although at times it comes along the shore and searches in the manner of the spoon-bill duck. Its usual fare consists of small shellfish, fry, and various kinds of seaweeds, along with which it swallows much sand and gravel.

Other writers say that it fed on shellfish which it obtained by diving on the sand shoals, whence it derived the common name of "sand shoal duck."

Mr. S. F. Cheney, of Grand Manan, wrote to William Dutcher (1891) in 1890:

The female Labrador duck I gave to Mr. Herrick was with some oldsquaws or long-tailed ducks when I shot it, and I think there were no others of the kind with it. This one had small shells in its crop. It dove to the bottom with the squaws.

Behavior.—Audubon (1840) wrote:

Its flight is swift, and its wings emit a whistling sound. It is usually seen in flocks of from 7 to 10, probably the members of one family.

Col. Nicholas Pike sent to William Dutcher (1891) the following interesting account of his experiences with the Labrador duck:

I have in my life shot a number of these beautiful birds, though I have never met more than two or three at a time, and mostly single birds. The whole number I ever shot would not exceed a dozen, for they were never plentiful. I rarely met with them. The males in full plumage were exceedingly rare; I think I never met with more than three or four of these; the rest were young males and females. They were shy and hard to approach, taking flight from the water at the least alarm, flying very rapidly. Their familiar haunts were the sandbars where the water was shoal enough for them to pursue their favorite food, small shellfish. I have only once met with this duck south of Massachusetts Bay. In 1858, one solitary male came to my battery in Great South Bay, Long Island, near Quogue, and settled among my stools. I had a fair chance to hit him, but in my excitement to procure it I missed it. This bird seems to have disappeared, for an old comrade, who has hunted in the same bay over 60 years, tells me he has not met with one for a long time. I am under the impression the males do not get their full plumage in the second year. I would here remark, this duck has never been esteemed for the table, from its strong, unsavory flesh.

Probably the Labrador duck was never abundant or even very common throughout its known winter range; certainly we have very little positive evidence to that effect. The statement, so often quoted, of Thomas Morton in his New English Canaan (1637) may not refer to this species at all. In writing of the birds noted by him in New England between 1622 and 1630, he says "Ducks there are of three kinds, pide ducks, gray ducks and black ducks in great abundance." It seems to be taken for granted that by the name "pide ducks" he referred to the Labrador duck. It seems to me much more likely that he referred to the goldeneye, which is still called the "pied duck" all along our northern coasts, or to one of several other species called by that name or, perhaps, to a number of species in general having more or less black and white plumages. Audubon (1840) considered it rather rare, although he says: "Along the coast of New Jersey and Long Island it occurs in greater or less number every year."

Dekay (1844), writing of this species in New York, says:

This duck, well known on this coast under the name of skunk head, and sand-shoal duck on the coast of New Jersey, is not, however, very abundant.

Walter J. Hoxie wrote to me a few years ago, as follows:

During my youthful experience among the ponds and creeks about the mouth of the Merrimac we sometimes got a duck which we called a "black-belly" and many of the gunners considered it a cross with the "sea coots." In the brackish ponds it was commonly found in company with the gadwall, or as we called it, the "gray duck." We rather disdained it, and I remember too it was hard to pick. Lots of down under the feathers that perhaps made us think it was akin to the scoters. One I remember in "Bushy Pond" with a gray duck on a frosty November evening. Did not seem to be as shy as its companion, but kept moving about watching me as I crawled down with a pine sapling for shelter. The old flintlock hung fire a little longer than usual, and though they were both in line when I sighted the gray was too quick. To-day that black-belly would not have been such a disappointment, though I had to wade for it and the water was almost freezing. It must have been in 1862. In 1870 I saw one—perhaps more—in Boston market. But one I know was tied up with an American merganser. I bought the merganser and stuffed it.

George N. Lawrence, in a letter to Mr. Dutcher (1891), wrote:

I recollect that about 40 or more years ago it was not unusual to see them in Fulton Market, and without doubt killed on Long Island; at one time I remember seeing six fine males, which hung in the market until spoiled for the want of a purchaser; they were not considered desirable for the table, and collectors had a sufficient number, at that time a pair being considered enough to represent a species in a collection. No one anticipated that they might become extinct, and if they have, the cause thereof is a problem most desirable to solve, as it was surely not through man's agency, as in the case of the great auk.

Dr. D. G. Elliot (1898) saw a considerable number of Labrador ducks, mostly females and young males, in the New York markets between 1860 and 1870, but full plumaged males were exceedingly rare.

George A. Boardman endeavored to get some specimens for Doctor Elliot from his collectors about Grand Manan, but found that these ducks had all gone; the last one taken in that vicinity was shot by S. F. Cheney in April, 1871; this specimen was sent, by Mr. Boardman, to John Wallace, of New York, to be mounted for the Smithsonian Institution, but, not knowing its value, Wallace parted with the skin, and all trace of it was lost. The last specimen taken and preserved was shot on Long Island in the fall of 1875, purchased, from J. G. Bell, by George N. Lawrence and presented by him to the Smithsonian Institution; it was a young male and possibly its parents or others of the same brood may have survived for a few years; but probably the Labrador duck became an extinct species at about that time.

Since then only one specimen has been recorded as taken; Dr. W. H. Gregg (1879) reported the capture of a Labrador duck, near Elmira, New York, on December 12, 1878; the duck had been eaten before he heard about it and he was able to procure and save only the head and neck; these remnants were preserved for some years, but finally lost; it is unfortuate that this record can not now be verified.

William Dutcher (1891, 1893, and 1894) has made a careful study of the records relating to the Labrador duck and a thorough investigation as to the number of specimens in existence, so far as known, in American and European collections. He published a number of papers on the subject and finally succeeded in locating, up to 1894, only 42 specimens, 31 of which were in American collections at that time. How many specimens have come to this country since, I have made no effort to determine. Many specimens were shipped abroad between 1840 and 1850, which have not been located, and some may turn up later in private collections. J. H. Gurney (1897) recorded a specimen in the museum at Amiens in France, which was apparently unknown to Mr. Dutcher; this, with one since discovered by Winthrop S. Brooks (1912) in the Boston Society of Natural History, brings the published record of specimens up to 44.

There has been considerable speculation among ornithological writers as to the causes which led to the disappearance of this species, which was apparently as well fitted to survive as several other species of ducks. It was a swift flyer, rather shy and difficult to approach in its offshore resorts; it was essentially a maritime species and seldom resorted to inland bays or rivers, though Audubon said that it was known to ascend the Delaware River as far as Philadelphia; it was not particularly popular as a table bird and often proved a drug in the market, when other more desirable ducks were obtainable; for the above reasons it is fair to assume that it was not exterminated by gunners and never was shot in very large numbers. What evidence we have goes to show that it never was a numerous species and that it probably had a very limited breeding range. If this breeding range was, as it appears, restricted to the southeast coast of Labrador, its disappearance may easily be charged to the wholesale destruction of bird life which took place on that coast during the last century. Continued persecution on its breeding grounds, where its nests and eggs were apparently conspicuous and where both young and old birds were easily killed in summer, when unable to fly, is enough to account for it. That certain other species, which are known to have wider breeding ranges, survived the same persecution is no proof that the Labrador duck did not succumb to it.

DISTRIBUTION

Breeding range.—Unknown. Supposed to have bred in Labrador, probably in some very restricted range on the south coast of the Labrador Peninsula.

Winter range.—On the Atlantic coast from Nova Scotia to New Jersey and probably to Chesapeake Bay. Most of the specimens with known data were taken near Long Island, New York.

Casual record.—A specimen, since lost, is said to have been taken at Elmira, New York, December 12, 1878.

POLYSTICTA STELLERI (Pallas)

STELLER EIDER

HABITS

This beautiful and oddly marked duck was first described by the Russian naturalist, Pallas, who named it after its discoverer. Steller obtained the first specimens on the coast of Kamchatka, which is near the center of its abundance and not far from its principal breeding grounds in northeastern Siberia. Illustrating the abundance of this species on the Siberian coast of Bering Sea, Dr. E. W. Nelson (1883) writes:

The first night of our arrival was calm and misty, the water having that peculiar glassy smoothness seen at such times, and the landscape rendered indistinct at a short distance by a slight mistiness. Soon after we came to anchor before the native village this body of birds arose from the estuary a mile or two beyond the natives' huts and came streaming out in a flock which appeared endless. It was fully 3 to 4 miles in length, and considering the species which made up this gathering of birds it was enough to make an enthusiastic ornithologist wild with a desire to possess some of the beautiful specimens which were seen filing by within gunshot of the vessel.

Mr. F. S. Hersey's notes of July 26, 1914, state:

As we steamed into St. Lawrence Bay there appeared in the distance a long low, sandy island known as Lutke Island. As we drew nearer we could see a cloud of birds hovering above it which our glasses showed us were Arctic terns. The island itself was very low, hardly above the sea level, and as we looked at it seemed to be strewn with small black rocks. With our glasses, however, we could see some movement among these black objects. At last we made them out to be birds, then suddenly they arose and swept out toward us, their black and white plumage flashing in the sunlight, and we saw that they were eiders. There were many kings and Pacifics among them, and these separated from the main flock and went out to sea, but the remainder, which were Steller eiders, returned to the farther side of the island. A boat was soon lowered and a party of us put off from the ship. When we landed and started to walk across the island the eiders again took flight but soon settled on the water a short distance offshore. They were not at all shy. While we stayed on the island small parties of from 2 or 3 to 8 or 10 were constantly flying back and forth, often close to us, although we were in plain sight at all times, for the island offered no concealment. We had no difficulty in obtaining all the specimens we wanted.

Spring.—From their winter home in the Aleutian Islands the main flight of the spring migration seems to pass westward through the Commander Islands, where they are very abundant in April, to the Siberian coast and northward. There is also a northward migration through Bering Straits to the Arctic coast of Alaska. Mr. John Murdoch (1885) found these eiders common at Point Barrow; he says:

Early in June they are to be found at the "leads" of open water at some distance from the shore, and perhaps the majority of them pass on in this way to their breeding grounds. From the middle to the end of June they appear on land in small parties scattered over the tundra. At this time they are in full breeding plumage, and the males are generally in excess in the flocks. They are generally to be found in small "pond-holes," frequently sitting on the bank asleep, and are very tame, easily approached within gunshot, and generally swimming together when alarmed, before taking wing, so that several can be secured at one discharge. I have stopped a whole flock of five with a single shot.

Mr. Alfred M. Bailey writes to me:

At Cape Prince of Wales, during the spring of 1922, the first Steller eiders were seen May 12. At this time the straits are still choked with pack ice and salt water freezes on the leads. On May 18 a few birds were seen and again on May 29, but the big migration past this westernmost point was on June 3. We had been walrus hunting in the straits for two days and were returning heavily loaded with meat when the wind suddenly died down and a slick calm prevailed—a very unusual occurrence. Immediately great strings of birds appeared on their northward journey, gulls, loons, ducks, and geese, and among them were many of this species. The natives said, " Plenty birds come from south, bime bye—mebbe one, two hours—plenty south wind." It was true ; the birds seemed to be going just ahead of the storm from the south. I learned to foretell a change in the wind by the migration of the birds, for invariably a large migration occurred just before a south wind. We feared a south wind, for if caught offshore, we could not sail back to Wales, and would be forced to drift into the Arctic, so the migration of birds was watched with interest.

Nesting.—Nothing seems to be known about the courtship of the Steller eider and very little has been published about its nesting habits, which is not strange considering the remote and inaccessible regions in which it makes its summer home.

The following brief references to the nesting habits of this species are given by John G. Millais (1913) :

Middendorff found nests on flat tundra in the moss, and describes them as deep, round, and lined with down. The male keeps in the vicinity of the female, who sits closely and leaves the nest unwillingly, and when disturbed flies off " with a harsh cry reminiscent of our teal, but still more harsh." Steller found a nest in Kamchatka amongst precipitous rocks near the coast.

Personally I have had no experience with this species, and Mr. Hersey never found its nest. I had five sets of eggs sent to me by my correspondent, T. L. Richardson, who collected them near Point Barrow, Alaska, during the summer of 1916. Unfortunately no data came with them, but one of the sets was accompanied by the nest, or rather the nest lining. This nest, which contains 10 eggs, consists of a bulky mass of curly, coarse grasses and various mosses and lichens, such as grow on the tundra, thoroughly mixed with considerable very dark brown down and a few feathers from the breast of the duck. Evidently the female plucks the down from her breast, together with such feathers as casually come with it, and mixes it with the coarser nesting material, as incubation advances. The nest is quite different from any other duck's nest that I have seen, and is easily identified by the peculiar breast feathers of the female Steller eider. The down varies in color from " benzo brown " to " fuscous."

Eggs.—The five sets referred to above consist of two sets of 6 eggs and one set each of 7, 8, and 10 eggs. They are typical eider's eggs in appearance. The prevailing shape is elliptical ovate, some are elongate ovate, and a few are nearly elliptical oval or approaching oval. The shell is smooth, with little or no gloss. The color varies from " light yellowish olive " to " water green " or from " deep olive buff " to " olive buff." Many of the eggs are clouded or mottled with darker shades of the above colors and many are quite badly nest stained.

The measurements of 75 eggs, in various collections, average 61.4 by 42 millimeters; the eggs showing the four extremes measure 70.5 by 45.5; 66.9 by 47.1, 55.5 by 40.5, and 59.2 by 37 millimeters.

Plumages.—The downy young Steller eider is easily recognizable, as it is quite different from the young of other species. The bill, even in the smallest specimens, shows the characteristic shape peculiar to the species, tapering evenly from forehead to tip, slightly compressed in the middle, with an overhanging upper mandible near the base and near the tip. The color is decidedly dark; the upper parts, including the crown, hind neck, back, and rump are very dark, glossy "bone brown" or "clove brown"; slightly lighter shades of the same colors extend downwards on the sides of the head to the chin and throat, on the sides of the body and across the chest; there is a "buffy brown" spot above the eye, a whitish spot below it and a stripe of "buffy brown" behind it; the throat and chin are "light vinaceous cinnamon" or "pinkish buff" in the youngest birds, grayer in older birds, the colors merging gradually into the darker colors above; the breast and belly are dull, silvery, grayish brown, invaded on the sides with darker browns. The bill and feet are black in dry skins.

In the juvenal plumage, during the first fall young males and females are very much alike and somewhat resemble the adult female except that they are lighter colored, redder, and more mottled below; in the young male the breast and flanks are heavily barred with rich reddish brown or "chestnut"; while in the young female the under parts are barred with paler browns; in the young male the wing is much like that of the adult female, with the curved tertials; but in the young female there is less blue in the speculum and the tertials are straighter, less curved. In both sexes the feathers of the back and scapulars have brownish buff edgings; and the under parts are wholly mottled or barred, instead of being uniform dark brown as in the adult female.

During the first winter and spring the sexes begin to differentiate more. The young male becomes lighter colored; the dusky throat patch and the black neck ring begin to show; the breast begins to assume a tawny shade; and in some forward birds some of the white-edged scapulars and long curved tertials appear before summer. But, on the whole, there is not much change until the summer molt occurs in July and August. This produces what might be called a first eclipse plumage, relatively similar to that of the common eider. The plumage is completely changed during this molt, after which old and young birds are practically indistinguishable.

Adults have one complete molt each year, which produces in the male a fairly complete double molt and eclipse plumage of the head, neck, and upper parts. It apparently occurs in July and August, as I have in my collection males in full nuptial plumage up to the end of June and a series of nine adult males, taken July 26, showing various stages of the eclipse plumage. In full eclipse the striking colors of the head and neck—white, green, and black—are wholly replaced by " bister " or " mummy brown," darker above and lighter below, with only a trace left on the hind neck of the purplish black collar. The back becomes dull black and the showy scapulars are replaced by plain " clove brown " feathers which over-hang the showy wings. The wings are still further concealed by " clove brown " feathers on the flanks and by a suffusion of dusky and brown barred feathers on the shoulders and chest, some of which invade the breast. The remainder of the under parts and the wings remain as they were and are apparently molted only once. Specimens showing the change into the full plumage are not available.

Food.—Referring to their feeding habits, Mr. Murdoch (1885) says:

When open water forms along shore, that is, in the latter part of July and early part of August, they are to be found in large flocks along the beach, collecting in beds at a safe distance from the shore, feeding on marine invertebrates, especially gephryean worms.

Mr. Bernard J. Bretherton (1896) says that at Kodiak Island in winter they feed largely on decapods and mollusks, which they obtain in deep water, seldom feeding near the shore. Mr. Millais (1913) writes:

They feed on fish spawn, young fish, crabs, and possibly on vegetable growths, but principally on conchylia and mussels. These they obtain by diving, and their favorite resorts are mussel banks lying at the same depths as those frequented by eiders and long-tailed ducks.

Behavior.—Referring to their behavior on the Siberian coast, Doctor Nelson (1883) writes:

Flocks of thousands were found about Cape Wankarem during our stay there the first of August, 1881, and, in company with an equal number of king eiders and a few of the Pacific eider, were seen passing out and in each evening to and from the large estuary back of the native village. This village was built upon the spit cutting this estuary from the sea at this place, and lay directly in the track of flight followed by these eiders as they passed to or from the sea. As these flocks passed back and forth the birds were being continually brought down by the slings thrown into the midst of the passing birds by the natives; yet, notwithstanding this, the birds continued from day to day the entire season to pass and repass this place. Their heedlessness in this respect may be accounted for from the fact that these people were without guns of any kind, and were thus unable to frighten them by the noise of the discharge. The birds were easily called from their course of flight, as we repeatedly observed. If a flock should be passing a hundred yards or more to one side, the natives would utter a long, peculiar cry, and the flock would turn instantly to one side and sweep by in a circuit, thus affording the coveted opportunity for bringing down some of their number. These flocks generally contained a mixture of about one-twentieth of the number of Pacific eiders, and the remainder about equally divided of stellers and the king eiders. At times the entire community of these birds, which made this vicinity their haunt, would pass out in a solid body, and the flock thus formed exceeded in size anything of the kind I ever witnessed.

Fall.—At Point Barrow, according to Mr. Murdoch (1885), the fall migration, or rather the movement away from their breeding grounds begins early.

Birds that have bred, judging from the looks of the ovaries, begin to come back from the first to the middle of July, appearing especially at Pergniak and flying in small parties up and down the coast. They generally keep to themselves, but are sometimes found associating with small parties of king ducks. They disappear from the first to the middle of August, and when gathered in large flocks are exceedingly wild and hard to approach.

The main migration route in the fall is southward along the Siberian coast of Bering Sea to their winter homes in the Kurile, Commander, and Aleutian Islands. But Doctor Nelson (1887) says that—

In autumn, as they pass south, stray individuals and parties are found in Norton Sound. Those taken there are usually young of the year. When found at St. Michael they usually frequented outlying rocky islets and exposed reefs, and fed in the small tide rips. The shallow turbid water of Norton Sound seems to be offensive to the majority of these birds, as their chosen haunts are along coasts where the water is clear and deep close to the shore.

Winter.—Steller eiders are almost as abundant in their winter resorts about the Aleutian Islands as they are in summer on the Siberian coast. Here they gather in large flocks, associated with king eiders, about the harbors which are free from ice. They resort to the vicinity of sunken ledges and rocky islets where they can obtain their food by diving to moderate depths, although they can dive in deep water if necessary. They are rather shy at this season when in large flocks. The winter range extends eastward to Kodiak Island, where this species is said to be abundant. Chase Littlejohn, in some notes sent to Major Bendire in 1892, writes:

These ducks are by far the most numerous of any duck during the winter, and a few were nesting at Morzhovia Bay in June. They are known locally as soldier ducks, from their habit of swimming single file and then as if by a given signal they all disappear beneath the surface in search of food, where they remain for some time, but when they arise they usually form a solid square or, in other words, a compact bunch, and then single file and repeat. Such chances are taken advantage of by men in search of game; if near shore they run to the nearest point where the ducks disappeared, and when they come to the surface shoot into the flock, sometimes killing a large number. The same tactics can be employed using a boat. They are not bad eating if the skin is removed.

Westward the winter range extends at least to the Commander and Kurile Islands. Probably all the birds which breed in eastern Siberia and Alaska winter in some of the resorts named above. But there is evidently a westward migration also, along the Arctic coast of Europe to a well-known winter resort in the unfrozen waters off the coast of Norway; this flight is probably made up of birds which breed in western Siberia or northern Europe.

DISTRIBUTION

Breeding range.—Coasts of northwestern America and northern Asia. East on the Arctic coast of America to Point Barrow, Alaska, and perhaps farther. South regularly, in the Bering Sea region, to St. Lawrence Island, Anadyr Bay, and Kamchatka; recorded as breeding on the Aleutian and Shumagin Islands and on the Alaska Peninsula, (Morzhovia Bay), but probably only sparingly and irregularly. The main breeding range is on the Arctic coast of Siberia from Bering Straits westward, at least as far as the Taimyr Peninsula, and perhaps on Nova Zembla.

Winter range.—The vicinity of the Aleutian Islands, eastward on the south side of the Alaska Peninsula to the Shumagin Islands and the Kenai Peninsula. Westward to the Commander and Kurile Islands. North in Bering Sea as far as open water extends. A few winter in northern Europe, as far west as Scandinavia, Heligoland, Denmark, and the Baltic Sea.

Spring migration.—Arrivals have been noted at Point Barrow, Alaska, as early as June 5 and at Nijni Kolymsk, northern Siberia, June 9. First seen at Cape Prince of Wales, May 12, and a heavy flight on June 3. The last birds leave the Commander Islands from May 25 to 31, and leave Nushagak, Alaska, about May 20.

Fall migration.—Early dates of arrival in the Bering Sea region: St. Michael, September 21; Nushagak, October 8; Commander Islands, November 1. Late dates of departure: Point Barrow, September 17; St. Michael, October 15; Ugashik, November 28. No dates are available for the migrations to and from the European winter range, which is probably occupied by birds breeding in western Siberia.

Casual records.—Accidental in Greenland (Disco Bay, August, 1878), Quebec (Godbout, February 17, 1898), England (Norfolk.

February 10, 1830 and Yorkshire, August 15, 1845), France, Germany and Japan (Yezzo, March 9, 1894 and May 3, 1894).

Egg dates.—Alaska: Eleven records, June 17 to July 10; six records, June 22 to July 6.

ARCTONETTA FISCHERI (Brandt)

SPECTACLED EIDER

HABITS

If the preceding life history was unsatisfactory, this will be more so, for still less is known about the habits of the oddly marked spectacled or Fischer eider, which occupies such a restricted breeding range in northwestern Alaska and northeastern Siberia. Few naturalists have ever seen it in life. Dr. E. W. Nelson (1887), to whom we are indebted for most of our knowledge of the habits of this species, says on this point:

Its restricted range has, up to the present time, rendered this bird among the least known of our waterfowl. Even in the districts where it occurs it is so extremely local that a few miles may lead one to places they never visit.

In Mr. Dall's paper upon the birds of Alaska he limits the breeding ground of the spectacled eider to the marshes between the island of St. Michael and the mainland. This, with the statement made to him by natives that they are never found north of St. Michael, is not borne out by my observations, for these eiders breed from the head of Norton Bay south to the mouth of the Kuskoquim, at least. St. Michael may be noted as the center of abundance. The spectacled eider is so restricted in its range and so local in its distribution, even where it occurs, that, like the Labrador duck and the great auk, it may readily be so reduced in numbers as to become a comparatively rare bird. A species limited in the breeding season to the salt marshes between the head of Norton Bay and the mouth of the Kuskoquim River occupies but a very small territory, and a glance at the map will show this coast line not to exceed 400 miles, even following its indentations. The width of the breeding ground will not exceed 1 or 2 miles, and there are long stretches where it does not breed at all.

In addition to the natural struggle for existence the species has to contend against thousands of shotguns in the hands of the natives. The diminution in all the species of waterfowl breeding along the coast is more and more marked each season; and while this may mean a desertion of one region for another in the case of the great majority of geese and ducks, yet for such narrowly limited species as the spectacled eider, and to a less extent the Emperor goose, this diminution is but the beginning of extermination. Moreover, the present scarcity of large game along the coast is having great effect in causing the natives to wage a continually increasing warfare upon the feathered game.

Apparently Doctor Nelson's fears have been realized, as the spectacled eider has nearly disappeared from the vicinity of St. Michael and from the Yukon delta. My assistant, Mr. Hersey, spent the season of 1914 at the mouth of the Yukon and the summer of 1915 in the vicinity of St. Michael with this species as one of the things especially wanted; and during the two seasons he succeeded in securing only one pair of the birds and did not find a single nest. I doubt very much if they breed there at all at the present time, for he saw only a few in the canal early in June, at which time they seemed to be already mated; they soon disappeared and were not seen again during the season. Wherever the center of abundance may have been in Doctor Nelson's time, it is now to be found somewhere in northeastern Siberia, where it is one of the commonest eiders.

Spring.—Doctor Nelson (1887) says:

Although living so far north, yet it is one of the last among the waterfowl to reach its breeding ground at the Yukon delta and the coast of Norton Sound. My observations show this species to be strictly limited to the salt marshes bordering the east coast of Bering Sea, and thus favoring the shallow, muddy, coast waters, which appear to be so distasteful to Steller's eider. Very soon after reaching their destination the flocks disband and the birds quietly pair, but the first eggs are rarely laid earlier than the first days of June.

When first paired the birds choose a pond on the marsh, and are thenceforth found in its vicinity until the young are hatched. Their love-making is very quiet. I have never heard any note uttered except by the female while conducting the brood out of danger. As the grass commences to show green and the snow and ice are nearly gone, although the other denizens of the marsh are already well along in their housekeeping, these ducks choose some dry, grassy spot close to the pond, and making a slight hollow with a warm lining of grass, they commence the duties of the season.

Nesting.—The same writer gives us the following account of the nesting habits of the spectacled eider:

One nest found on June 15 was on a bed of dry grass within a foot of the water on the border of the pond, and when the female flew off the single egg could be seen 20 yards away. Tussocks of dry grass, small islands in ponds, and knolls close to the water's edge are all chosen as nesting places, and as a rule the nest is well concealed by the dry grass standing about. If the nest contains but one or two eggs the female usually flies off and remains until the intruder is gone; but if the set is nearly completed or incubation is begun she will soon return, frequently accompanied by the male, and both circle about, showing the greatest uneasiness. The female will sometimes alight in the pond, within easy range, and both parents may be obtained by watching near the nest.

A set of 9 eggs of this species, sent me by Rev. A. R. Hoare, was collected at Point Hope, Alaska, on June 15, 1917, on a small islet, about 3 feet square, in a tundra pond, in which the water was from 3 to 4 feet deep; the nest was concealed in the long grass at the edge of the islet and was composed of grass and very little down; the eggs were fresh and more down would probably have been added later.

Mr. T. L. Richardson sent we several sets of spectacled eider's eggs from Point Barrow, Alaska. The nest shown in the accompanying photograph was evidently in plain sight, in a depression in the tundra moss and grass, about 10 feet from the shore of a small pond; it was lined with a little moss and down; the 5 eggs that it contained were collected on June 26, 1917. He says that down is added to the nest as incubation advances, so that there is a heavy lining of it before the eggs hatch. The down is soft and closely matted; it varies in color from "bister" to "sepia," with inconspicuous, slightly lighter centers; small mottled breast feathers and dusky tipped belly feathers are usually found in it.

Eggs.—The spectacled eider lays from 5 to 9 eggs, the smaller sets being apparently commoner than the larger ones. In shape they vary from ovate to elongate ovate, but the prevailing shape is elliptical ovate. The shell is smooth with a slight gloss. The color varies from " deep olive buff " or " olive buff " to " water green " or " yellowish glaucous." The measurements of 101 eggs in various collections average 65.4 by 44.6 millimeters; the eggs showing the four extremes measure **73** by 45.7, 70.5 by **47.8,** and **59.5** by **40.5** millimeters.

Young.—Doctor Nelson (1887) says of the young:

The male is rarely seen after the young are hatched, but the female shows the greatest courage in guarding her brood, as the following incident will show: A brood was swimming away from me, and the female tried to protect them by keeping between the young and myself. I fired two charges of No. 12 shot, killing all the young, yet, in spite of the fact that the parent received a large share of the charge each time, she refused to fly, and kept trying to urge her dead offspring to move on, until a charge of larger shot mercifully stretched her among her offspring. Upon removing the skin her back was found to be filled with fine shot, and her desperate courage in defense of her brood shows the strength of parental feeling. Other similar instances attest the courage and devotion of this species.

Mr. Koren, while collecting for me, near the Kolyma Delta in northeastern Siberia, on July 21, 1916, saw a female spectacled eider swimming in a tundra pool followed by two downy young white-fronted geese, which she had evidently adopted and was carefully guarding; she allowed him to come near enough to photograph them, after which he shot all three of them and sent them to me.

Doctor Nelson (1887) says:

The middle of August young birds are frequently seen from a few days old to those nearly ready to take wing. During this month the adult birds pass through the summer molt, and with the half-grown young desert the marshes and tide creeks for the seacoast and outlying rocky islands.

By September 1 scarcely a single individual can be found on the marshes, and by the 20th they are scarce along the coast.

Plumages.—The downy young is easily recognized by the shape of the bill and the feathering at its base, which are just as they are in the adult; the bill slopes gradually to a point, with straight edges; the nail at the tip is light colored, but the bill is black in dried skins; the feathering extends to the nostrils and beyond them to a point above. The "spectacles" also are conspicuous. The colors on the upper parts shade from "warm sepia" on the crown and rump to "snuff brown" on the mantle, hind neck, and flanks; the dark color of the crown extends down over the lores and auriculars; a circular space around the eye is "wood brown," surrounded by a broken circle of "cinnamon buff," forming the "spectacles"; the lower cheeks, chin, and throat are pale "cinnamon buff," shading off to dull grayish buff on the breast and belly, into which the darker colors of the upper parts blend.

In the juvenal plumage the sexes are much alike, but they are quite different from the adult female. In the young male the head and neck are much like those of the adult female, with the "spectacles" only indicated; but the upper parts are darker, the feathers of the back and scapulars being "warm sepia" or "bister," edged with "clay color" or "cinnamon buff"; the under parts are uniformly, but rather faintly, barred with dusky, not strongly barred, as in the adult female; the wings are brownish black, with brownish buffy edgings on the greater and lesser coverts, secondaries and tertials. In the young female the juvenal plumage is much the same, except that the under parts are spotted rather than barred; the wings are like those of the adult female, but more brownish, with more buffy-brown edging in the coverts.

Specimens are lacking to show the progress toward maturity during the first winter, but probably it is similar to what takes place in the young common eider. The young male assumes during the following summer a first eclipse plumage, quite different from that of the adult male. In this plumage the "spectacles," lower cheeks, and throat are pale buff fading off to grayish buff on the neck, faintly mottled with dusky; the rest of the head and neck are "hair brown" or "mouse gray," becoming "fuscous" on the crown and occiput and mottled with buffy shades on the sides of the head; the back, scapulars, and flanks are "hair brown" or "deep mouse gray"; the wings are like the juvenal wings until they are molted in August or September; and the under parts are as in the juvenal plumage.

I have not been able to trace the immature plumages beyond this stage, but probably the second winter plumage, as in other eiders, is not fully adult, but very much like it. The perfection of the adult plumage is probably acquired after the second eclipse, when the young bird is over 2 years old.

The adult male apparently has but one complete molt each summer, at which most, if not all, of the contour plumage is molted twice, involving a nearly complete eclipse plumage. The adult eclipse, and probably the second eclipse, can easily be distinguished from the first eclipse by the wings, which are molted but once, and by the under parts, both of which remain as in the fully adult plumage. During the spring the plumage of the male becomes very much worn and in June it begins to molt into the eclipse. The brilliant plumage of the head and neck entirely disappears; the "spectacles" become "mouse gray," mottled with buff, and the rest of the head and neck become mottled and variegated with various shades of gray, buff, and dusky; the white mantle is entirely, or nearly all, replaced by plain "wood brown" or "deep mouse gray" feathers; many feathers barred with dark brown and buffy shades appear on the chest and shoulders; the white rump spots disappear; the conspicuous white wing coverts and white curving tertials are concealed by the dark scapulars and flank feathers while the bird is not in flight.

Food.—All that I can find published as to the food of this species is the short statement by Doctor Nelson (1887) that: "Their food in summer consists of small crustacea, grass, seeds, and such other food as the brackish pools afford."

Behavior.—The same writer says:

They fly in small compact flocks, rarely exceeding 50 birds in a flock, and skim close along the surface of the ice or marsh with a flight very similar to that of other heavy-bodied sea ducks.

Winter.—The winter home of the spectacled eider does not seem to be well known, but, as it has been recorded in winter in both the western and the eastern Aleutian Islands, its main winter range is probably in the vicinity of these islands, where so many other northern sea fowl are known to spend the winter in the comparatively mild open water, tempered by the Japan current.

DISTRIBUTION

Breeding range.—Arctic coasts of Alaska and Siberia. East to Point Barrow at least. South to the Bering Sea coast of Alaska to the mouth of the Kuskokwim River. Westward along the north coast of Siberia to the mouth of the Lena River and to the New Siberia Islands.

Winter range.—Mainly in the vicinity of the Aleutian and Pribilof Islands, and more sparingly eastward along the south side of the Alaska Peninsula to Sanakh Island.

Spring migration.—Early dates of arrival in Alaska: St. Michael, May 6; Point Hope, May 4; Cape Prince of Wales, May 16; Wainwright, May 28; Point Barrow, May 26.

Fall migration.—Latest date of departure from Point Barrow is September 17.

Egg dates.—Alaska: Twelve records, June 8 to July 4; six records, June 15 to 26.

Spring.—Winter lingers on the outer coast of Labrador well into the summer months; all through the month of June and part of July the northeast winds and the Arctic current drive the drifting pack ice onto these exposed and barren rocky coasts. Long before the icy barriers yield to the soft west winds and as soon as the lanes of open water begin to break up the fields of ice, flocks of these heavy-bodied sea ducks may be seen wending their way northward in the opening leads, flying with slow and labored wings beats close to the cold, dark waves or resting in flocks on the larger pans of ice until the way opens for further progress. Many of them have been wintering just beyond the ice floes and are seeking the first opportunity to find open water near their northern breeding grounds.

Regarding their arrival in Cumberland Sound, Kumlien (1879) says:

As soon as there is any open water they are found in spring; still they are not common at Annanactook till the latter days of May. Eskimos from the south reported them on the floe edge near Niantilic early in May, and I saw a few on an iceberg near the Middliejuacktwack Island on the 30th of April. They can stand almost any temperature if they can find open water.

W. Elmer Ekblaw writes to me of their arrival in northern Greenland, as follows:

The all-winter residents are probably the first eiders to appear along the mainland shore in early spring, wherever open water may be found off the outermost capes and islands, usually about April 20. The number of eiders frequenting these open places gradually increases, but slowly, until the last week in May, when the immigration begins in earnest and continues until mid-June, when apparently the last comers have arrived. The females come later than the males, but the last females come with the last males. They are usually rather shy and wary and will not permit near approach.

By mid-June the mating season is usually at its height, but in years of heavy snow when the islets are covered until late, the season is retarded. The summer of 1914 was a summer of late melting of snow and the nesting season of the eiders had hardly begun by the 20th of June.

Courtship.—John G. Millais (1913) describes the courtship of the European subspecies, as follows:

The courtship of the eider is a very simple one, and somewhat undemonstrative. It is essentially in accordance with the gentle disposition of the bird. The female seems to be at least as amorous as the male, and pays considerable court to the object of her affections. Having selected a mate, she follows him round and round in all his movements, stretching her neck out and sinking low in the water, calling and pushing herself against his side until he responds. The male, on his part, makes a very slight "lift" in front, the bill being lowered and the neck drawn up. At the same time he inhales, and on releasing the air as he slightly sinks forward, he utters a gentle "*Pu-whoo*" or "*Aa-u*," almost a dove-like cry. At the moment the call is emitted, the mouth is slightly opened. The call of the male is repeatedly uttered and is often made without "lifting" in front. At such times the head is held forward, then erected to the normal position as the cry is given. At the moment of calling, the whole throat is somewhat distended. When a general display is in progress amongst a flock of eiders the males and females are in a constant state of movement and activity. The males often make half turns and bows toward their inamorata, and utter a high soft note like the syllable "whoop."

Lucien M. Turner found northern eiders very abundant in Hudson Straits; his notes say:

They were by far the most abundant duck, probably exceeding all others together. The islands of Ungava Bay are crowded with them. During the mating season the males are irascible and when the mate is chosen he carefully resents an intrusion from another male. Severe and, often fatal, encounters take place between rival males, resulting in complete defeat to the one or the other. They fight by seizing with the beak and slapping with the wings; more of a kind of wrestle in which they endeavor to get the head of the adversary under the water. When enjoying quiet the male is fond of uttering a cooing sound *Oo oo*, spreading one wing out while he rolls on his side, then recovering and kicking rapidly through the water that makes it fly on both sides. This note with a *curring* sound made in their contests are the only ones I have heard the males produce.

The immature males, during the breeding season, do not associate with the adults. They keep aloof and are usually solitary. Not until the fully adult plumage of the male is assumed does he enter into contest for the female.

Nesting.—The same observer describes two interesting nesting localities as follows:

A few miles below Mackay's Island, about 18 miles up the Koksoak River, is a deep cove on the left bank and nearly opposite "Pancake" point. I gave the name of Eider Cove to that locality from the number of eider's nests I discovered in it during my first visit there—June 17, 1883. The cove is about 400 yards deep and 75 yards wide, preserving a nearly uniform width to the head, where a lively stream dashes down over the jagged rocks. The south side is inaccessible, formed by a steep wall of granite sloping very slightly to the summit, which is about 400 feet high. The northern side or wall is composed of ledges and projections covered with rank grasses, weeds, and ferns. On these ledges and rocks 14 nests of the common eider were found. The first nest was at the base of the rock on a flat scarcely above high-tide mark. This nest contained 5 eggs. Near by were 2 other nests, one of 3, and the other of 1 egg. Farther within were 11 nests each containing from 3 to 11 eggs. Only in the nests containing the greater number of eggs were they unfitted for food. I secured 49 eggs perfectly fresh and about a dozen that were too far advanced to be eaten.

On that same trip I visited the islands off the mouth of Whale River. Here James Irvine and myself collected, in less than an hour and a half, over 500 eggs from a single island and could, doubtless, have obtained many more, but a storm was near by and and we had to make for a larger island where we could secure the heavy whaleboat we had with us. As we approached that island the number of male eiders in the surrounding water and occasional females flying from the water and settling on the land gave promise of a great nesting place. We hauled the boat on a shelving ledge and quickly scrambled to the top of the bank. Here an immense ice cake and drifted snow had collected on the edge of the bank and extended for several hundred feet in length and over 30 yards wide. The height of the seaward edge was then, June 29, over 4 feet. The dripping water and slippery rock made it difficult to surmount in our anxiety to get at the eiders, which had taken alarm and were scurring in hundreds by wing and walk from the land to the sea. In a moment a nest was found and then another and so on until hundreds were discovered. Some with 1 or 2 eggs, others with 6 or 7, these being the more numerous; others with as many as 12. Every grass patch in the depressions of the rocks was examined and the eggs put into piles to be taken to the boat. Several small ponds surrounded by high grasses which were given a luxuriant growth by the droppings of these birds where they had come to bathe or drink for many successive seasons. Among these patches were also the nests of a few Phalaropes, *Phalaropus lobatus,* which twittered and flitted before us. A single nest of a gull was also found. The nests of the eiders were so differently constructed even on this one island that it would be impossible to describe them all. The materials of which they were composed were grasses, weeds, stalks, and down. The amount of the vegetable matter depended on the particular situation of the nest, for if in the midst of plenty of such material, the nest was often several inches high, resting on a mound formed from the decayed mass of material used as a nest many years ago. At times merely a slight depression was cleared of vegetation and on the bare earth the egg was deposited and covered with down.

On my trip down the coast of Labrador in 1912 I found eiders common all along the coast from the Straits of Belle Isle northward, but generally they were so shy that it was impossible to shoot any. The largest breeding colony I saw was on one of the outer islands off the coast near Hopedale, which we visited on July 22. It was a small, low, rocky island with a very little grass and a few mosses growing in the hollows and crevices between the rocks. No male eiders were seen on or about the island, but the females began flying off as we landed and we flushed many from their nests as we walked over the flat rocks. We found between 20 and 30 nests with eggs, varying in number from 1 to 5. Some natives had visited the island a fortnight or more previously and had collected about 150 eggs; there must have been between 30 and 40 nests on the island at that time. The nests were on the ground, in the grass or moss, or in hollows between the rocks; some of them were well made, with a generous supply of pure down, but in most of them the down was mixed with grass and rubbish, and in some of the nests the supply of down was very scanty. Apparently these nests were second or third attempts at raising broods, and evidently the supply of down was becoming exhausted. A drizzling rain was falling all the time that we were on the island, so my attempts at photographing the nests were not as successful as they might have been. We shot five of the ducks as they flew from the nests, all of which proved to be the northern eider. A pair of great black-backed gulls were breeding on the island; we saw the old nest and a young gull running about, as well as the old birds flying overhead. There is generally a pair of these gulls on every island where the eiders are breeding. The natives, who rob the duck's nests regularly, never disturb the gull's nest, for they believe that if the gulls are driven off the ducks will not return to the island to lay again. They say that the black-backed gulls are good watch dogs, to warn the eiders of approaching danger and to keep away the ravens and other gulls which might rob the nests. The great black-backed gulls are notorious nest robbers and destroyers of young eiders elsewhere, but perhaps they do not indulge in highway robbery and murder so near home. Perhaps, however, the gulls do levy their toll in eggs and young eiders, which the latter are too stupid to avoid.

On the coast of Greenland the northern eider frequently nests on cliffs, according to J. D. Figgins, as the following quotation from his notes, published by Dr. Frank M. Chapman (1899) will illustrate:

It prefers the small islands lying some distance offshore, but also breeds on the mainland. Its nest is usually well up the cliffs, and in some cases quite a distance from shore. One nest containing 4 eggs was at an altitude of about 450 feet, and more than three-quarter of a mile from shore.

Dalrymple Rock is the favorite breeding place of this species, it is much broken, and the many ledges offer fine nesting sites. There is a heavy growth of grass on these ledges, and the nest, when it has been used for many years, is a depression in the sod, lined with the down from the breast of the female. As soon as incubation begins the male birds form into flocks of from 4 or 5 to 20, and seem to be always on the wing. There is a constant line of the male birds flying around Dalrymple Rock, all going in the same direction. As soon as incubation is completed, the young are transferred to the water, where they seem perfectly at ease, even when there is a heavy sea running.

Mr. Ekblaw thus describes, in his notes, a visit to one of the great breeding resorts of these birds in northern Greenland:

On June 23 and 25, 1914, we went in a whaleboat to the Eider Islands, between Wolstenholme Island and Saunders Island. These are favorite nesting places of the eiders. In normal years the islands are covered with thousands of nests, but we found a relatively small number of the birds at this time.

As we approached the largest islet of the group flock after flock of eiders flew about us, skimming fast and low over the water. The males and females seemed about equal in number. The bright-colored plumage of the male contrasts vividly in the sunlight with the dark, uniformly barred coat of the female, both awing and alight.

Numerous pairs of the eiders were swimming about in the sea or idly preening their feathers or wooing on the ice pans. Their wooing "song" very closely resembles the cooing of our domestic pigeons. The noise from a flock together in the mating season might readily be mistaken for the "music" from a dovecot. The sound is audible for a long distance; from the time we left Saunders Island until we returned we were not beyond reach of these "love songs."

As we set foot upon the islet hundreds of eiders flew about us. The snow still left on the ice foot and on the slopes of the low, rocky hills was beaten down by their footprints. We scrambled hastily over the islet in search of eggs, but found only a dozen all told, where last year on June 15 several thousand were collected. The fact that no nest held more than one egg indicated that the lateness of the season and the heavy snow on the islet had retarded the nesting season. On the other hand, it may have been that the heavy inroad upon the nests last year discouraged the return of the birds to the islet this year. They may have gone to some other, more remote islet to nest.

The eiders nest on all the small skerries and islets and many favorable places along the mainland. The Eider Islands, Dalrymple Rock, Lyttleton Island, McGarys Rock, the small islets in the bay south of Cape Hatherton, Sutherland Island, Hakluyt, and the Cary Islands are all frequented by large numbers of nesting eiders. They may nest in large numbers close together where conditions are favorable, but many nest alone far from any other companions, either on the mainland, sometimes far inland, though more frequently near the shore, or on the larger islands. Safety from depredations by foxes, jaegers, and ravens is a factor in the choice of nesting sites.

The nest of the eider is profusely lined, around, under, and sometimes over the eggs with a thick bed of soft, fluffy down, densely matted, a famous product of considerable commercial value; in color it is "drab," "light drab," or "drab gray," with poorly defined lighter centers and light tips; mixed with it are occasional bits of pure white down, dusky belly feathers, and barred breast feathers.

Eggs.—The northern eider raises but one brood in a season and lays ordinarily from 4 to 6 eggs; larger numbers have been found, even as many as 19, in one nest, but probably the larger numbers are the product of more than one female. In this connection the following notes from Mr. Turner are of interest:

The number of eggs in a nest is not always a safe index to the number of birds having made the deposit. It frequently happens that a single female will be attended by as many as five males; although it is scarcely probable that they all enjoy equal rights. One of the males is always the leader and the others appear to be entirely under his guidance. I have again, and on repeated occasions, known a single male to have as many as three females under his charge. It is, of course, difficult with these wild birds to determine whether under such circumstances two or more of these ducks have a nest in common or whether they make separate nests.

The eggs of all three of the large eiders, *mollissima, dresseri*, and *V-nigra*, are indistinguishable in size, shape, or color, so one description will serve for all three. In shape they vary from ovate to elliptical ovate. The shell is smooth, with only a slight gloss, which increases with incubation. The color varies from "olive" to "deep olive buff," or from "yellowish glaucous" to "vetiver green." The eggs are often mottled or clouded with darker shades of green, olive, or buffy olive, through which the ground color sometimes shows in washed-out spots. The measurements of 76 eggs, in various collections, average 75.4 by 50.4 millimeters; the eggs showing the four extremes measure **83** by **53**, **67.8** by 47, and 73.2 by **46** millimeters.

Young.—The period of incubation of the European eider has been ascertained by several observers to be about 28 days. It is performed wholly by the female. The males are said to desert the females at this time and form small flocks by themselves; but the following observation by Kumlien (1879) is interesting:

I have often lain behind a rock on their breeding islands and watched them for a long time. On one occasion we disturbed a large colony, and the ducks all left the nests. I sent my Eskimos away to another island, while I remained behind to see how the ducks would act when they returned. As soon as the boat was gone they began to return to their nests, both males and females. It was very amusing to see a male alight beside a nest, and with a satisfied air settle himself down on the eggs, when suddenly a female would come to the same nest and inform him that he had made a mistake—it was not his nest. He started up, looked blankly around, discovered his mistake, and with an awkward and very ludicrous bow, accompanied with some suitable explanation, I suppose, he waddled off in search of his own home, where he found his faithful mate installed.

Mr. Turner's notes state that:

The young leave the nest when about 36 hours old and immediately accompany the parent to the edge of the water. The distance to be traveled varies from a few feet to half a mile. I have not on the Atlantic coast found the nests so far from the water as were found at St. Michael, Alaska. In some instances the nest is placed on ledges that have no path by which the delicate young can reach the water excepting by plunging several feet to the next ledge or else be assisted by the parent. The latter I have not seen the old ones do or have I seen it so recorded. The young remain with the mother during the summer and probably do not leave her at all, but join with other broods to compose the flocks seen in the fall of the year. As soon as the young are hatched the males separate from the females and do not join them again until fall.

Mr. Ekblaw says in his notes:

The first nesting birds hatch their eggs soon after July 1. The most are hatched about July 15 to 20. On Sutherland Island as late as August 16, 1912, I found a nest of four eggs still hatching in a single isolated nest. In this nest one little fellow had hatched and dried, and when I flushed the mother he followed her to the water. Another little fellow just hatched was not yet dry, but even so, he sensed the alarm and tried to hide in the down with which the nest was lined. A third duckling was just cutting the shell; later in the evening when I came back to the nest he had come safely into the world. The fourth egg was not even cracked, but a vigorous peeping within the shell indicated that on the morrow the last of the brood would follow the mother into the water.

The downy little ducklings get into the water just as soon as they can. They paddle after their mothers like animated little black balls of fur, keeping always close to her. Even when tiny, they dive like a flash, and come up like a bubble. Like the oldsquaws, the eider mothers join their little flocks, and one mother leads the file while the other brings up the rear. From the time they are hatched until they leave for the South, they keep to the open sea, coming in to the shore sometimes to rest, but more frequently resting on ice floes.

While the young birds are developing in strength and ability to swim, the mothers constantly lead them southward. From mid-August to mid-September a constant procession of eiders swims outward from the bays and fjords and goes on southward. The southward flight migration is late, beginning about the 1st of September and continuing until the ice freezes, often in October. Even so, many of the young birds are still unable to fly when the fjords freeze over, and frequently flocks of them are caught by sudden freezes and imprisoned in little pools where they finally freeze tó death or fall prey to the foxes, bears, or Eskimo.

Plumages.—The downy young of the three eiders, *mollissima*, *dresseri*, and *V-nigra*, are all practically indistinguishable. The upper parts are " olive brown," deepening to " clove brown " on the crown and rump, and paling to " light drab " on the sides and to " pale drab-gray " on the throat and belly; there is a broad superciliary stripe of " light drab " or dull " wood brown " above the eyes and the cheeks, and lores are abruptly darker than their surroundings. Before the young bird is half grown the first dusky, brown-tipped feathers of the juvenal plumage appear on the flanks and scapulars; the tail feathers start next, then the breast plumage and the head; the young bird is nearly fully grown before the last of the down disappears from the upper back and rump; the wings appear last of all, so that both old and young birds are flightless together in August.

In the juvenal plumage the sexes are much alike; this plumage is worn by the young male through the fall and resembles that of the young female, but not that of the adult female. Sometimes as early as October, but more often not until December, the young male begins to differentiate by acquiring a few black feathers in the flanks and scapulars and a few white feathers on the lower neck or chest. These two colors increase in purity and extent by a practically continuous molt throughout the winter and spring, with considerable individual variation. The tail is molted during the winter, the time varying with different birds, and some white feathers appear in the scapulars and rump, in early spring or before that. By April many young males have the throat, neck, and chest almost wholly white, the back almost wholly black and white, and the head nearly all black above, but the wings and the under parts are still wholly immature; at this stage, the sea-green patch over and behind the ear coverts is often completely developed or intermixed with black and brown feathers of the first stage.

The next change takes place at the summer molt, in July and August. This is a complete molt involving a double molt of much of the contour plumage and producing a first-eclipse plumage, which Mr. Millais (1913) describes as follows:

The feathers of the whole head and neck are shed and replaced in a few days by a plumage resembling, but somewhat darker than, that of the juvenile; eye-stripe dull white with blackish markings; crown, upper parts of cheeks, and back of head and neck black; rest of cheeks and throat grey-brown; mantle and scapulars ‚ blackish-brown. In a bird killed on July 6 at Fitfulhead, Shetland, which has effected the above change, the wings, tail, and nearly all the lower parts are still in juvenile plumage, much worn and faded; the white-and-buff shield on the upper chest and its sides is replaced by a new set of feathers—white with brown-black bars, and edged with reddish-brown; the long faded scapulars are still unshed and sandy-yellow as well as the primaries.

During the fall this first eclipse plumage is replaced by the second winter plumage, which is not completed until November. This resembles the adult plumage in a general way, but it can be easily recognized by its imperfections. The center of the crown is mottled with grayish brown; the green areas on the head are paler and more restricted; the white of the back is broken by scattering dusky feathers; the lesser wing coverts are brownish and the greater wing coverts are edged with dusky, both of which are pure white in adults; the curving tertials are less developed and edged with dusky, instead of being pure white; and the under parts, which are clear, deep black in adults, are now dull, brownish black, with the anterior border broken and mottled. This plumage is worn without much change until the second eclipse plumage appears the next summer. This is less complete than the adult eclipse plumage and can be distinguished from the first eclipse by the wings. The fall molt out of this plumage produces the adult winter plumage, characterized by the pure white back, wing coverts, and curved tertials. The young bird thus becomes adult at an age of 28 or 30 months. A few birds, otherwise adult, retain signs of immaturity during their third winter, chiefly in the form of dusky-edged feathers in the cream-colored breast.

The adult male has one complete molt each year, reaching its climax in August; the plumage of the head and neck is all molted twice to produce and to replace the eclipse plumage, that of the breast and back partially twice and the rest of the plumage only once. The eclipse plumage is very striking and very interesting, as it is beautifully adapted to conceal the brilliant colors of the male during the time when he is quite incapable of flight and obliged to seek refuge by swimming and diving on the open sea. The bright colors of the head and neck are completely replaced by blacks and browns in mottled effect, a complete molt of these parts beginning in July; the white back is screened by a new growth of grayish white feathers, broadly tipped with dusky; and the breast is completely concealed by new feathers, subterminally barred with the black and tipped with brown. In the fall the winter plumage is reproduced by a complete new growth of feathers on the head and neck; the plumage of the back and the breast is restored partly by molt and partly by wearing away of the dark tips; the whole process is a beautiful illustration of the maximum of concealment with the minimum of molt.

Mr. Millais (1913) says the young female can be distinguished from the male, even in the downy stage, being "generally darker on the under parts and the eye stripe narrower and shorter." In the juvenal plumage she has a "smaller eye stripe, paler upper parts and darker upper breast." The young female remains largely in the juvenal plumage through much or all of the first winter; specimens collected in February show the molt into the first spring plumage in various stages; but by March most of the birds have acquired a semiadult plumage. In this the dull-brown feathers, with narrow sandy-brown edges, of the juvenal plumage have been replaced by the dusky or dusky-barred feathers, with broad edges of deeper and richer browns, of the adult plumage. But birds in this plumage can always be distinguished from adults by their juvenal wings, which still retain the old, worn, dusky secondaries, tertials, and long scapulars; the long, curved, brown-edged tertials and the white-tipped secondaries and secondary coverts of adults are lacking; the belly plumage also remains largely immature. At the next summer molt, which is complete, a second winter plumage is assumed, which is nearly adult; but the white tips of the secondaries and secondary coverts are smaller and narrower; and the birds are usually more heavily barred above and more uniformly dark brown below. At the next molt, when a little over 2 years old, the fully adult plumage is acquired. Some females probably breed during their second spring, but probably most of them do not do so until they are nearly 3 years old.

The foregoing account of the molts and plumages of this species will suffice equally well for the American eider and the Pacific eider, as the sequence is the same in all three species, or subspecies, and the immature plumages of all three are practically indistinguishable.

Food.—Eiders obtain their food almost wholly by diving to moderate depths; almost any kind of marine animal life is acceptable and easily digested in their powerful gizzards; most of it is found on or about the sunken ledges or submerged reefs off rocky shores, which support a rank growth of various seaweeds and a profusion of marine invertebrates. They prefer to feed at low tide when the food supply is only a few fathoms below the surface; they often dive to depths of 6 or 8 fathoms and sometimes 10 fathoms, but when forced by the rising tide to too great exertion in diving, they move off to some other feeding ground or rest and play until the tide favors them again. They are usually very regular in their feeding habits, resorting to certain ledges every day at certain stages of the tides, as long as the food supply lasts. They seem to prefer to feed by daylight and to roost on some inaccessible rock to sleep at night. Many other ducks are forced to feed at night, as they are constantly disturbed on their feeding grounds during the day; but the eider's feeding grounds are so rough and inaccessible that they are seldom disturbed. Even in rough weather these tough and hardy birds may be seen feeding about the ledges white with breakers; they are so strong and so expert in riding the waves and in dodging the breakers that they do not seem to care how rough it is. I have seen them feeding, off our eastern coasts in winter, in water so rough that no boat could approach them.

Their favorite food seems to be the common black mussel (*Mytelis edulis*), which grows in such extensive beds as to furnish abundant food for myriads of sea fowl; the eiders devour these in such large quantities that their crops are most uncomfortably distended. Periwinkles, limpets, and a great variety of other univalve and bivalve mollusks are eaten; their stomachs are crammed full of such hard-shelled food, mixed with pebbles, all of which is ground up by the strong muscular action of the stomach, assisted by the chemical action of the gastric juices; the soft parts are digested and the pulverized shells pass out through the intestines. They are said to eat small fish occasionally, as well as fish roe and that of crustaceans. Starfish, sea urchins, and crabs are eaten, even the great spider crab and other large crabs measuring 2 inches across the carapace. Mr. Millais (1913) says:

I remember once, in Orkney, running down to a flock of feeding eiders that for the moment had vanished beneath the waves. One rose near the boat with something like a thick stick projecting 5 or 6 inches from its mouth, which it was unable to close. I shot the bird, an old female, and found that the obstruction, when drawn out, was a razor shell (*Ensis siliqua*), 10 inches long and 3 inches in circumference. How any bird, even with the digestion of a sea duck, could assimilate so tough a morsel with a hard and thick shell seemed a marvel, but it is doubtless the case that they are able to break them up and eject the shells as pellets.

Kumlien (1879) writes:

Their food in autumn consists almost entirely of mollusks. I have taken shells from the oesophagus more than 2 inches in length; from a single bird I have taken out 43 shells, varying from one-sixteenth to 2 inches in length.

The adult birds in spring did not seem to be quite so particular; in them I found almost all the common forms of marine invertebrates, and sometimes even a few fish (*Liparis*, and the young of *Cottus scorpius*).

Mr. Andrew Halkett (1905) found the following material in the gizzards of some 20 eiders:

Numerous shells of *Acmaea testudinalis*, numerous fragments of valves of *Tonicella marmorata*, a few shells of *Margarita cinerea*, a number of shells of other small gastropods, a few opercula of a gastropod, egg capsules of a gastropod, numerous valves of *Crenella*, fragments of valves of various small and medium sized lamellibranchs, various parts of the shells of *Hyas* and other crustaceans, a few pieces of the arms of an ophiurian, a few bones of a very small teleost, fragments of alga, numerous small stones.

Behavior.—The flight of the northern eider is apparently slow, heavy, and labored, but in reality it is much stronger and swifter than it appears and exceedingly straight and direct. Its heavy head is held low, with the bill pointing slightly downward, a characteristic and diagnostic attitude. Eiders usually fly in small flocks, in Indian file, close to the water, often following the indentations of the shore line, but very seldom flying over the land. In rough weather a flock of eiders is apt to follow the trough of the sea and is often lost to sight between the waves. I have seen one, when shot at and perhaps wounded, dive out of the air into the water and not show itself again. It is an expert at diving and hiding below the surface; if there is only the slightest ripple on the water it can conceal itself and swim away with only a portion of its bill protruding and almost invisible.

As stated above, eiders are capable of diving to depths of 8 or 10 fathoms if necessary. In diving the wings are partially opened and used to a limited extent in swimming under water, but the wings are not wholly spread; progress seems to be made mainly by the use of the feet, and there is nothing like the full subaqueous flight practiced by some of the Alcidae. Mr. Millais (1913) relates the following interesting incident:

Personally I have the gravest doubts of the truth of the statement made by many writers that the eider and other sea ducks "hold on" to the seaweed at the bottom of the ocean rather than allow themselves to come to the surface and be shot. One morning in February, 1866, I pursued an old male eider, which I had winged from a flock, into some shallows off the island of Reisa Little, in the Orkneys. The white back of the bird could be plainly seen under water entering some dark weeds amongst small rocks near the shore. Presently it disappeared in the tangle, and as the bird did not again come to the surface I leaned over the side of the boat and made search for it. I had seen it enter a comparatively small area of dark ground round which there were sand spaces, so I concluded it must be hidden amongst the fronds, and after a short search I saw the white back gleaming beside a small rock, the head and neck being concealed under the seaweed. It occurred to me that it would be interesting to see whether the bird would voluntarily leave this position or not; so after waiting for a quarter of an hour, during which it did not move, I gave it a lift with my long seal gaff, when it at once floated to the surface quite dead. The mouth was half open; some thin weeds encircled the neck. Doubtless this bird allowed itself to be drowned, as its half-open bill showed; but that it was actually holding on to the weeds I could see no sign. I could narrate several instances of a similar character which would only tend to show that whilst the birds both voluntarily get into positions under water from which they will not move until death overtakes them and also into crannies and encircling weeds from which they can not escape owing to lack of strength, yet there is not actual proof that they hold on to the weeds at the bottom of the sea, as Naumann suggests.

Outside of the vocal performances indulged in during the mating season, eiders, particularly males, are decidedly silent birds. Mr. Turner says:

The females utter a grating croak while flying to or from their nests and a hiss while on the nest. This hissing sound gives rise to the Eskimo name of this species, Mitik.

Mr. Millais (1913) says:

In winter eiders are very silent birds, like all the sea ducks except the long-tail, and their voice is not often heard except when single individuals are searching for their friends. The male when swimming occasionally utters a hoarse, grating call like the words "*Kor-er-korkorr-kor*," and the female a slightly higher note, "*Kar-er-karkar-kaa*." The female also utters this call when she is flying.

Referring to the enemies of eiders, Mr. Millais (1913) writes:

In the winter eiders have few enemies except man, though sea eagles often attack them along the coast line in Norway, whilst the great black-backed gull has a wonderful eye for a "picked" bird and will hunt it until it falls a prey owing to exhaustion. In the summer eiders have many enemies in their Arctic home, and a few in our islands. Even in the Orkneys and Shetlands a few of the young fall a prey to both lesser and greater black-backed gulls; whilst Richardson's skua is not wholly above suspicion. In Unst the great skua has been seen to attack and swallow young eiders. In Iceland numbers of young eiders are killed by Richardson's skua, sea eagles, and a few by the Iceland falcons. Arctic foxes are not numerous here, as they are in the Russian islands, Greenland, and Labrador, where these animals levy heavy toll on the old birds on the nests as well as the young. Polar bears also kill quantities of young eiders, and will break and eat their eggs. In West Greenland the harp seal is said to catch eiders on the water, coming up and seizing them from below, and it is possible that the small whale, *Orca gladiator*, kills a few. In northeast Greenland the chief marauder of all sea birds is the glaucous gull, which creates much havoc amongst young ducks.

Dr. I. I. Hayes (1867) gives the following graphic account of the predatory habits of the glaucous gulls:

A rugged little ledge, which I named Eider Island, was so thickly colonized that we could hardly walk without treading on a nest. We killed with guns and stones over 200 birds in a few hours; it was near the close of the breeding season. The nests were still occupied by the mother birds; but many of the young had burst the shell, and were nestling under the wing, or taking their first lessons in the water pools. Some, more advanced, were already in the ice-sheltered channels, greedily waiting for the shellfish and sea urchins which the old bird busied herself in procuring for them. Near by was a low isolated rock ledge, which we called Hans Island. The glaucous gulls, those cormorants of the Arctic seas, had made it their peculiar homestead; their progeny, already fully fledged and voracious, crowded the guano-whitened rocks; and the mothers, with long necks and gaping yellow bills, swooped above the peaceful shallows of the eiders, carrying off the young birds, seemingly just as their wants required. The gull would gobble up and swallow a young eider in less time than it takes me to describe the act. For a moment you would see the paddling feet of the poor little wretch protruding from the mouth; then came a distension of the neck as it descended into the stomach; a few moments more and the young gulls were feeding on the ejected morsel.

J. D. Figgins (1902) says that, in northwest Greenland, " eider ducks are much prized by the natives and are killed by spearing from the kayak. The spear is simply a sharpened rod of iron set into the end of a light shaft. At 15 or 20 yards the hunter seldom misses his mark."

Referring to the food value of eider's eggs to the Eskimos, Dr. Donald B. MacMillan (1918) writes:

How impatiently we awaited the discovery of those first golden nuggets in the nests. Can we ever forget those annual pilgrimages to the shrine at historic Littleton and Eider Duck Islands and McGarys Rock. Here, among a laughing, jolly company of men, women, and children, we pitched our tents among the nests; we boiled eggs, and we fried eggs, and we scrambled eggs, and we shirred eggs, and we did everything to eggs. In a few hours 4,000 delicious fresh eggs were gathered from one small island alone. Cached beneath the rocks, away from the direct rays of the sun, they remain perfectly fresh; they become chilled in August; and freeze hard as so many rocks in September—a much-appreciated delicacy during the long winter months. The shells are often broken and the contents poured or squirted from the mouth of the Eskimo into the intestinal sheath of the bearded seal or the walrus, a most nutritious sausage to be eaten on the long sledge trips.

The Moravian missionaries of northern Laborador showed me some beautiful eider-down blankets which were made by the Eskimos of Greenland for sale in the Danish markets; they were made of the breasts of eiders from which the feathers had all been plucked, leaving the down on the skins, which had been cured so that they were very soft and pliable; the edges of the blankets were trimmed with the cured skins of the heads of many northern and king eiders, making very attractive borders. They were the softest, lightest, warmest, and most beautiful blankets I had ever seen, and I was told that they brought such fancy prices that they were beyond the reach of ordinary mortals. I believe the natives also use these plucked skins for winter underwear, wearing them with the down side next to the skin; eider-down underwear and Arctic-hare stockings must be very soft and warm.

The eider-down industry has never been so highly developed on the American side of the Atlantic as it has on the other side. It would undoubtedly prove a profitable industry and would also serve to protect the birds if properly conducted. The following account of how it is done in Iceland, written by C. W. Shepard, is published by Baird, Brewer, and Ridgway (1884) :

The islands of Vigr and Oedey are their headquarters in the northwest of Iceland. In these they live in undisturbed tranquility. They have become 'almost domesticated, and are found in vast multitudes, as the young remain and breed in the place of their birth. As the island (Vigr) was approached we could see flocks upon flocks of the sacred birds, and could hear their cooing at a great distance. We landed on a rocky, wave-worn shore. It was the most wonderful ornithological sight conceivable. The ducks and their nests were everywhere. Great brown ducks sat upon their nests in masses, and at every step started from under our feet. It was with difficulty that we avoided treading on some of the nests. On the coast of the opposite shore was a wall built of large stones, just above the high-water level, about 3 feet in height, and of considerable thickness. At the bottom, on both sides of it, alternate stones had been left out so as to form a series of square compartments for the ducks to nest in. Almost every compartment was occupied, and as we walked along the shore a long line of ducks flew out, one after the other. The surface of the water also was perfectly white with drakes, who welcomed their brown wives with loud and clamorous cooing. The house itself was a marvel. The earthen walls that surrounded it and the window embrasures were occupied by ducks. On the ground the house was fringed with ducks. On the turf slopes of its roof we could see ducks, and a duck sat on the door scraper. The grassy banks had been cut into square patches, about 18 inches having been removed, and each hollow had been filled with ducks. A windmill was infested, and so were all the outhouses, mounds, rocks, and crevices. The ducks were everywhere. Many were so tame that we could stroke them on their nests; and the good lady told us that there was scarcely a duck on the island that would not allow her to take its eggs without flight or fear. Our hostess told us that when she first became possessor of the island the produce of down from the ducks was not more than 15 pounds in a year; but that under her careful nurture of 20 years it has risen to nearly 100 pounds annually. Most of the eggs are taken and pickled for winter consumption, one or two only being left in each nest to hatch.

Fall.—By the middle of the summer, or as soon as the egg-laying season is over, the adult eiders desert their mates and begin to move away from their breeding grounds. This might be called the beginning of the fall migration. The immature males of the previous year keep by themselves all summer in large flocks and do not even now mingle with the old males; they spend the summer well out at sea near the drift ice. The young eiders often are late in hatching and are slow in developing, so that it is often quite late in the fall before they are able to fly away with their mothers and join the mixed flocks in their winter resorts. All have to undergo the annual summer double molt, which lasts well into the fall and delays migration, for they are absolutely flightless for a few weeks while the wing quills are molting. So the fall migration is very irregular and much prolonged; many birds spend the winter not far away from their breeding grounds, moving only far enough away to find open water and good feeding grounds.

Winter.—On the coast of Greenland many northern eiders spend the winter in the open waters of the fjords. Near Ivigtut, Hagerup (1891) observed that:

In October, 1886, the females began to come into the fjord singly, and in November they came in small flocks. As the weather grew colder the number increased, and it became still larger after Christmas, the period of greatest abundance being March and April. The males did not come in as great numbers into the fjord that winter. I saw, indeed, none at Ivigtut until March, while they were quite numerous at Christmas of the following year.

In the evening these birds generally go as far inland as there is open water, and during the night they are almost constantly on the move. Then their cries may be plainly heard, as also their splashing near the shore; but if a match be lit, they fly aloft with a great uproar.

Eiders are at all seasons essentially sea ducks, but especially so in winter. Low temperatures have no terrors for them; their winter resorts extend from Greenland to the coast of Maine, wherever they can find open water and plenty of food. Even in the roughest winter storms they brave the rigors of the open sea, riding at ease among the white caps, diving for food among the surf-swept ledges, safe from the molestation of the hardiest gunners, and retiring at night to rest on some lonely rock or drifting iceberg.

Mr. Ekblaw writes:

A few eiders stay all through the four months winter night in the open waters of Smith Sound. Like the guillemots, the eiders find sufficient food in the upwelling of the tidal currents about the Gary Islands to maintain themselves throughout the coldest winters. These strong swift tidal currents running back and forth through Smith Sound between Baffin Bay and Kane Basin prevent the formation of widespread ice, and are the controlling factor which permits a luxuriant far-Arctic plant and animal life, including a pleasant homeland for the polar Eskimo, in this habitat a thousand miles within the Arctic Circle, far beyond the usual northern limit of life.

The far northern coasts of Greenland afford a sanctuary for the eider, where this splendid species of the duck family may save itself from total extermination. To the lonely, inaccessible rocks and islets of these far northern shores, the egg hunters, and down gatherers are not likely to come in numbers enough or often enough to destroy the species. The natives are too few and the value of the eider in their economic needs is too small to constitute any serious menace to the species. Farther south, in Greenland, and elsewhere, the eider is threatened with extinction, though in Danish Greenland the Danes are vigilantly safeguarding the birds as far as it lies in their power to do so. It is fortunate that the eiders have their far northern habitats, relatively safe from man's devastation.

DISTRIBUTION

Breeding range.—Coastal islands of Greenland and northeastern America. South on the Atlantic coast of Labrador to the vicinity of Hamilton Inlet and, in the regions north of Hudson Bay, to Baffin

Land, Ungava Bay, Southampton Island, and Cape Fullerton, intergrading at these points with *dresseri*. West about 100° west longitude, where it may intergrade, somewhere in the Arctic Archipelago, with *V-nigra*. North to northern Ellesmere Land (81° 40′) and northern Greenland (82° on the west coast and 75° on the east coast). Represented in Iceland and Europe by closely allied forms.

Winter range.—South along the coast to Maine and rarely to Massachusetts. North to southern Greenland, as far as open water extends.

Spring migration.—Early dates of arrival: Labrador, Battle Harbor, May 1; Cumberland Sound, April 30; northern Greenland, Etah, April 20; Wellington Channel, latitude 76°, May 17; Cape Sabine, latitude 79°, May 28; Thank God Harbor, latitude 81°, June 4. Late dates of departure: Massachusetts, April 3; Maine, April 6.

Fall migration.—Early dates of arrival: Maine, October 19; Massachusetts, late October. Late dates of departure: Thank God Harbor, November 4; Etah, November 1; Cumberland Sound, November 17.

Egg dates.—Labrador: Eight records, June 15 to August 2. Greenland: Two records, June 23 and July 2.

SOMATERIA MOLLISSIMA DRESSERI (Sharpe)

AMERICAN EIDER

HABITS

Contributed by Charles Wendell Townsend

The eider is a duck of which the Americans should well be proud. Large and splendid in plumage, interesting in courtship display, pleasing in its love notes, susceptible to kind treatment by man, and capable of furnishing him with a product of great value; notwithstanding all this, the bird is so incessantly persecuted, especially on its breeding grounds, that it is rapidly diminishing in numbers. If the senseless slaughter is not stayed the eider will continue to diminish until it is extinct. Happily, even now there are signs of a better era. On the Maine coast—the bird's most southern breeding station—there were less than a dozen pair breeding in 1905. As a result of protection, however, through the efforts of the Audubon Society, their numbers are now increasing, and Bowdish (1909) in 1908 reported as many as 60 eiders breeding on Old Man Island alone. Farther north the persecution still goes on; on the Nova Scotia coast not more than two or three remain to breed, while on the coast of Newfoundland and of the Labrador Peninsula south of Hamilton Inlet, where they formerly bred in immense numbers, but a remnant is left. All the ornithologists from the time of Audubon to the present day who have visited the Labrador coast have bewailed the fact that the eider was singled out for destruction. In "A Plea for the Conservation of the Eider" (Townsend, 1914) occurs the following:

There is no reason why the eider, which furnishes the valuable eider down of commerce, should not be made a source of considerable income without any reduction of its natural abundance. The principle of conservation can as well be applied to the eider as to a forest. The conservation of the common eider of Europe (*Somateria mollissima*), a species that differs but very slightly from the American bird, has been practiced for many years in Iceland and Norway. The birds are rigidly protected during the nesting season and offered every encouragement. They are not allowed to be shot, and even the discharge of a gun in their vicinity is forbidden by law. Suitable nesting sites are furnished close to the houses and the birds become semi-domesticated, losing all fear of man. The people are allowed to take the eggs and down during the first of the season, but the birds are permitted to hatch out and rear a few young in order to keep up the stock. The last down is taken after the birds have left.

Many quotations are given from various authors showing what is being accomplished in Iceland and Norway. For example (Annandale, 1905):

The one offense against the Icelandic bird laws which a native can not commit with impunity is the slaughter of the eider duck. What is more important than many laws, namely public opinion, protects the species, and there seems to be a sentimental interest in it. Probably it is due to the great tameness of the bird, which appears actually to seek the vicinity of a human dwelling for its nesting place and to frequent those parts of the coast which are more frequented by man. The Icelandic eider farms are frequently situated on little islands off the coast. Small circular or oblong erections of rough stones are made among the hummocks, to protect the brooding ducks from wind and driving rain. All the sea fowl in these farms become exceedingly tame, as no gun is allowed to be fired and everything liable to disturb the ducks is carefully banished. Those who know how to handle them can even stroke the backs of the ducks as they sit on their eggs. On such farms there is a separate building or large room entirely devoted to cleaning the down. It was formerly the custom to take away all the down supplied by the female; but this practice was said to lead to great mortality among the ducks through exhaustion, and nowadays each nest is generally rifled only once before the eggs are hatched, and then again after the young have left it.

Townsend (1914) then goes on to say:

Eiderdown is not only extremely light and elastic but is also one of the poorest conductors of heat. It is therefore an ideal substance for preserving warmth and is the best material for coverlets, puffs, cushions, etc. Its money value is considerable, and there is always a demand for it in the markets of the world. The down obtained from dead eiders, however, soon loses its elasticity and is of little value. The retail price in Boston at the present time of well-cleaned Iceland or Norwegian eiderdown is $14 a pound. It is probable that each nest furnishes—as a very conservative estimate—from an ounce to an ounce and a third of down; therefore 12 to 16 nests or breeding females are needed for each pound. Burton states that the annual supply of down in Iceland rose from 2,000 pounds in 1806 to 7,000 pounds in 1870. One can easily understand the great value of this product even if the producer receives only one-half of the retail price. He could count on at least 50 cents a season for each breeding female in his eider fold.

Imagine the pleasure as well as the profit that could be obtained along the coast of Labrador, Newfoundland, Nova Scotia, and Maine if these birds were treated in the manner above described and flocked and nested about the habitations of man. Then, each dweller in suitable localities by the sea could have his own flock of these beautiful birds, for the female is as beautiful in her modest dress of shaded and pencilled brown as is the male in his striking raiment of jet black and cream and snow white, delicate sea green and dark navy blue. The cooing notes, so long few or absent in many places, would again resound over the waters, and best of all, to the practical minded, the birds would pay well for their protection by gifts of eggs and of valuable eider down.

How can the present senseless habit of destruction be stopped and this desirable state of affairs brought about? As a preliminary step in Labrador and Newfoundland, I would suggest that a few islands scattered along the coast should be made bird reservations, and carefully guarded by one or two families who live on or near the islands. These people should be allowed to take the first set of eggs and down, as well as the down left behind after the duck has hatched out the second set and has left for the season, but should not be allowed the use of firearms, and their Eskimo dogs must be confined during the nesting season. In other words, these people must not frighten the birds and must treat them kindly. The object of the experiment should be spread broadcast along the coast with the request for fair play, so as to restrain others from poaching and frightening the ducks on the reservation.

The rapidity with which the birds will respond to this treatment and the intelligence they will display in the recognition of the safety spots will surprise the people. This is the case wherever bird reservations are established. At Ipswich, Massachusetts, the shores of a small, protected pond are thronged with shore birds of many species which display almost no fear of man, while on the neighboring beaches, where they are shot, they are very wary. In the city of Boston the Charles River Basin and Jamaica Pond are the resort of numerous ducks that pay but little attention to the people, while in the sea and ponds near by, where shooting is allowed, the ducks show their usual wildness.

It is useless to pass laws if they are not observed or if the sentiment of the community is against them. This reform, which will be of such great value to our northern seacoast, can only be accomplished by education, and these bird reservations with their eider farms will be one of the best means to that end.

Spring.—The spring migration occurs on the New England coast in the latter part of March or early in April. The birds have been wintering south to Nantucket and in rare cases to Delaware and Virginia. The adult males go north two or three weeks or a month ahead of the females and immature. In the latter part of May and early in June we found them abundant on the southern coast of the Labrador Peninsula. Some of them were nesting, but it was probable that many of them were on their way farther north along the coast.

Courtship.—The courtship of the eider has a certain resemblance to that of the goldeneye, but it is not so spectacular. It can be observed during the latter part of May and in June along the southern coast of the Labrador Peninsula. It is thus described by Doctor Townsend (1910):

The actual courtship of the eider may be recognized from afar by the love note of the male, which can be expressed by the syllables *aah-ou* or *ah-ee-ou*, frequently repeated, and, while low and pleasing in tone, its volume is so great that it can be heard at a considerable distance over the water. On a calm day when there were many eiders about, the sound was almost constant. While the syllables *aah-ou* express very well the usual notes, there is much variation in tone, from a low and gentle pleading to a loud and confident assertion. In fact, the tones vary much as do those of the human voice, and there is a very human quality in them, so much so that when alone on some solitary isle I was not infrequently startled with the idea that there were men near at hand.

But the showy drake eider does not depend on his voice alone; he displays his charms of dress to best advantage and indulges in well-worn antics. It always seemed to me a pity that the magnificent black belly should disappear when the drake is swimming on the water, and the bird evidently shares my sentiment, for during courtship he frequently displays this black shield by rising up in front, so that at times in his eagerness he almost stands upon his tail. To further relieve his feelings he throws back his head and occasionally flaps his wings. The movements of the head and neck are an important part of the courtship, and although there is considerable variation in the order and extent of the performance, a complete antic is somewhat as follows: The head is drawn rigidly down, the bill resting against the breast; the head is then raised up until the bill points vertically upward, and at this time the bill may or may not be opened to emit the love notes. Directly after this the head is occasionally jerked backward a short distance, still rigidly, and then returned to its normal position. All this the drake does swimming near the duck, often facing her in his eagerness, while she floats about indifferently, or at times shows her interest and appreciation by facing him and throwing up her head a little in a gentle imitation of his forcefulness.

In walking around the shore of Eskimo Island, one of the Mingan group of southern Labrador, on June 3, 1909, we found the water everywhere dotted with these splendid birds, all intent on courtship. In one cove there were 104 birds, in another 80. Only one eider was in partially immature plumage. The birds were for the most part in pairs, but there were frequent groups of 3 or 4 males ardently courting 1 female. There were also occasional coteries of 15 or 20 where the sexes were about evenly divided.

Nesting.—It is evident that the eider prefers to nest in communities, but where diminished in numbers from persecution they nest singly. On some small islands off the southern coast of Labrador we found, in 1909, 20 or 30 nests in the space of an acre; this, too, when the birds were much harassed and evidently less numerous than in former years. The nests are placed on the ground, generally close to salt water and almost always on islands; we have found them, however, a hundred yards or more from the water. The nesting site may be open to the sky in a depression among the rocks of a barren island, but it is often partially or wholly concealed among and under spruce, alder, and laurel bushes or in the grass and rushes.

Mr. Harrison F. Lewis (1922) refers to a nest which he found in an unusual situation, as follows:

On June 24 I found an eider's nest with six eggs on a bush-covered rock in the midst of the second falls of the Kegashka River, more than a mile from the sea. In an expansion of the river near by I saw seven female eiders swimming about. Residents of the vicinity informed me that considerable numbers of young eiders descended this river each autumn. It would be interesting to know just how and at what age the young eiders from the nest which I found left their birthplace, situated as it was in the midst of a foaming cataract.

The nest itself is made of seaweeds, mosses, sticks, and grasses matted together, but is chiefly distinguished for the famous eider down which is plucked by the mother from her breast. The down is of a dull gray color, very soft, light, and warm, and is supplied in such liberal amounts that the eggs can be entirely covered when the sitting bird is absent. If the departure of the mother is sudden and forced, the eggs are left exposed. The female can supply plenty of down for two sets if the first is stolen, but the story that the male is called upon to supply down for the third set is not true, for he does not go near the nest. The down is rarely clean, as it generally contains bits of moss, twigs, and grasses. If the nests are repeatedly robbed of their down the poor bird is obliged to use other material in its place, and some of the nests under these circumstances at the end of the season are practically destitute of down.

Eggs.—Under normal circumstances only one set of eggs is laid. Five eggs constitute a setting which, however, varies from 4 to 6 and in one instance, that came under our observation, to 7 eggs.

The eggs are nearly oval in shape, of a rough and lusterless exterior, as if the lime had been put on with a coarse brush. Their color is a pale olive green with patches and splashes of dull white. Sometimes their color is pale brownish or olive. The measurements of 59 eggs in various collections average 76 by 50.7 millimeters; the eggs showing the four extremes measure **83.5** by **54.8, 65** by 44.5, and 66.4 by **41.5** millimeters.

[AUTHOR's NOTE.—As the eggs, young, and plumage changes of the common eider are exactly like those of the northern eider, no further attempt will be made to describe them here, and the reader is referred to what has been written on this subject under the fore-going subspecies.]

Young.—The period of incubation is 28 days, and the incubation is performed only by the female. The young as soon as hatched are led to the water by the female, who is also said to help them over difficult places by carrying them in her bill. From the first they are expert divers in shallow water, and are assiduously tended by the mother who draws them from danger, or acts the part of the wounded duck to distract attention while they hide among the rocks or in the grass. The downy young are of grayish brown color, lighter on the belly. There is a pale line along the side of the head over and under the eye.

Plumages.—In his full nuptial plumage the male eider is a splendid sight, a very conspicuous object. It has been said by Thayer that the drake's plumage is in reality concealing, as the white matches the snow, the green and dark blue the ice and the water, and the black the rocky cliffs. But to one who is familiar with the bird, either among snow and ice, on the open sea, or under the beetling crags, on rocks or among mosses and dwarf spruces of the northern bogs, such an idea does not appeal, for the bird is always conspicuous. The display he makes of his plumage in courtship, and the fact that he retires after this season is over into the eclipse plumage which is similar to that of the female, is good proof—if proof were needed—that the courtship dress is for show only and not for protection. The eclipse plumage worn by the males and the nearly similar brown plumage of the females and young is indeed an inconspicuous one, and the birds wearing this are to a large extent protectively colored. I have almost stepped on the nesting female and did not see her until she ran from the nest; and at a distance on the ocean, one may see a band of eiders of which only the males are visible until a nearer approach, when one is surprised to find an equal number of females.

After the nesting season is over the males retire to the outer islands and rocks, where they are for a time unable to fly owing to the extensive molt into the eclipse plumage. According to Audubon the sterile females molt at the same time, but the females with broods do not molt until fully two weeks later.

With rare exceptions all the eiders in the region of the Mingan Islands in southern Labrador we found to be in full adult plumage in the last half of May and the first half of June. In the first half of July, on the southern part of the eastern coast, many birds were seen that were molting from the nuptial drake plumage into the eclipse, while in the last part of July and early in August, in the Mingan region, we found nearly all the eiders to be in the brown plumage; only a very few showed traces of the brilliant nuptial dress of the drakes. Native hunters say that the drakes leave the coast about the last of July, but it is probable that this is apparent only, and that the brown birds are females and immature birds of both sexes, as well as adult drakes in the eclipse plumage. The change from the eclipse to the nuptial plumage occcurs in November and December and from the immature to the first nuptial dress in the spring, after the 1st of March. It probably takes three years before the full drake plumage is acquired, although there is considerable variation in this.

Eiders with V-shaped marks under the chin suggestive of *Somateria v-nigra* of the Pacific coast have been reported on the Atlantic coast by W. A. Stearns (1883). Arthur H. Norton (1897) says that "the black lancet is a character of frequent occurrence in the young drakes of *S. dresseri*, and there are strong reasons for the belief that it occurs in *S. mollisima borealis*." He describes four specimens where the mark occurs in *S. dresseri*. He states that they are all immature birds and "show nothing than can be considered as of a hybridic nature."

Food.—The favorite food of the eider is the edible mussel (*Mytelis edulis*), although various other mollusks, crustaceans, echinoderms, and worms are taken with avidity. Mr. Mackay (1890) reports the finding of sculpin spawn in the stomach of the eider. Such food is particularly abundant around rocky ledges, and the birds gather there from all sides during the day, but toward evening they fly out to sea to spend the night.

Behavior.—The eider is an expert diver and uses the wings under water. This is evident from the fact that it flaps open the wings for the first stroke. If alarmed when diving it often comes out of the water flying, merely changing from subaqueous to aerial flight.

Floating or swimming on the water, the head and neck are generally drawn down as if resting at ease. When on the alert the neck is stretched up and is much elongated. The tail is often cocked up at an angle.

The flight of the eider is generally close to the water, swift and powerful, but in the absence of a head wind the bird often flaps along the surface of the water for several yards before it is able to rise. The neck is stretched out and the bill is pointed obliquely downward at an angle of 45°, a field mark of some value in the recognition of the bird.

The speed of flight was estimated by Cartwright (1792), who recorded it in his Labrador Journal, as follows:

In my way hither I measured the flight of the eider ducks by the following method, viz, on arriving off Duck Island, 6 miles distant from Henry Tickle, I caused the people to lie on their oars, and when I saw the flash of the guns, which were fired at a flock of ducks as they passed through, I observed by my watch how long they were in flying abreast of us. The result of above a dozen observations ascertained the rate to be 90 miles an hour.

The male, aside from his courtship notes or love song already described, appears to be a silent bird. The female utters at times a rolling quack or a succession of sharp *kuk kuk kuks;* the latter is heard when she is suddenly disturbed at the nest.

The great black-backed gull is probably the greatest enemy of the eider, aside from the arch enemy, man. Nesting in the same region and having a voracious progeny to support this gull takes frequent opportunities of pillaging the nest and capturing the downy young. The raven also eats both eggs and young. Another enemy, which is now entirely extirpated from the Labrador region south of Hamilton Inlet, is the polar bear. Cartwright (1792) gives several instances of their depredations. He says in his Journal, under date of June 18, 1777:

On examining the paunches of the bears (an old bitch polar bear and her cub), found them well filled with eggs. I had often heretofore observed that all the nests upon an island had been robbed and the down pulled out, but I did not know till now how those things happened.

Winter.—In the fall migration eiders arrive on the New England coast late in November or early in December. The eider winters throughout its range wherever there is open water and as far south regularly as Nantucket, rarely as far as Delaware and Virginia. Along the Maine coast it is still abundant in winter, although its numbers are much reduced over those of former days. On the Massachusetts coast the eider may be found off Cape Ann and Cape Cod, and especially in the tempestuous and shallow seas about Nantucket.

Mackay (1890) records the shooting of 87 eiders in a December day in 1859 by one man near the Salvages, small rocky islands off Rockport, on the end of Cape Ann. I was told that in 1875 a hundred eiders were shot there by a gunner in January. Of late years one is lucky to find any, but on March 14, 1909, I saw a flock of 17 near the Salvages. Mackay (1890) says that as the birds come in to feed in the morning they alight some distance outside these rocks and swim in in a compact body. They dive for the mussels outside the breakers. On March 18, 1875, he saw a flock between Muskeget and Nantucket Islands that he estimated contained 12,000 birds, and a flock near the harbor of Nantucket in 1890 of about 1,500. In March, 1894, he estimated about 200 eiders near Muskeget and 2,000 near Cape Poge, Marthas Vineyard. Also between 4,000 and 5,000 near Woods Hole, attracted by the great beds of the edible mussel.

Game.—Eiders are shot in winter off the Maine coast from blinds among the rocks off the islands and occasionally from boats. Wooden decoys are used and the sport requires much energy and endurance in the winter seas. The birds are very shy, easily taking alarm, and with their strong flight and well-made armor of thick feathers and down are very difficult to kill. Cripples are rarely recovered, as they escape by rapid diving and long swimming under water. Their value for down should, however, preserve them from persecution at all seasons.

DISTRIBUTION

Breeding range.—Islands along the coasts of Labrador (south of Hamilton Inlet), Newfoundland, eastern Quebec (north shore of the Gulf of St. Lawrence), Nova Scotia, and Maine (west to Penobscot Bay). Also in the southern half of Hudson Bay and James Bay at least as far north as Richmond Gulf, Southampton Island, and Cape Fullerton. It intergrades with *borealis* at the northern limits of its breeding range.

Winter range.—Northeastern coasts, from Newfoundland and the Gulf of St. Lawrence south regularly to Massachusetts (Vineyard Sound and Nantucket), rarely to New Jersey, and casually farther south.

Spring migration.—Northward movement starts late in March or early in April. Usual date of departure from Massachusetts is about April 20; unusually late dates are, Connecticut, Milford, May 29; Massachusetts, May 18.

Fall migration.—Early dates of arrival in Massachusetts: Essex County, September 20; Cohasset, September 18; usual date of arrival is early in November.

Casual records.—Inland wanderings have occurred as far west as Wisconsin (Lake Koshkonong, November, 1891), Iowa (Sioux City, November 1, 1901), and Colorado (Loveland).

Egg dates.—Labrador Peninsula: Twenty-five records, May 26 to July 9; thirteen records, June 5 to 20. Maine, New Brunswick and Nova Scotia: Ten records, May 25 to July 5; five records, June 12 to July 1.

SOMATERIA V-NIGRA Gray

PACIFIC EIDER

HABITS

The common eider of the Pacific coast is closely related to the eiders of the Atlantic coast, perhaps more closely than its present status in nomenclature would seem to indicate. The ranges of the Pacific eider and the northern eider on the Arctic coasts of North

America come very close together and perhaps overlap, with a good chance for hybridizing or intergrading as subspecies.

Some interesting specimens have been taken in eastern waters which are worth considering. Hagerup (1891) mentions specimens of *Somateria mollissima*, taken by Holboell in Greenland, which showed the black lancet-shaped figure on the throat so characteristic of *S. v-nigra*. Holboell supposed that these were hybrids with *S. spectabilis* which also has this black **V**. Mr. Arthur H. Norton (1897) obtained several specimens of immature males of *S. dresseri* on the coast of Maine, from which he inferred "that the black lancet is a character of frequent occurrence in the young drakes of *S. dresseri;* and there are strong reasons for the belief that it occurs in *S. mollissima borealis*." Mr. W. A. Stearns (1883) obtained similar specimens on the coast of Labrador and even recorded the Pacific eider as of regular occurrence there. The occasional appearance of this mark in immature males might perhaps indicate an occasional cross between two species, but it seems more reasonable to regard it as a reversion to an ancestral type, which would mean that at some date, probably not very remote, these three eiders belonged to a single species and perhaps even now they are merely intergrading subspecies. In this connection I would refer the reader to Dr. Charles W. Townsend's (1916a) interesting paper and plate showing intergradation between *S. mollissma borealis* and *S. dresseri.*

Whatever the systematic status of the Pacific eider may prove to be, its habits and its lift history are practically the same as those of the Atlantic species, and nearly everything that has been written about the latter would apply equally well to the former. Therefore I shall not attempt to write a full life history of this species, which would be largely repetition.

Nesting.—By the time that we reached the Aleutian Islands, early in June, the vast horde of eiders that winter in the open waters of this region had departed, to return to their extensive breeding grounds farther north. But we found the Pacific eider well distributed, as a breeding bird, on all of the islands west of Unalaska. They were particularly abundant about Kiska Harbor in small flocks and mated pairs. They frequented the rocky beaches at the bases of the cliffs, where they sat on the loose rocks, fed in the kelp beds about them, and built their nests among the large boulders above high-water mark. Here on June 19, 1911, I examined two nests of this species; one, containing 5 fresh eggs, was concealed in a hollow under or between two tufts of tall, rank grass which grew back of a large boulder on the beach at the foot of a high grassy cliff; the other, containing 4 fresh eggs, was hidden in the long grass at the top of a steep grassy slope; both nests were well supplied with down.

A pair of Peale falcons were flying about some cliffs, and probably had a nest, not very far from where we found these eiders' nests. This reminds me of what Mr. Lucien M. Turner (1886) says, on this subject:

> Another peculiarity that was brought to my notice by a native, was that these birds (the eiders) usually seek some slope where the duck hawk has its nest on the high point forming one end of the slope. This was true in three instances that came under my observation. The eiders were more numerous in such localities than otherwise. The natives always are glad when the hawk comes screaming overhead, as the canoe is being paddled along the shore, for they know the nest of the hawk is near and that many nests of the eider will be found close by.

About St. Michael the nesting habits of the Pacific eider are some-what different. Dr. E. W. Nelson (1887) says:

> Their courtship must be conducted before the birds reach the breeding ground, as I have never seen any demonstrations such as are usual among mating birds. The small flocks seen at first glance give place at once to soli-tary pairs, which resort to the salt marshes. The nesting site is usually a dry spot close to a small pond or a tide creek and not often in close proximity to the seashore. The moss-grown slope of some small knoll, a grassy tussock, or a depression made on an open flat, but hidden by the thin growth of sur-rounding vegetation, are all chosen as nest sites.
> The first evening after my arrival at St. Michael I walked back on the flat about 200 yards from the fort and put up a female from 5 fresh eggs. The nest was thickly lined with down and concealed by dwarf willows and other low Arctic vegetation. This was the only instance noted by me where the nest was so near human habitations. The nest is usually lined with dead grasses and sometimes fragments of moss when the first egg is laid, and the down is added as the eggs multiply. The male is a constant attendant of the female until her eggs are nearly all deposited, when he begins to lose interest in family affairs, and dozens of them may be found at all hours sunning them-selves upon the long reefs about shore, and if we are behind the scenes on the marshes they may be seen flying silently back to their partners as the dusky twilight of night approaches from 8 to 10 in the evening.

Mr. F. Seymour Hersey contributes the following notes:

> Unlike the spectacled, Steller, and king eiders, which spend considerable time and frequently nest among the tundra ponds some distance back from salt water, I found the Pacific eider to be almost exclusively a bird of the seacoast during the breeding season. About St. Michael Bay, portions of the shore of which is covered by volcanic rocks, these birds were quite abundant and were often seen about the rocky island at the entrance to the "canal," swimming in the surf or resting on the rocks and preening their feathers. They were also frequently met with in pairs flying up or down the canal near the entrance, but did not seem to follow it farther than the point where it begins to narrow, a mile or so from the bay. The land at this point is 6 or 7 feet above the reach of normal high tides, level, and quite dry, and with very few ponds. The ground is thickly and softly carpeted with a growth of mosses, creeping vines, and such Arctic vegetation as is common to this region. Here the birds nest, making a deep cup-like hollow in the thick mosses, the edge flush with the surface and abundantly lined with a thick wall of soft gray down.

Apparently the most extensive breeding grounds of this species are in the vicinity of Franklin and Liverpool Bays, where MacFarlane (1891) collected and sent to Washington over a thousand eggs. He says:

The nest is usually a shallow cavity in the ground, more or less plentifully lined with down. We found some nests on a sloping bank at a distance of 300 or more feet from the sea. Others were also on the mainland, but the bulk of those secured by us were obtained from sandy islets in the bays.

Eggs.—The Pacific eider has been credited with laying anywhere from 5 to 10 eggs, but probably the larger sets are exceptional. The eggs are indistinguishable in every way from those of *mollissima borealis* and *dresseri*, so I will not attempt to describe them here. The measurements of 85 eggs in the United States National Museum and the writer's collections average 75.9 by 50.4 millimeters; the eggs showing the four extremes measure **86.5** by 52, 74.5 by **55.5**, **70** by 48.5 and 71.5 by **47** millimeters.

Young.—Although incubation is performed wholly by the female, and although the male usually deserts the female after the eggs are all laid, he sometimes remains near her during the process of incubation and may help to guard the nest or young.

Doctor Nelson (1887) says:

From the 15th to the 20th of June nearly all the males desert their partners and are thenceforth found at sea or about outlying reefs and islands in large flocks, as already described. Toward the end of June the first young appear, but the majority are not hatched until the first of July. As the young are hatched they are led to the nearest large pond or tide creek and thence to the sheltered bays and mouths of streams on the seacoast. About this time the females lose their quill feathers and, like the young, are very expert in diving at the flash of a gun. At this time the Eskimo amuse themselves by throwing spears at the young, but the latter are such excellent divers that they are rarely hit. As a rule the young do not fly before the 10th of September, and broods with the female are often seen unable to fly even later.

Mr. Hersey's notes on the young of this species say:

When the young are hatched the female leads her brood to some small pond or lagoon just back from the coast, and apparently they do not take to the open sea or even the outer bays until well grown. I never saw any young birds on St. Michael Bay until they had become strong on the wing. A female with a brood of young was found in a small lagoon just back from the beach on Stuart Island on July 8, 1915. In her endeavors to lead her brood to safety the mother bird was absolutely fearless. I stood on the bank within 30 feet of her and watched for about 20 minutes. She splashed about in the water, making quite a commotion, all the while calling in a low guttural tone. Some of the young swam around her while others dove. Those that went under seemed unable to stay down more than the smallest fraction of a minute and reappeared almost instantaneously, bobbing up as buoyantly as corks. After considerable difficulty she got her brood around her and started to swim away, but the young did not follow and, after swimming some 12 or 15 feet and calling, she returned and the performance was repeated.

Whether the actions of the young were due to panic or inability to realize the presence of danger I could not tell, but they appeared to me to be decidedly stupid. I know of no other duck, not excepting the oldsquaw, which at times seems to be devoid of any sense of danger, that would not have led her young to safety in a fraction of the time it took this eider.

Plumages.—The downy young are absolutely indistinguishable, so far as I can see, from those of either *mollissima* or *dresseri*, and the molts and plumages of all three are practically identical.

Mr. Hersey secured for me a fine specimen of an adult male in full eclipse plumage, of which he says, in his notes:

The molt of the males into eclipse plumage takes place during July, and by August 1 the birds are flightless. This flightless period is probably spent on the open sea where they are practically safe. On August 11, 1915, a bird in full eclipse plumage was secured on St. Michael Bay. The new primaries were about 3 inches long, but the bird was still unable to fly. Its diving and swimming powers fully compensated for its loss of flight, and it was captured only after more than four hours' pursuit, when a mistake in judgment brought it to the surface, after a long dive, within range of our boat.

Food.—The Pacific eider apparently does not differ from its Atlantic relative in its food and feeding habits.

Behavior.—Pacific eiders have similar enemies and as meekly submit to their depredations as do their eastern relatives. MacFarlane (1891) saw a snowy owl eating the eggs in an eider's nest. Mr. Turner (1886) writes:

The bird is very shy except when on land during boisterous weather. At that time the natives of the western islands of the Aleutian chain used small handnets to throw over the birds as they sat stupidly on the shore. A bright night with a hard gale of wind was the best time to secure them. The birds then sit in a huddle and many are caught at one throw of the net. The natives assert that the common hair seals catch these birds when on the water and drag them under to play with them; hence, these birds are constantly on the alert for seals and take flight as soon as a seal is discovered near .

Winter.—The Pacific eider has a more decided migration than the Atlantic species, for, though it breeds abundantly on the Arctic coast of Alaska and eastward to the Coppermine River, it is not known to winter north of Bering Straits, as there is no open water to be found in this portion of the Arctic Ocean. The main winter resort of the Pacific eider is in the vicinity of the Aleutian Islands, though it has been detected in winter as far north as the Diomedes. This means a migration route of about 2,000 miles from the remotest breeding grounds. On the other hand, the birds which breed in the Aleutian Islands and south of the Alaska Peninsula probably do not migrate far from their breeding grounds.

DISTRIBUTION

Breeding range.—Coasts of northwestern America and northeastern Asia. East to Coronation Gulf and west to Cape Irkaipij, Siberia. South on both coasts of Bering Sea to the Commander and Aleutian Islands, and eastward along the south side of the Alaskan Peninsula to Kodiak Island and Cook Inlet (Chugachick Bay). North to Banks Land (Cape Kellett) and Victoria Land (Walker Bay). It may intergrade with *borealis* at the eastern extremity of its breeding range, in the vicinity of 100° west longitude.

Winter range.—Mainly in the vicinity of the Aleutian Islands and the Alaska Peninsula, extending but little south of its breeding range and north as far as open water extends, sometimes as far as the Diomede Islands.

Spring migration.—Early dates of arrival: Alaska, Point Hope, April 15; Point Barrow, May 16; and Demarcation Point, May 26; northeastern Siberia, May 28. Usual date of arrival at St. Michael, Alaska, is from May 10 to 20.

Fall migration.—Birds which breed in Coronation Gulf leave in September and migrate about 2,000 miles. Last seen at Point Barrow November 4.

Casual records.—Has wandered as far south on the Pacific coast as Washington (Tacoma, January 6, 1906), and has been recorded a number of times in the interior of Canada, as follows: Severn House, 1858; Fort Resolution, 1861; Fort Good Hope, June 14 and 30, 1904; and Manitoba (Giroux, November 11, 1911, and Lake Manitoba, October 23, 1911).

Egg dates.—Arctic Canada: Thirty records, June 6 to July 15; fifteen records, July 2 to 8. Alaska: Sixteen records, June 10 to July 12; eight records, June 20 to 29.

SOMATERIA SPECTABILIS (Linnaeus)

KING EIDER

HABITS

Although generally regarded as one of the rarer ducks and although comparatively few naturalists have ever seen it in life, this beautiful and showy species is astonishingly abundant in certain portions of its northern habitat. Among the vast hordes of wild fowl which migrate in the spring from Bering Sea, through the straits, to their Arctic summer homes the king eider takes a prominent and a conspicuous place, as the following observations by Mr. John Murdoch (1885), at Point Barrow, will illustrate:

This is by all means the most abundant bird at Point Barrow. Thousands hardly describes the multitudes which passed up during the great migrations, within sight of the station, and yet equally great numbers passed up along the

" lead " of open water several miles off shore. They appear in the spring before there is any open water except the shifting " leads " at a distance from the shore, and travel steadily and swiftly past Cape Smythe to the northeast, following the coast. Some flocks cross to the eastward below Point Barrow, but the majority follow the barrier of grounded ice past the point. It is probable, however, that they turn to the east after passing Point Barrow, because all the returning flocks in the autumn come from the east, hugging the shore of the mainland.

The first ducks in the spring of 1882 were seen on April 27, a comparatively warm day, with a light southerly wind blowing. They were flying parallel to the coast over the barrier of grounded ice. The natives said they were all " kingaling," "nosy birds," or males (referring to the protuberance at the base of the bill), and the first flocks of the migration appear to be composed exclusively of males. There were six great flights in 1882, the first on May 12 and the last on June 11, and five in 1883, the first on May 17 and the last on June 4.

As a rule, these flights took place on comparatively warm days, with light westerly or southwesterly winds. On one day each year, however, there was a large flight with a light breeze from the east. A warm southwest wind is pretty sure to bring a large flight of eiders. The flight seldom lasts more than two or three hours, beginning about 8 or 9 in the morning, or between 3 and 4 in the afternoon. More rarely a flight begins about 10 in the morning and lasts till afternoon. During the flights, the great flocks in quick succession appear to strike the coast a few miles from the station, probably coming straight across from the Seahorse Islands, and then follow up the belt of level ice parallel to the coast toward Point Barrow, going pretty steadily on their course, but swerving a little and rising rather high when alarmed. Their order of flight was generally in long diagonal lines, occasionally huddling together so that several could be killed at one discharge. A few flocks in a great flight usually followed up the line of broken ice a mile or two from the shore, and a flock occasionally turned in at the mouth of the lagoon and proceeded up over the land.

He further says:

The majority of them are paired by the middle of May, and the flocks are made up of pairs flying alternately, ducks and drakes. If a duck is shot down, the drake almost immediately follows her to the ice, apparently supposing that she has alighted.

Mr. W. Elmer Ekblaw contributes the following notes on his observations in northern Greenland:

The most strikingly beautiful of all the Arctic birds is undoubtedly the male king eider. His regal plumage warrants fully his royal name. He is almost as rare as he is royal. Only a relatively small number of his gorgeous family appears to be left, if ever it was plentiful. His mate is soberly dressed, quite undistinguishable from her cousin, the female of the common eider.

The king eiders reach the Smith Sound shores somewhat later in the season than do the common eiders. Because the males are so conspicuous they attract immediate attention; and since my first record for them is June 22, I feel confident that they do not arrive much earlier than that date. Probably June 15 would be a reasonable date for their first appearance in the land of the polar Eskimo. I can not say with certainty that the females arrive as early as the males, but I am inclined to think that they do, because the first males that we recorded were apparently paired with females. I believe that the king eiders are paired when they arrive, and that the sexes arrive together.

When the king eiders arrive, the inland ponds are already open, and to these fresh-water pools the king eiders go at once. They do frequent the open sea somewhat, but their favorite haunts through the mating and nesting season are the inland lakelets.

Courtship.—Mr. W. Sprague Brooks (1915) describes the courtship of this species as follows:

Once I found this species courting. On June 14, when approaching a small lagoon, but still unable to see it owing to a slight elevation of the tundra before me, I heard a strange sound on the other side of the elevation. This peculiar noise came in series of three "*Urrr-urrr-URRR,*" the last being the loudest, a sort of drumming call as when one expels air forcibly through the mouth with the tongue lightly pressed against the palate. I had heard this noise once before during the winter made by an Eskimo and used with indifferent results for encouraging his dog team. I thought this call was an invention of his own at the time, but when in sight of the lagoon I found that the disturbance came from a small flock of king eiders, three females and five males. They were on the beach, and three males were squatted in a triangle about a female, each about a yard from her. They did much neck stretching, as many male ducks do in the spring, and frequently bowed the head forward. The males constantly uttered the above drumming note. During this time the female was very indifferent to the attentions of her suitors, doing nothing more than occasionally extending her head toward one of them. After a brief period of these tactics, one or more of the males would enter the water and bathe vigorously, with much bowing of heads and stretching of necks, to return to the beach in a few moments and repeat the foregoing performance. Finally they all took wing, uttering the croaking sound similar to the Pacific eider.

Nesting.—Although the eggs of the king eider are not rare in collections, I am surprised to find that remarkably little has been published regarding the details of its nesting habits. I have three sets in my collection from Point Barrow, Alaska, but unfortunately no particulars came with them. MacFarlane secured over 200 eggs from Franklin Bay and Liverpool Bay, and says in a letter that when on Island Point, as he was walking along the sea beach, a female of this species got up and flew violently away to a short distance, where she alighted on the ground. He at once discovered her nest, which was a mere hole or depression in the ground, about 50 yards from the beach, wholly composed of eider down, and containing 6 eggs. Other nests were found on the coast during several seasons, and also among the islands of the Arctic Sea. All appear to have been similar to the one described, and 6 is the largest number of eggs mentioned as having been found in any one nest.

Messrs. Thayer and Bangs (1914) report that:

On June 26 a nest was found (by John Koren) in a tuft of grass 10 feet from the edge of a small lake on one of the islands in the delta of the Kolyma (northeastern Siberia). It contained the broken shells of two fresh eggs, evidently destroyed by a pair of glaucous gulls that were nesting nearby. The pair of eiders were swimming about in the lake.

A. L. V. Manniche (1910), on his explorations in northeastern Greenland, found two nests "on the slopes of the low rocks by the coast not far from the mouth of the river. The fresh down and eggshells proved that they had lately been inhabited." Again he states that the king eider—

always stayed in the fresh waters on the mainland, on which it undoubtedly exclusively nests. I did not succeed in finding nests with eggs, but all the old nests I found at Stormkap proved that this bird nests singly. The nests were placed on the lower slopes, with luxuriant vegetation, or on small hills in the lowland, with large stones surrounded by grass. None of the observed nests were far from the bay (as a maximum 1 kilometer).

According to Rev. C. W. G. Eifrig (1905), this species breeds commonly on the islands north of Hudson Bay and "places its soft, down-lined nest on tussocks of grass along the shores and on islands of inland ponds."

In northern Greenland Mr. Ekblaw noted that:

About July 1 the breeding season is at its height. In one day's tramp over the lake-dotted valleys about North Star Bay I saw some 20 pairs swimming about the ponds or resting on the grassy banks, feeding on the abundant life of the pools, preening their feathers, or sleeping either on land or water with their bills tucked under their wings. The birds were all paired. The females were very shy, indeed, and both females and males were shier than the old-squaws and common eiders.

The nests are placed at some distance from the pools; the nearest I found was about 200 yards from any water and 2 miles from the sea; the farthest at least a mile from any pool and 4 miles from the sea. Some of the nests were concealed in the sedges and grasses of the wet swales, usually on a hummock; some were placed in small hollows in the gravel of old glacial moraines. The nest is well-lined with down, much lighter in color than the down from the oldsquaws, and somewhat lighter than the down from the common eiders.

Rev. F. C. R. Jourdain writes to me as follows:

It is very remarkable that, although the king eider is found in fair numbers in several districts in Spitsbergen, hardly anything was known as to its breeding habits there until quite recently. The reason seems to be that it was surmised that its breeding habits were similar to those of the common eider, whereas they are really very different. While the common eider generally nests in thickly populated colonies on low flat islands in the fjords or off the coast, the king eider prefers to nest among the moss and lichen-covered expenses of flat tundra on the mainland. Instead of 100, or several hundred, nests being found crowded together on an acre or two of ground, the female king eiders are scattered over the tundra, perhaps half a mile of monotonous moorland intervening between the nests, and, as they squat closely in the moss, in most cases they are invisible till approached within a few yards. On the eider holms, too, the drakes, with their boldly contrasted plumage of black and white, stand close to the hens and always accompany them when they leave the nest to wash and feed, while, on the other hand, the male king eiders are never seen in the vicinity of the nest, but after the ducks have begun to sit they congregate in flocks and haunt the open fjords. When the young are hatched out the female king eiders lead them to some fresh-water lake in the vicinity of the nest, unlike the common eiders, which at once take to the sea. On a moderate-sized lagoon or fresh-water lake on the tundra scores of broods of young eiders may be found congregated together late in the summer, accompanied by the ducks, and Doctor Van Oort observed that the ducks, by adroit splashing and feigned attacks, were able to preserve their young from the powerful sledge dogs which haunted the camp.

Summing up what little data we have on the subject, it seems that, whereas the other eiders of the north Atlantic nest on the seacoast exclusively, preferably on islands and often in densely populated colonies, the king eider seems to prefer to nest near the shores or on the islands of fresh-water ponds and streams, and its nests are usually widely scattered. Some writers have said that the nest resembles that of the common eider, and others have called attention to the darker down in the nests of the king eider. This character is very well marked in the only nest I have of this species, in which the down is dark " bone brown " or dark " clove brown "; mixed with the down are numerous bits of moss, lichens, and grass from the tundra, a few dry leaves of willows, and a few breast feathers of the duck.

Eggs.—The king eider lays from 4 to 7 eggs, usually 5. These resemble the eggs of the common species, but they are decidedly smaller, somewhat more elongated, and rather more pointed. The shape is elliptical ovate or elongate ovate. The shell is smooth, but without much gloss. The color varies from " dark olive buff " to " deep olive buff " or even " olive buff." The eggs are often clouded or mottled with darker shades of olive or brown and are frequently much nest stained, giving them a darker appearance.

The measurements of 152 eggs, in various collections, average 67.6 by 44.7 millimeters; the eggs showing the four extremes measure **79.5** by 47, 78.5 by **52, 61.3** by 45, and 62.5 by **41.5** millimeters.

Incubation is performed by the female alone. The males desert the females at this season and fly out to sea, where they form in large flocks, often far from land and about the edges of the sea. Mr. Manniche (1910) writes:

The females would, in the breeding season, sometimes leave the nest for a short while and fly to the nearest pond for the purpose of bathing and seeking food. Like many other birds, the king eider is irritable and quarrelsome at this period. One evening I observed a female which had just left her nest. She flew quickly straight toward me and so low that she seemed to touch the earth with the tips of her wings. I was standing on the beach of a pond with shallow water. Uttering an angry grunting she circled around and quite near to me and then flew to the pond. Having quenched her thirst and by a pair of quick bounds under the surface put her feathers in order, she swam straight toward me, all the while uttering a peculiar growling and hissing; the feathers on her head were erected, and she seemed to be very much displeased at my presence; now and then she cackled in the shallow water like a domestic duck, again to show her displeasure.

Young.—Referring to the care of the young, the same observer says:

On the arrival of the expedition at the ship's harbor on August 17 several females, accompanied by their still downy young ones, were lying in the small openings in the ice. Three days later I met with 5 broods of ducklings at the mouth of Stormelven; one of these broods was scarcely 1 week old. These broods all contained 5 ducklings—in one case 6 were seen. The old birds behaved very anxiously when I approached and swam, grunting, around quite near me and the coast, while the young ones, with a surprising rapidity, moved outwards, swimming and diving till they at last disappeared far out in the bay.

Immature birds do not breed during their first spring and perhaps not during their second, as the full plumage is not acquired until the third winter, or when the young bird is about 2½ years old. These young birds flock by themselves until they become of breeding age, and frequent different resorts. They do not go as far north in the summer, are never seen on or near the breeding grounds, and they usually winter farther south. Most of the straggling inland records are made by birds of this class. Kumlien (1879) saw in July large numbers of these immature birds in Cumberland Sound, on the west coast of Davis Straits, and around Disko Island. They were in various stages of immature plumage, and the sexual organs of those he examined were not developed. Apparently these are the summer resorts of the immature birds not yet ready to breed.

Plumages.—The downy young king eider bears a superficial resemblance to the young of the common eider, but it can be easily recognized by the shape of the bill, head, and feathered tracts at the base of the bill. The bill is longer and more slender; the forehead is more rounded and prominent, less sloping; the feathered points on the sides of the bill do not extend so far forward; and there is a long, slender feathered point extending out onto the culmen to the outer end of the nostrils. The under parts are more extensively lighter, and the upper parts are tinged with more yellowish buff. The color pattern of the head is also different; the crown is "bister," paling to "Saccardo's umber" on the hind neck; there is a broad superciliary stripe of "pinkish buff," and a paler tint of the same color extends down the sides of the head and neck, paling almost to white on the throat; there is a dark postocular stripe of "sepia," and the cheeks and lores are washed with a paler tint of the same, leaving the lower half of the pointed feather tract nearly white, as on the throat. The colors on the upper parts shade from "Saccardo's umber" anteriorly to "bister" on the rump. The under parts are grayish white.

The progress toward maturity in the young male king eider advances by similar stages and at the same rate as in the common eider.

The plumage changes are parallel, and yet the two species can be easily recognied at any age in both sexes. In the brown stage, during the first fall and early winter, the young male king eider is much darker above and the shape of the bill and its feathered borders are distinctive. During the late winter and early spring the back, scapulars, and flanks become nearly black; the crown and neck become darker brown; a variable amount of white appears in the chest, each feather tipped with dusky; and some white, dusky-bordered feathers appear in the rump patches. Some forward birds show considerable white on the neck and throat, with a suggestion of the black V during the first spring. The under parts remain dull mottled brown and the immature wings, with dusky, light-edged coverts, are retained until the complete summer molt.

This molt involves the first eclipse plumage, which does not entirely disappear until November. The young bird is then in its second winter plumage, which is similar to the adult winter plumage, but duller and less complete. This plumage can be easily recognized, however, by the wing; in the adult male the lesser wing-coverts, except for a dusky border around the bend of the wing, and the median wing-coverts are pure white; but in the second-winter male these white feathers are more or less margined or shaded with dusky. At the next summer molt these wings are shed and the young male becomes adult as soon as the second eclipse plumage disappears in the fall, when about 28 months old.

The eclipse plumage of the adult male king eider is very similar in appearance, extent, and duration to that of the common eider; it begins to appear early in July or even in June, with the growth of dull-brown feathers in the head and neck; dark-brown or blackish feathers in the white area of the back, and buffy brown feathers barred with dusky on the breast. The brilliant colors of the head, including the black V, disappear entirely; the white rump spots are nearly or quite obliterated; there is very little white left in the back; and the buff breast shield is nearly concealed by the barred feathers. In this plumage, which is complete in August, the wings and the rest of the plumage are molted. The adult winter plumage is completely renewed again by the end of November.

The plumage changes of the female king eider are similar to those of the common eider. This species can always be easily recognized by its smaller size, smaller head and bill, and by the pattern of the feathering at the base of the bill, the central feathered point extending down to the nostrils. The colors of young females are always duller, particularly on the under parts. Adults are richer brown in winter and paler in summer or spring, owing to the wear and fading of the brown edgings, particularly on the scapulars, wings, and flanks.

Food.—Referring to the food of this species on its breeding grounds, Mr. Manniche (1910) says:

In the season in which the king eider lives in fresh water its food consists principally of plants. In the stomachs which I examined I found, however, many remnants of insects, especially larvae of gnats. In the stomachs of downy young ones I found indeterminable remnants of crustaceans, plants, and small stones.

At other seasons king eiders are essentially salt-water birds and spend much of their time out on the open sea. They obtain their food by diving, generally at moderate depths, to the rocky shoals and ledges where they find the bulk of their food, which consists mainly of mollusks, conchylia, bivalve, and univalve shellfish of a great variety of species. They are also said to eat a number of crustaceans, shrimps, starfish, small fishes, and fish spawn. On the coast of Maine in winter, Arthur H. Norton (1909) found that one "had its gullet filled with large specimens of *Gammarus locusta*, the common sea flea of our shores. Another was similarly filled with young crabs (*Cancer irroratus*), in both instances to the exclusion of other food." Ora W. Knight (1908) says: "They are said to feed in rather deeper water than the other eiders, and Mr. Norton has recorded the fact that certain individuals had been eating sea cucumbers (*Pentacta frondosa*) to the practical exclusion of other material. While a few I have examined also evidenced some fondness for such a diet, they also had been eating great quantities of mussels." Apparently almost any kind of animal food to be found in the sea is a welcome addition to the food of this bird.

Behavior.—The flight of the king eider is similar to that of the other eiders, but the male can be easily recognized, even at a long distance, by the larger amount of black in the back and wings. The adults are usually very shy, but the immature birds are often very unsuspicious. As this species has to fly inland to its breeding places, it has less fear of the land than the common eider and does not object to flying over points of land which lie in its line of flight.

F. Seymour Hersey says, in his notes:

The flight of the king eider, like all the eiders with which I am familiar, is swift. The wings are moved very rapidly and the large heavy body is propelled with a speed and directness that is bulletlike. A bird shot on the wing will frequently strike the water and bound along the surface for a considerable distance before coming to a stop. A bird which I shot at Cape Dyer just as it was about to round a turn in a small inlet it was flying over at the time, continued straight ahead from the momentum it had acquired and struck the tundra several yards from the water, where I found it nearly hidden from sight in the tundra mosses into which the impact of its fall had embedded it.

It always seemed to me that with the exception of the yellow-billed loon the king eider is the strongest flyer of any of the northern waterfowl I met.

As a diver it is an expert and can penetrate to great depths; birds are said to have been taken in gill nets at a depth of 150 feet. In diving it partially opens its wings and probably uses them, as well as its feet, in swimming under water.

Referring to the behavior of this species in Greenland, Mr. Manniche (1910) writes: " Every day they used to fly from the lakes and ponds inland down to the bay, and especially to the mouth of Stormelven, in which they would lie and dive for food. They used to lie for hours on the grass-clad beaches of the lake in order to rest or to sleep, with their heads hidden under their wings. During their excursions in the field, they always flew very low and sometimes uttered a slight growling or grunting sound." Hagerup (1891) says that "its only note is a single cooing sound, heard especially at night."

Fall.—Mr. Murdoch (1885) says of the fall migration at Point Barrow:

By the second week in July, before the ice is gone from the sea or from Elson Bay, the males begin to come back in flocks from the east, and from that time to the middle of September there is a flight of eiders whenever the wind blows from the east. The flocks are all males at first, but mixed flocks gradually appear, and the young of the year were first observed in these flocks on August 30, 1882.

Most of the flight birds make no stay, but continue on to the southwest, generally a couple of miles out at sea, though they occasionally stop to rest, especially when there is much drifting ice. Between the regular flights they continue to straggle along, coming off the land, and occasionally sitting apparently asleep on the beach. Small flocks and single birds are to be seen till the sea closes, about the end of October, and in 1882 many were seen as late as December 2, when there were many holes of open water.

When the birds are flying at Pergniak, it is quite a lively scene, as there is a large summer camp of Eskimos close to the point where the ducks cross when the conditions are favorable. When the wind is east or northeast, and not blowing too hard, the birds come from the east and strike the land at a point which runs out on the shore of the bay about half a mile from Pergniak, close to where the lagoons begin.

They would be apt to turn and fly down these lagoons were it not for a row of stakes, set up by the natives, running round the semicircle of the bay to the camp. As soon as the flock reaches this critical point, all the natives, and there may be 50 of them on the watch, with guns and slings, just at the narrowest part of the beach above the tents, immediately set up a shrill yell. Nine times out of ten the flock will waver, turn, follow round the row of stakes, and naturally whirl out to sea at the first open place, where, of course, the gunners are stationed. With a strong wind, however, the ducks do not follow the land, but come straight on from the east and cross wherever they happen to strike the beach, so that the shooting can not be depended on.

The flocks during the fall flight are not so large and do not follow one another in such rapid succession as in the spring; and though they arrive from the east in the same stringing order, they huddle into a compact body as they whirl along the line of stakes and out over the beach.

Mr. Hersey contributes the following notes on the fall migration:

No one who has not observed the migration of the king eider along the Arctic coast of Alaska can realize the enormous abundance of this species in the north. The southward migration was well under way when we left Kotzebue Sound early in August, 1914, and started northward for Point Barrow. When we reached Icy Cape we encountered ice, and by the time we were off Wainwright Inlet the ice conditions were so bad and the wind so unfavorable that the captain decided it was not prudent to go further until the wind changed. We spent the time from August 10 to 20 lying off Wainwright Inlet waiting for a change of wind, and during these days migrating flocks of king eiders were constantly passing. The birds travel mostly in large flocks of 75 to 350 birds, following the shore line but keeping at least a mile from land. They spread out in a long line, the birds flying nearly abreast, but in the larger flocks quite a few will be bunched toward the center, or sometimes two or three small parties of 10 to 20 birds will follow directly in back of the main line. There is an undulating motion to these flocks when seen at a distance similar to that of a flock of Canada geese. They fly some 30 or 40 feet above the water or ice and follow in what appears to be the exact course of the flock that had passed a few moments before. During the 10 days that this migration was under observation there appeared to be no diminution in the numbers of birds coming out of the north. A flock would appear on the horizon to the northeast, fly steadily toward us to a certain point where they always swerved away from the ship, pass at a distance of a quarter of a mile, and a moment later disappear in the southwest. Turning our faces to the northeast again another flock would be seen coming into view at the same point on the horizon where the last birds had appeared and pressing steadily on along the same flight line. Throughout the entire 10 days there was hardly a quarter hour in which a flock of birds was not passing, and often more than one flock was in sight. The migration moved on without interruption from daybreak, which at this time of year takes place between 3 and 4 in the morning, until the sun sets, about 9 p. m. The flight of one of these migrating flocks seems slow, probably on account of the wavy motion of the line of birds, but when they finally sweep past it is seen that they are really flying swiftly, and there is a roar of wings audible for a long distance.

Winter.—To visit the winter haunts of the king eider on the New England coast, one must be prepared to brave the rigors of the cold, rough sea in the most exposed places; for these hardy birds do not come until wintry conditions have made offshore boating far from comfortable, and they prefer to frequent the outer ledges which at that season are almost always unapproachable. I can well remember a December morning on the coast of Maine, the first chance after a week of waiting for a day smooth enough to reach the outer islands, when we started long before daylight for a little eider duck shooting. Fifteen miles or more we had to go in our little launch to reach the ledges where we were to shoot. With the first signs of daylight and for an hour before sunrise we could see small flocks of scoters, darkly painted on the lightening sky, flying from their bedding grounds at sea up into Jericho Bay to feed on the mussel beds in shallow water With the coming of the dawn the gulls became active, and and their shadowy forms could be made out against the rosy clouds. The black figure of an occasional cormorant was seen flying high in the air, and scurrying flocks of oldsquaws flew past us at safe distances. We soon realized, as we began to reach the outer islands, that it was none too smooth; a heavy ocean swell was rolling in and breaking on the ledges; and the west wind, coming up with the sun, was stirring up a troublesome cross chop. As we approached Spirit Ledge, where we intended to do our shooting, all hope of landing was dispelled, for the waves were breaking over it with clouds of spray and all around it the submerged ledges were white with combing breakers. It was no place for us, this wild scene of ocean fury, but for the birds it held no terrors. There, just beyond our reach were hundreds of American eiders, surf and white-winged scoters, flocks of oldsquaws, and a few of the black-backed king eiders; flocks were going and coming, settling in the water among the breakers or circling about the rocks. It was a wild and attractive scene, but we could only view it from a distance, and we were finally obliged to retire to a more sheltered ledge where we succeeded in landing and setting out our decoys in the lee. Here only occasional flocks, pairs, or single birds came in to us, as we lay concealed among the rocks while our boatman was anchored at a distance. Off around the outer ledges we could still see the flocks of eiders feeding in the surf, riding at ease among the angry waves, paddling backwards or forwards to avoid the breaking crests, or diving under a combing breaker. There were both old and young birds in the flocks, but the latter decidedly in the majority; the old birds were too shy to come to us, but we secured young males in various stages of plumage. Before long it became too rough to stay even here, and our boatman insisted on our leaving before it was too late; as it was we lost one oar and nearly lost our skiff; we were glad to leave the sea ducks alone in their glory.

On the southern coasts of New England and Long Island the king eider is an irregular winter visitor, and during some seasons it is quite common. I have a small series of immature males and females taken in midwinter about Hen and Chickens Reef, partially submerged ledges a few miles off the coast of Westport, Massachusetts; here these birds are known as "cousins," owing to their resemblance to the common eiders, which are known as "wamps." On Long Island they are known as "Isle of Shoal ducks"; William Dutcher (1888) received, in January, 1887, a female king eider from

Capt. J. G. Scott, keeper of the lighthouse at Montauk Point, who reported them:

Living off the Point since early in November (11), when I saw a flock of 4; the next day I saw 10 at one time. They appear less shy than the other wild fowl and will permit a nearer approach in a boat. In this locality it is seen occasionally in the winter months on the ocean from one-quarter to one-half mile from shore. It is not a common duck, and I believe it is only a few years since they have been seen off Montauk Point, but this winter they have been more than usually common. There is a shoal, with a depth of water from 15 to 20 feet, about one-quarter of a mile off the Point, where I go to shoot ducks, but can only do so when the surf will permit. Every time I have visited this spot this winter I have seen from 4 to 20 king eiders.

The king eider spends the winter as far north as it can find open water; in southern Greenland it associates with the northern eider in the open water in the fjords, but probably the greater number spend the winter at sea on the edges of the ice packs or in the open leads. On the western side of the continent the principal winter resort of this species is in the vicinity of the Aleutian Islands, where so many other sea ducks find congenial surroundings and abundant food. Some few birds winter as far north as the Diomede Islands, and many resort to the islands south of the Alaska Peninsula.

DISTRIBUTION

Breeding range.—Arctic coasts of both hemispheres. On both coasts of Greenland, north to 82° 30′, less abundantly in southern Greenland. In North America south to northern Labrador (Nachvak), Hudson Straits (Wales Sound), northern Hudson Bay (Southampton Island and Cape Fullerton), and the entire Arctic coasts of Canada and Alaska. On St. Lawrence and St. Matthew Islands, in Bering Sea. All along the Arctic coast of Siberia, on Nova Zembla, and on Spitsbergen. North on Arctic islands to Melville Island and probably others up to at least 76° N.

Winter range.—South on the Atlantic coast more or less regularly to Massachusetts (Vineyard Sound) and New York (Long Island), more rarely to New Jersey, and casually farther south. South in the interior frequently to the Great Lakes (Ontario, Erie, and Michigan) and casually beyond. On the Pacific coast south to the Aleutian, Kodiak, and Shumagin Islands. North as far as open water extends in Bering Sea and around southern Greenland. In the Eastern Hemisphere it visits Iceland, the Faroes, Norway, Denmark, Great Britain, Holland, and the Baltic Sea, and has occurred in France (twice) and Italy (four times).

Spring migration.—Early dates of arrival: Greenland, Igloolik, latitude 69°, April 16, and Etah, May 1; Wellington Channel, latitude 76°, June 9; Fort Conger, latitude 82°, June 11. Late dates of departure: Georgia, Brunswick, May 5; New York, Long Island, June 8, and Waterford, April 30; Maine, May 29; Ontario, Ottawa, May 8. Dates of arrival in Alaska: Point Hope, March 17; Point Barrow, April 27; Humphrey Point, May 15. Arrival at Banks Land, Mercy Bay, June 1.

Fall migration.—Early dates of arrival: Massachusetts, October 21; New York, Cayuga, November 3; Pennsylvania, Erie, November 13; Ontario, Toronto, November 25; Ohio, Columbus, November 4: North Carolina, Dare County, December 3; Virginia, Cobb Island, December 19. Late dates of departure: Alaska, Point Barrow, December 2, and Wainwright, November 9; Mackenzie, Fort Simpson, October 25.

Casual records.—Has wandered south on the Atlantic coast to Georgia (Ossabaw Island, December 1, 1904, St. Catherine Island, December 3, 1904, and Brunswick, April 25 and May 5, 1890), on the Pacific coast to central California (San Francisco, winter of 1879–80), and in the interior to Alberta (Calgary, November 4, 1894), and to Iowa (Keokuk, November 18, 1894).

Egg dates.—Arctic Canada: Sixteen records, June 27 to July 8. Alaska: Twelve records, June 10 to July 5; six records, June 20 to July 3. Greenland: Four records, July 11 to 25.

OIDEMIA AMERICANA Swainson

AMERICAN SCOTER

HABITS

This is the least known and the rarest of the three species of scoters or "coots" which migrate up and down our coasts on both sides of the continent; it is also the hardest of the three to identify in life, as it has no distinctive marks visible at a distance; hence it is commonly referred to by nearly all observers in connection with the other two, and it is very difficult to separate much that is applicable to this species alone. This group as a whole seems to be rather unpopular among naturalists, as it is among sportsmen; consequently comparatively little effort has been devoted to the study of its habits.

Spring.—The spring migration of the American scoter, on the Atlantic coast, is eastward and northward along the seacoast; I can find no evidence of an overland flight to the interior, which is so conspicuous in the white-winged scoter. During April and the early part of May large numbers may be seen migrating eastward through Vineyard Sound and around Cape Cod. On the south coast of Labrador we saw them flying eastward during the latter part of May and the first half of June. While migrating the three species usually keep in flocks by themselves, but mixed flocks are occasionally seen; such mixed flocks are more apt to contain American and surf scoters than white-winged scoters.

Nesting.—Dr. E. W. Nelson (1887) writes:

At St. Michael these ducks are never seen in spring until the ice begins to break offshore and the marshes are dotted with pools of open water. May 16 is the earliest date of arrival I recorded. Toward the end of this month they leave the leads in the ice and are found in abundance among the salt and fresh water ponds on the great marshes from the Yukon mouth north and south. The mating is quickly accomplished and a nesting site chosen on the border of some pond. The spot is artfully hidden in the standing grass, and the eggs, if left by the parent, are carefully covered with grass and moss. At the Yukon mouth Dall found a nest of this species on June 17. The nest contained two white and rather large eggs, and was in a bunch of willows on a small island, and was well lined with dry grass, leaves, moss, and feathers.

Edward Adams (1878) found this species breeding in the same general region, and says of its nesting habits:

These birds were rather late in their arrival; I met with none until the 19th of May. Toward the end of the month several pairs had taken possession of the larger lakes near Michalaski; here they remained to breed, seldom going out to sea, but keeping together in small flocks in the middle of the lake. Their nests were well secreted in the clefts and hollows about the steep banks of the lakes, close to the water; they were built of coarse grass, and well lined with feathers and down. They had not laid when I last examined the nests.

Audubon's (1840) historic account of the nesting of the American scoter on the south coast of Labrador is interesting as showing that it once bred farther south than it now does and as illustrating its method of nesting in Labrador, where it probably still breeds abundantly in the more remote sections; he writes:

On the 11th of July, 1833, a nest of this bird was found by my young companions in Labrador. It was placed at the distance of about 2 yards from the margin of a large fresh-water pond, about a mile from the shore of the Gulf of St. Lawrence, under a low fir, in the manner often adopted by the eider duck, the nest of which it somewhat resembled, although it was much smaller. It was composed externally of small sticks, moss, and grasses, lined with down, in smaller quantity than that found in the nest of the bird just mentioned, and mixed with feathers. The eggs, which were ready to be hatched, were 8 in number, 2 inches in length, an inch and five-eighths in breadth, of an oval form, smooth, and of a uniform pale yellowish color.

We did not observe this species on the south coast of Labrador except as a migrant, but on the east coast we found it fairly common all summer all along the coast, at least as far north as Hopedale. Flocks made up entirely of males were seen in many of the inner bays and in the mouths of rivers in July and August; probably their deserted mates were incubating on their eggs or tending broods of young about the inland ponds a few miles back from the coast.

It is surprising that none of the numerous ornithologists who have visited Labrador have ever found and identified a nest of the American scoter since Audubon's time, but anyone who has ever attempted to explore into the interior of this discouraging country will appreciate why. The region is so vast, so hopelessly impassable, and so exceedingly poor in bird life that one soon gives it up in despair. This and all other species are so widely scattered that the chances of finding their nests are very small. I doubt if the American scoter migrates very far north to breed; we did not see it north of Hopedale, though we did see the surf scoter; it has never been found breeding abundantly about Hudson Bay in the northwest territories or on the Arctic coast, and Turner reported it as very scarce about Ungava Bay. Its main breeding grounds have apparently never been found. One would naturally infer then that the large numbers of this species which winter on our eastern coasts must breed in the interior of the Labrador peninsula, probably in the southern half of it, and perhaps near the marshy coasts of James Bay and the southern half of Hudson Bay; all of which regions are sadly in need of further exploration.

The American scoter undoubtedly breeds regularly, but not abundantly in Newfoundland. My friend, J. R. Whitaker, told me that he had seen this duck on Grand Lake with a brood of young, though his attempts to find a nest have proved unsuccessful. This is another vast region, difficult to travel in and largely unexplored.

I have a set of 9 eggs in my collection, said to be of this species, taken by Rev. C. E. Whitaker on Gary Island, Mackenzie Bay, on June 10, 1910; the nest is described as made of down in a tussock of grass. The down is rather dark in color, varying from "bone brown" to "dusky drab" and is flecked with bits of whitish down, uniformly mixed with the dark down; the down is mixed with bits of dry leaves, pieces of grass, and small sticks.

Eggs.—The American scoter is said to lay from 6 to 10 eggs. They vary in shape from ovate to elliptical ovate. The shell is clean and smooth, but without gloss. The color varies from "light buff" or "pale pinkish buff" to "cartridge buff." The measurements of 58 eggs, in various collections, average 61.9 by 41.7 millimeters; the eggs showing the four extremes measure 72.5 by 46, 63 by 46.2, and 53 by 33.6 millimeters.

Young.—Nothing seems to be known about the period of incubation. This duty is performed solely by the female, who is entirely deserted by the male at this season. Doctor Nelson (1887) writes:

As the set of eggs is completed, the male gradually loses interest in the female and soon deserts her to join great flocks of his kind along the seashore, usually keeping in the vicinity of a bay, inlet, or the mouth of some large stream. These flocks are formed early in June and continue to grow larger until the fall migration occurs. Males may be found in the marshes with females all through the season, but these are pairs which breed late. A set of fresh eggs was taken on August 3, and a brood of downy young was obtained on September 9. The habits of these flocks of males are very similar to those of the male eiders at this season. They are good weather indicators, and frequently, 10 or 20 hours in advance of a storm, they come into the sheltered bays, sometimes to the number of a thousand or more. At such times they show great uneasiness, and frequently pass hours in circling about the bay, sometimes a hundred yards high and again close over the water, the shrill whistling of their wings making a noise which is distinctly audible nearly or quite half a mile. Until the young are about half grown the female usually keeps them in some large pond near the nesting place, but as August passes they gradually work their way to the coast and are found, like the eiders of the same age, along the reefs and about the shores of the inner bays until able to fly.

Regarding the care of the young, Audubon (1840) says:

I afterwards found a female with seven young ones, of which she took such effectual care that none of them fell into our hands. On several occasions, when they were fatigued by diving, she received them all on her back, and swimming deeply, though very fast, took them to the shore, where the little things lay close among the tall grass and low tangled bushes. In this species, as in others, the male forsakes the female as soon as incubation commences.

Plumages.—The downy young, when first hatched, is dark colored above, varying from " Prout's brown " or " verona brown " to " bister," darkest on the crown and rump; the throat and cheeks, below the lores and the eyes, are white; the under parts are grayish white centrally, shading off on the flanks into the color of the upper parts; the bill is broadly tipped with dull yellow. The plumage appears first, when about half grown, on the breast and scapulars; the tail appears next and the wings are the last to grow.

The following remarks are based largely on two papers by Gurdon Trumbull (1892 and 1893) and one by Dr. Jonathan Dwight (1914) on the molts and plumages of the scoters, all of which are well worth reading, and to which I would refer the reader for details. In the juvenal plumage the sexes are practically alike, the female averaging slightly smaller. The upper parts, including the crown, back, wings, and tail, are deep, rich brown, varying from " Prout's brown " to " mummy brown," darkest on the scapulars and tertials and palest on the neck, chest, and flanks, where it fades into the light color of the under parts; the lower half of the head and the belly are grayish white, mottled with lighter browns. This is the plumage in which the birds are known to the gunners as " gray coots "; it is worn during the fall and often well into the winter without change. Sometimes as early as November, but more often not until January or later, the sexes begin to differentiate; a growth of black feathers begins in the head and neck of the young male and a similar growth of brown feathers appears in the young female. The growth of black feathers in the male increases during the winter and spring until some of the most advanced birds become nearly all black except on the belly and wings. Doctor Dwight (1914) says:

Shortly after new feathers appear, the bill of the young male begins to take on the colors of the adult and still more gradually assumes its shape. The colors may closely approximate, by the end of the winter, those of the adult, but the shape is not perfected for at least a year, the swelling of the hump not being marked in the first winter birds, although the yellow color may be brilliant. The bill of the female and the legs and feet of the male remain dusky, adults differing very little from young birds.

No matter how black the plumage may be nor how bright the colors of bill or feet, young males may infallibly be told from adults by the shape of the first primary, which is not replaced until the first postnuptial molt. The iris in *americana* is always brown in both sexes at all ages.

At the first complete postnuptial molt, the following summer, the young bird becomes practically adult; the plumage is wholly black in the male and wholly dark brown in the female. At this molt the adult wing is acquired, in which the outer primary is deeply emarginated; the broad tipped outer primary is worn by the young bird for one year only.

Adults have two molts each year, a partial prenuptial molt in March and April, involving the body feathers and the tail, and a complete postnuptial molt in August and September. There is no evidence of anything like an eclipse plumage in this or in the other scoters. The plumages described as such by European writers are probably produced by wear and fading or by left-over traces of a former plumage.

Food.—Writing of the feeding habits of the three species of scoters on the Massachusetts coast, George H. Mackay (1891) says:

These scoters are the most numerous of all the sea fowl which frequent the New England coast, collecting in greater or less numbers wherever their favorite food can be procured—the black mussel (*Modiola modiolus*), small sea clams (*Spisula solidissima*), scallops (*Pecten concentricus*), and short razor shells (*Siliqua costata*), about an inch to an inch and a half long, which they obtain by diving. Mussels measuring 2½ inches by 1 inch have been taken from them; but usually they select sea clams and scallops varying in size from a 5-cent nickel piece to a quarter of a dollar. They can feed in about 40 feet of water, but prefer less than half of that depth. As these mussels are frequently difficult to detach, and the sea clam lives embedded endwise in sand at the bottom with only about half an inch above the sand, the birds are not always successful in obtaining them, it requiring considerable effort on their part to pull the mussels off or to drag out the clams. Eight or ten of these constitute a meal, but the number varies according to the size. I have heard of a mussel closing on a scoter's tongue, which was nearly severed at the time the bird was shot (Muskeget Island, about 1854). The fishermen frequently discover beds of shellfish (scallops) by noticing where these birds congregate to feed. In the shoal waters adjacent to Cape Cod, Nantucket, and Marthas Vineyard, these mollusks are particularly abundant, and consequently we find more of the scoters in those localities than on any other part of the coast or perhaps than on all the rest of the coast combined.

E. H. Forbush (1912) writes:

Its food consists largely of mussels, and when feeding on fresh water it prefers the *Unios* or fresh-water clams to most other foods. Thirteen Massachusetts specimens were found to have eaten nearly 95 per cent of mussels; the remaining 5 per cent of the stomach contents was composed of starfish and periwinkles. It is a common belief that all scoters feed entirely upon animal food, but this is not a fact. Along the Atlantic coast they appear to subsist mostly on marine animals, but, in the interior, vegetable food also is taken. Mr. W. L. McAtee found the scoters in a Wisconsin lake living almost exclusively for a time on the wild celery, but he does not state definitely what species of scoter was represented there.

Dr. F. Henry Yorke (1899) says that, while on the lakes and ponds of the interior, this species eats minnows and small fish, slugs, and snails, larvae of insects, fish spawn, crawfish, small frogs, and polliwogs; also a variety of vegetable food such as duckweed, pondweed, flags, water milfoil, bladderwort, and several other water plants. Probably the young are fed largely on insect food.

Behavior.—The American scoter is not easily recognized in flight; its size, shape, gait, and general appearance are all much like those of the surf scoter, from which only the adult males can be distinguished by the head and bill markings at short range; the females and young of these two species can not be distinguished in life at any considerable distance, and many gunners do not recognize them in the hand. Its flight is not quite so heavy as that of the white-winged scoter. All the scoters fly more swiftly than they appear to be going, but at nothing like the speed at which they have been reported to fly; I doubt if they ever fly at over 60 miles an hour or even attain that speed except under the most favorable circumstances. Migrating flocks in the fall usually fly high in fair weather, but in stormy or very windy weather the flocks sweep along close to the water and usually well in shore, following the indentations of the coast line and seldom flying over the land, except on their occasional visits to inland ponds. The flocks vary greatly in size and form, some are great irregular masses or bunches, others are strung out in long straight or curving lines, and sometimes they form in more or less regular V or U shapes. The wings make a whistling sound in flight, which the gunners imitate to attract the attention of passing flocks.

All the scoters are strong, fast, and tireless swimmers, either on the surface or below it; they dive quickly and neatly and can remain under water for a long time. Mr. Mackay (1891) writes:

In these shallow waters the tide runs rapidly over the shoal ground and sweeps the scoters away from where they wish to feed, thus necessitating their flying back again to it; consequently there is at such times a continual movement among them as they are feeding. When wounded and closely pursued, they will frequently dive to the bottom (always using their wings as well as feet at such times in swimming under water) and retain hold of the rockweed with the bill until drowned, prefering thus to die than to come to the surface to be captured. As an instance of this, I may mention that on one occasion I shot a scoter when the water was so still that there was not even a ripple on its surface; after pursuing the bird for some time I drove it near the shore, when it dove and did not reappear. I knew it must have gone to the bottom, as I had seen the same thing repeatedly before. As the occasion was a favorable one for investigation, the water being clear and not more than 12 or 15 feet in depth, I rowed along carefully, looking continually into the water near the spot where the bird was last seen. My search was at last successful, for on getting directly over where the bird was I could look down and distinctly see it holding on to the rockweed at the bottom with its bill. After observing it for a time I took one of my oars, and aiming it at the bird sent it down. I soon dislodged it, still alive, and captured it. I have often seen these birds, when wounded and hard pressed, dive where the water was 40 to 50 feet deep, and not come to the surface again. I therefore feel much confidence in stating that it is no uncommon occurrence for them under such circumstances to prefer death by drowning to capture. This they accomplish by seizing hold of the rockweed at the bottom, holding on even after life has become extinct. I have also seen all three species when wounded dive from the air, entering the water without any splash. All are expert divers, it requiring considerable experience to retrieve them when wounded.

Scoters are usually silent birds; I can not remember having heard any notes from any of them, but Mr. Mackay (1891) says: "The American scoter makes a musical whistle of one prolonged note, and it can frequently be called to the decoys by imitating the note." Rev. J. H. Langille (1884) says: "The note of the scoter in spring is like *whe-oo-hoo*, long drawn out."

Maj. Allan Brooks (1920) writes:

In British Columbia this scoter is an exclusively maritime duck; at least I have not come across a single reliable inland record. Not only is it a maritime bird, but it is seldom found in the small bays and inlets where the other species swarm, but frequents the exposed shores and outer reefs together with the harlequin. It has many points in common with that duck, rising easily from the water and doing much flying about in small lots of four or five—mostly males—seemingly for the pleasure of flying, usually returning to the point they started from. In flight the silvery undersurface of the primaries, in both sexes, is very conspicuous. In fine, calm weather they call a great deal and their plaintive *cour-loo* is the most musical of duck cries, very different from the croaking notes of most diving ducks.

Fall.—The fall migration of the American scoter is somewhat earlier than that of the other two species. On the Massachusetts coast the flight begins in September, and during the latter half of that month there is often quite a heavy flight which consists almost entirely of adult birds. The young birds, which are known as "gray coots," come along with the other scoters in October. Each species usually flocks by itself, and flocks of adults are often separated from flocks of young birds; but mixed flocks are often seen, particularly of young American and surf scoters. The American scoter is more often seen in fresh-water ponds a few miles back from the coast than are the other two, though all three are often seen on our large inland lakes.

Game.—From the sportsman's standpoint the American scoter is a more desirable game bird than the other two scoters. The young birds particularly, when they first arrive from their northern feeding grounds in the interior, are fatter, more tender, and less strongly flavored than are the others. The value of " coots " as food has been much maligned and in my opinion unjustly; if young and tender birds are selected and if they are properly cooked their flesh is much more palatable than is generally supposed; the popular prejudice against them is largely due to an erroneous impression that they must be parboiled, which is a pernicious practice and will render any oily seaduck unfit for food by saturating the flesh with the oily flavor. There are only two proper ways to cook a sea duck; one is to skin it and broil it; and the other is to scrape as much oil out of the skin as possible and then roast it quickly in a hot oven, letting the oil run off.

The Massachusetts method of " coot shooting," in which I have often indulged, is described under another species, so I shall quote from Walter H. Rich (1907) as to the methods employed on the Maine coast; he writes:

Probably the least wary of the duck family, they may be approached quite readily as compared with other members of the tribe. Gunners use many methods for capturing the coots, but the greater number are killed óver decoys. A string of " tolers " is set in a promising place just off some rocky point or ledge in the deep water, the gunner is well hidden, and if the birds are flying there is every prospect of good shooting, for the coot is one of the best of birds to decoy. Often in the early part of the season, before the birds have become shy from constant peppering, the gunner may set his decoys on a line from his boat, only keeping below the gunwale when the flocks are coming in. And they *will* come in. I have often seen them fly close enough to be struck with an oar—I may say that they make it an invariable rule to do this when the gunner has taken the shells out of his gun or laid it aside to pick up his decoys after a morning's cootless waiting in the cold. One oddity in the gentle art of duck shooting is the practice of " hollerin' coots "—that is, of making a great noise when a flock is passing by out of shot—when they will often turn and come to the decoys. The report of a gun sometimes has the same effect, but we New Englanders are too thrifty to waste powder and lead where our vocal organs will serve as well.

Next to decoying, the use of the " gunning float " is the most effective method of killing coots. The " gunning float " is a long, low craft, drawing but little water and showing only a foot or so above the surface when properly trimmed down with ballast. In the fall, for use in the open water, they are " trimmed " with " rockweed "; in the marshes with " thatch." In the spring and winter months the proper thing is snow and ice to represent a drifting ice cake. It takes sharp eyes to detect the dangerous one among the many harmless pieces of ice when the gunner, clad in his white suit, is working his cautious way along toward the feeding flocks. The deception is so complete that I have known that crafty old pirate, the crow, to almost alight on the nose of a float when it was being pushed after a flock of sea fowl. This float gunning is the method most used for all duck and goose shooting on the eastern New England coast line.

Winter.—There is not a month in the year during which scoters may not be seen on the Massachusetts coast; straggling birds, crippled, sick, or nonbreeding birds are present more or less all summer; the heavy migration flights last all through the fall and during much of the spring; and in winter this is one of the main resorts of all three species. The waters lying south of Cape Cod and in the vicinity of Nantucket and Marthas Vineyard are particularly congenial to these birds in winter, where the numerous islands, bays, and reefs offer some shelter from the winter storms, where they are not much disturbed by gunners at that season, and where they can find extensive beds of mussels, scallops, clams, and quahogs within easy reach on the numerous shoals and ledges. Here they congregate in enormous numbers, the three species associated together and often with eiders and oldsquaws. They have their favorite feeding grounds, to which they resort regularly every day at daybreak, feeding, playing, and resting during the day and flying out again at night to sleep on the bosom of the ocean, or on some more sheltered portion of the sound, far enough from land to feel secure.

DISTRIBUTION

Breeding range.—Northern North America and northeastern Asia. East to the coast of Labrador (north of the Straits of Belle-Isle) and Newfoundland (Grand Lake). South nearly or quite to the Gulf of St. Lawrence, to James Bay, to an unknown distance in the interior of Canada and Alaska and to the base of the Alaska Peninsula (Lake Clark). On the Aleutian and Kurile Islands. West to the Bering Sea coast of Alaska and to northeastern Siberia (Gichiga). North to northern Alaska (Kowak River), northern Canada (Mackenzie Bay) and probably north in the Labrador Peninsula to Ungava Bay and perhaps Hudson Straits.

Winter range.—Mainly on the seacoast. On the Atlantic coast regularly south to Long Island Sound and New Jersey, rarely to South Carolina, and occasionally to Florida. North regularly to Maine and more rarely to the Gulf of St. Lawrence and Newfoundland. On the Pacific coast from the Pribilof and Aleutian Islands south to southern California (Santa Barbara Islands) and from the Commander Islands south to Japan and China. In the interior it winters on the Great Lakes more or less regularly and has occurred irregularly or casually as far west and south as Wyoming (Cheyenne), Colorado (Fort Collins), and Louisiana (Lake Catherine).

Spring migration.—Early dates of arrival: Gulf of St. Lawrence, March 25; Ontario, Ottawa, May 4; Alaska, St. Michael, May 16, and Bering Straits, May 8. Late dates of departure: South Carolina, Bulls Bay, May 7; Virginia, Cobb Island, May 19; New York, Shelter Island, June 5; Massachusetts, Woods Hole, June 10; Alaska, Admiralty Island, June 10.

Fall migration.—Early dates of arrival: Ontario, Ottawa, September 1; Massachusetts, September 8; Minnesota, Heron Lake, October 5; Colorado, Denver, October 2. Main flight passes Massachusetts in October. Late date of departure: Alaska, St. Michael, October 15.

Egg dates.—Arctic Canada: Five records, June 10 to 21. Alaska: Four records, June 2 to August 3. Labrador: Two records, June 10 and 17.

MELANITTA FUSCA (Linnaeus)

VELVET SCOTER

HABITS

This is strictly an Old World species which owes its somewhat questionable place on the American list to the fact that it has been recorded as a straggler in Greenland. I have never been able to understand why the birds of Greenland should be included in our North American fauna, while those of Cuba and the Bahamas, which are both geographically and faunally much closer to us, are excluded. Greenland both geographically and faunally is but a little nearer North America than Europe; it is intermediate. If we exclude cosmopolitan species, common to both hemispheres, about three-fifths of the breeding birds of Greenland are also North American and about two-fifths are also European.

As the velvet scoter is practically unknown, as an American bird, I can not do better than quote its life history from one of the best of the European writers, an eminent authority on ducks, Mr. John G. Millais (1913) as follows:

Nesting.—Velvet scoters arrive on the lakes of Norway and Sweden about the end of April, in fact, as soon as the ice breaks up, and even earlier on the lake swamps of Lithuania, which seems to be about the southern limit of nesting birds. The male and female are much devoted to one another and keep close together during the early part of the nesting season. It has often been noticed that if one of the pair is shot the other will fall to the water and dive or stay close to its fallen mate.

They seem to prefer inland lakes and small ponds on which to breed. Collett has found them breeding in large numbers in the hill lakes of Gudbrandsda, Valders, Osterdal, and north to Finmark, and I have myself seen females and young birds on the lakes of Valders and Trondhjem in September, the males having departed.

The nest is often found in a depression of the dry ground in the open; at other times sheltered by brushwood such as salix or juniper. C. E. Pearson found one nest in a clump of marram grass amongst sand hills. Others were placed deep down in cracks of the peat, overgrown by *Empetrum nigrum*, so that the sitting duck was carefully concealed. Seebohm found several nests in the Siberian tundra far from the water, whilst Knobloch says the velvet scoter sometimes breeds in forests. The nest is usually a deep hollow lined with grass and leaves. The earliest clutches are to be met with in the Baltic, and are to be found from May 25 onward, but in Lapland it is more usual to find eggs in June, and generally in the second half of that month. H. F. Witherby took a clutch of eggs on July 22 in Russian Lapland, and Seebohm found eggs on the Petschora in July. Six to ten eggs are usually laid, and incubation is by the female alone. As to the period of incubation no data are available.

Eggs.—Six to ten, as a rule, but clutches of 11 have been recorded. Simonson says that clutches of 10 to 14 may be met with. Oval in shape, creamy white with a warm "apricot" tinge when fresh, which fades after a time. Average size of 90 eggs, 70.8 by 47.9 mm. (2.78 by 1.88 inches). Max., 76.5 by 49.5 and 71.2 by 51.5; min., 64.3 by 46.9, and 68.3 by 44.8 mm. (F. C. R. Jourdain).

Young.—The males appear to desert the females about the time the young are hatching. E. F. von Homeyer says: " I have often seen flocks of 60 to 100, consisting of old males only, in the months of July and August, and these spent the day on the high sea and at dusk came to the shallower water on the coasts in the bays of the island of Rügen."

According to Pleske, they nest in such numbers in the island of Rugoe in Esthland (Russian Baltic Provinces), that the inhabitants make ornaments for their rooms with the blown eggs. All the habits of this duck, the upbringing of the young, and the early departure of the males for the sea, seem to be similar to other true sea ducks. Late in September, when the young are able to fly, the female takes them to the nearest seacoast, where she stays with them until the migration commences in late October.

Plumages.—The sequence of plumages from the downy stage to maturity and the subsequent molts and plumages are so similar to those of our white-winged scoter that it seems hardly necessary to describe them here. For a full account of the molts and plumages of the velvet scoter, I would refer the reader to the excellent work by Mr. Millais (1913).

Food.—On this he says:

The food of this species consists chiefly of conchylia and crustacea, which they gain from a considerable depth. I have found their stomachs filled with large numbers of the common mussel, which seems to be their principal food, mixed with quantities of sand and small pebbles. They are also very partial to the razor shell in Orkney. I have also seen them bring to the surface quite large crabs, which they break up before swallowing. The great blackbacked gull often waits on in attendance of feeding velvet scoters, and I have more than once seen these clever robbers swoop down and steal the crab, the duck merely gazing round in surprise when he finds his treasure gone.

Behavior.—I have never found the velvet scoter a very wild bird, except in rough weather, when it is easy for them to take to wing, and this is probably accounted for by the fact that their bodies are very heavy, and they seem to experience considerable difficulty in taking to flight if there is little or no headwind. They are as a rule much tamer than either the surf or common scoter; and if a boat is carefully maneuvered so as not to press them at first, a shot is certain. They rise head to wind with the usual run-up, and can not turn away from a boat until they have traveled some 30 to 50 yards. The flight is at first accompanied with much noise and flapping, and usually performed at a very low elevation. Unlike the other scoters, they usually adopt a "string" formation, and seldom move about in large flocks. It is most common to see single birds or flocks of from 3 to 15, each bird following the leader at a yard or so apart, and only 2 or 3 feet above the water. In the morning and evening these flocks or single birds may often be seen coming up the tideway from the deep sea, where they have been resting, preening, or sleeping during the hours of high tide, and moving toward their regular feeding grounds. On settling they seem to sink into the water with a heavy splash and glide for some distance over the element before coming to rest.

The velvet scoter has no superior in swimming and diving. Its powerful legs and feet enable it to pass rapidly beneath the water, and reach the bottom at depths of 40 feet, and even more. They seem to prefer to search for their food in deep places, probably because mussel beds situated in such spots are far offshore, and consequently safe. I do not think they use the wings under water, at any rate to the same extent as the eider.

Both the male and female velvet scoter make a hoarse guttural cry like the words "*kra-kra-kra.*" The male probably had a distinct call during courtship, but no one, so far as I know, has ever seen the mating display of these birds.

In our islands the velvet scoter is strictly a sea duck, is only very rarely killed on fresh water, and then only on migration. As a rule these birds frequent the neighborhood of mussel banks at some distance offshore, apparently caring little whether these situations are exposed or protected, for they come with the utmost regularity to the same places year after year. Most of the places known to me in Scotland and the islands where these birds spend the winter months are more or less protected by outlying islands or headlands, but in some cases, such as St. Andrews Bay and the Tay estuary, their feeding grounds are usually exposed to north and easterly winds. They seem to be capable, however, of standing as much buffeting by wind and weather as the hardy eiders and long-tailed ducks, and will ride out great storms at sea without coming in for protection.

Winter.—Herr Gätke (1895) gives the following account of the winter home of this and other sea ducks about Heligoland:

During the severe winter all the flocks of birds which, during ordinary winters, are in the habit of staying in the Gulfs of Bothnia and Finland, and under the shelter of the west coast of Holsten, now congregate on the open sea outside of this ice field. Wherever the eye roams it alights upon sea ducks of all possible species, near and far, high and low, in smaller or larger flocks, singly or in pairs. These consist of myriads of common and velvet scoters, flights of from 5 to 50 gay-colored red-breasted mergansers, smaller companies of the beautifully colored goosander, mixed with bands of from 20 to 100 or more scaups (*A. marila*), which flights again may be crossed by from 3 to 5 of the brilliant white, green-headed males of the goldeneye, and the still rarer and elegant eider duck; and travelling high overhead long chains of whooper swans send forth their loud and resonant trumpet calls. The wide surface of the sea presents a scene of aquatic bird life equally rich and varied. Velvet and common scoters assemble in dense crowds near the ice, while large flocks of scaups, all keeping close together, dive and swim about among the rocks off the eastern and western sides of the island.

DISTRIBUTION

Breeding range.—Northern Europe and Asia, from Norway eastward to northeastern Siberia (Marcova and Gichiga) and on Nova Zembla.

Winter range.—Temperate Europe and Asia, south to Spain, Morocco, Egypt, northern Persia, and Turkestan.

Casual records.—Accidental in the Faroe Islands and Greenland.

Egg dates.—Lapland: Five records, May 25 to July 22. Norway and Sweden: Two records, June 18 and July 4.

MELANITTA DEGLANDI (Bonaparte)

WHITE-WINGED SCOTER

HABITS

Spring.—The northward movement of scoters on the New England coast begins early in March, but the main flight comes along during the first half of May and continues in lessening numbers all through that month. It has long been known to gunners that a local westward flight of white-winged scoters takes place on the south coast of New England in May, consisting wholly of fully plumaged adult birds, recognized by the gunners as "May white wings." This undoubtedly indicates an overland migration route to their breeding grounds in the Canadian interior. I have seen several thousand of these birds gathered in large flocks in the waters about Seconnet Point, Rhode Island, early in May, preparing for this flight.

Mr. George H. Mackay (1891) refers to this flight as follows:

This movement is a peculiar one, inasmuch as it takes place about the middle of May, and after the greater portion of the migration of this group has passed by, as also ignoring the coast route accepted by all the rest. My attention was first directed to this unusual movement during the spring of 1870, while shooting at West Island, off Seconnet Point, Rhode Island, and it has occurred regularly every year since that date, as was undoubtedly the case earlier. These birds are apparently all adults and do not seem to heed the regular migration to the eastward of many of their own kind, which has no effect in hastening their own departure for the north. When the time arrives for them to set out on their migration, and the meteorological conditions are favorable—for it must be clear at the westward—they always start late in the afternoon, from 3 to 5 o'clock, and continue the flight during the night, passing by Marthas Vineyard, Woods Hole, Seconnet Point, Point Judith, and Watch Hill, quite a number frequently going over the land near the coast, they being very erratic at such times in their movements. This flight lasts for from three to seven days, according to the state of the weather. I have never heard of their starting before the 7th of May, which is unusually early; the customary time being from the 12th to the 15th, and the latest the 25th. They usually fly at a considerable altitude, say, from 200 to 300 yards, fully two-thirds of them being too high to shoot. They prefer to start during calm warm weather, with light southerly, southeasterly, or easterly winds; though they will occasionally fly when the wind is strong. They never fly in the forenoon; but when once they have determined to migrate they leave in large flocks, some of which number from five to six hundred birds, while as many as 10,000 have been estimated as passing in a single day, I have never heard of, or seen, any similar flight to the eastward after this western flight has taken place. A few of the other two scoters are seen with the white wings during this western movement. No perceptible difference is noted in their numbers from year to year, and I have never heard of a year when such a flight as above described did not take place.

On the south coast of Labrador we saw migrating flocks of scoters flying eastward all through the month of June, but probably some of these were not breeding birds. Flocks of nonbreeding scoters are frequently seen in summer on the coast of New England and from California northward. Probably the bulk of the breeding birds arrive on their nesting grounds early in June, although the nesting season does not begin until the middle or last of the month.

What becomes of the vast hordes of scoters that migrate along our coasts has long been a mystery to the gunners. Although they are widely distributed over an extensive breeding range, they have never been found breeding abundantly anywhere; probably their main breeding grounds have never been discovered. On the south coast of Labrador we saw no evidence of their breeding, and Audubon found them there but sparingly. Judging from what I saw and what I learned from other observers on the northeast coast of Labrador in 1912, I am inclined to think that this species breeds more or less commonly in the interior of that great peninsula. Among the vast flocks of scoters, seen all along that coast in summer, numerous flocks of this species were observed, but they were not nearly as abundant as the other two species. These flocks were composed almost entirely of adult males, which probably meant that the females were incubating or tending their broods of young in inland ponds. I was told that they breed far inland and at long distances from any water.

Nesting.—In the Devils Lake region, in North Dakota, Herbert K. Job found white-winged scoters breeding quite commonly; on June 27, 1898, he found several nests of this species on some small islands in Stump Lake, containing from 1 to 14 fresh eggs and one empty nest. I visited these islands with him in 1901, and on May 31 we did not find a single egg, although we saw a few of the birds flying about in pairs; evidently they had not yet laid. On June 15 we again explored the islands quite thoroughly, finding only one incomplete set of 5 eggs, cold and fresh. This nest was in the center of a small patch of rosebushes, where a hollow had been scraped in the ground and the eggs buried under a lot of dry leaves, sticks, soil, and rubbish, so as to be completely concealed from view. No attempt had been made to line the nest with down which is generally added after the set is complete. The scattered clumps of rosebushes on these islands, where they grew tall and thick among masses of large boulders, formed excellent nesting sites for the scoters and doubtless concealed several nests. One nest we certainly overlooked, which on June 22, was found to contain 12 eggs.

In the Crane Lake region in southwestern Saskatchewan we found a few pairs of white-winged scoters breeding in 1905 and 1906, but only one nest was found on June 28, 1906. While walking through an extensive patch of wild rosebushes near a small slough the female was flushed from the nest almost underfoot and shot by my companion, Dr. Louis B. Bishop. The nest consisted of a hollow in the ground under the rosebushes, profusely lined with dark-gray down; it contained 9 fresh eggs. All of the nests that Mr. Job and I have seen were placed under wild rosebushes or other small deciduous shrubs, but others have found them in somewhat different situations.

Macoun (1909) records a nest found by Walter Raine as follows:

On June 26, 1893, Mr. G. F. Dippie and myself found a nest containing 9 eggs on an island at the south end of Lake Manitoba. The nest was built between loose bowlders and consisted of a hollow in the sand lined abundantly with dark down. The eggs were very large and of a deep, rich, buff color. The bird sat very close upon the nest and did not fly up until I almost trod upon her. It appears to be a late breeder, nesting late in June on the islands of Lakes Manitoba and Winnipeg. Mr. Newman sent me an egg of this bird which he took from a female he had shot at Swan Lake, northern Alberta, on June 25, 1897.

The nest down of the white-winged scoter is larger than that of the American scoter; in color it varies from "clove brown" to "olive brown," with small and inconspicuous whitish centers.

Eggs.—As this scoter is a late breeder, probably some of the smaller sets referred to were incomplete. I think that the normal number of eggs in a full set varies from 9 to 14. The eggs are elliptical ovate in shape. The shell is smooth but not glossy; in some eggs it is very finely granulated or minutely pitted. When first collected, even after being blown, the color is a beautiful "pale ochraceous salmon" or "sea shell pink," but this color fades to "pale pinkish buff" or "cartridge buff" in cabinet specimens. The pitted eggs are minutely dotted with "pinkish cinnamon," giving them a darker appearance. The measurements of 71 eggs, in various collections, average 65.3 by 45.7 millimeters; the eggs showing the four extremes measure 72.5 by 47, 68.5 by 49, 55.4 by 37.7, and 58.9 by 35.7 millimeters.

Plumages.—The downy young of the white-winged scoter is thickly covered with soft, silky down. The upper parts, including the upper half of the head, down to the base of the lower mandible and a space below the eye, are uniform " clove brown," shading off to " hair brown " on the flanks and into a broad collar of " hair brown " which encircles the lower neck. The chin and throat are pure white, which shades off to grayish white on the lower cheeks and the sides of the neck. The under parts are silvery white, and there is an indistinct, tiny white spot under the eye. The feather outline at the base of the bill is much like that of older birds. Doctor Dwight (1914) mentions a " white patch of down, foreshadowing the white wing patch," but I can find no trace of it in my one specimen.

In the juvenal plumage the sexes are alike, dark brown above, lighter and more mottled brown below; there are conspicuous whitish patches on the lores and on the auriculars, varying in intensity and extent; the white secondaries, forming the speculum, are tipped with dusky, which often invades much of the inner web. This plumage is often worn without much change all through the winter and into the spring. But usually in December, or a little later, the sexes begin to differentiate by the growth of black feathers in the male and brown feathers in the female, starting in the head, obliterating the whitish head patches, and spreading to the back, scapulars, and flanks, the latter being dark brown in both sexes. The bill in the young male now begins to show color, about as in the adult female, but not the swollen shape of the older male.

A complete postjuvenal molt takes place during the next summer, July, August, and September, at which the black plumage of the male is assumed, with the white eye patches and the pure white secondaries; the flanks are still dark brown in this and in all subsequent plumages that I have seen; the bill now becomes highly colored and approaches the adult bill in shape. The bird is now practically adult, at an age of 14 or 15 months, but the full development of the bill and highest stage of plumage will not be perfected for about a year more. The iris, which is brown in young birds, becomes white at this age. The female also assumes a practically adult plumage, at this molt, which is uniform dark brown; and she will be ready to breed the following spring.

Adult birds have an incomplete prenuptial molt in early spring, involving the head and body plumage and tail, and a complete postnuptial molt in late summer, at which time they become incapable of flight. There is no real eclipse plumage, but the appearance of one is created by the mixture of old, worn, faded feathers with fresh, new ones. There is also no marked seasonal change in any of the scoters.

Food.—The food of the white-winged scoter includes a varied bill of fare, differing greatly in the various localities which it visits. On the New England coast, where it is so abundant in the winter, it is strictly maritime and seems to feed mainly on small mussels and other small mollusks which it obtains by diving about the submerged ledges, often to a depth of 40 feet, tearing, with its powerful bill, the shellfish from the rocks to which they are firmly attached. I have seen the crop of one of these birds crammed full of mussels nearly an inch long, and have often wondered whether the tough shells were ground up in their muscular stomachs or chemically dissolved; probably both actions are necessary. Some of our fishermen have claimed that scoters are injurious to the shellfish interests on our coast, accusing them of feeding on young scallops and clams but I doubt if they do much damage in this way; they certainly could not obtain many clams, which are usually buried in the sand. Sea clams, which are sometimes found on the surface of a sand flat, are probably more often taken by these birds. J. C. Cahoon (1889) recorded an instance where the clam was too big for the scoter, which was found floating on the water with a large sea clam firmly clasped on its bill; probably the weight of the clam had kept the bird's head under water until it was drowned. On inland lakes and ponds they live largely on crawfish, slugs, snails, and mussels. They have been known to eat, according to Dr. F. Henry Yorke (1889), small fishes, frogs, tadpoles, fish spawn, and the larvae of insects. On the western sloughs and marshes they evidently feed largely on vegetable food, such as flags, duckweed, pondweed, and pickerel weed. Doctor Yorke reports the following families of plants as identified among their foods: Lemnaceae, Naiadaceae, Selaginellaceae, Salviniaceae, Glatinaceae, Gentianaceae, Lentibulariaceae, Pontederiaceae, and Mayaceae; also the following genera: Iris, Myriophyllum, Callitriche, and Utricularia.

Behavior.—The flight of the white-winged scoter is heavy and apparently labored; it seems to experience considerable difficulty in lifting its heavy body from the surface of the water; except when facing a strong wind, it has to patter along the surface for some distance, using its feet to gain momentum. But, when well under way, it is much swifter than it seems, is strong, direct, and well sustained. Migrating flocks, in all sorts of irregular formations, fly high under favorable circumstances; but when flying against the wind or in stormy weather (northeast storms seem to be particularly favorable for the migration of the scoters) they fly close to the water and in rough weather they take advantage of the eddies between the waves. The flight is usually along the seacoast, following all the large indentations of the coast and crossing the smaller bays; but, where considerable distance is to be gained they often fly across capes or necks of land, usually all at about the same place. There is a regular crossing place on Cape Cod, Massachusetts, from Barnstable Harbor to Craigville beach, a distance of about 3 miles; this is one of the narrowest points on the cape and it saves them many miles of flight around the horn of the cape. Gunners take advantage of this confirmed habit and assemble there in large numbers to shoot at the passing flocks; when flying against a strong south wind here they usually fly low enough to shoot, but, if not, a loud shout from the gunners often brings them scurrying down to within range.

Edwin S. Bryant (1899) describes an interesting flight habit of this species, as follows:

This bird has some habits unlike those of other ducks. The most prominent habit is the morning flight. This does not occur so regularly as at first I supposed. But if a person is so fortunate as to be present when a great flight is in progress, he will witness what I consider to be a fascinating picture of bird life on the prairie.

Imagine if you can a body of water some 6 or 7 miles long and 2 miles wide where it leaves the main lake, extending northward, bounded on both sides by undulating prairie. Take for a background the steep hills on the far side of the lake, or the heavy timber of Grahams Islands—let the time be sunrise, with the dewdrop jewel accompaniment that the poets rave about. Fill the air with hundreds of scoters, circling and quartering after the manner of swallows, most of them fanning the weed tops in their flight. Flying by pairs, side by side, and in companies of pairs, they often circle about a person several times, within easy gunshot range; and if one is so disposed, he may shoot a pair with one discharge of the gun, so closely do they keep together. As would be supposed, the white wing patch is very conspicuously displayed as the birds glide around. In half an hour the performance is at an end.

In two minutes time the scene changes as if by magic. All the birds are making offshore together. With a glass I follow them. Their dark bodies stand out in contrast with the whitecaps, and the flash of a wing patch against a green wave is the last seen of them as they settle down far out in the lake. Later in the day they will swarm along shore or congregate on the numerous sandy points.

A. D. Henderson has sent me the following notes on the habits of this species in northern Alberta:

These birds are much esteemed by the halfbreed Indian population, and up to a few years ago residents in the northern part of the Province were allowed to kill them at any time for food by a special provision in the game act. They make the best wing shooting of all the ducks, as they seldom swerve from the gunner. They seem to be the most amorous of the ducks, readily decoying to a wounded female and chasing her on the water within easy range of a canoe in the breeding season. In spring they fly from daylight until about 9 o'clock, and it is then they are shot as they round the points on the lake or pass between narrows. Small flocks can be seen on the water, the males pursuing the females; then they will make a short flight and alighting again resume the sport with much splashing on the water. At this time they make a sound like tinkling ice, but whether this is made with their wings or voice I do not know. When flying during courtship their wings whistle like a goldeneye's, but much louder. They also utter a short croak while flying. Though hundreds of them breed here, I have never found a nest, but have heard of several being found, usually at quite a distance back from the large lakes and near smaller ones. It is said that Lac LaNoune takes it name from these ducks owing to the resemblance of their black and white coloring to the garb of the nuns.

J. M. Edson has sent me the following interesting notes:

This species is found at all seasons in the Puget Sound region, being particularly abundant during winter. Like *O. perspicillata*, this species has a habit of leaving the water and taking a daily flight off over the land, during the summer season. These flights are particularly noticeable in pleasant weather and in late afternoon. The birds rise in considerable flocks to an elevation of 200 or 300 feet, stringing out in line, or in converging lines, sometimes forming a V. The whistling of their wings can be heard for some distance. Often this sound is punctuated by the slapping together of interfering wings. They sometimes fly considerable distances inland before returning to the water. So far as known they do not nest in this region, although birds in the full adult plumage are frequently seen throughout the summer.

An instance of peculiar behavior of birds of this species came under my notice not long ago. Watching the sea birds from a bluff overlooking Bellingham Bay, on a calm evening in December (the 24th), my attention was attracted by unusual activity in a little group of white-winged scoters. They were about 50 yards from the beach. Ten of these birds were bunched together and actively swimming and plunging about within a circle of perhaps 10 or 12 feet in diameter. I was unable to distinguish the sexes with certainty, and have no knowledge to the effect that December is their courtship season. It looked like a game of tag of some sort. At the center of the group two birds would assume a pose as if billing and caressing each other, one with its head elevated, the other's depressed, the bills coming in contact. The pose would last only two or three seconds, till some other bird would approach one of them from behind, when the latter would suddenly turn upon it and chase it away, the pursued bird taking a circular course around the flock. Sometimes both the posing birds would be simultaneously approached, and each would turn upon his assailant. The other birds would hover close about, watching for a chance to tag the posers from behind. The two main actors would again come to the center and resume their pose, only to be promptly interrupted again with the same result. So far as I could observe, the same pair took the central part all the time. I watched them for perhaps half an hour, and the game was still in progress when I left. On February 11 I saw the same performance enacted at a greater distance from shore. There were about the same number of birds in the group and the play was as before. Although there were numerous other birds of the same species scattered about in the near vicinity, these paid no attention to the game.

Like the other scoters, this species is a strong swimmer and an expert diver. It dives to considerable depths for its food when necessary, though it prefers to feed at low tide when the mussel beds are nearer the surface. When wounded it can swim for such long distances under water that its pursuit is almost useless.

I have never heard any vocal sound from the white-winged scoter, but Dr. Charles W. Townsend has sent me the following notes from E. P. Richardson:

In regard to the bell note of the white-winged scoter, I have only as much as this to say: On still nights in the fall, when we might be listening for black ducks, we would occasionally hear the rush of a flock of ducks overhead, with an occasional bell-like, low whistle, recurring at intervals in series of six or eight notes, entirely distinct from the rush of wings. The old gunner who took charge of our place at Eastham used to say that these birds were old white wings, and would add, "some call them bell coots." The sound is rather more slowly repeated than the usual wing beat of the black duck, but the impression that it always gave me was that it was produced by the wings and not by the voice of the fowl. At any rate, it is a very clear and distinct sound, a series of low, bell-like sounds which might occur repeated two or three times and then be lacking. These birds were crossing Cape Cod on their fall migration. I have not heard it for some years now, but it used to be a frequent experience. As I said, these birds were going over in the night and we could never, of course, identify them.

Game.—The time-honored sport of coot shooting has for generations been one of the most popular and important forms of wildfowl hunting on the New England coast. Next to the black duck, which undoubtedly stands first in the estimation of our sportsmen, there are probably more scoters killed on our coasts than any other of the Anatidae. Aside from the fact that the scoters are not of much value for the table, coot shooting has much to recommend it; it is a rough and rugged sport, testing the strength, endurance, and skill of an experienced boatman; the birds are strong fliers and hard to kill, requiring the best of marksmanship, under serious difficulties, and hard-shooting guns; during good flights game is almost always within sight, giving the sportsman much pleasant anticipation; and chances are frequently offered to show his skill at difficult and long shots. I was born and bred to be a coot shooter, inheriting the instinct from three generations ahead of me, and I only wish that I could impart to my readers a small fraction of the pleasure we have enjoyed in following this fascinating sport.

Rudely awakened at an unseemly hour, soon after midnight it seems, the party of gunners are given an early breakfast before starting out. It is dark as midnight as we grope our way down to the beach, heavily laden with paraphernalia, launch our boats in a sheltered cove among the rocks, and row out onto the ocean. The crisp October air is cool and fresh, as the light northeast wind comes in over the ledges, fragrant with the odors of kelp and rockweed. There is hardly light enough at first to see the line of boats, strung out straight offshore from the point, but soon we find our

place in the line, anchor our several strings of wooden decoys, and
then anchor our dory within easy gunshot of the nearest decoys,
which if correctly placed are the smallest and most life-like; the
largest decoys are merely to attract the birds from long distances.
Perhaps before our decoys are set we have seen a few shadowy forms
flitting past us in the gloom, or heard the whistle of their wings in
the dark, the beginning of the morning flight; occasionally the flash
of a gun is seen along the line and the day's sport has begun. As
the gray of early dawn creeps upward from the sea we can clearly
distinguish the long line of boats, perhaps a dozen or fifteen, anchored at regular intervals, a little less than two gunshots apart so
that birds can not slip through the line, and extending for several
miles offshore, an effective barrier to passing flocks. Every eye is
turned northward, looking up the coast and straining to discover
the minute specks in the distance, as the first flock appears several
miles away. "Nor'ard," the warning signal is passed along the
line, as some keen eye has made the longed-for discovery, and every
gunner crouches in his boat to watch and wait and hope for a shot.
Soon we can make them out, an irregular, wavering bunch of black
specks, close to the water and well inshore. The boom of distant
guns tells us that other gunners up the coast have seen them and
perhaps taken their toll. On they come, now strung out in a long
line headed straight for us, big black birds with flashing white wing
patches, "bull white wings," as the males of this species are called;
we shall surely get a shot. But no, they have seen us and swerved,
flying along the line seaward; a shot from the next boat drops a
single bird and they pass through the line beyond, dropping two
more of their number. A bunch of young surf scoters, "gray coots,"
is headed for the next boat, and we try to attract their attention
by imitating the whistling of their wings; they turn and swing in
over our decoys, dropping their feet and preparing to alight; four
barrels are fired in quick succession and three of them drop in the
water. Two of them will die as they are lying on their backs with feet
kicking the air, but the other has its head up and is swimming
away. We throw over our anchor buoy and give chase, but cripples
are hard to hit in the water and we have a long pull and plenty of
shooting before we land him. Meantime we have missed a magni-
cent shot at a large flock of "skunk heads," surf scoters, which
circled over our decoys and escaped through the gap, and on our
return we find only one of our "dead" birds.

A temporary lull in the flight gives us a chance to rest and admire
the beauty of the scene around us; the delicate blush of dawn deepens
and brightens as the gorgeous hues of sunrise spread from the eastern
horizon over the broad expanse of sky and sea, a rapidly changing

play of colors until the sun itself appears over the water and bright daylight gilds the ocean. Bird life is not lacking in the scene; herring gulls are flying about on all sides, often coming near enough to tempt us to shoot at them, but never quite near enough to kill; they seem to know just how far a gun will shoot. Occasionally a black-backed or a few kittiwake gulls are seen. Loons are frequently passing, generally high in the air, with long outstretched necks, flying swiftly in a straight line, their bodies propelled by rapid wing strokes; they often fly within gunshot, but are tough and hard to kill. Large flocks of oldsquaws make interesting shooting, as they twist and turn and wheel in compact bunches; they are swift of wing and not easy to hit; their weird cries add a tinge of wildness to the scene. On rare occasions the sport is enlivened by a shot at a flock of brant, and our pulse runs high when we see a long line of big black birds with white bellies headed for our boat, flying close to the water; we are lucky if we get any for they are very shy.

The little "gray coots," the young of the American and the surf scoters, give the best shooting and are the best for the table; they decoy well, particularly when in small flocks, and are easily killed; a pair or a single bird will often circle about the decoys again and again, giving plenty of chances for long single shots. "Butter bills" and "skunk heads," the adults of these two species, decoy well in small flocks, but large flocks are usually wild and either pass the line high in the air or circle out around the end of it. Fifteen or twenty birds is considered a good day's sport, but as many as 135 birds have been killed in a day by two gunners in one boat, or over 90 by a single gunner. Although they are thus persecuted year after year throughout the whole length of their migration route, they do not seem to have diminished materially in numbers since the time of our earliest records, and vast numbers of them still migrate along our coast.

Fall.—The fall migration on the New England coast begins in September, a few early flocks sometimes appearing in August; the main flight is in October when, under favorable weather conditions, it is very heavy; before and during northeast storms large flocks of scoters are almost constantly in sight migrating southward; the flight is prolonged in lessening numbers during November, and by the end of that month they have reached their winter quarters.

Winter.—Their winter range extends from the Gulf of St. Lawrence southward along the Atlantic coast to South Carolina, and on the Pacific coast they winter from the Aleutian Islands to Lower California. White-winged scoters are particularly abundant in winter on the waters of Long Island and Vineyard Sounds, the center of their winter range, where they find an abundant food supply in the beds of shellfish which abound in this region. Great rafts of them may be seen bedded on the water way offshore where they sleep and rest. At certain stages of the tides, when the water is not too deep over their feeding grounds, they fly in regularly, day after day, to the same spot to feed on the mussel beds on the submerged ledges and sunken rocks along the shores and even in the harbors. Scallop fishermen are often guided by their movements in locating their quarry. Gunners soon learn to locate their feeding grounds and take advantage of their regular flights.

Winthrop Sprague Brooks (1915) described, under the subspecific name, *dixoni*, a subspecies of the white-winged scoter, the type of which was collected by Joseph Dixon at Humphrey Point, Alaska. He assumes that all of the white-winged scoters, which breed in Alaska and migrate down the Pacific coast, are referable to this subspecies, which he characterizes as "similar to *deglandi*, with the exception of the size and shape of bill, which in *dixoni* is shorter and broader in proportion to its length and more blunt at the tip, with the angles from its greatest width to the tip more abrupt." He says further: "On examining a large series of white-winged scoters from both sides of the continent there is no difficulty in separating Atlantic and Pacific birds by means of this character of the bill."

In order to establish a winter range for this subspecies I wrote Dr. Joseph Grinnell for his opinion on the status of California birds. He replied as follows:

I know nothing about *Oidemia deglandi dixoni*. I have not used this name for any of the birds in this museum, because the authenticity of the alleged race has not been verified by anyone else. I have just looked at our birds, with Brooks's drawings of bills before me. I see every sort of variation from the narrow extreme to the broad extreme among birds taken in California. There are only three eastern birds here, and each of them finds a counterpart among California-taken specimens.

From this statement I should infer that the subspecies is untenable and that the characters ascribed to it are due to individual variation. The study of more specimens from the supposed breeding range of *dixoni* might establish a local breeding race, which mingles in its winter range with the commoner form. A careful study of a large series from many localities is necessary to settle the question.

Dr. H. C. Oberholser and I have recently made a careful study of the large series of white-winged scoters in the collections of the United States National Museum and the Biological Survey, containing birds from many different parts of North America, and find that the characters on which *dixoni* are supposed to be based can be matched in many birds from the Atlantic coast, and that they are no more prevalent in birds from the Pacific coast or the interior than elsewhere. We therefore came to the conclusion that these characters represent merely individual variation and should not be regarded as establishing a subspecies.

DISTRIBUTION

Breeding range.—Northern North America. East to the Labrador coast (Hamilton Inlet and Nain), occasionally in Newfoundland (Gaff Topsail). South to the north shore of the Gulf of St. Lawrence, southern Manitoba (Shoal Lake), central North Dakota (Devils and Stump Lakes), and northeastern Washington (east of the Cascade Mountains). West to northwestern British Columbia (Stikine River) and sparingly to northwestern Alaska (Kotzebue Sound). Seen in summer and perhaps breeding in the Aleutian Islands as far west as Tanaga Island. North to the barren grounds of northern Alaska and Canada.

Winter range.—Mainly on the seacoasts. On the Atlantic coast from the Gulf of St. Lawrence southward to South Carolina and rarely to Florida. On the Pacific coast from the Commander, Pribilof, and Aleutian Islands southward to Lower California (San Quintin Bay). In the interior on the Great Lakes and irregularly or casually as far west and south as southern British Columbia (Okanogan Lake), Colorado (9 records), and Louisiana.

Spring migration.—Northward along the Atlantic coast to Labrador and northwestward from the coast to the interior; also northward in the interior and along the Pacific coast. Early dates of arrival: Ontario, Toronto, April 13; Ohio, Lorain, April 27; Kentucky, Bowling Green, April 6; Minnesota, April 5; Manitoba, Aweme, April 15; Alberta, Alix, May 10; Mackenzie, Fort Simpson, May 18. Late dates of departure: Connecticut, May 15; Massachusetts, May 25; Ontario, Ottawa, May 4, and Toronto, May 26; Pennsylvania, Pittsburgh, May 13; Ohio, Lorain, May 3. The main flight up the Pacific coast and across British Columbia to the interior is in May.

Fall migration.—Apparently a reversal of spring routes. Early dates of arrival: Massachusetts, September 6; Maryland, Baltimore, September 12; Ontario, Beamsville, October 8; Minnesota, Heron Lake, October 11; Colorado, Loveland, October 11; Idaho, Coeur d'Alene, October 22; Utah, Bear River, October 8. Late dates of departure: Mackenzie, Nahanni River, October 14; Ontario, Beamsville, November 26; Idaho, Coeur d'Alene, December 1.

Egg dates.—North Dakota: Thirteen records, June 18 to August 10; seven records, June 29 to July 19. Arctic Canada: Nine records, June 14 to July 10. Alberta, Saskatchewan, and Manitoba: Seven records, June 21 to July 6.

MELANITTA PERSPICILLATA (Linnaeus)

SURF SCOTER

HABITS

This is probably the most abundant and certainly the most widely distributed of the three American species of scoters. It is widely and well known on the Atlantic and Pacific coasts, and in some of the more northern localities it is exceedingly abundant. The enormous flights of scoters, or " coots," as they are called, which pour along our coasts in the spring and fall are made up mainly of surf scoters and white-winged scoters; every gunner knows them, and most of the residents along the New England coasts have tasted the delights of coot stew.

Spring.—The abundance of the surf scoter on the spring migration is well illustrated by the following quotation from Mr. Dresser, given by J. G. Millais (1913), based on observations made at Lepreaux Lighthouse, in the Bay of Fundy:

On my arrival there on April 25 myriads of ducks were flying past, among which surf scoters were more numerous than any other species. They followed the line of the coast at a short distance from the shore, and in passing the point generally steered close in or flew over the end of the point itself. On the 26th I spent the day among the rocks, and I never recollect seeing waterfowl in such countless numbers as I did on that day, all wending their way northward. Velvet, common, and especially surf scoters were the most numerous; but there were also many eiders, brent geese, long-tailed ducks, with a few harlequins, great northern divers, and some others. The surf scoters flew in large, compact flocks, from 8 to 10 deep. I estimated the length of the flocks by watching them as they passed certain points, the distance between which was known to me, and I found that one compact flock was at least half a mile in length, a second reaching from one point to another, distant nearly a mile and a quarter. I made several telling shots amongst them, knocking over 8 at one discharge and 6 and 4 at a double shot, though I was only using a light 15-bore gun. I found them, however, very hard to recover, for during the time the dog was retrieving them one or two were sure to come to and paddle off, and the sea was too rough to go out in a boat to pick up the cripples. The males proved to be far more numerous than the females, of which sex I only killed 3 during the whole day.

George H. Mackay (1891) writes:

In the spring mating begins before the northward migration commences, as I have taken eggs from females, between the 15th and 25th of April, which varied in size from a cherry stone to a robin's egg. During this period the duck when flying is always closely followed by the drake, and wherever she goes he follows; if she is shot, he continues to return to the spot until also killed. I have often on firing at a flock shot out a female; the moment she commences to fall she is followed by her mate; he remains with her, or flies off a short distance, only to return again and again until killed, regardless of previous shots fired at him. I have never seen any such devotion on the part of the female; she always uses the utmost speed in flying away from the spot, and never returns to it.

Courtship.—W. Leon Dawson (1909) thus describes the courtship.

I have seen a surf scoter courtship in mid-April. Five males are devoting themselves to one female. They chase each other about viciously, but no harm seems to come of their threats; and they crowd around the female as to force a decision. She in turn chases them off with lowered head and out-stretched neck and great show of displeasure. Now and then one flees in pretended fright and with great commotion, only to settle down at a dozen yards and come sidling back. If she will deign a moment's attention, the flattered gallant dips his head and scoots lightly under the surface of the water, showering himself repeatedly with his fluttering wings. One suitor swims about dizzily, half submerged, while another rises from the water re-peatedly, apparently to show the fair one how little assistance he requires from his feet in starting, a challenge some of his corpulent rivals dare not accept, I ween. I have watched them thus for half an hour, off and on, and the villains still pursue her.

Charles E. Alford (1920) describes another interesting perform-ance, as follows:

I once watched 8 male surf scoters wooing one female, and a most absurd spectacle it was. Immediately the female dived, down went all her admirers in pursuit. Then after a lapse of about 40 seconds the males would reappear one by one, the female, who was always the last to rise to the surface, being invariably accompanied by one male; but whether it was the same male on each occasion I was unable to distinguish. For a few seconds pandemonium would reign, the rejected suitors splashing through the water and pecking at their rivals in the most vicious manner, whilst the object of their desire floated serenely in their midst, apparently well pleased that she should be the object of so much commotion. Then she would dive again, and so the performance continued for over an hour, when they drifted out of sight.

He writes again (1921): "When displaying, the male surf scoter swims rapidly to and fro, keeping head and neck erect, and at inter-vals dipping its beak into the water. Should several males be pres-ent, the female swims from one to the other, bowing her head, or darting occasionally at some undesirable suitor." Maj. Allan Brooks (1920) says that he has "seen them vigorously courting in central British Columbia, well along in June; three or four males whirl-ing about a female on the water like whirling beetles, and uttering a curious low, liquid note, like water dropping in a cavern." Mr. Charles L. Whittle writes to me that he has seen active courtship in the fall, October 5, which he describes as follows:

The males would face the females and bow rapidly and repeatedly, even to the extent of emersing their heads, thereby spraying themselves with water, the females watching the operation with interest. Another pretty and characteristic maneuver on the part of the males was to fly away suddenly about 75 feet, their wings being raised over their backs till the tips nearly touched as they alighted on the water, and then to swim back to their mates with great velocity, only to repeat their bowing. The males chased each other away from their respective mates by lowering their heads and swimming fiercely at their offending neighbor. That the females were also parties to these courtship performances is shown by the fact that they also would similarly attack the male, paired to the other female, if he approached too near.

Nesting.—In spite of the abundance of this species over a wide breeding range very few naturalists have ever found its nest, and remarkably little has ever been published regarding its breeding habits. The reason for this is that the breeding grounds are usually in such inaccessible places in the marshy interior that few explorers have ever visited them; moreover, the nests are probably so widely scattered and so well hidden that few have been found. The following from Dr. E. W. Nelson (1887) shows how abundantly the surf scoter must breed in northern Alaska and yet he never found a nest. He says:

On August 23, 1878, I visited Stewart Island, about 10 miles to the seaward of St. Michael. As I neared the island in my kyak I found the water literally black with the males of this species, which were united in an enormous flock, forming a continuous band around the outer end of the island for a distance of about 10 miles in length and from one-half to three-fourths of a mile in width. As the boat approached them those nearest began to rise heavily, by aid of wings and feet, from the glassy surface of the gently undulating but calm water. The first to rise communicated the alarm to those beyond, until as far as could be seen the water was covered with flapping wings, and the air filled with a roar like that of a cataract. The rapid vibrations produced in the air by tens of thousands of wings could be plainly felt. In all my northern experience among the waterfowl which flock there in summer I never saw any approach to the number of large birds gathered here in one flock, nor shall I soon forget the grand effect produced by this enormous body of birds as they took wing and swept out to sea in a great black cloud and settled again a mile or so away.

MacFarlane (1891) found a number of nests of the surf scoter in the Anderson River region which he said were much like those of the white-winged scoter, " the only difference noted being that generally less hay and feathers was observed in the composition of its nest, while only one contained as many as 8 eggs, the usual number being from 5 to 7." Of the white-winged scoter's nests he said:

These were always depressions in the ground, lined with down, feathers, and dry grasses, and placed contiguous to ponds or sheets of fresh water, frequently amid clumps of small spruce or dwarf willow, and fairly well concealed from view.

In a letter to Professor Baird, dated July 16, 1864, he writes:

The surf duck is numerous, but as its nest is usually placed at a considerable distance from open water, and always well concealed underneath the low-spreading branches of a pine or spruce tree, we never get many of its eggs. The female never gets off the nest until very closely approached, and then invariably (so far as I had an opportunity of judging) makes off to the nearest lake, where it will remain for hours, and thus exhaust the patience of the finder, who is, when traveling, at least, obliged to secure the eggs without their parent.

Audubon (1840) gives an interesting account of the finding of a surf scoter's nest in southern Labrador, which is about the only detailed account we have of the nesting habits of this common species. He writes:

For more than a week after we had anchored in the lovely harbor of Little Macatina, I had been anxiously searching for the nest of this species, but in vain; the millions that sped along the shores had no regard to my wishes. At length I found that a few pairs had remained in the neighborhood, and one morning while in the company of Captain Emery, searching for the nests of the red-breasted merganser, over a vast oozy and treacherous fresh-water marsh, I suddenly started a female surf duck from her treasure. We were then about 5 miles distant from our harbor, from which our party had come in two boats, and fully 5½ miles from the waters of the Gulf of St. Lawrence. The marsh was about 3 miles in length and so unsafe that more than once we both feared as we were crossing it that we might never reach its margin. The nest was snugly placed amid the tall leaves of a bunch of grass and raised fully 4 inches above its roots. It was entirely composed of withered and rotten weeds, the former being circularly arranged over the latter, pro-ducing a well-rounded cavity 6 inches in diameter by 2½ in depth. The borders of this inner cup were lined with the down of the bird, in the same manner as the eider duck's nest, and in it lay 5 eggs, the smallest number I have ever found in any duck's nest. They were 2⅚ inches in length by 1⅝ in their greatest breadth; more equally rounded at both ends than usual; the shell perfectly smooth and of a uniform pale yellowish or cream color.

We saw no signs of breeding surf scoters in southern Labrador in 1909, and apparently the few which bred there in Audubon's time have long since ceased to breed there regularly. On the north-east coast of Labrador, however, or rather a few miles inland, they probably still breed regularly and abundantly. We saw large num-bers of males in the inner harbors and in the mouths of rivers at a number of places all along the coast in July and August, which suggested that probably the females were incubating sets of eggs or tending broods of young on the inland ponds or marshes. We hunted for nests in many suitable places, but never succeeded in find-ing one. Samuel Anderson, an intelligent observer and collector of birds at Hopedale, told me that surf scoters breed about the in-land ponds and lakes, making their nests in the grass or under bushes close to the edge of the water. There is a Labrador set of 7 eggs in the collection of Herbert Massey, of Didsbury, England, for which he has kindly given me the data; it was taken by R. S. Duncan on Akpatok Island on June 11, 1903, and the female was shot for identification.

Eggs.—The surf scoter evidently lays from 5 to 9 eggs, usually about 7. The eggs are, I think, usually recognizable by their shape, size, and color. They vary in shape from ovate to elliptical oval and are often quite pointed. The shell is smooth but not at all glossy.

The color is a very pale "cartridge buff," or a pinkish or buffy white. Mr. Millais (1913) describes the eggs in the Massey collection as "rather pointed in shape, creamy in color." The measurements of 33 eggs, in various collections, average 61.6 by 43 millimeters; the eggs showing the four extremes measure **67.5** by 43, 59 by **45**, **58** by 41, and 59 by **40.5** millimeters.

Plumages.—Strangely enough there does not seem to be a single specimen of the downy young surf scoter in any American or European collection, except two half-grown young in the Museum of Comparative Zoology, in Cambridge, Massachusetts, collected by Francis Harper on Athabasca Lake, on July 28, 1920. Although as large as teal, these birds are still wholly downy, with no trace of appearing plumage. The smaller, a female, has the crown, down to and including the eyes, a deep glossy " clove brown " in color; the color of the black varies from " olive brown " anteriorly to " clove brown " on the rump; the sides of the head and throat are grayish white, mottled with " clove brown "; the entire neck is pale " clove brown "; the colors of the upper parts shade off gradually into paler sides and a whitish belly. In younger birds these colors would probably be darker, brighter, and more contrasted, as they are in other species.

In the juvenal plumage the sexes are alike. The crown is very dark, blackish brown, conspicuously darker that the rest of the plumage; the upper parts are dark brown and the lower parts lighter brown and mottled; there is a whitish loral space and a smaller whitish auricular space; the tail feathers are square tipped; and there is no trace of the white nuchal patch. During the first winter, beginning sometimes as early as October but often not until February, the sexes differentiate by the growth of new black feathers in the male and brown feathers in the female; this growth begins on the head, scapulars, and flanks, whence it spreads, before spring, until it includes all the fore part of the body and much of the back, leaving only the juvenal wings, part of the back, and the central under parts, which fade out almost to white; the tail is molted during the winter and the new feathers are pointed at the tip. The white nuchal patch is acquired by the young male before spring, but not the frontal patch; the bill assumes its brilliant coloring and increases in size, but it does not reach its full perfection for at least another year.

A complete postnuptial molt takes place in August, September, or even later in young birds, which produces a plumage which is practically adult. The male acquires the white frontal patch and the female the white nuchal patch at this molt and the bills become more mature, but full perfection is probably not attained for another year.

Young birds probably breed the following spring and at the next postnuptial molt become fully adult, when 27 or 28 months old.

Adults have a partial prenuptial molt, involving mainly the head and flanks, in March and April, and a complete molt in August. There is no true eclipse plumage and no marked seasonal change. I have a highly plumaged adult male in my collection, collected October 4, in which the white nuchal patch is merely indicated by a narrow, broken outline and the frontal patch by a short row of small white feathers.

Food.—The food and feeding habits of the surf scoter are practically the same as those of the other scoters and other diving sea ducks. Their food consists almost entirely of various small mollusks, such as mussels, sea clams, scallops, and small razor clams. The large beds of the common black mussel which are so numerous and so extensive in the tidal passages of our bays and harbors or on outlying shoals are their favorite feeding grounds. Large flocks, often immense rafts, of scoters spend the winter within easy reach of such beds, which they visit daily at certain stages of the tide; although they can dive to considerable depths to obtain food if necessary, they evidently prefer to feed at moderate or shallow depths and choose the most favorable times to visit the beds which can be most easily reached. Their crops are crammed full of the small shellfish, which are gradually ground up with the help of small stones in their powerful stomachs and the soft parts are digested. A small amount of vegetable matter, such as eelgrass and algae, is often taken in with the other food, perhaps only incidentally. Dr. F. Henry Yorke (1899) says that, on the lakes of the interior, " it feeds on shellfish, especially mussels, crayfish, and fish spawn; besides a few bulbs of aquatic plants."

Behavior.—The flight of the surf scoter is not quite so heavy as that of the white-winged scoter; it is a smaller, lighter, and livelier bird on the wing, but it so closely resembles the American scoter in flight that the two can not be distinguished at any great distance. It rises heavily from the surface of the water and experiences considerable difficulty in doing so unless there is some wind, which it must face in order to rise. This necessity of rising against the wind is well understood by gunners, who take advantage of it to approach a flock of bedded birds from the windward, forcing the birds to rise toward the boat and thus come a little nearer. When once under way the flight is strong, swift, and well sustained. In calm weather or in light winds migrating birds fly high, but in windy or stormy weather they plod along close to the waves. They often fly in large flocks or irregular bunches without any attempt at regular formation, following the coast line, as a rule, but sometimes passing over capes or points to make short cuts. Mr. Mackay (1891) writes:

I have noticed during the spring migration northward in April that frequently the larger flocks of the surf scoter are led by an old drake. That the selection of such a leader is a wise precaution has frequently been brought to my notice, for on first perceiving such a flock coming toward me in the distance they would be flying close to the water; as they neared the line of boats, although still a considerable distance away, the old drake would become suspicious and commence to rise higher and higher, the flock following him, until the line of boats is passed, when the flock again descends to the water. When over the boats shots are frequently fired up at them, but so well has the distance been calculated that it is seldom a bird is shot from the flock.

As a diver the surf scoter is fully equal to the other sea ducks, depending on its diving powers in its daily pursuit of food and to escape from its enemies in emergencies. It dives with an awkward splash, but very quickly and effectively, opening its wings as it goes under, and using them in its subaqueous flight. It can remain under for a long time and swim for a long distance without coming up; it is useless to attempt to chase a slightly wounded bird. Mrs. Florence Merriam Bailey (1916) has graphically described the ability of this species to dive through the breaking surf, as follows:

It was a pretty sight when, under a gray sky, the beautiful long green rolls of surf rose and combed over and the surf scoters came in from the green swells behind to feed in front of the surf and do skillful diving stunts to escape being pounded by the white waterfalls. As the green wall ridged up over their heads they would sit unmoved, but just as the white line of foam began to appear along the crest they would dive, staying under till the surf had broken and the water was level again. When diving through the green rollers near the shore the black bodies of the scoters, paddling feet and all, showed as plainly as beetles in yellow amber.

I have never heard the surf scoter utter a sound; and Mr. Mackay (1891) says: "My experiences show that all the scoters are unusually silent and seem to depend entirely on their sight in discovering their companions. I have rarely heard the surf scoter make any sound, and then only a low, guttural croak, like the clucking of a hen; they are said to utter a low whistle." Doctor Nelson (1887) says: "In the mating season they have a low, clear whistle for a call note, and may be readily decoyed within gunshot by imitating it from a blind."

Fall.—Referring to the fall migration, Dr. Charles W. Townsend (1905) writes:

Although scoters fly most in stormy weather and are often found quietly feeding on calm days, still they sometimes go south in great numbers even in pleasant weather. This flight is greatest in the early morning, but may be continued all day. At times flock succeeds flock as far as the eye can see off the beach at Ipswich. Occasionally four or five exclusive ones go along together, but usually the flocks are much larger, up to five or six hundred. These sweep along at times in one long line close to the water. Anon they press together in a compact and solid square. Again they spread out into a long line abreast or form a **V**, and at all times they rush along with irresistible energy. On reaching the angle at Annisquam where Cape Ann juts out boldly, the birds are often at a loss what to do. Sometimes they fly first one way and then another, rising higher and higher all the time, and then strike out toward the end of the cape, over which they resume their southerly course at a considerable height. Another flock will turn at the angle without pausing and skirt the shore around the cape. Again, a flock will pause and fly high at the angle, and then along the coast, soon to descend to the original height above the water and round the end of the cape. All these are methods commonly adopted. Occasionally a flock will get discouraged on reaching the solid barrier of the cape, will turn back and drop into the water to talk it over. All this shows the dislike of the scoter to fly over the land.

As a result of many years of observation, Mr. Mackay (1891) says:

The old birds of the surf scoter appear about the middle of September, with a very large movement about the 20th, according to the weather, the young birds making their appearance the last of September or first of October. I have known a considerable flight to occur on the last day of September, the wind all day being very fresh from the southwest, which deflected them toward the land; such an early movement is, however, unusual. An easterly storm about the middle of August is likely to bring them along, the wind from this direction being particularly favorable for migration; if, on the other hand, the weather is mild and warm, it is not usual to see them so early.

From this time on they continue to pass along the coast until near the end of December, the main flight coming between the 8th and 20th of October, depending upon the weather, when the migration appears to be at an end. During such migration they are estimated to fly at a rate of about 100 miles an hour, but this rate is also governed by the weather. The greater part of these scoters pass around Cape Cod, as I have never heard of, nor seen, any of the immense bodies of "bedded" fowl north or east of it as occur south and west of the cape; probably because they are unable to find either the security or profusion of food north of it that they can obtain in the waters to the south. They therefore congregate here in large numbers.

Winter.—In the waters lying south of Cape Cod, Massachusetts, in the vicinity of Nantucket, Muskeget Island, and Marthas Vineyard, vast numbers of scoters spend the winter. Mr. Mackay (1891) writes:

Most of these places being inaccessible to ordinary sportsmen, the birds can live undisturbed during the late autumn, winter, and spring months, undoubtedly returning year after year to these same waters, which appear to have become their winter home.

Where there are large ponds adjacent to the coast, separated from the ocean by a strip of beach, all three of the scoters will at times frequent them to feed, and will collect in considerable numbers if the supply of food is abundant; in which case they are very unwilling to leave such ponds, and, although much harassed by being shot at and driven out, continue to return until many are killed. An instance of this kind occurred the 1st of November, 1890, when some 400 scoters collected in the Hummuck Pond on Nantucket Island; they were composed entirely of the young of the surf and white-winged scoters, only one American (a female) being obtained out of about 50 birds shot in one day (November 3) by a friend and myself. On March 18, 1875, I saw on a return shooting trip from the island of Muskeget to Nantucket a body of scoters, comprising the three varieties, which my three companions and myself estimated to contain 25,000 birds.

DISTRIBUTION

Breeding range.—Northern North America. East to the Atlantic coast of Labrador and probably Newfoundland. South nearly or quite to the Gulf of St. Lawrence, to James Bay (both sides), northern Manitoba (Churchill), northern Saskatchewan and Alberta (Athabasca Lake), perhaps northern British Columbia, and to southern Alaska (Sitka). West to the Bering Sea coast of Alaska (Yukon delta). North to northern Alaska (Kotzebue Sound), the barren grounds of Canada and northern Labrador. Said to have bred in northeastern Siberia (Tschuktschen Peninsula) and in Greenland (Disco Island).

Winter range.—Mainly on the sea coasts. On the Atlantic coast from the Bay of Fundy southward to Florida (St. Lucie, Jupiter, etc.), most abundantly from Massachusetts to New Jersey. On the Pacific coast from the Aleutian Islands southward to Lower California (San Quintin Bay). It winters commonly on the Great Lakes and more sparingly westward to southern British Columbia (Okanogan Lake) and southward rarely to Louisiana (New Orleans).

Spring migration.—Early dates of arrival: New Brunswick, April 10; Central Alberta, McMurray, May 14; Alaska, Kowak River, May 22. Late dates of departure: Louisiana, New Orleans, March 20; Georgia, Cumberland Island, May 6; North Carolina, Pea Island, May 15; Rhode Island, May 21; Massachusetts, May 9.

Fall migration.—Early dates of arrival: Massachusetts, September 4; Rhode Island, September 1; South Carolina, Mount Pleasant, October 24; Minnesota, Jackson County, October 1; Idaho, Fernan Lake, October 9; Colorado, Barr Lake, October 22; Utah, Bear River, October 24.

Casual records.—Three records for Bermuda (January 8, 1849, October 7, 1854 and November 17, 1874). Said to have occurred in Jamaica. There are numerous records for Great Britain and France, three for Finland and several others for western Europe; these may come from a Siberian breeding range.

Egg dates.—Arctic Canada: Twelve records, June 19 to July 8; six records, June 25 to July 1.

ERISMATURA JAMAICENSIS (Gmelin)

RUDDY DUCK

HABITS

This curious little duck is in a class by itself, differing in several peculiarities from any other North American duck. It is widely scattered over the most extensive breeding range of any of our ducks, from far north to far south and from our eastern to our western coasts. Its molts and plumages are unique, involving a complete seasonal change from the gaudy nuptial to the dull and somber autumn dress; even the seasonal changes in the oldsquaw are less striking. But its eggs furnish the greatest surprise of all; for, although this is one of our smallest ducks, it lays eggs which are about as large as those of the great blue heron or the wild turkey. In its appearance and behavior it is also unique and exceedingly interesting. One must see it on its breeding grounds, in all its glory, to appreciate what a striking picture is the male ruddy duck. In the midst of a sea of tall, waving flags a quiet, sheltered pool reflects on its glassy surface the dark green of its surroundings, an appropriate setting for the little gem of bird life that floats gently on its surface, his back glowing with the rich, red brown of his nuptial attire, offset by the pure white of his cheeks, his black crown, and above all his wonderful bill of the brightest, living, glowing sky blue. He knows he is handsome as he glides smoothly along, without a ripple, his saucy sprigtail held erect or even pointed forward till it nearly meets his upturned head; he seems to strut like a miniature turkey gobbler.

Courtship.—His mate knows that he is handsome, too, as she shyly watches him from her retreat among the flags, where perhaps she is already building her basketlike nest. As she swims out to meet him his courtship display becomes more ardent; he approaches her with his head stretched up to the full extent of his short neck and his eyes gleaming under two swollen protuberances above them like the eyes of a frog; with his chest puffed out like a pouter pigeon, he bows and nods, slapping his broad, blue bill against his ruddy breast; its tip striking the water and making a soft, clucking sound. Should a rival male appear upon the scene, he rushes toward him, they clash in an angry struggle, and disappear beneath the surface in desperate combat, until the vanquished one skulks away and leaves the victor to strut and display his charms with more pride than ever. Since the above was written, Dr. Alexander Wetmore (1920) has published an accurate description of what is apparently the same performance, but rather than repeat it here, I would refer the reader to it.

Mrs. Florence Merriam Bailey (1919) describes it more briefly, thus:

When I arrived only two pairs were in evidence, the puffy little drakes looking very cocky and belligerent, suggesting pouter doves with their air of importance and the curious muscular efforts by which they produced their strange notes. When I first saw one perform, not knowing about his tracheal air sac, I thought he might be picking at his breast or have something stuck in his throat and be choking. With quick nods of the head that jerked the chin in, he pumped up and down, till finally a harsh guttural cluck was emitted from his smooth, blue bill. Often in doing chin exercises the little drakes pumped up a labored *ip-ip-ip-ip-u-cluck; cluck*, producing it with such effort that the vertical tail pressed forward over the back, as if to help in the expulsion, afterwards springing erect again.

Nesting.—In the deep-water sloughs of North Dakota we found the ruddy ducks nesting in abundance; the ideal conditions found here are to be found in many places throughout the west, where the nesting habits of the species are probably similar. In these large sloughs there are extensive tracts of tall reeds, bullrushes, or flags, often higher than a man's head and growing so thickly that nothing can be seen through them at a little distance. In these excellent hiding places the ruddy duck conceals its nest, and so well is this done that even after the nest has once been located it is extremely difficult to find it again. The nests are basketlike structures, well made of the reeds, bullrushes, or flags, closely interwoven; the material always matches the surroundings of the nest, so sometimes the nest is made of the dry stalks only and sometimes partially or wholly of the green material, producing a very pretty effect. The nest is built up some 7 or 8 inches above the level of the water, which is often more than knee deep, and attached firmly to the growing reeds; a sloping pile of reeds is usually added as a stairway leading to the nest, down which the duck can quickly slide into the water on the approach of danger; and the growing reeds above are often arched over the nest in such a way as nearly to conceal it. There is no lining in the nest except a few finer bits of reeds and flags; and what little down is found there may be more accidental than an intentional lining. From such a well-concealed nest the departure of the duck could never be seen; she simply slides into the water and slinks away like a grebe. The female is particularly shy during the breeding season and seldom shows herself near the nest.

The man who found the first ruddy duck's nest must have been surprised and puzzled, for he would never suppose that such large eggs could belong to such a small duck. W. H. Collins (1881) mistook the first eggs of this species that he found at St. Clair Flats for brant's eggs, because the ruddy ducks kept out of sight and some brant happened to be flying about the marsh. But the next season, when no brant were to be seen, he succeeded in identifying the eggs by a careful study of the feathers in the nest, the parents keeping out of sight, as usual. He did finally succeed in seeing a female ruddy leave her nest and swim away under water to the nearest clump of rushes. According to Rev. J. H. Langille (1884), the nesting habits of this duck are somewhat different in this vicinity from what they are in North Dakota. He says:

> The nest, built some time in June, is placed in the sedges or marsh grass over the water, and may contain as many as 10 eggs, remarkably large for the size of the bird, oval or slightly ovate, the finely granulated shell being almost pure white, tinged with the slightest shade of grayish blue. The nest may be quite well built of fine colored grasses, circularly laid, or simply a mere matting together of the tops of the green marsh grass, with a slight addition of some dry, flexible material. I found one nest on a hollow side of a floating log. It consisted of a few dried grasses and rushes laid in a loose circle. Indeed, the bird inclines to build a very slight nest.

Robert B. Rockwell (1911) has found the ruddy duck nesting in still more open situations in Colorado. On May 31, 1907, he found a fine set of 10 eggs in an excavation in the side of a large muskrat house, without any downy lining whatever, and only a few inches above the water level. On June 8 this nest contained 11 eggs, 2 of which were canvasback's or redhead's; there was also a new nest of the canvasback, containing 8 fresh eggs, on the other side of the same muskrat house and only 4 feet away; and, moreover, a new ruddy duck's nest, containing 3 fresh eggs, was found on top of the house and about midway between the two nests. "This was a mere unlined depression in the litter composing the house, entirely without concealment of any kind, and the great snowy white eggs could be seen from a distance of many yards." Three ducks' nests on one muskrat house is certainly a remarkable record.

The ruddy duck has been known to use an abandoned nest of the American coot, which sometimes is not much unlike its own. Doctor Wetmore tells me that in the Bear River marshes in Utah the old nests of the redheads are commonly appropriated by the ruddy ducks. It also lays its eggs in other duck's nests and even in grebe's nests. At Crane Lake, Saskatchewan, I flushed a female ruddy duck from a clump of bulrushes in the midst of a large colony of western grebes; a careful search through the clump revealed only grebes' nests, but one of the nests held 2 eggs of the western grebe and 1 egg of the ruddy duck. I have found ruddy ducks' eggs in the nests of the redhead and the canvasback, and others have mentioned the same thing; the other two species often lay in the ruddy ducks' nests also, so that it is sometimes difficult to decide which was the original owner of the nest.

Eggs.—The ruddy duck is said to lay as many as 19 or 20 eggs, but such large sets are not common; the numbers usually run from 6 to 9 or 10. The eggs are often deposited in two layers and with the largest numbers in three layers; it is obviously impossible for so small a duck to cover any large number of such large eggs. The indications are that in the more southern portions of its range two broods may be raised in a season, which seems to be very much prolonged. William G. Smith says in his notes that he has taken young birds in the down as late as October 16 in Colorado. The eggs are distinctive and could hardly be mistaken for anything else. They vary somewhat in shape from short ovate to elongate ovate, or from oval to elliptical oval. The shell is thick and decidedly rough and granular, much more so than any other duck's egg. When first laid the eggs are pure, dull white or creamy white, but they become more or less stained during incubation. The measurements of 80 eggs, in the United States National Museum and the writer's collections, average 62.3 by 45.6 millimeters; the eggs showing the four extremes measure **67.6** by 44.5, 66.5 by **48**, **59.4** by 45.4, and 61.3 by **42.6** millimeters.

Young.—The period of incubation seems to be unknown, but it is probably not far from 30 days. It is apparently performed by the female alone, although the male does not desert the female at this season, and, contrary to the rule among ducks, he remains with the young family and helps care for them until they are fully grown. Dr. Alexander Wetmore writes to me as follows:

The male ruddy ducks in most instances remain with the females after the young hatch, and it is a common sight to see a male, with tail erect and breast and throat puffed out, swimming at the head of a brood of newly hatched young in a compact flock, while the female follows behind. When such families are approached the adults submerge quietly and disappear with no demonstration whatever, while the young, left to their own devices, make off as rapidly as possible, still maintaining their close formation. Only when seriously threatened do they dive and then scatter. As they grow older the young birds become more independent, and usually when half grown are found separated from their parents. Occasionally, however, well-grown young are found with the female. Young as well as adults are more or less helpless on land, resembling grebes in this respect. Young birds half grown were able to waddle a few steps, but fell on the breast almost at once and then usually progressed by shoving along in a prostrate position with both feet stroking together. These half-grown birds were sullen and ferocious, and none that I had became tame at all. They invariably snapped and bit at my fingers when handled, and with open mouths resented every approach. When first hatched, the feet of these birds are truly enormous in proportion to the size of the body and form a certain index to the future activities of the ducklings.

According to Maj. Allan Brooks (1903), the "young when first hatched are, as might be expected, very large, and dive for their food, unlike all other young ducks, which take their food from the surface for several weeks."

G. S. Miller, jr. (1891), published the following observations on the behavior of young ruddy ducks on Cape Cod, Massachusetts:

On August 11 I found four young, accompanied by the female parent, on a large shallow pond which lies between the towns of Truro and Provincetown. At the approach of my boat the old bird left her young and joined five other adults which were resting upon the water half a mile away; the young ones, however, were too young to fly, and so attempted to escape by swimming and diving to the shelter of a cat-tail island near which they happened to be when surprised. Two of them reached this place of safety, but the others were secured after a troublesome chase. They were very expert divers, remaining beneath the surface for a considerable length of time, and on appearing again exposing the upper part of the head only, and that for but a few seconds. As the water just here happened to be filled with pond weed (*Potamogeton pectinatus* and *P. perfoliatus*), it was not difficult to trace the motions of the birds when beneath the surface by the commotion which they made in passing through the thick masses of vegetation. The flock of old birds contained at least two adult males, which were very conspicuous among their dull-colored companions. They were all very shy, so that it was impossible to approach to within less than 100 yards of them. The adults, as well as the two remaining young, were seen afterwards on several visits to the pond.

Plumages.—The downy young, when first hatched is a large, fat, awkward, and helpless looking creature, covered with long coarse down, which on the upper parts is mixed with long hair-like filaments, longest and coarsest on the rump and thighs. The upper parts are "drab" or "hair brown," deepening to "Prout's brown" or "mummy brown" on the crown and rump, with two whitish rump patches, one above each thigh; the brown of the head extends below the eyes to the lores and auriculars, a broad band of grayish white separating this from a poorly defined malar stripe of "drab"; the under parts are mostly grayish white, shading into the darker colors on the sides and into an indistinct collar of "drab" on the lower neck. The colors fade out paler with increasing age. The young bird is almost fully grown before the juvenal plumage is complete; it comes in first on the flanks, scapulars and head; the down is replaced last on the center of the belly, back, and rump. In this plumage the upper parts are dark brown, "clove brown" or "bone brown" on the back and "blackish brown" on the crown; the feathers of the mantle are indistinctly barred, tipped, or sprinkled with fine dots of pale buffy shades; and the crown feathers are tipped with brownish buff. The flank feathers are more distinctly barred with dusky and grayish buff; the breast feathers are dusky, broadly tipped with buff and the rest of the plumage is more or less mottled with dusky, grayish, and buffy tints. There is no clear white on the side of the head which is mottled with dusky, the mottling forming a more or less distinct malar strip. The sexes are alike in this plumage, except that the female is decidedly smaller. This plumage is worn without much change until the spring molt begins. This molt is nearly complete, involving everything but the wings, and produces the decided seasonal change peculiar to this species.

Mr. A. J. van Rossem has sent me some notes on the molts and plumages of this unique duck, based on extensive studies, from which I quote as follows:

> The juvenal plumage is retained until about January or February, when it is replaced (including the tail) by a plumage closely resembling that of the winter adults. The male, at least, about the middle or end of May then assumes a red plumage in general resembling the midsummer adult, except that the reds are darker and apt to be obscured by an admixture of darker (similar to the winter) feathers. With the taking on of this first red plumage, the tail is again molted. It is molted again in the fall, at the time of the transition into winter plumage. Thus two years are required to attain the brilliant red plumage of the fully adult male.

The ruddy duck is one of very few species which have a strictly nuptial plumage and two extensive molts. The prenuptial molt in April and May produces the well-known nuptial plumage of the male, involving practically all of the contour plumage and the tail, and characterized by the brownish black crown, the white cheeks, the sky-blue bill, and the " chestnut " back. The nuptial plumage of the female is not so striking; it is much like that of the first winter, but the cheeks, chin, and throat become purer white.

There is no eclipse plumage. The summer molt, occurring from August to October, is complete, producing an adult winter plumage much like that of the first winter, except that the cheeks, chin, and throat are pure white, including the lores and nearly up to the eyes; the sexes are much alike in this plumage, but the male is decidedly larger, and many of the mottled feathers of the mantle and flanks are more or less washed with chestnut. Adults can always be distinguished from young birds by the white cheeks and throats.

Food.—Being decidedly a diving duck, the ruddy duck obtains most of its food on the bottom and subsists very largely on a vegetable diet, hence its flesh is usually well flavored. While living on the inland ponds, marshes, and streams, it feeds on the seeds, roots, and stems of grasses and the bulbs and leaves of aquatic plants, such as flags, teal moss, wild rice, pond lilies, duckweed, and wild rye. Dr. F. Henry Yorke (1899) says it also eats small fishes, slugs, snails, mussels, larvae, fish spawn, worms, and creeping insects. Prof. W. B. Barrows (1912) " once took from the crop and stomach of a single ruddy duck, at Middletown, Connecticut, 22,000 seeds of a species of pondweed (*Naias*), which at that time was growing in great abundance in the city reservoir, where the bird was shot." Dr. J. C. Phillips (1911) found in the stomachs of ruddy ducks, shot in Massachusetts, " seeds of bur reed, pondweed, bulrush, and *Naias*, and buds, etc., of wild celery," also " chironomid and hydrophilid larvae."

In the Currituck Sound region of North Carolina and Virginia I have found them feeding almost exclusively on the seeds of the fox-tail grass. Nuttall (1834) mentions " seeds and husks of the *Ruppia maritima*," which is apparently the same thing. Audubon (1840) says: " When on salt marshes they eat small univalve shells, fiddlers, and young crabs, and on the seacoast they devour fry of various sorts. Along with their food they swallow great quantities of sand or gravel."

Behavior.—In its flight, swimming, and diving habits the ruddy duck more closely resembles the grebes than does any other American duck. Its small, rounded wings are hardly sufficient to raise its chunky little body off the water, except with the aid of its large, powerful feet, pattering along the surface for several yards. But, when well under way, it makes good progress in flight, though it flies usually close to the water and seldom rises to any great height in the air, even when migrating. It has a peculiar, uneven, jerky gait in flight by which it can be easily recognized at a long distance, and it usually flies in good-sized or large flocks. Audubon (1840) says:

They alight on the water more heavily than most others that are not equally flattened and short in the body, but they move on that element with ease and grace, swimming deeply immersed, and procuring their food altogether by diving, at which they are extremely expert. They are generally disposed to keep under the lee of shores on all occasions. When swimming without suspicion of danger they carry the tail elevated almost perpendicularly and float lightly on the water; but as soon as they are alarmed, they immediately sink deeper, in the manner of the anhinga, grebes, and cormorants, sometimes going out of sight without leaving a ripple on the water. On small ponds they often dive and conceal themselves among the grass along the shore, rather than attempt to escape by flying, to accomplish which with certainty they would require a large open space. I saw this very often when on the plantation of General Hernandez in east Florida. If wounded, they dived and hid in the grass, but, as the ponds there were shallow, and had the bottom rather firm, I often waded out and pursued them. Then it was that I saw the curious manner in which they used their tail when swimming, employing it now as a rudder, and again with a vertical motion; the wings being also slightly opened, and brought into action as well as the feet.

Walter H. Rich (1907) writes:

The wings are small in proportion to their chunky little bodies, and their flight at the outset is heavy and labored, but once fairly going they fly fast, their wings making considerable noise from their rapid motion. With all these drawbacks the ruddy is wonderfully quick, either in the air or on the water. He is quite capable of taking care of himself once he gets it into his head that harm is intended. He can get under water with a celerity that falls little short of the marvelous. One of his tricks has always been a mystery to me: He will sink himself completely beneath the surface without div-ing—simply settles down like a sinking craft and beats a retreat under water, where he is as much at home as any duck of them all. I have seen black ducks, when they thought themselves undiscovered and their wit said it was dangerous to fly, sink themselves so that only the head showed above water, and have seen shell drakes settle down in the same style until only their heads were visible and so go darting and zigzagging away when they had flown in and settled among a bunch of decoys before discovering the cheat, but I have never seen any of these go completely below the surface without an attempt at diving as does the ruddy.

Audubon (1840) says: "Their notes are uttered in a rather low tone and very closely resemble those of the female mallard." Rev. J. H. Langille (1884) observes: "The ruddy duck is nearly noiseless, occasionally uttering a weak squeak." Doctor Wetmore tells me that the female is entirely silent and that the only note heard from the male is the courtship call, *tick tick tickity quo-ack.*

Fall.—On its migrations the ruddy duck follows the courses of the streams and the lakes, flying low and in large flocks, often close to water and below the level of the banks of the streams. The flights are made mainly early in the morning or during the dusk of evening, perhaps even during the night; they seem to appear suddenly in the ponds and small lakes and disappear as mysteriously; they are seldom seen coming or going. The flocks are made up largely of the dull-colored young birds, and even the old males have acquired their somber autumn dress. They are said to be unsuspicious and easily approached by gunners, but my experience has shown that they are well able to take care of themselves. When in a large flock on an open lake they are particularly difficult to approach, for they will fly long before the gunner can come within gunshot; I have chased them for hours in this way and seen them go spattering off close to the surface with a great whirring of little wings, only to drop into the water again at no great distance, without checking their speed, sliding along the surface and making the spray fly; only when cornered in some narrow bay and forced to fly past the boat do they give the gunner a chance for a shot. Even when suddenly surprised they can escape by diving in remarkably quick time and, swimming under the water for a long distance, come up at some unexpected place; often they seem to have vanished entirely until a careful search reveals one crawling out on a grassy bank to hide or skulking somewhere in the reeds. To chase a wounded bird is almost hopeless. When swimming under water the wings are closed and both feet work simultaneously. William G. Smith states in his notes that while hunting in a boat, where the water was clear, he has "often observed" a wounded ruddy duck "dive down, grasp a weed," and "remain in this position for 20 minutes"; but he does not say whether the duck was alive or not at the end of this remarkable performance.

Game.—Ruddy ducks resort in large numbers, late in the fall, to Back Bay, Virginia, where they are known as "boobies," and furnish good sport for the numerous duck clubs located in that famous resort for sportsmen. Here they spend the winter in the broad expanse of shallow fresh and brackish water bays and estuaries, with the hosts of other wild fowl that frequent that favored region, growing fat and tender on the abundance of foxtail grass, wild celery, and other duck foods. Their feeding grounds are mainly in the shallower, more protected parts of the bays and near the shores, where they are most intimately associated with the American coots which gather there in immense rafts. Large flocks of these sprightly little ducks are frequently seen flying back and forth and they are popular with the sportsman, as they are lively on the wing, decoy readily under proper conditions, and are excellent table birds when fattened on clean vegetable food. They are usually shot from the batteries, such as are used for canvasbacks, but, as they are a little shy about coming to the large rafts of canvasback decoys that are used for the larger ducks, better results are obtained by "tying out" the battery with a smaller number of "booby" decoys. Under favorable circumstances it does not take long for a gunner to secure his legal limit of 35 ducks a day. Another method of shooting them, which is often very succesful, is for a number of boats to surround a flock of birds or drive them into some small bay, where they are eventually forced to fly out past the boats, as they do not like to fly over the land.

DISTRIBUTION

Breeding range.—Mainly in the sloughs and marshes of central and western North America. East to southern Manitoba (Shoal Lake), west central Minnesota (Becker County), southeastern Wisconsin (Lakes Koshkonong and Pewaukee), and southeastern Michigan (St. Clair Flats). South to northern Illinois (Lake and Putnam Counties), northern Iowa (Hancock County), south central Texas (Bexar County), northern New Mexico (Lake Burford), central Arizona (Mogollon Mountains), and northern Lower California (latitude 31° N.). West to southern and central California (San Diego, Los Angeles, Monterey, and Siskiyou Counties), central Oregon (Klamath and Malheur Lakes), northwestern Washington (Seattle and Tacoma), and central British Columbia (Cariboo District). North throughout much of Alberta (Buffalo Lake and Belvedere), probably to Great Slave Lake (Fort Resolution) and to northern Manitoba (York factory).

Outlying, and probably casual, breeding stations have been recorded as far east as Ungava (Richmond Gulf), southeastern Maine

(Washington County), eastern Massachusetts (Cape Cod), southern Rhode Island (Seaconnet Point), and central New York (Seneca River). Extreme southern breeding colonies have been found in southern Lower California (Santiago), the Valley of Mexico, at the Lake of Duenas, Guatemala, and in the West Indies (Cuba, Porto Rico, the Grenadines, Carriacou, etc.), many of which are probably permanent colonies.

Winter range.—The northern portions of the breeding range are vacated in winter. It winters abundantly on the Atlantic coast as far north as Chesapeake Bay and more rarely north to Long Island and Massachusetts; south to Florida, the Bahamas, and the West Indies (Cuba, Porto Rico, Jamaica, Martinique, Grenada, Barbados, etc.). On the Pacific coast, from southern British Columbia (Boundary Bay) southward to Lower California, Guatemala, and Costa Rica (Irazu). In the interior north to central Arizona (Pecks Lake), southern Illinois, and western Pennsylvania (Erie).

Spring migration.—Early dates of arrival: Massachusetts, March 20; Utah, Bear River, March 30; Minnesota, Heron Lake, April 3; Ohio, Oberlin, April 7; Manitoba, southern, April 26; Alberta, Edmonton, May 1. Average dates of arrival: Pennsylvania, Erie, April 16; Ohio, Oberlin, April 15; Nebraska, April 7; Minnesota, Heron Lake, April 10; Wyoming, Cheyenne, April 21; Manitoba, southern, May 5.

Late dates of departure: Kentucky, Bowling Green, April 18; Lower California, Colnet, April 8.

Fall migration.—Early dates of arrival: Virginia, Potomac River, August 20 (average September 30); Massachusetts, Pembroke, September 5; West Indies, Barbados, September 13.

Casual records.—Accidental in Bermuda (November 24, 1846) and Alaska (Kupreanof Island, August 15; 1916). Rare straggler in Nova Scotia and New Brunswick.

Egg dates.—California: Thirty records, April 26 to August 11; fifteen records, May 22 to June 10. North Dakota: Twelve records, June 8 to July 19; six records, June 13 to July 9. Colorado: Nine records, May 31 to August 6. Porto Rico: December to March.

NOMONYX DOMINICUS (Linnaeus)

MASKED DUCK

HABITS

This curious little duck resembles the ruddy duck in many ways and has been placed by some writers in the same genus with it. It is a tropical species, with its center of abundance somewhere in eastern South America, found frequently if not regularly in some

of the West Indies, and with at least five well-established records
in five widely scattered localities within the United States.

Nesting.—A. H. Holland (1892) found it breeding at Estancia
Espartella, in Argentine Republic, where he speaks of it as—

> Rare, living singly or in pairs in the small lagoons, either open or contain-
> ing rushes. It is next to impossible to flush this peculiar duck, as it takes
> after the grebes and invariably dives when disturbed, so that I have never
> seen it on the wing. When swimming it holds its stiff tail spread out and
> erected, inclined somewhat toward its head, and as it swims very low in the
> water the duck is only visible by its head, tail, and the top of its back. It
> builds amongst the rushes early in November, making a nest of green rushes
> with scarcely any lining, being a very flat construction. The eggs are three
> in number and white in color, very rough and very round.

Eggs.—There is an egg of this species in the R. M. Barnes collection, in Lacon, Illinois, which I have examined. It was taken
from the oviduct of a bird in Yucatan on November 17, 1904. It
is ovate in shape and broadly rounded at both ends; the shell is
rough and granulated; and the color is a dirty white. It looks
very much like a ruddy duck's egg. It measures 63 by 45.8
millimeters.

Behavior.—According to Baird, Brewer, and Ridgway (1884):

> Léotaud mentions this duck as being one of the birds of Trinidad, where it
> is by no means rare. While to a certain extent it seems to be migratory
> some are always present on that island. It is social in its habits and seems
> more disposed than any other duck to keep to the water. Its flight is rapid,
> but is not so well sustained as that of most of the other kinds. When it is
> on the land it keeps in an upright position, its tail resting on the ground.
> Its movements on dry land are embarrassed by its claws, which are placed so
> far back as to disturb its equilibrium. Its flesh is excellent, and is held in
> high esteem in that island.

In a paper on the birds of Jamaica, W. E. D. Scott (1891) says:

> In the ponds about Priestmans River I met with this species on two occa-
> sions, and from native hunters learned that it was not at all uncommon,
> especially early in the fall. At Priestmans River, 9th February, 1891, I took
> an adult male, No. 11000, of *Nomonyx dominicus*. The bird was in a small
> and very shallow pond, and did not attempt to fly away upon being approached,
> but tried to hide in some thin grass growing where an old stump of a tree
> projected from the water, and remained so motionless as almost to escape
> notice, though not more than 20 feet away. It was killed with a light load of
> dust shot.
> These little ducks do not seem at all rare on the island, and have much the
> habits of the grebes, frequenting small fresh-water ponds and depending rather
> on hiding in the grass or diving than on flight to escape pursuit. They are
> said by the native gunners to breed at various points on the island.

T. M. Savage English (1916) writes:

> *Nomonyx dominicus* seems to be more or less abundant throughout the year,
> on the secluded ponds of salt water which are frequent among the tall black
> mangrove (*Avicennia*) woods in the north of Grand Cayman; it most probably

breeds somewhere near them—very possibly among the dense thickets of red mangrove (*Rhizophora*), by which they are mostly surrounded. Anyone who has ever been among red mangroves will appreciate the difficulty of finding the nest of a diving bird among them—except by a fortunate chance, which never came to the writer.

Most of the resident birds of Grand Cayman are remarkably fearless of man, very much as robins are in Europe, but these ducks are more wary, and when their pond is approached generally make their first appearance in the middle of it, having dived at the sight or sound of the intruder and, if near the shore, found their way under water to what they think is a safer place. When at rest they float very much as most waterfowl do, the water line being in about its usual place, but when swimming they are almost always deeply submerged, and if approaching or receding from the observer, seem to have a relatively enormous "beam." Of course this effect may be only due to the very low elevation of the bird's back above the water. Their method of diving is interesting. It has the appearance of being done without the movement of a muscle, just as if the bird were a leaking vessel which was going down on an even keel. This downward progress is often interrupted, when just the head, the neck, and the upper part of the upstanding tail are showing above the surface, or a little later, when only the head and part of the neck, which is habitually kept stiffly upright (as is the tail), are visible. In either of these positions the bird seems able to rest as well as to swim at some speed.

Nomonyx dominicus has at least two calls, one of them very like the clucking of a hen to her chickens and the other more reminiscent of a short note from a motor horn.

H. B. Conover writes to me, of the habits of this species in Venezuela, as follows:

We first saw the masked duck in a small pond on the edge of the savannah about 60 miles south of Maracaibo. Here one day I ran into a pair of males in the hen plumage. They were sitting a short way offshore and allowed us to walk up within 15 or 20 yards. The native with me shot at them, killing one, and the other bird jumped. This pair were probably stragglers; I was around there for a week and never saw any more. At Lagunillas in May these birds were abundant in the same marsh as the tree ducks. They sat around in open patches of water among the aquatic plants in small lots of about 5 to 15. They seemed to stay almost entirely in these open patches of water and rarely, if ever, were seen to alight among the floating aquatic plants. They would start to flush at about 75 yards and would rarely let one get within 50 yards of them in a boat. As a general rule, when the flock was approached, they would go off one or two at a time, not rising in a body. They would again alight within 200 or 300 yards. They rose fairly easily from the water, which was a great surprise to me, as they got off the surface very quickly and were not anywhere nearly as clumsy as the ruddy duck. A few birds were seen at this time which showed the red plumage, but the greater majority were in the brown stage. I tried my best to get an adult male, but the birds were so wild I was unsuccessful.

DISTRIBUTION

Breeding range.—In the West Indies (Cuba, Jamaica, Haiti, Porto Rico, St. Croix, Barbados, and Trinidad). Mainly in eastern South America, in Argentina, eastern and central Brazil, Guiana, Venezuela, etc.

Has been taken in Chile (Concepcion, June and September), Peru (Eten, October 11, 1899), Bolivia (Tatarenda and Lake Titacaca), Ecuador (Sarayacu and Peripa), Panama, Guatemala, Mexico (Orizaba, Jalapa, Matamoras, and Esquinapa), and southern Texas (Brownsville, July 22, 1891), and it may breed at some or all of these places.

Winter range.—Includes the breeding range. The records for western South America and Central America may represent winter wanderings.

Casual records.—Has wandered widely in North America to Maryland (Elkton, September 8, 1905), Massachusetts (Malden, August 27, 1889), Vermont (Albury Springs, September 26, 1857), and Wisconsin (near Newville, November, 1870). Some of these may be escapes from captivity.

CHEN HYPERBOREA HYPERBOREA (Pallas)

SNOW GOOSE

HABITS

As fully explained under the next subspecies, a careful study of the available specimens of birds and eggs, from various portions of the breeding range and the winter range of this species, has demonstrated that, while the greater snow goose (*nivalis*) occupies a limited breeding range in northern Greenland and adjacent lands and a narrow winter range on the Atlantic coast, the lesser snow goose (*hyperborea*) is a much more abundant bird of much wider distribution. It breeds along the entire Arctic coast of this continent and on the islands north of it, from Alaska to Baffin Land. Its winter range extends from the Atlantic to the Pacific, but it is very rare east of the Mississippi Valley and much more abundant from there westward. It is especially abundant in winter in California, Texas, and Mexico.

Spring.—The breeding grounds of the snow goose are so far north that we know very little about them in their summer home. They are known to us mainly as winter residents or as migrants. The lesser snow goose seems to have two main lines of flight in the spring, one from the Gulf coast directly northward through the Mississippi Valley and the Athabaska-Mackenzie region, or Hudson Bay route, to the Arctic coast, and the other from California northward, by an overland route west of the mountains, to northern Alaska and then eastward to the mouth of the Mackenzie River or beyond it. The Alaska route is not well known, and it may be that many, perhaps a majority, of the birds pass northeastward across the mountains to the Mackenzie Valley long before they reach northern Alaska. Illustrating these two lines of flight we have the following statements by E. A. Preble and Dr. E. W. Nelson; Mr. Preble (1908) says:

The valleys of the Athabaska and the Mackenzie lie in the path of migration of great numbers of snow geese of both the eastern and western forms. The rivers themselves, however, are seldom followed by the birds, except for short distances, since their general courses trend somewhat toward the west, while the lines of flight of the geese are usually nearly due north and south. Flocks of snow geese, leaving in spring the marshes at the delta of the Peace and Athabaska, a favorite stopping place, strike nearly due northward over the rocky hills, probably not again alighting until several hundred miles nearer their breeding grounds. Thus they press onward, close on the heels of retreating winter, feeding, when suitable open water is denied them, on the various berries which have remained on the stems through the winter.

Pursuing the course of the river northward, the next favorite goose ground is the delta of the Slave, where great numbers stop both spring and fall for rest and food. The low country about the outlet of Great Slave Lake is also a favorite resort. Leaving this point the geese in spring take a general northerly course, which suggests that their breeding grounds are north of the east end of Great Bear Lake.

Doctor Nelson's (1887) remarks would seem to indicate that only a small portion of the birds come as far north as St. Michael and Point Barrow before they turn eastward. He writes:

The handsome lesser snow goose is uncommon on the coast of Norton Sound and about the Yukon mouth. It arrives in spring from the 5th to the 15th of May, according to the season, and after remaining a very short time passes on to its more northern summer haunts. In the vicinity of Nulato, on the Yukon, Dall found them arriving about May 9, on their way up the Yukon; "they only stop to feed and rest on the marshes during the dusky twilight of the night, and are off with the early light of an Arctic spring."

According to Murdoch they are occasionally seen at Point Barrow in spring. This is all seen of these geese in spring throughout Alaska, except perhaps on the extreme northern border, for south of this none breed, and none are found after about May 25. They are far less numerous in spring than in fall along the coast of Bering Sea, and their spring migration is over so quickly that they are rarely killed at that season. Doctor Adams, while at St. Michael in 1851, noted the arrival of these birds from the south in spring and their departure to the north in fall, agreeing with my own observations, as noted elsewhere.

Nesting.—Although there are quite a number of sets of eggs of the snow goose in collections, the information we have regarding its nesting habits is scanty enough. MacFarlane (1891) apparently never found the nest of this bird himself, for he says:

The Esquimaux assured us that large numbers of "white waves" annually breed on the shores and islands of Esquimaux Lake and Liverpool Bay, but strange to say, we never observed any in the Barren Grounds proper or on the shores of Franklin Bay. The Esquimaux brought in to Fort Anderson about 100 eggs, which they claimed to have discovered among the marshy flats and sandy islets on the coast of the former, as well as from similar localities on and in the vicinity of the lake of that (Esquimaux) name.

There is a set of 7 eggs in the collection of Herbert Massey, Esq., taken for Bishop J. O. Stringer, on an island in the center of the mouth of the Mackenzie River on June 20, 1896; the nest is described as a depression in the ground, lined with a beautiful lot of gray down; it was collected by an Eskimo, but the bird was shot and the head, wings, and feet were sent with the eggs. I have a set of 5 eggs in my collection from the same missionary, taken on Garry Island in the mouth of the Mackenzie River on June 10, 1912.

Eggs.—The eggs of the snow goose vary in shape from ovate to elliptical ovate. The shell is thick and smoothly granulated, with a slight gloss on incubated specimens. The color is dull white or creamy white. They are usually much nest stained. The measurements of 103 eggs in various collections average 78.6 by 52.3 millimeters; the eggs showing the four extremes measure **88** by **55.5**, 79.6 by **57.2**, **63.2** by 42.4, and 67.8 by **41.8** millimeters.

Plumages.—In the small downy young snow goose, recently hatched, the color of the head shades from " olive buff " above to " pale olive buff " below, suffused with " colonial buff " or pale yellow on the throat, forehead, and cheeks; the down on the back is quite glossy and appears " hair brown," " light drab," or " light grayish olive " in different lights; the under parts are " pale olive buff," suffused on the breast and sides with pale yellow shades.

I have seen no specimens showing the change into the juvenile plumage. In this plumage in the fall the head and neck is mottled with brownish gray or dusky, faintly below, more heavily and thickly above; the mantle and wing coverts, and early in the season the breast are washed or finely sprinkled with grayish; the scapulars, tertials, and secondaries are heavily sprinkled and clouded with grayish; the primaries are more grayish black and not so extensively black tipped as in the adult.

During the first winter and spring much progress is made toward maturity by wear and molt. The dusky markings gradually disappear, much of the contour plumage is molted, as well as the wing coverts and tail, until by summer there is little left of the immature plumage, except a small amount of grayish mottling on the head and the juvenal wings. At the complete molt that summer young birds become practically indistinguishable from adults, when 14 or 15 months old.

Food.—The food of the snow goose is largely vegetable, in fact almost wholly so, during the greater part of its sojourn in its winter home. In the spring this consists largely of winter wheat and other sprouting grains and grasses; and in the fall the stubble fields are favorite feeding grounds, where large flocks are known to congregate regularly. According to Swainson and Richardson (1831) it " feeds on rushes, insects, and in autumn on berries, particularly those of the *empetrum nigrum*." Doctor Coues (1874) gives the best account of its feeding habits, as follows:

Various kinds of ordinary grass form a large part of this bird's food, at least during their winter residence in the United States. They gather it precisely as tame geese are wont to do. Flocks alight upon a meadow or plain, and pass over the ground in broken array, cropping to either side as they go, with the peculiar tweak of the bill and quick jerk of the neck familiar to all who have watched the barnyard birds when similarly engaged. The short, turfy grasses appear to be highly relished; and this explains the frequent presence of the birds in fields at a distance from water. They also eat the bulbous roots and soft succulent culms of aquatic plants, and in securing these the tooth-like processes of the bill are brought into special service. Wilson again says that, when thus feeding upon reeds, " they tear them up like hogs; " a questionable comparison, however, for the birds *pull* up the plants instead of *pushing* or " rooting " them up. The geese, I think, also feed largely upon aquatic insects, small mollusks, and marine invertebrates of various kinds; for they are often observed on mud flats and rocky places by the seaside, where there is no vegetation whatever; and it is probable that when they pass over meadows they do not spare the grasshoppers. Audubon relates that in Louisiana he has often seen the geese feeding in wheat fields, where they plucked up the young plants entire.

Behavior.—Dr. D. G. Elliot (1898) says that the snow geese fly—

very high in a long, extended curved line, not nearly so angular as the V-shaped ranks of the Canada and other geese. With their snowy forms moving steadily along in the calm air, the outstretched wings tipped with black, glowing in the sun's rays with the faint blush of the rose, they present a most beautiful sight. Usually they fly silently with hardly a perceptible movement of the pinions, high above

" * * * the landscape lying so far below
With its towns and rivers and desert places,
And the splendor of light above, and the glow
Of the limitless blue ethereal spaces."

Occasionally, however, a solitary note like a softened " *honk* " is borne from out the sky to the ear of the watcher beneath. Should they perceive a place that attracts them, they begin to lower, at first gradually, sailing along on motionless wings until near the desired spot, and then descend rapidly in zigzag lines until the ground or water is almost reached, when with a few quick flaps they gently alight.

Vernon Bailey (1902) writes:

They are oftenest seen on the wing high overhead in long diagonal lines or V-shaped flocks, flying rapidly and uttering a chorus of shrill falsetto cries.

Illustrating the sociability of the snow goose, in its relation to other species, W. Leon Dawson (1909) says:

Snow geese dispense shrill falsetto cries as they fly about in companies of their own kind, or else mingle sociably with other species. Doctor Newberry says he has often seen a triangle of geese flying steadily, high overhead, "composed of individuals of three species (*Chen hyperborea, Branta canadensis hutchinsii,* and *Anser albifrons gambelli*), each plainly distinguishable by its plumage, but each holding its place in the geometrical figure as though it was composed of entirely homogeneous material, perhaps an equal number of the darker speecies, with three, four or more snow-white geese flying together somewhere in the converging lines."

At Moses Lake and again on the Columbia River I have seen a single snow goose attach itself to a company of resident Canadas—in each case through several days' observation—appearing now alone and now in company with the larger birds. A specimen taken May 9, 1907, at Wallula was with three Canada geese (one pair and a presumed "auntie"), and these were very reluctant to leave their fallen companion.

Fall.—On the fall migration, when the vast hordes of snow geese begin to wing their way southward from their Arctic summer homes, we begin to realize the astounding abundance of the species. George Barnston (1862), of the Hudson's Bay Co., writes:

The snow goose, although it plays a less conspicuous part in the interior of the country, where it seldom alights, except along the margin of the larger lakes and streams, becomes, from its consolidated numbers, the first and greatest object of sport after the flocks alight in James Bay. The havoc spread throughout their ranks increases as the season advances and their crowds thicken, and even the Indian becomes fatigued with the trade of killing. In the fall of the year, when the flocks of young "wewais," or "wavies," as they are called, are numerous and on the wing between the low-tide mark and the marshes or are following the line of coast southerly, it is no uncommon occurrence for a good shot, between sunrise and sunset, to send to his lodge about 100 head of game.

These "wavies," or white geese, form the staple article of food as râtions to the men in James Bay and are the latest in leaving the coast for southern climes, an event which takes place toward the end of the month of September, although some weak broods and wounded birds linger behind until the first or second week in October. They are deliberate and judicious in their preparation for their great flight southward and make their arrangements in a very businesslike manner. Leaving off feeding in the swamps for a day or more, they keep out with the retreating ebb tide, retiring, unwillingly as it were, by steps at its flow, continually occupied in adjusting their feathers, smoothing and dressing them with their fatty oil, as athletes might for the ring or race. After this necessary preparation the flocks are ready to take advantage of the first north or northwest wind that blows, and when that sets in in less than 24 hours the coast that has been covered patchlike by their whitened squadrons and widely resonant with their petulant and incessant calls is silent as the grave—a deserted, barren, and frozen shore.

J. R. Forster (1772), the naturalist, who sailed with Captain Cook in this region, says:

The Indians have a peculiar method of killing all these species of geese, and likewise swans. As these birds fly regularly along the marshes, the Indians range themselves in a line across the marsh, from the wood to highwater mark, about musket shot from each other, so as to be sure of intercepting any geese which fly that way. Each person conceals himself, by putting round him some brushwood; they likewise make artificial geese of sticks and mud, placing them at a short distance from themselves, in order to decoy the real geese within shot; thus prepared they sit down, and keep a good lookout; and as soon as the flock appears they all lie down, imitating the call or note of geese, which these birds no sooner hear, and perceive the decoys, than they go straight down toward them; then the Indians rise on their knees, and discharge one, two, or three guns each, killing two or even three geese at each shot, for they are very expert. Mr. Graham says he has seen a row of Indians, by calling, round a flock of geese, keep them hovering among them, till every one of the geese was killed. Every species of geese has its peculiar note or call, which must gradually increase the difficulty of calling them.

Dr. George Bird Grinnell (1901) draws a pretty picture of migrating snow geese, as follows:

The spectacle of a flock of these white geese flying is a very beautiful one. Sometimes they perform remarkable evolutions on the wing, and if seen at a distance look like so many snowflakes being whirled hither and thither by the wind. Scarcely less beautiful is the sight which may often be seen in the Rocky Mountain region during the migration. As one rides along under the warm October sun he may have his attention attracted by sweet, faint, distant sounds, interrupted at first, and then gradually coming nearer and clearer, yet still only a murmur; the rider hears it from above, before, behind, and all around, faintly sweet and musically discordant, always softened by distance, like the sound of far-off harps, of sweet bells jangled, of the distant baying of mellow-voiced hounds. Looking up into the sky above him he sees the serene blue far on high flecked with tiny white moving shapes, which seem like snowflakes drifting lazily across the azure sky; and down to earth, falling, falling, falling, come the musical cries of the little wavies that are journeying toward the southland.

Winter.—Doctor Coues (1874) refers to the abundance of snow geese in the winter resorts in California, as follows:

On the Pacific coast itself, particularly that of California, the birds are probably more abundant in winter than anywhere else. Upon their arrival in October, they are generally lean and poorly flavored, doubtless with the fatigue of a long journey; but they find abundance of suitable food and soon recuperate. At San Pedro, in southern California, in November, I saw them every day, and in all sorts of situations—some on the grassy plain, others among the reeds of a little stream or the marshy borders of the bay, others on the bare mud flats or the beach itself. Being much harassed they had grown exceedingly wary and were suspicious of an approach nearer than several hundred yards. Yet with all their sagacity and watchfulness—traits for which their tribe has been celebrated ever since the original and classic flock saved Rome, as it is said—they are sometimes outwitted by very shallow stratagem—the same that I mentioned in speaking of the speckle-bellies. It is strange, too, that the noise and general appearance of a carriage should not be enough to frighten them, but such is the case. I have driven in a buggy along the open beach directly into a flock of snow geese that stood staring agape, "grinning" the while, till they were almost under the horse's hoofs; the laziest flock of tame geese that were ever almost run over in a country by-road were in no less hurry to get out of the way. Advantage is often taken of this ignorance to shoot them from a buggy; and, though they have not yet learned that anything is to be dreaded when the rattling affair approaches, yet no doubt experience will prove a good teacher, and its acquirements be transmitted until they become inherent. A wild goose of any species is a good example of wariness in birds, as distinguished from timidity. A timid bird is frightened at any unusual or unexpected appearance, particularly if it be accompanied by noise, while a wary one only flies from what it has learned to distrust or fear through its acquired perceptions or inherited instincts. Doctor Heermann's notice of this species gives an idea of the immense numbers of the birds in some localities, besides relating a novel method of hunting them. He says they "often cover so densely with their masses the plains in the vicinity of the marshes as to give the ground the appearance of being clothed in snow. Easily approached on horseback, the natives sometimes near them in this manner, then suddenly putting spurs to their animals, gallop into the flock, striking to the right and left with short clubs, and trampling them beneath their horses' feet. I have known a native to procure 17 birds in a single charge of this kind through a flock covering several acres."

Walter E. Bryant (1890), in comparing their status then with past conditions in California, writes:

There has not, so far as I am aware, been a very marked decrease in the number of geese which annually visit California, but the area over which they now feed is considerably less than in 1850. In the fall of that year, my father, while going from San Francisco to San Jose, met with acres of white and gray geese near San Bruno. They were feeding near the roadside, indifferent to the presence of all persons, and in order to see how close he could approach he walked directly toward them. When within 5 or 6 yards of the nearest ones they stretched up their necks and walked away like domestic geese; by making demonstration with his arms they were frightened and took wing, flying but a short distance. They seemed to have no idea that they would be harmed, and feared man no more than they did the cattle in the fields. The tameness of the wild geese was more remarkable than of any other birds, but it must be understood that in those days they were but little hunted and probably none had ever heard the report of a gun and few had seen men. This seems the most plausible accounting for the stupid tameness of the geese, 40 years ago. What the wild goose is to-day on the open plains of the large interior valleys of California those who have hunted them know. By 1853 the geese had become wilder and usually flew before one could get within shotgun range, if on foot, but in an open buggy or upon horseback there was no difficulty. There was a very marked contrast between the stupidly tame geese after their arrival in the fall and the same more watchful and shy birds before the departure in spring of the years 1852 and 1853. This is an important fact, showing not only the change in the instinct occurring within three years, but the more remarkable change, or it may be called the revival of the instinct of fear, which was effected within a few months; to this point I will refer again.

The following quotations from Grinnell, Bryant, and Storer (1918) will give a fair idea of present conditions in California:

There has been a more conspicuous decrease in the numbers of geese than in any other game birds in the State. Many observers testify that there is only 1 goose now for each 100 that visited the State 20 years ago, and some persons aver that in certain localities there is not more than 1 to every 1,000 which formerly occurred here. Not only have these birds been slaughtered for the market, but gangs of men have been paid to destroy them where they were feeding in grain fields. Until 1915 they were afforded no protection whatever, and as a natural result their ranks have been so often decimated that, comparatively speaking, only a remnant now remains.

In former years, when passing through the Sacramento or San Joaquin Valleys by train, great flocks of white geese, in company with other, dark-colored species, were often to be seen sitting on the grain fields or pasture lands almost within gunshot of the cars. The days are past and gone when a man has to drive geese from his grain field. In many places where formerly the ground was so covered with white geese as to look snowclad, not a single goose is now to be observed feeding and but few flying overhead. In spite of the extreme shyness and watchfulness of these geese, the ingenuity of the hunter and the increased efficiency of firearms has so far overbalanced the natural protection thus afforded that the birds are now actually threatened with extinction. Unless the protection now furnished proves adequate in the very near future, this State, which at one time appeared to have an inexhaustible supply of geese, will have entirely lost this valuable game resource.

That snow geese are abundant in winter in certain parts of Texas is well illustrated by the following note made by Herbert W. Brandt in Kleberg County:

On March 23, 1919, we went up to the Laureless Ranch headquarters and got Mr. Cody, the foreman, to go for a ride with us. He showed us a new road and took us to Laguna Larga, a great marshy tract 6 miles long in the plains. The water is not deep and grass grows up through it all over, and there are a few small patches of tules or cat-tails, but it all dries up if the summer is dry. As we approached it looked as if it was covered with snow, but it proved to be thousands upon thousands of snow geese and other wild geese. Here is their winter home, coming into the great pastures at night to feed on the abundant grass. Last year for the first time known a couple of large flocks remained the entire summer. It was the most wonderful sight in bird life I ever saw, and it will never be forgotten, as cloud after cloud of white and black birds took to wing and then settled down in a distant part of the marsh.

Mr. Kleberg told us that the geese we saw were just a few left from the great winter flocks, most of them having now departed for the northland. He has seen 500 acres of solid geese, he said, just one snow bank. He hunts them by taking his big Packard car and runs toward them on the prairies at 60 miles an hour. The wind is always blowing here and the geese must rise and fly against it; as they are overtaken they work the pump shotguns on them.

DISTRIBUTION

Breeding range.—Arctic America, along the coast from northern Alaska (Point Barrow) eastward to Hudson Bay (Southampton Island) and Baffin Land, and on Arctic lands and islands north of North America. Has been seen in summer on the Arctic coast of northeastern Siberia (Tchuktchen Peninsula), where it probably breeds. It may breed farther west in Siberia.

Winter range.—Includes the whole of temperate North America from the Atlantic to the Pacific, rare or straggling, mainly as a migrant, on the Atlantic coast, uncommon east of the Mississippi

Valley and most abundant in California, Mexico, Texas, and Louisiana. East rarely to Rhode Island (Narragansett Bay, January 10, 1909), more frequently to the coasts of Virginia and North Carolina and probably only casually to the West Indies. South regularly to the Gulf coasts of Alabama, Louisiana, and Texas, and to central Mexico (Tamaulipas and Jalisco). West to the Pacific coast States. North to southern British Columbia (Vancouver), Nevada, Utah, southern Colorado (San Luis Valley), southern Illinois, and sparingly to the coast of Virginia. South on the Asiatic coast to Japan.

Spring migration.—Mainly northward in the interior and northwestward or northeastward from the coasts to inland valleys. Early dates of arrival: Iowa, Sac County, March 28; Montana, Teton County, April 9; Manitoba, Aweme, April 5; Mackenzie, Fort Simpson, May 2, and Fort Anderson, May 20; Banks Land, Mercy Bay, 74° N., May 31; Alaska, St. Michael, May 5, Nulato, May 9, Kowak River, May 23, and Cape Prince of Wales, May 31. Late dates of departure: Southern Texas, Rio Grande River, March 29, and San Angelo, April 16; California, Gridley, May 1; Utah, Bear River, May 5; Montana, Teton County, April 23; Manitoba, Shoal Lake, April 30; Mackenzie, Fort Simpson, May 25.

Fall migration.—A reversal of spring routes, with more eastward wanderings (practically all New England records are in fall). Early dates of arrival: Maine, Cape Elizabeth, October 2; Massachusetts, Essex County, October 7; New York, Shinnecock Bay, October 8; Mackenzie, Providence, August 30; Alberta, Buffalo Lake, September 26; Manitoba, Aweme, September 24; Arkansas, Helena, October 19; Louisiana, Cameron County, October 7; Texas, San Angelo, October 1; Montana, Terry, September 12; Utah, Bear River, September 3; California, Stockton, September 28; Alaska, Wainwright, September 6, St. Michael, September 1, and Taku River, September 17. Late dates of departure: Banks Land, September 7; Alaska, St. Michael, October 10; Alberta, Buffalo Lake, October 26; Manitoba, October 31; Montana, Teton County, November 24; Massachusetts, Ipswich, December 7.

Casual records.—Snow geese, probably of this form, have wandered on migrations to Labrador (Independent Harbor, October 1, 1914), Florida (Wakulla County, October 30, 1916, and November 23, 1918, and Key West), Bermuda (October 19, 1848), South Carolina (Mount Pleasant, October 16, 1916), the Bahama Islands, Cuba, Jamaica, and Porto Rico. Said to have occurred in the Hawaiian Islands. It has been recorded in Iceland, Norway, Holland, Great Britain, Germany, Hungary, etc. The numerous European records suggest the probability of a more extended breeding range in Palaearctic regions than is now known, with a westward migration.

Egg dates.—Arctic Canada: Nineteen records, June 9 to July 6; ten records, June 15 to 23.

CHEN HYPERBOREA NIVALIS (J. R. Forster)

GREATER SNOW GOOSE

HABITS

When I first began to study the distribution of this large subspecies I was skeptical as to its status, for it did not seem to have any well-defined breeding range or winter range, and it looked very much as if the large birds could be nothing more than extra large individuals. My confusion was due to the fact that I did not know where to draw the line between the greater and the lesser snow geese. I found that my friend Frederic H. Kennard had been studying the same problem for some time, and while he had collected considerable data, which he placed at my disposal, he was waiting for additional data before publishing it.

For the purposes of this life history it will suffice to give merely the general conclusion I have arrived at and a brief statement of the steps which led to them. A collection of the measurements of over 250 birds from various parts of the country, when tabulated according to size, shows very clearly that an extra large subspecies, now called *nivalis*, occupies a very narrow winter range on the Atlantic coast, which it reaches by a decidedly eastern migration route from its breeding range in northern Greenland. All of the largest birds come from extreme eastern localities; I have seen only one bird from the interior that I should call *nivalis;* that is an immature bird in the United States National Museum, labeled Hudson Bay, which, if it came from there, is probably a straggler. All of the birds from Atlantic coast States and Provinces are *nivalis*, except a few very small ones which are doubtless stragglers from the westward and are referable to *hyperborea*. The average measurements of all the birds from Atlantic coast points, including the small birds referred to above, are decidedly larger than the average measurements of birds from the interior or from the Pacific coast States.

The average measurements of all the birds from the interior, from Hudson Bay to Texas, agree very closely with the average measurements of a series of birds from California. This shows conclusively that the birds of the interior are unquestionably referable to the smaller form, *hyperborea*, and that the larger birds from that region, which have been called *nivalis*, are merely large specimens of *hyper-*

borea, which can be nearly, if not quite, matched with birds from California. The measurements of the greater snow goose do not well illustrate its real superiority in size; it is a much heavier bird than its western relative, with a much more stocky build, thicker neck, and larger head. It is generally recognizable at a glance, in the flesh.

The breeding range of the greater snow goose must be determined largely by elimination, though it is clearly indicated by two specimens from northern Greenland; these are the only Greenland specimens of snow geese that we have; they are both typical *nivalis;* and one was the parent of a downy young. The average measurements of 26 birds from the Arctic coasts of Alaska, Canada, and Baffin Land agree very closely with those from California and the interior, and none of them are any larger than the largest birds from these localities. A study of the average measurements of 20 sets of eggs from Arctic America, collected at various points from Point Barrow to Baffin Land, shows no correlation of size with locality; the largest 2 sets came from Cape Bathurst and Franklin Bay; and the smallest 2 came from Mackenzie Bay and Point Barrow. Judging from the evidence shown in the measurements of both birds and eggs, it seems fair to assume that *nivalis* does not breed anywhere on the Arctic coast from Alaska to Baffin Land and that all the breeding birds of that region are referable to *hyperborea*. This leaves for *nivalis* a known breeding range in northern Greenland, which probably extends into Ellesmere Land, Grinnell Land, and Grant Land.

Spring.—Although we have very little data on the subject, what evidence we have seems to indicate that the greater snow geese, which spend the winter on the Atlantic coast, migrate overland across New England to the Gulf of St. Lawrence and then across the Labrador Peninsula to their Arctic summer home. William Brewster (1909) published a letter from M. Abbott Frazar giving an account of a large flock of snow geese which he saw migrating at Townsend, Massachusetts, on April 13, 1908. There were at least 75 birds in the flock. Although the subspecies is in doubt, the chances are that these were greater snow geese. The following note, published by Harrison F. Lewis (1921), throws some light on the subject:

Most recent writers on the waterfowl of northeastern North America speak of the greater snow goose (*Chen hyperboreus nivalis* [Forst.]) as a rare bird in that area and appear to pay little or no attention to the fact that Mr. C. E. Dionne, on pages 109–110 of his book, "Les Oiseaux de la Province de Quebec" (1906), states of this subspecies that it "is very common and often occurs in considerable flocks in spring and fall in certain places on our shores, notably at St. Joachim, where I have seen flocks of three or four thousand individuals, on the Island of Orleans, and as far as the Sea-Wolves' Batture." The three points mentioned by Mr. Dionne are within sight of one another. In their vicinity probably all the greater snow geese in existence in a wild state gather each spring and autumn. From the independent statements of various careful observers, I should conclude that their number is now about five or six thousand. When I visited St. Joachim on March 31, 1921, I saw about 2,000 greater snow geese there and was told that the maximum number would be present about 10 days later. They are well protected by a resident warden maintained by the Cap Tourmente Fish and Game Club.

Kumlien (1879) "saw a few specimens in early spring and late autumn" at Cumberland Sound, where it was apparently "rare and migratory."

W. Elmer Ekblaw has sent me the following notes on the arrival of these geese on their breeding grounds in northern Greenland:

June is almost gone when the first snow geese arrive in northwest Greenland. The land is almost bare of snow, the inland lakelets are open, and rushing streams are flush to the brim with clear, cold water. Spring is at its height when the snow geese come. The first notice of their arrival is a high-pitched *honk-honk*, almost resembling the call of the domestic guinea fowl, that rings out clear and sharp from the swales and valleys of the inland slopes. The birds fly low and swift, their gleaming white plumage dazzlingly conspicuous against the dark-brown hills. When they fly near, the black tips of their wings are easily recognizable. They stalk regally about the lakelets and along the streams like the snow king's soldiers, stately and dignified. They are mated when they arrive in the North, and though they stay in flocks most of the time, they pair as soon as they alight, either on land or in water. Wherever they appear they grace the landscape.

On July, 2, 1914, I watched a flock of 10 at close range while they fed in a small shallow pool in which *Pleuropogon* and *Hippuris* grew abundantly. There were 5 pairs in the flock, and though they did not separate far, the pairs kept somewhat to themselves as they floated idly about in the pool or marched about the shore. They apparently found food on the bottom of the pool, because they dipped under much like canvasbacks feeding on wild celery. I watched them for at least an hour, delighted with their grace and quiet beauty. Their calm behavior contrasted strongly with the wild antics of the oldsquaws in near-by pools.

Nesting.—A long time ago Dr. Witmer Stone (1895) published a list of birds collected by the Peary expedition of 1891 and 1892 in northern Greenland, in which were included an "adult female in worn plumage and one young gosling entirely in down" of the greater snow goose. These birds were collected by Langdon Gibson, the ornithologist of the expedition, in the vicinity of McCormick Bay, latitude 77° 40' north. The measurements of this bird clearly indicate that it is a typical specimen of *Chen hyperborea nivalis* and this constitutes the only definite breeding record we have for this subspecies. Recently Mr. Gibson (1922) has published his notes on this collection, from which I quote as follows:

It was my good fortune to record, for the first time, the breeding of this species in north Greenland. A family was found in Five Glacier Valley on

July 11, 1892. The male disputed my advance with head lowered and much hissing, quite after the fashion of the barnyard goose, and before I was aware of the existence of goslings I shot the female. Then I took two of the goslings, that were about 2 weeks old, leaving the gander to rear the remaining six. The birds were on the nest at the time of capture. The nest itself was well lined with grasses and placed near a pile of broken stone beside a marshy spot some acres in extent and about 100 yards from a shallow pond.

On August 21, when again passing through the valley, I was happy to see the male proudly marching at the head of his family of six at least 10 miles from the nest. As he had a broken wing and his family then had every indication of being able to shift for themselves, I reluctantly, and in the interest of science, dispatched him.

A brief note in the report of the Greeley (1888) expedition to Grinnell Land indicates that this goose probably breeds on this and other lands west of northern Greenland, as a pair was seen June 12, 1882, near Fort Conger, latitude 82° north, and another June 13, 1882, on the shore of Sun Bay. The snow geese found breeding in northern Greenland by the Crocker Land Expedition were undoubtedly greater snow geese, but unfortunately no specimens of birds or eggs were preserved. Mr. Ekblaw's notes state:

The geese nested in the grassy swales and flats along the lake-dotted flood plain of the streams which empty into North Star Bay. The nests are placed in depressions among the tussocks so that the brooding birds are not readily detected; built up somewhat with mud and grass and dead vegetation and lined with white feathers and down, they are much better constructed than are the nests of the eider and the oldsquaw.

The first eggs are laid soon after July 1. A full clutch is 6 or 7 eggs. In about four weeks they hatch. The mothers and the young frequent the larger inland lakes until the young are able to walk and swim and dive fairly well, and then they take to the open sea. In late August or early September the fall molting season comes on. The geese then repair to the most remote and isolated lakes to be safe and free from disturbance while their wing feathers are renewed. At this time they are relatively helpless and the Eskimo find them easy prey. By mid-September the molting season is over and the geese leave at once.

Eggs.—Apparently there are no eggs of the greater snow goose in collections. All the eggs in collections came from regions where this subspecies is not known to breed and are almost certainly referable to the smaller race.

Plumages.—The downy young, referred to above, is described by Dr. D. G. Elliot (1898) as follows:

Lores, dusky. Two black stripes from bill, passing above and beneath the eye. Top of head, dark olive brown. Sides of head, neck, and entire under parts, light yellow. Upper parts, dark olive brown. Bill, black; nail, yellowish white.

The subsequent molts and plumages are apparently the same as those of the lesser snow goose.

Food.—The food and the feeding habits of the greater snow goose are very much like those of its western relative. It has less opportunity, in the Eastern States, to feed in grain and stubble fields, as such cultivated areas are scarcer and more restricted. Perhaps for this reason these geese seem to be more often seen on the seacoast marshes and beaches in the East than they are in the West. Mr. Elisha J. Lewis (1885) the veteran sportsman, writes:

Snow geese are numerous on the coast of Jersey and in the Delaware Bay. They frequent the marshes and reedy shores to feed upon the roots of various marine plants—more particularly that called sea cabbage. Their bills being very strong and well supplied with powerful teeth, they pull up with great facility the roots of sedge and all other plants.

Harold H. Bailey tells me that on the coast of Virginia they come into the hollows on the sandy beaches to pull up the beach grass and other scanty sand-dune plants to feed on the roots; they do not come into the fresh-water bays with the Canada geese to feed on the fox-tail grass.

Behavior.—Audubon (1840) writes:

The flight of this species is strong and steady, and its migrations over the United States are performed at a considerable elevation, by regular flappings of the wings, and a disposition into lines similar to that of other geese. It walks well, and with rather elevated steps; but on land its appearance is not so graceful as that of our common Canada goose. Whilst with us they are much more silent than any other of our species, rarely emitting any cries unless when pursued on being wounded. They swim buoyantly, and when pressed, with speed. When attacked by the white-headed eagle, or any other rapacious bird, they dive well for a short space. At the least appearance of danger, when they are on land, they at once come close together, shake their heads and necks, move off in a contrary direction, very soon take to wing, and fly to a considerable distance, but often return after a time.

Winter.—Regarding its winter habits Doctor Elliot (1898) says:

On the northern portion of the Atlantic coast the snow goose can not be said to be common, and in many parts is seldom seen. Small flocks are occasionally met with on the waters of Long Island, but the species becomes more abundant on the shores of New Jersey and the coasts of Virginia and North Carolina, where, in the latter State in the vicinity of Cape Hatteras and along the beaches and inlets of Albemarle Sound, it sometimes congregates in great multitudes. Occasionally flocks of considerable size may be seen on the inner beach of Currituck Sound where the water is brackish, but the birds do not remain any length of time in such situations. They present a beautiful sight as they stand in long lines upon the beach, their pure, immaculate plumage shining like snow in the sun, against the black mud of the marshes or the dingy hues of the shore. It is very difficult to approach them at such times, as they are exceedingly watchful and wary, but occasionally a few may leave the main body and, if flying by, will draw perhaps sufficiently near to geese decoys or live geese tied out in front of a blind to afford an opportunity for a shot. The chances are better, however, for the sportsman when these geese are moving in small flocks of six or seven, as they are then more apt to come near the shore looking for favorable feeding places or spots on the beach to sand themselves.

H. H. Bailey tells me that these geese are not now as common on the Virginia coast as formerly, that they do not come until cold weather in midwinter, and that they spend most of their time in Chesapeake Bay or on the ocean, resorting to the hollows among the sand dunes of the outer beaches when these are partially covered with snow and ice.

DISTRIBUTION

Breeding range.—Positively known to breed only in northern Greenland (McCormick Bay, latitude 77° 40′ north, and North Star Bay). Probably breeds also in Ellesmere Land, Grinnell Land (Fort Conger), and Grant Land.

Winter range.—Mainly, if not wholly, on the Atlantic coasts of Maryland, Virginia, and North Carolina, from Chesapeake Bay to Core Sound. Probably all the birds from farther south are referable to *hyperborea*.

Spring migration.—Directly north, overland across New England and the Labrador Peninsula. Early dates of arrival: New York, Shelter Island, April 3; Massachusetts, Townsend, April 13; Maine, Scarborough, April 4; Quebec, St. Joachim, March 31, and Hatley, April 6; Greenland, Etah, June 10. Late dates of departure: North Carolina, Currituck Sound, March 6; Maine, Georgetown, April 25, and Lubec, April 30.

Fall migration.—A reversal of spring route. Early dates of arrival: Quebec, St. Lawrence River, October 12; Massachusetts, Westfield, November 24; Connecticut, Portland, November 20; North Carolina, Currituck Sound, December 11.

Casual records.—An immature bird in the United States National Museum is labeled Hudson Bay, with no further data. Probably all records for Bermuda and the West Indies are referable to *hyperborea*, as that is the wider-ranging form, but some records may refer to *nivalis*.

CHEN CAERULESCENS (Linnaeus)

BLUE GOOSE

HABITS

The blue goose is one of the few North American birds which we know only as a migrant and a winter resident, and within the narrowest limits. It has generally been regarded as a rare species, but it is really astonishingly abundant within the narrow confines of its winter home on the coast of Louisiana. Its apparent rarity is due to the fact that on its migrations to and from this favorite resort its seldom straggles far from its direct route to and from its unknown breeding range. To find the breeding resorts of the blue goose is one of the most alluring of the unsolved problems in American ornithology. It is really surprising that such a large and conspicuous species, which is numerically so abundant, can disappear so completely during the breeding season.

Spring.—Numerous records from various observers indicate a heavy spring migration northward through the Mississippi Valley and over the Great Lakes to James Bay and Hudson Bay, but beyond there the species vanishes completely. No one knows where the blue goose goes to spend the summer and none of the numerous Arctic explorers have ever found its breeding grounds.

The blue goose migrates generally in flocks by itself and usually the old white-headed birds are in separate flocks from the young birds; but occasionally one or more dark-blue geese may be seen leading a flock of pure white-snow geese, which makes a striking picture. The main flight in the spring seems to pass up the east side of James Bay.

Owen Griffith says, in a letter published by Mr. W. E. Saunders (1917):

About 3 miles north of Fort George Post there is a big bay (salt water) with lots of mud and grass at low tide, and in the spring almost every flock of wavies and other geese feed in this bay on their way north; the Indians never hunt them on their arrival in this bay, but gather on a long hill on the other side and then shoot at the birds as they are going off; they generally get up in small flocks, and as they have to rise considerably to clear the hill they can be seen getting up some time before they get to the hill, and then everyone runs along a path and tries to get right under where the flock is going to pass; of course, if three or four flocks get up at the same time, there is shooting on different parts of the hill and the hunters are apt to spoil one another. The Indians say that once these birds leave this bay that they do not feed again till they get far north (Hudson Straits or Baffin Land) in fact a wavey's nest is a great rarity. Strange to say they do not feed in this bay in the fall.

Dr. Donald B. MacMillan, who spent the spring and part of the summer of 1921 at Bowdoin Harbor in southern Baffin Land, says that the blue geese and snow geese migrate from Cape Wolstenholme across to southern Baffin Land. He was told by the natives of that country that both of these geese breed in immense numbers in the marshy lands near some lakes in the interior, a region too difficult to reach and too remote from where his ship was frozen in until August.

Nesting.—There seems to be no authentic record of the finding of a nest of the blue goose and, so far as I know, the nest and eggs in a wild state are unknown to science. All that has been published on the breeding habits or the probable breeding range of the species seems to be based on speculation or hearsay. George Barnston (1862), one of the best authorities on the geese of the Hudson Bay region, says that:

According to Indian report a great breeding ground for the blue wavy is the country lying in the interior of the northeast point of Labrador, Cape Dudley Digges. Extensive swamps and impassible bogs prevail there, and the geese incubate on the more solid and the driest tufts dispersed over the morass, safe from the approach of man. * * * In May it frequents only James Bay and the Eastmain of Labrador, and it is probably the case that its hatching ground is on the northwest extremity of that peninsula and the opposite and scarcely known coast of Hudson Straits.

Eggs.—Hon. R. M. Barnes has kept blue geese on his estate at Lacon, Illinois, for a number of years and has succeeded in raising them to maturity in confinement. He says in a letter to Mr. Frederic H. Kennard that the eggs of the blue goose are quite different from those of the snow goose. He describes the eggs of the snow goose as " more elongated and of a slightly yellowish color," whereas the eggs of the blue goose " are pyriform, of thicker diameter, shorter in proportion to their length, and have a very slight bluish cast," the eggs of both appearing white at first glance; moreover, the eggs of the blue goose have " more minute pit holes and apparently most of these pit holes have a very small deep black center, which can only be disclosed by a microscope." An egg in Mr. Kennard's collection is pure white and very finely granulated. It measures 78 by 51 millimeters.

The measurements of four eggs, laid by one of Mr. Barnes's birds, are 81 by 54.2, 84.6 by 56, 81.2 by 55.8, and 81 by 60.2 millimeters. The nest was lined with " the purest of white down."

Plumages.—Mr. Barnes says that the downy young of the blue goose " is of a deep smoky or slaty bluish color." F. E. Blaauw, who has also raised this species in captivity, describes it as " olive green, darkest on the upper side and yellowish on the belly," with " a little white spot under the chin."

In the fresh juvenile plumage of the first fall, October, the chin is white, the entire head and neck are uniform bluish gray, the back very dark gray, with brownish edgings, and the under parts dull gray, almost whitish on the belly; the wings show a dull reflection of the adult color pattern, the lesser coverts are more or less edged or tipped with brownish, the greater wing coverts are plain pale gray, the primaries and secondaries are duller and browner black than in adults, and the tertials and scapulars are either plain dusky brown or are less conspicuously patterned than in adult birds.

During the first winter there is a nearly continuous molt, with a gradual advance toward maturity. White feathers appear in the head and neck early in the winter, and by spring these have become nearly all white in some birds, but there is generally more or less black on the crown and hind neck. The bluish-gray feathers of the adult plumage invade the lower neck and breast, much new plumage comes in on the back, and new scapulars are partially or wholly acquired. The tail is molted in the spring, beginning sometimes as early as the last of February, but not the wings. Before the birds go north in the spring many of the first-year birds are practically indistinguishable from adult birds except for the immature wings.

What takes place during the following summer we can only guess at, as summer specimens are lacking, but apparently a complete summer molt produces the second winter plumage, which is practically adult. The head and neck become wholly white, or nearly so. The wing is practically adult, with the pure gray lesser coverts and the pale gray primary coverts; the greater coverts have black centers, shading off into silvery gray, and broad, white edges; the scapulars and tertials have the adult color pattern; and the primaries and secondaries are deep black. The under parts are mainly bluish gray, and the rump and upper tail coverts are clear pale gray.

Subsequent molts produce similar plumages, and probably third-year and older birds show greater perfection of plumage and more brilliant color patterns. Many adult birds show more or less white on the under parts, in strong contrast with the bluish gray, varying from a small spot to a large area covering nearly all of the belly; this may be the result of crossing with the snow goose or it may be a character which develops and increases with age. Some observers believe that the blue goose is a dark-color phase of the snow goose. Mr. Blaauw, who has bred both species for some 22 years, has come to this conclusion. On the other hand, Mr. Barnes, who has also bred both, has come to the opposite conclusion; in addition to the difference in the eggs and young, he says that the " build of the two birds is very different, and their physical appearance is very distinct. The call notes are not very similar." It seems to me that they are too unlike in many ways to be color phases of one species, and I can find no conclusive evidence to prove that they are. They are very closely related; so that, like the mallard and black duck, they can interbreed and raise fertile hybrids, which they probably frequently do.

Food.—The feeding habits of the blue goose have been well described by W. L. McAtee (1910), as follows:

In the Mississippi Delta the blue geese rest by day on mud flats bordering the Gulf. At the time of my visit (January 29 to February 4, 1910) these were entirely destitute of vegetation, a condition to which the geese had reduced them by their voracious feeding. Every summer these flats are covered by a dense growth of " cut grass " (the local name for *Zizaniopsis mili-*

acea), "goose grass" (*Scirpus robustus*), "oyster grass" (*Spartina glabra*), "Johnson grass" (*Panicum repens*), and cat-tails or "flag grass" (*Typha augustifolia*), and every fall are denuded by the blue geese, or brant, as they are called in the Delta. The birds feed principally upon the roots of these plants, but the tops of all are eaten at times, if not regularly. Each goose works out a rounded hole in the mud, devouring all of the roots discovered, and these holes are enlarged until they almost touch before the birds move on. They maintain themselves in irregular rows while feeding, much after the manner of certain caterpillars on leaves, and make almost as clean a sweep of the area passed over.

In the Belle Isle region the method of feeding is the same except that the birds feed by day, but the places frequented are what are locally known as "burns"; that is, areas of marsh burned over so that new green food will sooner be available for the cattle. These pastures, for the most part, are barely above water level, so that the holes dug by the geese immediately fill with water. Continued feeding in one area produces shallow, grass-tufted ponds, where formerly there was unbroken pasture. Some of these ponds are resorted to for roosting places, in which case the action of the birds' feet further deepens them, and veritable lakes are produced, which the building-up influence of vegetation can not obliterate for generations, and never, in fact, while the geese continue to use them.

The numbers of the blue geese are so great that these effects are not local but general. At Chenjere-au-Tigre, one proprietor formerly hired from two to four men at a dollar a day, furnishing them board, horses, guns, and ammunition, and keeping them on the move constantly in the daytime to drive the geese away. The attempt was unsuccessful, however, and fully 2,000 acres of pasture were abandoned. Other proprietors had similar experience and suffered loss of the use of hundreds of acres.

The stomachs and crops of the birds in my collection were sent to the Biological Survey for examination by Mr. McAtee, who reported that the contents consisted entirely of the stems of spikerush (*Eleocharis*), of which those in the crops were whole and those in the gizzards finely ground.

Mr. Hersey was told, while collecting blue geese for me in Louisiana, that they also feed on the duck potato, one of the principal duck foods in that vicinity. In his notes on their feeding habits he states:

In reviewing my experience with the blue geese it seems that *normally* they begin to feed about 2 p. m. and continue to do so until dark. They then fly to their roosting ground, where they spend the night. Some time before daylight the flocks again begin to feed, and do so until about 9 or 10 o'clock. They then rest until the afternoon, usually without leaving the feeding ground.

While feeding, small parties are continually flying into the air and moving to a new spot on the outskirts of the flock. If they see anyone approaching at such times, they at once warn their companions and the whole flock takes wing with great clamor.

Behavior.—O. J. Murie has sent me some interesting notes on this species in which he says:

The blue geese are apparently not as prone to fly in the V formation as the Canada geese. The flocks are often broken in a mixture of V's, bars, curves, and irregular lines. Perhaps this is due to the immense numbers in the flocks noted on James Bay. When a flock of "waveys" is passing, the Indian hunter will imitate their call by a single, high-pitched "*guop*"—very different from the double "*au-unk*" in the case of Canada geese. As the blue geese approach with answering calls, an accompanying undertone is heard, a conversational "*ga-ga-ga-ga-ga-ga*," with an occasional clear "whistle." The whistling note is the call of young birds. The Indian makes use of all these sounds, employing the "cackling" notes and an occasional whistle when the birds are near enough to hear it.

On one occasion, while lying in a blind, I heard a peculiar, startled "squawk." Looking up I saw a single blue goose pursued by a duck hawk. The goose ducked and swerved here and there in his flight, with the duck hawk swooping after. The chase continued some distance down the marsh, when finally the duck hawk turned aside and gave it up.

Fall.—Mr. Murie says of the fall flight:

The extensive salt-water marshes around the south and part of the west shore of James Bay furnish an excellent feeding place for shore birds and various ducks and geese, including thousands of blue geese. I was told that blue geese are seen as early as August. By September at least they begin to arrive in James Bay, and during this month and most of October they congregate in immense flocks, principally in Hannah Bay, at the extreme south end of James Bay. Here the Indians go for their annual goose hunting. A blind of willows is placed at a favorite feeding spot, often beside a small streamlet cutting its way by several channels over the mud flat. For decoys, lumps of mud or sod are turned up with a wooden spade. In the top of each lump is thrust a small stick or twig, at the end of which is fastened a piece of folded paper, or, better yet, a small bundle of white quills from a snow goose is stuck in to represent the white head. These crude decoys are very realistic at a distance and prove effective.

The blue geese feed on the open tide flats, while the Canada geese are often found in the swamps or open muskegs well within the margin of the forest. The birds become extremely fat, sometimes bursting open in the fall to the ground when shot. According to native information they do not feed at all the last few days before they begin their flight farther south. In 1914 the blue geese were seen leaving for the south, up the Moose River, on November 1. The following autumn they went south October 21 and 22. In each case snow was falling, with a north or northeast wind.

Winter.—Few people, who have not seen them, appreciate the astonishing abundance of blue geese in the narrow confines of their winter home on the coast of Louisiana.

Mr. Hersey states in his notes:

I am told that before going north most of the flocks congregate in the vicinity of Great and Little Constance Lakes on the Gulf coast west of Vermilion Bay. These flocks are said to be enormous, but the estimates I heard of their numbers were too vague to be of use. One game warden, a very conservative man, told me, however, that he once saw a spot 5 miles long and 1 mile wide (approximately), covered with blue geese, all standing as close together as they could get. Three men fired 5 shots into this flock and picked up 84 dead birds.

Mr. McAtee (1910 and 1911) found these geese exceedingly abundant in a very restricted area on the Louisiana coast. He writes:

The center of abundance of the species is a narrow strip extending along the coast of Louisiana from the Delta of the Mississippi to a short distance west of Vermilion Bay. To the eastward the bird is known only as a straggler, and to the west it diminishes gradually in numbers, being scarce on the extreme western coast of Louisiana and rare on the Texas coast. * * * Being so localized in their winter range, it might seem that the blue geese are in danger of extermination. But they are so wary and so few hunters molest them that at present there is no appreciable reduction in their numbers by man. The same is true, I feel sure, of the winter colonies of snow geese and swans on Currituck Sound, North Carolina. So long as conditions remain the same, the birds being very wary, and having little market value, there is no incentive to kill them, nothing occurring during their stay in the United States will materially lessen their numbers, nor even interfere with the increase of these fine birds. However, if they should become an object of pursuit, it is equally true that they would diminish very rapidly.

DISTRIBUTION

Breeding range.—Recently reported as breeding in large numbers in the interior of southern Baffin Land. Breeding range otherwise unknown.

Winter range.—Mainly in a very restricted area on the coast of Louisiana; from the mouth of the Mississippi River to Vermilion Bay, decreasing very rapidly in abundance eastward and more gradually westward to the coast of Texas (Rockport, Corpus Christi, and Brownsville). Has been recorded in winter as far north as Nebraska, southern Illinois, and Ohio (New Bremen, January 17, 1916), but probably only casually.

Spring migration.—Northward through the Mississippi Valley up the east coasts of James Bay and Hudson Bay. Early dates of arrival: New York, Amagansett, March 21; Rhode Island, Westerly, March 16; Illinois, Lacon, March 23; Iowa, March 28; Manitoba, Aweme, April 9; Ontario, Kingsville, April 6. Late dates of departure: New York, Miller Place, April 28; Manitoba, Shoal Lake, May 29.

Fall migration.—Southward across the eastern United States; more easterly than in the spring. Early dates of arrival: Ontario, Ottawa, October 11; Maine, Umbagog Lake, October 2; Massachusetts, Gloucester, October 20; Rhode Island, Charlestown Beach, October 16; Manitoba, Shoal Lake, October 1; Illinois, Gary, October 21; Louisiana, November 1. Late dates of departure: James Bay, Moose River, November 1; Ontario, Thames River, November 16; Maine, Little Spoon Island, November 13; Rhode Island, Dyers Island, November 9; New York, Amityville, November 22; Manitoba, Aweme, October 24.

Casual records.—Rare in Atlantic coast States, but records are too numerous to be regarded as casuals. Has been recorded in North and South Carolina, the Bahama Islands, and Cuba. There are two good records for California (Stockton, February 1, 1892, and Gridley, December 15, 1910).

EXANTHEMOPS ROSSII (Cassin)

ROSS GOOSE

HABITS

The smallest and the rarest of the geese which regularly visit the United States is this pretty little white goose, hardly larger than our largest ducks, a winter visitor from farthest north, which comes to spend a few winter months in the genial climate of California.

Spring.—Whither it goes when it wings its long flight northeastward across the Rocky Mountains in the early spring no one knows, probably to remote and unexplored lands in the Arctic regions. At certain places it is abundant at times, as the following account by Robert S. Williams (1886), of Great Falls, Montana, will illustrate; he writes:

On the 17th of April, 1885, after several days of stormy weather, with wind from the northwest, accompanied at times by heavy fog and rain, there appeared on a bar in the Missouri River at this place a large flock of Ross's snow geese. In the afternoon of the same day, procuring a boat, we rowed toward the flock, which presented a rather remarkable sight, consisting as it did of several thousand individuals squatting closely together along the edge of the bar. Here and there birds were constantly standing up and flapping their wings, then settling down again, all the while a confused gabble, half gooselike, half ducklike, arising from the whole flock. We approached to within a hundred yards or so, when the geese lightly arose to a considerable height and flew off over the prairie, where they soon alighted and began to feed on the short, green grass. While flying, often two or three birds would dart off from the main flock, and, one behind the other, swing around in great curves, quite after the manner of the little chimney swift in the East. Apparently these same birds remained about till the 26th of April, long after the storm was over, but they became broken up into several smaller flocks some time before leaving. Some five or six specimens were shot during their stay.

Mr. Roderick MacFarlane (1891) never succeeded in finding its breeding grounds or learning anything definite about where it goes in summer; he says:

A male bird of this species was shot at Fort Anderson on 25th May, 1865, where it is by far the least abundant of the genus during the spring migration. The Esquimaux assured us that it did not breed in Liverpool Bay, and it may therefore do so, along with the great bulk of the two larger species, on the extensive islands to the northwest of the American continent. At Fort Chipewyan, Athabasca, however, it is the last of the geese to arrive in spring, but among the first to return in the autumn.

Nesting.—Absolutely nothing seems to be known about its breeding habits in a wild state. Probably nothing will be known until some of the vast unexplored areas in the Arctic regions are better known. But these regions are so inaccessible that their exploration would involve more time, greater expense, and more enthusiasm than even the valuable results to be attained are likely to warrant. Therefore this and several other similar problems are likely to remain for a long time unsolved.

For all that we know about the nesting habits of the Ross goose, we are indebted to F. E. Blaauw (1903) who has succeeded in breeding this species in captivity on his place at Gooilust in Holland. He writes:

At a meeting of the British Ornithologists' Club on March 20, 1901, I exhibited an egg of the rare Ross's snow goose (*Chen rossi*) laid in captivity by a solitary female kept by me at Gooilust. A year later, through the courtesy of Doctor Heck, of Berlin, I received a second specimen of this species, which fortunately proved, as I hoped it would, to be a male. The birds soon paired, and in the beginning of May, 1902, the female made a nest under a bush in her inclosure. The nest was, as is usual with geese, a small depression in the soil, lined with dry grass and grass roots.

Toward the end of the month the female began to lay, and on the 30th, when the full complement of 5 eggs had been deposited, she began to sit, having in the meantime abundantly lined her nest with down from her own breast. The two birds had always been of a very retiring disposition, but after the female had laid her eggs the male, who nearly always kept watch close by the nest, became quite aggressive. He would fearlessly attack anybody that approached.

Eggs.—There is an egg in the collection of Adolph Nehrkorn, probably one of Mr. Blaauw's eggs, which is described as white and which measures 74 by 47 millimeters.

Young.—Mr. Blaauw's bird had incubated for only 21 days when he was surprised to find the eggs hatched. "All the 5 eggs had hatched, and the little birds were still in the nest when I noticed them, forming a most charming group, ever watched as they were by their anxious parents." Another season, when 3 eggs were set under a hen, the period of incubation proved to be 24 days.

Plumages.—Mr. Blaauw (1903) describes the downy young as follows:

The chicks are of a yellowish gray, darker on the upper side and lighter below, and have, what makes them most conspicuously beautiful, bright canary-yellow heads, with the most delicate grayish sheen over them, caused by the extremity of the longer down hairs being of that color. The bill is black, with a flesh-colored tip. A little spot in front of each eye is also blackish. The legs are olive green. The down is wonderfully full and heavy, and it seems almost incredible how such large birds can have come out of such small eggs. Three of the chicks were as described above, but two of them had the part white which in the others was yellow. All that I can add is that, as usual with chicks, the intensity of the coloration gradually diminished as they got older, and in particular the brightness of the yellow of the head and the depth of the black in front of the eyes slowly diminished, so that even when a week old the delicate glory of it had largely disappeared.

The young birds described above all died in the downy stage, but another season he raised one young bird, in which he describes (1905) the development of the plumage as follows:

I am now able to give a complete account of the development of Ross's goose, *Chen rossi*. This season my female laid three eggs, and, as in previous years, she had proved to be a bad mother, I took the eggs away and put them under a common hen. The period of incubation was 24 days this time, and the eggs were hatched on the 10th of July. All the three eggs were hatched, but unfortunately the hen in some way or other killed two of the chicks the same day that they were born. The third escaped this fate and was tenderly cared for by its foster mother. I have described in detail the color of the down in a previous letter (*Ibis*, 1903, p. 245), so that it will suffice to say that the chick was a fluffy object with gray down and a bright canary-yellow head.

The little bird grew very rapidly, and when 2 weeks old was about the size of a Japanese bantam hen. The bill was still black at this stage, with a pink tip (the nail), and the legs were greenish. When 3 weeks old the feathers began to appear on the shoulders, the flanks, the tail, and the wings. When 4 weeks old the bird was about the size of a small hen. The body was almost entirely feathered, but the head and neck were still in down. The legs were bluish and the bill was getting lighter in color. When 5 weeks old the whole body was feathered, and when 6 weeks old even the flight feathers were of their full length. The first plumage may be described as follows: General color, white. A brownish-gray spot on the occiput, which runs down along the back of the neck. The base of the neck and the mantle brownish gray, forming a crescent of that color, of which the points are turned forward on each side of the base of the neck. The smaller wing coverts are of the palest brownish gray, with a dark spot at the tip of each feather. The flanks are gray, the large flight feathers black. The first five secondaries have a dark spot in the center; those that follow are white, with only a very slight sprinkling of brownish; the three innermost have dark centers, and the white edges are finely spotted with gray. The tail is white, with only a suspicion of a grayish tint on the middle feathers. The legs are greenish gray with pink shining through. The bill is pinkish, the lores are blackish gray, which color extends over and behind the eyes. When 10 weeks old the bird began to molt, and the gray feathers of the juvenile dress were rapidly replaced by white ones. Also the large tail feathers were molted, the central rectrices being dropped first. The legs now began to turn pink in earnest, and the bill assumed its double coloration of a greenish base and a pink tip.

From the above account one would infer that the Ross goose acquires its fully adult plumage at its first prenuptial molt, when about 10 months old. As this molt probably involves the tail, all the contour plumage, and the wing coverts, it would leave only the secondaries and tertials to be replaced at a complete postnuptial molt the following summer.

Winter.—The principal winter home of the Ross goose within our limits seems to be in the central valleys of California, where it associates with the snow goose in the stubble fields and is often quite common. It seems to be tamer than other species of geese which visit that region; hence many are shot for the market and quite a number have found their way into scientific collections. Often the wing-tipped birds are kept in captivity and become easily domesticated; I have seen some interesting photographs illustrating the tameness of such captured birds.

DISTRIBUTION

Breeding range.—Entirely unknown, probably on some unexplored Arctic lands.

Winter range.—The main winter range is in California, in the interior valleys (Sacramento and San Joaquin) and nearer the coast farther south (Ventura and Orange Counties). A few may winter occasionally in neighboring States or in Mexico, but probably only casually.

Spring migration.—Northeastward to the Athabasca-Mackenzie region and beyond into Arctic regions. Early dates of arrival: Montana, Lewistown, March 14; Oregon, Camp Harney, April 12; Alaska, Wrangell, April 15; Mackenzie, Fort Anderson, May 25. Average dates of arrival in Montana are April 7 and 8 and of the departure April 24. Later dates of departure: California, Merced County, April 2; Montana, Teton County, May 8; Alberta, Athabasca River, June 4; Arctic coast, Kent Peninsula, June 2.

Fall migration.—A reversal of the spring route. Early dates of arrival: Great Slave Lake, September 1; Alberta, Buffalo Lake, September 6; Montana, Columbia Falls, October 10; California, Stockton, October 6; Utah, Bear River, October 22. Late dates of departure: Alberta, Buffalo Lake, October 10 and Athabasca Lake, October 18; Montana, Columbia Falls, October 28.

Casual records.—Outside of regular migration, it has occurred in Manitoba (Winnipeg, September 20, 1902), Louisiana (Little Vermilion Bay, February 23, 1910), Arizona (Fort Verde, October 24, 1887), Mexico (Bustillos Lake, Chihuahua) and British Columbia (Comox, January, 1894, and Lumby, May, 1920).

ANSER ALBIFRONS ALBIFRONS (Scopoli)

WHITE-FRONTED GOOSE

HABITS

Two forms of the white-fronted goose have long stood on our Check List unchallenged—a smaller European form (*albifrons*) and a larger American form (*gambelli*). The status of the European form as an American bird was based on a somewhat doubtful record for eastern Greenland, where it was supposed to occur only as a straggler. It was supposed to be entirely replaced in North

America by the larger form, where all the American geese of this species were called *gambelli*. This was not a very satisfactory arrangement, for the two forms were so much alike that it was very difficult to distinguish them, and some European writers refused to recognize them. Recently Messrs. Swarth and Bryant (1917) have demonstrated that there are probably two subspecies of white-fronted geese which spend the winter in California between which there is a striking difference in size, and there are some other differences. They have also shown that Hartlaub's name, *gambelli*, belongs to the larger and the rarer of the two and that all of the smaller white-fronted geese, which are far commoner, should be called *albifrons*.

The white-fronted goose has a wide distribution; in the eastern half of this continent it is everywhere rare, but on migrations and in its western winter range it is locally abundant; in much of its breeding range in the far northwest it is one of the commonest and best known of the geese.

Spring.—In writing of this species at Fort Klamath, Oregon, Dr. J. C. Merrill (1888) says:

Very common in April, the main flight occurring between the 20th and 30th, and many flocks stopping to feed in the grassy meadows bordering the marsh. The upper part of the valley is inclosed on the west and north by the main divide of the Cascade Mountains and on the east by a spur from the same range, all averaging a height of over 6,500 feet. On stormy days, if the wind was not blowing from the south, geese flying low up the valley had great difficulty in rising sufficiently to cross the abrupt divide, and most of them would return to the marsh and its vicinity to wait for a more favorable opportunity. At such times geese of this and the next species gathered by thousands and afforded great sport. The immense numbers of these birds that migrate through western Oregon can not be appreciated until one has seen their spring flight, which, I am informed, extends in width from the coast inland about 250 or 300 miles. About 50 of this species were seen at the marsh on May 23 and 20, on May 27 and June 3, after which none were observed; their remaining so late excited general remark among the settlers.

Nesting.—Of the arrival and nesting of this goose at St. Michael, Alaska, Dr. E. W. Nelson (1887) writes:

When the white-fronted goose first arrives in the north the lakes are but just beginning to open and the ground is still largely covered with snow. The last year's heath berries afford them sustenance, in common with most of the other wild fowl at this season. As the season advances they become more numerous and noisy. Their loud call notes and the cries of the males are heard everywhere.

The mating season is quickly ended, however, and on May 27, 1879, I found their eggs at the Yukon mouth. From this date on until the middle of June fresh eggs may be found, but very soon after this latter date the downy young begin to appear. These geese choose for a nesting site the grassy border of a small lakelet, a knoll grown over with moss and grass, or even a flat, sparingly covered with grass. Along the Yukon, Dall found them breeding gregariously, depositing their eggs in a hollow scooped out in the sand. At the Yukon mouth and St. Michael they were found breeding in scattered pairs over the flat country. Every one of the nests examined by me in these places had a slight lining of grass or moss, gathered by the parent, and upon this the first egg was laid; as the complement of eggs is approached the female always plucks down and feathers from her breast until the eggs rest in a soft warm bed, when incubation commences.

John Murdoch (1885) says that at Point Barrow—

the eggs are always laid in the black, muddy tundra, often on top of a slight knoll. The nest is lined with tundra moss and down. The number of eggs in a brood appears subject to considerable variation, as we found sets of 4, 6, and 7, all well advanced in incubation. The last-laid egg is generally in the middle of the nest and may be recognized by its white shell unless incubation is far advanced, the other eggs being stained and soiled by the birds coming on and off the nest.

Roderick MacFarlane (1891) writes:

A considerable number of nests of this "gray wavy" was discovered in the vicinity of fresh-water lakes in timber tracts, as well as along the Lower Anderson River to the sea. Some were taken on the Arctic coast, and several also on islands and islets in Franklin Bay. In all, about 100 nests were secured. The nest, which was always a mere shallow cavity in the ground, in every observed and reported instance had more or less of a lining of hay, feathers, and down, while the maximum number of eggs in no case exceeded 7. On the 5th of July, 1864, on our return trip from Franklin Bay we observed 30 molting ganders of this species on a small lake in the Barrens. Our party divided, and by loud shooting and throwing stones at them they were driven to land, where 27 of them were run down and captured. Their flesh proved excellent eating; it is seldom, indeed, that I have come across a gray wavy that was not in good condition in the far North.

A nest of the white-fronted goose in the writer's collection was taken near Point Barrow, Alaska, on June 27, 1916. It consists of a mass of pale gray and white down, thoroughly mixed with breast feathers of the goose, bits of dry, coarse grasses, lichens, mosses, dead leaves of the dwarf willow, and other rubbish found on the tundra; it is quite different in appearance from the nests of other geese. It contained four eggs advanced in incubation.

Eggs.—The white-fronted goose lays from 4 to 7 eggs, usually 5 or 6. These vary in shape from elliptical oval or elliptical ovate to elongate ovate. The color varies from "light buff" to creamy white or pale pinkish white. I have never seen any tinge of greenish in the eggs of this goose. The eggs often become very much stained with buffy or reddish brown stains, such as "cinnamon buff" or "ochraceous buff," which rub off or scratch off in irregular patches, exposing the original color; there are often several degrees of color in the same set of eggs, the freshest egg being quite clean and the oldest eggs decidedly dark colored. The measurements of 109 eggs, in various collections, average 79 by 52.5 millimeters; the eggs showing the four extremes measure **89.6** by 48, 82 by **58**, **70** by 52, and 77.2 by **46.7** millimeters.

Young.—The period of incubation does not seem to be positively known, but probably it is about 28 days. The male does not desert the female during the process, and both sexes help in caring for and protecting the young. Mr. Hersey, while collecting for me on the Yukon delta, encountered a family of these birds, about which he wrote in his notes for June 21, 1914, as follows:

On the edge of a little pond on the tundra about 5 miles back from the mouth of the river I found a pair of these geese and a brood of five young. The birds had been resting under a clump of dwarf willows, and on my approach the old birds came out into the open and attempted to lead the young away over the open tundra. The young, although not more than a day or two old, could run as fast as a man could travel over the rough ground. I had to remove my coat before I could overtake them. They did not scatter, but ran straight ahead, keeping close together, one of the parents running by their side and guiding them and the other flying along above them and not more than 3 feet above the ground. The young kept up a faint calling, and the old birds occasionally gave a low note of encouragement.

Doctor Nelson (1887) says:

The young are pretty little objects and are guarded with the greatest care by the parents, the male and female joining in conducting their young from place to place and in defending them from danger. The last of June, in 1877, I made an excursion to Stewart Island, near St. Michael, and while crossing a flat came across a pair of these geese lying prone upon the ground in a grassy spot, with necks stretched out in front and their young crouching prettily all about them. Very frequently during my visits to the haunts of these birds the parents were seen leading their young away through the grass, all crouching and trying to make themselves as inconspicuous as possible. At Kotzebue Sound, during the *Corwin's* visit in July, 1881, old and young were very common on the creeks and flats at the head of Eschscholtz Bay.

John Koren collected for me in northeastern Siberia a strange family party consisting of a female spectacled eider and two downy young white-fronted geese.

Plumages.—The downy young white-fronted goose is a beautiful creature, thickly covered with long, soft down and brightly colored. It somewhat resembles the young Canada goose, but the upper parts are a trifle duller in color, and the bill is brown with a light-colored nail, instead of all black as in the Canada. The colors of the upper parts, including the central crown, back, wings, rump, and flanks, vary from " buffy olive " to " ecru olive," darkest on the crown and rump and palest on the upper back, with a yellowish sheen; there is a faint loral and postocular stripe of olive; on the remainder of the head and neck the colors shade from " olive ocher " on the forehead, cheeks, and neck to " colonial buff " on the throat; the colors on the under parts shade from " mustard yellow " on the breast to "citron yellow" on the belly. The colors become duller and browner with increasing age; large downy young are "olive brown" above and grayish or "deep olive buff" below.

I have seen no specimens showing the development of the juvenal plumage. This is much like the adult plumage, except that the " white front " is lacking and there are no black spots on the under parts, which are mottled with whitish and gray; the upper parts are duller colored with lighter edgings; the tail feathers are more pointed and narrower and the wing coverts are narrower than in adults. This plumage is worn without much change during the first winter and spring; but more or less white appears in the " white front," and sometimes a few black spots appear in the breast. The tail is molted in the spring, and during the next summer a complete postnuptial molt produces a plumage which is practically adult.

Food.—Lucien M. Turner (1886) says, of the food of this species: " It inhabits the fresh-water lagoons, and is essentially a vegetarian. The only animal food found in their crops was aquatic larvae and insects. I am not aware that it eats shellfish at any season of the year. The young grass shoots found in the margins of the ponds form its principal food." Doctor Nelson (1887) says: " During August and September the geese and many other wild fowl in the north feed upon the abundant berries of that region and become very fat and tender." In the interior valleys of California, where it spends the winter, and on its migrations through agricultural districts, it feeds in the grain fields on fallen grain in the fall and on the tender shoots of growing grain in the spring. In some places where these geese were formerly abundant they did so much damage to the young crops that the farmers hired men to drive them away.

Audubon (1840) says:

In feeding they immerse their necks, like other species; but during continued rains they visit the cornfields and large savannahs. While in Kentucky they feed on the beech nuts and acorns that drop along the margins of their favorite ponds. In the fields they pick up the grains of maize left by the squirrels and racoons, and nibble the young blades of grass. In their gizzards I have never found fishes nor water lizards, but often broken shells of different kinds of snails.

Behavior.—The flight of the white-fronted goose is similar to that of the Canada goose, for which it might easily be mistaken at a distance. It flies in V-shaped flocks, led by an old gander, and often very high in the air. Its flight has been well described by Neltje Blanchan (1898) as follows:

A long clanging cackle, *wah, wah, wah, wah,* rapidly repeated, rings out of the late autumn sky, and looking up, we see a long, orderly line of laughing geese that have been feeding since daybreak in the stubble of harvested grain fields, heading a direct course for the open water of some lake. With heads thrust far forward, these flying projectiles go through space with enviable ease of motion. Because they are large and fly high, they appear to move slowly; whereas the truth is that all geese, when once fairly launched, fly rapidly, which becomes evident enough when they whiz by us at close range. It is only when rising against the wind and making a start that their flight is actually slow and difficult. When migrating, they often trail across the clouds like dots, so high do they go—sometimes a thousand feet or more, it is said—as if they spurned the earth. But as a matter of fact they spend a great part of their lives on land; far more than any of the ducks.

On reaching a point above the water when returning from the feeding grounds the long defile closes up into a mass. The geese now break ranks, and each for itself goes wheeling about, cackling constantly, as they sail on stiff, set wings; or, diving, tumbling, turning somersaults downard, and catching themselves before they strike the water, form an orderly array again, and fly silently, close along the surface quite a distance before finally settling down upon it softly to rest.

The peculiar laughing cry of this bird has given it the name of "laughing goose." Its cries are said to be loud and harsh, sounding like the syllable *wah* rapidly repeated; the note is easily imitated by striking the mouth with the hand while rapidly uttering the above sound.

The following, taken from Mr. MacFarlane's unpublished notes, illustrates the methods employed by the natives to capture these and other geese during the flightless molting season:

On 12th July we observed about 30 geese (*Anser gambelli*) on the edge of a small lake (in the water) in the Barren Grounds; they were all ganders, and molting. On our approach they went sailing (swimming) across the lake, which was about 2 miles in extent. Our party then divided—half taking one side, and half the other side of the lake—and by the time we reached the spot where the geese had quitted the water, they had all concealed themselves as well as the scant grass and low tangled willows in the vicinity would admit. After we discovered their whereabouts there was some sport and a lively chase after them, and we soon succeeded in securing 27 out of the 30— the remaining 3 having escaped beyond our reach, although followed for some distance into the water. They were all in good condition, in fact, gray wavies are always fat and excellent eating, while it is but seldom in spring and never in summer that a really good Canada goose is met with. The Indians inform me that when they observe a flock of swans or geese on a lake, during the molting season, they at once make a fire on the shore, and they state that this course on their part never fails to drive the geese, etc., on land, where most of them easily fall a prey to the hunter. If they were only wise enough to remain in the water at a proper distance they would be safe enough.

Fall.—The white-fronted goose does not start to migrate until driven south by cold weather. Doctor Nelson (1887) says:

All through September, old and young, which have been on the wing since August, gather in larger flocks, and as the sharp frosts toward the end of September warn them of approaching winter, commence moving south.

The marshes resound with their cries, and after some days of chattering, flying back and forth, and a general bustle, they suddenly start off in considerable flocks, and a few laggards which remain get away by the 7th or 8th of October.

There is a southward migration through the Mississippi Valley to the Gulf coast of Louisiana and Texas, but the main flight trends more to the southwestward to the principal winter home of the species in California. Doctor Coues (1874) writes:

The "speckle-bellies," as they are called in California, associate freely at all times with both the snow and Hutchins geese, and appear to have the same general habits, as well as to subsist upon the same kinds of food. Their flesh is equally good for the table. As is the case with other species, they are often hunted, in regions where they have become too wild to be otherwise successfully approached, by means of bullocks trained for the purpose. Though they may have learned to distrust the approach of a horse, and to make off with commendable discretion from what they have found to be a dangerous companion of that animal, they have not yet come to the same view with respect to horned cattle, and great numbers are slaughtered annually by taking advantage of their ignorance. The bullock is taught to feed quietly along toward a flock, the gunner meanwhile keeping himself screened from the birds' view by the body of the animal until within range. Though I have not myself witnessed this method of hunting, I should judge the gunners killed a great many geese, since they talk of its "raining geese" after a double discharge of the tremendous guns they are in the habit of using. Man's ingenuity overreaches any bird's sagacity, no doubt, yet the very fact that the geese, which would fly from a horse, do not yet fear an ox, argues for them powers of discrimination that command our admiration.

Winter.—Dr. L. C. Sanford (1903) has given us a good account of hunting white-fronted and snow geese in their winter haunts, as follows:

The large bodies of water that are found at rare intervals in northern Mexico are the resort through the winter of countless numbers of geese; not the Canada goose of the East and Middle West, but the snow goose and the white-fronted goose. In early October the hordes arrive, announcing their coming with discordant clamor. They choose as a resting place the shallow alkali waters, and as a feeding ground the neighboring corn stubble, if such there be. A short distance from Minaca is one of these lakes, some 20 miles in length. In the Mexican summer rains replenish the scanty water supply left over from the spring, and October finds it a paradise for waterfowl. Shut in by the rolling hills of the mesa, yellow with wavy grass, its blue surface reflects a bluer sky. All around, as far as the eye can reach, are herds of cattle, for some 6 miles away is a ranch; and at this spot one fall recently we stopped. Early in the morning a breakfast of tortillas and coffee was served, and before it was finished a Mexican boy appeared with the horses. Guns were slipped into the saddle cases. Our attendant found room for most of our ammunition in his saddlebag, and we started for the lake. It was a ride of about 6 miles over an open country, but the horses were fast, and in less than half an hour we looked down from a knoll on the sheet of water some 2 miles away. Along the farther shore was a bank of white, shining in the light of sunrise—a solid bank of snow geese. Scattered over its surface everywhere were flocks of ducks and geese, black masses of them. We hurried on, passing through herd after herd of cattle, which increased in numbers as the water was approached. A coyote stopped to take a fleeting glance from the top of a hill opposite, then disappeared. A jack rabbit scurried from in front. A familiar cry overhead caused us to look up. It came from a flock of sand-hill cranes, far out of reach, which were sailing on toward their feeding ground in the stubble. We reached the edge of the lake, and hundreds of ducks rose as the horses neared them, mostly shovelers and teal, but mallard, widgeon, and pintail were all there. The geese were across the lake, thousands in one band. Every now and then a white line jointed the resting birds, and at the approach of a flock their discordant cries could be heard a mile away. How to get a shot seemed more or less of a problem, owing to lack of cover. Finally we noticed a few bunches of rushes extending well out into the lake, the only possible chance to hide. We waded out and took a position in the farthest clump. The Mexican led off the horses and started on a tour to the farther shore. It was a long way off, almost 4 miles, but there was plenty to watch. Every few minutes flocks of ducks would pass over us in range, but we let them go. Gulls circled around, crying at the unusual sight of two men with guns. We looked over at the geese. At times cattle seemed almost among them; yet the white assembly did not move, and we only heard them when a flock was about to alight to those on the ground. The horses were getting closer, and finally a part of the body started, to settle down a little farther on. But presently a tumultuous clamor, and the entire company was in motion. Line after line separated and led out into the lake. Some followed the opposite shore; an immense flock led toward our clump, and we crouched in the water. On they came, scarcely a hundred yards off. But geese are uncertain, even in Mexico, and for some reason best known to themselves they turned when just out of range and led toward the shore beyond us. In a few minutes they were reassembled and the immediate prospect of a shot gone. The Mexican, with his string of horses, continued down the opposite side, evidently after birds we could not see. Ducks were around us all the time, and flocks drifted by within easy range, unmolested. Before long we heard the familiar cry and looked to see a mass of white heading for the flock on the shore; our blind was right in their line, and they came on, low down over the water, nearer and nearer; finally, 50 or more seemed directly over us, so close we could see their red bills and legs. This was the chance; back to back we raked them, four barrels; 3 birds fell on one side, 2 on the other. The reports started all of the wild fowl in the country. In a few minutes part of the first flock came over us from the opposite direction, and 2 dropped. A flock of geese swung in range over the dead birds, and we killed 2 more. For an hour the shots were frequent, but the birds became wiser every minute and kept to the middle of the lake or else came over the blind out of range. We picked up 18, a dozen white, the rest white-fronted—all one Mexican could pack on a horse.

DISTRIBUTION

Breeding range.—Nearly circumpolar. On the barren grounds and Arctic coasts of North America, east at least as far as the Anderson River and Beechey Lake, in the district of Mackenzie, and west as far as the Yukon Valley (Fort Yukon, Lake Minchumina and the Yukon delta). On the west coast of Greenland, mainly between 66° and 72° N. In Iceland, Lapland, Nova Zembla, Kola, Kolguev, and along the Arctic coast of Siberia to Bering Straits. The only gap in the circumpolar breeding range seems to be between the district of Mackenzie and Greenland; this may prove to be the breeding range of the large tule goose, now called *gambelli*.

Winter range.—In North America, mainly in western United States and Mexico. East to the Mississippi Valley, rare east of that, and hardly more than casual on the Atlantic coast. South to the coast of Louisiana and Texas and to central western Mexico (Jalisco and Cape San Lucas). West to the Pacific coasts of Mexico and United States. North to southern British Columbia, southern Illinois, and perhaps Ohio. In the Eastern Hemisphere, south to Japan, China, India, the Caspian, Black, and Mediterranean Seas and northern Africa.

Spring migration.—Early dates of arrival: Manitoba, Aweme, April 5; Mackenzie, Fort Simpson, May 11, Fort McMurray, May 15, and Fort Anderson, May 16; Coronation Gulf, May 31. Alaska dates of arrival: Forrester Island, April 24, St. Michael, April 25, Kuskokwim River, April 29, Kowak River, May 10, Wainwright, May 27, Point Barrow, May 16. Late dates of departure: California, Stockton, May 2; Washington, Grays Harbor, May 5; Manitoba, Shoal Lake, May 26; Alaska, Kuiu Island, May 6; Oregon, Fort Klamath, June 3.

Fall migration.—Early dates of arrival: Manitoba, Aweme, September 7 (average October 2); Alberta, Red Deer River, September 12; Alaska, Sitka, September 29; British Columbia, Porcher Island, September 6; Washington, Tacoma, October 1; Colorado, Brighton, October 1; Utah, Bear River, October 10; California, Stockton, September 7. Late dates of departure: Mackenzie, Great Bear Lake, October 9; Alaska, St. Michael, October 8, and Craig, November 8; Manitoba, Aweme, November 1.

Casual records.—Has wandered east to Labrador (Hopedale, May, 1900), Massachusetts (Essex County, October 5, 1888, Plymouth, November 26, 1897, and Ipswich, August, 1907), North Carolina (Currituck Sound, January 1897), and Cuba. Said to have occurred in the Hawaiian Islands.

Egg dates.—Arctic Canada: Seventeen records, June 2 to July 10; nine records, June 24 to July 6. Alaska: Twelve records, May 23 to July 25; six records, June 5 to 24. Greenland: Five records June 4 to July 26.

ANSER ALBIFRONS GAMBELLI Hartlaub

TULE GOOSE

HABITS

The above scientific name has been in use for many years to designate the North American race of the white-fronted goose, which was understood to be slightly larger and to have a decidedly larger bill than the European bird. But the characters were not sufficiently well marked and not constant enough to fully satisfy all the European writers, many of whom questioned the validity of the race. Recently, however, Messrs. Swarth and Bryant (1917) have established the fact "that two well-defined subspecies of *Anser albifrons* occur in California during the winter months, instead of the single race heretofore recognized." Tule goose is the common name they have proposed for the newly discovered larger race, and they seem to have shown that Hartlaub's name, *gambelli*, refers to the larger rather than to the smaller and commoner race. In addition to a marked difference in size between the two races, comparable to that existing between the Canada and the Hutchins geese, "the larger birds are of a browner tint, and the smaller ones more gray. This is especially noticeable in the heads and necks. In some individuals of the larger race the head is extremely dark brown, almost black." Also the larger bird is said to have the "naked skin at edge of eyelid, yellow or orange," whereas in the smaller bird it is "grayish brown."

At present the tule goose is known only from its limited winter range in California. Its center of abundance seems to be in Butte and Sutter Basins in the Sacramento Valley, but there are persistent rumors among hunters that it occurs also in the Los Baños region in the San Joaquin Valley and at Maine Prairie in Solano County. I have examined and measured perhaps half a dozen large specimens of white-fronted geese in eastern collections, taken at widely scattered localities in the Mississippi Valley, Hudson Bay, and even on the Atlantic coast, that measured well up within the range of measurements of the tule goose, but they have not been compared with typical large birds from California, nor have they been examined by anyone who is familiar with the characteristics of the tule goose; they may be stragglers of the larger race or they may be only extra large individuals of the smaller race.

Nesting.—In my attempt to establish a breeding range for the larger race I find nothing but negative evidence. There are very few specimens of breeding birds in American collections, and all of those that I have seen are referable to the smaller race. I have collected the measurements of 109 eggs, taken in various localities in northeastern Siberia, Alaska, northern Canada, and Greenland, and they show no correlation of size with locality; the largest two sets came from Greenland and Siberia and the smallest two from Point Barrow and Greenland; average measurements from one locality are not materially different from those from another locality. Moreover, the average measurements of the 109 eggs are very close to the average measurements of 81 eggs of European birds; and the extremes in our series are inclusive. From the above we can infer only that the breeding range of the larger race has never been found and that none of its eggs are in existence. The breeding range of the species, *Anser albifrons*, is circumpolar, except for a decided gap between Greenland and the district of Mackenzie. Somewhere in this gap, or in the Arctic regions north of it, may be the breeding grounds of the big tule goose. An interesting parallel is seen in the case of the Ross goose, which also is found in a restricted winter range in California; the breeding grounds of both are entirely unknown; perhaps some day both may be found breeding somewhere in the vast unexplored regions of the Arctic Archipelago.

Behavior.—Messrs. Swarth and Bryant (1917) have referred to certain characteristic habits of the tule goose, as follows:

> It is said that the two kinds flock separately, for the most part; and that the larger race is never seen in such big flocks as is customary with the other, but is most frequently noted singly or in pairs. Also that while the smaller variety is a common frequenter of grain fields and uplands generally the larger one is preeminently a denizen of open water or of ponds and sloughs surrounded by tules and willows. The predilection of the latter species for such localities has given rise to the local names by which it is known, " tule goose," or " timber goose," as contrasted with the upland-frequenting " speckle-belly."

The notes of the tule goose are said to be " coarser and harsher " than those of the smaller bird.

DISTRIBUTION

Breeding range.—Unknown. It may fill in the gap in the known breeding range of *albifrons*, between the district of Mackenzie and Greenland, where much far northern land is unexplored.

Winter range.—Mainly in California (Sacramento Valley). It may also occur in other central valleys of California and perhaps rarely elsewhere.

ANSER FABALIS (Latham)

BEAN GOOSE

HABITS

Because this common European species has been recorded as a straggler in northern Greenland it has been included in our American list. It was named the bean goose because of its well-established habit of arriving in England with great regularity during bean-harvesting time in October; beans were very extensively cultivated in certain districts, to which these geese resorted in large numbers to feed on the remains of the harvest. John Cordeaux (1898) says on this subject:

We learn from Arthur Young's Agricultural Survey (1798) that the small country towns and villages in the middle-marsh and sea-marsh districts of Lincolnshire were surrounded by vast open fields, arable lands, cow and horse pastures, and furze; on strong land the rotation was fallows, wheat, beans, and again fallows. The area under beans in the low country was enormous, the wheat stubbles being plowed once, and the beans sown broadcast in the spring and never cleaned. These were harvested late in the autumn, usually got with much loss from the jaws of winter. These were the days of the gray goose, which our observant forefathers called the bean goose (*Anser segetum*), coming in great flocks in the later autumn to feast on the shelled beans in the open fields; and this continued till the change in cultivation and general inclosure banished them from their ancient haunts.

Most of the old wild-fowl shooters, who have long since gone over to the majority, used to assert that these autumn flights fed regularly in the bean fields as long as the old system of agriculture continued—a system in which quite one-third of the cultivated land was under that crop.

Nesting.—Rev. F. C. R. Jourdain writes to me that in Nova Zembla the nests of the bean goose are found on grassy tussocks on low ground, and that in Lapland it breeds in the partly wooded marshes where a few birch trees grow, nesting generally on the top of a grassy hummock.

Witherby's Handbook (1920) says that its main breeding haunts are in more wooded districts than those of most geese; that it nests "on islets in rivers or swamps, sheltered by rank vegetation and sometimes by willows or other bushes," and that the nest is "composed of down mixed with grass, moss, etc."

Eggs.—Mr. Jourdain says of the eggs:

They are large as compared with other geese, bulky in appearance, creamy white when first laid, but rapidly becoming nest stained with yellowish, which becomes more pronounced as incubation advances.

The set usually consists of 4 or 5 eggs, occasionally 6. The measurements of 51 eggs, as given in Witherby's Handbook (1920), average 84.2 by 55.6 millimeters; the eggs showing the four extremes measure 91 by 57.2, 84 by 59, and 74.5 by 53.3 millimeters.

Food.—Mr. Cordeaux (1898) says:

The bean goose is very partial to all sorts of grain, and, in this respect, differs from the gray lag, whose chief food is grass. A local name is "corngoose," in France "harvest-goose," and in Transylvania it is known as the "growing-grain goose"; it will, however, eat grass and clover as readily as its congeners when the stubbles are exhausted.

Behavior.—Seebohm (1901) describes the flocking habits of old and young birds in Siberia, as follows:

I then skirted the margin of a long, narrow inlet, exactly like the dried-up bed of a river, running some miles into the tundra, bending round almost behind the inland sea. I had not gone more than a mile when I heard the cackle of geese; a bend of the river bed gave me an opportunity of stalking them, and when I came within sight I beheld an extraordinary and interesting scene. At least 100 old geese, and quite as many young ones, perhaps even twice or thrice that number, were marching like a regiment of soldiers. The vanguard, consisting of old birds, was halfway across the stream, the rear, composed principally of goslings, was running down the steep bank toward the water's edge as fast as their young legs could carry them. Both banks of the river, where the geese had doubtless been feeding, were strewn with feathers, and in five minutes I picked up a handful of quills. The flock was evidently migrating to the interior of the tundra, molting as it went along.

Yarrell (1871) quotes Sir Ralph Payne-Gallwey as saying that in Ireland—

It is by far the commonest species, and may be seen in enormous "gaggles" for six months of every year. It is essentially an inland feeder on bogs and meadows, but will fly to the mud banks and slob of the tide at dusk to pass the night. These geese frequent every bog and marsh in Ireland which afford food and security from molestation. They are always found inland in large numbers save in frost, when they fly down to the meadows and soft green reclaimed lands that lie near the tide. A small proportion will, in the wildest weather, frequent the mud banks to feed and rest. They usually quit their inland haunts at dusk, disliking to remain on land by night when dogs, men, or cattle may disturb them, and accordingly fly to the estuaries to rest and feed. At first dawn they again wing inland and pass the day in open, unapproachable ground.

DISTRIBUTION

Breeding range.—Northern Palaearctic region. East in northern Siberia to the Taimyr Peninsula. South to about 64° N. in Siberia, Russia, Kola, Finland, and Scandinavia. Also on Kolguev and Nova Zembla. Replaced in eastern Siberia by closely allied forms.

Winter range.—Europe and western Asia. South to northern China, casually northern India, Persia, the Mediterranean Sea, and rarely to northern Africa. West to Great Britain.

Casual record.—A specimen in the Zoological Museum of Copenhagen is said to have come from northern Greenland.

Egg dates.—Northern Europe: Eight records, April 29 to June 20. Novaya Zemlia: One record, July 9.

ANSER BRACHYRHYNCHUS Baillon

PINK-FOOTED GOOSE

HABITS

An accidental occurrence of this Old World species in eastern Greenland had long been the slim excuse we had for including the pink-footed goose in the list of American birds, until recently, September 25, 1924, one was taken in Essex County, Massachusetts.

This and the bean goose resemble each other so closely in general appearance and habits that much confusion has arisen as to the distribution and comparative abundance of the two species. It has even been suggested that they may be only subspecies or varieties, as the characters on which the description of the pink-footed goose was based are not very constant. It seems to be now conceded, however, that they are distinct species and that the latter is now the commonest of the gray geese in Great Britain.

Nesting.—Rev. F. C. R. Jourdain has kindly sent me the following notes on his experiences with the pink-footed goose in Spitsbergen:

Although it is probable that this species breeds in Iceland, there is as yet no definite proof, and the only certainly known breeding place is Spitsbergen, so that perhaps the following notes may have some interest.

The pink-footed goose is still a fairly common bird along the west coast of Spitsbergen. Here it has only two enemies—man and the Arctic fox. In former years the Arctic fox was the more dangerous foe, and the habits of the goose have been gradually evolved to contend with this wily little enemy, while the only men to be feared were the few trappers and sealers who robbed the nests occasionally in the spring and shot the molting birds in the summer. Now the foxes have been greatly thinned down, but the little sealing sloops, no longer dependent on their sails, but filled with noisy little oil engines, penetrate everywhere, so that the birds are badly harried. Still the eggs of the geese can not be as readily collected as those of the eider and in consequence have less value, and to discover the isolated nests on the tundra and shingle banks in marketable numbers would be a hopeless task. But during the season of molt the goose has only its speed of foot to trust to, and no doubt large numbers are killed from time to time.

While the brent have found security from the foxes by breeding on the islets round the coast and the barnacle has attained the same end by nesting on steep cliffs, the pink foot, which is a much larger and stronger bird, has to a certain extent managed to hold its own on the open tundra, though it is much more usual to find the nest in somewhat similar sites to those used by the barnacle. I think it is quite possible for a couple of pink-footed geese to keep a prowling fox at bay, though a single bird might have a very unpleasant time, and probably a fair proportion of nests come to grief in this way every year. Like the other species which breed here, the male pink foot is an excellent father and stands by his mate during the incubation period. The first nest we met with was about 10 miles up a wide valley running into Ice Fjord. Here on a slightly raised mossy ridge, which gave a wide view over the snow-sodden flats, we put up a pair of pink-footed geese from the nest, which contained 2 eggs, highly incubated on June 26. This was a curiously small clutch, and yet there is no reason to suppose that the birds had been already robbed. Subsequently we found another nest with 2 incubated eggs on a grassy cliff, and this, too, was in a locality which had not been disturbed. Koenig, who examined a very large number of nests of this species, only met with full sets of 2 on two occasions and considers 4 as the normal number, while sets of 3 and 5 occur commonly. He also met with an instance of 7 eggs in one nest and believed them to be the product of one female, but in another case where 9 eggs were found, the stages of incubation proved that two females had laid together. Curiously enough we never met with more than 4 eggs or young, but the number of eggs taken in 1921 was not large.

Like the brent and barnacle the pink-footed shows a decided tendency to sociability in the breeding season, though many nests are also quite isolated.

Along the west side of Prince Charles Foreland, where the mountains rise steeply from the sea and are almost perpetually wrapped in drifting mists and fogs, there are low grassy slopes and bluffs which lie at the foot of the main range. Here many pink-footed geese breed in hollows on the green ledges, sometimes two or three pairs nesting not far from one another, and nesting hollows which have been used in previous years are quite plentiful; sometimes four or five being visible close together. Most of these nests can be reached by a scrambling climb from below, but there may be a sheer drop of 15 or 20 feet below the nest. In one case we saw four newly hatched goslings in a nest, and the most enterprising of them scrambled over the side of the nest for about a foot. The others, however, did not follow, and it was only by repeated efforts that the youngster was able, after several attempts, to regain its place in the nest. By next day every one of the young birds had disappeared completely. On a subsequent occasion we saw an old goose at the foot of a cliff, attending closely to something on the ground below. Little by little it descended the slope, guiding and helping with its bill something which looked like a downy young bird. One of our party coming from another direction shot the old goose, and going to the spot discovered the young which was evidently being conducted to the shore. The empty nest was on the cliff exactly above where we had first seen the bird, and I have no doubt that it had fallen from the top without suffering any injury, for we took the bird back with us to the ship and attempted to rear it. On another occasion we put up two geese from a vast expanse of shingle at the mouth of one of the valleys, and going to the spot found three addled eggs and a newly hatched gosling. The little bird had already left the nest and made off for us with wonderful speed over the shingle. It was not the least use replacing it, for immediately it was released it set off again in pursuit of the nearest of our party. On returning later with cameras, the young bird was not to be found.

One nest was in a curious position, quite close to the sea, on some sloping ground, sheltered by big bowlders which had fallen from the rocks above.

By July 7 many of these geese had already shed their primaries and were unable to fly in North Spitsbergen. Great numbers of their feathers lay strewn along the shore, while the birds made off at top speed directly they sighted us.

Eggs.—Witherby's Handbook (1920) describes the eggs of the pink-footed goose as "dull whitish." The measurements of 292 eggs average 78.2 by 52.3 millimeters; the eggs showing the four extremes measure **88** by 52.6, 82.6 by **56.7, 69** by 51, and 77 by **47.4** millimeters, according to the same authority.

Food.—John Cordeaux (1898) says:

Geese, on reaching their feeding grounds, whirl in wide circles over the selected spot and, when satisfied that all is safe, sweep suddenly downwards with considerable velocity, and commence feeding at once on alighting.

When, through the depth of snow on the high wolds, food is not to be got, geese entirely change their habits, loafing about on the coast and sand banks during the day, and in the evening flying and dropping anywhere in the low country where they can get green food; the snow seldom lies long in coast districts, and there are always places which the winds have left bare, and the ground is more or less uncovered. I have often seen their paddlings and droppings in pasture, corn, and turnip fields, near the coast. If the neighborhood is quiet and retired, they come inland just as readily in the daytime as at night

Geese feed very greedily anywhere at the break up of a snowstorm, and they are then least difficult to approach, being too much engrossed in eating to heed slight indications of disturbance or interruption. The pink-footed geese, when associated with other species on a feeding ground, keep apart and are not inclined to be sociable. In the day they are visible on a hillside at a very considerable distance and, if a yellow stubble, look like a blue cloud on the land. They are also very conspicuous objects on the sands of the coast, lining the tide edge in long extended line, like a regiment on parade.

In the dusk of evening or at night geese are not so wide-awake as in the day, or they do not see so well, and I have sometimes walked into a flock to our mutual astonishment.

Behavior.—The same writer says of the habits of this species:

The habits of the pink-footed goose so closely. resemble those of the bean goose that much which has been written of the one will hold good of the other. They arrive in the Humber district the last week in September and early in October; the earliest dates in my notebook are September 26, October 3, October 5 (twice), October 10. Mr. Haigh has known them appear as early as August 26, in 1893, in excessively hot weather. During the day they haunt the stubbles and clover fields on the wolds and open districts, rising about the same hour in the evening and wend their way, in the long extended order, to the islands and sand banks in the Humber, to return as punctually to their feeding grounds at the break of day. They are the wildest and most unapproachable of all the geese.

Within the recollection of certainly three generations and probably since the inclosure of the wolds, if not before, flocks of wild geese, coming up from the coast, have been in the habit of passing over the town of Louth in the early morning on their way to their feeding grounds on the high wolds. The large barley walks are the places which are most frequented, not so much, as I have found by an examination of the stomach, for scattered grain as young white clover and trefoil plants, of which they are immoderately fond. Considering the persistency with which geese day by day resort to the same locality it is surprising so few are shot. The fields on the wolds are very extensive, and geese keep near the center; on coming in from the coast they fly high, and it is only in stormy weather that their flight is low enough for a shot from a heavy gun to do execution, fired from the vantage ground of a solitary barn, shed, or stack on a hilltop, where at the same time the shooter remains concealed till the skein of geese are well above him.

Mr. Howard Saunders says: "The voice of the pink-footed goose differs from that of the bean goose in being sharper in tone, and the note is also repeated more rapidly." It is extremely difficult to express the note or the difference between the calls of birds on paper. I can, however, testify from experience that there is a very distinct difference between the call note of these two species.

DISTRIBUTION

Breeding range.—Breeds in Spitsbergen, probably in Franz-Josef Land and possibly in Iceland.

Winter range.—Northern Europe, Scandinavia, Holland, Belgium, Great Britain, Iceland, France, Germany, and northern Russia.

Casual records.—Accidental in eastern Greenland and Massachusetts.

Egg dates.—Spitsbergen: Six records, June 16 to 27.

BRANTA CANADENSIS CANADENSIS (Linnaeus)

CANADA GOOSE

HABITS

The common wild goose is the most widely distributed and the most generally well known of any of our wild fowl. From the Atlantic to the Pacific and from the Gulf of Mexico nearly to the Arctic coast it may be seen at some season of the year, and when once seen its grandeur creates an impression on the mind which even the casual observer never forgets. As the clarion notes float downward on the still night air, who can resist the temptation to rush out of doors and peer into the darkness for a possible glimpse at the passing flock, as the shadowy forms glide over our roofs on their long journey? Or, even in daylight, what man so busy that he will not pause and look upward at the serried ranks of our grandest wild fowl, as their well-known honking notes announce their coming and their going, he knows not whence or whither? It is an impressive sight well worthy of his gaze; perhaps he will even stop to count the birds in the two long converging lines; he is sure to tell his friends about it, and perhaps it will even be published in the local paper, as a harbinger of spring or a foreboding of winter. Certainly the Canada goose commands respect.

Spring.—The Canada goose is one of the earliest of the water birds to migrate in the spring. Those which have wintered farthest south are the first to feel the migratory impulse, and they start about a month earlier than those which have wintered at or above the frost line, moving slowly at first but with a gradually increasing rate of speed. Prof. Wells W. Cooke (1906) has shown, from his mass of accumulated records, that beginning with an average rate of 9 miles a day, between the lowest degrees of latitude, the speed is gradually increased through successive stages to an average rate of 30 miles a day during the last part of the journey. Following, as it does, close upon the heels of retreating ice and snow, the migration of these geese may well be regarded as a harbinger of spring; for the same reason it is quite variable from year to year and quite dependent on weather conditions.

The first signs of approaching spring come early in the far south, with the lengthening of the days and the increasing warmth of the sun; the wild geese are the first to appreciate these signs and the first to feel the restless impulse to be gone; they congregate in flocks and show their uneasiness by their constant gabbling and honking, as if talking over plans for their journey, with much preening and oiling of feathers in the way of preparation; at length a flock or two may be seen mounting into the air and starting off northward, headed by the older and stronger birds, the veterans of many a similar trip; flock after flock joins the procession, until the last have gone, leaving their winter homes deserted and still. The old ganders know the way and lead their trustful flocks by the straightest and safest route; high in the air, with the earth spread out below them like a map, they follow no coast line, no mountain chain, and no river valley; but directly onward over hill and valley, river and lake, forest and plain, city, town, and country, their course points straight to their summer homes. Flying by night or by day, as circumstances require, they stop only when necessary to rest or feed, and then only in such places as their experienced leaders know to be safe. A thick fog may bewilder them and lead them to disaster or a heavy snowstorm may make them turn back, but soon they are on their way again, and ultimately they reach their breeding grounds in safety.

Courtship.—The older geese are paired for life, and many of the younger birds, which are mating for the first time, conduct their courtship and perhaps select their mates before they start on their spring migration. Audubon (1840) gives a graphic account of the courtship of the Canada goose, as follows:

It is extremely amusing to witness the courtship of the Canada goose in all its stages; and let me assure you, reader, that although a gander does not strut before his beloved with the pomposity of a turkey, or the grace of a dove, his ways are quite as agreeable to the female of his choice. I can imagine before me one who has just accomplished the defeat of another male after a struggle of half an hour or more. He advances gallantly toward the object of contention, his head scarcely raised an inch from the ground, his bill open to its full stretch, his fleshy tongue elevated, his eyes darting fiery glances, and as he moves he hisses loudly, while the emotion which he experiences causes his quills to shake and his feathers to rustle. Now he is close to her who in his eyes is all loveliness; his neck bending gracefully in all directions, passes all round her, and occasionally touches her body; and as she congratulates him on his victory, and acknowledges his affection, they move their necks in a hundred curious ways. At this moment fierce jealousy urges the defeated gander to renew his efforts to obtain his love; he advances apace, his eye glowing with the fire of rage; he shakes his broad wings, ruffles up his whole plumage, and as he rushes on the foe hisses with the intensity of anger. The whole flock seems to stand amazed, and opening up a space, the birds gather round to view the combat. The bold bird who has been caressing his mate, scarcely deigns to take notice of his foe, but seems to send a scornful glance toward him. He of the mortified feelings, however, raises his body, half opens his sinewy wings, and with a powerful blow, sends forth his defiance. The affront can not be borne in the presence of so large a company, nor indeed is there much disposition to bear it in any circumstances; the blow is returned with vigor, the aggressor reels for a moment, but he soon recovers, and now the combat rages. Were the weapons more deadly, feats of chivalry would now be performed; as it is, thrust and blow succeed each other like the strokes of hammers driven by sturdy forgers. But now, the mated gander has caught hold of his antagonist's head with his bill; no bulldog can cling faster to his victim; he squeezes him with all the energy of rage, lashes him with his powerful wings, and at length drives him away, spreads out his pinions, runs with joy to his mate, and fills the air with cries of exultation.

Nesting.—Reaching their breeding grounds early in the season and being in most cases already paired, these geese are naturally among the earliest breeders; their eggs are usually hatched and the nests deserted before many of the other wild fowl have even laid their eggs, the dates varying of course with the latitude. When I visited North Dakota in 1901 there were still quite a number of Canada geese breeding there; probably many of them have since been driven farther west or north, as they love solitude and retirement during the nesting season. We found them nesting on the islands in the lakes and in the marshy portions of the sloughs, building quite different nests in the two locations. On May 31 we found a nest on an island in Stump Lake, which had evidently been deserted for some time; the island was also occupied by nesting colonies of double-crested cormorants and ring-billed gulls and by a few breeding ducks; the goose nest was merely a depression in the bare ground among some scattered large stones lined with a few sticks and straws and a quantity of down. In a large slough in Nelson County we found, on June 2, a deserted nest containing 3 addled eggs, the broken shells of those that had hatched being scattered about the nest. It was in a shallow portion of the slough where the dead flags had been beaten down flat for a space 50 feet square. The nest was a bulky mass of dead flags, 3 feet in diameter and but slightly hollowed in the center. Within a few yards of this, and of a similar nest found on June 10, was an occupied redhead's nest; the proximity of these two ducks' nests to those of the geese may have been merely accidental, but the possibility is suggested that they may have been so placed to gain the protection of the larger birds. This suggestion was strengthened when I saw a skunk foraging in the vicinity; undoubtedly these animals find an abundant food supply in the numerous nests of ducks and coots in these sloughs.

Somewhat similar nests were found by our party in Saskatchewan, including two beautiful nests on an island in Crane Lake, found on June 2, 1905. The largest of these was in an open grassy place on the island, about 25 yards from the open shore; it consisted of a great mass of soft down, " drab gray " in color, measuring 16 inches in outside diameter, 7 inches inside, and 4 inches in depth; it was very conspicuous and contained 6 eggs. As I approached it and when about a hundred yards from it, the goose walked deliberately from the nest to the shore and began honking; her mate, away off on the lake answered her and she flew out to join him. Both of these nests had been robbed earlier in the season and the birds had laid second sets.

According to Milton S. Ray (1912) the Canada goose nests quite commonly at Lake Tahoe in California; he found a number of nests there in 1910 and 1911. The nesting habits in this region are not very different from what we noted in northwest Canada. Referring to the nests found in 1910, Mr. Ray writes:

Anxious to learn something of their nesting habits, and hoping I might be in time to find a nest or so, May 23 found me rowing up the fresh-water sloughs of the marsh, unmindful of the numerous terns, blackbirds, and other swamp denizens, in my quest for a prospective home of the goose. Nor was I long without reward, for when about 100 feet from a little island that boasted of a few lodge-pole pine saplings and one willow, a goose rose from her nest, took a short run, and rising with heavy flight and loud cries, flew out to open water, where she was joined by her mate. The cries of the pair echoed so loudly over the marsh that it seemed the whole region must be awakened. Landing on the island I found on the ground, at the edge of the willow, a large built-up nest with 7 almost fresh eggs. The nest was composed wholly of dry marsh grasses and down, and measured 22 inches over all, while the cavity was 11 inches across and 3 inches deep.

After a row of several miles I noticed a gander in the offing, whose swimming in circles and loud honking gave assurance that the nesting precincts of another pair had been invaded. A heavily timbered island, now close at hand, seemed the most probably nesting place. This isle was so swampy that most of the growth had been killed, and fallen trees, other impedimenta, and the icy water, made progress difficult. I had advanced but a short distance, however, when a goose flushed from her nest at the foot of a dead tree. This nest was very similar to the first one found, and, like it, also held 7 eggs, but these were considerably further along in incubation. On the homeward journey, while returning through the marsh by a different channel, I beheld the snake-like head of a goose above the tall grass (for the spring had been unusually early) on a level tract some distance away. Approaching nearer, the bird took flight, and on reaching the spot I found my third nest. As it contained 5 eggs all on the point of hatching, I lost no time in allowing the parent to return.

Of his experiences the following year, he says:

I found the goose colony to consist of but a single nest, placed on the bare rock at the foot of a giant Jeffrey pine near the water's edge. It was made entirely of pine needles, with the usual down lining, and held an addled egg, while numerous shells lay strewn about. The parents were noticed about half a mile down the bay. Two days later at Rowlands Marsh I located another goose nest with the small compliment of 2 eggs, 1 infertile and 1 from which the chick was just emerging. The nest was placed against a fallen log, and besides the lining of down was composed entirely of chips of pine bark, a quantity of which lay near. From the variety of material used in the composition of the nests found, it seems evident that the birds have little or no preference for any particular substance, but use that most easily available.

A long day's work at the marsh on June 9 revealed three more nests. The first of these, one with 6 eggs, well incubated, was the most perfectly built nest of the goose that I have ever seen, being constructed with all the care that most of the smaller birds exercise. It was made principally of dry marsh grasses. The second nest held a set of 5 eggs, and was placed by a small willow on a little mound of earth rising in a tule patch in a secluded portion of the swamp. Dry tules entered largely into its composition. In this instance the bird did not rise until we were within 25 feet, although they usually flushed at a distance varying from 40 to 100 feet.

In the Rocky Mountain regions of Colorado and Montana the Canada goose has been known to build its nest, sometimes for successive seasons, on rocky ledges or cliffs at some distance from any water or even at a considerable height. In the northwestern portions of the country it frequently nests in trees, using the old nests of ospreys, hawks, or other large birds; it apparently does not build any such nest for itself, but sometimes repairs the nest by bringing in twigs and lining it with down. John Fannin (1894) says that in the Okanogan district of British Columbia, " Canada geese are particularly noted for nesting in trees, and as these valleys are subject to sudden inundation during early spring, this fact may have something to do with it." He also relates the following interesting incident:

Mr. Charles deB. Green, who spends a good deal of his spare time in making collections for the Museum, writes me from Kettle River, Okanogan district, British Columbia, to the effect that while climbing to an osprey's nest he was surprised to find his actions resented by not only the ospreys but also by a pair of Canada geese (*Branta canadensis*), the latter birds making quite a fuss all the time Mr. Green was in the tree. On reaching the nest he was still further surprised to find 2 osprey eggs and 3 of the Canada goose. He took the 2 osprey's eggs and 2 of the geese eggs. This was on the 1st of May. On the 12th of May he returned and found the osprey setting on the goose egg; the geese were nowhere in sight. Mr. Green took the remaining egg and sent the lot to the Museum.

A. D. Henderson has sent me the following notes on the nesting habits of the Canada goose, in the Peace River region of northern Alberta, as follows:

The geese breed on the small gravelly islands in the Battle River and its two tributaries, known at that time as the Second and Third Battle Rivers. Another favorite breeding place is in old beaver dams, where they nest on the old sunken beaver houses, which in course of time have flattened down into small grass-covered islets. Even inhabited beaver houses are used as nesting sites, as my half-breed hunting partner, on one of our trips, took 5 eggs from a nest on a large beaver house in an old river bed of the Third Battle, which we repeatedly saw entered and left by a family of beaver, showing that the geese and beaver live together in unity.

On May 18 I found a nest containing 7 eggs on a low grassy islet, probably a very old beaver house, in the same flooded beaver meadow. The nest was made of grass lined with finer grasses and feathers. The sitting bird permitted a near approach, with her head and neck stretched out straight in front of her and lying flat along the ground, watching my approach. This appears to be the usual behavior when the nest is approached during incubation. We saw two other nests on this day, one on a small grassy islet in the same beaver meadow, containing 3 eggs, and another on an island in the Third Battle with 6 eggs.

Eggs.—The Canada goose lays from 4 to 10 eggs, usually 5 or 6. They vary in shape from ovate to elliptical ovate, with a tendency in some specimens toward fusiform. The shell is smooth or only slightly rough, but with no gloss. The color is creamy white or dull, dirty white at first, becoming much nest stained and sometimes variegated or nearly covered with "cream buff." The measurements of 84 eggs, in various collections average 85.7 by 58.2 millimeters; the eggs showing the four extremes measure **99.5** by 56, 87.6 by **63.6, 79** by 56.5, and 86.5 by **53.5** millimeters.

Young.—The period of incubation varies from 28 to 30 days; probably the former is the usual time under favorable circumstances. The gander never sits on the nest, but while the goose is incubating he is constantly in attendance, except when obliged to leave in search of food. He is a staunch defender of the home and is no mean antagonist. Audubon (1840) relates the following:

It is during the breeding season that the gander displays his courage and strength to the greatest advantage. I knew one that appeared larger than usual, and of which all the lower parts were of a rich cream color. It returned three years in succession to a large pond a few miles from the mouth of Green River, in Kentucky, and whenever I visited the nest it seemed to look upon me with utter contempt. It would stand in a stately attitude until I reached within a few yards of the nest, when suddenly lowering its head and shaking it as if it were dislocated from the neck, it would open its wings and launch into the air, flying directly at me. So daring was this fine fellow that in two instances he struck me a blow with one of his wings on the right arm, which for an instant I thought was broken. I observed that immediately after such an effort to defend his nest and mate he would run swiftly toward them, pass his head and neck several times over and around the female, and again assume his attitude of defiance.

The same gifted author writes regarding the care of the young as follows:

The lisping sounds of their offspring are heard through the shell; their little bills have formed a breach in the inclosing walls; full of life and bedecked with beauty they come forth, with tottering steps and downy covering. Toward the water they now follow their careful parent; they reach the border of the stream; their mother already floats on the loved element; one after another launches forth and now the flock glides gently along. What a beautiful sight. Close by the grassy margin the mother slowly leads her innocent younglings; to one she shows the seed of the floating grass, to another points out the crawling slug. Her careful eye watches the cruel turtle, the garfish, and the pike that are lurking for their prey, and, with head inclined, she glances upward to the eagle or the gull that are hovering over the water in search of food. A ferocious bird dashes at her young ones; she instantly plunges beneath the surface, and in the twinkling of an eye her brood disappear after her; now they are among the thick rushes, with nothing above water but their little bills. The mother is marching toward the land, having lisped to her brood in accents so gentle that none but they and her mate can understand their import, and all are safely lodged under cover until the disappointed eagle or gull bears away.

More than six weeks have now elapsed. The down of the goslings, which at first was soft and tufty, has become coarse and hairlike. Their wings are edged with quills and their bodies bristled with feathers. They have increased in size and, living in the midst of abundance, they have become fat, so that on shore they make their way with difficulty, and as they are yet unable to fly, the greatest care is required to save them from their numerous enemies. They grow apace, and now the burning days of August are over. They are able to fly with ease from one shore to another, and as each successive night the hoarfrosts cover the country and the streams are closed over by the ice, the family joins that in their neighborhood, which is also joined by others. At length they spy the advance of a snowstorm, when the ganders with one accord sound the order for their departure.

Samuel N. Rhoads (1895) published the following interesting note, based on the observations of H. B. Young in Tennessee:

At Reelfoot Lake the goose nearly always builds in the top of a blasted tree over the water, sometimes nesting as high as 50 feet or even higher. When the young are hatched the gander soon gets notice of it and swims around the foot of the tree uttering loud cries. On a signal from mother goose he redoubles his outcries and, describing a large circle immediately beneath the nest, beats the water with his wings, dives, paddles, and slashes about with the greatest fury, making such a terrible noise and commotion that he can be heard for several miles. This effectually drives away from that spot every catfish, spoonbill, loggerhead, hellbender, moccasin, water snake, eagle, mink, and otter that might take a fancy to young goslings, and into the midst of the commotion mother goose, by a few deft thrusts of her bill, spills the whole nestful. But a few seconds elapse ere the reunited family are noiselessly paddling for the shores of some secluded cove with nothing to mark the scene of their exploits but a few feathers and upturned water plants and above them the huge white cypress with its deserted nest.

While the family party is moving about on the water the gander usually leads the procession, the goslings following, and the goose acting as rear guard. The old birds sometimes lead their young for long distances over large bodies of water. While cruising on Lake Winnipegosis on June 18, 1913, we came upon a family party fully 5 miles from shore and evidently swimming across the lake. The two old birds when hard pressed finally took wing and flew away, leaving the three half-grown young to their fate. The young were still completely covered with down, and their wings were not at all developed, although their bodies were as large as mallards. They could swim quite fast on the surface, could dive well, and could swim for a long distance under water. They were surprisingly active in eluding capture, and when hard pressed they swam partly submerged, with their necks below the surface and their heads barely above it, in a sort of hiding pose.

P. A. Taverner (1922) describes an interesting pose assumed by a family party on Cypress Lake, Saskatchewan. When pursued by a motor boat—

they put on more speed and arranged themselves in a long single file, one parent leading, the other bringing up the rear, swimming low, and both with their long necks outstretched and laid down flat on the water, making themselves as inconspicuous as possible. The young, coaxed from ahead and urged from behind, paddled along vigorously between, one close behind the other. From our low and distant point of view the effect was interesting. They looked like a floating stick. Certainly they would not impress the casual eye as a family of Canada geese, and if we had not first seen them in a more characteristic pose they would undoubtedly have been passed without recognition.

Dr. Alexander Wetmore tells me that, in the Bear River marshes in Utah where these geese breed, both old and young birds resort during the summer to the seclusion of the lower marshes. Here he found numerous places where the thick growth of bullrushes had been beaten down to form roosting places for family parties, well littered with cast-off feathers and other signs of regular occupancy. Here they live in peace and safety while the young are attaining their growth and their parents are molting. Before the shooting season begins they gather into larger flocks, now strong of wing and ready for their fall wanderings.

James P. Howley (1884) gives the following account of the behavior of these geese in Newfoundland:

During the breeding season they molt the primary wing and tail feathers, and are consequently unable to fly in the months of June, July, and the early part of August. They keep very close during this molting season and are rarely seen by day; yet I have frequently come across them at such times in the far interior and on many occasions have caught them alive. When surprised on some lonely lake or river side they betake themselves at once to the land and run very swiftly into the bush or tall grass to hide. But they appear somewhat stupid, and if they can succeed in getting their heads out of sight under a stone or stump imagine they are quite safe from observation. When overtaken in the water and hard pressed they will dive readily, remaining a considerable time beneath, swimming or running on the bottom very fast. About the 15th of August the old birds and most of the young ones are capable of flight, and from thence to the 1st of September they rapidly gain strength of wing. Soon after this they betake themselves to the seaside, congregating in large flocks in the shallow estuaries or deep fiords, to feed during the nighttime, but are off again to the barrens at earliest dawn, where they are generally to be found in daytime. Here they feed on the wild berries, of which the common blueberry, partridge berry, marsh berry, and a small blackberry (*Empetrum nigrum*) afford them an abundant supply. They are exceedingly wary at this season, and there is no approaching them at all on the barrens.

Mr. Henderson has given the following observation regarding the young:

On June 4, while walking up the river bank looking for bear, we met a pair of geese and four goslings on shore and got within 20 yards before they moved. The old birds made a great fuss and flew down to the foot of a rapid and waited on the still water about 60 yards below. The goslings took to the water, which was tumbling and boiling over the stones; swimming and diving, they went down the rapid, under water most of the time, and joined their fond parents below.

On the 28th, while walking up the gravel banks of the Third Battle, hunting bear, I came on a pair of geese with six goslings, also three other geese about 100 yards upstream from them. The three geese flew on my approach, and the female took her brood across the stream to about 30 yards distant. Her mate went upstream, flopping along the water pretending to be crippled. He would allow me to approach to about 40 yards and then flap along the water again for a few yards and wait for me again. He repeated this performance several times, until he thought he had enticed me far enough around the next bend, when he had a marvelous recovery, flying away and giving me the merry honk! honk! for being so easy. I am sure he enjoyed the ease with which he fooled me, and I enjoyed watching him and letting him think so.

Plumages.—The downy young when recently hatched is brightly colored and very pretty. The entire back, rump, wings, and flanks are "yellowish olive," with a bright, greenish-yellow sheen; a large central crown patch is lustrous "olive"; the remainder of the head and neck is bright yellowish, deepening to "olive ocher" on the cheeks and sides of the neck and paling to "primrose yellow" on the throat; the under parts shade from "deep colonial buff" on the breast to "primrose yellow" on the belly; the bill is entirely black. Older birds are paler and duller colored, "drab" above and grayish white below.

When about 4 weeks old the plumage begins to appear, the body plumage first and the wings last; they are fully grown when about 6 weeks old, and they closely resemble their parents in their first plumage. There is, however, during the first summer and fall at least a decided difference. The plumage of young birds looks softer and the colors are duller and more blended. The head and neck are duller, browner black; the cheeks are more brownish white, and the edges of the black areas are not so clearly cut; the light edgings above are not so distinct; and the sides of the chest and flanks are indistinctly mottled, rather than clearly barred. During the fall and winter these differences disappear by means of wear and molt, so that by spring the young birds are practically indistinguishable from adults.

Food.—Canada geese live on a variety of different foods in various parts of their habitat and at different seasons, but they seem to show a decided preference for vegetable foods where these can be obtained. They usually feed in flocks in certain favored localities where suitable food can be found in abundance, feeding during the daytime if not too much disturbed, or at night, if necessary, in localities where it would be unsafe to feed in daylight. The feeding flocks are guarded by one or more sentinels, which are ever on the alert until they are relieved by some of their companions and allowed to take their turns at feeding. Their eyesight is very keen and their sense of hearing very acute. They are very wary at such times and among the most difficult of. birds to approach; at a warning note from the watchful sentry every head is raised and with eyes fixed on the approaching enemy they await the proper time for taking their departure. Geese are very regular in their feeding habits, resorting day after day to the same feeding grounds if they are not too much disturbed; they prefer to feed for a few hours in the early morning, flying in to their feeding grounds before sunrise and again for an hour or two before sunset, spending the middle of the day resting on some sandbar or on some large body of water.

While on their spring migration overland wild geese often do considerable damage to sprouting grain, such as wheat, corn, barley, and oats; nipping off the tender shoots does no great harm, but they are not always content with such careful pruning and frequently pull up the kernel as well. They also nibble at the fresh shoots of growing grasses and other tender herbage, nipping them off sideways, cleanly and quickly.

Aububon (1840) says that "after rainy weather, they are frequently seen rapidly patting the earth with both feet, as if to force the earthworms from their burrows." Farther north, where they meet winter just retreating, they find the last year's crop of berries uncovered by the melting snow in a fair state of preservation and various buds are swelling fresh and green. Later on some animal food becomes available, insects and their larvae, crustaceans, small clams and snails, and probably some small fishes. In the marshes they feed on wild rice, arrowhead, sedges, marsh grasses, and various aquatic plants, eating the roots as well as the leaves and shoots. On the fall migration they again frequent the grain fields to pick up the fallen grain, pull up the stubble, and nibble at what green herbage they can find. They resort to the shallow ponds and borders of lakes to feed after the manner of the surface-feeding ducks, reaching down to the bottom with their long necks and even tipping up with their feet in the air, in their attempts to reach the succulent roots and the tender water plants. On the coast in winter they prefer to feed in fresh or brackish water on the leaves, blades, and fruits of marine plants, such as *Zostera marina*, the sea lettuce (*Ulva lactuca*) and various *Algae*. Probably some small mollusks, crustaceans, and other small marine animals are taken at the same time.

Behavior.—In flight, Canada geese impress one as heavy, yet powerful birds, as indeed they are. In rising from the water or from the land they run along for a few steps before rising, but Audubon (1840) says that " when suddenly surprised and in full plumage, a single spring on their broad webbed feet is sufficient to enable them to get on the wing." When flying about their feeding grounds or elsewhere on short flights, they fly in compact or irregular bunches. Their flight then seems heavy and labored, but it is really much stronger and swifter than it seems, and for such heavy birds they are really quite agile. It is only when traveling long distances that they fly high in the air in the well-known V-shaped flocks, which experience has taught them is the easiest and most convenient for rapid and protracted flight. In this formation the leader, cleaving the air in advance, has the hardest work to perform; the lead is taken by the strongest adult birds, probably the ganders, which change places occasionally for relief; the others follow along in the diverging lines at regular intervals, so spaced that each has room enough to work his wings freely, to see clearly ahead, and to save resistance in the wake of the bird ahead of him. As the wing beats are not always in perfect unison, the line seems to have an undulatory motion, especially noticeable when near at hand; but often the flock seems to move along in perfect step. Flight is not always maintained in the stereotyped wedge formation; sometimes a single, long, sloping line is formed or more rarely they progress in Indian file. The speed at which geese fly is faster than it seems, but it has often been overestimated; the following statement by J. W. Preston (1892) is of interest in this connection:

The Canada goose presses onward, borne up by strong and steady pinions. For forceful, solid business he has few rivals. I remember once, while traveling by rail at a rate of 30 miles an hour, our way lay for a time along the course of a swollen creek. A flock of geese, among them one little teal, came alongside the train and kept almost within gunshot for fully 10 miles, seemingly at an ordinary rate; and the teal was at no loss to keep his place among his larger companions.

There are exceptions to the orderly method of procedure outlined above. Audubon (1840) says that:

When they are slowly advancing from south to north at an early period of the season, they fly much lower, alight more frequently, and are more likely to be bewildered by suddenly formed banks of fog, or by passing over cities or arms of the sea, where much shipping may be in sight. On such occasions great consternation prevails among them, they crowd together in a confused manner, wheel irregularly, and utter a constant cackling resembling the sounds from a disconcerted mob. Sometimes the flock separates, some individuals leave the rest, proceed in a direction contrary to that in which they came, and after awhile, as if quite confused, sail toward the ground, once alighted on which they appear to become almost stupefied, so as to suffer themselves to be shot with ease, or even knocked down with sticks. Heavy snowstorms also cause them great distress, and in the midst of them some have been known to fly against beacons and lighthouses, dashing their heads against the walls in the middle of the day. In the night they are attracted by the lights of these buildings, and now and then a whole flock is caught on such occasions.

When preparing to alight the whole flock set their wings and drift gradually down a long incline until close to the surface, then scaling or flying along they drop into the water with a splash. They swim gracefully on the water after the manner of swans and can make rapid progress if necessary. That they can dive and swim under water, if need be, is well illustrated by the following incident, related by Audubon (1840):

I was much surprised one day, while on the coast of Labrador, to see how cunningly one of these birds, which, in consequence of the molt, was quite unable to fly, managed for awhile to elude our pursuit. It was first perceived at some distance from the shore, when the boat was swiftly rowed toward it, and it swam before us with great speed, making directly toward the land; but when we came within a few yards of it, it dived, and nothing could be seen of it for a long time. Every one of the party stood on tiptoe to mark the spot at which it should rise, but all in vain, when the man at the rudder accidentally looked down over the stern and there saw the goose, its body immersed, the point of its bill alone above water, and its feet busily engaged in propelling it so as to keep pace with the movements of the boat. The sailor attempted to catch it while within a foot or two of him, but with the swiftness of thought it shifted from side to side, fore and aft, until delighted at having witnessed so much sagacity in a goose, I begged the party to suffer the poor bird to escape.

Mr. Henderson describes in his notes an interesting habit of pose assumed by this species, as follows:

I rode down the river a short distance to where I had noticed a pair of geese alight and soon saw one standing on a gravelly island. Making a short detour and riding closer, I saw both birds lying flat on the gravel, head and neck outstretched along the ground, precisely as they do on the nest. They were hiding right in the open without the slightest cover. Though I have what is called the hunter's eye pretty well developed, it is doubtful if I would have noticed them if I had not previously known they were there. They remained perfectly motionless and resembled pieces of water-worn driftwood so perfectly that I now understand how it was that in descending rivers in a canoe I had so often failed to observe them until they took wing. It was the most beautiful example of protective coloring I have ever seen. As I rode up to the river bank in plain sight and making a good deal of noise, one bird remained perfectly still and the other moved its head slightly to watch me. I then rode out into the river to within 35 yards before they broke the pose and took to flight.

M. P. Skinner has noticed similar habits in Yellowstone Park. He says in his notes:

Geese have a curious habit of "playing possum." Instead of flying away, they squat flat with head and neck stretched out straight before them in a most ungooselike attitude. After one has passed by three or four hundred yards they raise their heads slowly an inch or two at a time and finally get to their feet again. They do this on the ice, on stony banks of streams, on bowlders, on sandbars, in the grass, and I have even seen a sitting bird do it on her nest. On the ice it makes them inconspicuous, on stony shores or bowlders the deception is perfect, for the rounded gray back looks just like a stone; as sand beaches may have stones, the method is good hiding there; but on the grass "playing possum" fails because of the contrast. In the water's edge the deception is good, as the inert, idly rocking body looks very little like a live bird. And this method is carried even further, for I have seen geese swim the Yellowstone River with heads and necks at the surface and have had them sneak off through the grass in the same way. This subterfuge is used more in spring than in summer, but is practiced sometimes in September and October.

Geese are social and like to be together, although the flocks are usually small unless there is strong reason for their gathering temporarily. Pages can be written of the sagacity and wisdom of these birds. Wary as they are, they are one of the first to realize the protection given them and are quick to lose their suspicions of man and his ways. But it is interesting to observe that although they pay no attention to autos passing along a road near them, they are at once on the alert and suspicious if a car stops near. Often we find the geese tamer than the pintail and mallard they are associating with. And their sagacity extends to wild animals as well; they know just how near it is safe to let a coyote approach, and one September day I watched a flock on a meadow seemingly indifferent to a black bear near by, although they never let him get within 20 feet, first walking away, then flying, if he came too near.

The well-known resonant honking notes of a flock of geese flying overhead on the migration are familiar sounds to every observant person; they are characteristic and distinctive of such migrating flocks and are sometimes almost constant. The Canada goose is also a noisy bird at other times, indulging freely in softer, lower-toned, conversational honking or gabbling notes while feeding or in other activities. Ora W. Knight (1908) gives a very good description of the notes of this species, as follows:

The cry uttered when on the wing is a clear trumpetlike "honk," seemingly uttered by various individuals in the flock. When the weather is foggy their "honk" seems uttered more frequently and in a querulous tone. When a flock has alighted and is sporting in the water without apprehension of trouble they swim gracefully about, plunging their heads and necks under the water to feed. Now and then some lusty or exuberant individual (probably a gander) will stretch itself up in the water, flap its wings over its back, and utter a series of resonant honks, the first loudest, longest drawn out, and highest pitched, and gradually lessening in loudness and length and decreasing in pitch, about as follows: "h——o——n——k, h——o——n——k, h—o—n—k, h–o–n–k, honk, onk, uf," the last note being a mere expelling of the breath. This proceeding I have only observed with one flock, never having been able to observe others while they were unconscious of my whereabouts and feeding, but judge that it is a characteristic habit.

The attitude of the Canada goose toward other species seems to be one of haughty disdain; although it often frequents the same breeding grounds and the same feeding resorts with various other species of geese, ducks, and other waterfowl, it never seems to mingle with them socially or to allow them to join its flocks. Toward man and other animals it shows remarkable sagacity in discriminating between harmless friends and dangerous enemies, and the latter must be very crafty to deceive it. On this point Audubon (1840) writes:

At the sight of cattle, horses, or animals of the deer kind, they are seldom alarmed, but a bear or a cougar is instantly announced, and if on such occasions the flock is on the ground near water, the birds immediately betake themselves in silence to the latter, swim to the middle of the pond or river, and there remain until danger is over. Should their enemies pursue them in the water, the males utter loud cries, and the birds arrange themselves in close ranks, rise simultaneously in a few seconds, and fly off in a compact body, seldom at such times forming lines or angles, it being in fact only when the distance they have to travel is great that they dispose themselves in those forms. So acute is their sense of hearing that they are able to distinguish the different sounds or footsteps of their foes with astonishing accuracy. Thus the breaking of a dry stick by a deer is at once distinguished from the same accident occasioned by a man. If a dozen of large turtles drop into the water, making a great noise in their fall, or if the same effect is produced by an alligator, the wild goose pays no regard to it; but however faint and distant may be the sound of an Indian's paddle, that may by accident have struck the side of his canoe, it is at once marked, every individual raises its head and looks intently toward the place from which the noise has proceeded, and in silence all watch the movements of their enemy.

These birds are extremely cunning also, and should they conceive themselves unseen, they silently move into the tall grasses by the margin of the water, lower their heads, and lie perfectly quiet until the boat has passed by. I have seen them walk off from a large frozen pond into the woods, to elude the sight of the hunter, and return as soon as he had crossed the pond. But should there be snow on the ice or in the woods, they prefer watching the intruder, and take to wing long before he is within shooting distance, as if aware of the ease with which they could be followed by their tracks over the treacherous surface.

Fall.—The beginning of the fall migration in Ungava is described by Lucien M. Turner, in his unpublished notes, as follows:

The birds first seen in the fall in the vicinity of Fort Chimo are those asserted to have been reared in the Georges River district and repair to this locality in search of fresh feeding grounds. They appear about August 12 to 20, but are in very lean condition. By the first of September the earlier birds hatched north of the strait begin to appear and become quite numerous by the latter week of September. By this time they are in tolerable condition and rapidly become fat by the first of October, feeding on vegetable matter growing in the ponds, in the swamps and flats along the river banks. They remain until the latter part (24th) of October and follow up the rivers which flow from the south. In the year 1882 immense numbers of these geese flew southward on the 19th of October. Hundreds of flocks of various sizes, from 15 to 80 birds, passed over. A cold snap immediately succeeded, although a flock of 6 settled in the river a few yards from the houses on October 24.

From the foregoing it will be seen that the fall movement from the breeding grounds begins early in the season, the flocks gradually gathering on the coasts or on the larger bodies of water in large numbers, moving about slowly and deliberately and reveling in the milder temperatures and abundant food to be found in such places. But the shortening days and the sharpening frosts of autumn accelerate their movements and they prepare for their long journey; at length the leaders summon their hosts to meet on high; and forming in two long converging lines, pointing toward the already feeble rays of the noonday sun, they start. High in the air they travel on, cheered by the clarion call of the leader, answered at frequent intervals by his followers, far above all dangers and straight along the well-known path. When bewildered by fogs or storms or when overtaken by darkness the flight is lower and full of dangers. But usually toward night a resting place is sought; perhaps some well-known lake is sighted and the weary birds are glad to answer the call of some fancied friend below them; so setting their wings the flock glides down in a long incline, circling about the lake for a place to alight, and greeting their friends with loud calls of welcome. Too often their friends prove to be domesticated traitors, trained to lure them to the gunner's blind, and it is a wary goose indeed that can detect the sham. But, if all goes well, they rest during the hours of darkness and are off again at daybreak, for now they must push along fast until they reach their winter haven. Dr. John C. Phillips (1910 and 1911a) has published two very interesting papers on the migrations of Canada geese in Massachusetts which are well worth reading; but as they are principally of local interest and are too lengthy to quote in full, I would refer the reader to them rather than attempt to quote from them.

Game.—Many and varied are the methods employed by gunners to bring to bag the wily wild goose. On account of its large size and generally good table qualities it has always been much in demand as a game bird; it is so wary, so sagacious, and so difficult to outwit that its pursuit has always fascinated the keen sportsman and taxed his skill and his ingenuity more than any other game bird. According to Henry Reeks (1870) the settlers of Newfoundland were formerly adepts in tolling geese with the help of a dog; he describes the method, as follows:

The sportsman secretes himself in the bushes or long grass by the sides of any water on which geese are seen, and keeps throwing a glove or stick in the direction of the geese, each time making his dog retrieve the object thrown; this has to be repeated until the curiosity of the geese is aroused, and they commence swimming toward the moving object. If the geese are a considerable distance from the land, the dog is sent into the water, but as the birds approach nearer and nearer the dog is allowed to show himself less and less; in this manner they are easily tolled within gunshot. When the sportsman has no dog with him he has to act the part of one by crawling in and out of the long grass on his hands and knees, and sometimes this has to be repeated continuously for nearly an hour, making it rather a laborious undertaking, but I have frequently known this device to succeed when others have failed. The stuffed skin of a yellow fox (*Vulpes fulvus*) is sometimes used for tolling geese, and answers the purpose remarkably well, especially when the geese are near the shore, by tying it to a long stick and imitating the motions of a dog retrieving the glove or stick.

On the coast of New England in winter geese have been successfully pursued by sculling upon them among the drift ice in a duck float. The float sits low in the water, with pieces of ice on her bow and along her sides; the gunner, clad in white clothing, crouches out of sight, and if properly handled the whole outfit can scarcely be distinguished from a floating ice cake. But a much more successful and more destructive, though less sportsmanlike, method is used on the inland lakes and larger ponds of eastern Massachusetts. This is the duck-stand method, which I have so fully described under the black duck that it is necessary only to refer to it here. Perhaps it should have been described under this species, for, although more ducks than geese are usually killed in such stands, the goose-shooting part of it is the more highly developed. Large numbers of live decoy geese are raised and trained for annual use in these stands and the most efficient teamwork is employed. The old mated pairs and their young are separated and made to call to each other in such a way that the wild birds are attracted. An old gander may be tethered out on the beach, while its young are kept in a " flying pen " back of the stand; when wild geese appear the goslings are released by pulling a cord; they fly out to meet the incoming flock; their parents call to them and they return to the beach, bringing the wild birds with them. When the geese are near enough and properly bunched a raking volley from a battery of guns is poured into them and other shots are fired as the survivors rise, with the result that very few are left to fly away. Even some of these may return and be shot at again if the leaders or the parents of the young birds have been killed. Such slaughter can hardly be regarded as sport.

Farther south on the Atlantic coast, in Virginia and North Carolina, geese are shot from open blinds in a much more sportsmanlike manner. A box, large enough for a man to lie down in or deep enough for a man to sit in and barely look over the top, is sunken into the ground on some sand spit or bar where the geese are wont to come for gravel or to rest, or perhaps it is placed on some marshy point on their feeding grounds where it can be concealed in the tall grass or covered with grass to match its surroundings. The decoys, either live birds or wooden imitations, are strung out in front of the blind, and the hunter crouching in the box eagerly awaits the inspiring sight of a flock of oncoming birds. At last a long line of dark, heavy birds in a wedge-shaped phalanx is seen approaching, with apparently labored flight. The well-known challenge note of the leader, repeated along the line of his followers, arouses the decoys to answering notes of invitation to alight. The flock wheels and swings in to the decoys, anxiously scanning the surroundings for any suspicious object. Seeing nothing to alarm them, they all set their wings and scale down to join their fellows. This is the sportman's opportunity for a flight shot; the pothunter would prefer to wait until they had all alighted and gathered in a dense bunch near the decoys. But in either case the birds have a better chance than in front of a concealed battery of heavy guns.

Goose shooting on the western grain fields is perhaps the most sportsmanlike method, as it is practically all wing shooting. The birds frequent the grain fields in large numbers to feed on the tender shoots of growing grain in the spring or on the stubble and fallen grain in the autumn. They are very regular in their feeding habits, flying in to the fields from their roosting grounds on the lakes and sloughs about daylight and feeding for a few hours after sunrise; they rest during the middle of the day and come in again to feed for a few hours before sunset. Gunners take advantage of these regular habits to shoot them on their lines of flight. A hole is dug in the ground deep enough to conceal the gunner entirely, and the decoys, usually wooden ones, are set out around it. Or a convenient and effective blind is made by hollowing out the center of a corn shock, with which the geese are already familiar. Concealed in such a blind before daylight, the hunter is well prepared for some excellent shooting when the flight begins, especially if he is an expert in calling the birds by imitating their notes. It must be exciting sport to shoot these large birds flying over and often within easy range.

I suppose that the Canada goose has been more persistently hunted, over a wider range of country and for a longer period of years, than any other American game bird, for in the earlier days, when all game was so abundant, only the largest species were considered worth the trouble. In spite of this fact it has shown its ability to hold its own and is even increasing in numbers in many places to-day. Messrs. Kumlien and Hollister (1903) report it in Wisconsin as—

abundant, increasing rather than diminishing in numbers during the fall, winter, and spring. To such an extent has this species changed its habits that it is no longer looked upon as a sure harbinger of spring, as in most sections of southern and even south-central Wisconsin it remains all winter, flying back and forth from its favorite cornfields to some lake or large marsh for the night. When snow is plenty it even remains in the fields for days at a time. Twenty-five to fifty years ago the flocks which first made their appearance were noted by everyone, and spring was not far distant. Now, the flocks which return from the north in October are continually added to until they are often several hundred strong, and remain thus until the beginning of spring.

On a recent (1916) visit to the great shooting resorts on the coasts of Virginia and North Carolina, I was told by the members of some of the gun clubs that geese were more abundant than ever before and are increasing every year. I certainly saw more geese in the north end of Currituck Sound on one of the rest days than I had ever seen in my life before; great rafts of them were gathering to feed in the shallow water on the fox-tail grass and wild celery which abounds in that region; the water was black with them as far as I could see; flock after flock was constantly coming in from the sea; and sometimes it seemed as if they came in flocks of flocks. They winter here in large numbers; probably this vicinity is the greatest winter resort on the Atlantic coast, for here they find abundant food in the fresh-water bays and sounds and ample security from pursuit on the broad waters of Chesapeake Bay or even on the open sea in calm weather. They feed largely at night, as they are often driven out of the bays during the days when shooting is allowed.

Winter.—Canada geese spend the winter quite far north in the interior, where they can find suitable food and large bodies of open water.

M. P. Skinner says in his notes:

In winter the reduced number remain at the outlet of Yellowstone Lake and on numerous waters kept open by hot springs and geysers. A number of our meadows are underlain by springs sufficiently warm to melt the snow and even furnish a little green grass all winter. These are frequented by geese as well as mallard and green-winged teal.

On the coast they winter abundantly as far north as Massachusetts; probably the greatest winter resort on the New England coast is on Marthas Vineyard, where the large fresh-water ponds are not always frozen and where there are open salt-water ponds which never or very rarely freeze.

That the Canada goose winters abundantly in northern Florida is well illustrated by the following notes sent to me by Charles J. Pennock:

The numerous shallow bays, bayous, and broad river mouths of the counties of Wakulla, Jefferson, and Taylor, lying south and southeast from Tallahassee, offer attractive feeding for winter visiting *Branta canadensis canadensis*, while not infrequently a short distance inland, just back of the bordering salt marshes, numerous sand flats and burnt-over semimarsh areas afford irresistible attractions to a hungry goose. Fresh shoots of grass with plenty of gravel and a clear, clean sand bed on which to take a siesta seems to be a combination most alluring, and in February and early March, with weather conditions favorable, numerous bands of these sturdy birds may be found constantly on the move, flying in as the tide rises and stops their feeding along shore or, if undisturbed after a hearty feeding on the freshly grown grass, they betake them to a long stretch of bare sand, where they evidently feel secure from surprise by virtue of sentinels most alert with keenest senses of sight and hearing, some hunters even claiming them to have a like keen sense of smell; at any rate they are most difficult to approach at such times and usually beat off up wind just before an approaching hunter gets within range.

DISTRIBUTION

Breeding range.—Northern North America, south of the barren grounds. East to Labrador (Okak, Nain, Hopedale, etc.), and Newfoundland (Grand Lake). South to the Gulf of St. Lawrence (Anticosti Island), James Bay, South Dakota, northern Colorado (Boulder County), northern Utah (Bear River), northern Nevada (Halleck), and California (Lake Tahoe). Formerly, and perhaps occasionally now, as far south as western Tennessee (Reelfoot Lake) and northeastern Arkansas (Walker Lake). West to northeastern California (Eagle Lake and Lower Klamath Lake), central Oregon (Lake County), central Washington (Douglas County), central British Columbia (Cariboo District), probably to the coast in southern Alaska, and to the upper Yukon (Fort Yukon). North to the northern limit of trees in Mackenzie (Providence and Fort Anderson) and northern Quebec (Whale River).

Winter range.—Nearly all of the United States. East to the Atlantic coast. South to Florida (Wakulla and Marion Counties), the Gulf coasts of Louisiana and Texas, Mexico (San Fernando, Matamoras, etc.), and southern California (San Diego). West nearly or quite to the Pacific coast. North to southern British Columbia (Chilliwack, Shuswap Lake, and the Okanogan Valley), northwestern Wyoming (Yellowstone Park), South Dakota, southern Wisconsin (Sauk County), southern Ohio, southern New England (Long Island and Marthas Vineyard), and northeastward to Nova Scotia (Barrington Bay, Port Joli, etc.).

Spring migration.—Early dates of arrival: Rhode Island, Block Island, February 21; central Massachusetts, February 25; southern New Hampshire, March 11; southern Maine, March 5; Quebec City, March 1; Prince Edward Island, March 9; Labrador, Sandwich Bay, April 30; southern Iowa, February 4; Minnesota, Heron Lake, February 23; North Dakota, Argusville, March 8; Manitoba, Aweme, March 9; Saskatchewan, Reindeer Lake, April 17; Mackenzie, Fort Simpson, April 22, and Fort Anderson, May 15. Average dates of arrival: Central Pennsylvania, March 17; central New York, March 13; central Massachusetts, March 17; southern Maine, March 24; Quebec City, March 27; southern Iowa, March 1; southern Wisconsin, March 13; southern Ontario, March 16; Manitoba, Aweme, March 29; Mackenzie, Fort Simpson, April 28. Late dates of departure: Florida, Marion County, May 22; Texas, Grapevine, April 15; southern Mississippi, April 20; Kentucky, Bowling Green, May 7; central Maryland, April 22; central New Jersey, May 9; Massachusetts, Cape Cod, May 26; California, Gridley, April 11.

Fall migration.—Early dates of arrival: Central Massachusetts, September 4; Long Island, Montauk Point, September 30; Virginia, Alexandria, October 5; South Carolina, Anderson, October 10; Florida, Wakulla County, October 9; northern Nebraska, September 7; central Iowa, September 16; central Missouri, September 23; Kentucky, Bowling Green, September 22; California, Gridley, November 5. Average dates of arrival: Central Massachusetts, October 11; Long Island, Montauk Point, October 20; central New Jersey, October 18; Virginia, Alexandria, October 20; northern Nebraska, October 7; central Wisconsin, October 12; central Indiana, October 19; southern Mississippi, November 12. Late dates of departure: Quebec, Hatley, November 25; Prince Edward Island, December 22; southern Ontario, November 10; southern Michigan, November 25; central Minnesota, December 1; Manitoba, Aweme, December 2; Montana, Columbia Falls, November 24.

Casual records.—Accidental in Bermuda (fall, 1874, and January and February, 1875) and the West Indies (Jamaica).

Egg dates.—Northern Canada: Eighteen records, May 18 to July 14; nine records, June 19 to July 9. Utah and Nevada: Sixteen records, March 29 to May 19; eight records, April 18 to 27. North Dakota and Saskatchewan: Thirteen records, April 29 to July 19; seven records, May 9 to June 3. Labrador and Newfoundland: Eleven records, May 24 to July 7; six records, June 4 to 13.

BRANTA CANADENSIS HUTCHINSI (Richardson)

HUTCHINS GOOSE

HABITS

After writing such a full life history of the Canada goose, it seems unnecessary to go over the same ground again in writing about this small northern subspecies, which, though it differs somewhat in habits from its larger relative, has many characteristics in common with it. There seems to be little doubt that *hutchinsi* is a true subspecies of the *canadensis*, for it seems to be exactly like it except in size, and perhaps in the number of tail feathers, which is variable in both forms. The other two, so called, subspecies can not be so satisfactorily placed.

Spring.—The Hutchins goose is a later migrant than the Canada goose, probably because it goes so much farther north to breed. It is said to pass through the Hudson Bay region at about the same time that the snow geese are migrating; probably both of these hardy northerners know enough not to migrate until their summer homes become habitable. The migration is about due northward on both sides of the Rocky Mountains, through the interior valleys to the Arctic coast, and along the Pacific slope to northern Alaska.

Nesting.—MacFarlane (1891) found this goose breeding abundantly on the Arctic coast, of which he says:

A large number (50) of nests of the smaller Canada goose was found on the Lower Anderson, as well as on the shores and islands of the Arctic Sea. All but one were placed on the earth, and, like that of the preceding species, it was composed of hay, feathers, and down, while 6 was the usual number of eggs. The exceptional case was a female parent shot while sitting on 4 eggs in a deserted crow's or hawk's nest built on the fork of a pine tree at a height of about 9 feet. At the time the ground in the vicinity thereof was covered with snow and water, and this may have had something to do with her nesting in so unusual a place.

In a letter to the Smithsonian Institution he writes:

I have no doubt about Hutchins goose being a good species; its mode of nesting alone would go far to prove it distinct from the Canada goose, which it so greatly resembles. The former, so far as I have been able to ascertain, *invariably* nests on the small islands which occur on the small lakes of the islands situated on the shores of the Arctic Sea, while the latter generally builds in the neighborhood of the lakes and rivers of the wooded country. The former also scoops a hole in the sand or turf, lining its sides with down, while the nest of the latter is composed of a large quantity of feathers and down placed on or supported by some dry twigs or willow branches.

I have had several sets of eggs of the Hutchins goose sent to me from Point Barrow, which were evidently taken from nests on the tundra, for the nesting down, which came from them, was mixed with tundra mosses, bits of grass, leaves, and other rubbish. Nests of the Canada goose generally contain pure, clean down.

Eggs.—The Hutchins goose lays from 4 to 6 eggs, usually 5. These are in no way distinguishable from the eggs of the Canada goose except that they are smaller, as they should be. The measurements of 83 eggs, in various collections, average 79.2 by 53.1 millimeters; the eggs showing the four extremes measure **85.4** by 57, 78.5 by **58**, **72.1** by 53.1, and 76 by **50** millimeters.

Food.—The food and feeding habits of this goose are similar to those of its well-known relative. Nuttall (1834), however, calls attention to the fact that their habits " are dissimilar, the Canada geese frequenting the fresh-water lakes and rivers of the interior, and feeding chiefly on herbage; while the present species are always found on the seacoast, feeding on marine plants, and the mollusca which adhere to them, whence their flesh acquires a strong fishy taste." Dr. J. G. Cooper (1860) says: " They feed principally on the mud flats at low tide, eating vegetable and animal food which they find there," during their annual visits to the coasts of Oregon and Washington.

Dr. Joseph Grinnell (1909) was informed by the natives of Alaska "that some years these geese stop in large numbers for a short time to feed upon the herring spawn which is to be seen all along the beach at low tide, where it sticks to the rocks."

While sojourning in California these geese associate with the white-fronted and snow geese and feed largely in the grain fields and grassy plains. In spring they do considerable damage by pulling up freshly sprouting grain; formerly, when they were much more abundant, it was customary for farmers to hire men and furnish them with guns and ammunition to keep the geese away from the grain; but the geese have decreased in numbers so decidedly in recent years that this is no longer necessary.

Game.—The importance of this bird as a game bird in California is well illustrated by the following statement made by Grinnell, Bryant, and Storer (1918):

The Hutchins goose, although not quite so desirable a bird for the table as are some other species, is the goose which has afforded the greatest amount of sport for the hunter because of its abundance. It has usually been a common goose on the market, where it is known as the "brant." In 1909–10 one transfer company in San Francisco sold the following numbers of brant: October, 1,442; November, 2,196; December, 1,592; January, 1,479; February, 1,226; March, 251. Cackling as well as Hutchins geese are probably included in these numbers. This makes a total of over 8,000 geese of only two varieties sold by the one transfer company. That season the same company sold more than 20,000 geese of all kinds. In 1906–7, it sold only 7,431. In 1895–96 there were sold on the markets of San Francisco and Los Angeles 48,400 geese, of which 16,319 were brant. There is little wonder that geese have decreased in numbers more than most other game birds. The markets of San Francisco during 1910–11 paid from $2.50 to $8 a dozen for geese other than the snow geese. On the Los Angeles markets during 1912–13 the same geese sold at from 65 cents to $1 a pair.

Winter.—A very good account of the winter home and habits of this goose is given by Coues (1874), as follows:

We must, however, visit the regions west of the Rocky Mountains to find the Hutchins goose plentiful in its favorite winter residences, and observe it under the most favorable circumstances. On river, lake, and marsh, and particularly along the seacoast, it is found in vast numbers, being probably the most abundant representative of its family. It enters the United States early in October, or sometimes a little earlier, according to the weather, and in the course of that month becomes dispersed over all its winter feeding grounds. It is generally in poor condition on its arrival, after the severe journey, perhaps extending from the uttermost Arctic land; but it finds abundance of food and is soon in high flesh again. During the rainy season in California the plains and valleys, before brown and dry, become clothed in rich verdure, and the nourishing grasses afford sustenance to incredible numbers of these and other geese. Three kinds, the snow, the white-fronted, and the present species, have almost precisely the same habits and the same food during their stay with us, and associate so intimately together that many, if not most, of the flocks contain representatives of all three. At least, after considerable study of the geese in Arizona and southern California, I have been unable to recognize any notable differences in choice of feeding grounds.

The following extract on Hutchins goose, from Doctor Heermann's report, will be found interesting: "While hunting during a space of two months in the Suisun Valley I observed them, with other species of geese, at dawn, high in the air, winging their way toward the prairies and hilly slopes, where the tender young wild oats and grapes offer a tempting pasturage. Their early flight lasted about two hours, and as far as the eye could reach the sky was spotted with flock after flock, closely following in each other's wake, till it seemed as though all the geese of California had given rendezvous at this particular point. Between 10 and 11 o'clock they would leave the prairies, first in small squads, then in large masses, settling in the marshes and collecting around the ponds and sloughs, thickly edged with heavy reeds. Here, swimming in the water, bathing and pluming themselves, they keep up a continual but not unmusical clatter. This proves the most propitious time of the day for the hunter, who, under cover of the tall reeds and guided by their continual cackling, approaches closely enough to deal havoc among them. Discharging one load as they sit on the water and another as they rise, I have seen 23 geese gathered from two shots, while many more, wounded and maimed, fluttered away and were lost. About 1 o'clock they leave the marshes and return to feed on the prairies, flying low, and affording the sportsman again an opportunity to stop their career. In the afternoon, about 5 o'clock, they finally leave the prairies, and, rising high up in the air, wend their way to the roosting places whence they came in the morning. These were often at a great distance, as I have followed them in their evening flight until they were lost to view. Many, however, roost in the marshes. Our boat, sailing one night down the sloughs leading to Suisun Bay, having come among them, the noise they made as they rose in advance of us, emitting their cry of alarm (their disordered masses being so serried that we could hear their pinions strike each other as they flew), impressed us with the idea that we must have disturbed thousands. Such are the habits of the geese during the winter. Toward spring they separate into small flocks and gradually disappear from the country, some few only remaining, probably crippled and unable to follow the more vigorous in their northern migration."

DISTRIBUTION

Breeding range.—Barren grounds of North America. East to southern Baffin Land. South to Southampton Island, west coast of Hudson Bay (Cape Fullerton and Churchill), northern Mackenzie (Fort Anderson and Fort Good Hope) and northern Alaska (northern coast and south to Kowak River). Said to breed on the Bering Sea coast of Alaska and on the Aleutian Islands, but such reports need confirmation; it may, however, breed on the extreme western Aleutians (Agattu Island) as it is reported as breeding on the Commander and Kurile Islands. North to Victoria Land (Cambridge Bay) and Boothia Peninsula (Felix Harbor). Intergrades with *minima* in Alaska and with *canadensis* in northern Canada.

Winter range.—Mainly western United States. East regularly to the Mississippi Valley, rare in the Eastern States, and only casual on the Atlantic coast. South regularly to the Gulf coasts of Louisiana and Texas and probably Mexico and Lower California (San Rafael Valley). West nearly or quite to the Pacific coast. North to southern British Columbia (mouth of Fraser River), northern Colorado (Barr Lake), Nebraska, southern Illinois, and rarely to southern Wisconsin. On the Asiatic coast south to Japan.

Spring migration.—Early dates of arrival: Manitoba, Aweme, April 2 (average April 12); Saskatchewan, Indian Head, April 29; British Columbia, Sumas, April 10; Alaska, Admiralty Island, April 18, Kuskokwim River, April 30, and Kowak River, May 14. Late dates of departure: Texas, Houston, April 18; California, Gridley, April 26; British Columbia, May 20.

Fall migration.—Early dates of arrival: Manitoba, Aweme, September 13; Montana, Terry, September 22; British Columbia, Sumas, October 4; Wisconsin, Delavan, October 12; Utah, Bear River, October 9; California, Gridley, October 9. Late dates of departure: Hudson Straits, Wales Sound, September 6; Great Bear Lake, September 25; Mackenzie, Fort Wrigley, October 12; Manitoba, Aweme, November 20; Alaska, Kowak River, September 14; British Columbia, November 25.

Casual records.—Has wandered east to Greenland (Disco and Godhaven), Maine (Cape Elizabeth, November 13, 1894), and Virginia (Cobb Island, winter of 1888–89), and south to Florida (Wakulla County, March 12, 1918), and Mexico (Vera Cruz and probably Lake Chapala, Jalisco).

Egg dates.—Arctic Canada: Eighteen records, May 17 to July 14; nine records, June 14 to July 5. Alaska: Thirteen records, May 25 to June 28; seven records June 1 to 11.

BRANTA CANADENSIS OCCIDENTALIS (Baird)

WHITE-CHEEKED GOOSE

HABITS

This large, dark-breasted form of the Canada goose seems to be a well-marked race of decidedly local distribution, occupying the northwest coast region from Prince William Sound, Alaska, to British Columbia. It is practically nonmigratory and does not wander far inland at any season. It is another one of the many saturated forms confined to this humid coast strip. Its specific status has been much discussed and is by no means definitely settled; this will be referred to under the next subspecies. It was formerly recorded by several observers as breeding in the lakes of the interior as far south as northern California, but these records have been shown to refer to the eastern Canada goose. The breeding range of the white-cheeked goose is now known to lie wholly north of the United States boundary.

Nesting.—Although the white-cheeked goose is quite common throughout its restricted range, and even numerous in certain parts of it, its nest has not often been found and very little has been published about its habits. The published reports of the Alexander expeditions to southern Alaska contain the most important contributions to its life history, and even these are meager enough.

Joseph Dixon (1908), a member of this expedition, writes:

The country about Canoe Passage on Hawkins Island was low and rolling, with large open parks bordered by wooded creeks. There were a number of lagoons almost shut off from the bay by long grassy gravel bars. One mountain in the interior of the island was 1,900 feet above the sea, according to the aneroid. Hutchins geese were nesting about these lagoons, and about the 20th of June goslings were everywhere. It was strange how they all hatched out so near the same time. I was wandering home one evening about 10 o'clock. It was just after sundown, but the deeper woods were beginning to darken slowly. It was high tide, so that I had to make a cut clear around the head of a slough. Just as I came out of the thick huckleberry underbrush in the strip of timber I stumbled over a log and almost fell on top of an old goose that was sitting on a nestful of eggs. She made a terrible racket as she went flopping and squawking off the nest, and I do not know which of us was the worst scared for a minute. The nest was placed in the open close to the trunk of a large tree just at the edge of the wood. It was lined with moss and down and held 6 eggs, which I afterwards regretted were almost ready to hatch.

Although he called them Hutchins geese at that time, the geese of that region all proved to be of the present form.

Eggs.—A set of five eggs of this subspecies in the United States National Museum was collected by Dr. Wilfred H. Osgood on Prince of Wales Island, Alaska, on May 22, 1903. These eggs are practically indistinguishable from average eggs of the eastern Canada goose. They measure 86 by 59, 87.4 by 59.4, 86 by 55.8, 87.2 by 57.8, and 87 by 58.2 millimeters.

Young.—Dr. Joseph Grinnell (1910) refers to two broods of young as follows:

On June 21, also on Hawkins Island, Miss Kellogg flushed an old goose from a nest in the tall grass near the beach. There were five newly hatched young. One of these, taken as a specimen (No. 1131), is identical in coloration with a downy young one from the Sitkan district. On June 22, Dixon records as follows: " In crossing some marshy flats we came upon six geese, five of which flew noisily away; but the sixth came gabbling toward us. We soon saw that her unusual tameness was due to her anxiety in regard to six or eight newly hatched goslings that scrambled from under our feet and disappeared with a splash into a near-by pond. I walked up to within 25 feet of the mother as she came with her head down in the usual manner of an irate goose. She followed us for some distance when we left."

Plumages.—Doctor Grinnell has kindly loaned me two specimens of the downy young of this subspecies. These and a specimen of downy young cackling goose in the United States National Museum resemble each other very closely, but are quite unlike the downy young of the Canada goose. The young of the eastern birds when first hatched are bright greenish olive above and bright yellow below, with no dark markings on the sides of the head. On the other hand, the young of the two western forms, at the same age, are much browner above and much duller and more buffy below, with more or less distinct head markings. The central crown patch and the upper parts of the body are lustrous "brownish olive," darkest on the head and rump; the lores are washed or striped with the same dark color, which surrounds the eye and extends in a postocular stripe down the neck; the under parts, including the forehead and the sides of the head and the neck, are dull yellowish or "colonial buff,"washed on the sides of the head and neck with "honey yellow" or "yellow ocher," paling on the belly and flanks to "ivory yellow" and deepening on the breast to "deep colonial buff."

Judging from what little material there is available for study, I should say that the molts and plumages are similar to those of the Canada goose.

Behavior.—Very little has been published about the habits of this goose and practically nothing about its food. Doctor Grinnell (1909) gives the following general account of it, taken from Mr. Littlejohn's notes:

When Mole Harbor, Admiralty Island, was reached, on April 16, large flocks were seen about the creek mouth at the head of the bay. On the 18th many were found at Windfall Harbor, and by the 27th nearly all had paired and could be seen passing back and forth to the inland waters every day, remaining a good share of the time in the open water, where their loud notes could be heard at all times, but when night came on I think most, if not all, came to land to roost. They seemed to feed about the shores, especially where small streams and springs were flowing across the gravel. One large creek near our camp was a favorite place to assemble, and each evening they could be seen coming in from all directions to pass the night. At low tide they would remain on the gravel flats at the creek mouth, but when the tide came in they would retreat to the acres of ice inland, which had been formed during the winter; here they remained until morning if not disturbed, and then would break up in pairs, as a rule, and go off again for the day. Several pairs had chosen the lakes back of Mole Harbor for a nesting ground and were seen together when we first went there; but a few days later some old gander was apt to be seen in a secluded cove, or as happened several times, flushed from the thick timber at some distance from the water. At such times he would fly about, scolding away at a great rate, as if he were alarmed at our presence so near his mate, who was undoubtedly near by, but in the almost impenetrable forest and underbrush was not to be found.

Harry S. Swarth (1922) found these geese abundant at the mouth of the Stickine River in southeastern Alaska; he writes:

In our descent of the river, the first white-cheeked geese were seen at the boundary, August 16. From there on down an occasional small flock was noted, but not until the mouth of the river was reached were they seen in any numbers. At Sergief Island they were abundant. Flocks of large size frequented the marshes at that point, changing their feeding ground as the tides advanced and receded. These local movements covered but a few miles at most, and, of course, were gone through with daily as regularly as the tides. Aside from this hourly shifting, which kept some flocks on the wing practically throughout the day, there was no appearance of migration. Flocks of white-cheeked geese were never seen to depart in a manner suggestive of the beginning of along flight, nor were any seen arriving as though from a distance.

During the last two weeks in August the geese were still molting extensively. In some the breast and belly were almost entirely devoid of feathers, only the down remaining, and nearly all were renewing the tail feathers. Flight feathers were fully grown, or at any rate sufficiently so for flying. Presumably the birds would not gather upon these open and exposed marshes until they could fly; nesting and the beginning of the molt, including loss of the remiges, probably takes place in more sheltered localities.

Winter.—Of their winter habits he (1913) says:

Since so many of the water birds of the coast of southern Alaska and British Columbia are resident the year through in that general region, it is very probable that the white-cheeked goose belongs in the same category. In a letter recently received from Mr. Allen E. Hasselborg, a resident of Juneau, Alaska, and familiar with the native birds and mammals, he confirms this view, saying that the geese are about as abundant in the Sitkan district in winter as in summer. During the winter they frequent the more sheltered south and west facing bays and inlets, avoiding localities exposed to the cold land winds, while in summer they are of more general distribution. That this subspecies does not perform as extensive migrations as other members of the group is evident from its nonoccurrence in California. If it occurs in this State at all it should be found along the extreme northern coast.

DISTRIBUTION

Breeding range.—Pacific coast region of southeastern Alaska, from the vicinity of Prince William Sound southward, to British Columbia (Queen Charlotte Islands). Intergrades on the north with *minima* and on the east and south with *canadensis.*

Winter range.—Apparently the same as the breeding range. This seems to be a local form of very restricted habitat and non-migratory.

Egg dates.—Southern Alaska: Three records, May 22 to June 18.

BRANTA CANADENSIS MINIMA Ridgway

CACKLING GOOSE

HABITS

The characters which warrant the separation of the Canada goose group into four subspecies have been so generally misunderstood and so poorly designated in most of the manuals, and the nomenclature of the group has been so variable and puzzling, that much confusion has existed as to the true relationships of the various forms and their distribution. Various theories have been advanced, none of which seem to fit the known facts exactly. Rather than attempt to discuss this complicated systematic question, which would require more space than is warranted in a work on life histories, I would refer the reader to the interesting papers on the subject published by Harry S. Swarth (1913) and J. D. Figgins (1920 and 1922). It seems best, under the circumstances, to follow the classification and nomenclature of the American Ornithologists' Union Check List until some better arrangement is suggested and proven to be correct by the collection of large enough series of breeding birds to demonstrate the relationships and to outline the breeding ranges of the four forms. It is, however, difficult to explain, under this generally accepted theory, why the breeding ranges of *hutchinsi* and *minima* should overlap so extensively in Alaska and the Aleutian Islands, as they are said to do, which is contrary to the rule with subspecies. It is also of interest to note that the downy young of *occidentalis* and *minima* resemble each other very closely and are quite different from the downy young of *canadensis;* this suggests the possibility of a distinct, dark-breasted, western species. But perhaps both of these matters will be cleared up when more material is collected.

Spring.—Dr. E. W. Nelson (1887) gives the following interesting account of the arrival of these geese at St. Michael, Alaska:

As May advances and one by one the ponds open, and the earth looks out here and there from under its winter covering, the loud notes of the various wild fowl are heard, becoming daily more numerous. Their harsh and varied cries make sweet music to the ears of all who have just passed the winter's silence and dull monotony, and in spite of the lowering skies and occasional snow squalls everyone makes ready and is off to the marshes.

The flocks come cleaving their way from afar, and as they draw near their summer homes raise a chorus of loud notes in a high-pitched tone like the syllable "luk," rapidly repeated, and a reply rises upon all sides, until the whole marsh reechoes with the din, and the newcomers circle slowly up to the edge of a pond amid a perfect chorus raised by the geese all about, as in congratulation.

Even upon first arrival many of the birds appear to be mated, as I have frequently shot one from a flock and seen a single bird leave its companions at once and come circling about, uttering loud call notes. If the fallen bird is only wounded, its mate will almost invariably join it, and frequently allow itself to be approached and shot without attempting to escape. In some, instances I have known a bird thus bereaved of its partner to remain in the vicinity for two to three days, calling and circling about. Although many are mated, others are not, and the less fortunate males fight hard and long for possession of females. I frequently amused myself while at the Yukon mouth by watching flocks of geese on the muddy banks of the river, which was a favorite resort. The females kept to one side and dozed or dabbed their bills in the mud; the males were scattered about and kept moving uneasily from side to side, making a great outcry. This would last but a few minutes, when two of the warriors would cross each other's path, and then began the battle. They would seize one another by the bill, and then turn and twist each other about, their wings hanging loosely by their sides meanwhile. Suddenly they would close up and each would belabor his rival with the bend of the wing, until the sound could be heard two or three hundred yards. The wing strokes were always warded off by the other bird's wing, so but little damage was done; but it usually ended in the weaker bird breaking loose and running away. Just before the males seize each other they usually utter a series of peculiar low growling or grunting notes.

Nesting.—Of their breeding habits in that vicinity he writes:

The last week of May finds many of these birds already depositing their eggs. Upon the grassy borders of ponds, in the midst of a bunch of grass, or on a small knoll these birds find a spot where they make a slight depression and perhaps line it with a scanty layer of grasses, after which the eggs are laid, numbering from 5 to 8. These eggs, like the birds, average smaller than those of the other geese. As the eggs are deposited the female gradually lines the nest with feathers plucked from her breast until they rest in a bed of down. When first laid the eggs are white, but by the time incubation begins all are soiled and dingy. The female usually crouches low on her nest until an intruder comes within a hundred yards or so, when she skulks off through the grass or flies silently away, close to the ground, and only raises a note of alarm when well away from the nest. When the eggs are about hatching, or the young are out, both parents frequently become perfectly reckless in the face of danger.

Both the cackling goose and the Hutchins goose are said to breed on the Aleutian Islands, but it seems hardly likely that these two subspecies should occupy the same breeding range. It seems more likely that some of the records are based on erroneous identifications or on misunderstandings as to the characters, both puzzling and variable, which separate these two forms. Lucien M. Turner (1886) reported both forms as breeding abundantly on the western islands of this chain, mainly on Agattu and Semichi, but I can not find any specimens of *hutchinsi* to substantiate his claim.

Mr. Austin H. Clark (1910) reported that the Hutchins goose—

is the most abundant bird on Agattu, where it breeds by thousands. When we approached the shore we saw a number of geese flying about the cliffs and bluffs and soaring in circles high in air. On landing I walked up the beach to the left and soon came to a small stream which enters the sea through a gap in the high bluffs, when I saw 50 or more of these birds along the bank preening their feathers. From this point I walked inland over the rough pasture-like country toward a lake where this stream rises. Geese were seen on all sides in great abundance, walking about the grassy hillsides in companies of six or eight to a dozen, or flying about from one place to another. When on the ground they were comparatively shy; at about 100 yards distant they would stop feeding and watch my movements; at about 50 yards they generally took wing, but instead of flying away they would circle about and fly toward me, often not more than 10 feet over my head, as if to see what sort of a strange beast it was which thus intruded on their domains.

He shot nine of the birds, but unfortunately was unable to preserve any of them; he did, however, write down descriptions and take the measurements of four of them. Although the measurements are rather large for *minima*, the descriptions seem to fit this form rather than *hutchinsi*, and perhaps if we had the specimens before us we might decide to refer them to the former subspecies.

On our expedition to the Aleutian Islands in 1911 we saw geese of this group on Kiska, Adak, Atka, and Attu Islands, but the only specimen taken was a female *minima* shot by R. H. Beck as she flew from her nest on Attu Island. The nest was located on the slope of a grassy hillside; it consisted of a mass of down in a hollow in the ground and contained 4 eggs on June 23.

Mr. Turner (1886) says that "the clutch of eggs varies from 7 to 13 and are laid in a carelessly arranged nest composed of dead grasses and few feathers."

Eggs.—There are 13 sets of eggs of the cackling goose in the United States National Museum, in which the numbers vary from 4 to 7; there are also four nests collected by C. H. Townsend on Agattu Island on June 5, 1894. The nests are large masses of "light drab" or "drab-gray" down, mixed with bits of white or whitish down, numerous breast feathers and bits of straw. The eggs are similar to those of the Canada goose, but smaller. The measurements of 110 eggs, in various collections, average 72.7 by 48 millimeters; the eggs showing the four extremes measure **85** by 55, 78.5 by **55.5**, and **60.3** by **37** millimeters.

Young.—Mr. Turner (1886) says:

The young remain with the parents until the latter molt, by the 20th of August, by which time the young are able to fly. This date witnesses a few of the older young and adult males coming from the breeding grounds on the Semichi Islands to the island of Attu. The geese have exhausted, by that time, the food supply of that place and repair to Attu to feast on the berries of the *Vaccineum* that are rapidly ripening. Attu Island has a great many blue foxes (*V. lagopus*) on it, hence is resorted to only by adult birds. The birds arrive poor and lean, but by the 10th of September they abound in thousands and are very fat at this time. The birds usually alight on the hillsides, and quickly strip the lower areas of the berries that have ripened earlier. Toward the evening the geese resort to the shallow pools (destitute of vegetation, with gravelly bottoms) on the sides of the mountains.

Plumages.—The downy young is exactly like that of *occidentalis*. The molts and plumages are probably similar to those of the other subspecies of this group. Doctor Nelson (1887) says:

The first plumage of this bird is a dull grayish umber-brown; the head and neck almost uniform with the rest of the body and without any trace of the white cheek patches. As is common to the young of many waterfowl, the feathers of head, neck, and much of the rest of body are bordered with a lighter shade than the main part of the feathers. The old birds molt their quill feathers from the 20th of July until late in August, and flocks begin forming as soon as the birds are on the wing again. From that time until the last of September and first of October, when they migrate, they are found scattered over the country, feeding on various berries, which are ripe on the hillsides.

Behavior.—Very little has been published about the habits of this subspecies, but they are probably similar in the main to those of its close relatives. Mr. Turner (1886) writes:

As an illustration of the parental solicitude exhibited by these birds, I will relate that several years ago a heavy fall of snow occurred in the latter part of June at the islands of Agattu and Semichi and covered the ground with more than 3 feet of snow. At that date the geese were incubating. The geese did not quit their nests and were suffocated. The natives found scores of the birds sitting dead on their nests after the snow had melted.

During the summer the geese are not molested. The natives take many of the young and domesticate them. I have seen as many as 50 young ones at a time at Attu Island owned by the natives, to whom the goslings become much attached, especially those who attend them. The goslings remain at large during the winter, but have to be fed during severe spells of weather. The housetops being covered with sod, the excessive heat within causes the grass roots to continually send out new blades of grass. The geese are constantly searching every housetop to find the tender blades. One man had a pair of adult geese which he assured me had been reared from goslings, and that they were then entering the sixth year of their captivity. These two geese did not breed the second year of their life, but that every year thereafter they had reared a brood of young and brought them home as soon as hatched. The wings and half of the tail feathers had to be clipped every season to prevent them migrating.

Messrs. Grinnell, Bryant, and Storer (1918) say: "The high pitch of its call note, which resembles the syllables *luk-luk*, is about the best character to use in the field after recognizing the bird to be of the Canada type." This note is "oft repeated" and has caused the bird to be called the cackling goose. It is easily distinguished from the notes of the Canada goose and the Hutchins goose.

The same writers say further:

In habits the cackling goose so nearly resembles the Hutchins goose that no one has been able to point out differences. As with the latter species, the cackling goose feeds largely on grass and grain during its stay in California.

Along with other geese, this species used to do much damage to young wheat in Colusa, Butte, Sutter, and Uba Counties. But the ranks of the birds are so thinned at the present time that the injury they inflict now is negligible.

On the market this species is usually classified along with the Hutchins goose as " brant." Very large numbers of cackling geese are to be found at times in the markets of our larger cities. The cackling goose, once just as numerous, if not more so, than the Hutchins goose, is, like the Hutchins, rapidly decreasing in numbers from year to year. Old residents in some parts of the Sacramento Valley say that now there is " not more than one of these geese present where formerly there were hundreds." To the work of the market hunter can be attributed much of this decrease, for this goose is one which is easily procured and which finds a ready sale on the market. While still rated as common in restricted portions of the State, this goose is in a fair way to disappear completely unless enough of the birds are left each winter to guarantee the return of an adequate stock in the spring to the breeding grounds in the north.

Game.—The primitive hunters of the Aleutian Islands formerly killed large numbers of these geese by catching them in long nets set on the edges of ponds where they fed. Some of the natives were also quite expert at throwing at the passing flocks a bolas made of three stones attached to leather thongs, which became entangled with the necks and wings of the birds, bringing sometimes two and even three birds down to the ground. The birds were salted away for future use during the winter and must have served as an important addition to the food supply of the natives.

Mr. Turner (1886) describes the more modern method of shooting geese on Attu Island as follows:

The manner of shooting geese at Attu Island is different from that pursued in other localities. In the evening the geese repair to the shallow pools to preen their feathers and be secure from the attacks of foxes. These resorts leave unmistakable signs of the presence of geese of preceding nights. The native wanders over the hills until he finds a lake where " signs " are abundant. A hut is generally to be found near the favorite night haunts of the geese. To this one journeys in a canoe, and on arriving the *chynik* (teakettle) is hung on the soon-kindled fire to boil, as the *chypeet* (tea drinking) is a certain concomitant of all Alaskan jaunts, either of pleasure or of profit. The chypeet over, the approach of dusk is awaited. The hunters then seek the chosen ponds and secrete themselves in a gully or on the hillside near the place to watch the geese as they come in for the evening, for during the day the geese have been feeding on the smooth, sloping hillsides.

The hunter is careful to approach these lakes lest he leave a footprint or other sign of his presence, as the goose is ever on the alert for such traces and forsakes any lake that is suspected. They will in such cases hover round and round endeavoring to discover the danger, and when satisfied that the lake has been visited by man or that he is present their loud cries give warning to all the geese within hearing as they quickly stream off and away to the head of the ravine from which they came. After such an occurrence the hunter would just as well go home or seek some other locality, for no more geese will visit that lake until the next night.

A night on which the sky is partly clouded and a light wind is blowing is the best. If the air is calm and the night bright, the still water reflects too strongly the outlines of the surrounding hills, making the water inky black, and renders it impossible to distinguish a goose sitting on the water.

At the time the geese are expected each person has selected his place and remains quiet. On the approach of the first flock for the night a low whistle from the hunter to his companions gives signal. A low *hunk hunk* of the geese and a swirl of wings announce their approach. A straight dash or a few circles round the pond and they settle. Shoot just as they alight and again as they rise. Sometimes they become so confused as to enable the holder of a breechloader to get four shots at a single flock. The dead geese serve as decoys and soon many are added to those already killed. The gentle wind slowly blows them ashore while you are waiting for others. In a short time a sufficient number is obtained. At an appointed time another native comes from the hut to help bear home the geese.

Winter.—Cackling geese are abundant winter residents in the interior valleys of California, where they frequent the grain fields in company with Hutchins, snow, Ross, and white-fronted geese. As their habits are evidently similar, it is unnecessary to repeat what has already been written about the others.

DISTRIBUTION

Breeding range.—The Bering Sea coast of Alaska and the Aleutian Islands. South to the north side of the Alaskan Peninsula (Bristol Bay and Nushagak River). West to the western Aleutians (Agattu and Attu Islands). North to Norton Sound (St. Michael), probably Kotzebue Sound (Kowak River) and possibly as far as Wainwright, where it has been taken in July. Intergrades with *hutchinsi* in northern and with *occidentalis* in southern Alaska.

Winter range.—Western North America, west of the Rocky Mountains from southern British Columbia to southern California (San Diego County).

Spring migration.—Arrives at St. Michael, Alaska, April 25 to 30. Latest date of departure from California, Stockton, April 25. Taken on St. Paul Island, Alaska, May 14.

Fall migration.—Earliest date of arrival in California, Gridley, October 1. Late dates of departure in Alaska, Yukon Delta, October 1, Aleutian Islands, November 15; British Columbia, Okanogan, November 20.

Casual records.—Said to wander on migrations as far east as Wisconsin and Colorado (Loveland, April 10, 1898), but identifications are doubtful.

Egg dates.—Alaska: Eighteen records, May 20 to June 30; nine records June 5 to 15.

BRANTA BERNICLA BERNICLA (Linnaeus)

BRANT

HABITS

For the past 25 years the American brant has been called *Branta bernicla glaucogastra* (Brehm); white-bellied brant, ever since Dr. Elliott Coues (1897) called our attention to the supposed subspecific distinction between the common European brant and the North American bird of the Atlantic coast and proposed the adoption of Brehm's name for our bird. The European bird was supposed to breed in Spitsbergen, Franz-Josef Land, Nova Zembla, and the Taimyr Peninsula, and the American bird, *glaucogastra*, was supposed to breed in western Greenland and westward as far as the Parry Islands. Recent investigations and explorations have shown that this theory is untenable, that the European and the American birds are not separable, and that *Branta bernicla glaucogastra* (Brehm) is a *nomen nudum*. Even if there were such a subspecies as the white-bellied brant, the name, *glaucogastra*, could not be used for it, as it was applied by Brehm to a dark-bellied bird shot on the coast of Germany.

Rev. F. C. R. Jourdain, who has made two recent visits to Spitsbergen, in 1921 and 1922, writes to me:

The pale-breasted form is the one which breeds in Spitsbergen. We got over 20 birds in 1921 and they were all pale, as also were all those examined in 1922. Chapman got 30 or more, and they were all pale too. Koenig speaks of getting dark-breasted birds there, but he figures what he calls the dark-breasted bird, and it does not in the least resemble the uniformly slaty-breasted individuals which visit us in winter. There is some variation among the light-breasted birds, and it is quite evident that the "dark" birds which Koenig refers to are merely specimens in which the brownish-gray markings extend over the whole of the lower breast to the vent, instead of being confined to the breast only. The only really dark-breasted *breeding* bird I have seen came from Franz-Josef Land, but we get lots of them here (England) in winter. I am inclined to think that the pale-breasted bird extends from America to Spitsbergen in breeding time, and that perhaps farther east the darker-breasted form predominates.

The two so-called species of brant, *Branta bernicla* and *B. nigricans*, together have a complete circumpolar breeding range. The western limit of *nigricans* on the Siberian coast is not definitely known, and future investigation may show that it intergrades with the so-called dark-bellied form of *bernicla* somewhere in the palaearctic region. This would explain the occurrence of both light and dark birds in western Europe in winter, for it is well known that certain birds, such as the yellow-billed loon and the Steller eider, migrate from their breeding grounds in Arctic Siberia to the Scandinavian coasts to spend the winter, and the brant might well be expected to do the same.

In later communications Mr. Jourdain refers to a third form, darker than our so-called *glaucogastra* but lighter than *nigricans*, breeding in western Siberia, Kolguev, and Nova Zembla. Such birds, it seems to me, are intermediates, and show intergradation between *bernicla (glaucogastra)* and *nigricans*.

There is considerable evidence which points to intergradation between *bernicla* and *nigricans* in Arctic America. P. A. Taverner writes to me that they have specimens of both forms from Melville Island and that he obtained two specimens at Comox, British Columbia, which are halfway between the two forms and furnish "almost positive proof of complete intergradation between them." Dr. R. M. Anderson writes to me:

> I have seen the natives shoot a good many brant (supposed to be black brant) around the Mackenzie delta and in Arctic Alaska, and they were quite variable as to paleness. The females and young are lighter in color than the males as a rule, and, if my memory serves me right, some were as light as so-called *glaucogastra* which I have since seen.

Alfred M. Bailey writes to me regarding birds collected in northern Alaska:

> The majority of our specimens taken in the fall were dark bellied and would be referable to the so-called *nigricans*, although we got many light-colored birds. In the spring at Wales and Wainwright the birds collected averaged considerably lighter than those taken in the fall, with the dark breasts sharply defined in many cases. The white collar was practically continuous in both the spring and fall birds.

I notice that European writers are now recognizing *nigricans* as a subspecies of *bernicla*, and I believe that they are correct in doing so.

Spring.—The brant which have spent the winter farthest south begin to move northward in February, joining the birds which have wintered on the Virginia coast late in February, and moving on to Great South Bay, Long Island, in March. By the middle of April they have moved farther east and are congregated in large numbers off Monomoy, on the south side of Cape Cod. In the old days before spring shooting was abolished this was a famous resort for brant shooting in April. Monomoy Island, now joined to the mainland, extends for 9 or 10 miles southward from the elbow of Cape Cod; the eastern or outer side is a long, high, sandy beach washed by the surf of the broad Atlantic; on the western or inner side, beyond the sand dunes, are large grassy meadows or salt marshes, invaded by shallow bays; at low tide broad mud flats, more or less covered with eelgrass, extend for miles along the shore, furnishing ideal feeding grounds for brant and other sea fowl. Between here and the flats around Muskeget Island, a few miles south, immense numbers of brant congregate in the spring; they have been moving gradually northward from their winter resorts, gaining in numbers, by picking up those that have wintered farther north, as they went along. The spring flight is leisurely and largely dependent on the weather and the direction of the wind; cold, northerly, or easterly winds hold them back; but warm days and favorable southwest winds are sure to start them moving. Dr. Leonard C. Sanford (1903) has well described the departure of the brant from the Monomoy flats, which usually takes place in the latter part of April, as follows:

Some time in April comes a pleasant day, warm and sunny, with a southwest wind. The several thousand brant in Chatham Bay feed greedily until the rising tide removes their food from reach. Now they assemble in deep water in the center of the bay, study the weather, and discuss the advisability of journeying toward their summer home. Soon 15 or 20 birds take wing, fly back and forth over the others, honking loudly, and circling ever higher until they have reached a considerable altitude; then the long line swings straight, headed northeast. Out over the beach, over the ocean it goes, and the birds in it will not be seen again. Then another flock follows, taking exactly the same course; flock after flock succeeds and the movement is kept up until dark. You may sit in the blind next day or sail across the bay, you will see no brant save a few stragglers; branting is through for the year.

Up to this time the flight has been wholly coastwise, marshaling the hosts for the main flight. But here there is apparently an occasional, if not a regular, offshoot from the main flight, which migrates overland from Long Island Sound to the St. Lawrence River, for Dr. Louis B. Bishop (1921) writes:

Prof. A. E. Verrill informed me that on May 17, 1914, he saw, with Mr. G. E. Verrill, many flocks of brant flying north up the Housatonic Valley near the mouth of the Housatonic River; that most were high in the air, but some almost within gunshot; also that he saw others flying northwest while at Outer Island, Stony Creek, about May 22.

But the main flight, when it leaves Cape Cod, flies northeastward to the Bay of Fundy, across the neck of Nova Scotia to the Gulf of St. Lawrence, in the vicinity of Prince Edward Island. Here, according to E. H. Forbush (1912) —

about June 1 those in the district around Charlottetown (which probably comprise a great part of the Atlantic coast flight) begin to assemble in Hillsborough Bay, outside of Charlottetown Harbor, on the south side of the island. Here they gather, between St. Peters and Governors Island, in preparation for their northern journey. From June 10 to 15 they leave in large flocks. Sometimes four or five such flocks follow one another, about a mile apart.

Richard C. Harlow writes to me that—

during the last half of May the brant fairly swarm in the sheltered bays and channels along the coast of Northumberland County, New Brunswick. Here in certain favored places are channels from 1 to 5 miles wide, lying between the mainland and the sandy coastal islands. Where the water is shallow an abundant growth of eelgrass occurs, and here, protected from the open seas beyond the islands, the brant find an ideal haven. There is a noticeable increase of the birds since spring shooting was abolished, and during the last 10 days of May I have seen the water dotted with them in flocks ranging from three or four to hundreds. During a 10-mile run in this region flocks were rising every few minutes, and the din from their honking was terrific, especially in the early morning and evening. The main flocks leave in a body about June 1, though stragglers linger up until June 10. As the time draws near for their departure they gather into larger flocks and grow still more noisy, but no premature mating tendencies are observed.

Harrison F. Lewis has sent me the following notes on the movements of brant on the north shore of the Gulf of St. Lawrence:

Warden P. G. Rowe, of Prince Edward Island, was sent to the Bay of Seven Islands last spring (1922) to protect the brant while they passed there, as they do every spring. He arrived there on May 17 and found at that time some hundreds of brant in the bay. He was unable to get near them. Natives of Seven Islands told him that they had arrived there about the 1st of May; that they came into the bay from the southwest by a "pass" never used by the great brant flight, as though they had descended the St. Lawrence; and that the same thing occurred each spring. These brant all left the bay some days before the usual big flight of brant began to arrive.

This may be the flight, referred to above, which migrates overland from Long Island Sound and which naturally would arrive earlier. When Dr. Charles W. Townsend and I reached the Bay of Seven Islands, May 23, 1909, no brant were there, nor did we see any on our cruise farther eastward down the coast; but when we returned to Seven Islands on June 22 we were told by several observers that there had been a big flight there in the meantime and all had gone but one. They came the last of May and were practically all gone, in the direction of Hudson Bay, before June 20. Mr. Lewis's notes confirm these statements very well, as follows:

I may also say that the big flight of brant from Prince Edward Island passed the Bay of Seven Islands in the early days of June (5–15) this year. They all enter the bay by the two easternmost "passes," chiefly by the most eastern "pass" of all. The number entering the bay was checked carefully by Warden Rowe, who was able to count them very well, as they passed at a low elevation, chiefly in flocks of two or three hundred or less. He sets the total number at at least 60,000. I believe that this includes practically the entire species.

Their route overland to Hudson Bay and from there to their northern Arctic breeding places is not so easily traced. They have not been noted in spring on the west coast of Hudson Bay, where they are reported as common in the fall. They may migrate up the east coast or they may fly straight north overland to Ungava Bay. Mr. Lucien M. Turner's notes, which seem to point to the overland route, say:

At Fort Chimo they arrive from the 20th of May to the 20th of June. They fly past the station of Fort Chimo over the water in the Koksoak. At times they are as high as 100 yards, and oftener only a few feet above the water or running ice. They come at a time when it is almost impossible to get at them on account of ice, and if this is not present they fly too high. They follow the sinuosities of the river and only cross such points that they can see over. Thousands of them are seen every spring and never one of them in the fall. They are reported by the Eskimo to fly southward over Hudson Bay. The route taken in the spring is to the west of Anticosti Island, thence north to the "Height of land" where the Koksoak River descends, along which they fly northward. They appear fatigued when they reach Hudson Strait, but with rapid beat of wing they pursue their course to the unknown regions beyond.

From here they apparently pass to the westward of Baffin Land and spread out over their breeding grounds from Melville Island to northern Greenland. Dr. Donald B. MacMillan tells me that they appear in large numbers in spring on the southwest coast of Baffin Land and apparently cross the center of that land, over a chain of lakes, to Baffin Bay and fly straight north to Ellesmere Land and northern Greenland, arriving at Etah about June 1. These early arrivals must be the vanguard of the earliest flight. He says that Sverdrup has seen them in Eureka Sound and Peary has seen them at the north end of Axel Heiberg Land, Cape Thomas Hubbard, and on the north coast of Grant Land, the northernmost land known.

Nesting.—The best account I have of the nesting habits of this species comes in some notes sent to me by the Rev. F. C. R. Jourdain; he writes:

Although closely allied to the barnacle goose, the brant differs widely from it in its breeding habits. While the barnacle goose has attained security from marauders by placing its nest in inaccessible spots on mountain sides, the brant prefers as a rule to breed on the little holms and outlying islets which fringe the coast. Here for centuries they have bred undisturbed save for an occasional visit from a sealing sloop, but of late years, since most of these vessels have been fitted with auxiliary oil engines, the sloops have taken to working systematically the eider holms for eggs and down, and the geese in consequence have been driven from many of their old haunts by indiscriminate shooting during the breeding season. No doubt a good many pairs still breed on some of the less accessible islands, but apparently many birds now nest also on the mainland, especially on the grassy islands formed by the many channels into which the rivers tend to divide when the valleys open out. The diminution in the number of Arctic foxes by trapping has probably rendered this type of site less dangerous than formerly, but we had evidence of nests of this kind being destroyed by foxes.

On Moffen Island, which is practically a huge shingle bed, we found several pairs breeding among the shingle and in one case on the "slob-land" not far off. As in the case of the other geese, incubation is performed by the goose alone, but the gander mounts guard by her side and is generally to be found on duty. The normal clutch is apparently 3 to 5, but Koenig records one instance of 6 and Kolthoff 7. Several cases of 2 and even 1 incubated egg occurred, but are probably due to the fact that a previous clutch had been taken. The nests vary a good deal in appearance. On low islets they may be found among the eider ducks' nests, and are substantially built of mosses, lichens, and other vegetable matter, with a plentiful lining of light grayish down. When flushed from incubated eggs, both birds show great anxiety, flying round and round with anxious "gaggling." On shingle banks, where little nesting material is available, the nest may be little more than a hollow among the stones, lined with down and perhaps a few bits of seaweed or lichen. While hiding in order to watch the bird back to the nest, it was interesting to notice the head and upper neck of the goose silently watching us from behind a bank of shingle, and all the time keeping as much as possible out of sight, so that the contest resolved itself into one of endurance.

The nests found by Doctor MacMillan's (1918) party in northern Greenland were apparently similar in location and construction. W. Elmer Ekblaw writes to me:

The brant, whether it comes from Europe or from America, arrives in northwest Greenland about mid-June. It appears in rather large flocks, from about 15 to 50 in number, generally sweeping along the coast in low, long files. When they arrive the ice is well broken and open, so that they find no lack of feeding grounds. Either they are mated when they arrive, or they mate soon after, without any distinct mating season, because they proceed at once to the business of nesting and incubation. They gather along the shores of the rocky islets, and usually group their nests somewhat gregariously. Lyttleton Island, McGarys Rock, and Sutherland Island are favorite nesting places. The nests, like those of the eiders, are placed among the tussocks of grass or sedge growing on the low flat ledges of the islets where they nest. The nests are heavily lined with dark down, and the full clutch of eggs seems to vary considerably. Some nests held but 4 eggs, while a few had 11 or 12. The period of incubation is between three and four weeks.

Col. John E. Thayer (1905) has a nest and four eggs taken by J. S. Warmbath on Ellesmere Land, of which he says:

The nest was found June 17, 1900, on a ledge of rock, 20 feet from the ground, among elder ducks' and glaucous gulls' nests. Both birds were shot. The female was shot on a slight elevation above the nest and the male in the water near it.

Eggs.—The brant ordinarily lays from 3 to 5 eggs, though as many as 6 or 8 have been recorded. The 4 eggs in the Thayer (1905) collection, referred to above, are described as "dull creamy white and smaller than eggs of the black brant." Four eggs in the author's collection, taken on Eider Duck Island, northern Greenland, June 18, 1917, by W. Elmer Ekblaw, are creamy white in color, clean and smooth, but not glossy, and elliptical ovate in shape. The measurements of 54 eggs, in various collections, average 71.7 by 47.1 millimeters; the eggs showing the four extremes measure 81.1 by 49.4, 77 by 51.3, 60.4 by 38.8, and 61.8 by 36.5 millimeters.

Young.—The period of incubation is not definitely known, but it is probably about four weeks. The female alone incubates, but the male stands guard near by and helps defend the nest. Mr. Jourdain says, in his notes:

We first met with the pretty ashy gray goslings on July 14, but Koenig mentions having seen them on July 4 and 10, so that probably the normal time for fresh eggs is during the first fortnight of June. The sailors on our boat succeeded in rearing one gosling, providing freshly cut pieces of turf daily and allowing the bird to feed itself.

On July 17 a flock of about 60 geese, which had shed their flight feathers and were temporarily unable to fly, was met with on a lagoon up the Sanen River. They kept close together in a compact body, the barnacles usually leading and the brent and pink-footed following. When the flock had been fired at several times and about 18 specimens secured, the pink-footed geese separated themselves from the rest of the party and led the way toward land, running with considerable speed and soon putting themselves out of danger, an example soon followed by the rest.

Mr. Ekblaw writes to me:

As soon as the young are hatched they hurry to sea. They dive and swim agilely almost as soon as they reach the water. Several broods of young are wont to congregate together, the mothers aiding one another in vigilant guidance and guard over the flock. They are exceedingly shy, and it is well-nigh impossible to approach them except by surprise. They grow and develop fast, so that by mid-September they are ready for their departure. As soon as the ice begins to form in the fjords the brant begin to leave. By October 1 the last long, low-flying files of migrating brant have passed the outer capes; almost nine months slip by before they appear again.

Plumages.—I have never seen the downy young of the brant, but it is described in Witherby's Handbook (1921) as follows:

Down of crown, center of nape, upper parts and sides of body pale mouse gray, some tipped grayish white; patch on lores and lines above eye sepia; chin, throat, and rest of neck white; remaining under parts ashy white, down with dusky-brown bases.

The juvenal plumage during the first fall is similar in a general way to that of the adult, except that the black areas are duller and more brownish, the white neck patches are lacking, the feathers of the scapulars, and median wing coverts are broadly edged with buffy white, and those of the back and other coverts are more narrowly edged with the same; the secondaries are also narrowly edged with white. Molting and wear of the contour feathers, especially about the head and neck, during the winter produce an advance toward maturity; the white neck patches appear in January, but the wings retain the juvenal characters until the following summer. A complete molt in summer produces a plumage indistinguishable from that of the adult.

Food.—According to Witherby's Handbook (1921) the food of the brant on its breeding grounds consists of "grass, algae, moss, and stalks and leaves of arctic plants (*Eriophorum, Ranunculus, Cerastium, Oxyria,* and *Saxifraga*)." The "young feed on *Gramineae* and *Oxyria.*"

While on our coasts their chief food is eelgrass (*Zostera marina*), which grows so extensively in our shallow bays and estuaries. At

certain stages of the tides, the last half of the ebb or the first half of
the flood, when the beds of eelgrass are uncovered or covered with
shallow water, the brant resort to them in large numbers to feed.
They prefer the roots and the whitish lower stems, but they eat the
green fronds also. As soon as the water is shallow enough for
them to reach the grass by tipping up they begin to feed, and they
keep at it until the tide again covers the flats too deeply. While
most of the birds are feeding with heads and necks below the surface
there are always a few sentinels on watch to warn them of approaching danger. They pull up much more eelgrass than they can eat
at once; this floats off with the tide and often forms small floating
islands, far off from shore, to which the brant resort at high tide
to feed again. John Cordeaux (1898) says that the longer pieces of
Zostera " are neatly rolled up, like ribbons, in their stomachs "; they
also devour the fronds of some species of algae, crustaceans, mollusca, worms, and marine insects. Gätke says that at Heligoland,
when the sea is calm, small companies will approach the cliffs and
pick off the small mollusca and crustaceans.

I have at times been greatly entertained in watching a flock of brant feeding in shallow water, close inshore, the greater portion of the birds upside
down, their rumps and tails showing the white coverts, only visible as they
greedily tear at the blades and roots of the grass wrack, whilst others are
seizing the floating fragments of the plant, broken off and dislodged by
their mates; and on the outside there are always some with heads held high,
ever on the watch, and ready to give alarm. All the time they keep a continuous, noisy gabbling and grunting, the rear birds constantly swimming forward
to get in advance of their fellows, a procedure which I have known, more
than once, bring them within range of an ordinary sporting gun.

Brant in captivity are especially fond of barley and will eat corn
and other grains. George H. Mackay (1893) says:

Two wing-tipped birds I have in confinement eat with avidity the alga
(*Ulva lactuca*). They also eat *Zostera marina*, preferring the white portion
farthest from the extremity of the blade. They cut this up by chewing first
on one side and then on the other of their mandibles, which cuts the grass
as clean as if scissors had been used. The motion reminds one strongly of
a dog eating, the bird turning its head much the same way. They are fond
of whole corn and common grass. These confined birds drink after almost
every mouthful, from a pan of fresh water. The wild birds living in this
neighborhood have no opportunity of obtaining fresh water.

Doctor MacMillan tells me that he has seen brant, when they first
arrive in Baffin Land in the spring, feeding on the black lichens
which grow on the rocks on the uplands.

Behavior.—Brant do not ordinarily fly in V-shaped flocks, like
Canada geese, but in long undulating lines, spread out laterally in
straight company-front formation, or in a curving line, or in an
irregular bunch, and without a definite leader. When migrating

overland they fly high, but when traveling along the coast they usually fly within a few feet of the water. Their flight is apparently slow and heavy, but it is really swifter than it seems. A flock of on-coming brant is a thrilling sight to the expectant gunner; he can recognize afar the long wavy line of heavy black birds; as they draw near, the white hind parts show up in marked contrast to the black heads and necks; and soon he can hear their gabbling, grunting notes of greeting to his well-placed decoys. They are naturally shy birds, and we seldom got a shot at the passing flocks when anchored off the shore in small boats. But on their feeding grounds they are more fearless and will decoy well to live or even wooden decoys around a well-concealed blind. Brant can swim well, but do not dive unless hard-pressed. They prefer to skulk and hide by stretching the neck out on the water or in the grass. They are very fond of sand and like to rest on sandy points and sand bars.

Mr. Cordeaux (1898) describes the voice of the brant very well, as follows:

The common cry or call note of the brant is a loud metallic *chronk, chronk.* The confused gabbling and mixed cries of a flock can be heard at an immense distance at sea. They have another, and double, note, which has been likened to the word *torock,* constantly repeated on the wing; and the alarm cry is a single word, *wauk.*

Dr. D. G. Elliott (1898) says:

It has a peculiar guttural note, which is frequently uttered, resembling *car-r-r-rup,* or *r-r-r-rouk,* or *r-r-rup,* and with a rolling intonation, and, when a large number of these birds are gathered together, the noise they make is incessant and deafening. I have been in the vicinity of a bar on which were congregated many thousands of brant, and their voices made such a din that it was difficult to hear one's own in speaking, and when they rose at the report of a gun the sound of their myriad wings was as the roar of rushing waters.

Fall.—Winter comes early in the far North, and the brant are forced to start on their fall migration early in September or even late in August. The route differs only slightly from that taken in the spring. They now migrate down the west coast of Hudson Bay, cross eastern Canada to the Gulf of St. Lawrence, which they reach late in September, cross the neck of Nova Scotia to the Bay of Fundy, and then head straight for Cape Cod, where they usually begin to arrive about the middle of October. So far their flight has been more rapid than in the spring, but from here on their movements are more leisurely and they scatter along the coast, lingering at favorable spots until well into the winter.

Game.—From the standpoint of the epicure the brant is one of our finest game birds, in my opinion *the* finest, not even excepting the far-famed canvasback. I can not think of any more delicious bird than a fat, young brant, roasted just right and served hot, with a bottle of good Burgundy. Both the bird and the bottle are now hard to get; alas, the good old days have passed.

A few brant are shot, as they migrate along the coast, by gunners anchored offshore for coot shooting; the long undulating line of big black birds with white hind quarters is easily distinguished from the irregular flocks of the scoters; a thrill of anticipation runs along the line as word is passed from boat to boat; the brant will not decoy to the wooden blocks of coot shooters, but they may pass over or near one of the boats or swing and fly along the line near enough for a shot; but more often they give the boats a wide berth, and the disappointed gunner fires in vain at the coveted birds, which are probably farther away than they seem to be.

Real brant shooting may be had at only a few favored localities where the birds are wont to congregate, and then only with an elaborate equipment. It was a sorry day for the brant shooter when spring shooting was abolished, for the brant is the one bird above all others for which spring seems to be the natural shooting season. Brant seem to be more plentiful in the spring than in the fall and to linger longer on their favorite feeding grounds at that season. April brant shooting at Monomoy has long been famous in the annals of Massachusetts sportsmen, when formerly splendid sport could be enjoyed. E. H. Forbush (1912) says:

Hapgood gives a record of 44 birds killed from one of these boxes *at one shot*, and states that 1,000 or 1,500 were killed in a season. This was many years ago, before the formation of the brant clubs. No such number has been killed in recent years. The average number killed by the members of the Monomoy Branting Club for 34 years, during the Hapgood régime, is a trifle over 266 birds per year.

Now that we can shoot only in the fall, no such sport is obtainable; there are still plenty of brant, as the spring flights are enormous, but on the Monomoy Flats, where my limited experience has been gained, the brant seem to be comparatively scarce in the fall, and they are so constantly disturbed by the busy fleet of scallop fishermen's power boats that they do not remain to feed.

On Monomoy our brant shooting is done from boxes located on favorable points or sand bars near the feeding grounds. The box is well made and water-tight, 6 feet long, 4 feet wide, and 4 feet deep; big enough for three men; it is sunken into the sand deep enough to be covered at high tide; numerous bags, sometimes 50 or 60, of sand are piled around it to hold it in place; and if it is in a grassy place, which helps to conceal it, the sloping sides of the pile may be thatched with marsh grass woven into the meshes of poultry netting, held in place by stakes and weighted with sand. Unless there is a natural sand bar near the box, one must be made, on which the live decoys are located and where the wild birds may alight. Live decoys are preferable, but brant will come to good wooden decoys if properly placed; a supply of both is desirable. The brant feed at low tide away off on the eelgrass beds; but as the rising tide covers the grass too deeply, they are driven to seek other feeding grounds or sanding places, and in flying about will often come to the decoys. The best shooting then is for a short time only at about half-flood tide and again at about half ebb, while the birds are moving. The morning tides are considered the best, so it is often quite dark when we tramp down through the marsh to our box, heavily laden with decoys, guns, and ammunition and encumbered with rubber boots and oilskins, for it is cold and wet work. We set out the decoys, bale out the box, and sit low on a wet seat, our eyes just above the rim of the box, and scan the flats for distant flocks of brant. Occasional shots at passing birds or small bunches on their way seem like fair sport. But when a large flock swims up to the decoys on the rising tide or flies up and settles on the bar among them, it is exciting enough, but it seems like wanton slaughter to fire a battery of guns at a given signal into a dense mass of birds. Perhaps a dozen or a score of birds are killed or wounded and we jump out of the box and go splashing off through the mud and water to retrieve the cripples. When the rising tide finally drives us out of our box, we may have a large bunch of birds to lug back to the club house, but have we given them a fair show for their lives?

Brant shooting in Great South Bay, Long Island, and in southern waters is usually done from batteries, such as are used for canvas-back-duck shooting. As this means wing shooting most of the time, it seems more sportsmanlike. The battery may be anchored near their feeding ground or near a floating mass of eelgrass, known as a " seaweed bank," to which the brant resort to feed.

Winter.—The winter home of the brant is along the Atlantic coast from New Jersey southward. Probably most of the birds spend the winter on the coast of Virginia and North Carolina. T. Gilbert Pearson (1919) writes:

In Pamlico Sound the long extended lines of submerged sandbars and mud-flats, with their abundant supplies of eelgrass, make an ideal winter resort for the brant. They arrive from the north usually early in November, but the exact date depends much upon weather conditions. In flight they usually go in compact flocks without any apparent leader. They move slowly and often appear loath to leave a favorite feeding ground, even returning to it many times after being disturbed.

On clear winter days, as one sails along the reefs in the region about Ocracoke or Hatteras, flocks of brant, disturbed from their feeding areas, arise in almost constant succession for miles, their numbers running far into the tens of thousands. When heavy winds arise these large rafts are broken up.

and later when the birds are flying singly or in small companies they readily
draw to decoys. It is then that the gunners get in their most telling work,
bags of 75 or 100 birds being sometimes taken in a day. Near Cape Hatteras
I once lay in a battery near a local gunner, who shot 50 brant between the
hours of 10 a. m. and 2 p. m., and the size of his kill in four hours occasioned
no particular comment in the neighborhood.

DISTRIBUTION

Breeding range.—Arctic regions north of eastern North America,
Europe, and Western Asia. East to Spitsbergen, Franz Joseph
Land, Nova Zembla, Kolguev, and the Taimyr Peninsula. On
both coasts of Greenland, south to about 70° N., and north to at
least 81° or 82° N. South to about 74° on islands around the Gulf
of Boothia, Prince Regent Inlet, and Wellington Channel. West
to about 100° or 110° W. Seen in summer and probably breeding
as far north as explorers have been, on the Parry Islands, Axel
Heiberg Land, Grant Land, and Greenland. Probably intergrades
with *nigricans* at both the eastern and the western limits of its
range.

Winter range.—Atlantic coast of United States. Regularly from
New Jersey to North Carolina; more rarely eastward to Long
Island and Massachusetts (Marthas Vineyard); and rarely south
to Florida. Coasts of northwestern Europe, from the Baltic and
North Seas, to the British Isles and France; occasionally to Morocco, the Mediterranean, and Egypt. Occurs more or less regularly on the Pacific coasts of Canada and United States.

Spring migration.—Fully described above. Early dates of arrival: New York, Long Island, February 15; Rhode Island, Block
Island, March 8; Massachusetts, Vineyard Sound, March 10; Maine,
Englishman Bay, April 22; Quebec, Bay of Seven Islands, May 1;
latitude 79° N., May 30; northern Greenland, Etah, June 1; Grinnell Land, latitude 82°, N., June 7; Boothia Peninsula, June 8;
Wellington Channel, June 2.

Late dates of departure: North Carolina, first week in April;
Rhode Island, April 28; Massachusetts, Cape Cod, May 17; Prince
Edward Island, June 12; Quebec, Bay of Seven Islands, June 15.

Fall migration.—Early dates of arrival: Massachusetts, Cape
Cod, September 11; Rhode Island, September 17; New York, Long
Island, September 8; New Jersey, Barnegat Bay, October 14. Main
flight reaches the Gulf of St. Lawrence late in September and New
England in October. Late dates of departure: Maine, December
8; Massachusetts, Cape Cod, December 14; New York, Long Island,
December 20.

Casual records.—Has wandered east on the fall migration to
Labrador (Nain, October, 1899) and Nova Scotia (Sable Island,

November 7, 1908). Stragglers, probably from a Hudson Bay migration route, have been recorded from Ontario (Toronto, December 2, 1895, and November 12, 1899), Manitoba (Shoal Lake and Lake Manitoba), Michigan (Monroe, November 8, 1888), Wisconsin (Hoy's record), and Nebraska (Omaha, November 9, 1895). Occurs often, perhaps regularly, on the Pacific coast: British Columbia (Comox, December 13, 1903), and California (Humboldt County, January 30, 1914). Brooks (1904) says that " about 8 per cent of the brant in Comox Bay are the eastern species." Accidental in the West Indies (Barbados, November 15, 1876), Louisiana, and Texas.

Egg dates.—Greenland: Four records, June 14 to July 13. Ellesmere Land: One record, June 17.

BRANTA BERNICLA NIGRICANS (Lawrence)

BLACK BRANT

HABITS

It seems strange that this bird (which is apparently only a subspecies of the eastern brant), so abundant on the Pacific coast and such a rare straggler on the Atlantic coast, should have been first recognized in New Jersey and described from a specimen taken at Egg Harbor. George N. Lawrence (1846), who described it, says:

When on a shooting excursion some years since, at Egg Harbor, I noticed a bird flying at some distance from us which our gunner said was a black brant. This was the first intimation I had of such a bird. Upon further inquiry of him, he informed me he had them occasionally, but they were not common. I have learned from Mr. Philip Brasher, who has passed much time at that place, that, speaking to the gunners about them, they said they were well known there by the name of black brant, and one of them mentioned that he once saw a flock of five or six together. Since then two others have been obtained at the same place, one of which I have in my possession.

Spring.—Chase Littlejohn, in some notes sent to Major Bendire, says of the migration of black brant across the Alaska Peninsula:

Thousands of these geese pass a mile or two offshore each spring on their way north; they follow the coast line from the eastward until they come to Morzhovia Bay, where they sheer off for the Bering Sea. There bay and sea almost meet, and as they have a great aversion to flying over the land they select a narrow portage from the bay to a long lake, which is separated from the Bering Sea by a very narrow sand bar, not over 100 yards wide, and instead of crossing the bar they fly to the opposite end of the lake, fully 2 miles, and follow the outlet of the lake into Bering Sea and back to where you would suppose they would have crossed in the first place, and then continnue on their way north. In years gone by I think there was a passage through, but by the action of the sea it has been closed. But the geese do not care to forsake their old route and consequently break through their aversion of flying over the land and cross the narrow portage. A few birds go farther on and fly through False Pass and probably passes farther on, but the great majority take the Morzhovia Bay route.

The spring migration of the black brant in northern Alaska and the circumstances surrounding it have been so attractively portrayed by Dr. E. W. Nelson (1881) that I can not refrain from quoting parts of what he says about it, as he observed it at St. Michael, Alaska; he writes:

The long reign of ice and snow begins to yield to the mild influence of the rapidly lengthening days; the middle of May is reached, and the midnight sky over the northern horizon blushes with delicate rose tints, changing to purple toward the zenith. Fleecy clouds passing slowly across the horizon seem to quiver and glow with lovely hues, only to fade to dull leaden again as they glide from the reach of fair Aurora. The land, so lately snow-bound, becomes dotted with pools of water, and the constantly narrowing borders of the snow soon make room for the waterfowl which, with eager accord, begin to arrive in abundance, some upon lagging wings, as if from far away, others making the air resound with joyous notes as they recognize some familiar pond where, for successive seasons, they have reared their young in safety, or, perhaps a favorite feeding ground. At this time the white-fronted and Hutchins geese take precedence in numbers, though, to be sure, they have been preceded for two weeks by the hardy pintail duck, the common swan, and, lastly, that ornithological harlequin, the sandhill crane, whose loud rolling note is heard here and there as it stalks gravely along, dining upon the last year's berries of *Empetrum nigrum*, when, meeting a rival, or perchance one of the fair sex, he proceeds to execute a burlesque minuet.

A few days later, upon the mirror-like bosoms of myriads of tiny lakelets, the graceful northern Phalaropes flit here and there or swim about in pretty companies. At length, about the 20th of May, the first barn swallow arrives, and then we begin to look for the black brant, the "*nimkee*," as it is called by the Russians, the "*luk-lug-u-nuk*" of the Norton Sound Eskimo. Ere long the *avant-courier* is seen in the form of a small flock of 10 or 15 individuals which skim along close to the ice, heading directly across Norton Sound to the vicinity of Cape Nome, whence their route leads along the low coast to Port Clarence where, I am told by the natives, some stop to breed; but the majority press on and seek the ice-bordered northern shore of Alaska and even beyond to unknown regions far to the north.

The 22d of May a native came in bringing a lot of geese and reporting plenty of black brant up the "canal." For the benefit of the unfortunate few who have not been at St. Michael I may explain that the "canal" is a narrow and shallow tidal channel which separates St. Michael Island from the mainland and is bordered on either side by a stretch of low, flat land abundantly dotted with brackish ponds and intersected by numerous small tide creeks. As would be surmised, this forms a favorite haunt for various kinds of waterfowl.

Preparing the tent and other paraphernalia, two of us, accompanied by a couple of natives, started out the next morning with a sled and team of five large dogs, driven tandem, just as the sun gilded the distant hilltops and gave a still deeper tint to the purple haze enveloping their bases. The sharp, frosty air and the pleasurable excitement of the prospective hunt, after months of inactivity, causes an unusual elation of spirits, and with merry jests we speed along until, in a short time, we approach a low, moundlike knoll rising in the midst of innumerable lakelets. A strange humming, for which we were at first unable to account, now becomes more distinct, and we perceive its origin in the united notes of scores of flocks of brant which are dispersed here and there over the half bare ground. Some sit along the edges of the snow banks or upon the ground, still sleeping, while others walk carelessly about or plume themselves in preparation for the work before them. Their low, harsh, gutteral *gr-r-r-r*, *gr-r-r-r* rises in a faint monotonous matinal whose tone a week later may waken the weird silence in unknown lands about the Pole.

Reaching the knoll before mentioned, we pitch our tent, and after tieing the dogs to keep them within bounds we separate to take positions for the morning flight. Each of the party is soon occupying as little space as possible behind some insignificant knoll or tuft of grass that now and then breaks the monotonous level. The sun rises slowly higher and higher until at length the long, narrow bands of fog hovering over the bare ground are routed. Now we have not long to wait, for, as usual at this season, the lakes, which are frozen over nightly, open under the rays of the sun between 7 and 9 in the morning and start the waterfowl upon their way. The notes, which until now have been uttered in a low conversational tone, are raised and heard more distinctly and have a harsher intonation. The chorus swells and dies away like the sound of an aeolian harp of one or two heavy bass strings, and as we lie close to the ground the wind whispers among the dead plants in a low undertone as an accompaniment; but while we lay dreaming the sun has done its work; the lakes have opened, and suddenly a harsh *gr-r-r-r*, *gr-r-r-r*, *gr-r-r-r* causes us to spring up, but too late, for, gliding away to the northward, the first flock goes unscathed. After a few energetic remarks upon geese in general and this flock in particular, we resume our position, but keep on the alert to do honor to the next party.

Soon, skimming along the horizon, flock after flock is seen as they rise and hurry by on either side. Fortune now favors us, and a large flock makes directly for the ambush, their complicated and graceful evolutions leading us to almost forget why we are lying here upon our face in the bog with our teeth rattling a devil's tattoo in the raw wind. On they come, only a few feet above the ground, until, when 20 or 30 yards away, we suddenly rise upon one knee and strike terror into the hearts of the unsuspecting victims. In place of the admirable order before observed, all is confusion and, seemingly in hope of mutual protection, the frightened birds crowd into a mass over the center of the flock, uttering, the while, their ordinary note raised in alarm to a higher key. This is the sportsman's time, and a double discharge as they are nearly overhead will often bring down from 4 to 10 birds. Scarcely have the reports died away when they once more glide along close to the ground; the alarm is forgotten; order is again restored, and the usual note is heard as they swiftly disappear in the distance. Thus they continue flying until 1 or 2 o'clock in the afternoon when, after a pause of three or four hours, they begin again and continue until after sundown.

Nesting.—At Point Barrow, Alaska, according to John Murdoch (1885)—

the black brant appear at the end of the main spring migrations of the waterfowl, but in no very considerable numbers, following the same track as the eiders. A few remain to breed and are to be seen flying about the tundra during June. The nest is placed in rather marshy ground and is a simple depression lined with down, with which the eggs are completely covered when the birds leave the nest. The birds sometimes begin to sit on 4 eggs and sometimes lay as many as 6.

MacFarlane (1891) sent to Washington 650 eggs of this brant from Fort Anderson, obtained by the Eskimos on the Arctic coast of Liverpool Bay, where it was exceedingly abundant, but he adds little to our scanty knowledge of its breeding habits. He wrote to Professor Baird, concerning a visit to an island in Liverpool Bay on July 4, 1864, as follows:

> *Bernicla brenta* breeds on small islands on the small lakes occurring on this island. It scoops a hole in the sand or turf composing the island and lines it with down taken from the body of the female. They frequently nest in small parties, but a pair will sometimes select an island for themselves. Very few specimens were seen, though numerous nests containing broken eggs were met with; these had evidently been destroyed by white foxes, gulls, owls, and crows. But for the depredations committed by them we should have made a superb collection of eggs of *Somateria, Bernicla hutchinsii, Anser gambelli, Columbus articus,* gulls, and terns. A great many nests of each and all of these species were found without eggs, their contents having been destroyed. The entire damage inflicted on the poor birds in one season must be enormous.

Rev. A. R. Hoare sent me a fine nest and 5 eggs of the black brant, taken at Tigara, near Point Hope, Alaska, in June 1916; it consisted of a great mass of down on a small low island in an extensive marsh; judging from the two photographs, which came with it, it must have been quite conspicuous. He found other nests sunken in moss and grass near the lakes out on the tundra. There is a nest and 5 eggs in the collection of Herbert Massey, Esq., taken by W. E. Snyder, at Admiralty Bay, Alaska, on June 16, 1898; the nest which consists of a large quantity of down, was in a depression in the dry tundra. I received 11 sets of black brant's eggs, all consisting of 5 eggs, with the nests, from Point Barrow, Alaska, in 1916. The nests of this species are the most beautiful nests I have ever seen of any of the ducks and geese; they are great, soft, thick beds of pure, fluffy down, unmixed with the tundra rubbish so common in nests of other species; the down is a rich, handsome shade of "benzo brown" or "deep brownish drab," flecked with whitish; it must make a warm and luxurious blanket to cover the eggs.

Eggs.—The black brant lays from 4 to 8 eggs, but 5 seems to be by far the commonest number. The prevailing shapes are elliptical ovate or elliptical oval; some are elongate ovate and a few are nearly ovate, rounded at the small end. The colors are " cartridge buff," " ivory yellow," " pale olive buff," or " cream color." The original color is often much obscured by stains or mottlings of various buffy or brownish shades, such as "cinnamon buff" or "ochraceous buff"; some of the eggs seem to be wholly of these darker shades; in others the stains have apparently worn off or been scratched off, exposing the original color. The shell is smooth and sometimes quite glossy.

The measurements of 107 eggs in the United States National Museum and the author's collections average 71.1 by 47.4 millimeters; the eggs showing the four extremes measure 79 by 47.5, 68 by 51, 66 by 45 and 75.5 by 43.5 millimeters.

Plumages.—The downy young black brant is thickly covered with soft down in dark colors; the upper half of the head, including the lores, to a point a little below the eyes is "fuscous" or "benzo brown"; the chin is white; the back varies from "benzo brown" to "hair brown," darkest on the rump; the flanks and chest shade from "hair brown" to "light drab," fading off nearly to white on the belly and throat.

I have seen no specimens showing the change from the downy to the juvenal plumage. But a bird in the juvenal plumage, taken September 5, has the whole head, neck and breast plainly colored, "fuscous" to "fuscous black," with only faint traces of the white markings on the neck; the feathers of the back are edged with grayish white or buffy white; the juvenal wing has broad, conspicuous, pure white edgings on the lesser and the greater coverts, the secondaries, and the tertials, broadest on the greater coverts; the belly and flanks are plain "fuscous," with no barring.

Molting begins first on the head and neck; the white neck patches are often, but not always, conspicuous in October; they are well developed by spring. Aside from a partial molt of body and tail feathers there is not much change during the winter and spring. Young birds in May and June are still decidedly juvenal, much worn and faded. At the following post-nuptial molt, when a little over a year old, the young bird undergoes a complete molt and becomes practically adult in plumage, with white neck patches, barred flanks, and plain dark wings without any light edgings.

Food.—The black brant, like its eastern relative, is a decidedly maritime bird, living on salt water and feeding on the grassy mud flats; it never comes in to the uplands to feed. It seems to feed almost entirely on the leaves and roots of various marine grasses, mainly *Zostera*. In connection with its vegetable food it picks up various small mollusks, crustaceans, and other forms of marine animals. Mr. W. Leon Dawson (1909) says that they "not only dip but dive as well."

Behavior.—Doctor Nelson (1881) gives such a good account of the flight of the black brant that I quote it in full, as follows:

The flight of this species is peculiar among North American geese and bears a close resemblance to that of the eider and other species of heavy-bodied short-winged sea ducks. It has a parallel in the flight of the emperor goose except that the latter is a far heavier bird and, in consequence, the wing strokes are less rapid. In *B. nigricans* the strokes are short, energetic, and repeated with great rapidity, carrying the bird with a velocity far greater than that attained by any other goose with which I am acquainted, though probably its eastern prototype equals it in this respect.

But this is not the point upon which the mind rests when the birds are in view, for then the eye is held in involuntary admiration of the varied and graceful evolutions of the flocks, which have a protean ability to change their form without ever breaking the array or causing confusion. They are very gregarious, and two flocks almost invariably coalesce when they draw near each other. This frequently occurs until, as I have seen, it results in a single flock numbering between 400 and 500 birds. The usual size is considerably less, generally comprising from 20 to 50 or more, and it is rare to see less than 10 or 15 in a party. At times 4 or 5 individuals become detached, and until they can unite with a stronger party they fly irregularly about as though bewildered, continually uttering their harsh notes, and hurry eagerly away to join the first flock that comes in view. The order of flight is invariably a single rank, the birds moving side by side in a line at right angles to their course so that the entire strength of a flock is to be seen at a glance along its front, which at times covers several hundred yards. There is barely room enough between the individuals to allow a free wing stroke. Thus ranged, the flock seems governed by a single impulse, which sends it gliding along parallel and close to the ground, then, apparently without reason, careering 30 or 40 yards overhead, only to descend to its former level as suddenly as it was left; now it sways to one side and then to the other, while at short intervals swift undulations seem to run from one end of the line to the other. These movements are repeatedly taking place; they are extremely interesting to observe but difficult, I fear, to convey an adequate idea of in words.

The entire flock, consisting of perhaps over a hundred birds arranged in single line, is hurrying on, straight as an arrow, toward its destination, when, without warning, it suddenly makes a wide curving detour of several hundred yards, then resumes its original course only to frequently repeat the maneuver, but always with such unison that the closest scrutiny fails to reveal the least break or irregularity in the line; nor does the front of the flock swerve, excepting an occasional slight obliquity which is corrected in a few seconds.

In addition to this horizontal movement is a still more interesting vertical one which often occurs at the same time as the other but generally by itself. A bird at either end of the flock rises or descends a few inches or several feet, as the case may be, and the movement is instantly followed in succession by every one of its companions till the extreme bird is reached and the entire flock is on the new level; or it may be that a bird near the middle of the line changes its position, when the motion extends in two directions at once. These latter changes are made so regularly and with such rapidity that the distance between the birds does not appear altered in the least, while a motion exactly like a graceful undulation runs the length of the flock, lifting or depressing it to the level of the originator of the movement. These changes present to one's eye as the flocks approach, keeping close to the ground, the appearance of a series of regular and swift waving motions such as pass along a pennant in a slight breeze.

The black brant never wings its way far up in the sky, as many other geese have the habit of doing, but keeps, as a rule, between 10 and 30 yards above the ground, with more flocks below these limits than above them.

Another idiosyncrasy of this bird is its marked distaste for passing over low ranges of hills which may cross its path. A striking case of this is shown here where a low spur runs out from the distant hills in the form of a grass-covered ridge projecting several miles into the flat marshy land. This ridge is from 50 to 200 feet above the surrounding country and bars the course of the black brant. So slight an obstacle as this is enough to cause at least 95 per cent of the flocks to turn abruptly from their path and pass along its base to round the end several miles beyond, and then continue their passage. In consequence of this habit it has been a regular practice for years for the hunters to occupy positions along the front of this ridge and deal destruction to the brant, which still hold as pertinaciously as ever to their right of way.

Doctor Nelson (1887) says:

While upon the ground or in flight they have a low guttural note something like the syllables *gr-r-r-r-r*, When alarmed this note, repeated often and with more emphasis, was the only cry heard.

W. Leon Dawson (1909) writes:

From the esthetic standpoint the most interesting phase of brant life is the mellow *cronk, cronk, cronk,* which the birds frequently emit whether in flight or at rest. From the back bay near Dungeness in April rises a babel like the spring offering of a giant frog-pond, a chorus of thousands of croaking voices, among which the thrilling basso of bullfrogs predominates.

Mr. Hoare writes me that, at Point Hope, the brant "suffer very much from the depredations of the gulls and hawks." He "found many eggs scattered and broken." He says:

This summer I witnessed a battle between a male brant and three gulls. The female brant was on the nest and did not move. The gulls kept returning to the attack and were very fierce. Usually they are cowardly. Eventually the brant drove them away, although badly mauled. I could not find it in my heart to disturb the female on the nest.

Fall.—According to Mr. Murdoch (1885) the fall migration at Point Barrow begins early; he writes:

After the middle of August they begin to fly across the isthmus at Pergniak, coming west along the shore of Elson Bay, crossing to the ocean, and turning southwest along the coast. Whenever during August the wind is favorable for a flight of eiders at Pergniak the brant appear also. They, however, frequently turn before reaching the beach at Pergniak, follow down the line of lagoons and cross to the sea lower down the coast. The adults return first. No young of the year were taken till the end of August. During the first half of September, a good many flocks cross the land at the inlets as well as at Pergniak, and are to be seen resting and feeding along the lagoons and pond holes. At this season they are very shy and hard to approach, and all are gone by the end of September.

Doctor Nelson (1887) says:

Some old whaling captains assured me that they have frequently seen these birds coming from over the ice to the north of Point Barrow in fall; and to the hardy navigators of these seas this is strong evidence in support of the theory that bodies of land lie beyond the impenetrable icy barrier which heads off their advance in that direction. Perhaps it was the droppings of this bird which we found on the dreary shores of Wrangel Island, when our party from the *Corwin* were the first human beings to break in upon its icy solitude. Mr. Dall writes that on his return to the coast of California in the latter part of October enormous flocks of these birds were seen about 100 miles offshore. They were flying south and frequently settled in the water near the ship.

Along much of the route followed by the brant in the spring in such enormous numbers, they are comparatively scarce in the fall, indicating that a different route is followed. In the spring, when open water shows first near the land, they would naturally follow the coast line; but in the fall, when Bering Sea is all open, they evidently prefer to migrate far from land, stopping to rest and perhaps to feed on the open sea.

Game.—Grinnell, Bryant, and Storer (1918) say of the game qualities of this bird:

The black brant evades the devices of the hunter better than any other duck or goose. In very early days on San Diego Bay it was never seen to alight on the shore or near it. By 1875 it was almost impossible to obtain a shot at the bird from a boat, and even with a box sunk in the mud and concealed by seaweed a good bag was secured with difficulty. In 1883 a floating battery with plenty of decoys alone would enable a hunter to obtain this much-prized bird. A few years later many of the birds failed to put in an appearance at all off San Diego, probably going farther south, along the Mexican coast. Because of its habit of occasionally cutting across low sand spits to avoid a long detour in its flight, most of the hunting has been done from blinds situated beneath such a line of flight. On Tomales Bay hunters have sailed down on flocks with " blind boats," when the birds were at rest during a fog, their whereabouts being disclosed by their " gabbling " noises.

The black sea brant has not been sold on the markets to any extent for a good many years. About 20 years ago consignments were shipped to San Francisco from Humboldt Bay, and the birds sold for as little as 25 cents each. Even the high price that the bird would bring at the present time does not attract it to the market because of the difficulty now attached to obtaining it.

Winter.—The black brant winters abundantly on the Pacific coast from the Puget Sound region southward, living entirely on salt water, in the larger bays and channels. Mr. Dawson (1909) writes:

Black brants are the only geese one is quite sure of seeing from the deck of a steamboat on an average winter day on Puget Sound. While they have their favorite feeding grounds upon the mud flats and in shallow bays, they are widely distributed over the open water also, and their numbers during the spring migrations are such that not all other wild geese put together are to be mentioned in comparison. They sit the water in small companies; and although they are exceedingly wary in regard to rowboats, they often permit an approach on the part of steamers which is very gratifying to the student. An exaggerated use of their long wings as the birds get under way gives the beholder the impression of great weight—an impression which is not sustained in the hand, where the bird is seen to disappointingly light; all feathers, in fact, as compared with a chunky scoter, which does not equal it in extent of wing by a foot or more.

Mr. S. F. Rathbun has sent me the following notes in regard to the black brant, as seen on the coast of Washington:

Some time during November the arrival of the black brant may be expected in the Strait of Juan de Fuca and the lower Sound. During the winter months however, it will be found in all the waters of Puget Sound, but not so commonly as in the first mentioned localities, for it appears to prefer the open waters, in such at times assembling in large flocks. And this statement may be qualified to an extent, for there are certain spots to which the bird seems partial.

In and near the eastern end of the strait lies Smiths Island, this being an abrupt bit of land not many acres in extent. Running eastward from the island is a long ledge or spit almost a mile in length, an extension as it were, parts of which are exposed only at the times of low tides, and to the north is a wide expanse of water having numerous kelpbeds. This locality is a much favored one by the black brant, and here almost any time during the winter and early spring months it may be seen in large numbers. Another place where it may invariably be found is in the general vicinity of Dungeness on the strait, and here also kelpbeds exist, for this bird appears to favor the spots where this marine growth is to be found. These localities are favorite ones in which to hunt this bird, but even so this hunting involves at times considerable work and exposure, to say nothing of the time required. One never knows what character of weather will be experienced, for sometimes a number of days will elapse before one arrives on which sport can be had. As a rule the black brant is an easy bird to decoy, and when hunting it one needs but little concealment. Often the blind used is simply some log or uprooted tree that has drifted ashore, over which will be draped in a careless way seaweed or kelp, or both, the flotsam of the beach. On the windward side the decoys are placed in the water, to be changed from time to time according to the run of tide. If the brant are flying, ordinarily but little time will elapse before some passing flock sights the decoys and almost invariably comes to them. And frequently such birds that escape the fire will—as if governed by mere fatuousness—return to be shot at again, sometimes the result being that the entire flock is killed.

This species appears to be restricted to the salt water, and its food being in the nature of marine vegetation and the smaller forms of marine life, gives somewhat of a clue to the reason why it exhibits the partiality shown for the vicinity of the beds of kelp.

DISTRIBUTION

Breeding range.—Arctic coasts of western North America and eastern Asia. East on Arctic islands to about 110° or 100° W. (Melville Island, Banks Land, etc.) and on the mainland to Coronation Gulf. Westward along the coasts of Canada, Alaska, and Siberia to the Taimyr Peninsula and New Siberia Islands. North to Banks Land (Cape Kellett, etc.) and Melville Island (Winter Harbor). Probably intergrades with *bernicla* at the eastern and the western limits of its range.

Winter range.—Mainly on the Pacific coast of the United States. North to British Columbia (Comox, Vancouver Island). South to

Lower California (San Quintin Bay and Cerros Island). Inland in Oregon (Malheur and Klamath Lakes) and in Nevada (Pyramid and Washoe Lakes). On the Asiatic coast south to northern China (Tsingtau) and Japan.

Spring migration.—Main flight is northward along the coast, but some fly overland across Alaska to the Mackenzie Valley. Early dates of arrival in Alaska: St. Michael, May 5; Point Hope, May 15; Wainwright, May 24; Demarcation Point, May 20; Point Barrow, June 5. Late dates of departure: Lower California, Cerros Island, May 10; California, San Francisco, April 24; Alaska, Yukon delta, May 22.

Fall migration.—A reversal of the spring routes. Migrants pass through Bering Sea during the last half of September and first half of October and reach California in October and November. Latest date for Point Barrow is September 21, and Kolyma River, Siberia, October 5.

Casual records.—Has wandered east to New York (3 records), Massachusetts (Chatham, spring of 1883 and April 15, 1902), and New Jersey (Great Egg Harbor, January, 1846, and Long Beach, April 5, 1877); and from the Pacific coast as far inland as Utah (Bear River). Accidental on the Hawaiian Islands (Maui).

Egg dates.—Arctic Canada: Fifteen records, June 8 to July 7; nine records, June 20 to July 6. Alaska: Eleven records, June 15 to July 4; six records, June 22 to 26.

BRANTA LEUCOPSIS (Bechstein)

BARNACLE GOOSE

HABITS

This Old World species, which probably resorts regularly to Greenland for the purpose of breeding, has been taken a number of times at various places in eastern North America and is therefore well worthy of a place on our list, as a straggling migrant, mainly in the fall.

Spring.—It is a very common bird on the west coast of Scotland, whence it takes its departure about the end of April or beginning of May. John Cordeaux (1898) quotes Robert Gray, concerning its departure as follows:

Previous to leaving, the barnacle geese assemble in immense flocks on the open sands, at low tide, in the sounds of Benbecula and South Uist; and as soon as one detachment is on the wing it is seen to be guided by a leader, who points the way with a strong flight northwards, maintaining a noisy bearing until he gets the flock into the right course. After an hour's interval, he is seen returning, with noisy gabble, alone, southwards to the main body, and taking off another detachment as before, until the whole are gone.

Nesting.—The breeding grounds of the barnacle goose have only recently been found; the following quotation from A. L. V. Manniche (1910) seems to indicate that the species breeds abundantly in northeastern Greenland. He writes:

June 8 and 9, 1908, I got my first opportunity to study the barnacles in their real nesting territory. Up to this time the geese had led a comfortable and by me unsuspected existence in a lonely marsh and moor territory far up country— 10 to 15 kilometers from the nearest salt water—east of Saelsoen, imposing by its extent and grandness of scenery. This territory, the farthest extent of which is in a northerly direction, comprises an area of some 20 square kilometers; on the north it is bordered by a mountain range, the lower slopes of which are covered by a vegetation more luxuriant than I saw in any other place in northeast Greenland.

To the east and north the marshes lose themselves in barren stony plains sprinkled with sandy spots and a few deep lying fresh-water basins bare of all vegetation. To the south the steep and barren mountain of Trekroner rises to a height of 360 meters in small terraced projections.

In the marsh and moor itself the vegetation was extremely luxuriant; as well the alpine willow as other plants reached here a relatively gigantic size. All over the snow had melted, though it was early in the season, and the place offered an increased allurement to the swimmers and waders by the countless ponds of melting snow. The influence of the powerful sunlight on the dark turfy soil surely accounts for the unusually early melting of the snow in this place.

At my arrival the barnacles were standing in couples or in small flocks in the ponds or they were grazing near these; some were high up the mountain slopes. Almost all the geese used to leave the marsh every day at certain times and disappeared southwards toward the high middle part of Trekroner. I set out in this direction, thinking that a larger lake was lying near the mountain, and that the geese retired to this after their meal. I really found a pair of larger fresh-water basins and saw in these a few geese, which being frightened flew farther toward the mountains. Having come within a distance of one kilometer from Trekroner I solved the riddle. The barnacles were swarming to and fro along the gigantic mountain wall like bees at their hive, and I heard a continuous humming, sounding like a distant talk. I took a seat at the foot of the mountain and observed the behavior of the geese for some hours. Using my field glass I could without difficulty notice even the smallest details.

While some of the geese would constantly fly along the rocky wall and sometimes mounted so high in the air that they disappeared on the other side of the rocks, the majority of the birds were sitting in couples upon the shelves of the rocky wall, some of which seemed too narrow to give room for the two birds—much less for a nest. It was only on the steep and absolutely naked middle part of the mountain wall that the geese had their quarters and in no place lower than some 200 meters from the base of the cliff. As the wall was quite inaccessible, I had to content myself by firing some rifle balls against it in order to frighten the birds and thus form an idea of the size of the colony. The birds which were "at home" then numbered some 150 individuals. As far as I could judge, breeding had not yet commenced.

I feel sure that some of the geese resorted to the mountain without intending to breed. A pair of females, which I later on secured in the marsh, had but undeveloped eggs in their ovaries. In the mountain the geese were not very shy and paid no attention to my shots; the great height at which the birds always stayed made them confident. In the marsh, however, they were very wary and almost always had sentinels posted while they were seeking food.

The Oxford expeditions to Spitsbergen in 1921 and 1922 succeeded in locating a number of nests of this species and collecting a series of eggs. The Rev. F. C. R. Jourdain has kindly sent me the following interesting notes on the subject:

The barnacle goose in Spitsbergen seems to have its main breeding haunts in the valleys opening into Ice Fjord. We saw nothing of it on the north coast or at Liefde Bay, but met with it at Advent Bay, Sassen Bay, Klaas Bitten Bay, and Dicksons Bay during the breeding season, and have good reason to believe that it breeds in all three localities. Probably in order to escape the attentions of the Arctic foxes this species has acquired the habit of nesting on ledges and hollows in precipitous bluffs, and even on the tops of isolated pinnacles of rock. In many of the valleys in Spitzbergen one finds a continuous succession of steep outcrops of rock running along the side of the valley, and in some cases more than one tier running parallel with one another and separated by a steeply sloping range of hillside or talus. It is on these projecting masses of rock that the barnacle nests, and as the goose sits closely and is not readily disturbed from below, a nest halfway up the hillside on a projecting rock may escape notice altogether on the part of those traversing the bottom of the valley. The gander stands close by his mate on watch, and his white face may be detected with a good glass from a considerable distance. Even when approached from above both male and female are slow to leave the nest when the eggs are much incubated, and the gander in some cases will look up inquiringly at the intruder from 20 or 30 yards below before taking wing, while the goose will allow of even closer approach. In one case where a goose was shot from the nest, the report failed to flush another bird, which was also sitting on eggs, not more than 20 yards farther on. Evidently the same breeding places are resorted to year after year, as it is often possible to detect the sites of several old nests in the immediate neighborhood of that in use. The sites varied to some extent, some nests were on gently sloping declivities, sparsely covered with lichens and mosses, at the foot of a low cliff or on ledges on its face, and with a drop of 10 to 20 or 30 feet below; others were on projecting spurs of rocks reached by a narrow "knife-edge" from the main face of the cliff; one was in a small cave overhung from above and with a sheer drop below; and a bird was observed sitting on the flat top of a mushroom-shaped pinnacle of rock, at the very top of a high cliff. In practically every case where the female was incubating eggs, the male was standing close beside her, and the ground near the nest was covered with the accumulation of droppings from the parent birds, which evidently spend most of the incubation period here.

In 1922 we renewed our acquaintance with this species, but found to our disappointment that none of the sites occupied in 1921 were tenanted. This was probably due to shooting and egg collecting by the residents prior to our arrival; but anyhow the birds had disappeared and the high winds had removed all traces of the nests. A range of hills some 1,500 to 1,700 feet high, with bold cliffs and conspicuous stony ridges running down from the top, seemed likely to produce the desired result, so we proceeded to make our way up a steep gulley till at last we reached the top of the ridge. Working our way along the top we could look down on the steep slopes below and could see two or three pairs of barnacle geese, some 300 or 400 feet from the top, the geese quietly incubating while the ganders stood close at hand. The usual nesting place was a sort of saddle on a stony ridge where a space of a few feet of mossy ground was comparatively flat. We had brought with us ropes and with their help were enabled to reach a point about 150 feet above the sitting bird. By careful stalking, with camera and rope in hand, the leading climber descended the ridge till only 20 paces from the sitting bird. The gander had already taken wing, but, as the goose still sat steadily, he tried another stealthy approach and was within 15 paces before the goose, which had previously shown signs of restlessness, rose from the nest and joined her mate. Within the down-clad nest hollow was a clutch of 5 eggs, and below was a range of cliffs, steep screes and bluffs, reaching for quite 1,200 feet by aneriod to the innumerable streams at the foot of the valley. The other three nests we examined in 1922 were all in very similar positions.

Eggs.—According to Mr. Jourdain (1922), who has published an interesting paper on the nesting habits of this species and sent me some extensive notes on the subject, the barnacle goose lays from 3 to 6 eggs, usually 4 or 5. He describes the eggs and the down as follows:

When fresh laid they are pure white, and bear a great resemblance to eggs of the pink-footed goose, but are somewhat smaller. They are, however, larger than those of the brant on the average, besides being considerably heavier. The amount of down in the various nests varied considerably; probably in some cases a certain amount remained in the nest hollow from the previous year. We found no black feathers in the nest; all were either white or had only a faint grayish tinge.

The measurements of 49 eggs, furnished by Mr. Jourdain, average 76.35 by 50.32 millimeters; the eggs showing the four extremes measure 82.7 by 46.4, 78.4 by 53.6, 68.7 by 49.5, and 82.7 by 46.4 millimeters.

Young.—Referring in his notes to the young he says:

Piecing together the information we obtained, it is clear that the goslings remain in the nest only long enough for their down to become thoroughly dry. They must then scramble or fall down the cliffs, probably being to some extent helped by the strong updraft of wind sweeping up the side of the valley, and then make their way down the screes till they reach the flat ground at the foot of the valley, when they take to the water and are carried down to the marshes at the head of the bay. As there is no vegetation except a few lichens and mosses near the nest, it is obvious that the young can not feed till they reach the foot of the valley, and from what we saw of the pink-footed goose in somewhat similar circumstances the goslings are quite capable of surviving a perpendicular drop of considerable height without injury. There seems however, to be no evidence that the parents give them any assistance, though it would seem improbable for a newly hatched bird to descend a perpendicular cliff nearly 100 feet in height.

Food.—Mr. Cordeaux (1898) says:

The food of the barnacle goose is both vegetable and animal; it is remarkably fond of the short sweet grasses which cover the holms and islets off the western coasts of Scotland, at low water also resorting to saltings, fitties, mud flats, and foreshores, left uncovered by the sea, and is as much a land feeder as its congener, the brent, is a sea goose. Mr. C. M. Adamson, of North Jesmond, had some tame barnacles which in the spring would eat worms, as exceptional diet.

The stomachs and crops of birds taken in Greenland by Mr. Manniche (1910) were "filled with twigs, leaves, and catkins of alpine willow, with seeds of different plants and also grasses."

Behavior.—Mr. Cordeaux (1898) quotes Macpherson and Duckworth, as follows:

It is interesting to wait upon the point of Burgh marsh, before daybreak, and listen to the cries of the barnacles, feeding upon the point of Rockcliffe marsh, just opposite. About an hour after daybreak they rise *en masse* from their feeding ground, and after wheeling up and down the Solway for a few moments, displaying their pretty barred gray, black, and white plumage against the mud flats, they fly seawards to the estuary of the Wampool, or, circling round, pitch in a long line upon the exposed mud half a mile to windward. Barnacle geese are constantly vociferous, especially when feeding, and Mr. A. Smith compares the volume of sound produced by a flock of several hundred feeding at night together, as heard at a distance, to a pack of harriers in full cry.

Witherby's Handbook (1921) says:

Favorite feeding localities are wide stretches of "machar" land of firm springy turf inside sandhills. A common trait in all geese, but more noticeably so in this species, is a continual series of friendly quarrels amongst a feeding flock. Less inclined to associate with other geese than any other species, and never nearly so unapproachable, it is the "fool" amongst geese, and only one which on occasion will fail to take alarm after having seen and distrusted a moving object within 100 yards. Occasionally goes to sea to rest on very calm days, but as a rule as much land loving as any "gray" goose. Note a series of rapidly repeated short barks—some higher than others. Combined chorus produced by big flock of any geese has been likened to "music" of pack of hounds running. Taking that comparison, barnacle's cry is represented by one end of scale, gray lag's by other; gray lag's is full-mouthed music of pack of foxhounds, barnacle's that of host of small terriers. Almost if not quite insensitive to scent of man, and rarely if ever takes alarm from it.

DISTRIBUTION

Breeding range.—Known to breed only in northeastern Greenland (Scoresby Land, Trekones) and on Spitsbergen. Said to breed also on Nova Zembla, the Lofoten Islands, and in northwestern Siberia.

Winter range.—Northwestern Europe. South regularly to the Baltic and North Seas and the British Isles, occasionally inland to Switzerland and Austria and exceptionally south to the Azores, Spain, Morocco, and Italy. Occurs on migrations in western Greenland and Iceland.

Casual records.—There are about 9 North American records: Labrador (Okak), James Bay (Rupert House), Massachusetts (Chatham, November 1, 1895), Long Island (Jamaica Bay, October 20, 1876, Great-South Bay, October 16, 1919, and Farmingdale, November 28, 1922), North Carolina (Currituck Sound, October 31, 1870, and November 22, 1892), and Vermont (Marshfield, 1878).

Egg dates.—Spitsbergen: Nine records, June 25 to 28.

PHILACTE CANAGICA (Sevastianoff)

EMPEROR GOOSE

HABITS

The handsomest and the least known of American geese is confined to such narrow limits, both in its breeding range and on its migrations, that it has been seen by fewer naturalists than any other goose on our list. On the almost inaccessible, low, marshy shores of Alaska, between the mouths of the Yukon and Kuskokwim Rivers, it formerly bred abundantly; but recent explorations in that region indicate that it has been materially reduced in numbers during the past 30 years. My assistant, Mr. Hersey, who spent the season of 1914 at the Yukon delta, saw less than a dozen birds, where Doctor Nelson found it so abundant in 1879. The decrease is partially, if not wholly, due to the fact that large numbers are killed every year and their eggs taken by the natives, even within the limits of what is supposed to be a reservation.

Spring.—For what we know about the life history of the emperor goose we are almost wholly indebted to that pioneer naturalist, Dr. Edward W. Nelson, who fortunately has given us a very good account of the habits of this species. I shall quote freely from his writings, mainly from his educational leaflet on this species, in which he (1913) writes:

At the border of the Yukon delta, Esquimos familiar with the country were employed to lead us to the desired nesting ground of the emperor goose. Nearly half a day's journey among the maze of ice-covered channels of the delta brought us to a low, flat island, where our guide assured me many *nachau-thluk* would soon arrive to rear their young. It was a bare, desolate spot, with only a few scattered alders on the upper side of the islands, and an unbroken view out over the frozen sea to the west. A tent was put up on a slight rise and, after a stock of driftwood had been gathered, the guides took the sledge and left me with my Esquimo companion to await the arrival of the birds. Later, when the ice went out, they returned for me with kyaks.

A few white-fronted and cackling geese gave noisy evidence of their presence, but it was not until May 22 that the Esquimo brought in the first emperor goose—a male in beautiful spring plumage. After this, small flocks came in rapidly until they were plentiful all about us. They arrived quietly, skimming along near the ground, quite unlike the other geese, which appeared high overhead with wild outbursts of clanging cries, which were answered by those already on the ground. The river channels and the sea were still covered with ice, and the tundra half covered with snow, at the time of the first arrivals.

Courtship.—Almost at once after their arrival on the islands, the emperor geese appeared to be mated, the males walking around the females, swinging their heads and uttering low love notes, and incoming flocks quickly disintegrated into pairs which moved about together, though often congregating with many others on flats and sand bars. The male was extremely jealous and pugnacious, however, and immediately resented the slightest approach of another toward his choice; and this spirit was shown equally when an individual of another species chanced to come near. When a pair was feeding, the male moved restlessly about, constantly on the alert, and at the first alarm the pair drew near one another, and just before taking wing uttered a deep, ringing *u-lugh, u-lugh;* these, like the flight notes, having a peculiar deep tone impossible to describe.

At low tide, as soon as the shore ice disappeared, the broad mud flats along shore were thronged with them in pairs and groups numbering up to 30 or 40 individuals. They were industriously dabbling in the mud for food until satisfied, and then congregated on bars, where they sat dozing in the sun or lazily arranging their feathers. By lying flat on the ground and creeping cautiously forward, I repeatedly approached within 30 or 40 yards of parties near shore without their showing any uneasiness.

Nesting.—The first of June they began depositing eggs in the flat marshy islands bordering the sea all along the middle and southern part of the delta. The nests were most numerous in the marshes, a short distance back from the muddy feeding grounds, but stray pairs were found nesting here and there farther inland on the same tundra with the other species of geese and numerous other waterfowl. Near the seashore, the eggs were frequently laid among the bleached and wave-torn scraps of driftwood lying along the highest tide marks. On June 5, a female was found on her eggs on a slight rise in the general level. A small gray-bleached fragment of driftwood lay close by. The goose must have lain with neck outstretched on the ground, as I afterward found was their custom when approached, for the Esquimo and I passed within a few feet on each side of her; but, in scanning the ground for nesting birds, the general similarity in tint of the bird and the obvious stick of driftwood had complete misled our sweeping glances. We had gone some 20 steps beyond when the sitting bird uttered a loud alarm note and flew swiftly away. The ground was so absolutely bare of any cover that the 3 eggs on which she had been sitting were plainly visible from where we stood. They were lying in a slight depression without a trace of lining. The same ruse misled us a number of times; but on each occasion the parent betrayed her presence by a startled outcry and hasty departure soon after we had passed her and our backs were presented. They usually flew to a considerable distance, and showed little anxiety over our visit to the nests. The nests I examined usually contained from 3 to 5 eggs, but the full complement ranged up to 8. When first laid, the eggs are pure white, but soon become soiled. They vary in shape from elongated oval to slightly pyriform, and are indistinguishable in size and shape from those of the white-fronted goose. As the complement approaches completion, the parent lines the depression in the ground with a soft, warm bed of fine grass, leaves, and feathers from her own breast. The males were rarely seen near the nest, but usually gathered about the feeding grounds with others of their kind, where they were joined now and then by their mates.

Eggs.—The emperor goose lays from 3 to 8 eggs; probably 5 or 6 is the usual number. The eggs that I have seen are elliptical ovate in shape, with variations toward ovate and toward elongate ovate. The shell is smooth or very finely granulated and not at all glossy. The color is creamy white or dull white at first, becoming nest stained or variegated or finely speckled with buff. The measurements of 96 eggs, in various collections, average 78.6 by 52.1 millimeters; the eggs showing the four extremes measure **86** by 49, 80.2 by **56.2, 70.3** by 50.3, and 75.8 by **48.3** millimeters.

Young.—The period of incubation is 24 days, according to F. E. Blaauw (1916), who has succeeded in raising this species in captivity. Doctor Nelson (1913) says of the young:

The young are hatched the last of June or early July, and are led about the tundras by both parents until, the last of July and the first of August, the old birds molt their quill feathers and with the still unfledged young become extremely helpless. At this time, myriads of other geese are in the same condition, and the Esquimos made a practice of setting up long lines of strong fishnets on the tundras to form pound traps, or inclosures with wide wings leading to them, into which thousands were driven and killed for food. The slaughter in this way was very great, for the young were killed at the same time and thrown away in order to get them out of the way of the next drive. The Esquimos of this region also gather large numbers of eggs of the breeding waterfowl for food and, with the demand for them at the mining camps of the north, a serious menace to the existence of these and other waterfowl might ensue.

Plumages.—Mr. Blaauw (1916) says: " The chick in down is of a beautiful pearl-gray, darkest on the head and upper side and lighter below. The legs and bill are black." A larger downy young, about the size of a teal, in the United States National Museum, has probably faded some; the upper parts vary in color from " bister " to " buffy brown " and the under parts from " smoke gray " to " olive buff."

Mr. Blaauw (1916) says:

The chicks grew very fast, and in a few weeks were completely feathered. In the first feather dress the bird resembles the adults, but the gray is not so bluish. The black markings on the feathers are only indicated, and the coverts on the upper side are not so square, but more pointed. The black throat is wanting, and so is the white head and neck, these parts being gray like the rest of the body. The tail is white.

The bill is dusky bluish, flesh color at the base and black at the tip. The legs are yellowish black. As soon as the birds are full grown they begin to molt, shedding all the feathers except the large flight feathers. The tail feathers are also molted.

At the end of October the young birds are quite grown, and similar to the old birds. By this time the upper mandible has got the beautiful blue and flesh colors of the old birds, whilst the lower mandible has become black. The legs are now orange. When the bird is molting, the first white feathers of the head to appear are near the base of the bill.

The above gray-headed plumage must be the juvenal plumage, which I have never seen, and which is probably not worn for more than a few weeks. Evidently the change into the first winter plumage must be very rapid. All the young birds which I have seen, collected between September 9 and November 17 of their first year, are in the first winter plumage. In this the head and neck are largely white above and black below, much as in the adult, but the black area is browner and the white area is much obscured by dusky mottling, especially on the forehead, lores, and neck; the juvenal wing is similar in color pattern to the adult, but it has narrower, buffy white edgings instead of broad white edgings and dull, brownish-dusky, subterminal markings instead of pure clear black; the feathers of the back are similarly marked with dull patterns and narrow buffy edgings, which soon wear away; the under parts are dull and mottled; and the tail is largely white, as in the adult. This plumage is worn for a very variable length of time by different individuals. I have seen birds taken in November in which the adult plumage was well advanced on the back and scapulars; and I have seen others which were just begininng the molt in June. Perhaps both of these were exceptional; and probably a more or less continual molt of the body plumage takes place all through the winter and spring. I have a fine young male in my collection, taken June 30, which is just completing this molt and is practically adult. The wings are molted during the coming summer, July and August, after which young birds, during their second fall, become indistinguishable from adults.

Food.—Lucien M. Turner (1886) says that "the emperor goose visits the vicinity of Stewart and St. Michael Islands in great numbers to feed on the shellfish exposed by the low water." Grinnell, Bryant, and Storer (1918) say that "at times it resorts to heath berries, which are available on the tundras closely adjacent to the seashore." Other writers speak of it as feeding on mussels and other shellfish and, as it is known to feed on the beaches and mud flats, rather than on the grassy marshes or uplands, its food is probably mainly animal. Its flesh is said to be rank and strongly flavored, which is generally not the case with vegetable feeders.

Behavior.—Doctor Nelson (1913) says, of the flight and notes of this species:

When on the wing, they were easily distinguished from the other geese, even at considerable distances, by their proportionately shorter necks and heavier bodies, as well as by their short, rapid wing strokes, resembling those of the black brant. Like the latter, they usually flew near the ground, rarely more than 30 yards high, and commonly so close to the ground that their wing tips almost touched the surface on the down stroke. While flying from place to place, they give at short intervals a harsh, strident call of two syllables, like *kla-ha, kla-ha, kla-ha,* entirely different from the note of any other goose I have ever heard. A group of them on a sand bar or mud flat often utter lower, more cackling notes in a conversational tone, which may be raised to welcome new arrivals. They are much less noisy than either the white-fronted or cackling geese, which often make the tundra resound with their excited cries. Occasionally I could cause a passing flock to leave its course and swing in close to my place of concealment by imitating their flight notes.

Again (1887) he writes:

While a pair is feeding, the male keeps moving restlessly about, with eyes constantly on the alert, and at the first alarm they draw near together and just before they take wing both utter a deep, ringing *u-lugh, u-lugh*. As in the case of the call note, this has a peculiar, deep hoarseness, impossible to describe.

Game.—Mr. Turner (1886) says that these geese—

Form an important article of food in the Yukon district, alike to the white and native population. They are mostly obtained by means of the gun. The best localities near St. Michael are toward the western end of the canal, along the edge of the low grounds bordering the hills of the mainland, and near the village of Stephansky (Athwik, native name), on the western side of St. Michael Island. This area is low, intersected with innumerable swamps and connecting streams, forming a fine feeding ground for all kinds of water-fowl.

A regular camping outfit is taken by sledge and dogs to a chosen locality. In the early morning a site is selected where the geese fly around some ending of a hill range, for they fly low and prefer to sweep around the hills rather than mount over them. They are frequently so low in their flight that the hunter has to wait until the geese are well past before he can shoot them to an advantage. A nearly constant stream of geese fly around a certain point, just to the left of the Crooked Canal, on a slight eminence, formed from the deposit of soil torn up by some immense ice cake, which the high tides of some December in years long gone by had left as the water receded and the warm weather of spring had melted; now overgrown with patches of rank vegetation.

By 10 o'clock the geese were done flying for that morning. The low character of the ground did not favor approach to the geese feeding at the ponds. During the middle of the day a quiet sleep invigorated the hunter for the late evening shooting, the latter generally affording a less number of geese than the morning's shooting.

By the next morning a sufficient number of geese were obtained to heavily load a sledge; drawn by six lusty Eskimo dogs, assisted by two sturdy natives. This sport generally lasts from the arrival of the geese until the first week of June. At this time they repair to the breeding grounds. During the summer the geese are not hunted. The eggs are eagerly sought by the natives and whites and take the place of meat of the birds. In the latter part of August or the early part of September the fall shooting begins, as the geese have molted, the young are able to fly, and they are fattening on the ripening berries. The geese are now obtained by watching the ponds, or as they fly over in small flocks or singly. Should a flock not fly sufficiently near, a favorite method to attract their attention is for the hunter to lie on his back, swing his arms and hat, kick up his legs, and imitate the call of the geese. It rarely fails to bring them within distance, and may, if several be just shot from their ranks, be repeated, and even a third time. Later in the season, when cool and frosty nights are regular, great numbers of the geese are killed and disemboweled for freezing to keep throughout the winter. The feathers are left on the birds, for the flesh is said to keep in better condition. The body is washed out and the bird hung up by the neck in the icehouse to keep, even until the geese have arrived the next spring. The flesh, when thawed out slowly, has lost all the rank taste, and, in my opinion, is much improved by the freezing process.

I have eaten the flesh of all the various kinds of geese, frequenting those northern regions, and place them in value of flesh as follows: white-fronted goose, *A. albifrons gambelli;* white-cheeked goose, *B. canadensis hutchinsii* and *B. canadensis minima;* Canada goose, *B. canadensis;* black brant, *B. nigricans,* is always tough and lean, fit food only for a Russian; snow goose, *Chen hyperboreus,* is scarcely fit for food, except in cases of necessity. Its flesh is coarse, rank, and has a decidedly unpleasant odor; the emperor goose, *P. canagica,* is scarcely to be thought of as food. There is a disgusting odor about this bird that can only be removed in a degree, and then only by taking off the skin and freezing the body for a time. Even this does not rid the flesh entirely of strong taste.

Winter.—According to Grinnell, Bryant, and Storer (1918) :

The principal winter home of the emperor goose is on the seacoast of southwestern Alaska, and only stragglers reach California. But it is probable that if all the emperor geese ever observed in California had been recorded, it would be found that almost every year one or two of the birds had made their way within our borders. At least 10 definite instances of the occurrence of the emperor goose in this state are known. In spite of the fact that this is a marine species, most of the records are from the interior valleys. Mr. Vernon Shepherd, a taxidermist of San Francisco, informs us that he has known of the capture of at least a dozen specimens of this goose since 1906.

The emperor goose flies in pairs or in small flocks of 4 or 5. A juvenile killed at Gridley, Butte County, was alone, being the second in a flock of white-fronted geese. One taken near Modesto, Stanislaus County, came to the blind alone. Another taken near Davis, Yolo County, had been noted alone in the same pond for three weeks previous to capture. This species is said to be shyer than any other goose except the black sea brant.

DISTRIBUTION

Breeding range.—On the northwest coast of Alaska, from the mouth of the Kuskokwim River northward to the north side of the Seward Peninsula (Cape Prince of Wales, Cape Espenberg, and Deering). On St. Lawrence Island and on the northeast coast of Siberia, from East Cape westward at least as far west as Koliutschin Bay.

Winter range.—Mainly in the Aleutian Islands. East along the Alaska Peninsula at least as far as Sanakh Island and Bristol Bay and probably to Cook Inlet, straggling farther south and casually to California. West to the Commander Islands and perhaps Kamchatka.

Spring migration.—Early dates of arrival in Alaska: Pribilof Islands, St. George, April 26; Nushagak River, May 5; Yukon Delta, May 22; Cape Prince of Wales, May 19.

Fall migration.—Early dates of arrival: Pribilof Islands, St. George Island, September 22; Aleutian Islands, August 31; Oregon, Willamette River, September 30; California, San Francisco market, October 8.   Latest date for St. Michael is November 15.

Casual records.—Rare south of Alaska, but frequently wanders south to Washington (Snohomish County, January 1, 1922), Oregon (Netarts Bay, December 31, 1920), and California (10 or more records).   One record for the Hawaiian Islands (Kalapan, December 12, 1902), and one doubtful record for the Great Slave Lake region.

Egg dates.—Alaska: Fifteen records, May 26 to July 4; eight records, June 2 to 20.

DENDROCYGNA AUTUMNALIS (Linnaeus)

BLACK-BELLIED TREE DUCK

HABITS

As I have never seen either of the tree ducks in life, I shall have to quote wholly from the writings of others; and very little has been published about this species, which is to be found in only a very limited area north of the Rio Grande.   Writing of its habits near Fort Brown, Texas, Dr. J. C. Merrill (1878) says:

This large and handsome bird arrives from the south in April, and is soon found in abundance on the river banks and lagoons. Migrating at night, it continually utters a very peculiar chattering whistle, which at once indicates its presence. Called by the Mexicans *patos maizal*, or cornfield duck, from its habit of frequenting those localities. It is by no means shy, and large numbers are offered for sale in the Brownsville market. Easily domesticated, it becomes very tame, roosting at night in trees with chickens and turkeys. When the females begin to lay, the males leave them, and gather in large flocks on sandbars in the river.

Nesting.—Mr. George B. Sennett (1879) writes:

First noticed early in May, in pairs, at Lomita, looking for nesting places. Soon after it became quite common. During the mating season it is found about in trees of open woodland, and very tame. It nests in hollow trees without regard to nearness of water. I was shown the nest from which a set of 12 eggs was taken the season before. It was in an ebony tree in an open grove, near the houses of the ranch, and much frequented; was about 9 feet from the ground, in a hollow branch, with no lining but the chips from the rotten wood.

Four sets of eggs in the United States National Museum, collected near Brownsville, Texas, were taken from nests in holes in elms and willows, 10 or 12 feet from the ground.   Another set is said to have been taken from a nest on the ground, among rushes, weeds, and grass, on the edge of a lake.   The tree nests were mostly in " big woods," usually near a lake or creek, and no lining was found in the nests except the rotten wood in the hollows.   Doctor Merrill (1878) says that " the eggs are deposited in hollow trees and branches, often at a considerable distance from water (2 miles), and from 8 to 30 feet or more from the ground."

Eggs.—Doctor Merrill (1878) says that " two broods are raised," but Mr. Sennett (1879) was " of the opinion that but one brood is reared in a season." By reference to the egg dates, given below, it will be seen that the nesting season is very much prolonged, which suggests the possibility that two broods might be raised.

The black-bellied tree duck does not lay such large sets of eggs as its relative, the fulvous tree duck; from 12 to 16 eggs usually constitute a full set, the smaller number being more often found. The eggs are ovate or short ovate in shape, the shell is sometimes smooth and not at all glossy, but in other specimens it is highly glossy and very finely pitted; the color is white or creamy white, with occasional nest stains. The measurements of 99 eggs, in various collections, average 52.3 by 38.3 millimeters; the eggs showing the four extremes measure **58.5** by 39.5, 54.2 by **42.5**, **41.5** by 28.7 and 43.7 by **28.6** millimeters.

Young.—According to Doctor Merrill (1878) " the parent carries the young to water in her bill." And Mr. George N. Lawrence (1874) quotes Col. A. J. Grayson as saying: " The young are lowered to the ground one at a time in the mouth of the mother; after all are safely landed she then cautiously leads her young brood to the nearest water."

Plumages.—Baird, Brewer, and Ridgway (1884) describe the downy young as follows:

Above, blackish brown, varied by large areas of sulphury buff, as follows: A supraloral streak extending over the eye; a wide stripe from the bill under the eye and extending across the occiput, the blackish below it extending forward only about as far as directly beneath the eye, and confluent posteriorly with the nuchal longitudinal stripe of the same color; a pair of sulphury buff patches on each side of the black, and another on each side of the rump; posterior half of the wing whitish buff, the end of the wing blackish; the black of the upper parts sends off two lateral projections on each side, the first on each side of the crop, the second over the flanks to the tibiae; the buff of the abdomen extending upward in front of this last stripe as far as the middle portion of the buff spot on the side of the back. Lower parts wholly whitish buff, paler and less yellowish along the middle.

A bird in my collection, taken September 11, is apparently in the juvenal or first winter plumage. The bright rufus of the upper parts is replaced by duller shades of pale browns; and the under parts are uniform pale grayish buff, with no traces of the rufous breast or black belly; the bill is dusky. I have seen a bird in similar plumage, collected February 7, in which the color pattern of the under parts of the adult is faintly indicated. Apparently this immature plumage is worn at least through the first fall and winter and perhaps until the first postnuptial molt, the next summer.

Food.—This species is locally known as the "cornfield duck," on account of its habits of frequenting the cornfields to feed on the corn, where it is said to do considerable damage. Mr. Sennett (1878) writes:

Late in August, the young not full grown are seen about the corncribs picking up the refuse corn, at which time Mr. Bourbois says they afford most excellent eating. This bird does not alight in the water as do other ducks but on the land, and wades about in shallow water for food. When corn is nearly ripe, it alights on the stalks, strips the ears of their husks, and pulls the grain from the cob, making this its chief food during the season. I never saw it skulk in the grass for cover, but always take wing and fly to the woods, or to some removed open point by the water. It is a pretty sight to see this bird on some dead stub, pluming itself, its color and shape being very handsome.

Behavior.—Colonel Grayson, in his notes, quoted by Mr. Lawrence (1874), says:

This duck perches with facility on the branches of trees, and when in the cornfields, upon the stalks, in order to reach the ears of corn. Large flocks of them spend the day on the bank of some secluded lagoon, densely bordered with woods or water flags, also sitting among the branches of trees, not often feeding or stirring about during the day. When upon the wing they constantly utter their peculiar whistle of *pe-che-che-né*, from which they have received their name from the natives. (The other species is called Durado.) I have noticed that this species seldom lights in deep water, always prefering the shallow water edges, or the ground; the cause of this may be from the fear of the numerous alligators that usually infest the lagoons.

When taken young, or the eggs hatched under the common barnyard hen, they become very domestic without being confined; they are very watchful during the night, and, like the goose, give the alarm by their shrill whistle when any strange animal or person comes about the house. A lady of my acquaintance possessed a pair which she said were as good as the best watchdog; I also had a pair which were equally as vigilant, and very docile.

Doctor Sanford (1903) writes:

In April, 1901, I found these birds abundant in the vicinity of Tampico, Mexico. They were most often seen in small flocks of from 4 to 10 on the banks at the edge of the lagoon. Their long legs gave them an odd look. At our approach they would run together, raising their long necks much like geese. The flight was peculiar and characteristic, low down and in a line, their large wings with white bands presenting a striking aspect, and giving the impression of a much larger bird. We saw them occasionally on the smaller ponds, and shot several, all of them males. In one or two instances the appearance of the breast indicated the bird had been sitting on eggs. While the males of this species are supposed to attend to their own affairs during the period of incubation, it would seem as if they occasionally assisted in nesting duties. Once or twice I saw them near small ponds in woods, apparently nesting, flying from tree to tree with perfect ease, exhibiting some concern at our presence.

Winter.—Prof. W. W. Cooke (1906) says:

It winters in Mexico at least as far north as central Vera Cruz (Vega del Casadero) and Mazatlan. North of this district it is strictly migratory, and throughout most, if not all, of its ranges in Central America there seems to be a shifting of location between the winter and the summer homes, but no data are available to determine the movements with accuracy.

Since writing the above life history I have visited the Browns-ville region in the lower Rio Grande Valley and made a special effort to learn something about the two tree ducks, which were formerly so abundant there. I did not see a specimen of either species. Capt. R. D. Camp, who has spent some 13 years in studying and collecting birds in that region, told me that the black-bellied tree duck had entirely disappeared from the Brownsville region and that the fulvous tree duck had become very scarce. He took me to a resaca where he had seen a pair of the latter this spring, 1923, but we saw no trace of the birds.

DISTRIBUTION

Breeding range.—East to the Gulf coasts of Texas and Mexico. South to Panama (River Truando). West to the Pacific coast of Mexico (Mazatlan). North to southern Texas (lower Rio Grande Valley) and irregularly north to Corpus Christi and perhaps Kerrville. Known to breed in Porto Rico and Trinidad and probably breeds in some of the other West Indies.

Winter range.—Resident in most of its range. Winters at least as far north as Vera Cruz and Mazatlan.

Migrations.—Arrives in Texas in April and leaves in September, October, and November.

Casual records.—Has wandered to Arizona (Tucson, May 5, 1899) and southern California (Imperial Valley, fall, 1912).

Egg dates.—Texas: Sixteen records, May 3 to October 18; eight records, June 20 to July 14.

DENDROCYGNA BICOLOR (Vieillot)

FULVOUS TREE-DUCK

HABITS

Messrs. Grinnell, Bryant, and Storer (1918) introduce this species in a few well-chosen words as follows:

The term tree duck, as applied to the fulvous tree duck, seems to be an almost complete misnomer for the bird. As regards structure this species seems to be more closely related to the geese than to the ducks, and, at least in California, it seldom nests in trees but chooses the extensive tule marshes of our interior valleys. Birds apparently belonging to the same species of tree duck that occurs in this State are found in South America, in southern Uruguay and Argentina, and also in South Africa and in India—a very striking case of what is known as interrupted or discontinuous distribution. In North America the chief breeding ground of the species is in Mexico, but a considerable number of birds breed in the southwestern United States. The latter contingent is migratory, moving south for the winter season.

Spring.—Col. A. J. Grayson, in his notes quoted by Mr. George N. Lawrence (1874), says:

Although its geographical range is confined within the limits of the Tropics, yet this species has its seasons of periodical migrations from one part of the country to the other; during the month of April their well-known and peculiar whistle may be heard nightly as they are passing over Mazatlan in apparently large flocks, going northward. At first this phenomenon puzzled me not a little, as I well knew that they are not often found far north of the Tropics, except an occasional straggler. But I was at length enlightened as to their point of destination; by frequent inquiries of the natives, I was satisfied that they went no farther north than the Mayo and Yaqui Rivers, in Sonora, and the adjacent lakes and lagoons, where they breed. Some, however, remain and breed in the State of Sinaloa, and the adjoining localities.

Referring to the migration in South America, W. H. Hudson (1920) writes:

This duck, the well-known *Pato silvon* (whistling duck) of the eastern Argentine country, is found abundantly along the Plata and the great streams flowing into it, and northwards to Paraguay. Along this great waterway it is to some extent a migratory species, appearing in spring in Buenos Aires in very large numbers, to breed in the littoral marshes and also on the pampas. They migrate principally by night, and do not fly in long trains and phalanxes like other ducks, but in a cloud; and when they migrate in spring and autumn the shrill confused clangor of their many voices is heard from the darkness overhead by dwellers in the Argentine capital; for the ducks, following the eastern shore of the sealike river, pass over that city on their journey.

Nesting.—One of the best accounts of the nesting habits of the fulvous tree duck in California is given by A. M. Shields (1899), as follows:

Starting early next morning to search a different locality, the place selected was an extensive strip of high grass growing in the damp swampy ground and sometimes in several inches of water. The grass was from 2 to 3 feet high, of a variety commonly known as "sword" or "wire" grass, and covered an area of perhaps 100 acres of low land between the deep water and the higher ground a few hundred yards back. Just as we were alighting from the wagon on the edge of the swampy area I saw a fulvous tree duck flying from the swamp. After a few circles she dropped down among the dense grass not 300 yards distant, and I, not stopping to put on my wading boots but keeping my eye on the spot where she had settled, quickly approached and when within a few yards I was delightfully shocked by a flutter of wings and the sight of the old bird rising and winging a hasty retreat. I reached the nest and what a thrill at the sight, there in the midst of a little vacant square of 4 or 5 feet was a beautifully built nest, composed entirely of grass, about 6 inches in height and containing 19 beautiful white eggs. I immediately saw by comparison that my surmise as to the identity of the strange parasite eggs found the day before was correct.

The nest was situated in the center of a little open spot in the grass; the open area had evidently been created by the bird in her quest for building material, for she had proceeded to pull up or break off the grass immediately adjacent as her nest grew higher and larger, until the nest finally occupied a position in broad daylight as it were, although it is not improbable that when the spot was selected it was well hidden by overhanging and surrounding grass. I was not long in securing this nest and eggs, after which we began a systematic search through the high grass and in a short time I had found my second nest, constructed similarly to the first but a little better hidden, being under an overhanging bunch of grass which furnished a slight covering. This nest contained 30 eggs, deposited in a double layer; and if the first set of 19 was a surprise, what shall I say of this?

Dr. Harold C. Bryant (1914) describes other nests, similarly located, as follows:

One of our most interesting finds was a nest of the fulvous tree duck, discovered on May 12, 1914. The nest was situated on a hummock in the middle of a marsh between two ponds. The nest was a well-woven one of dry sedges placed about 6 inches above the ground in a tall clump of sedge and weeds. The cavity was about 5 inches deep and in it lay 12 ashy white eggs. A few days later the nest was raided by some predacious animal and all the eggs destroyed. On May 18 we discovered a second nest in the same swamp. This one was built about 6 inches above the water in a small clump of sedge and contained but 4 eggs. The sedges were arched over the cavity in such a way as to conceal it effectively. Two days later when we visited this nest we found it also raided. The only other nest of this species noted was a new one found on June 23. No attempt had been made at special construction of a nest, the two eggs simply lying in a crushed-down place among tall sedges.

The method of nesting described above seems to be the method regularly followed in California. I have two sets of fulvous tree duck's eggs in my collection from Merced County, California; one nest is described as made of grass and small tules, lined with fine grass and a little down, and placed on the ground among high grass in a swamp; the other nest was made of grass and tules and was placed in a clump of grass and tules in a ditch with 2½ feet of water under it; there were 29 eggs in the latter nest, 10 of which were in the upper layer.

That this duck probably does nest occasionally in trees in California, as it certainly does elsewhere, is suggested by the following observation by W. Otto Emerson, published by Mr. Shields (1899), in his paper referred to above:

On May 23, 1882, while collecting with William C. Flint at Lillie's ranch near Tulare Lake I noticed a fulvous tree duck sitting in the entrance hole of a large white oak near one of the ditches, but it was out of the question to reach it. Again on May 26 another was located sitting on the edges of a hole high up in a white oak.

Mr. D. B. Burrows found this species nesting in hollow trees, at heights varying from 4 to 30 feet, in the valley of the lower Rio Grande, near Roma, Texas. He says in his notes:

The fulvous tree duck is a common species in some localities along the Rio Grande River. In the breeding season the birds are frequently seen singly, perched in large trees in the heavily timbered bottom lands.

I secured two sets of their eggs, one of which contained 14 and the other 11 eggs. Both of these nests were found by Mexicans, and one of them I visited and examined. This nest was a natural cavity in the large trunk of a mesquite tree and about 4 feet from the ground; the cavity was about 2 feet in depth and the eggs, 11 in number, were placed on rotten chips at the bottom.

The eggs are deposited at a warm time of the year, and I am informed by the Mexicans that the birds are in the habit of leaving the nests for the greater part of the day, the heat of the sun continuing their incubation, but they return and remain upon the nest during the night and the cool part of the morning. How true this is I am not able to say, as I had no opportunity of watching them, but it seems quite reasonable. The nest was more than half a mile from the Rio Grande River, in a broad mesquite bottom.

Eggs.—Either the fulvous tree duck lays an extraordinary number of eggs or several females lay in the same nest. Mr. Shields (1899) says:

We subsequently found about a dozen nests, all similarly situated, and most of them containing from 17 to 28, 30, 31, and 32 eggs. The smallest set found was of 9 and another of 11 eggs, both evidently being incomplete, as the nests were not finished and incubation had not commenced.

Authentic sets of as many as 36 eggs are in existence and probably much larger numbers have been found according to F. S. Barnhart (1901), who writes:

From time to time since 1895 pothunters have told wonderful stories of finding large numbers of eggs piled up on bunches of dead grass and on small knolls that rose above the water in the swamps. The number of eggs in these nests ranged from 30 to 100 or more, according to report, and in not a few cases the finder has brought the eggs with him in order to prove that what he said was true.

Probably the large numbers referred to by Mr. Barnhart are surplus eggs laid by various individuals and never incubated; and perhaps some of the large sets in collections are the product of more than one female. Evidently the fulvous tree duck is careless in its laying habits, for Mr. Shields (1899) speaks of finding eggs of this species in the nests of the redhead and the ruddy duck. All of the slough-nesting ducks seem to be careless about laying in each other's nests and to have the habit of using "dumping nests" in which large numbers of eggs are laid and forgotten.

In shape the eggs are bluntly ovate, short ovate, or oval. The shell is usually smooth and without gloss, but in many specimens, probably those that have been incubated, the shell is quite glossy and minutely pitted. The color varies from white to buffy white, but the eggs are often much stained with deep shades of buff. The measurements of 212 eggs, in various collections, average 53.4 by 40.7 millimeters; the eggs showing the four extremes measure **59.9** by 40.4, 52.5 by **44.03**, 49.1 by 39.7 and 51.7 by **37.6** millimeters.

Plumages.—The downy young of the fulvous tree duck is described by Grinnell, Bryant, and Storer (1918) as follows:

Top of head clove brown; chin, throat, and sides of head dull white, a streak of the same color extending around back of head on each side and meeting its fellow on hind head; a short, dull white streak on each side of head from side of bill to above eye; bill (dried) dusky brown with prominent yellowish nail; hind neck clove brown, a streak of same color invading side of head below streak of white which encircles head; rest of upper surface of body uniform bister brown; whole under surface of body dull white; feet (dried) grayish yellow.

A series of young birds in my collection, about two-thirds grown, are strikingly like adults, except that the colors are all duller, the brown edgings on the back are narrower, there is less chestnut in the wing coverts, and the upper tail coverts are tipped with brown. I have no data as to subsequent molts and plumages, but suppose that the adult plumage is assumed at the first postnuptial molt when the young bird is a little over a year old.

Food.—Mr. Shields (1899) says that these ducks "are equally at home in an alfalfa patch (about dusk) or in a lake of water, and are entirely at home in an oak forest not far from the breeding swamp, where they are said to assemble for the purpose of feeding on acorns."

Referring to the food of this species, Grinnell, Bryant, and Storer (1918) write:

The fulvous tree duck feeds largely on the seeds of grasses and weeds. In Mexico and Texas it is said to visit the cornfields at night where it finds palatable provender. When feeding in muddy or marshy situations the birds thrust their bills deep in the soft mud on both sides and in front of them as they walk along. The stomach of an individual obtained at Los Banos, Merced County, in May, 1914, and examined by us, contained finely cut up grass and other vegetable matter.

Behavior.—The same writers say on this subject:

The fulvous tree duck is more easily approached than many other waterfowl, but nevertheless is often difficult to find as it congregates among the dense tules or far out on the marshy ponds. On occasion a flock has been easily approached and a number killed at one shot. Sometimes, when tree ducks are surprised on grassy ground, they simply stand rigidly with their heads and long necks straight up in the air, and at a distance look more like stakes than birds. When wounded they are said to escape not only by diving but also by running at great speed and hiding in the grass, and thus often baffle entirely the hunter's efforts to recover them.

Game.—Regarding its status as a game bird, they say:

The flesh of the fulvous tree duck is light colored and juicy, and also free from the rank flavor possessed by sea-faring ducks and geese. On their arrival in California the birds are fat and eminently fit for the table; but since they are here in greatest numbers during the close season, they largely escape the slaughter levied on other wild fowl. The numbers of this species are, at best, small in comparison with many other ducks and geese. They could ill afford a heavy toll by the hunter during the period of their stay here. Any levy upon them during the actual breeding season would be contrary to all recognized principles of game conservation and humanity. As it is, but a few tree ducks are to be shot each year at the opening of the season, October 15. Those who are anxious to hunt the fulvous tree duck in numbers must go to Mexico, where the birds are to be found regularly in winter and where a certain toll may be levied with safety.

Winter.—On the winter habits of the fulvous tree duck in Mexico Mr. Lawrence (1874) quotes Colonel Grayson as follows:

At the conclusion of the rainy season, or the month of October, they make their appearance in the vicinity of Mazatlan, San Blas, and southward, in large flocks; inhabiting the fresh-water ponds and lakes in the coast region, or *tierra caliente*, during the entire winter, or dry months, subsisting principally upon the seeds of grass and weeds, and often at night visiting the cornfields for grain. During these months I have found them in the shallow grass-grown ponds in very large numbers, affording excellent sport to the hunter, and a delicious game for the table; their flesh is white, juicy, and, feeding upon grain and seed, is free from the strong or rank flavor of most other ducks; they are rather heavy or bulky and usually fat. They are more easy to approach than our northern species; I have shot as many as 15 with the two discharges of my double-barrel. When only winged they are almost sure to make their escape, which their long and stout legs enable them to do, running and springing with extraordinary agility, and ultimately eluding pursuit by dodging into the grass or nearest thicket; if the water is deep they dive, and as they rise to breathe, having only the head above water, and that concealed among the water plants, they are soon abandoned by the hunter.

Mr. H. B. Conover writes to me, of the haunts of this species in Venezuela, as follows:

The only place we saw this duck was at Lagunillas. Here on a large savannah or swamp we saw thousands of tree ducks, about 5 per cent of which were fulvous and the rest gray breasted. The fulvous tree duck was very much wilder than the other, and when polling through the marsh, would be the first to leave, generally rising 100 to 150 yards away. On the water these birds were very easy to distinguish from the gray breasted because of their whitish rump, which showed up plainly. They flocked by themselves, as I never noticed them mixed in with flocks of gray breasted or vice versa. This marsh was a shallow place, I believe not over 3 feet deep in any spot, and consisted of large pieces of open water with patches and islands of high grass on the sides. The open water was covered for the most part with floating aquatic plants somewhat similar to our lily. It was in these open places, among the floating aquatic plants, that the tree ducks could be seen. This bird was well known to the natives there and went by the name of Llaguasa Colorado as against the plain Llaguasa for the gray-breasted tree duck.

DISTRIBUTION

Breeding range.—Southwestern North America, parts of South America, and southern Africa and India. In North America east to Louisiana (Lake Catharine and the Rigolets). South to central Mexico (Jalisco and Valley of Mexico). North to central California

(Merced County), central Nevada (Washoe Lake), southern Arizona (Fort Whipple), and eastern Texas (Nueces County). In South America from central Argentina (near Buenos Aires and in Ajo district), northwards to northern Argentina (Tucuman Fort, in Donovan), central Paraguay (Asuncion), and southern Brazil. Occurs in northern South America (Colombia, Venezuela, and British Guiana); it probably breeds in these localities and casually on the island of Trinidad.

Winter range.—Includes the breeding range and extends southwards in Mexico to Guerrero and Chiapas and northwards in California to the Sacramento Valley (Marysville) and Marin County (Inverness).

Migrations.—Migratory movements are not well marked, but occur mainly in April and October.

Casual records.—Has wandered east to North Carolina (Currituck Sound, July, 1886) and Missouri (New Albany, fall, 1890) and north to British Columbia (Alberni, Vancouver Island, September 29, 1905.

Egg dates.—California: Twenty-three records, April 28 to July 13; twelve records, June 7 to 25. Texas: Nine records, May 16 to September 10; four records, June 16 to July 12.

CYGNUS CYGNUS (Linnaeus)

WHOOPING SWAN

HABITS

The status of this fine swan as an American bird has rested mainly on its former occurrence as a breeding bird of southern Greenland, of which Andreas T. Hagerup (1891) says: "Formerly nested in South Greenland, but is now only a rare visitor." It is said to have been exterminated in Greenland by the natives, who pursued and killed the young birds and the adults, when molting and unable to fly. Probably what few stragglers now occur there are wanderers from Iceland, where it is known to breed regularly.

The whooping swan is a Palearctic bird of wide distribution across the northern portions of Europe and Asia, breeding mainly north of the Arctic Circle.

Nesting.—John Cordeaux (1898) writes:

"It is the earliest of the Arctic breeding birds to move toward its nesting quarters, and its loud trumpet calls are the first notice to the dwellers in high latitudes that the long dreary winter is nearing its end. Swans arrive at their nesting quarters as early as the end of March. The nest is a round mass of water plants and moss, fragments of turf and peat, of considerable elevation and often visible at a long distance. It is placed in some vast wilderness of bog or marsh, and sometimes on a small island in a lake. The eggs, from 3 to

5, and 7, are creamy white, and small for the great size of the parent. They are buried in down from the bird's breast, with which the nest is also lined.

The following account of the breeding of this species in the West Highlands of Scotland is published by Mrs. Audrey Gordon (1922), as follows:

On May 21, 1921, my husband and I went to a certain loch in the West Highlands hoping to photograph a black-throated diver whose nest we had located on May 16. However, to our great disappointment the diver's eggs had been washed out of the nest during the flood in the night of May 19–20. Near a neighboring island, where many herons nested on low birch trees, we saw a pair of whooper swans (*Cygnus cygnus*) swimming. Suspecting a nest, a search was made, and soon revealed the swan's nest with 4 eggs. It was situated on a patch of green grass amid a mass of hummocks of blueberry and heather and about 4 yards from the edge of the loch. The nest was composed of dead grasses and weeds and was raised some 15 inches from the ground level. A "hide" was constructed among the hummocks and from it a watch was kept on the 22d and 23d.

The swan always landed at exactly the same place, on a tiny sandy beach, and approached the nest slowly, drying her breast feathers by rubbing them with her head. While sitting she spent a good deal of time building up the nest by pulling the grasses up and around her from the base of the nest. Several times she stood up and laboriously turned the great eggs completely over. Once she left the nest to feed and before doing so carefully covered the eggs with the nesting material. On returning, however, she did not remove the covering but wriggled it off the eggs with her body. Often she went to sleep on the nest, her long neck lying along her back in tortuous curves. The photograph shows clearly the distinguishing features of the whooper swan— the large size, long straight neck held erect and not curved as in the mute species, and the absence of knob or berry on the bill. Further proof of the identity of the species was given by the hearing of the repeated calling of both birds, a musical call, rather resembling that of the wigeon.

Eggs.—This swan is said to lay from 3 to 7 eggs, but usually from 4 to 6. They are creamy or yellowish white at first but soon become nest stained. The measurements of 75 eggs, as given in Witherby's Handbook (1921) average 112.8 by 72.6 millimeters; the eggs showing the four extremes measure **126.3** by 71.3, 114 by **77.4, 105.2** by 72, and 117 by **68.1** millimeters. The period of incubation is given as from 31 to 42 days, or as about five weeks.

Food.—Mr. Cordeaux (1898) says on this subject:

Swans feed on vegetable substances, as grass, and shoots of shrubs and trees, and the roots and leaves of water plants, which their long necks enable them to tear up from the bottom of the rivers and shallows of the lakes they frequent. They will also eat grain when it can be got.

Witherby's Handbook (1921) adds to the list of food taken in summer, "fresh-water mollusca, worms, and acquatic insects."

Behavior.—Rev. F. O. Morris (1903) writes:

They fly in a long line, at times divaricated in the form of a wedge, and go in flocks or teams of from 4 or 5 to 30, which unite together to the number of several hundreds, at the times of migration. Their flight is easy and well sustained and usually conducted at a great height. It is exercised without much noise, except on first rising or alighting, when the sound may be heard to a considerable distance. It is said that they can fly at the rate of above 100 miles an hour. They walk well and can also run with considerable rapidity. In swimming about, except when feeding, the neck is carried in an upright posture and seldom in the arched manner characteristic of the other species. In walking the neck is bent backward over the body and the head lowered as if to preserve a proper balance.

The note resembles the word " *hoop*," repeated ten or a dozen times; hence the name of the bird. It is both loud, clear, and sonorous, and sounds aloft like the clang of a trumpet. Other inflections of their voice are expressed by Meyer, by the syllables " *hang, hang*," " *grou, grou*," and " *killelee*." Montagu writes that having killed one of these species out of a flock of 10 or 12 its companions flew around several times making a most melancholy cry before they flew off.

Mr. Cordeaux (1898) refers to the notes of this swan as follows:

There is no sound in nature more likely to attract attention than the aerial music of a herd of migrating swans passing high overhead; some speak of it as exhilarating to the highest degree, but to me there is always a touch of sadness in the sound—the sadness of Highland music in those long drawn, melancholy, and plaintive notes, which seem suggestive of the illimitable wilds of the great lone lands where the birds have passed the long day of the short Arctic summer.

He further says:

Mr. St. John has seen them arrive on Loch Spynie as early as September 30. He says: " While they remain with us, they frequent and feed in shallow pieces of water, of so small a depth that in many places they can reach the bottom with their long necks and pluck off the water grasses on which they feed. While employed in tearing up these plants, the swans are generally surrounded by a number of smaller water fowl, such as wigeon and teal, who snatch at and carry off the pieces detached by their more powerful companions. The rapidity of the flight of a swan is wonderful; one moment they are far from you, the next they have passed you like an arrow. This speed, however, is only attained when at a considerable height above the ground." Swans are most powerful swimmers and will swim out from the seashore in the teeth of a considerable gale with the greatest ease.

DISTRIBUTION

Breeding range.—Palearctic region. East to northeastern Siberia (Anadyr and Kamchatka) and the Commander Islands. West to Great Britain. South to about 65° N. in northern Siberia and about 62° N. in northern Europe. North of the Arctic Circle in Finland and Scandinavia. West to Iceland, and formerly to Greenland.

Winter range.—South to southern Europe (rarely to northern Africa), central Asia, Persia, China, and Japan.

Casual records.—Now only casual in Greenland (Atangmik, Godthaab, Ingtuk, and Arsuk).

Egg dates.—Iceland: Ten records, May 1 to June 18. Great Britain: Five records, April 20 to June 21.

CYGNUS COLUMBIANUS (Ord)

WHISTLING SWAN

HABITS

I had lived to be nearly 50 years old before I saw my first wild swan, but it was a sight worth waiting for, to see a flock of these magnificent, great, snow-white birds, glistening in the sunlight against the clear blue sky, their long necks pointing northward toward their polar home, their big black feet trailing behind, and their broad translucent wings slowly beating the thin upper air, as they sped onward in their long spring flight. If the insatiable desire to kill, and especially to kill something big and something beautiful, had not so possessed past and present generations of sportsmen, I might have seen one earlier in my life and perhaps many another ornithologist, who has never seen a swan, might have enjoyed the thrill of such an inspiring sight. No opportunity has been neglected to kill these magnificent birds, by fair means or foul, since time immemorial; until the vast hordes which formerly migrated across our continent have been sadly reduced in numbers and are now confined to certain favored localities. Fortunately the breeding grounds of this species are so remote that they are not likely to be invaded by the demands of agriculture; and fortunately the birds are so wary that they are not likely to be exterminated on migrations or in their winter resorts.

Spring.—Dr. D. G. Elliot (1898) says of the start on the spring migration:

At the advent of spring the swan begin to show signs of uneasiness, and to make preparations for their long journey to the northward. They gather in large flocks and pass much of their time preening their feathers, keeping up a constant flow of loud notes, as though discussing the period of their departure and the method and direction of their course. At length all being in readiness, with loud screams and many *who-who's*, they mount into the air, and in long lines wing their way toward their breeding places amid the frozen north. It has been estimated that swan travel at the rate of 100 miles an hour with a moderate wind in their favor to help them along. The American swan is monogamous, and once mated the pair are presumed to be faithful for life. The young keep with their parents for the first year, and these little families are only parted during that period by the death of its members.

Being early migrants, swans are often overtaken by severe storms with disastrous results, as the following incident, related by George B. Sennett (1880), will illustrate:

An unusual flight of swans occurred in northwestern Pennsylvania on the 22d of last March (1879). On the day mentioned, as well as the previous day and night, a severe storm prevailed, the rain and snow freezing as they fell. The swans, on their migration north, were caught in the storm and, becoming overweighted with ice, soon grew so exhausted that they settled into the nearest ponds and streams, almost helpless. Generally a single one was seen in some mill pond or creek, and the fowling piece, loaded with large shot, and not infrequently the rifle, was used to bring to bag the noble game, though, considering the plight they were in, in all probability anyone might have paddled up to the birds and taken them alive. In fact, in a number of instances they were reported as thus taken alive. Large flocks were seen in some districts in the same pitiable condition. A flock of from 33 to 35 American or whistling swans surprised the inhabitants of Plumer on Saturday forenoon by alighting in the waters of Cherry Run. One of the swans was almost immediately shot at and killed, and, to the surprise of the now large crowd of men and boys, the remainder of the flock, on account of the ice accumulating on their wings, was unable to fly, and a general rush was then made for the poor birds, and 25 were captured alive by the eager fellows.

The late E. S. Cameron has sent me some very full notes on the whistling swan, which seems to be a regular spring and fall migrant through central Montana. He mentions a flock of 344 birds seen by W. R. Felton on Mallard Lake on April 4, 1912, and a still larger flock of about a thousand birds seen by J. H. Holtman on Marshy Lake on April 10, 1911. He says:

The swans come in small flocks, at short intervals, until they sometimes aggregate several hundred individuals. While the swans are usually the earliest birds to arrive, geese may be still earlier, and this year a small flock of six Canada geese (*Branta canadensis canadensis*) preceded the swans. In 1913 the first swans were observed on April 4 by Bob Morrow (one of Mr. Williams's men), who counted 26. On April 6 W. P. Sullivan, of the Square Butte Ranch, enumerated 25 in one flock and saw another smaller bunch of about half that number, which were too far away to count without glasses. At the present time (April 8), when we reached the lake side there were 125 swans, as we ascertained after frequent counts. These were grouped upon the southwest shore of the lake immediately below the ranch where the fine mountain stream called Alder Creek flows in. Some were standing upon one leg in 2 or 3 inches of water, others floated asleep behind these, with their heads under their wings, and farther away watchful birds, constituting a rear guard, were sailing about. With very few exceptions the swans held one leg along the side either when swimming or resting upon the water. They allowed us to examine them through binoculars for a few minutes and then all began swimming slowly for the center of the lake. Mr. Williams informed us that no matter how much the swans might be disturbed they would always return to this place, on account of the fresh water running in from the mountains. He also said that unless shot at (when they would probably leave altogether) the swans might possibly remain until May 1.

Doctor Nelson (1887) writes:

This fine bird arrives on the shore of Bering Sea in the vicinity of St. Michael early in May, and in some seasons by the 27th of April, as in 1878, when several were seen on that date about a spring hole in the ice. At this time the ground was clothed with over a foot of snow, and the sea covered, as far as could be seen, with unbroken ice. During the next few days a terrible storm of wind and snow swept over the country, but did these birds no harm, as was seen directly after the storm ceased by their presence at the water hole as usual. Mr. Dall records their arrival on the Yukon about May 1, and notes the fact of their descending that stream in place of going up the Yukon, as most of the geese do at this season.

Courtship.—Alfred M. Bailey has sent me the following account of this ceremony which he witnessed in Alaska:

At Wales I saw swans rarely, the first noted being on June 5, when I witnessed as pleasing a performance as it has been my privilege to see. The tundra was still clothed in its winter's coat of white, although pools of brilliant colors had formed here and there by the melting snow. It was in the height of the spring migration, with hundreds of snow geese, little brown cranes, and shore birds in sight continually. Then, far out on the tundra I heard a different call, a clamoring, quavering call, first full and loud and gradually dying down. With the aid of the glasses I made out three swans, possibly two males performing for the benefit of the female. They walked about with arched necks proudly lifted, taking high steps, with wings outstretched, two birds occasionally bowing to each other, and as they performed, they continually kept calling. After a few minutes in a given place, they took to wing and drifted across the tundra a hundred yards, where the ceremony was then repeated.

Nesting.—Doctor Nelson (1887) describes the nest, as follows:

The birds arrive singly or in small parties on the coast, and directly after scatter to their summer haunts. The nest is usually upon a small island in some secluded lakelet, or on a rounded bank close to the border of a pond. The eggs are deposited in a depression made in a heap of rubbish gathered by the birds from the immediate vicinity of the nest, and is composed of grass, moss, and dead leaves, forming a bulky affair in many cases. On June 14, 1880, a swan was seen flying from the side of a small pond on the marsh near St. Michael, and a close search finally revealed the nest. The eggs were completely hidden in loose moss, which covered the ground about the spot, and in which the bird had made a depression by plucking up the moss and arranging it for the purpose. The site was so artfully chosen and prepared that I passed the spot in my search, and one of my native hunters, coming close behind, called me back, and thrusting his stick into the moss exposed the eggs. I may note here that whenever the Eskimo of Norton Sound go egging on the marshes they invariably carry a stick 3 or 4 feet long, which they thrust into every suspicious tussock, bunch of grass, or spot in the moss, and if a nest is there it is certain to be revealed by the stick striking the eggs. They are very expert in detecting places likely to be chosen by the ducks and geese. I have seen my hunters examine the borders of a lake, after I had given it what I considered a thorough search, and unearth in one instance three geese nests and one duck's. This was after I had acquired considerable skill in finding eggs, so it may readily be seen that the birds are very cunning in placing their nests.

Swainson and Richardson (1831) say of this species:

This swan breeds on the seacoast within the Arctic Circle, and is seen in the interior of the fur countries on its passage only. It makes its appearance amongst the latest of the migratory birds in the spring, while the trumpeter swans are, with the exception of the eagles, the earliest. Captain Lyon describes its nest as built of moss peat, nearly 6 feet long and 4¾ wide, and 2 feet high exteriorly; the cavity a foot and a half in diameter. The eggs were brownish-white, slightly clouded with a darker tint.

According to Rev. C. W. G. Eifrig (1905) the Canadian Neptune Expedition to Hudson Bay found this swan common on Southampton Island;

also in the flat land north of Repulse Bay. They breed in lowlands with lakes, where their nests, constructed of seaweed, grass, and moss, are very conspicuous. They are very bulky affairs, about 3 feet in diameter at the base, tapering to 18 inches at the top, and 18 inches high. A set of 2 eggs was taken on Southampton, July 4, 1904.

Mr. Bailey has contributed the following notes on a nest he found in Alaska:

While collecting near Mint River, which empties into Lopp Lagoon about 20 miles north of Cape Prince of Wales, I found a nest of this species with three downy young. It was early in the morning that we discovered it, on July 12. Both adults were seen sitting close to the edge of a pond, and, as we approached, they flew majestically away, only to circle and sail back directly over our heads. The female was more stained than the male. There, near the water's edge, from where the parent birds had taken flight, were three beautiful little downy young, which had just left the nest, some 25 feet away, and were doubtless ready to undertake their first swim. They were as fluffy as balls of yarn, with dark brown eyes, and bills and feet of pink flesh-color. They showed no fear, and cuddled contentedly when we held them in our hands.

The nest was a conspicuous, built-up mound of moss on a ridge overlooking the little lagoon, and was unlined with down. From the size of the young, it was evident that the swans made their nest on the first bit of bare tundra. The swans are probably among the first birds to nest in the vicinity of Wales; the geese eggs were but half incubated at this time, while the loons' eggs were fresh.

The swans owe their present-day numbers to the fact that they nest over a wide stretch of barren country, uninhabited even by natives. They are continually persecuted on their breeding grounds, and were it not for their habit of nesting early, when the snow is deep and too soft for traveling, they would have been exterminated long ago.

Eggs.—The foregoing brief accounts are about all we have regarding the nesting habits of this well-known species. MacFarlane collected about 20 sets of eggs, but said very little about the nests. The usual number of eggs seems to be 4 or 5, though as few as 2 and as many as 7 have been reported. The eggs resemble goose eggs except that they are much larger. In shape they are elliptical ovate or elliptical oval, with a tendency toward fusiform in some specimens. The shell is fairly smooth or finely granulated and not glossy. The color is creamy white or dull white at first, becoming much nest stained. The measurements of 94 eggs, in various collections, average 106.9 by 68.2 millimeters; the eggs showing the four extremes measure 115.7 by 68.5, 115 by 73, and 90 by 58.7 millimeters.

Young.—The period of incubation is said to be from 35 to 40 days. Doctor Nelson (1887) says of the young:

The last of June or first of July the young are hatched, and soon after the parents lead them to the vicinity of some large lake or stream, and there the old birds molt their quill feathers and are unable to fly. They are pursued by the natives at this season, and many are speared from canoes and kyaks. Although unable to fly, it is no easy task single handed to capture them alive. The young men among the Eskimo consider it a remarkable exhibition of fleetness and endurance for one of their number to capture a bird by running it down.

Plumages.—The downy young is described by Dr. D. G. Elliot (1898) as " pure white, bill, legs, and feet yellow "; but the young of European swans are all either pale grayish-white or grayish-brown.

Doctor Nelson (1887) describes a young bird taken in September, apparently in juvenile plumage, as follows:

The young birds of the year frequently retain the immature plumage until the last of September. A specimen in this plumage, taken on September 19, had its bill purplish flesh color, the nail and a border along the gape black; the iris hazel, and the feet and tarsi livid flesh color. The plumage of this bird, which is now before me, is sooty brownish with a plumbeous shade about the top and sides of the head; neck and throat all around dull plumbeous ashy of a light shade; back, tertials, and wing coverts dull plumbeous ashy with a silvery gray luster, especially upon the wings. Rump white, lightly washed with ashy, which increases to dull plumbeous ashy on the tail coverts and rectrices. Quills white, heavily mottled with ashy gray on their terminal third, but almost immaculate toward bases. Under surface white, washed with dingy gray.

Doctor Sharpless, quoted by Audubon (1840), says:

The swan requires five or six years to reach its perfect maturity of size and plumage, the yearling cygnet being about one-third the magnitude of the adult, and having feathers of a deep leaden color. The smallest swan I have ever examined, and it was killed in my presence, weighed but 8 pounds. Its plumage was very deeply tinted, and it had a bill of a very beautiful flesh color, and very soft. This cygnet, I presume, was a yearling, for I killed one myself the same day, whose feathers were less dark, but whose bill was of a dirty white; and the bird weighed 12 pounds.

Doctor Elliot (1898) also writes:

The young of this species is gray, sometimes lead color during its first year, and the bill is soft and reddish in hue. In the second year the plumage is lighter, and the bill white, becoming black in the third year, when the plumage, though white, is mottled with gray; the head and neck especially showing but little white. It is probable that it takes fully five years before the pure white dress is assumed and the bird becomes such an ornamental object.

Although Baird, Brewer, and Ridgway (1884) make a similar statement, I can not believe that it takes a swan any such length of time to acquire its full plumage. Witherby's Handbook (1921) seems to imply that the pure white plumages of the whooping swan and the Bewick swan are acquired before the second winter.

Hon. R. M. Barnes tells me that young swans, reared by him in confinement, acquired their full plumage during the second summer or fall, when 14 or 15 months old. I believe that this is usually the case with wild birds, though some traces of immaturity may not disappear until some time during the following winter or even spring.

Food.—The food of the whistling swan is largely vegetable, which it obtains by reaching down with its long neck in shallow water, occasionally tipping up with its tail in the air when making an extra long reach. While a flock of swans is feeding in this manner, one or more birds are always on guard watching for approaching dangers, as the feeding birds often keep their heads and necks submerged for long periods. It apparently never dives for its food except in cases of great extremity. In Back Bay, Virginia, and in Currituck Sound, North Carolina, the swans feast on the roots of the wild celery and fox-tail grass; they are now (1916) so numerous that they do considerable damage by treading great holes in the mud and by rooting and pulling up the celery and grass; they thus waste large quantities of these valuable duck foods, much more than they consume, and consequently spoil some of the best feeding grounds for ducks, much to the disgust of the sportsmen in the various clubs, who are not allowed to shoot the swans and have to submit to this interference with their duck shooting. The swans are really such a nuisance in this particular locality that a reasonable amount of shooting might well be allowed; these birds are so wary that there is little danger of any great number being killed.

Major Bendire (1875) found in the stomach of a whistling swan, shot in Oregon, "about 20 small shells, perhaps half an inch in length, quite a quantity of gravel, and a few small seeds." Mr. Cameron in his Montana notes, says:

The swans were engaged in feeding upon the soft-shelled fresh-water snails which abound in this lake and explain its great attraction for them. During the several days that I watched the swans I never saw them eat anything else, but doubtless they pick up vegetation as well, being accustomed to walk about in the grass at the mouth of Alder Creek. Marshy Lake is so shallow (only 2 feet deep over most of it, and 4 feet in the deepest part) that the long-necked birds can generally reach the mollusca without much tilting of their bodies in characteristic swan fashion.

Dr. F. Henry Yorke (1891) says: "They feed upon corn, and upon tender roots of wheat, rye, and grass, and upon bulbous roots, pushing about for them in the mud at the bottom of lakes and rivers. They also catch and eat tadpoles, frogs, and even fish." Other writers have mentioned, among the food of this species, the roots of the *Equisetacae*, *Sagittaria*, various grasses, and other succulent water plants, also worms, insects, and shellfish.

Behavior.—Considering its size and weight, a swan rises from the water with remarkable ease and celerity; it runs along the surface for 15 or 20 feet, flapping its wings and beating the water with its feet alternately, until it has gained sufficient headway to launch into the air; like all heavy-bodied birds it must face the wind in rising. When well awing it flies with considerable speed and power, with the long neck stretched out in front and the great black feet extending beyond the tail; the wing beats are slow, but powerful and effective. It has been said to fly at a speed of 100 miles an hour; probably no such speed is attained, however, except when flying before a heavy wind; it undoubtedly flies faster than it appears to on account of its great size, and it certainly flies faster than any of the ducks and geese. When traveling long distances swans fly in V-shaped wedges, in the same manner as geese and for the same reason; the resistance of the air is less, as each bird flies in the widening wake of its predecessor; the leader, of course, has the hardest work to do, as he "breaks the trail," but he is relieved at intervals and drops back into the flock to rest. On shorter flights they fly in long curving lines or in irregular flocks. They usually fly rather high, and when traveling are often way up above the clouds. Audubon (1840) quotes Doctor Sharpless, as follows:

In flying, these birds make a strange appearance; their long necks protrude and present, at a distance, mere lines with black points, and occupy more than one-half their whole length, their heavy bodies and triangular wings seeming but mere appendages to the prolonged point in front. When thus in motion, their wings pass through so few degrees of the circle that, unless seen horizontally, they appear almost quiescent, being widely different from the heavy semicircular sweep of the goose. The swan, when migrating, with a moderate wind in his favor, and mounted high in the air, certainly travels at the rate of 100 miles or more an hour. I have often *timed* the flight of the goose, and found one mile a minute a common rapidity, and when the two birds, in a change of feeding ground, have been flying near each other, which I have often seen, the swan invariably passed with nearly double the velocity.

Mr. Cameron, in his notes, refers to the powers of flight of swans, as follows:

Small parties of the swans on the water spread their long wings at regular intervals and took lengthy flights, presumably to keep themselves in practice for their forthcoming journey. The control which such large birds (weighing from 17 to 20 pounds) possess over their flight on a perfectly calm day is to me quite marvelous, and must be seen to be appreciated. A compact flock of from 4 to 6 swift-flying swans will circle the whole basin of the lake several times, and then, as if tied together, alight in the closest proximity to each other, yet never collide. They will pitch upon the water in the most graceful manner imaginable, without bringing their long legs forward, or making any splash. At exceptional times, however, the swans do make a loud splash when t' alight.

The ease and grace with which a swan swims on the surface of the water is too well known and too far famed to need any further comment; there is no prettier picture, no grander picture, than a party of these beautiful birds floating undisturbed on the mirror surface of some northern mountain lake against the rugged background of one of nature's wildest spots. But few people realize the speed and power of the swan as a swimmer until they have tried to chase one in a boat and seen how easily he escapes, even against wind and waves, without recourse to flight.

The notes of the whistling swan are varied, loud and striking at times and again soft and musical trumpetings. To me they are suggestive of the Canada goose's call in form, but are more like soft musical laughter, suggested by the syllables "*wow-how-ou*," heavily accented on the second note. Mr. Cameron says, in his notes:

Mr. Skelton describes the sounds uttered by his tame swan as "long whoops, or clucking croaks, according to its mood." The wild swans upon taking wing, or when arriving on migration, produce sounds like a slow shake of two notes upon a clarinet. If the flock is large, as in the present instance, so many throats yield a great volume of musical sound. When the quiescent swans become suddenly alarmed, and contemplate flight, a subdued chorus runs through the flock like different modulations from an orchestra of reed instruments. Under no circumstances could the swan voices be compared to brass instruments (such as a trumpet or hunting horn) in my opinion, and herein concur Mr. Felton, Mr. Williams, and Mr. Skelton, who have had frequent opportunities for listening to them. We could distinctly hear the swan cries at the ranch a mile from the lake, and they might have been heard at a much greater distance.

The old saying that "a swan sings before it dies" has generally been regarded as a myth, but the following incident, related by so reliable an observer as Dr. D. G. Elliot (1898), is certainly worthy of credence:

I had killed many swan and never heard aught from them at any time, save the familiar notes that reach the ears of everyone in their vicinity. But once, when shooting in Currituck Sound over water belonging to a club of which I am a member, in company with a friend, Mr. F. W. Leggett, of New York, a number of swan passed over us at a considerable height. We fired at them, and one splendid bird was mortally hurt. On receiving his wound the wings became fixed and he commenced at once his song, which was continued until the water was reached, nearly half a mile away. I am perfectly familiar with every note a swan is accustomed to utter, but never before nor since have I heard any like those sung by this stricken bird. Most plaintive in character and musical in tone, it sounded at times like the soft running of the notes in an octave, and as the sound was borne to us, mellowed by the distance, we stood astonished, and could only exclaim, "We have heard the song of the dying swan."

Fall.—Referring to the beginning of the fall migration, Mr. Lucien M. Turner (1886) says:

The young are able to leave the nest by the first week in July, and fly by the middle of September. They migrate about the middle of October, and at this time the migration is invariably to the northward from St. Michael,

and directed toward the head of Norton Sound. As many as 500 may form
a single line, flying silently just over the shore line at a height of less than
600 feet. I always suspected that these birds flew to the northward as far as
the Ulukuk Portage, in about 65° 30′ north latitude, so as to get to the Yukon
River at Nulato, about 120 miles in the interior of the Territory, and continue their flight up the Yukon River, which would in its course let these
birds more easily cross the Rocky Mountain ridge with least effort. This is supposed by the fact that I never saw swans, at any season of the year, migrating
to the southward.

From this statement and similar observations by Dall and Nelson,
one would infer that the swans which breed in northern Alaska cross
the Rocky Mountains to join the main migration route of the species,
which is southward through the interior of Canada; perhaps the
birds which breed in southern Alaska and in Canada west of the
Rockies migrate down the coast to their winter homes on the Pacific
coast. Swans are very abundant in the interior of Canada and the
northern States in the fall migration. Large numbers were formerly
killed by the fur traders for their skins which were dealt in as regular
articles of commerce. The Hudson's Bay Co. sold 17,671 swan skins
between the years 1853 to 1877; the number steadily decreased, however, from 1,312 in 1854 to 122 in 1877, and during the next two
or three years the traffic practically ceased.

From the vicinity of the Great Lakes the heaviest flight seems to
take a southeastward direction to the Atlantic coast, but there is
also a southward flight to the Gulf of Mexico and probably a limited
southwestward flight to the Pacific coast.

A striking example of the disasters which may befall even one
of our largest and strongest species of wild fowl is shown in the
destruction of swans in the Niagara swan trap. In one instance
over 100 of these great birds met their death; being caught in the
rapids they were swept over the falls; many were killed by the fall,
others were killed or maimed by the rough treatment they received
in the whirlpools and rapids, where they were hurled against the
rocks or crushed in the ice; a few probably escaped by flying back
over the falls, but most of them were unable to fly at all on account
of their injuries or were too exhausted to rise high enough to clear
the falls. But eventually many of them would have escaped if they
had not been attacked by a crowd of men and boys, who shot, beat,
and clubbed the poor struggling birds until not a living bird remained. For full accounts of two such catastrophes I would refer
the reader to Mr. J. H. Fleming's (1908 and 1912) interesting papers
on the subject.

Game.—As game birds, swans have never held a prominent place.
They are not abundant anywhere except in a few favored spots,
as migrants or winter sojourners. They have always been so wary
and shy that attempts to shoot them in any considerable numbers

generally resulted in making them wilder than ever or in driving them away altogether. The flesh of the younger birds is comparatively tender and palatable, but the older birds are very tough. Swans always have been attractive marks for sportsmen on account of their large size and spectacular appearance, but comparatively few have ever enjoyed the privilege of shooting at them. Swans are now protected in their winter resorts on the Atlantic coast, but formerly they were shot in considerable numbers in the vicinity of Chesapeake Bay and Currituck Sound. They were shot mainly from the marshy points where blinds were built for duck shooting; the swans were wont to feed along the shores of the marshy coves and bays; and in passing from one cove to another they frequently flew close around or over these points, offering tempting shots. It was an exciting moment for the sportsman when he saw a flock of these great white birds approaching and few could resist the temptation to shoot at them. On windy, stormy days it was often possible to creep up to them through the marsh near enough to get a shot at them when they rose. Approaching swans on the open water of the bay was a different proposition, especially if they were surrounded, as they often were, by the watchful geese. But even this was successfully accomplished by sailing down the wind upon them, which made it necessary for them to rise toward the boat. In winter, boats covered with blocks of ice and manned by gunners dressed in white could sometimes be paddled or allowed to drift within gunshot of a feeding flock.

Winter.—Doctor Sharpless, in his interesting account of this species published by Audubon (1840), thus describes the arrival of the swans in their principal winter home on the coasts of Virginia and North Carolina:

The swans, in traveling from the northern parts of America to their winter residence, generally keep far inland, mounted above the highest peaks of the Allegheny, and rarely follow the watercourses like the geese, which usually stop on the route, particularly if they have taken the seaboard. The swans rarely pause on their migrating flight, unless overtaken by a storm, above the reach of which occurrence they generally soar. They have been seen following the coast in but very few instances. They arrive at their winter homes in October and November, and immediately take possession of their regular feeding grounds. They generally reach these places in the night, and the first signal of their arrival at their winter abode is a general burst of melody, making the shores ring for several hours with the vociferating congratulations whilst making amends for a long fast, and pluming their deranged feathers. From these localities they rarely depart unless driven farther south by intensely cold weather, until their vernal excursion.

The Chesapeake Bay is a great resort for swans during the winter, and whilst there they form collections of from 100 to 500 on the flats, near the western shores, and extend from the outlet of the Susquehanna River almost to the Rip Raps. The connecting streams also present fine feeding grounds.

They always select places where they can reach their food by the lengths of their necks, as they have never, so far as I can learn, been seen in this part of the world to dive under the water, either for food or safety.

Whistling swans are still abundant in winter on Bay Back, Virginia, and Currituck Sound, North Carolina, where, according to recent accounts, they are holding their own or even increasing in numbers. I have seen from 1,000 to 1,500 birds there in a day, as recently as 1916, standing in long white lines along the grassy shore of some marshy island, or feeding in large flocks, sometimes of two or three hundred birds, in the shallow waters of the bay, always conspicuous as striking features of these great wild-fowl resorts. Their chief companions here are the Canada geese, with whom they are intimately associated on their feeding grounds and on whom they depend largely, as sentinels to warn them of approaching danger, for the geese are even more watchful than the swans. But here, as well as on the lakes visited on their migration, they are also associated with the various ducks which resort to similar feeding grounds. They usually flock by themselves, however, when on the wing and do not mingle in the flocks of geese and ducks. They move about largely in family parties of 6 or 7 birds, but often gather together in large flocks to feed or to rest; large flocks are also often seen moving about, sometimes high in the air, calling to their fellows with loud mellow trumpetings in their search for quiet and safe feeding or resting places.

Nathan L. Davis (1895), writing of their winter habits on the coast of Texas, says:

I first saw them on Galveston Bay on January 1, and observed them every day until March 20, when there seemed to be but a very few left; all remaining on that date I think were crippled birds, being unable to stand the fatigue in their long journey to the north. It is a great sight to watch a flock of these birds assembled on the water, curling their long necks around each other, all making a strange honking noise, peculiar to themselves. This they continue for some time, then all turn with military precision and form in line; when they swim up and down the coast, proudly swaying their heads from side to side. In this manner they spend most of the bright days. They can be easily seen far out on the bay, their large white bodies glistening in the sun, as the restless waves toss their corklike forms above the level of the water. At first sight I could not distinguish whether the silvery spots rising on the waves were swans or the water breaking over some treacherous sandbar, which are common both in Galveston and San Jacinto Bays. Each day as the sun begins to go down they turn and slowly approach the shore, each keeping a sharp lookout ahead. If frightened any way they will either turn and swim quietly away or all take wing and survey the country for miles around before they will again settle on the water. Often small flocks may be seen in company with ducks, geese, pelicans, and gulls, but usually they will be found alone at some distance from all other birds, as well as human habitation. They are very hard to approach on a bright day, and hunting for them in clear weather is like fishing for trout in a thunderstorm. The dense fogs which prevail along the coast are no doubt the worst enemies these birds have, for then if the hunter is careful he can approach within easy range before they attempt to escape.

In stormy weather they are very restless and are continually flying from place to place as if hunting for a quiet spot, where they may rest in peace till the storm passes. In this continuous change of positions they often come too near the shore, and many are killed by the hunters who lay hidden, awaiting their approach. I once saw five of these large birds killed at a single discharge of a heavy double gun.

The tragic end of a belated cripple on a Montana lake is thus described in Mr. Cameron's notes:

In the fall of 1908, a member of a large flock of whistling swans, which settled upon Marshy Lake, was slightly wounded in the wing by a bullet (or, as is more probable, had a flight feather cut away by it) and could not leave with its frightened companions. Mr. Sullivan observed the swan about a dozen times when driving cattle to another Milner ranch near Shonkin, and when returning by the same route. He informed me that after the lake became frozen over, the swan, which was an adult in pure white plumage, by constantly swimming in a circle, kept open a small pond, about 25 feet wide. Until December 1 he regularly saw the swan upon this pond, which it was able to maintain open even when the ice was 3 inches thick upon the rest of the lake. The swan frequently dived, but was, of course, always obliged to come up in the same place on account of the ice; and Mr. Sullivan supposed that the poor bird eked out a scanty subsistence by means of the weeds or other food which it found at the bottom of the lake. The fate of this swan, though not absolutely known, can easily be surmised. Numerous coyotes, which crossed upon the ice, persistently menaced, and would have devoured the unfortunate bird but for its self-made asylum; hence, with the advent of colder weather, and consequent freezing up of the water, it would have undoubtedly become their prey. The above suggests a wintry scene which would be a fitting subject for an artists's brush; the famished prisoner swimming around the dark refuge pool, the scarcely less hungry jailers patrolling the ice edge and licking their expectant lips, the white world, and the onward creeping ice, grim with inexorable fate.

DISTRIBUTION

Breeding range.—Nearctic region, mainly north of the Arctic Circle. East to Baffin Land. South to Nottingham and Southampton Islands, the barren grounds of northern Canada, the Alaska Peninsula (Becharof Lake, Chulitna River and Morzhovia Bay), and St. Lawrence Island in Bering Sea. Northward in Alaska to the Arctic coast (Cape Prince of Wales and probably Point Barrow). North on the Arctic islands to about 74°, the North Georgia Islands, and Victoria Land (Cambridge Bay).

Winter range.—Mainly on the seacoasts of United States. On the Atlantic coast most abundantly from Maryland (Chesapeake Bay) to North Carolina (Currituck Sound); less commonly north to New Jersey; rarely north to Long Island (Shinnecock) and Massachusetts (Nantucket). Rarely south to Florida and the Gulf coasts of

Louisiana and Texas. On the Pacific coast from southern Alaska (Dall, Long, and Prince of Wales Islands) southward to southern California (San Diego). A few may winter irregularly in the interior as far north as large bodies of open water may be found.

Spring migration.—Toward the interior and generally northward. Early dates of arrival: Pennsylvania, Erie, March 11, and Williamsport, March 20; New York, Lockport, March 20; Ontario, Toronto, April 8; Michigan, Detroit, March 14; Wisconsin, Delavan, April 1; Minnesota, Heron Lake, March 31 and Elk River, April 8; Manitoba, Shoal Lake, April 30; northern Alberta, Athabasca Lake, May 17; Mackenzie, Fort Simpson, May 5, and Fort Anderson, May 18; Melville Island, May 31. Dates of arrival in Alaska: St. Michael, April 27; Kowak River, May 11; Point Hope, May 21. Late dates of departure: Maryland, Baltimore, May 4; Pennsylvania, Williamsport, May 30.

Fall migration.—Reversal of spring routes. Early dates of arrival: Mackenzie, Great Bear Lake, September 15, and Mackenzie River, October 6; Quebec, Cape St. Ignace, October 11; Maine, Crawford Lake, September 10; New Hampshire, Seabrook, October 18; Massachusetts, Nantucket, October 16; Rhode Island, Quonocontaug Pond, November 9; Maryland, Baltimore, September 26; Virginia, Alexandria, October 15; South Carolina, Cooper River, November 21; Alaska, Sitka, September 28; Washington, Thurston County, October 25; Montana, Teton County, October 31. Late dates of departure: Alaska, St. Michael, October 8, and St. George Island, October 17.

Casual records.—Accidental in Bermuda (1835 or 1836) and Commander Islands (Bering Island, November 3, 1882). Casual in Mexico (near Colonia Diaz, Chihuahua, January 18, 1904, and at Silao, Guanajuato).

Egg dates.—Arctic Canada: Thirteen records, May 29 to July 5; seven records, June 15 to July 1. Alaska: Ten records, May 17 to July 4; five records, June 4 to 12.

TRUMPETER SWAN

CYGNUS BUCCINATOR Richardson

HABITS

This magnificent bird, the largest of all the North American wild fowl, belongs to a vanishing race; though once common throughout all of the central and northern portions of the continent, it has been gradually receding before the advance of civilization and agriculture; when the great Central West was wild and uncultivated it was known to breed in the uninhabited parts of many of our Central States, even as far south as northern Missouri; but now it probably does not breed anywhere within the limits of the United States, except possibly in some of the wilder portions of Montana or Wyoming; civilization has pushed it farther and farther north until now it is making its last stand in the uninhabited wilds of northern Canada. E. H. Forbush (1912) has summed up the his-tory of its disappearance very well, as follows:

The trumpeter has succumbed to incessant persecution in all parts of its range, and its total extinction is now only a matter of years. Persecution drove it from the northern parts of its winter range to the shores of the Gulf of Mexico; from all the southern portion of its breeding range toward the shores of the Arctic Ocean; and from the Atlantic and Pacific slopes toward the interior. Now it almost has disappeared from the Gulf States. A swan seen at any time of the year in most parts of the United States is the signal for every man with a gun to pursue it. The breeding swans of the United States have been extirpated, and the bird is pursued, even in its farthest northern haunts, by the natives, who capture it in summer, when it has molted its primaries and is unable to fly. The swan lives to a great age. The older birds are about as tough and unfit for food as an old horse. Only the younger are savory, and the gunners might well have spared the adult birds, but it was "sport" to kill them and fashion called for swan's-down. The large size of this bird and its conspicuousness have served, as in the case of the whooping crane, to make it a shining mark, and the trumpetings that were once heard over the breadth of a great continent, as the long converging lines drove on from zone to zone, will soon be heard no more. In the ages to come, like the call of the whooping crane, they will be locked in the silence of the past.

The late E. S. Cameron prepared for me, in 1913 and 1914, some very elaborate notes on the history of this species in Montana, which Mrs. Cameron very kindly sent to me after her husband's death. They are interesting and valuable enough to print in full, but my space will permit only a few quotations and references. Regarding recent records he says:

The trumpeter swan, which 20 years ago was quite common in Montana, has now become exceedingly scarce, and is probably on the verge of extinction everywhere. My investigations during 1912–13 and 1914, show that trumpeters are almost unrepresented among the large numbers of migrant swans which biannually pass over Montana. It seems to be the melancholy fact that thou-sands of whistling swans are seen to one trumpeter, and at the time of writ-ing I have only two authenticated records of trumpeter swans for the three years above mentioned, the specimens from St. Marys Lake and Cut bank. Mr. J. H. Price informed me that an adult male trumpeter was shot by a boy on the Yellowstone, near Miles City, Custer County, on October 27, 1905, and I have since seen the mounted bird in a saloon keeper's window. At the time of writing the finest specimen of a trumpeter swan, within my knowledge, is the one killed by Mr. Robert Sloane, of Kalispell, when duck shooting on the shore of Flathead Lake. We left Kalispell before daylight on the morning of November 15, 1910, on our way to where the Flathead River debouches from the flat alluvial floor of the valley through a fair-sized delta into Flathead Lake. The morning was chilly, with occasional snow flurries, and we knew that the ducks would be on the move. Leaving the spring wagon behind the strip of brush which fringes the lake shore at this point, we built blinds, set our decoys, and were soon in the midst of a good flight of canvasbacks, redheads, and mallards. The sport was the best in my experience, as the birds, in passing from the lake to the sloughs or bayous inshore, offered fine shots. At this place there is a sandy beach a hundred yards in width, while here, and for some miles on either side, it is possible to wade into the lake for another 200 yards without becoming wet above the knees. About 3 o'clock in the afternoon a violent snow squall arose, and in the thick of it my attention was drawn to some white objects which were rising and falling on the waves about a mile offshore. At times these appeared like small sailing boats, but when they drew nearer I distinguished a flock of eight swans led by a splendid snow-white bird whose every movement was followed by the others. Two more of the swans were white and the remaining five dark colored. I left my blind and, running along a cattle trail through the brush to the wagon, took my 30–30 Winchester and returned to the edge of the beach. I then fired at the big leading swan, and struck it fairly in the neck at the first shot, although the bird was some 200 yards distant. Upon the death of their leader the rest of the flock momentarily bunched up in bewilderment, but, recovering their wits, made a great commotion in their efforts to rise from the water. Having once cleared the lake with their wings, however, they departed at great speed, while I waded through the shallows to retrieve my coveted trophy. The swan was found to weigh a full 31 pounds.

He describes at considerable length the capture of a trumpeter swan by a shepherd employed by G. B. Christian, of Augusta, Montana, in November, 1907. The man fired a rifle at a passing flock and brought down a bird, which he captured unhurt except for one broken pinion. The bird was kept for a year alive and then presented to the Great Falls Park; but, as it was not pinioned, it escaped after the next molt and was shot by a boy and all trace of it was lost. It was a pure white adult of very large size and was supposed to have weighed about 35 pounds.

In 1913 an Indian offered for sale at Kalispell an immense trumpeter swan from St. Marys Lake, Glacier National Park. It was poorly skinned, not properly poisoned, became infested with beetles, and was burned. Dr. Jonathan Dwight has the head and legs of this swan.

A female trumpeter swan, now in the collection of Dr. Jonathan Dwight, was shot by a saloon keeper, Ben Schannberg, at Cutbank, Teton County, Montana, in the first week of November, 1913. This was also an immature bird, supposed to have been about 18 months old, and was in a much emaciated condition, but it weighed 20 pounds.

Henry K. Coale (1915) has published an excellent paper on the present status of this swan, in which he mentions three of the above records, but he does not include them in the list of specimens to which he refers, as follows:

Of the great multitudes of trumpeter swans which traversed the central and western portion of north America 60 years ago, there are 16 specimens preserved in museums which have authentic data. These were collected between the years 1856 and 1909. There are besides the type, five other Canadian records, Toronto 1863, Fort Resolution 1860, Lake St. Clair 1878, St. Clair Flats 1884, and Manitoba 1887; and one from Wyoming 1856, Idaho 1873, Michigan 1875, Wisconsin 1880, Ohio 1880, Oregon 1881, North Dakota 1891, Minnesota 1893, Montana 1902, and Mexico 1909.

Nesting.—Prof. Wells W. Cooke (1906) says:

In early times it probably bred south to Indiana, Wisconsin, Iowa, Nebraska, Montana, and Idaho; it nested in Iowa as late as 1871, in Idaho in 1877, in Minnesota in 1886, and in North Dakota probably for a few years later. It is not probable that at the present time the trumpeter nests anywhere in the United States, and even in Alberta no nests seem to have been found later than 1891. The vast wilderness of but a generation ago is now crossed by railroads and thickly dotted with farms. The species is supposed still to breed in the interior of British Columbia at about latitude 53°.

Dr. R. M. Anderson (1907) writes:

The only definite record of the nesting of the trumpeter swan in Iowa which I have been able to trace was received from the veteran collector, J. W. Preston, in a letter dated March 22, 1904: "A pair of 'trumpeters' reared a brood of young in a slough near Little Twin Lakes, Hancock County, in the season of 1883, not many miles from where some good finds in the way of sets of whooping cranes were made. This was positively *Olor buccinator*. The nest was placed on a large tussock in a marshy slough or creek, and had been used for years by the swans, as I was credibly informed; but the nest mentioned above, so far as I am aware, was the last in that locality."

Roderick MacFarlane (1891) reported:

Several nests of this species were met with in the Barren Grounds, on islands in Franklin Bay, and one containing 6 eggs was situated near the beach on a sloping knoll. It was composed of a quantity of hay, down, and feathers intermixed, and this was the general mode of structure of the nests of both swans. It usually lays from 4 to 6 eggs, judging from the noted contents of a received total of 24 nests.

Mr. Cameron says that trumpeter swans formerly bred in western Montana, but his diligent investigations have failed to discover any recent nesting sites. " Some birds made great nests of tules, but many more built them on muskrat houses which they flattened out for the purpose." He describes a nest, found in 1871 on the Thompson River, on " a large deserted beaver lodge. On this mound, which measured at least 5 feet across, was a great pile of grass and feathers." The two eggs, which it contained, were concealed under a bunch of down. Of the latest two obtainable records he says:

A Kootenai Indian woman, while hunting with her husband and father-in-law, in the year 1889, saw a pair of swans with two cygnets on a small lake toward the headwaters of the South Fork of the Flathead River. Shortly after this she took two eggs from a swan's nest by the same lake, but can not give the exact year, although it was probably 1890.

The latest information I have comes in a letter from M. P. Skinner, of Yellowstone Park, and is very encouraging; he writes:

Early in the summer of 1919, I noted a swan in the vicinity of Heart Lake. A little later the nest was found on a low island in a lagoon northeast of Lewis Lake, containing five whitish eggs, the nest being made of leaves and grass. On August 14 I returned and then found the tail and flight feathers molted by the adults, but the birds were too far away and too wary to determine the species. On September 6, I again visited this section and found five trumpeter swan (the two parents and three young so nearly grown as to be able to fly well). While I did not feel justified in sacrificing one of these rare birds, there can be no mistake as to identification. I have been familiar since November of 1912 with both of our swans, the whistling swan occuring in comparatively large numbers from October 31 (earliest date ever noted by me) to May 3, the latest date. I saw the trumpeter swans several times, and once within an estimated distance of 50 yards under a pair of 12 X binoculars. Bill and lores of all the birds lacked the yellow spot; they were markedly superior in size to the whistling swans; and their cries were unmistakable. The breeding range of the smaller swan is given as "far northward and probably in British Columbia," whereas the trumpeter has been known to breed as far south as Iowa.

Mr. H. M. Smith, United States Fish Commissioner, reports that on July 16, 1919, he visited a small, unnamed lake lying south of Delusion Lake and found there a pair of swans with six cygnets about the size of teal swimming actively about. Mr. Smith could not identify these as *buccinator*, but in view of my own discovery I believe they were of this variety.

Eggs.—The trumpeter swan has been said to lay from 2 to 10 eggs in a set; the latter number must be very unusual and was probably the product of two birds; probably the usual set consists of from 4 to 6 eggs. Mr. Cameron says that the number of eggs varies from 2 to 8 according to the age of the birds and other circumstances, the smaller sets being laid by the younger birds; at least this is the general opinion among the Indians. The eggs are like those of the whistling swan, but larger. In shape they vary from elliptical ovate or elliptical oval to nearly elliptical. The shell is rough or granulated and more or less pitted. The color is creamy white or dull white, becoming much nest stained. The measurements of 25 eggs, in various collections, average 110 by 71.1 millimeters; the eggs showing the four extremes measure 119.5 by 76, 115 by 76.5, and 101 by 62.8 millimeters.

Young.—P. M. Silloway (1903) records the following incident which a friend of his witnessed in Montana:

A friend told me of seeing an old swan and a young one upon the "Highland" lakes. The two were in flight between the lakes, and the cygnet flew only a few feet directly above the elder, so that it could drop on the parent's back at frequent intervals. The younger swan would fly 50 or 60 yards alone, then drop lightly upon the parent's back to rest, being carried for 50 to 60 yards in this manner; then it would rise upon its own pinions and flap along above the elder bird until it again became weary of its own exertions.

Mr. Cameron sent me the following statement from Ed. Forbes a rancher of Kalispell:

I punched cows in the Centennial Valley in Beaverhead County from 1883 to 1888. During that time I saw quantities of swans, and killed many young birds which we thought good to eat. We used to paddle after them among the tules (bullrushes) and rope them, as they never seemed to learn to fly until ice formed around the shores, and were fearless, big, and awkward. Even then it took them a long, flapping flight to clear the water. The young birds would dive, and come up at a distance of 600 feet when chased with a boat.

Plumages.—I have never seen a downy young trumpeter swan and can find no description of it in print. We know very little of its molts and plumages. Audubon (1840) describes the first winter plumage as follows:

In winter the young has the bill black, with the middle portion of the ridge, to the length of an inch and a half, light flesh-color, and a large elongated patch of light dull purple on each side; the edge of the lower mandible and the tongue dull yellowish flesh-color. The eye is dark brown. The feet dull yellowish brown, tinged with olive; the claws brownish black; the webs blackish brown. The upper part of the head and the cheeks are light reddish brown, each feather having toward its extremity a small oblong whitish spot, narrowly margined with dusky; the throat nearly white, as well as the edge of the lower eyelid. The general color of the other parts is grayish white, slightly tinged with yellow; the upper part of the neck marked with spots similar to those on the head.

How long it takes for the young bird to reach maturity we do not know, but he speaks of two young birds, seen in captivity, that were about 2 years old and were pure white.

Food.—Audubon (1840) says of the feeding habits of the trumpeter swan:

This swan feeds principally by partially immersing the body and extending the neck under water, in the manner of fresh-water ducks and some species of geese, when the feet often seen working in the air, as if to aid in preserving the balance. Often, however, it resorts to the land, and then picks at the herbage, not sidewise, as geese do, but more in the manner of ducks and poultry. Its food consists of roots of different vegetables, leaves, seeds, various aquatic insects, land snails, small reptiles, and quadrupeds. The flesh of a cygnet is pretty good eating, but that of an old bird is dry and tough.

Behavior.—Referring to the behavior of this species, with which he seems to have been quite familiar, he writes:

The flight of the trumpeter swan is firm, at times greatly elevated and sustained. It passes through the air by regular beats, in the same manner as geese, the neck stretched to its full length, as are the feet, which project beyond the tail. When passing low, I have frequently thought that I heard a rustling sound from the motion of the feathers of their wings. If bound to a distant place, they form themselves in angular lines, and probably the leader of the flock is one of the oldest of the males; but of this I am not at all sure, as I have seen at the head of a line a gray bird, which must have been a young one of that year.

To form a perfect conception of the beauty and elegance of these swans, you must observe them when they are not aware of your proximity, and as they glide over the waters of some secluded inland pond. On such occasions, the neck, which at other times is held stiffly upright, moves in graceful curves, now bent forward, now inclined backward over the body. Now with an extended scooping movement the head becomes immersed for a moment, and with a sudden effort a flood of water is thrown over the back and wings, when it is seen rolling off in sparkling globules, like so many large pearls. The bird then shakes its wings, beats the water, and as if giddy with delight shoots away, gliding over and beneath the surface of the liquid element with surprising agility and grace. Imagine, reader, that a flock of 50 swans are thus sporting before you, as they have more than once been in my sight, and you will feel, as I have felt, more happy and void of care than I can describe.

When swimming unmolested the swan shows the body buoyed up; but when apprehensive of danger, it sinks considerably lower. If resting and basking in the sunshine, it draws one foot expanded curiously toward the back, and in that posture remains often for half an hour at a time. When making off swiftly, the tarsal joint, or knee as it is called, is seen about an inch above the water, which now in wavelets passes over the lower part of the neck and along the sides of the body, as it undulates on the planks of a vessel gliding with a gentle breeze. Unless during the courting season, or while passing by its mate, I never saw a swan with the wings raised and expanded, as it is alleged they do, to profit by the breeze that may blow to assist their progress; and yet I have pursued some in canoes to a considerable distance, and that without overtaking them, or even obliging them to take to wing. You, reader, as well as all the world, have seen swans laboring away on foot, and therefore I will not trouble you with a description of their mode of walking, especially as it is not much to be admired.

The notes of the trumpeter swan are described as loud, resonant trumpetings; differing in tone and volume from those of the whistling swan; the windpipe of the larger species has one more convolution, which enables it to produce a louder and more far-reaching note on a lower key, with the musical resonance of a French horn.

Winter.—For an account of its winter habits, we must again quote Audubon (1840) as follows:

The trumpeter swans make their appearance on the lower portions of the waters of the Ohio about the end of October. They throw themselves at once into the larger ponds or lakes at no great distance from the river, giving a marked preference to those which are closely surrounded by dense and tall canebrakes, and there remain until the water is closed by ice, when they are forced to proceed southward. During mild winters I have seen swans of this species in the ponds about Henderson until the beginning of March, but only a few individuals, which may have stayed there to recover from their wounds. When the cold became intense, most of those which visited the Ohio would remove to the Mississippi, and proceed down that stream as the severity of the weather increased, or return if it diminished; for it has appeared to me, that neither very intense cold nor great heat suit them so well as a medium temperature. I have traced the winter migrations of this species as far southward as Texas, where it is abundant at times.

Whilst encamped in the Tawapatee Bottom, when on a fur-trading voyage, our keel boat was hauled close under the eastern shore of the Mississippi, and our valuables, for I then had a partner in trade, were all disembarked. The great stream was itself so firmly frozen that we were daily in the habit of crossing it from shore to shore. No sooner did the gloom of night become discernible through the gray twilight than the loud-sounding notes of hundreds of trumpeters would burst on the ear; and as I gazed over the ice-bound river, flocks after flocks would be seen coming from afar and in various directions, and alighting about the middle of the stream opposite to our encampment. After pluming themselves awhile they would quietly drop their bodies on the ice, and through the dim light I yet could observe the graceful curve of their necks, as they gently turned them backward, to allow their heads to repose upon the softest and warmest of pillows. Just a dot of black as it were could be observed on the snowy mass, and that dot was about half an inch of the base of the upper mandible, thus exposed, as I think, to enable the bird to breathe with ease. Not a single individual could I ever observe among them to act as a sentinel, and I have since doubted whether their acute sense of hearing was not sufficient to enable them to detect the approach of their enemies. The day quite closed by darkness, no more could be seen until the next dawn; but as often as the howlings of the numerous wolves that prowled through the surrounding woods were heard, the clanging cries of the swans would fill the air. If the morning proved fair, the flocks would rise on their feet, trim their plumage, and as they started with wings extended, as if racing in rivalry, the pattering of their feet would come on the ear like the noise of great muffled drums, accompanied by the loud and clear sounds of their voice. On running 50 yards. or so to windward, they would all be on wing. If the weather was thick, drizzly, and cold, or if there were indications of a fall of snow, they would remain on the ice, walking, standing, or lying down, until symptoms of better weather became apparent, when they would all start off.

Mr. Hoyes Lloyd has recently written to me about a flock of wild trumpeter swans that have for several years been spending the winter in a lake in southern British Columbia under the protection of the Canadian National Parks Branch. So there is hope that the species may survive.

DISTRIBUTION

Breeding range.—Probably still breeds sparingly in the wilder portions of Wyoming (Yellowstone Park), western Montana, Alberta, British Columbia (Skeena River), and northwestern Canada. Has bred in the past east to James Bay (Norway House), Manitoba (Shoal Lake, 1893 and 1894), Minnesota (Heron Lake, 1883), and Indiana. South to Iowa (Hancock County, 1883), Nebraska, and Missouri west to British Columbia (Chilcoten) and Alaska (Fort Yukon).

Winter range.—Western United States. South to the Gulf of Mexico and southern California. North to west-central British

Columbia (Skeena River) and the central Mississippi Valley. Now too rare everywhere to outline its range more definitely.

Spring migration.—Average dates of arrival: Nebraska, March 16; South Dakota, April 2; Minnesota, Heron Lake, April 4; Saskatchewan, April 16; British Columbia, April 20. Late date of departure: Arkansas, Helena, April 29, 1891; British Columbia, Osoyoos, April 25.

Fall migration.—Fall dates: Minnesota, Spicer, October 8, 1913; Michigan, St. Clair Flats, November 20, 1875; Washington, Douglas County, November 9, 1912; Colorado, Fort Collins, November 18, 1897, and November 25, 1915.

Egg dates.—Arctic Canada: Five records, June 17 to July 9. Alaska: One record, June 28. Alberta: One record, April 7. Dakota: One record, June 4.

REFERENCES TO BIBLIOGRAPHY

ADAMS, EDWARD.
   1878—Notes of the Birds of Michalaski, Norton Sound. The Ibis, 1878,
      pp. 420–442.
ALFORD, CHARLES E.
   1920—Some Notes on Diving Ducks. British Birds, vol. 14, pp. 106–110.
   1921—Diving Ducks—Some Notes on their Habits and Courtship. British
      Birds, vol. 15, pp. 33–38.
ANDERSON, RUDOLPH MARTIN.
   1907—The Birds of Iowa. Proceedings of the Davenport Academy of
      Sciences, vol. 11, pp. 125–417.
ANNANDALE, NELSON.
   1905—The Faroes and Iceland.
AUDUBON, JOHN JAMES
   1840—The Birds of America. 1840–44.
BAILEY, FLORENCE MERRIAM.
   1916—A Populous Shore. The Condor, vol. 18, pp. 100–110.
   1919—A Return to the Dakota Lake Region. The Condor, vol. 21, pp. 3–11.
BAILEY, VERNON.
   1902—Notes in Handbook of Birds of the Western United States, by Flor-
      ence Merriam Bailey.
BAIRD, SPENCER FULLERTON; BREWER, THOMAS MAYO; and RIDGWAY, ROBERT.
   1884—The Water Birds of North America.
BARNHART, F.
   1901—Evolution in the Breeding Habits of the Fulvous Tree-Duck. The
      Condor, vol. 3, pp. 67–68.
BARNSTON, GEORGE.
   1862—The Swans and Geese of Hudson Bay. The Zoologist, 1862, p. 7831.
BARROWS, WALTER BRADFORD.
   1912—Michigan Bird Life.
BENDIRE, CHARLES EMIL.
   1875—Notes on seventy-nine species of Birds observed in the neighborhood
      of Camp Harney, Oregon. Proceedings of the Boston Society
      of Natural History, vol. 18, pp. 153–168.
BEYER, GEORGE EUGENE; ALLISON, ANDREW; KOPMAN, HENRY HAZLITT.
   1907—List of the Birds of Louisiana. The Auk, vol. 23, pp. 1–15 and 275–
      282; vol. 24, pp. 314–321; vol. 25, pp. 173–180 and 439–448.
BISHOP, LOUIS BENNETT.
   1921—Notes from Connecticut. The Auk, vol. 38, pp. 582–589.
BLAAUW, FRANS ERNST.
   1903—Notes on the Breeding of Ross's Snow-Goose in Captivity. The
      Ibis, 1903, pp. 245–247.
   1905—Letter in The Ibis, 1905, pp. 137, 138.
   1916—A Note on the Emperor Goose (*Philacte canagica*) and on the Aus-
      tralian Teal (*Nettion castaneum*). The Ibis, 1916, pp. 252–254.
BLANCHAN, NELTJE. (Mrs. F. N. DOUBLEDAY.)
   1898—Birds that Hunt and are Hunted.

BOWDISH, BEECHER SCOVILLE.
   1909—Ornithological Miscellany from Audubon Wardens. The Auk, vol.
      26, pp. 116–128.
BRETHERTON, BERNARD J.
   1896—Kadiak Island, A Contribution to the Avifauna of Alaska. The
      Oregon Naturalist, vol. 3, pp. 45–49; 61–64; 77–79; 100–102.
BREWER, THOMAS MAYO.
   1879—The Rocky Mountain Golden-eye (*Bucephala islandica*). Bulletin
      of the Nuttall Ornithological Club, vol. 4, pp. 148–152.
BREWSTER, WILLIAM.
   1900—Notes on the Breeding Habits of the American Golden-eyed Duck
      or Whistler. The Auk, vol. 17, pp. 207–216.
   1909—Snow Geese in Massachusetts. The Auk, vol. 26, pp. 188–189.
   1909a—Barrows Golden-eye in Massachusetts. The Auk, vol. 26, pp.
      153–164.
   1911—Courtship of the American Golden-eye or Whistler. The Condor,
      vol. 13, pp. 22–30.
BROOKS, ALLAN.
   1903—Notes on the Birds of the Cariboo District, British Columbia. The
      Auk, vol. 20, pp. 277–284.
   1920—Notes on some American Ducks. The Auk, vol. 37, pp. 353–367.
BROOKS, WINTHROP SPRAGUE.
   1912—An Additional Specimen of the Labrador Duck. The Auk, vol. 29,
      pp. 389–390.
   1915—Notes on Birds from East Siberia and Arctic Alaska. Bulletin of
      the Museum of Comparative Zoology at Harvard College.
BRYANT, EDWIN S.
   1899—The White-winged Scoter in North Dakota. The Osprey, vol. 3,
      pp. 132–133.
BRYANT, HAROLD CHILD.
   1914—A Survey of the Breeding Grounds of Ducks in California in 1914.
      The Condor, vol. 16, pp. 217–239.
BRYANT, WALTER (PIERCE) E.
   1890—An Ornithological Retrospect. Zoe, vol. 1, pp. 289–293.
BUTLER, AMOS WILLIAM.
   1897—The Birds of Indiana. Department of Geology and Natural Re-
      sources, Twenty-second Annual Report.
CAHOON, JOHN CYRUS.
   1889—A Quahaug Captures a Tern, and a Sea Clam Drowns a Scoter.
      Ornithologist and Oologist, vol. 14, p. 36.
CARTWRIGHT, GEORGE.
   1792—A Journal of Transactions and Events during a Residence of nearly
      Sixteen Years on the Coast of Labrador.
CHAPMAN, FRANK MICHLER.
   1899—Report of Birds Received through the Peary Expeditions to Green-
      land. Bulletin of the American Museum of Natural History,
      vol. 12, pp. 219–244.
CLARK, AUSTIN HOBART.
   1910—The Birds collected and observed during the Cruise of the United
      States Fisheries Steamer "Albatross" in the North Pacific Ocean,
      and in the Bering, Okhotsk, Japan, and Eastern Seas, from April
      to December, 1906. Proceedings of the U. S. Nat. Museum, vol.
      38, pp. 25–74.

COALE, HENRY KELSO.
    1915—The Present Status of the Trumpeter Swan (*Olor buccinator*).
        The Auk, vol. 32, pp. 82–90.
COLLINS, WILLIAM H.
    1881—Those "Brants"—Corrections. Ornithologist and Oologist, vol. 6,
        p. 55.
COOKE, WELLS WOODBRIDGE.
    1906—Distribution and Migration of North American Ducks, Geese, and
        Swans. U. S. Department of Agriculture, Biological Survey, Bul-
        letin No. 26.
COOPER, JAMES GRAHAM.
    1860—The Natural History of Washington Territory and Oregon, by Suck-
        ley and Cooper.
CORDEAUX, JOHN.
    1898—British Birds with their Nest and Eggs. Order Anseres, vol. 4,
        pp. 52–203.
COUES, ELLIOTT.
    1861—Notes on the Ornithology of Labrador. Proceedings of the Phila-
        delphia Academy of Natural Sciences, 1861, pp. 215–257.
    1874—Birds of the North-West.
    1897—Branta bernicla glaucogastra. The Auk, vol. 14, pp. 207–208.
CURRIER, EDMONDE SAMUEL.
    1902—Winter Water Fowl of the Des Moines Rapids. The Osprey, vol. 6,
        pp. 71–75.
DAVIS, NATHAN L.
    1895—Notes on Whistling Swan *Olor columbianus*. The Museum, vol. 1
        pp. 114–116.
DAWSON, WILLIAM LEON.
    1909—The Birds of Washington.
DEKAY, JAMES ELLSWORTH.
    1844—Zoology of New York, Part 2, Birds.
DICE, LEE RAYMOND.
    1920—Notes on some Birds of Interior Alaska. The Condor, vol. 22,
        pp. 176–185.
DIONNE, CHARLES EUSEBE.
    1906—Les Oiseaux de la Province de Quebec.
DIXON, JOSEPH.
    1908—Field Notes from Alaska. The Condor, vol. 10, pp. 139–143.
DUTCHER, WILLIAM.
    1888—Bird Notes from Long Island, N. Y. The Auk, vol. 5, pp. 169–183.
    1891—The Labrador Duck—A Revised List of the Extant Specimens in
        North America, with some Historical Notes. The Auk, vol. 8,
        pp. 201–216.
    1893—Notes on some Rare Birds in the Collection of the Long Island
        Historical Society. The Auk, vol. 10, pp. 267–277.
    1894—The Labrador Duck—Another Specimen, with Additional Data
        Respecting Extant Specimens. The Auk, vol. 11, pp. 4–12.
DWIGHT, JONATHAN.
    1914—The Moults and Plumages of the Scoters—Genus Oidemia. The
        Auk, vol. 31, pp. 293–308.
EATON, ELON HOWARD.
    1910—Birds of New York.

EIFRIG, CHARLES WILLIAM GUSTAVE.
    1905—Ornithological Results of the Canadian "Neptune" Expedition to
        Hudson Bay and Northward. The Auk, vol. 22, pp. 233–241.
ELLIOT, DANIEL GIRAUD.
    1898—The Wild Fowl of North America.
ENGLISH, T. M. SAVAGE.
    1916—Notes on some of the Birds of Grand Cayman, West Indies. The
        Ibis, 1916, pp. 17–35.
FANNIN, JOHN.
    1894—The Canada Goose and Osprey laying in the same Nest. The Auk,
        vol. 11, p. 322.
FIGGINS, JESSE DADE.
    1902—Some Food Birds of the Eskimos of Northwestern Greenland. Ab-
        stract of the Proceedings of the Linnaean Society of New York
        for the year ending March 11, 1902, pp. 61–65.
    1920—The Status of the Subspecific Races of *Branta canadensis*. The
        Auk, vol. 37, pp. 94–102.
    1922—Additional Notes on the Status of the Subspecific Races of *Branta
        canadensis*. Proceedings of the Colorado Museum of Natural
        History, vol. 4, No. 3.
FLEMING, JAMES HENRY.
    1908—The Destruction of Whistling Swans (*Olor columbianus*) at Niagara
        Falls. The Auk, vol. 25, pp. 306–309.
    1912—The Niagara Swan Trap. The Auk, vol. 29, pp. 445–448.
FORBUSH, EDWARD HOWE.
    1912—A History of the Game Birds, Wild-Fowl and Shore Birds of Massa-
        chusetts and Adjacent States.
FORSTER, JOHANN REINHOLD.
    1772—An Account of the Birds sent from Hudson's Bay; with Observa-
        tions relative to their Natural History; and Latin Descriptions
        of some of the most uncommon. Philosophical Transactions,
        vol. 62, p. 382.
GÄTKE, HEINRICH.
    1895—Heligoland as an Ornithological Observatory.
GIBSON, LANGDON.
    1922—Bird Notes from North Greenland. The Auk, vol. 39, pp. 350–362.
GORDON, AUDREY.
    1922—Nesting of the Whooper Swan in Scotland. British Birds, vol. 15,
        p. 170.
GORDON, SETON PAUL.
    1920—Periods of Dives made by Long-tailed Ducks. British Birds, vol.
        13, pp. 244–245.
GREELY, ADOLPHUS WASHINGTON.
    1888—Report on the Proceedings of the United States Expedition to
        Lady Franklin Bay, Grinnell Land.
GREGG, WILLIAM HENRY.
    1879—The American Naturalist, vol. 13, p. 128.
GRINNELL, GEORGE BIRD.
    1901—American Duck Shooting.
GRINNELL, JOSEPH.
    1909—Birds and Mammals of the 1907 Alexander Expedition to South-
        eastern Alaska. University of California, Publications in Zo-
        ology, vol. 5, pp. 171–264.
    1910—Birds of the 1908 Alexander Alaska Expedition. University of Cali-
        fornia Publications in Zoology, vol. 5, pp. 261–428.

GRINNELL, JOSEPH; BRYANT, HAROLD CHILD; and STORER, TRACY IRWIN.
1918—The Game Birds of California.

GURNEY, JOHN HENRY.
1897—Labrador Duck. The Auk, vol. 14, p. 87.

HAGERUP, ANDREAS THOMSEN.
1891—The Birds of Greenland.

HALKETT, ANDREW.
1905—A Naturalist in the Frozen North. The Ottawa Naturalist, vol. 19, pp. 104–109.

HANNA, G. DALLAS.
1916—Records of Birds New to the Pribilof Islands Including two New to North America. The Auk, vol. 33, pp. 400–403.

HAYES, ISAAC ISRAEL.
1867—The Open Polar Sea.

HAYNES, WILLIAM B.
1901—The Oldsquaw Duck. The Wilson Bulletin, No. 32, pp. 12–13.

HOLLAND, ARTHUR H.
1892—Short Notes on the Birds of Estancia Espartilla, Argentine Republic. The Ibis, 1892, pp. 193–214.

HOWLEY, JAMES P.
1884—The Canada Goose (*Bernicla canadensis*). The Auk, vol. 1, pp. 309–313.

HUBBARD, SAMUEL, Jr.
1893—A Tragedy in Bird Life. Zoe, vol. 3, pp. 361–362.

HUDSON, WILLIAM HENRY.
1920—Birds of La Plata.

HULL, EDWIN D.
1914—Habits of the Oldsquaw (*Harelda hyemalis*) in Jackson Park, Chicago. The Wilson Bulletin, No. 88, pp. 116–123.

JOURDAIN, FRANCIS CHARLES. ROBERT.
1922—The Breeding Habits of the Barnacle Goose. The Auk, vol. 9, pp. 166–171.

KING, WILLIAM ROSS.
1866—The Sportsman and Naturalist in Canada.

KNIGHT, ORA WILLIS.
1908—The Birds of Maine.

KUMLIEN, LUDWIG.
1879—Contributions to the Natural History of Arctic America. Bulletin of the United States National Museum, No. 15.

KUMLIEN, LUDWIG, and HOLLISTER, NED.
1903—The Birds of Wisconsin. Bulletin of the Wisconsin Natural History Society, vol. 3, new series, Nos. 1, 2, and 3.

LANGILLE, JAMES HIBBERT.
1884—Our Birds and Their Haunts.

LAWRENCE, GEORGE NEWBOLD.
1846—Description of a New Species of Anser. Annals of the Lyceum of Natural History, New York, vol. 4, pp. 171–172.
1874—Birds of Western and Northwestern Mexico. Memoirs of the Boston Society of Natural History, vol. 2, pp. 265–319.

LEWIS, ELISHA JARRETT.
1885—The American Sportsman.

LEWIS, HARRISON F.
1921—The Greater Snow Goose. The Canadian Naturalist, vol. 25, p. 35.
1922—Notes on some Labrador Birds. The Auk, vol. 39, pp. 507–516.

MACARTNEY, WILLIAM NAPIER.
1918—Golden-eye Duck carrying Young. Bird-Lore, vol. 20, pp. 418–419.
MACFARLANE, RODERICK ROSS.
1891—Notes on and List of Birds and Eggs Collected in Arctic America, 1861–1866. Proceedings of the United States National Museum, vol. 14, pp. 413–446.
MACKAY, GEORGE HENRY.
1890—*Somateria dresseri*, The American Eider. The Auk, vol. 7, pp. 315–319.
1891—The Scoters in New England. The Auk, vol. 8, pp. 279–290.
1892—Habits of the Oldsquaw (*Clangula hyemalis*) in New England. The Auk, vol. 9, pp. 330–337.
1893—Stray Notes from the vicinity of Muskeget Island, Massachusetts. The Auk, vol. 10, pp. 370–371.
MACMILLAN, DONALD BAXTER.
1918—Four Years in the White North.
MACOUN, JOHN.
1909—Catalogue of Canadian Birds. Second Edition.
MANNICHE, A. L. V.
1910—The Terrestrial Mammals and Birds of North-East Greenland. Medelelser om Gronland, vol. 45.
McATEE, WALDO LEE.
1910—Notes on Chen coerulescens, Chen rossi, and other Waterfowl in Louisiana. The Auk, vol. 27, pp. 337–339.
1911—Winter Ranges of Geese on the Gulf Coast; Notable Bird Records for the same Region. The Auk, vol. 28, pp. 272–274.
MERRIAM, CLINTON HART.
1883—Breeding of the Harlequin Duck. Bulletin of the Nuttall Ornithological Club, vol. 8, p. 220.
MERRILL, JAMES CUSHING.
1878—Notes on the Ornithology of southern Texas, being a List of Birds observed in the Vicinity of Fort Brown, Texas, from February, 1876, to June, 1878. Proceedings of the United States National Museum, vol. 1, pp. 118–173.
1888—Notes on the Birds of Fort Klamath, Oregon. The Auk, vol. 5, pp. 139–146.
MICHAEL, CHARLES W., and ENID.
1922—An Adventure with a Pair of Harlequin Ducks in the Yosemite Valley. The Auk, vol. 39, pp. 14–23.
MILLAIS, JOHN GUILLE.
1913—British Diving Ducks.
MILLER, GERRIT SMITH, Jr.
1891—Further Cape Cod Notes. The Auk, vol. 8, pp. 117–120.
MORRIS, FRANCIS ORPEN.
1903—A History of British Birds. Fifth Edition.
MORTON, THOMAS.
1637—New English Canaan.
MUNRO, JAMES ALEXANDER.
1918—The Barrow Golden-eye in the Okanagan Valley, British Columbia. The Condor, vol. 20, pp. 3–5.
MURDOCH, JOHN.
1885—Report of the International Polar Expedition to Point Barrow, Alaska. Part 4, Natural History.

NELSON, EDWARD WILLIAM.
    1881—Habits of the Black Brant in the Vicinity of St. Michaels, Alaska.
        Bulletin of the Nuttall Ornithological Club, vol. 6, pp. 131–138.
    1883—The Birds of Bering Sea and the Arctic Ocean. Cruise of the
        Revenue-Steamer Corwin in Alaska and the N. W. Arctic Ocean
        in 1881.
    1887—Report upon Natural History Collections made in Alaska.
    1913—The Emperor Goose. Educational Leaflet, No. 64. Bird-Lore, vol.
        15, pp. 129–132.
NEWTON, ALFRED.
    1896—A Dictionary of Birds.
NORTON, ARTHUR HERBERT.
    1897—A Noteworthy Plumage observed in the American Eider Drake. The
        Auk, vol. 14, pp. 303–304.
    1909—The Food of Several Maine Water Birds. The Auk, vol. 26, pp.
        438–440.
NUTTALL, THOMAS.
    1834—A Manual of the Ornithology of the United States and Canada,
        Water Birds.
PALMER, WILLIAM.
    1899—The Avifauna of the Pribilof Islands. The Fur-Seals and Fur-Seal
        Islands of the North Pacific Ocean, Part 3, p. 355.
PEARSON, THOMAS GILBERT; BRIMLEY, CLEMENT SAMUEL; and BRIMLEY, HER-
BERT HUTCHINSON.
    1919—Birds of North Carolina. North Carolina Geological and Economic
        Survey, vol. 4.
PHILLIPS, JOHN CHARLES.
    1910—Notes on the Autumn Migration of the Canada Goose in Eastern
        Massachusetts. The Auk, vol. 27, pp. 263–271.
    1911—Ten years of Observation on the Migration of Anatidae at Wenham
        Lake, Massachusetts. The Auk, vol. 28, pp. 188–200.
    1911a—Two Unusual Flights of Canada Geese Noted in Massachusetts
        during the Fall of 1910. The Auk, vol. 28, pp. 319–323.
PREBLE, EDWARD ALEXANDER.
    1908—A Biological Investigation of the Athabaska-Mackenzie Region.
        North American Fauna, No. 27.
PRESTON, JUNIUS WALLACE.
    1892—Notes on Bird Flight. Ornithologist and Oologist, vol. 17, pp. 41–42.
RAY, MILTON SMITH.
    1912—Nesting of the Canada Goose at Lake Tahoe. The Condor, vol. 14,
        pp. 67–72.
REEKS, HENRY.
    1870—Notes on the Birds of Newfoundland. The Canadian Naturalist,
        vol. 5, pp. 38–47, 151–159, 289–304, and 406–416.
RHOADS, SAMUEL NICHOLSON.
    1895—Contributions to the Zoology of Tennessee, No. 2, Birds. Proceed-
        ings of the Academy of Natural Sciences of Philadelphia, 1895,
        pp. 463–501.
RICH, WALTER HERBERT.
    1907—Feathered Game of the Northeast.
ROCKWELL, ROBERT BLANCHARD.
    1911—Nesting Notes on the Ducks of the Barr Lake Region, Colorado. The
        Condor, vol. 13, pp. 121–128 and 186–195.

SANFORD, LEONARD CUTLER; BISHOP, LOUIS BENNETT; and VAN DYKE, THEODORE STRONG.
    1903—The Waterfowl Family.
SAUNDERS, WILLIAM ERWIN.
    1917—Wild Geese at Moose Factory. The Auk, vol. 34, pp. 334–335.
SCOTT, WILLIAM EARL DODGE.
    1891—Observations on the Birds of Jamaica, West Indies. The Auk, vol.
        8, pp. 249–256 and 353–365
SEEBOHM, HENRY.
    1901—The Birds of Siberia.
SENNETT, GEORGE BURRITT.
    1878—Notes on the Ornithology of the Lower Rio Grande of Texas.
        Bulletin of the United States Geological and Geographical
        Survey, vol. 4, pp. 1–66.
    1879—Further Notes on the Ornithology of the Lower Rio Grande of
        Texas. Bulletin of the United States Geological and Geographical Survey, vol. 5, pp. 371–440.
    1880—An unusual Flight of Whistling Swans in Northwestern Pennsylvania. Bulletin of the Nuttall Ornithological Club, vol. 5, pp. 125–126.
SHIELDS, ALEXANDER MCMILLAN.
    1899—Nesting of the Fulvous Tree Duck. Bulletin of the Cooper Ornithological Club, vol. 1, pp. 9–11.
SILLOWAY, PERLEY MILTON.
    1903—Birds of Fergus County, Montana. Bulletin No. 1, Fergus County Free High School.
STANSELL, SIDNEY SMITH STOUT.
    1909—Birds of Central Alberta. The Auk, vol. 26, pp. 390–400.
STEARNS, WINFRED ALDEN.
    1883—Notes on the Natural History of Labrador. Proceedings of the United States National Museum, vol. 6, pp. 111–137.
STONE, WITMER.
    1895—List of Birds Collected in North Greenland by the Peary Expedition of 1891–2 and the Relief Expedition of 1892. Proceedings of the Academy of Natural Sciences of Philadelphia, 1895, pp. 502–505.
SWAINSON, WILLIAM; and RICHARDSON, JOHN.
    1831—Fauna Boreali-Americana, vol. 2, Birds.
SWARTH, HARRY SCHELWALDT.
    1913—A Study of a Collection of Geese of the *Branta canadensis* Group from the San Joaquin Valley, California. University of California Publications in Zoology, vol. 12, pp. 1–21.
    1922—Birds and Mammals of the Stikine River Region of Northern British Columbia and Southeastern Alaska. University of California Publications in Zoology, vol. 24, pp. 125–314.
SWARTH, HARRY SCHELWALDT; and BRYANT, HAROLD CHILD.
    1917—A Study of the Races of the White-fronted Goose (*Anser albifrons*), occurring in California. University of California Publications in Zoology, vol. 17, pp. 209–222.
TAVERNER, PERCY ALGERNON.
    1922—Adventures with the Canada Goose. The Canadian Field Naturalist, vol. 36, pp. 81–83.

THAYER, JOHN ELIOT.
1905—Brant's Nest. The Auk, vol. 22, p. 408.
THAYER, JOHN ELIOT and BANGS, OUTRAM.
1914—Notes on the Birds and Mammals of the Arctic Coast of East Siberia—Birds. Proceedings of the New England Zoological Club, vol. 5, pp. 1–66.
TOWNSEND, CHARLES WENDELL.
1905—The Birds of Essex County, Massachusetts. Memoirs of the Nuttall Ornithological Club. No. 3.
1910—The Courtship of the Golden-eye and Eider Ducks. The Auk, vol. 27, pp. 177–181.
1913—Some More Labrador Notes. The Auk, vol. 30, pp. 1–10.
1914—A plea for the Conservation of the Eider. The Auk, vol. 31, pp. 14–21.
1916—The Courtship of the Merganser, Mallard, Black Duck, Baldpate, Wood Duck, and Bufflehead. The Auk, vol. 33, pp. 9–17.
1916a—Notes on the Eider. The Auk, vol. 33, pp. 286–292.
TRUMBULL, GURDON.
1892—Our Scoters. The Auk, vol. 9, pp. 153–160.
1893—Our Scoters. The Auk, vol. 10, pp. 165–176.
TURNER, LUCIEN McSHAN.
1886—Contributions to the Natural History of Alaska.
WETMORE, ALEXANDER.
1920. Observations on the Habits of Birds at Lake Burford, New Mexico. The Auk, vol. 37, pp. 221–247 and 393–412.
WHITFIELD, ROBERT PARR.
1894—The Food of Wild Ducks. The Auk, vol. 11, p. 323.
WILLIAMS, ROBERT STATHAM.
1886—A Flock of Chen rossii East of the Rocky Mountains. The Auk, vol. 3, p. 274.
WITHERBY, HARRY FORBES.
1913—Barrow's Goldeneye and the Common Goldeneye. British Birds, vol. 6, pp. 272–276.
WITHERBY, HARRY FORBES, and OTHERS.
1920–22.—A Practical Handbook of British Birds.
YARRELL, WILLIAM.
1871—History of British Birds, Fourth Edition, 1871–85. Revised and enlarged by Alfred Newton and Howard Saunders.
YORKE, F. HENRY.
1891—Shooting Canada Geese and Swans. Days with the Waterfowl of America. No. 25. The American Field, vol. 35, No. 26, pp. 641–643.
1899—Our Ducks.

INDEX

Page

Adams, Edward, on American scoter_____ 120
albeola, Charitonetta_____ 24
albifrons, Anser albifrons_____ 188
albifrons, Anser gambelli_____ 196
Alford, Charles E.—
    on American goldeneye_____ 2
    on surf scoter_____ 144
American eider_____ 94
American goldeneye_____ 1
American scoter_____ 119
americana, Glaucionetta clangula_____ 1
americana, Oidemia_____ 119
Anderson, R. M.—
    on brant_____ 238
    on trumpeter swan_____ 296
Annandale, Nelson, on American eider_____ 95
Anser albifrons albifrons_____ 188
Anser albifrons gambelli_____ 196
Anser brachyrhynchus_____ 200
Anser fabalis_____ 198
Arctonetta fischeri_____ 74
Atlantic harlequin duck_____ 50
Audubon, J. J.—
    on American scoter_____ 120, 122
    on Atlantic harlequin duck_____ 51, 52
    on bufflehead_____ 28
    on Canada goose_____ 205, 209, 214, 215, 217
    on greater snow goose_____ 177
    on Labrador duck_____ 63, 64, 65
    on oldsquaw_____ 36
    on ruddy duck_____ 158, 159
    on surf scoter_____ 146
    on trumpeter swan_____ 298, 299
    on white-fronted goose_____ 192
autumnalis, Dendrocygna_____ 269
Bailey, Alfred M.—
    on brant_____ 238
    on Steller eider_____ 68
    on whistling swan_____ 283, 284
Bailey, Florence Merriam—
    on ruddy duck_____ 153
    on surf scoter_____ 149
Bailey, Vernon, on snow goose_____ 167
Baird, Brewer, and Ridgway—
    on black-bellied tree duck_____ 270
    on masked duck_____ 162
barnacle goose_____ 258
Barnes, R. M., on blue goose_____ 180
Barnhart, F. S., on fulvous tree duck_____ 275
Barnston, George—
    on blue goose_____ 180
    on snow goose_____ 168
Barrow goldeneye_____ 14
Barrows, W. B., on oldsquaw_____ 44
bean goose_____ 198
bernicla, Branta bernicla_____ 237
bernicla, Branta nigricans_____ 249
bicolor, Dendrocygna_____ 272
Bingaman, W. H., on bufflehead_____ 26
Bishop, Louis B., on brant_____ 239

Page

Blaauw, Frans Ernst—
    on emperor goose_____ 265
    on Ross.goose_____ 186, 187
    black-bellied tree duck_____ 269
    black brant_____ 249
Blanchan, Neltje—
    on bufflehead_____ 28
    on white-fronted goose_____ 192
blue goose_____ 178
borealis, Somateria mollissima_____ 79
brachyrhynchus, Anser_____ 200
Brandt, Herbert W., on snow goose_____ 171
brant_____ 237
brant, black_____ 249
Branta bernicla bernicla_____ 237
Branta bernicla nigricans_____ 249
Branta canadensis canadensis_____ 204
Branta canadensis hutchinsi_____ 223
Branta canadensis minima_____ 231
Branta canadensis occidentalis_____ 227
Branta leucopsis_____ 258
Bretherton, B. J., on Pacific harlequin duck_ 58, 61
Brewer, T. M., on Barrow goldeneye_____ 15
Brewster, William, on American goldeneye__ 2
Brooks, Allan—
    on American scoter_____ 125
    on Barrow goldeneye_____ 16
    on bufflehead_____ 26
    on ruddy duck_____ 155
Brooks, W. Sprague, on king eider_____ 109
Brown, D. E., on Pacific harlequin duck____ 60
Bryant, Edwin S., on white-winged scoter___ 136
Bryant, Harold C., on fulvous tree duck____ 274
Bryant, Walter E., on snow goose_____ 170
buccinator, Cygnus_____ 293
bufflehead_____ 24
Burrows, D. B., on fulvous tree duck_____ 275
cackling goose_____ 231
caerulescens, Chen_____ 178
Cameron, E. S.—
    on trumpeter swan_____ 294, 298
    on whistling swan_____ 282, 286, 287, 288, 292
Camptorhynchus labradorius_____ 62
Canada goose_____ 204
canadensis, Branta canadensis_____ 204
canadensis, Branta hutchinsi_____ 223
canadensis, Branta minima_____ 231
canadensis, Branta occidentalis_____ 227
Cartwright, George, on American eider_____ 100, 101
Charitonetta albeola_____ 24
Chen caerulescens_____ 178
Chen hyperborea hyperborea_____ 164
Chen hyperborea nivalis_____ 173
clangula, Glaucionetta americana_____ 1
Clangula hyemalis_____ 32
Clark, Austin H., on cackling goose_____ 232
Coale, Henry K., on trumpeter swan_____ 295
columbianus, Cygnus_____ 281
Conover, H. B.—
    on fulvous tree duck_____ 277
    on masked duck_____ 163

Page

Cooke, W. W.—
  on black-bellied tree duck............. 272
  on trumpeter swan.................... 296
Cooper, J. G., on bufflehead................ 29
Cordeaux, John—
  on barnacle goose................. 258, 261
  on bean goose...................... 199
  on brant.......................... 245
  on pink-footed goose............. 202, 203
  on whooping swan............. 278, 279, 280
Coues, Elliott—
  on Barrow goldeneye............... 14
  on Hutchins goose................. 225
  on Labrador duck.................. 63
  on snow goose.................. 167, 169
  on white-fronted goose............ 194
Currier, E. S., on American goldeneye....... 11
Cygnus buccinator...................... 293
Cygnus columbianus..................... 281
Cygnus cygnus.......................... 278
cygnus, Cygnus......................... 278
Davis, Nathan L., on whistling swan....... 291
Dawson, W. Leon—
  on American goldeneye.............. 8
  on black brant................. 255, 256
  on bufflehead..................... 30
  on snow goose..................... 167
  on surf scoter.................... 144
deglandi, Melanitta.................... 131
DeKay, James E., on Labrador duck........ 65
Dendrocygna autumnalis................. 269
Dendrocygna bicolor.................... 272
Dice, L. R., on bufflehead.............. 30
Dixon, Joseph, on white-cheeked goose...... 228
dominicus, Nomonyx..................... 161
dresseri, Somateria mollissima........... 94
duck, Atlantic harlequin............... 50
  black-bellied tree............... 269
  fulvous tree...................... 272
  Labrador.......................... 62
  masked............................ 161
  Pacific harlequin................. 58
  ruddy............................. 152
Dutcher, William, on Labrador duck....... 63, 64
Dwight, Jonathan, on American scoter...... 123
Eaton, E. H., on oldsquaw............... 44
Edson, J. M., on white-winged scoter........ 137
eider, American........................ 94
  king.............................. 107
  Northern.......................... 79
  Pacific........................... 102
  spectacled........................ 74
  Steller........................... 67
Eifrig, C. W. G., on whistling swan.......... 284
Ekblaw, W. Elmer—
  on brant....................... 242, 243
  on greater snow goose.......... 175, 176
  on king eider.................. 108, 110
  on northern eider............ 79, 82, 84, 93
  on oldsquaw.......... 34, 36, 38, 40, 46
Elliot, D. G.—
  on Barrow goldeneye............... 20
  on brant.......................... 245
  on bufflehead..................... 30
  on greater snow goose.......... 176, 177
  on Pacific harlequin duck......... 59

Page

Elliot, D. G.—Continued.
  on snow goose..................... 167
  on whistling swan........... 281, 285, 288
emperor goose.......................... 263
English, T. M. Savage, on masked duck...... 162
Erismatura jamaicensis................. 152
European goldeneye..................... 12
Exanthemops rossii..................... 185
fabalis, Anser......................... 198
Fannin, John, on Canada goose.......... 208
Figgins, J. D., on northern eider........... 82, 91
fischeri, Arctonetta................... 74
Forbush, E. H.—
  on American scoter................ 124
  on brant....................... 239, 246
  on trumpeter swan................. 294
Forster, J. R., on snow goose.......... 168
fulvous tree duck...................... 272
fusca, Melanitta....................... 128
gambelli, Anser albifrons............. 196
Gätke, Heinrich—
  on brant.......................... 244
  on velvet scoter.................. 130
Gibson, Langdon, on greater snow goose...... 175
Gilbert, R. A., on American goldeneye....... 5
Glaucionetta clangula americana........... 1
Glaucionetta islandica................. 14
goldeneye, American.................... 1
  Barrow............................ 14
  European.......................... 12
goose, barnacle........................ 258
  bean.............................. 198
  blue.............................. 178
  cackling.......................... 231
  Canada............................ 204
  emperor........................... 263
  greater snow...................... 173
  Hutchins.......................... 223
  pink-footed....................... 200
  Ross.............................. 185
  snow.............................. 164
  tule.............................. 196
  white-cheeked..................... 227
  white-fronted..................... 188
Gordon, Mrs. Audrey, on whooping swan.... 279
Gordon, Seton, on oldsquaw............. 45
Gray, Robert, on barnacle goose........... 258
Grayson, A. J.—
  on black-bellied tree duck........ 270, 271
  on fulvous tree duck........... 273, 277
greater snow goose..................... 173
Griffith, Owen, on blue goose.......... 179
Grinnell, Bryant, and Storer—
  on black brant.................... 256
  on cackling goose................. 234
  on emperor goose.............. 266, 268
  on fulvous tree duck........... 272, 276
  on Hutchins goose................. 225
  on snow goose..................... 170
Grinnell, George Bird, on snow goose......... 169
Grinnell, Joseph—
  on white-cheeked goose......... 228, 229
  on white-winged scoter............ 141
Hagerup, Andreas T.—
  on northern eider................. 93
  on whooping swan.................. 278

Page

Halkett, Andrew, on northern eider_____ 89
Hanna, G. Dallas, on European goldeneye__ 12
harlequin duck, Atlantic_____ 50
harlequin duck, Pacific_____ 58
Harlow, Richard C., on brant_____ 239
Hayes, I. I., on northern eider_____ 90
Haynes, William B., on oldsquaw_____ 43
Henderson, A. D.—
   on Canada goose_____ 208, 212
   on white-winged scoter_____ 136
Hersey, F. S.—
   on blue goose_____ 182, 183
   on king eider_____ 114, 116
   on oldsquaw_____ 35, 39
   on Pacific eider_____ 104, 105, 106
   on Steller eider_____ 68
   on white-fronted goose_____ 191
Histrionicus histrionicus histrionicus_____ 50
histrionicus, Histrionicus histrionicus_____ 50
Histrionicus histrionicus pacificus_____ 58
histrionicus, Histrionicus pacificus_____ 58
Hoare, A. R., on black brant_____ 255
Holland, A. H., on masked duck_____ 162
Howley, James P., on Canada goose_____ 211
Hoxie, Walter J., on Labrador duck_____ 65
Hubbard, Samuel Jr., on bufflehead_____ 29
Hudson, W. H., on fulvous tree duck_____ 273
Hull, Edwin D., on oldsquaw_____ 43
Hutchins goose_____ 223
hutchinsi, Branta canadensis_____ 223
hyemalis, Clangula_____ 32
hyperborea, Chen hyperborea_____ 164
hyperborea, Chen nivalis_____ 173
islandica, Glaucionetta_____ 14
jamaicensis, Erismatura_____ 152
Jourdain, F. C. R.—
   on barnacle goose_____ 260, 261, 262
   on bean goose_____ 199
   on brant_____ 237, 241, 243
   on king eider_____ 110
   on pink-footed goose_____ 201
king eider_____ 107
King, W. Ross, on Labrador duck_____ 64
Knight, Ora W.—
   on bufflehead_____ 28
   on Canada goose_____ 216
Kumlien and Hollister, on Canada goose____ 220
Kumlien, Ludwig, on northern eider_____ 79, 84, 88
Labrador duck_____ 62
labradorius, Camptorhynchus_____ 62
Langille, J. H.—
   on oldsquaw_____ 45
   on ruddy duck_____ 154, 159
Lawrence, George N.—
   on black brant_____ 249
   on Labrador duck_____ 65
leucopsis, Branta_____ 258
Lewis, Elisha J., on greater snow goose_____ 177
Lewis, Harrison F.—
   on American eider_____ 98
   on brant_____ 240
   on greater snow goose_____ 174
Littlejohn, Chase—
   on black brant_____ 249
   on Steller eider_____ 72
Macartney, W. N., on American goldeneye__ 6

MacFarlane, R.—
   on black brant_____ 252
   on Hutchins goose_____ 224
   on Pacific eider_____ 105
   on Ross goose_____ 185
   on snow goose_____ 165
   on surf scoter_____ 145
   on trumpeter swan_____ 296
   on white-fronted goose_____ 190, 193
   on white-winged scoter_____ 145
Mackay, George H.—
   on American scoter_____ 123, 124
   on brant_____ 244
   on oldsquaw_____ 43, 44, 48
   on surf scoter_____ 143, 149, 150
   on white-winged scoter_____ 131
MacMillan, Donald B., on northern eider___ 91
Macoun, John—
   on American goldeneye_____ 4
   on white-winged scoter_____ 133
Manniche, A. L. V.—
   on barnacle goose_____ 259
   on king eider_____ 110, 111, 112, 114
masked duck_____ 161
McAtee, W. L., on blue goose_____ 181, 184
Melanitta deglandi_____ 131
Melanitta fusca_____ 128
Melanitta perspicillata_____ 143
Merriam, C. Hart, on Atlantic harlequin
   duck_____ 51
Merrill, J. C.—
   on black-bellied tree duck_____ 269, 270
   on white-fronted goose_____ 189
Michael, Charles W., on Pacific harlequin
   duck_____ 59, 60
Millais, John G.—
   on American goldeneye_____ 6, 9
   on Atlantic harlequin duck_____ 51, 53, 54, 55, 56
   on Barrow goldeneye_____ 17, 18, 19, 21
   on northern eider_____ 79, 86, 88, 89, 90
   on oldsquaw_____ 35, 39, 41, 42, 46
   on Steller eider_____ 69, 71
   on surf scoter_____ 143
   on velvet scoter_____ 128, 129
Miller, G. S., jr., on ruddy duck_____ 156
minima, Branta canadensis_____ 231
mollissima, Somateria borealis_____ 79
mollissima, Somateria dresseri_____ 94
Morris, F. O., on whooping swan_____ 279
Munro, J. A.—
   on Barrow goldeneye_____ 14, 15, 16, 18, 19, 20, 23
   on bufflehead_____ 27
Murdoch, John—
   on black brant_____ 251, 255
   on king eider_____ 107, 115
   on oldsquaw_____ 46
   on Steller eider_____ 68, 71, 72
   on white-fronted goose_____ 190
Murie, O. J.—
   on Atlantic harlequin duck_____ 53
   on brant_____ 182, 183
Nelson, E. W.—
   on American scoter_____ 120, 121
   on black brant_____ 250, 253, 255
   on cackling goose_____ 231, 232, 234
   on emperor goose_____ 263, 265, 266, 267

Page

Nelson, E. W.—Continued.
 on oldsquaw_____ 34, 46
 on Pacific eider_____ 104, 105
 on Pacific harlequin duck_____ 59
 on snow goose_____ 165
 on spectacled eider_____ 74, 75, 76, 78
 on Steller eider_____ 67, 71, 72
 on surf scoter_____ 145, 149
 on whistling swan_____ 282, 283, 285
 on white-fronted goose_____ 189, 191, 192, 193
Newton, Alfred, on Labrador duck_____ 63
nigricans, Branta bernicla_____ 249
nivalis, Chen hyperborea_____ 173
Nomonyx dominicus_____ 161
northern eider_____ 79
occidentalis, Branta canadensis_____ 227
Oidemia americana_____ 119
oldsquaw_____ 32
Pacific eider_____ 102
Pacific harlequin duck_____ 58
pacificus, Histrionicus histrionicus_____ `58
Palmer, William, on oldsquaw_____ 37
Payne-Gallwey, Ralph, on bean goose_____ 200
Pearson, T. Gilbert, on brant_____ 247
Pennock, Charles J., on Canada goose_____ 221
perspicillata, Melanitta_____ 143
Philacte canagica_____ 263
pink-footed goose_____ 200
Polysticta stelleri_____ 67
Preble, E. A.—
 on oldsquaw_____ 33
 on snow goose_____ 165
Preston, J. W., on Canada goose_____ 214
Rathbun, S. F., on black brant_____ 257
Ray, Milton S., on Canada goose_____ 207
Reeks, Henry, on Canada goose_____ 218
Rhoads, Samuel N., on Canada goose_____ 210
Rich, Walter H.—
 on American scoter_____ 126
 on Atlantic harlequin duck_____ 56
 on oldsquaw_____ 47
 on ruddy duck_____ 158
Richardson, E. P., on white-winged scoter__ 138
Ross goose_____ 185
rossii, Exanthemops_____ 185
ruddy duck_____ 152
Sanford, Leonard C.—
 on black-bellied tree duck_____ 271
 on brant_____ 239
 on bufflehead_____ 31
 on white-fronted goose_____ 194
Saunders, Aretas A.—
 on Atlantic harlequin duck_____ 57
 on Pacific harlequin duck_____ 60
scoter, American_____ 119
 surf_____ 143
 velvet_____ 128
 white-winged_____ 131
Scott, J. G., on king eider_____ 118
Scott, W. E. D., on masked duck_____ 162
Seebohm, Henry, on bean goose_____ 199
Sennett, George B.—
 on black-bellied tree duck_____ 269, 270, 271
 on whistling swan_____ 281
Sharpless, Dr., on whistling swan____ 285, 287, 290
Shepard, C. W., on northern eider_____ 92

Page

Shields, A. M., on fulvous tree duck___ 273, 274, 275
Silloway, P. M., on trumpeter swan_____ 297
Skinner, M. P.—
 on American goldeneye_____ 12
 on Barrow goldeneye_____ 15, 22, 23
 on bufflehead_____ 30
 on Canada goose_____ 215, 221
 on trumpeter swan_____ 297
snow goose_____ 164
snow goose, greater_____ 173
Somateria mollissima borealis_____ 79
Somateria mollissima dresseri_____ 94
Somateria spectabilis_____ 107
Somateria V. nigra_____ 102
spectabilis, Somateria_____ 107
spectacled eider_____ 74
Steller eider_____ 67
stelleri, Polysticta_____ 67
surf scoter_____ 143
Swainson and Richardson, on whistling swan_ 283
swan, trumpeter_____ 293
 whistling_____ 281
 whooping_____ 278
Swarth and Bryant, on tule goose_____ 197, 198
Swarth, Harry S., on white-cheeked goose___ 230
Taverner, P. A., on Canada goose_____ 211
Thayer and Bangs, on king eider_____ 109
Thayer, John E., on brant_____ 242
Townsend, Charles W.—
 on American eider_____ 94, 95, 97
 on American goldeneye_____ 1, 6
 on bufflehead_____ 25
 on surf scoter_____ 149
tree duck, black-bellied_____ 269
 fulvous_____ 272
trumpeter swan_____ 293
tule goose_____ 196
Turner, Lucien M.—
 on Atlantic harlequin duck_____ 50
 on Barrow goldeneye_____ 21
 on brant_____ 241
 on cackling goose_____ 233, 234, 235
 on Canada goose_____ 217
 on emperor goose_____ 266, 267
 on northern eider_____ 80, 83, 84, 90
 on oldsquaw_____ 33, 37, 38, 45
 on Pacific eider_____ 104, 106
 on Pacific harlequin duck_____ 59
 on whistling swan_____ 288
 on white-fronted goose_____ 192
van Rossem, A. J., on ruddy duck_____ 157
velvet scoter_____ 128
V. nigra, Somateria_____ 102
Wetmore, Alexander, on ruddy duck_____ 155
whistling swan_____ 281
white-cheeked goose_____ 227
white-fronted goose_____ 188
white-winged scoter_____ 131
Whitfield, R. P., on Atlantic harlequin duck_ 55
Whittle, Charles L., on surf scoter_____ 144
whooping swan_____ 278
Williams, Robert S., on Ross goose_____ 185
Witherby's Handbook—
 on barnacle goose_____ 262
 on bean goose_____ 199
Yorke, F. Henry, on bufflehead_____ 25
 on whistling swan_____ 286

PLATES

PLATE 1. SNOW, BLUE, AND CANADA GOOSE. Mixed flock of snow, blue, and Canada geese on a Louisiana Wild Life Refuge, presented by Mr. Stanley Clisby Arthur.

PLATE 2. AMERICAN GOLDENEYE. *Upper:* Nesting site of American goldeye, Devils Lake, North Dakota, June 22, 1898, presented by Mr. Herbert K. Job. *Lower:* Nesting tree of American goldeneye, Nelson County, North Dakota, June 1, 1901, a photograph by the author, referred to on page 3.

PLATE 3. AMERICAN GOLDENEYE. *Upper*: Nesting tree of American goldeneye, near Eskimo Point, Quebec, June 10, 1909, referred to on page 2, presented by Dr. Charles W. Townsend. *Lower*: A pair of adult American goldeneyes feeding, a photograph purchased from Mr. Bonnycastle Dale.

PLATE 4. AMERICAN GOLDENEYE. *Upper:* Nesting tree of American goldeneye, Lake Winnipegosis, Manitoba, June 9, 1913, referred to on page 4. *Lower:* Another nest tree, in the same locality, showing a mass of down clinging to the bark near the opening. Both photographs by the author.

PLATE 5. AMERICAN GOLDENEYE. *Upper:* Female American goldeneye leaning far out of the nesting hole, 25 feet up in a white poplar, near Fort Chipewyan, Alberta. A photograph taken by Mr. Francis Harper, presented by the Biological Survey and Dr. John C. Phillips. *Lower:* Downy young American goldeneyes, Lake Winnipegosis, Manitoba, June, 1913, presented by Herbert K. Job.

PLATE 6. BARROW GOLDENEYE. Nesting stub of Barrow golden-eye, Okanogan, British Columbia, presented by Mr. James A. Munro.

PLATE 7. BARROW GOLDENEYE. Winter resort of Barrow golden-eyes, Yellowstone National Park, Wyoming, presented by Mr. M. P. Skinner.

PLATE 8. BUFFLEHEAD. *Left*: Nesting tree of bufflehead, Buffalo Lake, Alberta, June 8, 1920. The lower hole contained 12 fresh eggs. *Right*: Another nesting tree in the same locality, June 2, 1920. "The photograph shows how far the eggs were below the entrance hole." Both photographs presented by Mr. G. H. Lings.

PLATE 9. BUFFLEHEAD. Nesting stub of bufflehead, Alberta, June 11, 1906, presented by Mr. Walter Raine. The stub also contained the nest and eggs of desert sparrow hawk.

PLATE 10. OLDSQUAW. *Upper:* Nest and eggs of oldsquaw, broken up by gulls, near St. Michael, Alaska, July 5, 1915, from a negative taken by Mr. F. Seymour Hersey for the author, referred to on page 38. *Lower:* Nest and eggs of oldsquaw, Lopp Lagoon, near Cape Prince of Wales, Alaska, July 5, 1922, presented by Mr. Alfred M. Bailey, by courtesy of the Colorado Museum of Natural History.

PLATE 11. OLDSQUAW. *Upper:* Nest and eggs of oldsquaw, Iceland, June, 1911, presented by Mr. C. H. Wells. *Lower:* Pair of adult oldsquaws, a photograph purchased from Mr. Bonnycastle Dale.

PLATE 12. OLDSQUAW. *Upper:* Nest of oldsquaw, with eggs covered with down. Cape Prince of Wales, Alaska, July 5, 1922. *Lower:* Same nest, with eggs uncovered. Both photographs presented by Mr. Alfred M. Bailey, by courtesy of the Colorado Museum of Natural History.

PLATE 13. PACIFIC HARLEQUIN DUCK. *Upper:* Male Pacific harlequin duck, Yosemite Valley, California. *Lower:* A pair of the same. Both photographs presented by Mr. Charles W. Michael and referred to on page 59.

PLATE 14. SPECTACLED EIDER. *Upper:* Nesting site of spectacled eider, Point Hope, Alaska, June 15, 1917, from a negative taken by Rev. A. R. Hoare for the author and referred to on page 75. *Lower:* Nest and eggs of spectacled eider, Point Barrow, Alaska, June 26, 1917, from a negative taken by Mr. T. L. Richardson for the author and referred to on page 75.

PLATE 15. NORTHERN EIDER. *Upper:* Two nests of northern eider, near Hopedale, Labrador, July 22, 1912. *Lower:* Another nest, same locality and date. Both photographs by the author, referred to on page 81.

PLATE 16. NORTHERN EIDER. *Upper:* Nest and eggs of northern eider, Sutherland Island, Greenland. *Lower:* Another nest of same, near Etah, Greenland. Both photographs taken by Dr. Donald B. MacMillan and presented by the American Museum of Natural History.

PLATE 17. EIDER. *Upper:* Nest, eggs and young of eider. *Lower:* Female eider on her nest. Both photographs taken in Iceland and presented by Mr. C. H. Wells.

PLATE 18. AMERICAN EIDER. *Upper:* Nesting site of American eider, on an island off the north shore of the Gulf of St. Lawrence, May 26, 1909, referred to on page 97. *Lower:* Closer view of the nest in the same spot. Both photographs by the author.

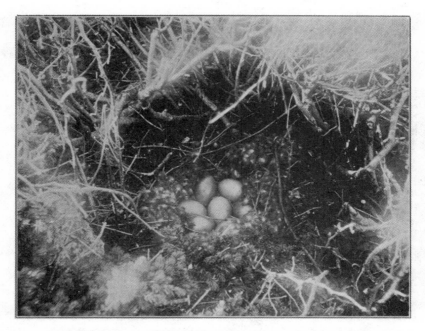

PLATE 19. AMERICAN EIDER. *Upper:* Nest and 7 eggs of American eider on an island off the north shore of the Gulf of St. Lawrence, May 29, 1909, a photograph by the author, referred to on page 98. *Lower:* Young male American eider in first winter plumage beginning to acquire the first white plumage, a photograph purchased from Mr. Bonnycastle Dale.

PLATE 20. PACIFIC EIDER. *Upper:* Nesting site of Pacific eider, Kiska Island, Alaska, June 19, 1911, referred to on page 103. *Lower:* Closer view of the nest in the same spot. Both photographs by the author.

PLATE 21. PACIFIC EIDER. Nest and eggs of Pacific eider, Cape Prince of Wales, Alaska, July 1, 1922, presented by Mr. Alfred M. Bailey, courtesy of the Colorado Museum of Natural History.

PLATE 22. KING EIDER. *Upper:* Nest and eggs of king eider, Spitsbergen, July, 1921. *Lower:* Nesting site of king eider, Spitsbergen, July, 1921. Both photographs taken by Mr. J. S. Huxley, purchased from the Oxford University Expedition to Spitsbergen and referred to on page 110.

PLATE 23. WHITE-WINGED SCOTER. *Upper:* Nest and eggs of
white-winged scoter, Stump Lake Reservation, North Dakota, June 27,
1898. *Lower:* Another nest, same locality and date. Both photographs
presented by Mr. Herbert K. Job and referred to on page 132.

PLATE 24. WHITE-WINGED SCOTER. *Upper:* Nest and eggs of white-winged scoter, Lake Manitoba, Manitoba, July 4, 1912. *Lower:* Downy young white-winged scoters, St. Marks, Manitoba, July, 1912. Both photographs presented by Mr. Herbert K. Job.

PLATE 25. WHITE-WINGED SCOTER. A flock of migrating white-winged scoters, off Manomet Point, Plymouth, Massachusetts, October 25, 1904, presented by Mr. Herbert K. Job.

PLATE 26. RUDDY DUCK. *Upper:* Pair of adult ruddy ducks, Lake Manitoba, Manitoba, July, 1912. *Lower:* Nest and eggs of ruddy duck, same locality, July 8, 1912. Both photographs presented by Mr. Herbert K. Job.

PLATE 27. RUDDY DUCK. *Upper:* Nest and eggs of ruddy duck, Steele County, North Dakota, June 13, 1901. *Lower:* Another nest, same locality, June 10, 1901. Both photographs by the author, referred to on page 153.

PLATE 28. RUDDY DUCK. *Upper:* Downy young ruddy duck, St. Marks, Manitoba, July, 1912, presented by Mr. Herbert K. Job. *Lower:* Young ruddy ducks, a photograph of dried skins, presented by Mr. Joseph Mailliard.

PLATE 29. SNOW GOOSE. *Upper:* Adult snow goose, Louisiana. *Lower:* Another view of same. Both photographs presented by Mr. Stanley Clisby Arthur.

PLATE 30. BLUE AND SNOW GOOSE. *Upper:* Flock of blue and snow geese, Vermilion Bay, Louisiana, January 3, 1916. *Lower:* Another flock, same locality and date. Both photographs presented by Mr. Herbert K. Job.

PLATE 31. BLUE GOOSE. Adult and young blue geese, same locality and date as preceding plate, presented by Mr. Herbert K. Job.

PLATE 32. BLUE AND SNOW GOOSE. Flock of blue and snow geese, same locality and date as preceding plate, presented by Mr. Herbert K. Job.

PLATE 33. WHITE-FRONTED GOOSE. *Upper:* Nesting site of white-fronted goose, Kolyma Delta, Siberia, July 1, 1917. *Lower:* Closer view of nest in same spot. Both from negatives taken by Mr. Johan Koren for the author.

PLATE 34. PINK-FOOTED GOOSE. *Left*: Nest and eggs of pink-footed goose, Spitsbergen, July, 1922, taken by Mr. W. M. Congreve. *Right*: Another nest of same, Prince Charles Foreland, 1921, taken by Mr. T. G. Longstaff. Both photographs purchased from the Oxford University Expedition to Spitsbergen and referred to on page 201.

PLATE 35. PINK-FOOTED GOOSE. Nest and eggs of pink-footed goose, Bruce City, Spitsbergen, July, 1921, a photograph taken by Mr. J. D. Brown and purchased from the Oxford University Expedition to Spitsbergen.

PLATE 36. CANADA GOOSE. *Upper:* Pair of Canada geese nesting under semi-wild conditions, Taunton, Massachusetts, April 27, 1918. *Lower:* Deserted nest of Canada goose in a slough, Steele County, North Dakota, June 10, 1901, referred to on page 206. Both photographs by the author.

PLATE 37. CANADA GOOSE. *Upper:* Nest and eggs of Canada goose, on an island in Crane Lake, Saskatchewan, June 2, 1905. *Lower:* Another nest on the same island. Both photographs by the author, referred to on page 206.

PLATE 38. CANADA GOOSE. *Upper:* Immature Canada geese. *Lower:* Downy young Canada goose. Both photographs taken on Klamath River, Oregon, and presented by Messrs. H. T. Bohlman and William L. Finley.

PLATE 39. CANADA GOOSE. Nest of Canada goose in an old red-tailed hawk's nest, Alberta, April 25, 1896, presented by Mr. Walter Raine.

PLATE 40. HUTCHINS GOOSE. *Upper:* Nest and eggs of Hutchins goose, Point Barrow, Alaska, June 20, 1917, from a negative taken by Mr. T. L. Richardson for the author. *Lower:* Adult Hutchins goose, Louisiana, presented by Mr. Stanley Clisby Arthur.

PLATE 41. BRANT. *Upper:* Nest and eggs of brant, Eider Duck
Island, Greenland. *Lower:* Another nest, same locality. Both photo-
graphs taken by Dr. Donald B. MacMillan, presented by the American
Museum of Natural History and referred to on page 242.

PLATE 42. BRANT. *Upper:* Nest and eggs of brant, Moffen Island, Spitsbergen, July 8, 1921, a photograph taken by Mr. J. D. Brown. *Lower:* Another nest, same locality and date, a photograph taken by Mr. Seton P. Gordon. Both photographs purchased from the Oxford University Expedition to Spitsbergen and referred to on page 241.

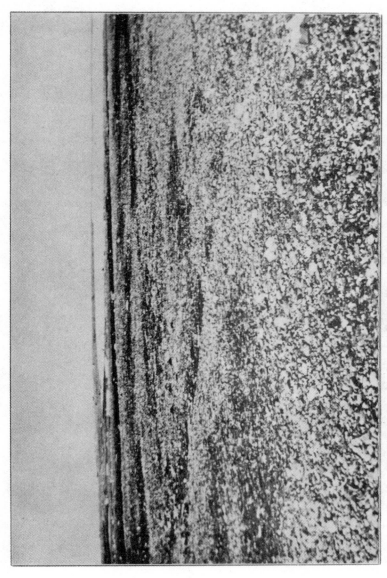

PLATE 43. BRANT. Nesting site of brant, Moffen Island, 80° N., Spitsbergen, July 8, 1921, a photograph taken by Mr. J. D. Brown and purchased from the Oxford University Expedition to Spitsbergen.

PLATE 44. BLACK BRANT. *Upper:* Nesting site of black brant, Point Hope, Alaska, June 15, 1917. *Lower:* Closer view of the nest in the same spot. Both photographs from negatives taken by Rev. A. R. Hoare for the author and referred to on page 252.

PLATE 45. BARNACLE GOOSE. *Upper:* Barnacle goose on its nest, 1,200 feet above the bed of the valley, Spitsbergen, June, 1922. *Lower:* Same nest as above. Both photographs taken by Mr. W. M. Congreve, purchased from the Oxford University Expedition to Spitsbergen and referred to on page 260.

PLATE 46. BARNACLE GOOSE. Nest and eggs of barnacle goose, Advent Bay, Spitsbergen, June 28, 1921, a photograph purchased from the Oxford University Expedition to Spitsbergen and referred to on page 260.

PLATE 47. EMPEROR GOOSE. *Upper:* Nest of emperor goose, with eggs concealed, Cape Prince of Wales, Alaska, July 5, 1922. *Lower:* Another nest of same. Mint River, Cape Prince of Wales, Alaska, July 12, 1922. Both photographs presented by Mr. Alfred M. Bailey, by courtesy of the Colorado Museum of Natural History.

PLATE 48. EMPEROR GOOSE. Nesting site of emperor goose, nest on small islet to right of stump, Lopp Lagoon, near Cape Prince of Wales, Alaska, July 5, 1922, presented by Mr. Alfred M. Bailey, by courtesy of the Colorado Museum of Natural History.

PLATE 49. FULVOUS TREE-DUCK. Nest of fulvous tree-duck, concealed in thick tules, Los Banos, California, June 4, 1914, presented by Mr. W. Leon Dawson, by courtesy of the South Moulton Company.

PLATE 50. FULVOUS TREE-DUCK. Closer view of same nest shown on previous plate, presented by Mr. W. Leon Dawson, by courtesy of the South Moulton Company.

PLATE 51. FULVOUS TREE-DUCK. Fulvous tree-ducks flying, near Santa Barbara, California, May 2, 1912, presented by Mr. W. Leon Dawson, by courtesy of the South Moulton Company.

PLATE 52. FULVOUS TREE-DUCK. Nesting site of fulvous tree-duck, Kern County, California, presented by Mr. Donald R. Dickey.

PLATE 53. FULVOUS TREE-DUCK. Nest and eggs of fulvous tree-duck, Kern County, California, presented by Mr. Donald R. Dickey.

PLATE 54. FULVOUS TREE-DUCK. Another nest and eggs of fulvous tree-duck, Kern County, California, presented by Mr. Donald R. Dickey.

PLATE 55. WHOOPING SWAN. *Right*: Nest, eggs and young of whooping swan, Iceland, June, 1911, presented by Mr. C. H. Wells. *Left*: Adult whooping swan standing over its nest, West Highlands, Scotland, presented by Mrs. Audrey Gordon, and referred to on page 279.

PLATE 56. WHISTLING SWAN. Nesting site of whistling swan, Mint River, Cape Prince of Wales, Alaska, July 13, 1922, presented by Mr. Alfred M. Bailey, by courtesy of the Colorado Museum of Natural History.

PLATE 57. WHISTLING SWAN. Nest and downy young of whistling swan, Mint River, Cape Prince of Wales, Alaska, July 13, 1922, presented by Mr. Alfred M. Bailey, by courtesy of the Colorado Museum of Natural History.

PLATE 58. WHISTLING SWAN. Pair of whistling swans, Fergus County, Montana, presented by Mr. E. S. Cameron.

PLATE 59. WHISTLING SWAN. Flock of wild whistling swans, Point Pelee, Ontario, April 13, 1924, presented by Mr. Walter E. Hastings.

PLATE 60. TRUMPETER SWAN. Adult trumpeter swan, Louisiana State Wild Life Reserve, February, 1915, presented by Mr. Stanley Clisby Arthur.

A CATALOG OF SELECTED
DOVER BOOKS
IN ALL FIELDS OF INTEREST

A CATALOG OF SELECTED DOVER
BOOKS IN ALL FIELDS OF INTEREST

DRAWINGS OF REMBRANDT, edited by Seymour Slive. Updated Lippmann, Hofstede de Groot edition, with definitive scholarly apparatus. All portraits, biblical sketches, landscapes, nudes. Oriental figures, classical studies, together with selection of work by followers. 550 illustrations. Total of 630pp. 9⅛ × 12¼.
21485-0, 21486-9 Pa., Two-vol. set $25.00

GHOST AND HORROR STORIES OF AMBROSE BIERCE, Ambrose Bierce. 24 tales vividly imagined, strangely prophetic, and decades ahead of their time in technical skill: "The Damned Thing," "An Inhabitant of Carcosa," "The Eyes of the Panther," "Moxon's Master," and 20 more. 199pp. 5⅜ × 8½. 20767-6 Pa. $3.95

ETHICAL WRITINGS OF MAIMONIDES, Maimonides. Most significant ethical works of great medieval sage, newly translated for utmost precision, readability. Laws Concerning Character Traits, Eight Chapters, more. 192pp. 5⅜ × 8½.
24522-5 Pa. $4.50

THE EXPLORATION OF THE COLORADO RIVER AND ITS CANYONS, J. W. Powell. Full text of Powell's 1,000-mile expedition down the fabled Colorado in 1869. Superb account of terrain, geology, vegetation, Indians, famine, mutiny, treacherous rapids, mighty canyons, during exploration of last unknown part of continental U.S. 400pp. 5⅜ × 8½. 20094-9 Pa. $6.95

HISTORY OF PHILOSOPHY, Julián Marías. Clearest one-volume history on the market. Every major philosopher and dozens of others, to Existentialism and later. 505pp. 5⅜ × 8½. 21739-6 Pa. $8.50

ALL ABOUT LIGHTNING, Martin A. Uman. Highly readable non-technical survey of nature and causes of lightning, thunderstorms, ball lightning, St. Elmo's Fire, much more. Illustrated. 192pp. 5⅜ × 8½. 25237-X Pa. $5.95

SAILING ALONE AROUND THE WORLD, Captain Joshua Slocum. First man to sail around the world, alone, in small boat. One of great feats of seamanship told in delightful manner. 67 illustrations. 294pp. 5⅜ × 8½. 20326-3 Pa. $4.50

LETTERS AND NOTES ON THE MANNERS, CUSTOMS AND CONDITIONS OF THE NORTH AMERICAN INDIANS, George Catlin. Classic account of life among Plains Indians: ceremonies, hunt, warfare, etc. 312 plates. 572pp. of text. 6⅛ × 9¼. 22118-0, 22119-9 Pa. Two-vol. set $15.90

ALASKA: The Harriman Expedition, 1899, John Burroughs, John Muir, et al. Informative, engrossing accounts of two-month, 9,000-mile expedition. Native peoples, wildlife, forests, geography, salmon industry, glaciers, more. Profusely illustrated. 240 black-and-white line drawings. 124 black-and-white photographs. 3 maps. Index. 576pp. 5⅜ × 8½. 25109-8 Pa. $11.95

THE BOOK OF BEASTS: Being a Translation from a Latin Bestiary of the Twelfth Century, T. H. White. Wonderful catalog real and fanciful beasts: manticore, griffin, phoenix, amphivius, jaculus, many more. White's witty erudite commentary on scientific, historical aspects. Fascinating glimpse of medieval mind. Illustrated. 296pp. 5⅜ × 8¼. (Available in U.S. only) 24609-4 Pa. $5.95

FRANK LLOYD WRIGHT: ARCHITECTURE AND NATURE With 160 Illustrations, Donald Hoffmann. Profusely illustrated study of influence of nature—especially prairie—on Wright's designs for Fallingwater, Robie House, Guggenheim Museum, other masterpieces. 96pp. 9¼ × 10¾. 25098-9 Pa. $7.95

FRANK LLOYD WRIGHT'S FALLINGWATER, Donald Hoffmann. Wright's famous waterfall house: planning and construction of organic idea. History of site, owners, Wright's personal involvement. Photographs of various stages of building. Preface by Edgar Kaufmann, Jr. 100 illustrations. 112pp. 9¼ × 10. 23671-4 Pa. $7.95

YEARS WITH FRANK LLOYD WRIGHT: Apprentice to Genius, Edgar Tafel. Insightful memoir by a former apprentice presents a revealing portrait of Wright the man, the inspired teacher, the greatest American architect. 372 black-and-white illustrations. Preface. Index. vi + 228pp. 8¼ × 11. 24801-1 Pa. $9.95

THE STORY OF KING ARTHUR AND HIS KNIGHTS, Howard Pyle. Enchanting version of King Arthur fable has delighted generations with imaginative narratives of exciting adventures and unforgettable illustrations by the author. 41 illustrations. xviii + 313pp. 6⅛ × 9¼. 21445-1 Pa. $5.95

THE GODS OF THE EGYPTIANS, E. A. Wallis Budge. Thorough coverage of numerous gods of ancient Egypt by foremost Egyptologist. Information on evolution of cults, rites and gods; the cult of Osiris; the Book of the Dead and its rites; the sacred animals and birds; Heaven and Hell; and more. 956pp. 6⅛ × 9¼. 22055-9, 22056-7 Pa., Two-vol. set $20.00

A THEOLOGICO-POLITICAL TREATISE, Benedict Spinoza. Also contains unfinished *Political Treatise*. Great classic on religious liberty, theory of government on common consent. R. Elwes translation. Total of 421pp. 5⅜ × 8½. 20249-6 Pa. $6.95

INCIDENTS OF TRAVEL IN CENTRAL AMERICA, CHIAPAS, AND YUCATAN, John L. Stephens. Almost single-handed discovery of Maya culture; exploration of ruined cities, monuments, temples; customs of Indians. 115 drawings. 892pp. 5⅜ × 8½. 22404-X, 22405-8 Pa., Two-vol. set $15.90

LOS CAPRICHOS, Francisco Goya. 80 plates of wild, grotesque monsters and caricatures. Prado manuscript included. 183pp. 6⅝ × 9⅝. 22384-1 Pa. $4.95

AUTOBIOGRAPHY: The Story of My Experiments with Truth, Mohandas K. Gandhi. Not hagiography, but Gandhi in his own words. Boyhood, legal studies, purification, the growth of the Satyagraha (nonviolent protest) movement. Critical, inspiring work of the man who freed India. 480pp. 5⅜ × 8½. (Available in U.S. only) 24593-4 Pa. $6.95

ILLUSTRATED DICTIONARY OF HISTORIC ARCHITECTURE, edited by Cyril M. Harris. Extraordinary compendium of clear, concise definitions for over 5,000 important architectural terms complemented by over 2,000 line drawings. Covers full spectrum of architecture from ancient ruins to 20th-century Modernism. Preface. 592pp. 7½ × 9⅜. 24444-X Pa. $14.95

THE NIGHT BEFORE CHRISTMAS, Clement Moore. Full text, and woodcuts from original 1848 book. Also critical, historical material. 19 illustrations. 40pp. 4⅝ × 6. 22797-9 Pa. $2.25

THE LESSON OF JAPANESE ARCHITECTURE: 165 Photographs, Jiro Harada. Memorable gallery of 165 photographs taken in the 1930's of exquisite Japanese homes of the well-to-do and historic buildings. 13 line diagrams. 192pp. 8⅜ × 11¼. 24778-3 Pa. $8.95

THE AUTOBIOGRAPHY OF CHARLES DARWIN AND SELECTED LETTERS, edited by Francis Darwin. The fascinating life of eccentric genius composed of an intimate memoir by Darwin (intended for his children); commentary by his son, Francis; hundreds of fragments from notebooks, journals, papers; and letters to and from Lyell, Hooker, Huxley, Wallace and Henslow. xi + 365pp. 5⅜ × 8. 20479-0 Pa. $5.95

WONDERS OF THE SKY: Observing Rainbows, Comets, Eclipses, the Stars and Other Phenomena, Fred Schaaf. Charming, easy-to-read poetic guide to all manner of celestial events visible to the naked eye. Mock suns, glories, Belt of Venus, more. Illustrated. 299pp. 5¼ × 8¼. 24402-4 Pa. $7.95

BURNHAM'S CELESTIAL HANDBOOK, Robert Burnham, Jr. Thorough guide to the stars beyond our solar system. Exhaustive treatment. Alphabetical by constellation: Andromeda to Cetus in Vol. 1; Chamaeleon to Orion in Vol. 2; and Pavo to Vulpecula in Vol. 3. Hundreds of illustrations. Index in Vol. 3. 2,000pp. 6⅛ × 9¼. 23567-X, 23568-8, 23673-0 Pa., Three-vol. set $36.85

STAR NAMES: Their Lore and Meaning, Richard Hinckley Allen. Fascinating history of names various cultures have given to constellations and literary and folkloristic uses that have been made of stars. Indexes to subjects. Arabic and Greek names. Biblical references. Bibliography. 563pp. 5⅜ × 8½. 21079-0 Pa. $7.95

THIRTY YEARS THAT SHOOK PHYSICS: The Story of Quantum Theory, George Gamow. Lucid, accessible introduction to influential theory of energy and matter. Careful explanations of Dirac's anti-particles, Bohr's model of the atom, much more. 12 plates. Numerous drawings. 240pp. 5⅜ × 8½. 24895-X Pa. $4.95

CHINESE DOMESTIC FURNITURE IN PHOTOGRAPHS AND MEASURED DRAWINGS, Gustav Ecke. A rare volume, now affordably priced for antique collectors, furniture buffs and art historians. Detailed review of styles ranging from early Shang to late Ming. Unabridged republication. 161 black-and-white drawings, photos. Total of 224pp. 8⅜ × 11¼. (Available in U.S. only) 25171-3 Pa. $12.95

VINCENT VAN GOGH: A Biography, Julius Meier-Graefe. Dynamic, penetrating study of artist's life, relationship with brother, Theo, painting techniques, travels, more. Readable, engrossing. 160pp. 5⅜ × 8½. (Available in U.S. only) 25253-1 Pa. $3.95

HOW TO WRITE, Gertrude Stein. Gertrude Stein claimed anyone could understand her unconventional writing—here are clues to help. Fascinating improvisations, language experiments, explanations illuminate Stein's craft and the art of writing. Total of 414pp. 4⅝ × 6⅜. 23144-5 Pa. $5.95

ADVENTURES AT SEA IN THE GREAT AGE OF SAIL: Five Firsthand Narratives, edited by Elliot Snow. Rare true accounts of exploration, whaling, shipwreck, fierce natives, trade, shipboard life, more. 33 illustrations. Introduction. 353pp. 5⅜ × 8½. 25177-2 Pa. $7.95

THE HERBAL OR GENERAL HISTORY OF PLANTS, John Gerard. Classic descriptions of about 2,850 plants—with over 2,700 illustrations—includes Latin and English names, physical descriptions, varieties, time and place of growth, more. 2,706 illustrations. xlv + 1,678pp. 8½ × 12¼. 23147-X Cloth. $75.00

DOROTHY AND THE WIZARD IN OZ, L. Frank Baum. Dorothy and the Wizard visit the center of the Earth, where people are vegetables, glass houses grow and Oz characters reappear. Classic sequel to *Wizard of Oz*. 256pp. 5⅜ × 8. 24714-7 Pa. $4.95

SONGS OF EXPERIENCE: Facsimile Reproduction with 26 Plates in Full Color, William Blake. This facsimile of Blake's original "Illuminated Book" reproduces 26 full-color plates from a rare 1826 edition. Includes "The Tyger," "London," "Holy Thursday," and other immortal poems. 26 color plates. Printed text of poems. 48pp. 5¼ × 7. 24636-1 Pa. $3.50

SONGS OF INNOCENCE, William Blake. The first and most popular of Blake's famous "Illuminated Books," in a facsimile edition reproducing all 31 brightly colored plates. Additional printed text of each poem. 64pp. 5¼ × 7. 22764-2 Pa. $3.50

PRECIOUS STONES, Max Bauer. Classic, thorough study of diamonds, rubies, emeralds, garnets, etc.: physical character, occurrence, properties, use, similar topics. 20 plates, 8 in color. 94 figures. 659pp. 6⅛ × 9¼. 21910-0, 21911-9 Pa., Two-vol. set $14.90

ENCYCLOPEDIA OF VICTORIAN NEEDLEWORK, S. F. A. Caulfeild and Blanche Saward. Full, precise descriptions of stitches, techniques for dozens of needlecrafts—most exhaustive reference of its kind. Over 800 figures. Total of 679pp. 8⅛ × 11. Two volumes. Vol. 1 22800-2 Pa. $10.95
Vol. 2 22801-0 Pa. $10.95

THE MARVELOUS LAND OF OZ, L. Frank Baum. Second Oz book, the Scarecrow and Tin Woodman are back with hero named Tip, Oz magic. 136 illustrations. 287pp. 5⅜ × 8½. 20692-0 Pa. $5.95

WILD FOWL DECOYS, Joel Barber. Basic book on the subject, by foremost authority and collector. Reveals history of decoy making and rigging, place in American culture, different kinds of decoys, how to make them, and how to use them. 140 plates. 156pp. 7⅞ × 10¾. 20011-6 Pa. $7.95

HISTORY OF LACE, Mrs. Bury Palliser. Definitive, profusely illustrated chronicle of lace from earliest times to late 19th century. Laces of Italy, Greece, England, France, Belgium, etc. Landmark of needlework scholarship. 266 illustrations. 672pp. 6⅛ × 9¼. 24742-2 Pa. $14.95

ILLUSTRATED GUIDE TO SHAKER FURNITURE, Robert Meader. All furniture and appurtenances, with much on unknown local styles. 235 photos. 146pp. 9 × 12. 22819-3 Pa. $7.95

WHALE SHIPS AND WHALING: A Pictorial Survey, George Francis Dow. Over 200 vintage engravings, drawings, photographs of barks, brigs, cutters, other vessels. Also harpoons, lances, whaling guns, many other artifacts. Comprehensive text by foremost authority. 207 black-and-white illustrations. 288pp. 6 × 9. 24808-9 Pa. $8.95

THE BERTRAMS, Anthony Trollope. Powerful portrayal of blind self-will and thwarted ambition includes one of Trollope's most heartrending love stories. 497pp. 5⅜ × 8½. 25119-5 Pa. $8.95

ADVENTURES WITH A HAND LENS, Richard Headstrom. Clearly written guide to observing and studying flowers and grasses, fish scales, moth and insect wings, egg cases, buds, feathers, seeds, leaf scars, moss, molds, ferns, common crystals, etc.—all with an ordinary, inexpensive magnifying glass. 209 exact line drawings aid in your discoveries. 220pp. 5⅜ × 8½. 23330-8 Pa. $3.95

RODIN ON ART AND ARTISTS, Auguste Rodin. Great sculptor's candid, wide-ranging comments on meaning of art; great artists; relation of sculpture to poetry, painting, music; philosophy of life, more. 76 superb black-and-white illustrations of Rodin's sculpture, drawings and prints. 119pp. 8⅜ × 11¼. 24487-3 Pa. $6.95

FIFTY CLASSIC FRENCH FILMS, 1912–1982: A Pictorial Record, Anthony Slide. Memorable stills from Grand Illusion, Beauty and the Beast, Hiroshima, Mon Amour, many more. Credits, plot synopses, reviews, etc. 160pp. 8¼ × 11. 25256-6 Pa. $11.95

THE PRINCIPLES OF PSYCHOLOGY, William James. Famous long course complete, unabridged. Stream of thought, time perception, memory, experimental methods; great work decades ahead of its time. 94 figures. 1,391pp. 5⅜ × 8½. 20381-6, 20382-4 Pa., Two-vol. set $19.90

BODIES IN A BOOKSHOP, R. T. Campbell. Challenging mystery of blackmail and murder with ingenious plot and superbly drawn characters. In the best tradition of British suspense fiction. 192pp. 5⅜ × 8½. 24720-1 Pa. $3.95

CALLAS: PORTRAIT OF A PRIMA DONNA, George Jellinek. Renowned commentator on the musical scene chronicles incredible career and life of the most controversial, fascinating, influential operatic personality of our time. 64 black-and-white photographs. 416pp. 5⅜ × 8¼. 25047-4 Pa. $7.95

GEOMETRY, RELATIVITY AND THE FOURTH DIMENSION, Rudolph Rucker. Exposition of fourth dimension, concepts of relativity as Flatland characters continue adventures. Popular, easily followed yet accurate, profound. 141 illustrations. 133pp. 5⅜ × 8½. 23400-2 Pa. $3.50

HOUSEHOLD STORIES BY THE BROTHERS GRIMM, with pictures by Walter Crane. 53 classic stories—Rumpelstiltskin, Rapunzel, Hansel and Gretel, the Fisherman and his Wife, Snow White, Tom Thumb, Sleeping Beauty, Cinderella, and so much more—lavishly illustrated with original 19th century drawings. 114 illustrations. x + 269pp. 5⅜ × 8½. 21080-4 Pa. $4.50

SUNDIALS, Albert Waugh. Far and away the best, most thorough coverage of ideas, mathematics concerned, types, construction, adjusting anywhere. Over 100 illustrations. 230pp. 5⅜ × 8½. 22947-5 Pa. $4.00

PICTURE HISTORY OF THE NORMANDIE: With 190 Illustrations, Frank O. Braynard. Full story of legendary French ocean liner: Art Deco interiors, design innovations, furnishings, celebrities, maiden voyage, tragic fire, much more. Extensive text. 144pp. 8⅞ × 11¾. 25257-4 Pa. $9.95

THE FIRST AMERICAN COOKBOOK: A Facsimile of "American Cookery," 1796, Amelia Simmons. Facsimile of the first American-written cookbook published in the United States contains authentic recipes for colonial favorites—pumpkin pudding, winter squash pudding, spruce beer, Indian slapjacks, and more. Introductory Essay and Glossary of colonial cooking terms. 80pp. 5⅜ × 8½. 24710-4 Pa. $3.50

101 PUZZLES IN THOUGHT AND LOGIC, C. R. Wylie, Jr. Solve murders and robberies, find out which fishermen are liars, how a blind man could possibly identify a color—purely by your own reasoning! 107pp. 5⅜ × 8½. 20367-0 Pa. $2.00

THE BOOK OF WORLD-FAMOUS MUSIC—CLASSICAL, POPULAR AND FOLK, James J. Fuld. Revised and enlarged republication of landmark work in musico-bibliography. Full information about nearly 1,000 songs and compositions including first lines of music and lyrics. New supplement. Index. 800pp. 5⅜ × 8¼. 24857-7 Pa. $14.95

ANTHROPOLOGY AND MODERN LIFE, Franz Boas. Great anthropologist's classic treatise on race and culture. Introduction by Ruth Bunzel. Only inexpensive paperback edition. 255pp. 5⅜ × 8½. 25245-0 Pa. $5.95

THE TALE OF PETER RABBIT, Beatrix Potter. The inimitable Peter's terrifying adventure in Mr. McGregor's garden, with all 27 wonderful, full-color Potter illustrations. 55pp. 4¼ × 5½. (Available in U.S. only) 22827-4 Pa. $1.75

THREE PROPHETIC SCIENCE FICTION NOVELS, H. G. Wells. *When the Sleeper Wakes, A Story of the Days to Come* and *The Time Machine* (full version). 335pp. 5⅜ × 8½. (Available in U.S. only) 20605-X Pa. $5.95

APICIUS COOKERY AND DINING IN IMPERIAL ROME, edited and translated by Joseph Dommers Vehling. Oldest known cookbook in existence offers readers a clear picture of what foods Romans ate, how they prepared them, etc. 49 illustrations. 301pp. 6⅛ × 9¼. 23563-7 Pa. $6.00

SHAKESPEARE LEXICON AND QUOTATION DICTIONARY, Alexander Schmidt. Full definitions, locations, shades of meaning of every word in plays and poems. More than 50,000 exact quotations. 1,485pp. 6½ × 9¼. 22726-X, 22727-8 Pa., Two-vol. set $27.90

THE WORLD'S GREAT SPEECHES, edited by Lewis Copeland and Lawrence W. Lamm. Vast collection of 278 speeches from Greeks to 1970. Powerful and effective models; unique look at history. 842pp. 5⅜ × 8½. 20468-5 Pa. $10.95

THE BLUE FAIRY BOOK, Andrew Lang. The first, most famous collection, with many familiar tales: Little Red Riding Hood, Aladdin and the Wonderful Lamp, Puss in Boots, Sleeping Beauty, Hansel and Gretel, Rumpelstiltskin; 37 in all. 138 illustrations. 390pp. 5⅜ × 8½. 21437-0 Pa. $5.95

THE STORY OF THE CHAMPIONS OF THE ROUND TABLE, Howard Pyle. Sir Launcelot, Sir Tristram and Sir Percival in spirited adventures of love and triumph retold in Pyle's inimitable style. 50 drawings, 31 full-page. xviii + 329pp. 6½ × 9¼. 21883-X Pa. $6.95

AUDUBON AND HIS JOURNALS, Maria Audubon. Unmatched two-volume portrait of the great artist, naturalist and author contains his journals, an excellent biography by his granddaughter, expert annotations by the noted ornithologist, Dr. Elliott Coues, and 37 superb illustrations. Total of 1,200pp. 5⅜ × 8.
Vol. I 25143-8 Pa. $8.95
Vol. II 25144-6 Pa. $8.95

GREAT DINOSAUR HUNTERS AND THEIR DISCOVERIES, Edwin H. Colbert. Fascinating, lavishly illustrated chronicle of dinosaur research, 1820's to 1960. Achievements of Cope, Marsh, Brown, Buckland, Mantell, Huxley, many others. 384pp. 5¼ × 8¼. 24701-5 Pa. $6.95

THE TASTEMAKERS, Russell Lynes. Informal, illustrated social history of American taste 1850's–1950's. First popularized categories Highbrow, Lowbrow, Middlebrow. 129 illustrations. New (1979) afterword. 384pp. 6 × 9.
23993-4 Pa. $6.95

DOUBLE CROSS PURPOSES, Ronald A. Knox. A treasure hunt in the Scottish Highlands, an old map, unidentified corpse, surprise discoveries keep reader guessing in this cleverly intricate tale of financial skullduggery. 2 black-and-white maps. 320pp. 5⅜ × 8½. (Available in U.S. only) 25032-6 Pa. $5.95

AUTHENTIC VICTORIAN DECORATION AND ORNAMENTATION IN FULL COLOR: 46 Plates from "Studies in Design," Christopher Dresser. Superb full-color lithographs reproduced from rare original portfolio of a major Victorian designer. 48pp. 9¼ × 12¼. 25083-0 Pa. $7.95

PRIMITIVE ART, Franz Boas. Remains the best text ever prepared on subject, thoroughly discussing Indian, African, Asian, Australian, and, especially, North-ern American primitive art. Over 950 illustrations show ceramics, masks, totem poles, weapons, textiles, paintings, much more. 376pp. 5⅜ × 8. 20025-6 Pa. $6.95

SIDELIGHTS ON RELATIVITY, Albert Einstein. Unabridged republication of two lectures delivered by the great physicist in 1920–21. *Ether and Relativity* and *Geometry and Experience*. Elegant ideas in non-mathematical form, accessible to intelligent layman. vi + 56pp. 5⅜ × 8½. 24511-X Pa. $2.95

THE WIT AND HUMOR OF OSCAR WILDE, edited by Alvin Redman. More than 1,000 ripostes, paradoxes, wisecracks: Work is the curse of the drinking classes, I can resist everything except temptation, etc. 258pp. 5⅜ × 8½. 20602-5 Pa. $3.95

ADVENTURES WITH A MICROSCOPE, Richard Headstrom. 59 adventures with clothing fibers, protozoa, ferns and lichens, roots and leaves, much more. 142 illustrations. 232pp. 5⅜ × 8½. 23471-1 Pa. $3.95

PLANTS OF THE BIBLE, Harold N. Moldenke and Alma L. Moldenke. Standard reference to all 230 plants mentioned in Scriptures. Latin name, biblical reference, uses, modern identity, much more. Unsurpassed encyclopedic resource for scholars, botanists, nature lovers, students of Bible. Bibliography. Indexes. 123 black-and-white illustrations. 384pp. 6 × 9. 25069-5 Pa. $8.95

FAMOUS AMERICAN WOMEN: A Biographical Dictionary from Colonial Times to the Present, Robert McHenry, ed. From Pocahontas to Rosa Parks, 1,035 distinguished American women documented in separate biographical entries. Accurate, up-to-date data, numerous categories, spans 400 years. Indices. 493pp. 6½ × 9¼. 24523-3 Pa. $9.95

THE FABULOUS INTERIORS OF THE GREAT OCEAN LINERS IN HISTORIC PHOTOGRAPHS, William H. Miller, Jr. Some 200 superb photographs capture exquisite interiors of world's great "floating palaces"—1890's to 1980's: *Titanic, Ile de France, Queen Elizabeth, United States, Europa,* more. Approx. 200 black-and-white photographs. Captions. Text. Introduction. 160pp. 8⅞ × 11¾. 24756-2 Pa. $9.95

THE GREAT LUXURY LINERS, 1927–1954: A Photographic Record, William H. Miller, Jr. Nostalgic tribute to heyday of ocean liners. 186 photos of Ile de France, Normandie, Leviathan, Queen Elizabeth, United States, many others. Interior and exterior views. Introduction. Captions. 160pp. 9 × 12. 24056-8 Pa. $9.95

A NATURAL HISTORY OF THE DUCKS, John Charles Phillips. Great landmark of ornithology offers complete detailed coverage of nearly 200 species and subspecies of ducks: gadwall, sheldrake, merganser, pintail, many more. 74 full-color plates, 102 black-and-white. Bibliography. Total of 1,920pp. 8⅝ × 11¼. 25141-1, 25142-X Cloth. Two-vol. set $100.00

THE SEAWEED HANDBOOK: An Illustrated Guide to Seaweeds from North Carolina to Canada, Thomas F. Lee. Concise reference covers 78 species. Scientific and common names, habitat, distribution, more. Finding keys for easy identification. 224pp. 5⅜ × 8½. 25215-9 Pa. $5.95

THE TEN BOOKS OF ARCHITECTURE: The 1755 Leoni Edition, Leon Battista Alberti. Rare classic helped introduce the glories of ancient architecture to the Renaissance. 68 black-and-white plates. 336pp. 8⅜ × 11¼. 25239-6 Pa. $14.95

MISS MACKENZIE, Anthony Trollope. Minor masterpieces by Victorian master unmasks many truths about life in 19th-century England. First inexpensive edition in years. 392pp. 5⅜ × 8½. 25201-9 Pa. $7.95

THE RIME OF THE ANCIENT MARINER, Gustave Doré, Samuel Taylor Coleridge. Dramatic engravings considered by many to be his greatest work. The terrifying space of the open sea, the storms and whirlpools of an unknown ocean, the ice of Antarctica, more—all rendered in a powerful, chilling manner. Full text. 38 plates. 77pp. 9¼ × 12. 22305-1 Pa. $4.95

THE EXPEDITIONS OF ZEBULON MONTGOMERY PIKE, Zebulon Montgomery Pike. Fascinating first-hand accounts (1805–6) of exploration of Mississippi River, Indian wars, capture by Spanish dragoons, much more. 1,088pp. 5⅜ × 8½. 25254-X, 25255-8 Pa. Two-vol. set $23.90

A CONCISE HISTORY OF PHOTOGRAPHY: Third Revised Edition, Helmut Gernsheim. Best one-volume history—camera obscura, photochemistry, daguerreotypes, evolution of cameras, film, more. Also artistic aspects—landscape, portraits, fine art, etc. 281 black-and-white photographs. 26 in color. 176pp. 8⅜ × 11¼. 25128-4 Pa. $12.95

THE DORÉ BIBLE ILLUSTRATIONS, Gustave Doré. 241 detailed plates from the Bible: the Creation scenes, Adam and Eve, Flood, Babylon, battle sequences, life of Jesus, etc. Each plate is accompanied by the verses from the King James version of the Bible. 241pp. 9 × 12. 23004-X Pa. $8.95

HUGGER-MUGGER IN THE LOUVRE, Elliot Paul. Second Homer Evans mystery-comedy. Theft at the Louvre involves sleuth in hilarious, madcap caper. "A knockout."—Books. 336pp. 5⅜ × 8½. 25185-3 Pa. $5.95

FLATLAND, E. A. Abbott. Intriguing and enormously popular science-fiction classic explores the complexities of trying to survive as a two-dimensional being in a three-dimensional world. Amusingly illustrated by the author. 16 illustrations. 103pp. 5⅜ × 8½. 20001-9 Pa. $2.00

THE HISTORY OF THE LEWIS AND CLARK EXPEDITION, Meriwether Lewis and William Clark, edited by Elliott Coues. Classic edition of Lewis and Clark's day-by-day journals that later became the basis for U.S. claims to Oregon and the West. Accurate and invaluable geographical, botanical, biological, meteorological and anthropological material. Total of 1,508pp. 5⅜ × 8½.
21268-8, 21269-6, 21270-X Pa. Three-vol. set $25.50

LANGUAGE, TRUTH AND LOGIC, Alfred J. Ayer. Famous, clear introduction to Vienna, Cambridge schools of Logical Positivism. Role of philosophy, elimination of metaphysics, nature of analysis, etc. 160pp. 5⅜ × 8½. (Available in U.S. and Canada only) 20010-8 Pa. $2.95

MATHEMATICS FOR THE NONMATHEMATICIAN, Morris Kline. Detailed, college-level treatment of mathematics in cultural and historical context, with numerous exercises. For liberal arts students. Preface. Recommended Reading Lists. Tables. Index. Numerous black-and-white figures. xvi + 641pp. 5⅜ × 8½.
24823-2 Pa. $11.95

28 SCIENCE FICTION STORIES, H. G. Wells. Novels, *Star Begotten* and *Men Like Gods,* plus 26 short stories: "Empire of the Ants," "A Story of the Stone Age," "The Stolen Bacillus," "In the Abyss," etc. 915pp. 5⅜ × 8½. (Available in U.S. only)
20265-8 Cloth. $10.95

HANDBOOK OF PICTORIAL SYMBOLS, Rudolph Modley. 3,250 signs and symbols, many systems in full; official or heavy commercial use. Arranged by subject. Most in Pictorial Archive series. 143pp. 8⅛ × 11. 23357-X Pa. $5.95

INCIDENTS OF TRAVEL IN YUCATAN, John L. Stephens. Classic (1843) exploration of jungles of Yucatan, looking for evidences of Maya civilization. Travel adventures, Mexican and Indian culture, etc. Total of 669pp. 5⅜ × 8½.
20926-1, 20927-X Pa., Two-vol. set $9.90

DEGAS: An Intimate Portrait, Ambroise Vollard. Charming, anecdotal memoir by famous art dealer of one of the greatest 19th-century French painters. 14 black-and-white illustrations. Introduction by Harold L. Van Doren. 96pp. 5⅜ × 8½.
25131-4 Pa. $3.95

PERSONAL NARRATIVE OF A PILGRIMAGE TO ALMANDINAH AND MECCAH, Richard Burton. Great travel classic by remarkably colorful personality. Burton, disguised as a Moroccan, visited sacred shrines of Islam, narrowly escaping death. 47 illustrations. 959pp. 5⅜ × 8½. 21217-3, 21218-1 Pa., Two-vol. set $17.90

PHRASE AND WORD ORIGINS, A. H. Holt. Entertaining, reliable, modern study of more than 1,200 colorful words, phrases, origins and histories. Much unexpected information. 254pp. 5⅜ × 8½. 20758-7 Pa. $4.95

THE RED THUMB MARK, R. Austin Freeman. In this first Dr. Thorndyke case, the great scientific detective draws fascinating conclusions from the nature of a single fingerprint. Exciting story, authentic science. 320pp. 5⅜ × 8½. (Available in U.S. only) 25210-8 Pa. $5.95

AN EGYPTIAN HIEROGLYPHIC DICTIONARY, E. A. Wallis Budge. Monumental work containing about 25,000 words or terms that occur in texts ranging from 3000 B.C. to 600 A.D. Each entry consists of a transliteration of the word, the word in hieroglyphs, and the meaning in English. 1,314pp. 6⅜ × 10.
23615-3, 23616-1 Pa., Two-vol. set $27.90

THE COMPLEAT STRATEGYST: Being a Primer on the Theory of Games of Strategy, J. D. Williams. Highly entertaining classic describes, with many illustrated examples, how to select best strategies in conflict situations. Prefaces. Appendices. xvi + 268pp. 5⅜ × 8½. 25101-2 Pa. $5.95

THE ROAD TO OZ, L. Frank Baum. Dorothy meets the Shaggy Man, little Button-Bright and the Rainbow's beautiful daughter in this delightful trip to the magical Land of Oz. 272pp. 5⅜ × 8. 25208-6 Pa. $4.95

POINT AND LINE TO PLANE, Wassily Kandinsky. Seminal exposition of role of point, line, other elements in non-objective painting. Essential to understanding 20th-century art. 127 illustrations. 192pp. 6½ × 9¼. 23808-3 Pa. $4.50

LADY ANNA, Anthony Trollope. Moving chronicle of Countess Lovel's bitter struggle to win for herself and daughter Anna their rightful rank and fortune—perhaps at cost of sanity itself. 384pp. 5⅜ × 8½. 24669-8 Pa. $6.95

EGYPTIAN MAGIC, E. A. Wallis Budge. Sums up all that is known about magic in Ancient Egypt: the role of magic in controlling the gods, powerful amulets that warded off evil spirits, scarabs of immortality, use of wax images, formulas and spells, the secret name, much more. 253pp. 5⅜ × 8½. 22681-6 Pa. $4.00

THE DANCE OF SIVA, Ananda Coomaraswamy. Preeminent authority unfolds the vast metaphysic of India: the revelation of her art, conception of the universe, social organization, etc. 27 reproductions of art masterpieces. 192pp. 5⅜ × 8½.
24817-8 Pa. $5.95

CHRISTMAS CUSTOMS AND TRADITIONS, Clement A. Miles. Origin, evolution, significance of religious, secular practices. Caroling, gifts, yule logs, much more. Full, scholarly yet fascinating; non-sectarian. 400pp. 5⅜ × 8½.
23354-5 Pa. $6.50

THE HUMAN FIGURE IN MOTION, Eadweard Muybridge. More than 4,500 stopped-action photos, in action series, showing undraped men, women, children jumping, lying down, throwing, sitting, wrestling, carrying, etc. 390pp. 7⅞ × 10⅝.
20204-6 Cloth. $19.95

THE MAN WHO WAS THURSDAY, Gilbert Keith Chesterton. Witty, fast-paced novel about a club of anarchists in turn-of-the-century London. Brilliant social, religious, philosophical speculations. 128pp. 5⅜ × 8½.
25121-7 Pa. $3.95

A CEZANNE SKETCHBOOK: Figures, Portraits, Landscapes and Still Lifes, Paul Cezanne. Great artist experiments with tonal effects, light, mass, other qualities in over 100 drawings. A revealing view of developing master painter, precursor of Cubism. 102 black-and-white illustrations. 144pp. 8¾ × 6⅝.
24790-2 Pa. $5.95

AN ENCYCLOPEDIA OF BATTLES: Accounts of Over 1,560 Battles from 1479 B.C. to the Present, David Eggenberger. Presents essential details of every major battle in recorded history, from the first battle of Megiddo in 1479 B.C. to Grenada in 1984. List of Battle Maps. New Appendix covering the years 1967–1984. Index. 99 illustrations. 544pp. 6½ × 9¼.
24913-1 Pa. $14.95

AN ETYMOLOGICAL DICTIONARY OF MODERN ENGLISH, Ernest Weekley. Richest, fullest work, by foremost British lexicographer. Detailed word histories. Inexhaustible. Total of 856pp. 6½ × 9¼.
21873-2, 21874-0 Pa., Two-vol. set $17.00

WEBSTER'S AMERICAN MILITARY BIOGRAPHIES, edited by Robert McHenry. Over 1,000 figures who shaped 3 centuries of American military history. Detailed biographies of Nathan Hale, Douglas MacArthur, Mary Hallaren, others. Chronologies of engagements, more. Introduction. Addenda. 1,033 entries in alphabetical order. xi + 548pp. 6½ × 9¼. (Available in U.S. only)
24758-9 Pa. $11.95

LIFE IN ANCIENT EGYPT, Adolf Erman. Detailed older account, with much not in more recent books: domestic life, religion, magic, medicine, commerce, and whatever else needed for complete picture. Many illustrations. 597pp. 5⅜ × 8½.
22632-8 Pa. $8.50

HISTORIC COSTUME IN PICTURES, Braun & Schneider. Over 1,450 costumed figures shown, covering a wide variety of peoples: kings, emperors, nobles, priests, servants, soldiers, scholars, townsfolk, peasants, merchants, courtiers, cavaliers, and more. 256pp. 8⅜ × 11¼.
23150-X Pa. $7.95

THE NOTEBOOKS OF LEONARDO DA VINCI, edited by J. P. Richter. Extracts from manuscripts reveal great genius; on painting, sculpture, anatomy, sciences, geography, etc. Both Italian and English. 186 ms. pages reproduced, plus 500 additional drawings, including studies for *Last Supper, Sforza* monument, etc. 860pp. 7⅞ × 10¾. (Available in U.S. only) 22572-0, 22573-9 Pa., Two-vol. set $25.90

THE ART NOUVEAU STYLE BOOK OF ALPHONSE MUCHA: All 72 Plates from "Documents Decoratifs" in Original Color, Alphonse Mucha. Rare copyright-free design portfolio by high priest of Art Nouveau. Jewelry, wallpaper, stained glass, furniture, figure studies, plant and animal motifs, etc. Only complete one-volume edition. 80pp. 9⅜ × 12¼. 24044-4 Pa. $8.95

ANIMALS: 1,419 COPYRIGHT-FREE ILLUSTRATIONS OF MAMMALS, BIRDS, FISH, INSECTS, ETC., edited by Jim Harter. Clear wood engravings present, in extremely lifelike poses, over 1,000 species of animals. One of the most extensive pictorial sourcebooks of its kind. Captions. Index. 284pp. 9 × 12. 23766-4 Pa. $9.95

OBELISTS FLY HIGH, C. Daly King. Masterpiece of American detective fiction, long out of print, involves murder on a 1935 transcontinental flight—"a very thrilling story"—NY Times. Unabridged and unaltered republication of the edition published by William Collins Sons & Co. Ltd., London, 1935. 288pp. 5⅜ × 8½. (Available in U.S. only) 25036-9 Pa. $4.95

VICTORIAN AND EDWARDIAN FASHION: A Photographic Survey, Alison Gernsheim. First fashion history completely illustrated by contemporary photographs. Full text plus 235 photos, 1840–1914, in which many celebrities appear. 240pp. 6½ × 9¼. 24205-6 Pa. $6.00

THE ART OF THE FRENCH ILLUSTRATED BOOK, 1700–1914, Gordon N. Ray. Over 630 superb book illustrations by Fragonard, Delacroix, Daumier, Doré, Grandville, Manet, Mucha, Steinlen, Toulouse-Lautrec and many others. Preface. Introduction. 633 halftones. Indices of artists, authors & titles, binders and provenances. Appendices. Bibliography. 608pp. 8⅜ × 11¼. 25086-5 Pa. $24.95

THE WONDERFUL WIZARD OF OZ, L. Frank Baum. Facsimile in full color of America's finest children's classic. 143 illustrations by W. W. Denslow. 267pp. 5⅜ × 8½. 20691-2 Pa. $5.95

FRONTIERS OF MODERN PHYSICS: New Perspectives on Cosmology, Relativity, Black Holes and Extraterrestrial Intelligence, Tony Rothman, et al. For the intelligent layman. Subjects include: cosmological models of the universe; black holes; the neutrino; the search for extraterrestrial intelligence. Introduction. 46 black-and-white illustrations. 192pp. 5⅜ × 8½. 24587-X Pa. $6.95

THE FRIENDLY STARS, Martha Evans Martin & Donald Howard Menzel. Classic text marshalls the stars together in an engaging, non-technical survey, presenting them as sources of beauty in night sky. 23 illustrations. Foreword. 2 star charts. Index. 147pp. 5⅜ × 8½. 21099-5 Pa. $3.50

FADS AND FALLACIES IN THE NAME OF SCIENCE, Martin Gardner. Fair, witty appraisal of cranks, quacks, and quackeries of science and pseudoscience: hollow earth, Velikovsky, orgone energy, Dianetics, flying saucers, Bridey Murphy, food and medical fads, etc. Revised, expanded In the Name of Science. "A very able and even-tempered presentation."—The New Yorker. 363pp. 5⅜ × 8. 20394-8 Pa. $5.95

ANCIENT EGYPT: ITS CULTURE AND HISTORY, J. E Manchip White. From pre-dynastics through Ptolemies: society, history, political structure, religion, daily life, literature, cultural heritage. 48 plates. 217pp. 5⅜ × 8½. 22548-8 Pa. $4.95

SIR HARRY HOTSPUR OF HUMBLETHWAITE, Anthony Trollope. Incisive, unconventional psychological study of a conflict between a wealthy baronet, his idealistic daughter, and their scapegrace cousin. The 1870 novel in its first inexpensive edition in years. 250pp. 5⅜ × 8½. 24953-0 Pa. $4.95

LASERS AND HOLOGRAPHY, Winston E. Kock. Sound introduction to burgeoning field, expanded (1981) for second edition. Wave patterns, coherence, lasers, diffraction, zone plates, properties of holograms, recent advances. 84 illustrations. 160pp. 5⅜ × 8¼. (Except in United Kingdom) 24041-X Pa. $3.50

INTRODUCTION TO ARTIFICIAL INTELLIGENCE: SECOND, EN-LARGED EDITION, Philip C. Jackson, Jr. Comprehensive survey of artificial intelligence—the study of how machines (computers) can be made to act intelligently. Includes introductory and advanced material. Extensive notes updating the main text. 132 black-and-white illustrations. 512pp. 5⅜ × 8½. 24864-X Pa. $8.95

HISTORY OF INDIAN AND INDONESIAN ART, Ananda K. Coomaraswamy. Over 400 illustrations illuminate classic study of Indian art from earliest Harappa finds to early 20th century. Provides philosophical, religious and social insights. 304pp. 6⅜ × 9⅜. 25005-9 Pa. $8.95

THE GOLEM, Gustav Meyrink. Most famous supernatural novel in modern European literature, set in Ghetto of Old Prague around 1890. Compelling story of mystical experiences, strange transformations, profound terror. 13 black-and-white illustrations. 224pp. 5⅜ × 8½. (Available in U.S. only) 25025-3 Pa. $5.95

ARMADALE, Wilkie Collins. Third great mystery novel by the author of *The Woman in White* and *The Moonstone*. Original magazine version with 40 illustrations. 597pp. 5⅜ × 8½. 23429-0 Pa. $7.95

PICTORIAL ENCYCLOPEDIA OF HISTORIC ARCHITECTURAL PLANS, DETAILS AND ELEMENTS: With 1,880 Line Drawings of Arches, Domes, Doorways, Facades, Gables, Windows, etc., John Theodore Haneman. Sourcebook of inspiration for architects, designers, others. Bibliography. Captions. 141pp. 9 × 12. 24605-1 Pa. $6.95

BENCHLEY LOST AND FOUND, Robert Benchley. Finest humor from early 30's, about pet peeves, child psychologists, post office and others. Mostly unavailable elsewhere. 73 illustrations by Peter Arno and others. 183pp. 5⅜ × 8½. 22410-4 Pa. $3.95

ERTÉ GRAPHICS, Erté. Collection of striking color graphics: *Seasons, Alphabet, Numerals, Aces* and *Precious Stones*. 50 plates, including 4 on covers. 48pp. 9⅜ × 12¼. 23580-7 Pa. $6.95

THE JOURNAL OF HENRY D. THOREAU, edited by Bradford Torrey, F. H. Allen. Complete reprinting of 14 volumes, 1837–61, over two million words; the sourcebooks for *Walden*, etc. Definitive. All original sketches, plus 75 photographs. 1,804pp. 8½ × 12¼. 20312-3, 20313-1 Cloth., Two-vol. set $80.00

CASTLES: THEIR CONSTRUCTION AND HISTORY, Sidney Toy. Traces castle development from ancient roots. Nearly 200 photographs and drawings illustrate moats, keeps, baileys, many other features. Caernarvon, Dover Castles, Hadrian's Wall, Tower of London, dozens more. 256pp. 5⅜ × 8¼. 24898-4 Pa. $5.95

AMERICAN CLIPPER SHIPS: 1833–1858, Octavius T. Howe & Frederick C. Matthews. Fully-illustrated, encyclopedic review of 352 clipper ships from the period of America's greatest maritime supremacy. Introduction. 109 halftones. 5 black-and-white line illustrations. Index. Total of 928pp. 5⅜ × 8½.
25115-2, 25116-0 Pa., Two-vol. set $17.90

TOWARDS A NEW ARCHITECTURE, Le Corbusier. Pioneering manifesto by great architect, near legendary founder of "International School." Technical and aesthetic theories, views on industry, economics, relation of form to function, "mass-production spirit," much more. Profusely illustrated. Unabridged translation of 13th French edition. Introduction by Frederick Etchells. 320pp. 6⅛ × 9¼. (Available in U.S. only)
25023-7 Pa. $8.95

THE BOOK OF KELLS, edited by Blanche Cirker. Inexpensive collection of 32 full-color, full-page plates from the greatest illuminated manuscript of the Middle Ages, painstakingly reproduced from rare facsimile edition. Publisher's Note. Captions. 32pp. 9⅜ × 12¼.
24345-1 Pa. $4.50

BEST SCIENCE FICTION STORIES OF H. G. WELLS, H. G. Wells. Full novel *The Invisible Man*, plus 17 short stories: "The Crystal Egg," "Aepyornis Island," "The Strange Orchid," etc. 303pp. 5⅜ × 8½. (Available in U.S. only)
21531-8 Pa. $4.95

AMERICAN SAILING SHIPS: Their Plans and History, Charles G. Davis. Photos, construction details of schooners, frigates, clippers, other sailcraft of 18th to early 20th centuries—plus entertaining discourse on design, rigging, nautical lore, much more. 137 black-and-white illustrations. 240pp. 6⅛ × 9¼.
24658-2 Pa. $5.95

ENTERTAINING MATHEMATICAL PUZZLES, Martin Gardner. Selection of author's favorite conundrums involving arithmetic, money, speed, etc., with lively commentary. Complete solutions. 112pp. 5⅜ × 8½.   25211-6 Pa. $2.95

THE WILL TO BELIEVE, HUMAN IMMORTALITY, William James. Two books bound together. Effect of irrational on logical, and arguments for human immortality. 402pp. 5⅜ × 8½.   20291-7 Pa. $7.50

THE HAUNTED MONASTERY and THE CHINESE MAZE MURDERS, Robert Van Gulik. 2 full novels by Van Gulik continue adventures of Judge Dee and his companions. An evil Taoist monastery, seemingly supernatural events; overgrown topiary maze that hides strange crimes. Set in 7th-century China. 27 illustrations. 328pp. 5⅜ × 8½.   23502-5 Pa. $5.00

CELEBRATED CASES OF JUDGE DEE (DEE GOONG AN), translated by Robert Van Gulik. Authentic 18th-century Chinese detective novel; Dee and associates solve three interlocked cases. Led to Van Gulik's own stories with same characters. Extensive introduction. 9 illustrations. 237pp. 5⅜ × 8½.
23337-5 Pa. $4.95

Prices subject to change without notice.
Available at your book dealer or write for free catalog to Dept. GI, Dover Publications, Inc., 31 East 2nd St., Mineola, N.Y. 11501. Dover publishes more than 175 books each year on science, elementary and advanced mathematics, biology, music, art, literary history, social sciences and other areas.